Social Studies and the Elementary School Child

FOURTH EDITION

GEORGE W. MAXIM
West Chester University

Merrill, an imprint of
Macmillan Publishing Company
New York

Maxwell Macmillan Canada, Inc.
Toronto

Maxwell Macmillan International Publishing Group
New York   Oxford   Singapore   Sydney

Cover photo by Les and Viola Van
Editor: Sally Berridge MacGregor
Production Editor: Gloria Schneider Jasperse
Art Coordinator: Mark D. Garrett
Text Designer: Debra A. Fargo
Cover Designer: Russ Maselli
Production Buyer: Pamela D. Bennett

This book was set in Italia.

Macmillan Publishing Company
866 Third Avenue, New York, NY 10022

Maxwell Macmillan Canada, Inc.

Library of Congress Cataloguing-in-Publication Data 90–43812
International Standard Book Number: 0–675–21271–5

Photos: pp. 3, 40, 46, 77, 177, 198, 257, 261, 271, 289, 324, 345, 354, 407, 424, 445, 448, 482, Elizabeth Maxim; 97, 106, Bruce Johnson, Macmillan; 130, 358, Keven Fitzsimmons, Macmillan; 390, Pat McKay; 426, National Aeronautics and Space Administration

Printing: 4   5   6   7   8   9   Year: 2   3   4

To Moy, Garibaldi, and Capitan
"Happily ever after!"
Your stories in my heart always end that way.

Preface

The fourth edition of *Social Studies and the Elementary School Child* is designed to help prospective teachers extend to the classroom the wonder and excitement elementary school children naturally bring to the process of investigating their social world. It is based on the most current research and theory related to subject matter content and instructional processes. Varied approaches for both of these curricular considerations are presented.

Many changes were made for this new edition. Four new chapters have been added. Chapter 10 focuses on the newer trends in literacy and offers practical suggestions about how the language arts can be effectively utilized in the social studies classroom. Chapter 13 addresses the valuable contributions of history to the social studies program. Chapter 14 offers sound ideas about how to implement the study of special topics: current affairs instruction, global education, environmental education, multicultural education, career education, law-related education, AIDS education, and drug/alcohol abuse prevention. Chapter 15 presents informative suggestions for evaluating teaching and learning in the social studies classroom.

You will also find new or expanded discussions on cultural literacy, cooperative learning, thinking skills, scope and sequence, unit and lesson planning, mastery learning (Madeline Hunter), Taba strategies, guided problem solving, values analysis, reading and writing in the social studies classroom, literature, the arts, "modern" geography, history, and evaluation.

I redesigned this edition into four thematic sections. The first section describes the evaluation of social studies as a major curricular mission in the elementary school and the qualities needed by teachers planning to teach it. The second section examines the processes of planning effective sequences of instruction and the alternative instructional techniques from which teachers may choose to enhance student learning. In the third section are suggestions for managing whole-group, small-group, and individualized instruction. The final section presents an overview of the major sources of content from which contemporary social studies experiences grow.

Finally, this edition offers a developmental approach to social studies instruction. Each chapter presents its recommendations in a developmental framework so that teachers at all grade levels will understand and appreciate their roles in providing the kinds of experiences that allow upper-elementary students to develop and learn successfully. There are specific examples, vignettes, and practical suggestions throughout the text.

As a teacher, your classroom practices should help prepare children to face the challenges of today's world and the unique conditions of the future. You must become a concerned decision maker and a master of the techniques for guiding children in the social studies. As you use this text, you will realize that there is no single correct way to teach social studies. You will be asked to consider old theories and new ones. Though you may be tempted to look more favorably on new theories because of their freshness, it is important to examine each option carefully to choose the one that is likely to produce the desired result. Even the most innovative teaching technique can make the classroom dull and lifeless if it is not suitable for the children. You will also need to adjust or abandon techniques that bore or frustrate children or produce insignificant results. This text is designed as a sourcebook and guide to help you interpret and apply different teaching options.

The importance of alternative teaching styles and the role of the teacher as decision maker form the central themes of the fourth edition of *Social Studies and the Elementary School Child*. This book is for use by both preservice and in-service teachers.

Acknowledgments

Writing a book is never an individual accomplishment; an author can never take complete credit for the finished product. This is especially true in my case. Many people have made valuable contributions to this book.

This fourth edition reflects the benefit of valuable comments from the many readers and users of the third edition who have offered specific ideas and asked challenging questions. That was one of the most exciting parts of the revision process.

My deepest appreciation goes to my wife, Libby. Her patience was certainly pushed to the breaking point a number of times, but she never let me know. Her understanding and encouragement sustained me through many long hours of writing. Without her help, I never would have been able to finish the book. My sons, Michael and Jeffrey, also contributed, even if they didn't know it. Their cheerfulness and affection picked up my spirits whenever the "writing blues" descended.

Jeff Johnston, editor-in-chief, must be singled out for his faith in the book and positive support throughout its revision. I also wish to thank Colin Kelly, sales representative at Macmillan, for his enthusiasm toward the project. His spirit and energy served as a major inspiration for my work, too.

Thanks also go to Doug Lantry and Gloria Jasperse, production editors, and Mark Garrett, art coordinator, for their efforts in bringing this text to its completion.

My colleagues at West Chester University warrant special recognition for their support: Kenneth L. Perrin, President; Michael Haines, Dean of the School of Education; Joan Hasselquist, Chair of the Department of Childhood Studies and Reading; and others involved in the teaching of elementary social studies methods—A. Scott Dunlap and E. Riley Holman.

Last, I thank the reviewers of the manuscript for their excellent suggestions. Their insights and expertise have improved this edition and guided my efforts to describe the ways teachers can help young children understand and appreciate this marvelous world in which we live. Those reviewers are: Kenneth Craycraft, Sam Houston State University; Phillip A. Heath, The Ohio State University—Lima; D. Rosalind Hammond, Bowling Green State University; Harvey Allen, University of South Carolina—Columbia; Mary E. Haas, West Virginia University.

Contents

1 *Examining the Social Studies Curriculum* *1*

Curriculum Controversy   3

The Social Sciences   6

    History   7
    Geography   7
    Civics   9
    Economics   11
    Sociology   12
    Anthropology   14

Organizing Content Selected from the Social Sciences   15

    The Expanding Environment Approach   15
    A Call for More History   18
    Recommendations for More Geography   20
    Suggestions for Expanding Civics   21

Designing a Thinking Skills Framework   26

Developing Good Citizens   28

    Categories of Social Studies Instructional Objectives   30

Lifelong Learning   30

2 *Becoming a Social Studies Teacher* *37*

Personal Characteristics of Good Social Studies Teachers   39

    Personality Differences   39
    Concern for Children   42
    Influence of Teachers on Children's Lives   42

Professional Characteristics of Good Social Studies Teachers   43

Importance of Your Professional Program   44
Apprenticeship by Participation   45
Professional Standards for Social Studies Teachers   46
Competency-based Programs   47

The Need for Continuous Growth   49

3

Planning for Social Studies Instruction   *55*

Planning for Individuals   56

Influences on Program Planning   58

Curriculum Guides   58
Textbooks   58

Planning for Instruction   59

Children's Choices   61
Teacher's Choices   66

Unit Plans   67

Selecting a Topic or Theme   67
Objectives   71
Learning Activities   75

Lesson Plans   81

Evaluation   84

4

Using Direct Instruction to Promote Thinking Skills   *87*

The Formal Approach   89

Concepts and Generalizations   90
Directed Teaching as an Active Process   90
Mastery Learning   93

Directed Learning Episodes   96

The Introductory Stage   96
The Learning Experience   102
Processing Information   102
Follow-Up and Extension Activities   117

A Sample DLE   118

5

*Enhancing Thinking Skills Through Guided
Problem Solving and Inquiry*   *123*

The Nature of Children's Learning   124

Active Learning in the Social Studies   124

Guided Problem Solving   125
Initiating Independent Research   133
Inquiry   137
A Sample Inquiry Episode   144

Cognitive Style and the Inquiry Process   146

Planning for Open-Ended Inquiry   150

6   *Thinking Skills Applied to Valuing Processes*   157

What Are Values?   159

Affective Prerequisites to Values Programs   160

The Magic Circle   161
The DUSO Kit   165

Values Inculcation   166

The Values Clarification Approach   167

Seven Subprocesses   168
Clarifying Responses   169
Values Clarification and Social Studies Content   171

Values Analysis   173

Climbing a Decision Tree   174
Using Stories   176

Moral Reasoning   178

Kohlberg's Cognitive-Developmental Model   178
Involving Children in Moral Dilemmas   180
Smooth Classroom Management   181

7   *Grouping for Instruction*   187

Cooperative Learning   189

Implementing Cooperative Learning Strategies   190

Whole-Group Orientation   190
Informal Experiences With Small Groups   198
Cooperative Learning Groups   204
Determining Group Composition   207
Behaviors in Cooperative Groups   207
Assigning Roles   208
A Sample Cooperative Learning Episode   208
Interest Groups   210
Research Groups   212
Ability Groups   214

Difficulties of Group Work   218

Initiating Grouping   218
Children's Readiness for Group Work   218
Dominating the Group   219

8

Enriching Instruction with Learning Centers   *223*

Types of Centers   224

Reinforcement Center   224
New Information Center   225
Creativity Center   225
Attitudes Center   225

Constructing Learning Centers   225

Pupil's Needs and Interests   226
Activities and Materials   226

Introducing Centers   230

Using the Centers   232

Organizing Routines and Student Assignments   234
Scheduling   234
Record Keeping   237
Initiating the Learning Center Experience   238

9

Selecting Instructional Resources   *249*

Intake of Information   250

Ways of Knowing   250

Enactive Learning   252

Activities Within the School   253
Realia   253
Field Trips   254
Resource Persons   259

Iconic Learning   262

Models or Replicas   262
Simulation Games   263
Motion Pictures, Videotapes, Slides, and Filmstrips   266
Computers   267
Pictures and Study Prints   270
Graphic Materials   272

Symbolic Learning   278

Lectures   279
Using a Variety of Activities   281

10 Integrating Social Studies with the Language Arts 285

A Social Studies-Language Arts Connection 286
Utilizing Children's Literature 287

Reading and Telling Stories 288
Children's Literature in Broader Contexts 290
Storytelling Techniques 294

Writing in the Social Studies Classroom 296

The Writing Process 298
Recognizing Children's Writing Efforts 298
Types of Writing in the Social Studies 303

11 Integrating the Arts into the Social Studies Program 317

The Arts in the Schools 318
Alternatives in Teaching the Arts 318

Providing Spaces in the Classroom 319
Integrating the Arts with the Social Studies 320

Creative Expression in the Classroom 323

Art Activities 323
Construction Activities 326
Creative Dramatics 327

Music and Dance 333

12 Incorporating Modern Geography into the Social Studies Curriculum 339

Geographic Literacy 340

Promotion of Geographic Literacy 341

Maps 342
Pre-Mapping Activities 343

Physical Features 343
The Earth 344
Representation 344

Perceptual Factors 345

Egocentrism and Conservation 345
Informal Play with Blocks 346

Beginning Map Instruction 349

Beginning Map Activities 349
The Globe 356
Map and Globe Reinforcement 358

Maps and Globes in the Subsequent Elementary Grades   362

Place Location   362
Latitude and Longitude   364
Relative Location   367
Map Symbols   369
Direction   370
Scale   370
Reading a Globe   372

Map Selection for the Classroom   374

Outline Maps   375
Relief Maps   376
Puzzle Maps   377
Topographic Maps   377
Outdoor Maps   378

Geographic Skills and Understandings   379

13   *Examining the Role of History in the Social Studies Curriculum*   *385*

Can Elementary School Children Learn History?   386

History Scope and Sequence   387

Sources of Historical Data   387

Physical Remains   387
Oral or Written Records   389

The Concept of Time   390

The Time Capsule   391
Classroom Calendars   393
Daily Schedule   394
Building a Calendar   394
Extending Time Concepts with Calendars   396
Calendar-Based Job Chart   397

History as Experience   400

Biographies   400
Oral History   400
Historical Panorama   401
Field Trips and Historical Investigation   401
Family History   402

Other Sources of Historical Data   404

Original Documents   406
Bringing Historical Figures to Life   408

Using Good Children's Literature   409
Time Lines   412

14 Utilizing Supplementary Sources of Social Studies Content   417

Current Affairs Instruction   419

Reading Newspapers   420
Sharing News Items   421
Current Affairs Periodicals   423
Supplementing the Regular Program   425

Global Education   425

Problems Shared by All People   425
Global Education Programs   427
Teacher's Role   428

Environmental Education   432

Learning About the Environment   433

Multicultural Education   438

Career Education   445

Primary Grades   447
Intermediate Grades   447

Law-related Education   448

Establishing Rules   449
The Making of Laws   451
Teacher Effectiveness Training   451
Classroom Constitution   456

AIDS Education   458

Drug and Alcohol Education   460

15 Evaluating Teaching and Learning   467

Standardized Achievement Tests   468

Criterion-Referenced Tests   470

Teacher-Made Achievement Tests   472

Constructing Teacher-Made Tests   473

Testing Early Primary Grade Children   478

Descriptive Reports   479
Checklists   480
Time Sampling   481

Event Sampling   482
Work Samples   483

Intelligence Tests   484

The Gifted   484
Students Requiring Special Help   488

Some final Thoughts   493

Index   *494*

About the Author   *528*

*Social Studies and the
Elementary School Child*

"We had the best of educations—in fact, we went to school every day—"
 "I've been to school, too," said Alice. "You needn't be so proud as all that."
 "With extras?" asked the Mock Turtle, a little anxiously.
 "Yes," said Alice.

—Lewis Carroll
Alice in Wonderland

Examining the Social Studies
1 *Curriculum*

KEY CONCEPTS

As you read, reflect on the following matters:

- What is the major purpose for teaching social studies?
- How is the social studies area defined?
- On what three instructional issues do most social studies educators tend to agree?
- What is a social science? Describe the six disciplines that contribute content and methods of inquiry to the social studies.
- What is meant by scope and sequence? Identify and describe the traditionally accepted pattern of organizing scope and sequence in the social studies.
- From what three disciplines do contemporary content innovators recommend we draw in order to improve social studies instruction? What is the justification for stressing each? How does each help us achieve our goal of "good citizenship"?
- Why is the refinement of effective thinking skills a major goal of social studies instruction?
- What is meant by "citizenship education"? What "essentials" for effective instruction does the National Council for the Social Studies recommend for exemplary social studies programs?

"What do *I* recall about my elementary school social studies experiences? I don't know; it's hard for me to remember *anything* from that far back." This is a typical response of college students who are asked to think about their early schooling. After some gentle prodding, however, some begin to piece together vague recollections: "Let's see, there was Mr. Otto, who always led us in memorization drills—the capitals of states, the order of presidential terms of office, where major cities and countries were located on a map, the dates of historical events, and lots of other facts. We even had to memorize the Gettysburg Address! Most of the time we just sat in our seats and listened to him talk, or else we read from our textbook and wrote the answers to questions at the end of the chapter. On the whole, social studies was a pretty rigorous subject as I remember it."

Others differ markedly from the preceding response: "I had an elementary teacher—Mrs. Dunbar—who made it one of my favorite subjects. We learned a lot because Mrs. Dunbar always had something interesting for us to do. Once, in fifth grade, we were studying prehistoric life. Mrs. Dunbar asked us to clean off and bring in bones left over from our dinner at home. You could probably guess that the next day we had a pile of all kinds of bones—fish, chicken, steak, and the like. Our first job was to clean them thoroughly with a scrubber, boil them in vinegar water, soak them in a bleach and water solution to make them white, and put them in a large box called 'the boneyard.' We were then organized into groups and given the freedom to choose any of the bones we wanted to be glued or wired together in the general shape of the dinosaurs we were studying. We gave our dinosaurs their scientific names and displayed an information card next to the models. Mrs. Dunbar called us 'paleontologists.' I still remember the word because it was a real thrill to be given such an impressive-sounding title at the time. Elementary school social studies were great fun, at least in Mrs. Dunbar's room. As a matter of fact, she has had as much influence on my choice of teaching as a career as any other single factor."

Social studies is one area of the elementary school curriculum that often evokes such disparate memories. Nearly all of us have had engaging experiences that brought life to the social studies content—building a tepee, publishing a colonial period newspaper, churning butter, creating a salt-and-flour relief map of the United States, or searching through books and articles to complete a report on the Aztec Indians. Our spirit of romanticism may have been captured while hearing absorbing yarns of life on the high seas, and our citizenship inspired by reading biographical sketches of famous Americans. But at the same time, we might be able to revive memories of less engrossing incidents—reading pages 79 to 81 in the text and writing answers to the questions that followed (while the teacher corrected the weekly spelling tests at his desk), listening to the teacher describe how an oil pump works (without the benefit of a diagram or model), or being required to memorize facts about the early explorers of our country: where they came from, when they left their homeland, the date they arrived here, and where they explored.

Which experiences dominate your perception of social studies from your elementary school days? Compare your responses with those of your peers. How many individuals described their elementary school social studies experiences as lively and

Good social studies teachers are careful to offer meaningful activity that provides depth to learning.

enjoyable? How many thought the subject was drab and boring? It is important to consider these questions, for our recollections have a major influence on the way we view the subject. If our memories are positive, we usually like the subject and often approach teaching it in an enjoyable, interesting way. If unkind memories dominate our thoughts, we may develop disinterest or dislike toward the subject and spend less time and energy on it. Understanding your feelings about elementary school social studies, then, is an important challenge for you to face at the beginning of this course. Some of you feel good about the subject; you will find it rewarding to strengthen and enlarge your enthusiasm. Others have ambivalent or unfavorable attitudes; you will need to overcome the displeasure imposed upon you by the mistakes of others, analyze alternative experiences, and determine for yourselves the full meaning of a teacher's contribution toward student learning.

CURRICULUM CONTROVERSY

With all this discussion about our past social studies experiences, one might be prompted to ask, "Just what *are* children supposed to be learning in their social studies classes, anyway?" "How *should* teachers teach whatever it is they're supposed to teach in the elementary school studies curriculum?" It is specifically within these two areas that controversy among social studies educators has become especially heated today: "What knowledge is of most value? How can that knowledge be made most useful and usable to the learner?" These questions are not new; they have captivated the thoughts of curriculum developers since the early history of our nation's schools. Throughout our educational history, social studies along with reading, writing, and arithmetic (regarded as the basics of a sound educational program), has traditionally been included in the curriculum as a valued basic subject. The worth of reading, writing, and arithmetic is apparent; they have been the cornerstone of basic skills instruction for many years. We continue to support fully the role of our schools in teaching literacy and computational skills as competencies essential in a modern society. Social studies, too, has been a basic subject over the years, one that is responsible for helping prepare children to exercise their rights and responsibilities as citizens. We value social studies instruction because we are a proud nation—a democratic republic of 250 million citizens, each of whom is part of one of the most unique political ventures in history. We prize our political processes, institutions, heritage, and the freedom of our citizens. To preserve and protect this prized inheritance, we expect our schools to effectively prepare our youngsters with a wide range of information, skills, and values as essentials of *good citizenship.* There is no question today that good citizenship is the most widely recognized goal of social studies education, but disagreements have arisen over the years about the nature of "good citizens" and how the social studies program could best contribute to their evolvement.

Perhaps no area of the elementary school curriculum is as open to debate about its true identity as the social studies. Presently, it is defined by the National Council for the Social Studies (NCSS) Task Force on Early Childhood/Elementary Social Studies as "the study of political, economic, cultural, and environmental aspects of societies in the past, present, and future."[1] This definition was fashioned in 1988 by a group of prestigious educators assigned the responsibility to discuss the definition, rationale, and goals for social studies during the early childhood/elementary years. It was a significant charge, for at no previous time has the NCSS (the primary professional organization for social studies educators in the United States) exerted such direct energy toward the topic of social studies for young children. Because of the significance of its work, the task force's interpretation has been chosen as the working definition of social studies for the elementary grades for this text. That choice, however, does not imply that a general consensus exists about what social studies is or what it should be for the elementary years.

Social studies educators have attempted to clarify the term *social studies* ever since it was first proposed as a subject area for our nation's schools in 1916. That year, the National Education Association (NEA) established various subject matter committees to study the curricula of our nation's schools; one of those committees was the Committee on Social Studies. Its main purpose was to determine whether the traditional history-dominated curriculum adequately addressed the needs and problems of a nation experiencing rapid change; multitudes of poor immigrants were crowding into our cities and trying to acclimate themselves to a new culture. Other than assisting high school students in their efforts to meet college entrance requirements and helping them exercise their brains (educational theorists of the time thought the brain was much like a muscle), the committee found little justification for the domination of history; it simply did not serve to meet the pressing needs of a changing society in any productive way. Instead, the committee supported the educational innovators of the time (such as John Dewey) who proposed that the work of our schools was to guarantee *social efficiency;* i.e., adjustment to the realities of life—readiness for the job market or the development of practical skills related to health, hygiene and nutrition. They recommended that school subjects should be practical: What point was there in teaching history to children when most of them would never go to college? The committee considered these concerns and proclaimed a new curricular area—social studies—as the major school experience responsible for promoting "social efficiency." The committee envisioned the social studies as "the subject matter related directly to the organization and development of human society, and to individuals as members of social groups."[2]

It recommended that the social studies be molded into a unique new subject area by integrating content from among the three prevailing social sciences of the time (systematized bodies of knowledge derived from methods of inquiry): history, geography, and civics. How was this integration of the social sciences to be accomplished? An answer to that question was as difficult to arrive at in 1916 as it is today. For about 75 years since they first addressed the issue, social studies educators have labored on a suitable answer acceptable to all factions in the field. They have constructed nothing

FIGURE 1–1

What to Include in the Social Studies Curriculum? The Search for Identity (Source: National Council for the Social Studies)

more than an endless maze of ambiguity, inconsistency, and contradiction. Barr, Barth, and Shermis explain:

> For the social studies the problem has been that there has been a lack of consensus among scholars as to what the field of social studies is or should be. Scholarly definitions of the social studies have been characterized by conflict rather than consensus. If the social studies is what the scholars in the field say it is, it is a schizophrenic bastard child.[3]

Author Bestor commented on the continuing turmoil, "This label [social studies] has itself contributed so greatly to educational confusion and stultification that it ought to be abandoned forthwith."[4]

Students introduced to the field are often incredulous when informed of its years of deep internal conflict: "Why can't social studies educators agree on the nature of this school subject?" To gain some perspective on that question, you must understand that, as with every education reform movement, attempts to reshape the social studies are sparked by experts holding strong opinions about such volatile issues as how students learn best and what learnings are of most worth. Resolutions to disagreements about these issues cannot be expected instantaneously; years of controversy, disagreement, and debate are to be expected when societal complexities cause theoreticians and curriculum specialists to examine regularly what is meant by "educating good citizens." However, out of the confusing maze of reform efforts, patterns of agreement finally appear to be emerging. Barr, Barth, and Shermis explain:

> It is similar to one of those puzzles found in introductory psychology textbooks. After gazing at length at a hopeless tangle of lines or colors, suddenly the perceptual gears slip into place, and out of the confusion emerge insight and clarity. Out of careful and patient observation of the seemingly incoherent, tangled, and contradictory practices . . . patterns have begun to appear.[5]

After decades of disagreement, there is now a pattern of general agreement that (1) the content of the social studies should be drawn from history and the social sciences, (2) the basic educational objectives should be varied, but should emphasize the acquisition of high-order thinking skills, and (3) the overall goal of social studies instruction should be the development of good citizens. Each of these trends will be examined in the following material.

HISTORY AND THE SOCIAL SCIENCES

Inherent in all discussions of the social studies are content decisions: "From which disciplines should the social studies draw its content?" Today, there appears to be common agreement that six disciplines offer the content foundation for elementary school social studies programs: history, geography, civics, economics, sociology, and anthropology. While the field may have drifted through the years, emphasizing one or more of the disciplines, proposals introduced during the past five years have been dominated by an emphasis on history, geography, and civics. We'll learn why after the social sciences are described.

History

We study history when we examine how people lived in the past. Our goal is not simply to require students to accumulate name/date/event knowledge, but to help them understand and deal with the enormous changes that will occur over their lifetime. Shirley Crenshaw and her associates advise:

> In order for students to grasp the full and true significance of the present, they must first have an understanding of the past—the context from which contemporary issues evolve. Only when they have made these crucial connections between the past and present will students be well-equipped to carry on important traditions of civic pride and responsibility.[6]

Historians integrate concepts from other disciplines into their investigations; history, by its nature, is an interdisciplinary subject. The Bradley Commission on History in Schools affirms that history

> should never be reduced to a thin recital of successive dates and facts, but carry what has been called "thick narrative," which combines lively storytelling and biography with [concepts] drawn from every relevant discipline.[7]

Because its scope is so immense, history can be the study of many things: local heritage, America's past, the evolution of Western civilization, and so on. But in order to provide more focus for emerging programs centered on history, the Bradley Commission (comprised of historians and master teachers) identified six vital organizational themes appropriate for any study of history, from the primary grades to graduate school. The themes are shown in Figure 1–2.

History is viewed today as one of the most important disciplines to be included in the social studies program because its portrayals of the human condition over time help citizens develop a sense of civic pride in and responsibility for their heritage. This idea meets with very little criticism today. However, there is disagreement as to whether history should be classified as a social science: references to the disciplines comprising the social studies often specify "history and the social sciences."

Geography

Geography contributes to the elementary school curriculum by providing the substance through which children learn about people and places, the natural environment, and the capacity of the earth to support life. "As a subject for study in the schools . . . geography provides an effective method for asking questions about places on the earth and their relationships to the people who live in them. It involves a pattern of inquiry that *begins* with two essential questions: *Why* are such things located in those particular places and *how* do those particular places influence our lives?"[8] The Joint Committee on Geographic Education advises that these two essential questions are effectively addressed through systematic study of five recurring central themes: *location, place, relationships within places, movement,* and *regions.* The Joint Committee defined those five areas as shown in Figure 1–4.

In carrying out programs in the elementary grades, children should have opportunities to explore and understand their own life space as well as the features of more

FIGURE 1–2

Six Vital Themes of Any Study of History (Source: Bradley Commission on History in Schools, Building a History Curriculum, *pp. 10–11.)*

Conflict and cooperation.
The many and various causes of war, and of approaches to peacemaking and war prevention. Relations between domestic affairs and ways of dealing with the outside world. Contrasts between international conflict and cooperation, between isolation and interdependence. The consequences of war and peace for societies and their cultures.

Comparative history of major developments.
The characteristics of revolutionary, reactionary, and reform periods across time and place. Imperialism, ancient and modern. Comparative instances of slavery and emancipation, feudalism and centralization, human successes and failures, of wisdom and folly. Comparative elites and aristocracies; the role of family, wealth, and merit.

Patterns of social and political interaction.
The changing patterns of class, ethnic, racial, and gender structures and relations. Immigration, migration, and social mobility. The effects of schooling. The new prominence of women, minorities, and the common people in the study of history, and their relation to political power and influential elites. The characteristics of multicultural societies; forces for unity and disunity.

Civilization, cultural diffusion, and innovation.
The evolution of human skills and the means of exerting power over nature and people. The rise, interaction, and decline of successive centers of such skills and power. The cultural flowering of major civilizations in the arts, literature, and thought. The role of social, religious, and political patronage of the arts and learning. The importance of the city in different eras and places.

Human interaction with the environment.
The relationships among geography, technology, and culture, and their effects on economic, social, and political developments. The choices made possible by climate, resources, and location, and the effect of culture and human values on such choices. The gains and losses of technological change. The central role of agriculture. The effect of disease, and disease-fighting, on plants, animals, and human beings.

Values, beliefs, political ideas, and institutions.
The origins and spread of influential religions and ideologies. The evolution of political and social institutions, at various stages of industrial and commercial development. The interplay among ideas, material conditions, moral values, and leadership, especially in the evolution of democratic societies. The tensions between the aspirations for freedom and security, for liberty and equality, for distinction and commonality, in human affairs.

remote areas of the world. The learning they acquire can satisfy their deep need to know about and help them become more sensitive toward the quality of human life on our planet. The Joint Committee on Geographic Education elaborates:

> The first task in geography is to locate places, describing and explaining their physical (natural) and human characteristics. Geographic inquiry continues by exploring the relation-

FIGURE 1–3

Characteristics of the Disciplines That Contribute to Contemporary Social Studies Programs

HISTORY
Gathers and eval-
uates relevant
traces of past
events.

ECONOMICS
Examines people's
attempts to satisfy
their wants with
limited resources.

GEOGRAPHY
Investigates the
ways in which the
physical charac-
teristics of the
earth affect its
people and people
affect the earth.

SOCIOLOGY
Probes people's
membership in
groups
such as family,
neighborhood,
community.

POLITICAL
SCIENCE
Studies people's
attempts to estab-
lish, maintain
order and bring about
peaceful change through
government.

ANTHROPOLOGY
Studies all of
the factors which
contribute to a
culture, such as beliefs,
customs, traditions, and
language.

ships that develop as people respond to and shape their physical and natural environments. It permits us to compare, contrast, and comprehend the regions of the world and its various physical and human features and patterns. This knowledge helps us to manage the world's resources and to analyze a host of other significant problems in terms of the *spaces* they occupy and how these spaces interact with each other on the earth's surface.[9]

Although geography is not commonly taught as a separate subject in our elementary schools, its content and processes are vitally important for the preparation of informed citizens. It should be an essential ingredient in all good social studies programs.

Civics

Traditionally, civics has been defined as a discipline involving studies of people's attempts to maintain order by establishing governing institutions and processes. The emphasis of civic study has been to examine the structure and functions of government—how people get power, what their duties are, and how they carry out their duties. Newer programs recognize the value of such knowledge, but many educators now

FIGURE 1–4

The Five Themes of Modern Geography (Source: Joint Committee on Geographic Education, Guidelines for Geographic Education *(Washington, DC: The Association of American Geographers, 1984), pp. 3–8.)*

Five geography themes

1. Location
Describes where specific points are located on the earth's surface and where certain points are in relation to others.

2. Place
Identifies the distinctive characteristics of areas (physical or human) that distinguish them from other places.

3. Relationships within places
Characterizes the ways people react to and sometimes change their environment.

4. Movement
Characterizes how people travel from one place to another, communicate with each other, or rely on products, information, or ideas from other places.

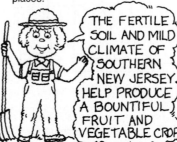

5. Regions
Classifies areas that display similarities of selected features—(landform, climate, natural vegetation, religions, land use, culture, etc.)

believe that limiting the social studies program to that single knowledge dimension is inappropriate for meeting contemporary citizenship needs. Benjamin R. Barber argues, "For the most part . . . civic education has been associated with *civic knowledge*. . . . [Y]et if democracy is to sustain itself, a richer conception of citizenship is required."[10] Barber refers to the new conceptualization of civics as "strong democracy." He describes strong democracy as "not simply a system whereby people elect those who govern them, but a system in which every member of the community participates in self-governance."[11] Citing public apathy toward such current crises as drug abuse and crime, Barber's goal is to create a civic virtue whereby individuals involve themselves in rigorous examination of real problems, past and present. Walter C. Parker agrees with Barber's concept, but refers to it as "participatory citizenship."[12] Parker advises that participatory citizenship experiences should be made a regular part of school life because they lay the foundation for students to participate in democratic life as they become adult citizens. He identifies three forms of participatory citizenship basic to the social studies program:

> One is democratic classroom and school meetings. Here real problems of school life are discussed openly and perhaps resolved. Meanwhile, students are learning the arts of discussion on public controversies and the challenge of formulating fair and wise public policy . . .
>
> A second form of participatory citizenship also relies on open and disciplined discussion of the heart of civic life, but deals with academic controversies rather than controversies drawn from school life . . . Issues can [include such topics as] deciding . . . whether the Constitution was really needed (many good citizens opposed it) . . .
>
> A third form draws discussion topics from contemporary public controversies.[13]

The mission of participatory citizenship, then, is to offer direct experiences in civic life that can evolve into deepened understandings of law, public policy, and democratic principles. Debate, discussion, and formulation of public judgments must all be a part of the process.

Economics

Economics affects all our lives. From the youngsters who save their allowance for a special toy to the college students who must scrape together enough money for tuition, through the newlyweds who apply for a mortgage as they buy their first home, all people face situations where they attempt to satisfy unlimited wants with limited resources. Referred to as the *scarcity concept,* it is from this idea that a family of economics learnings emerges. Because of scarcity, humans have attempted to develop methods to produce more in less time with less material, by which *specialization of labor* was discovered. From specialization has emerged the idea of *interdependence,* a reliance of people upon one another that necessitates monetary, transportation, and communication systems. From interactions of these factors, a *market system* developed through which buyers and sellers produce and exchange goods or services. Finally, governments are responsible for controlling segments of the market system to assure the welfare of all its citizens. Information about the economy helps one assess pressing issues of the day. This area includes the study of taxation, consumer economics, economic growth and development, and policies toward business.

W. Lee Hansen advises that economic education should begin in the elementary grades and have as its primary objective the understanding of both *economic analysis* and *economic policy*.

> Economics is the study of how goods and services we want get produced, and how they are distributed among us. This part we call economic analysis. Economics is also the study of how we can make the system of production and distribution work better. This part we call economic policy. Economic analysis is the necessary foundation for sound economic policy.[14]

The essence of economics lies in being able to make sense out of an array of economic concepts and issues. Four concepts basic among the many concepts in economics are *production, distribution, exchange,* and *consumption.* These are appropriate for elementary school classrooms because teachers can find a variety of concrete examples to illustrate them; Table 1–1 shows how these concepts can be integrated into the elementary school social studies curriculum.

Economics is a crucial discipline that needs to be included in social studies programs for today's youth. As they enter the twenty-first century, our students will not only be subject to the traditional questions of how best to ensure economic prosperity, but also challenged with a competitive global economy requiring deeper understanding, responsible citizenship, and effective decision making.

Sociology

The sociologist studies humans by examining their interactions with one another in groups or organizations such as the family, government, church, or school. Sociologists analyze the values and norms these groups hold in common to discover how they become organized (or disorganized) or why they behave as they do. They study how groups form, how they operate, and how they change.

Sociologists organize their study of groups around many questions, such as, "What kinds of groups do people in any given society form? What are the expectations of each group member? What problems do the group members face? How does the group control its members?"

To answer these questions, sociologists may visit a particular group, observe what the people in that group do, interview group members, or even live with a group for a short time to more completely understand its nature. This firsthand information is enough to get sociologists started, but they must check the validity of their information. By studying written material, television, films, radio programs, and a variety of other resources, they determine whether their original impressions contained inaccurate generalizations or unwarranted stereotypes. Sociologists share their findings with others through various means, of which one of the most popular is the *case study.* Case studies are reports of individuals or groups describing day-to-day conditions of their lives during a certain period. They frequently appear in elementary school social studies

TABLE 1–1
Economics Concepts and Examples

Concept	Example
Production (study of goods and services provided by others	*Bakery* (Grade 2) 1. Bakers use goods furnished by other workers. 2. The bakery is a source for many goods. 3. Work in a bakery is divided into specialized tasks for more efficient production. 4. Not all bakeries produce goods of the same variety or of equal quality.
Distribution (study of how goods and services are made available to consumers, i.e., selling, advertising, and shipping)	*Automobile Industry* (Grade 5) 1. Automobile dealers get the cars they sell from an automobile factory. 2. Many different workers help get the automobiles from the factory to the dealer and ready for the buyer. 3. Automobile dealers use attractive advertisements to encourage people to buy their goods. 4. Some automobile dealers are able to sell cars at a lower price than others.
Exchange (study of money and other mediums of exchange that enhance exchange of goods or services between producer and consumer)	*Bank* (Grade 4) 1. Banks are safe places in which to save money. 2. Banks lend to people who may not have enough money to buy what they want. 3. Banks provide checks for people who wish to pay without handling real money. 4. Banks pay people for the use of their money.
Consumption (study of needs and wants of the buyer and of the agencies responsible for protecting the buyer)	*Consumerism* (Grades 2–5) 1. Each person decides what to buy after evaluating what he needs most. 2. We buy some items because they satisfy basic needs and others because they bring us enjoyment. 3. Shoppers should examine the goods sold by several stores so they can select those that give them the most for their money. 4. The government protects the buyer from false claims and promises.

textbooks to provide children with real-life episodes that furnish clues to others' behavior.

The content of social studies programs, especially in the primary grades, is selected largely from the field of sociology as children are encouraged to investigate areas of group activity—a social characteristic especially meaningful in their own lives. Units usually center on *socialization,* the activities through which children are led to accept the folkways and mores of our society. By examining and accepting natural and artificial differences among individuals, children learn to predict human behavior in families, neighborhoods, cities, and the world.

Study of the family during the primary grades is usually followed by a study of neighborhood groups, community groups, special interest groups (such as a group of friends), and school groups. Progressing through the grades, children increase their study of groups in cultures other than their own.

Anthropology

Anthropologists study people to find out what they were like from earliest existence and what changed their lives throughout the years. They learn how people have existed—in their civilization's approach to language, literature, folklore, music, religion, art, law, and social institutions. When we study a society's contributions to existence, we refer to that society's *culture*—things its people do that are similar or dissimilar to the ways other people behave. Because of this great scope of study, anthropology has often been described as a universal social science—one that comprehensively studies people by looking at all aspects of their civilization.

Anthropologists examine a culture by visiting the lands of the people, living with the people, and recording what they do. This investigation is a *field study,* one of the most effective means of uncovering information about people. Of course, anthropologists support their findings by searching for additional information about a culture: conducting library research to discover what others have observed; examining artifacts (such as stone tools); or studying films, slides, or tapes of others' field studies. Also of great interest are a people's legends and stories. These stories often help anthropologists get a better idea of a culture they are studying, but may also lead them astray. For example, Navajo mythology implies that they have always lived in the Southwest, but years of accumulating other anthropological evidence suggests that they arrived there from the north about seven hundred years ago. Children are fascinated by the legends and myths of other cultures, however, so they should be included as a source of information whenever possible. Sometimes these stories influence a person's whole life, as in the case of amateur archaeologist Heinrich Schliemann. When Schliemann was young, he enjoyed listening to myths about Greece and Rome and was particularly fascinated with the Trojan War and how the gods and goddesses took sides with the Greeks and Trojans. When Schliemann was growing up, most people believed the story of Troy's burning was just a myth. But Schliemann was not convinced. He had an opportunity to find out later in his life when he visited Asia Minor to investigate stories of buried cities in the area. After much looking, he finally found a huge mound of earth close to the Aegean Sea—an area where the ancient city of Troy was believed to have existed. Schliemann dug into the earth and discovered that the site had been the location of many cities, each built upon the other as the previous city had been completely destroyed—nine separate cities altogether. Archaeologists were summoned to use their special equipment and methods to search the area. They now think the Troy made famous in stories was the city found in the seventh layer of Schliemann's mound.

Of course, not every child will become a Heinrich Schliemann, but children's curiosity and willingness to pursue areas of interest should be capitalized on when studying people. Allow the children to examine artifacts, for example, and guess how they were used. Have them support their guesses by visiting museums, reading books, searching through pictures, asking resource persons, or talking to anthropologists. The exciting contribution anthropology brings to the elementary school program is an understanding of and respect for cultures that are non-Western. Children are able to discover that all civilizations have things in common and that all peoples have used their abilities to think and create to shape their environments and build their cultures.

ORGANIZING CONTENT SELECTED FROM THE SOCIAL SCIENCES

Figure 1–5 summarizes the content characteristics of each of the disciplines as they might be applied to a study of Africa. Although some school programs approach instruction by maintaining the separate identities of each of the disciplines, most advocate an *interdisciplinary approach*, which combines two or more into one program. Children develop a more realistic picture of all the forces that influence human behavior with this approach.

Once the source of content has been agreed upon, curriculum developers must face two difficult questions: "*What* specific learnings from the disciplines should be taught?" and "*When* is the most desirable time to teach them?" When developers address the first question, they are determining the *scope* of the program; when they address the second, they are establishing the *sequence*.

The Expanding Environment Approach

Traditionally, social studies educators have addressed scope and sequence issues for the elementary grades with the *expanding environment* approach to curriculum organization. No one knows for sure how the approach actually began, but sometime during the 1930s, an organizational pattern emerged similar to that shown in Table 1–2. The plan starts during the early grades with what is closest to the child's own life experiences (home and family) and expands outward as the child matures to increasingly remote areas during the upper grades (Western Hemisphere). The expanding environment approach was popularly accepted throughout the country and became so widespread during the 1930s and through the 1970s that many considered it a national curriculum. Paul R. Hanna [15] reaffirmed the strength of the expanding environment approach when, in 1963, he published an influential article reinforcing its dominance in the social studies

FIGURE 1–5

An Interdisciplinary Approach to a Study of Africa

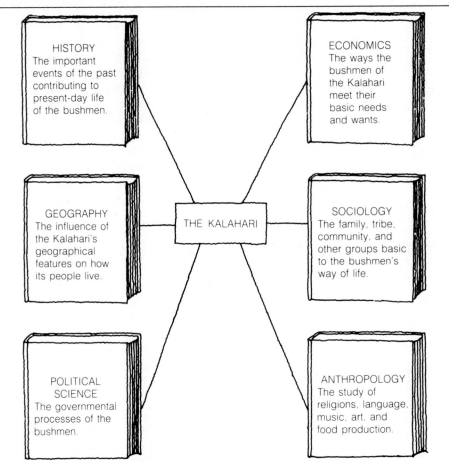

curriculum. So, from the 1930s through the 1970s, the elementary school social studies curriculum was based nearly exclusively on the expanding environment approach.

In 1983, the Task Force on Scope and Sequence of the NCSS met to determine a curriculum design suitable for contemporary times. The Task Force made this comment about its responsibility:

> The Task Force does not recommend that a social studies sequence rely solely on the expanding environment principle. The life space of today's children is greatly affected by modern methods of communication and transportation. Who would claim that the life space of a six-year-old is the local environment when each evening the child views television accounts of events *in progress* from anywhere in the world? Therefore, the social studies curriculum should not move sequentially from topics that are near at hand to

TABLE 1–2
The Expanding Environment Approach

Level	Topic of Study
Kindergarten–Grade 1	Home, Family, School
Grade 2	Neighborhoods, Neighborhood Helpers
Grade 3	Communities–Local and Regional
Grade 4	The State
Grade 5	The United States (geography, history, civics)
Grade 6	The World
Grade 7	American History and Government
Grade 8	Greek and Roman History

those that are far away for the purpose of expanding the environment. The purpose of extending content outward, away from a self-centric focus, is to illustrate how people and places interact; how people of different areas depend on each other; how people are part of interlocking networks that sustain the life of modern societies; and how people and places everywhere fit into a global human community.[16]

Despite their apparent desire to alter traditional scope and sequence of the expanding environment approach, the Task Force's broad recommendations actually reaffirmed it, at least for the elementary grades. (See Figure 1–6.) The Task Force met again in 1989 to examine whether its proposal was relevant for the 1990s; it reaffirmed its 1983 decisions.

Reaction to the report of the Task Force on Scope and Sequence was divided. On one hand, it was heartily commended by educators such as Ronald G. Helms, who stated, "[T]he report is needed by those educators and school districts that have neither the time nor the resources to develop good alternatives. Those more fortunate districts will be able to review the report as a launching point before beginning curriculum revision.[17] R. Freeman Butts commented, "[I]t takes seriously the oft-proclaimed social studies goal of education for citizenship. It thus reaffirms a long-held traditional purpose of social studies, but does so by explicit and persuasive attention to the common core of civic values and citizenship in a democratic society."[18] Critics of the report noted that very little was proposed for the elementary grades that was different from the traditional scope and sequence plans originating during the 1930s. Geraldine Hellman-Rosenthal commented, "If we really support the goals of the NCSS, we cannot base our scope and sequence on the perceived needs, make-up, and motivations of a client population of 60 to 80 years ago . . . [W]e require a broader scope and consideration of a more developmentally oriented sequence."[19] Diane Ravitch circulated the report to leading cognitive psychologists and child development authorities. She reported, "None knew of any research justifying the expanding environments approach; none defended it. All deplored the absence of historical and cultural content in the early grades."[20] Other critics of the status quo in elementary social studies education have voiced their objections as well. Most are concerned about low student achievement in history and geography as well as an increasing sense of individualism and apathy toward govern-

FIGURE 1–6

Recommendations of the Task Force on Scope and Sequence (Source: Task Force on Scope and Sequence, "In Search for a Scope and Sequence for Social Studies," Social Education 48, no. 4 (April 1984): pp. 376–385.)

Kindergarten—Awareness of Self in a Social Setting
  Providing socialization experiences that help children bridge their home life with the group life of school.

Grade 1—The Individual in Primary Social Groups: Understanding School and Family Life
  Continuing the socialization process begun in kindergarten, but extending to studies of families (variations in the ways families live, the need for rules and laws)

Grade 2—Meeting Basic Needs in Nearby Social Groups: The Neighborhood
  Studying social functions such as education, production, consumption, communication, and transportation in a neighborhood setting

Grade 3—Sharing Earth-Space with Others: The Community
  Focusing on the community in a global setting, stressing social functions such as production, transportation, communication, distribution, and government

Grade 4—Human Life in Varied Environments: The Region
  Emphasizing the region, an area of the earth defined for a specific reason; the home state is studied as a political region where state regulations require it

Grade 5—People of the Americas: The United States and Its Close Neighbors
  Centering on the development of the United States as a nation in the Western Hemisphere, with particular emphasis on developing affective attachments to the principles on which the nation was founded; Canada and Mexico also studied

Grade 6—People and Cultures: The Eastern Hemisphere
  Focusing on selected people and cultures of the Eastern Hemisphere, directed toward an understanding and appreciation of other people through development of such concepts as language, technology, institutions, and belief systems

Grade 7—A Changing World of Many Nations: A Global View
  Providing an opportunity to broaden the concept of humanity within a global context; focus is on the world as the home of many different people who strive to deal with the forces that shape their lives

Grade 8—Building a Strong and Free Nation: The United States
  Studying the "epic of America," the development of the United States as a strong and free nation; emphasis is on social history and economic development, including cultural and aesthetic dimensions of the American experience

---

ment that are thought to be indicative of a decline of civic life. As a result, sweeping new proposals are being advanced for returning to prominence three social sciences: history, geography, and civics.

A Call for More History

Of the three components of the movement to improve the social studies, none has captured more attention than efforts to bring history into the limelight. Led by such proponents as Diane Ravitch and E. D. Hirsch, Jr., the push to restore history to prominence is founded on concern about students whose knowledge of history is inadequate. (See, for example, the 1989 survey of college seniors conducted by the Gallup Organization for the National Endowment for the Humanities.)[21] This lack of basic historical knowledge has often been associated with the concept of "cultural literacy." The best way to introduce this concept is to offer specific examples. Take a few moments to examine the items in this list; then try to jot down definitions for each term:

non sequitur	wampum	totemism
Cotton Mather	Golan Heights	manifest destiny
Veni, vidi, vici	Doppler effect	beatniks

Did you know them all? Advocates of the cultural literacy movement say that you should. They were taken from a controversial best-selling book, *Cultural Literacy: What Every American Needs to Know* by E. D. Hirsch, Jr.[22] The author argues that there is a basic core of content needed to succeed in our modern world and has compiled a list of 4,662 names, phrases, concepts, historical events, books, and other facts that he believes all Americans should know. Hirsch believes that most youth cannot meaningfully interpret what they are learning in school because they simply lack a background of common general knowledge to help them fill in important gaps.

Hirsch does not stand alone in his insistence that all children should be required to master a common core curriculum. Diane Ravitch and Chester E. Finn[23] analyzed a 1986 assessment of over 7,000 high school juniors and found that U.S. students were ignorant of the most basic facts of American history and literature. Because history and literature are seen by Ravitch and Finn as being the essential studies that help us to interpret the human experience, and it is too late to begin appropriate instruction in high school, the authors recommend that elementary school social studies classes be centered around myths, legends, biographies, and historical literature as sources of rich academic content. They offer no concrete suggestions, but challenge educators to recognize the importance of helping children achieve cultural literacy through the study of history and literature:

> The challenge is to enable students of all backgrounds to understand the relevance of history and literature to the world today and to their own lives; to help them recognize universal themes and dilemmas in literary works written in other ages and other societies; to encourage them to see the significance of historical decisions that were made a hundred or a thousand years ago. You don't have to be Jewish to weep for the men, women, and children who were shepherded into gas chambers during the Holocaust; you don't have to be black to share the despair of the men, women, and children who were crammed into slave ships, bound for a lifetime of slavery in an unknown land. Not only history, but great literature has the capacity to carry us beyond our own ancestry, our immediate sphere.[24]

Adding to the call for a common social studies curriculum rich in history and the humanities is the Bradley Commission on History in Schools.[25] Calling the current social studies curriculum "seriously inadequate," the Commission declared in 1988 that history should have a more vital place in education. To that end, it recommended that the social studies curriculum of grades K–6 be history-centered. The Commission further urged that textbook publishers stop overloading their books with facts and substitute selections of quality literature.

Another major influence causing educators to engage in serious dialogue about the nature of the social studies program is former Education Secretary William Bennett's model curriculum proposal for grades K–8, released in 1987.[26] Entitled *James Madison Elementary School: A Curriculum for Elementary School,* the report chastises the entire elementary school curriculum for its superficial treatment of content. Specifically related to the social studies, Bennett's study cites a lack of coherent structure in programs and calls for acceptance of more traditional content from history, geography, and civics. "No child can think critically or conceptually about American history . . . if he doesn't yet know who George Washington was, or what took place at the Constitutional Convention of 1787," he wrote in an appeal to get back to the basics. "Information—basic content—must come first." Bennett offers a lengthy list of topics for each grade level. History, for example, would be introduced in the primary grades through the study of holidays, customs, important people, and daily life. Curriculum materials would include folk tales, legends, traditional and patriotic songs, and biographies of famous U.S. leaders, scientists, inventors, and explorers. A systematic study of U.S. history was proposed by Bennett for the middle grades, followed by the study of important topics in world history.

The proposals discussed up to this point are considered conceptual in nature; they exist only on paper and have not yet evolved into actual elementary social studies programs. One significant model that has arisen from the "more history, better taught" appeal is the new *California History-Social Science Framework,*[27] a curriculum model offering a common content core rich in history, geography, and the humanities that emphasizes readings from history, mythology, biography, legends, and other forms of literature.

The framework calls for early American history to be offered in grade 5; grade 8 focuses upon the period 1783–1914, and grade eleven centers on the years 1900–present. A 3-year world history sequence covers successive periods in the same way. The temporal interruptions between American and world history courses draw some criticism of the approach. Gilbert Sewall believes that the framework will be so influential as to force publishers to change their products: "California, by turning the searchlight back toward history, will undoubtedly have influence on the ways publishers create social studies and American history textbooks."[28] Sewall's comment reflects the power that large, populous states have, as major consumers of textbooks, to affect content.

Recommendations for More Geography

Reformers have not stopped at an effort to get more history into the social studies curriculum. Although history appears to be making the headlines, those concerned about the lack of geographic knowledge among our youth say that, by some measures, geography has experienced a more serious decline than history. Gilbert M. Grosvenor, president of the National Geographic Society, pointed to an informal quiz that compared the level of geographic knowledge demonstrated by college students of 1984 to those of 1950.[29] Here are some of the findings: In 1950, 46% could name all the Great Lakes; in 1984, the result was 12%. Responding to the question, "In what country is the Amazon River mainly found?" only 27% correctly named Brazil in 1984, as compared to 78% in 1950. Overall, 95% of college students tested in 1984 scored below the passing grade of 70, while three-fourths scored below 50%. If we realize the world according to some of the 1984 responses, Africa would be in North America, the USSR would border Panama, and the "state" of Atlanta would abut North Carolina. "You have to realize just how bad the situation is," says Bill Honig, California Superintendent of Public Instruction. "Our students are more illiterate in geography than in anything else."[30] Adding to this disturbing array of data, in 1988 the Gallup Organization found that of nine nations studied, Americans aged 18–24 ranked last on a test of geographic literacy.[31] The National Geographic Society (NGS) has spearheaded efforts to improve and extend the role of geography in our nation's elementary school programs. In 1988 the NGS initiated a $40 million effort to improve geographic study in the schools. As part of this initiative, the NGS has sponsored a national "Geography Bee" that began in 1989. Similarly, the National Council for Geographic Education sponsors the National Geographic Olympiad, open to students in grades 4–8. To promote geography awareness nationally, Congress in 1988 created Geography Awareness Week by joint resolution, a result of legislation initiated by Senator Bill Bradley of New Jersey. Geography Awareness Week occurs in the month of November. Additionally, two major geography organizations (the National Council for Geographic Education [NCGE] and the Association of American Geographers [AAG]) have combined their efforts to provide a model of what content needs to be taught.

Their blueprint is contained in the joint committee's publication *Guidelines for Geographic Education.*[32] Another critical contribution to the improvement of geography instruction has come from the Geographic Education National Implementation Project (GENIP),[33] an organization involving all of the professional groups discussed so far. Their "themes" were described in Figure 1–4. Their suggested "learning opportunities" for each theme furnish a helpful guide for geography instruction (see Chapter 12).

Although geographic educators have been bemoaning the status of geography in our social studies programs for many years, it was not until the late 1980s that the educational system in general was ready to address the deficiencies. GENIP's feeling of rejection must now be tempered with optimism, for if the California framework can be used as an indication of where we are headed, many programs will be guided by its assertion that history and geography are the two great integrative studies of the field.

Suggestions for Expanding Civics

The fervent cry to establish history and geography as the organizing core of social studies instruction is based on a strong concern for our students' dismal performance on tests of geography and history. Civics, too, has been singled out as a fundamental social science, but its advocacy is based not so deeply in test results as it is in the failure of our country's citizens to respond directly to such critical civic problems as drug abuse, crime, and dishonesty in government. Walter C. Parker says that near the heart of the problem is a pervading condition of "individualism."[34] Parker cites de Tocqueville's 150-year-old description of individualism to define what he means:

> Individualism is a calm and considered feeling which disposes each citizen to isolate himself from the mass of his fellows and withdraw into the circle of family and friends; with this little society formed to his taste, he gladly leaves the greater society to look after itself.[35]

Parker believes that the demise of civic life today is directly linked to individualism. Where can such an attitude lead? According to Parker, "no one knows to what it may lead. Political chaos, economic collapse, urban warfare, a quiet lapse into tyranny, or something less dramatic—anything is possible."[36] Fred M. Newman agrees with this outlook and warns that our schools must change: "Only recently have we come to understand how the dominant conception of . . . teaching civics . . . weakens civic culture. . . . [It] threatens the very survival of the human species and the planet."[37] These critiques of civic life send educators powerful messages about the nature of their social studies program. Educators are challenged today with the idea that democracy cannot exist without its citizenry assuming an active role: serving in civic or political office (PTA, town council, etc.), writing letters to the editor, deliberating and debating public policy, working for public interest groups, and voting. John J. Cogan maintains that active participation as adult citizens begins in school when "students and their teachers [become] active participants in the society. . . . How else does one ensure active participation as adults if this is not learned naturally in the living laboratory represented by the school . . .?"[38] Walter C. Parker recommends that schools move toward this mission on three fronts: "(1) they can help students acquire in-depth knowledge of history and politics, (2) they can conduct themselves as communities, continually exploring what community entails, and (3) they can provide rich opportunities for students to participate in democratic practices, such as rigorous discussion of real public problems, past and present."[39] JoAnn Shaheen has developed an impressive program of participatory citizenship for elementary students called SAC V (Student Advisory Council, Fifth Grade).[40] The program is based on the philosophy of involving students actively in a democratic classroom where real problems in school life are discussed openly and resolved during group meetings. Peggy Cahoon, an elementary school principal, reflected on the number and types of social problems her children encountered at school, and created the Mediator Program.[41] The program gives students opportunities to serve as mediators to solve small problems before they escalate into more cumbersome ones.

These issues and initial attempts to create classroom strategies are based on the belief that democratic society flourishes only when its citizens are active, involved, and knowledgeable about the process of government. The goal of these programs, and others that will surely emerge during the 1990s, is to help students reflect on their civic commitments—to generate excitement about the quest for public good and to diminish the pervasive apathy about democratic participation that some have labeled "individualism."

There have been no definitive data indicating the impact of these appeals on curriculum reform in our nation's elementary schools at the time of this writing. Whether or not these programs, or those that follow, result in significant change in the way social studies is taught depends upon the willingness of teachers and school districts to implement them. You may be interested in learning more about them. If so, the following sources will be of help.

Diane Ravitch and Chester Finn, Jr., *What Do Our 17-Year-Olds Know?* (New York: Harper & Row, 1987).

E. D. Hirsch, Jr., *Cultural Literacy: What Every American Needs to Know* (Boston: Houghton Mifflin, 1987).

Bradley Commission on History, "Building a History Curriculum," Educational Excellence Network, 1112 16th Street, N.W., Suite 500, Washington, DC 20036 (1988).

James Madison Elementary School, Superintendent of Documents, U.S. Government Printing Office, Washington, DC 20402 (1987).

California History - Social Science Framework, Bureau of Publications Sales, California State Department of Education, P.O. Box 271, Sacramento, CA 95802-0271 (1988).

National Commission on Social Studies in the Schools, *Charting a Course: Social Studies for the 21st Century* (Washington, DC: National Commission on Social Studies in the Schools, 1989).

Recommendations for Social Studies Programs for the Twenty-first Century

The educational reforms of recent years have awakened educators and the public to substantial weaknesses in our current social studies programs. Most reform programs have been supported by the National Council for the Social Studies and other influential professional groups, but some, as noble as their efforts were, have "fragmented and often marginalized the field of social studies"[42] with their emphases on teaching the separate disciplines (history, geography, civics) without considering their relationship to the whole curriculum. Concern over this lack of coherence led the governing bodies of the American Historical Association and the National Council for the Social Studies to call for a national commission to recommend ways to strengthen the teaching of social studies. These two organizations and others established the National Commission on Social Studies in the Schools. The commission examined the content and effectiveness of social studies instruction, determined goals for social studies curricula, and established priorities for the field. In 1989, the commission's Curriculum Task Force disseminated its findings to the educational community and the general public. Its vision for a comprehensive social studies program for the twenty-first century is shown in Figure 1–7.

Emphasizing Content and Process

Popular curriculum revision efforts are based on the idea that the traditional expanding environment approach is outdated; our youngsters are growing up without acquiring the essential knowledge needed for informed, thinking citizenship in a democratic

FIGURE 1–7

Recommendations from the National Commission on Social Studies (Source: National Commission on Social Studies in the Schools, Charting a Course: Social Studies for the 21st Century *(Washington, DC: National Commission on Social Studies in the Schools, 1989.)*

- A well-developed social studies curriculum must instill a clear understanding of the roles of citizens in a democracy and provide opportunities for active, engaged participation in civic, cultural, and volunteer activities designed to enhance the quality of life in the community and in the nation.
- A complete social studies curriculum provides for *consistent* and *cumulative* learning from *kindergarten* through *12th grade.* At each grade level, students should build upon knowledge and skills already learned and should receive preparation for the levels yet to come.
- Because they offer the perspectives of time and place, history and geography should provide the matrix or framework for social studies; yet concepts and understandings from political science, economics, and the other social sciences must be integrated throughout all social studies courses so that by the end of 12th grade, students will have a firm understanding of their principles and methodologies.
- Selective studies of the history, geography, government, and economic systems of the major civilizations and societies should together receive

attention at least equal to the study of the history, geography, government, economics, and society of the United States.

- Social studies provides the obvious connection between the humanities and the natural and physical sciences. Integration of other studies should be encouraged whenever possible in order to help students see the interrelationships among branches of knowledge.
- Content knowledge from the social studies should not be treated merely as received knowledge to be accepted and memorized, but as the means through which open and vital questions may be explored and confronted. Students must be made aware that just as contemporary events have been shaped by actions taken by people in the past, they themselves have the capacity to shape the future.
- Reading, writing, observing, debating, role-play in mock trials or simulations, working with statistical data, and using appropriate critical thinking skills should be an integral part of social studies instruction. Teaching strategies should help students become both independent and cooperative learners who develop skills of

problem solving, decision making, negotiation, and conflict resolution.

- Learning materials must incorporate a rich mix of written matter, including original sources, literature, and expository writing; a variety of audiovisual materials including films, television, and interactive media; a collection of items of material culture including artifacts, photographs, census records, and historical maps; and computer programs for writing and analyzing social, economic, and geographic data. Social studies coursework should teach students to evaluate the reliability of all such sources of information and to be aware of the ways in which various media select, shape, and constrain information.
- The core of essential knowledge to be incorporated in the instructional program at every level must be selective enough to provide time for extended in-depth study and must be directed toward the ultimate goal of social studies education—the development of thoughtful Americans who have the capacities for living effective personal and public lives.

society. These innovators take the position that all children in our country need to be brought together within a common core curriculum. Walter C. Parker summarizes their thoughts:

> Their argument is a cultural and moral one: because our society is democratic, *everybody must* be educated. Furthermore, this education must have a common content core. Once they have acquired it, new members of a democracy (both children and immigrants) are equipped for continued learning and for responsible participation in the community life of the nation.[43]

To content innovators, good citizens are those individuals who master a predetermined core of content; their pleas have been so forcefully made that some have interpreted them as calls for patriotic drill and memorization of core content. Thomas H. Estes, Carol J. Gutman, and Elise K. Harrison warn against such narrow interpretations:

> The hardest lesson for any educator . . . to learn is that *telling* is not *teaching, told* is not *taught*. The conception of teaching as transmission . . . ignores the central role of the learner in learning.
>
> Meaning derives from the learner's participation in learning. Most students today undoubtedly view the purpose of their education as information acquisition, while most teachers view their work as information transmission. As a result, students are graduating to the worlds of work and higher education in possession of varying amounts of knowledge but without the understandings that would make the content of instruction memorable. . . . Students will not remember this content when they have not attached meaning to it.[44]

What can teachers do to make their social studies instruction more effective? They must provide opportunities for students to go beyond the simple acquisition of knowledge; they must offer situations where students use what they know to reason, to analyze, to create, and to evaluate. The NCSS Task Force on Early Childhood/Elementary Social Studies supports this curriculum consideration:

> For children to develop citizenship skills appropriate to a democracy, they must be capable of thinking critically about complex societal problems and global problems. Teachers must arrange the classroom environment to promote data gathering, discussion, and critical reasoning by students. Another important aspect of citizenship is that of decision maker. Children must acquire the skills of decision making, but also study the process that occurs as groups make decisions. Continually accelerating technology has created and will continue to create rapid changes in society. Children need to be equipped with the skills to cope with change.[45]

Elementary school social studies programs are strongly concerned with the development of thinking skills, that is, the ability to use information to find order in the world and solve problems. This is proper, because the social studies curriculum possesses the richness of content so basic for effective thinking skills acquisition. *Thinking and content* are clearly an inseparable combination in quality elementary social studies programs.

DESIGNING A THINKING SKILLS FRAMEWORK

Although the emphasis on thinking skills instruction is a valid instructional goal, the actual attainment of that goal is not so easy as one might hope. One of the greatest impediments to a thinking skills program is that we are missing a common description of an organizing framework for teaching thinking upon which teachers can organize their instructional strategies. It is virtually impossible for teachers to gain insight into the various dimensions of thinking proficiency when educational psychologists and educators remain unsettled in their descriptions of the specific thinking attributes considered central to effective teaching.

Barry K. Beyer has proposed a specific framework of thinking operations that are repeatedly used in all subject areas, commonly used outside of school, and often identified by experts as significant thinking operations. These delineations are shown in Table 1–3. Do not be confused or discouraged by the long list; it is shown only to illustrate the array of skills associated with effective thinking.

Bloom's taxonomy[46] (see Chapter 3) is another popular system that has served as a guide for developing thinking skills in the social studies classroom for nearly 30 years. These are but two of the frequently cited explanations of the thinking processes involved in social studies instruction. Which is the most usable and useful? Roger Farr and Sam Weintraub respond:

> Psychologists have been attempting to get a hold on the thinking process for decades . . . Yet, for all their efforts, we still have but a limited understanding of only some of the more superficial behaviors related to thinking. Inasmuch as this is true, we are naive to expect educational research to provide us with answers to teach a specific kind of thinking behavior.[47]

In other words, despite all the valiant efforts to describe what goes on in one's mind as an individual tries to make sense of our fascinating world, we do not have at this time a conclusive description of the thinking process. Recognizing this limitation, I have chosen to synthesize Beyer's and Bloom's theories discussed so far into these special thinking skills operations:

1. *Content Acquisition*—a thinking skill that involves an intake of information and the processing of that information into higher-order concepts and generalizations.
2. *Problem Solving*—a thinking skill that calls for recognizing problems, hypothesizing about the problem, executing a plan of attack, collecting, analyzing, and using appropriate data and evaluating the results to form accurate conclusions.
3. *Critical Thinking*—a thinking skill that helps students analyze information carefully, examine valid evidence, and reach sound conclusions.
4. *Evaluative Thinking*—a thinking skill that involves personal feelings or attitudes. Values are achieved after analyzing alternatives, ranking alternatives, and choosing the best alternative.

Chapters 4 through 8 will be topically arranged so that these four thinking skills will each be highlighted within separate thematic discussions. This organizational pattern has been chosen so that you can more clearly distinguish how thinking skills can be

TABLE 1–3
Major Thinking Skills and Strategies

I. Thinking Strategies

Problem-Solving
1. Recognize a problem
2. Represent the problem
3. Devise/choose solution plan
4. Execute the plan
5. Evaluate the solution

Decision-Making
1. Define the goal
2. Identify alternatives
3. Analyze alternatives
4. Rank alternatives
5. Judge highest ranked alternatives
6. Choose "best" alternative

Conceptualizing
1. Identify examples
2. Identify common attributes
3. Classify attributes
4. Interrelate categories of attributes
5. Identify additional examples/ nonexamples
6. Modify concept attributes/ structure

II. Critical Thinking Skills

1. Distinguishing between verifiable facts and value claims
2. Distinguishing relevant from irrelevant information, claims, or reasons
3. Determining the factual accuracy of a statement
4. Determining the credibility of a source
5. Identifying ambiguous claims or arguments
6. Identifying unstated assumptions
7. Detecting bias
8. Identifying logical fallacies
9. Recognizing logical inconsistencies in a line of reasoning
10. Determining the strength of an argument or a claim

III. Information Processing Skills

1. Recall
2. Translation
3. Interpretation
4. Extrapolation
5. Application
6. Analysis (compare, contrast, classify, seriate, etc.)
7. Synthesis
8. Evaluation
9. Reasoning (inferencing): inductive deductive analogical

Source: Barry K. Beyer, "Developing a Scope and Sequence for Thinking Skills Instruction," *Educational Leadership, 45,* no. 7 (April 1988): p. 27.

developed within the social studies curriculum. Overall, the goal of such arrangement is to recognize the plea of such philosophers as John H. Chambers, who writes:

> What we require are teachers who know their disciplines in depth . . . who understand the structure of their particular discipline and how it is different from other disciplines and who can pass on such awareness to their students . . . [To do this, we] do not require a new breed of specialist teachers of an illusory "discipline" called "thinking skills." We need good teachers who can make children *think in the particular discipline the teacher is teaching.*[48]

The future of effective social studies instruction is in the hands of dedicated teachers filled with a desire to make learning interesting. Much of the current discussion of thinking skills involves a perception that this is a new area of knowledge and that to be able to carry it out in the classroom, one must scrap all that has been done and create something quite different from the curriculum we have been teaching. In effect, we might be coerced into the idea that a course in "thinking skills" needs to establish a niche in the school curriculum alongside traditional subjects such as reading or math. But thinking skills do not exist separately; they must be introduced and extended within particular disciplines, such as those in the social studies, having particular structures of knowledge and techniques of investigating problems. Thinking provides the skeletal framework upon which young citizens can mold the knowledge, skills, and attitudes necessary for becoming responsible members of a democratic society.

DEVELOPING GOOD CITIZENS

The primary reason for educating our youth, even from the earliest days of schooling in our nation, has been the development of good citizens. Walter C. Parker reasons that today especially, all other purposes are secondary:

> Schools must remember that they are *not* primarily for helping children acquire jobs, get into college, or develop a better self-concept. As worthy as these goals may be, they are less important than the school's distinctly *civic* mission: to educate students to be capable of—and passionately committed to—meeting the challenges of the democratic way of life.[49]

Despite this common agreement on the goal of citizenship, social studies educators had failed for well over one hundred years to reach agreement on what a "good citizen" should be. In the past, the social studies field has vacillated among three teaching traditions to achieve this noble goal: citizenship transmission, social studies taught as a social science, and social studies taught as reflective inquiry (see Table 1–4).

Clearly, the oldest and most frequently used teaching tradition is *citizenship transmission*. Nearly all cultures use this approach, especially if they have a particular vision of citizenship they wish all students to share in order to guarantee the survival of their political system. Therefore, the common core knowledge, beliefs, and values of a culture are identified and then transmitted to the young.

In our democracy, for example, many of our schools teach the mechanics of government, the heritage of our nation, an appreciation of our rich multi-ethnic character, and loyalty to our leaders, and they involve the children in such rituals as reciting the pledge of allegiance or singing the national anthem.

The *social science* tradition is also firmly entrenched, with historical roots that go back before 1900 when historians argued impressively that their discipline contained the most fruitful knowledge and processes of inquiry to guarantee effective citizenship. Through the years, geographers, political scientists, sociologists, anthropologists, and economists all have evolved special techniques to help students perceive the world from their viewpoint. Students are expected to use methods of inquiry associated with each social science to think and reason in a manner closely approximating the mature social scientists.

TABLE 1–4
The Three Social Studies Traditions

	1. Social Studies Taught as Citizenship Transmission	2. Social Studies Taught as Social Science	3. Social Studies Taught as Reflective Inquiry
Purpose	Citizenship is best promoted by inculcating right values as a framework for making decisions.	Citizenship is best promoted by decision making based on mastery of social science concepts, processes, and problems.	Citizenship is best promoted through a process of inquiry in which knowledge is derived from what citizens need to know to make decisions and solve problems.
Method	Transmission: Transmission of concepts and values by such techniques as textbook, recitation, lecture, question and answer sessions, and structured problem-solving exercises.	Discovery: Each of the social sciences has its own method of gathering and verifying knowledge. Students should discover and apply the method that is appropriate to each social science.	Reflective Inquiry: Decision making is structured and disciplined through a reflective inquiry process which aims at identifying problems and responding to conflicts by means of testing insights.
Content	Content is selected by an authority interpreted by the teacher and has the function of illustrating values, beliefs, and attitudes.	Proper content is the structure, concepts, problems, and processes of both the separate and the integrated social science disciplines.	Analysis of individual citizen's values yields needs and interests which, in turn, form the basis for student self-selection of problems. Problems, therefore, constitute the content for reflection.

Source: Robert D. Barr, James L. Barth, and Samuel S. Shermis, *Defining the Social Studies* (Washington, DC: National Council for the Social Studies, 1977), p. 67. Reprinted from *NCSS Bulletin No. 51.*

The *reflective inquiry* tradition is also steeped in history. It is based on an idea that good citizens should be able to make good decisions. The assumption is that a democracy presents its citizens with unique responsibilities and problems (e.g., choosing leaders, drug abuse) that must be faced together. The goal of reflective inquiry is to develop decision-making skills necessary to resolve such issues in an informed way. Content is not selected from the social sciences per se, but evolves as students delve into solving personal or social problems such as, "What can our community do about its trash disposal problem?" or "Why was the voter turnout so low for this election?"

Categories of Social Studies Instructional Objectives

Today, these three traditions appear to be drawing together rather than moving apart. After decades of heated disagreement, there is general (but not unanimous) agreement that the traditions offer a framework for organizing the essentials of social studies instruction. Examine the "Essentials of Exemplary Social Studies Programs" in Figure 1–8. They were conceived by the NCSS in 1979 to identify the major objectives of social studies programs deemed appropriate for good citizenship. Try to associate to each of the three traditions we have just examined the four objectives categories of the Exemplary Social Studies Programs document: (1) knowledge, (2) democratic beliefs, (3) thinking skills, and (4) participation skills.

LIFELONG LEARNING

By engaging children in positive social studies experiences that offer them opportunities to interact productively with the subject matter and among themselves, we are working toward the fulfillment of our primary responsibility of helping children attain the understandings, skills, and attitudes that will last a lifetime. For, as presented in *A Nation at Risk,* a critical educational report of the 1980s,

> educational reform should focus on the goal of creating a learning society. At the heart of such a society is the commitment to a set of values and to a system of education that affords all members the opportunity to stretch their minds to full capacity, from early childhood through adulthood, learning more as the world changes. . . . In our view, formal schooling in youth is the essential foundation for learning throughout one's life. But without lifelong learning one's skills will become rapidly dated.[50]

At the roots of a democracy are knowledgeable and thoughtful citizens comprising a learning and learned society. Of course, they have many other qualities, too, but high on the list of behavior for democratic citizens is *thinking for themselves.* Democracy requires individuals who are able to search for and examine the facts whenever they must make up their minds about important issues. Those issues might be related to one's personal life or to complex international concerns; regardless, the protection of our freedoms lies in the hands of rational people. Such skills must be started during the early years with a flexible social studies curriculum that offers meaningful experiences to all. All youngsters must find something to excite their interest and stimulate their thinking. A one-dimensional approach to social studies instruction cannot do this. We fail our children with our narrowness; if our myopic view of teaching has caused them to feel stupid or to be bored, we have lost. Learning for an informed citizenry is too important to be thought of as something that everyone must be able to do in any single way. The danger to our future is great when we restrict the adventuresome, "can-do" spirit of childhood. Therefore, our social studies program for the 1990s must be one that prizes lifelong learning through the use of various teaching strategies that promote functional thinking skills. The probing, wondering mind of childhood must be freed. Our society of tomorrow starts in your classroom today.

FIGURE 1–8 (pp. 31–32)

Essentials of Exemplary Social Studies Programs (Source: "Essentials of the Social Studies," Social Education, 45, *no. 3 (March 1981): 163–164.)*

Citizen participation in public life is essential to the health of our democratic system. Effective social studies programs help prepare young people who can identify, understand and work to solve the problems that face our increasingly diverse nation and interdependent world.

KNOWLEDGE

Students need knowledge of the world at large and the world at hand, the world of individuals and the world of institutions, the world past, the world present and future. An exemplary social studies curriculum links information prsented in the classroom with experiences gained by students through social and civic observation, analysis and participation.

Classroom instruction which relates content to information drawn from the media and from experience focuses on the following areas of knowledge:

History and culture of our nation and the world.

Geography—physical, political, cultural and economic.

Government—theories, systems, structures and processes.

Economics—theories, systems, structures and processes.

Social institutions—the individual, the group, the community and the society.

Intergroup and interpersonal relationships.

Worldwide relationships of all sorts between and among nations, races, cultures and institutions.

From this knowledge base, exemplary programs teach skills, concepts and generalizations that can help students understand the sweep of human affairs and ways of managing conflict consistent with democratic procedures.

DEMOCRATIC BELIEFS

Fundamental beliefs drawn from the Declaration of Independence and the United States Constitution with its Bill of Rights form the basic principles of our democratic constitutional order. Exemplary school programs do not indoctrinate students to accept these ideas blindly, but present knowledge about their historical derivation and contemporary application essential to understanding our society and its institutions. Not only should such ideas be discussed as they relate to the curriculum and to current affairs, they should also be mirrored by teachers in their classrooms and embodied in the school's daily operations.

These democratic beliefs depend upon such practices as due process, equal protection and civic participation, and are rooted in the concepts of:

Justice

Equality

Responsibility

Freedom

Diversity

Privacy

THINKING SKILLS

It is important that students connect knowledge with beliefs and action. To do that, thinking skills can be developed through constant systematic practice throughout the years of formal schooling. Fundamental to the goals of social studies education are those skills which help assure rational behavior in social settings.

In addition to strengthening reading and computation, there is a wide variety of thinking skills essential to the social studies which can be grouped into four major categories:

FIGURE 1–8
Continued

Data-Gathering Skills. Learning to:

    Acquire information by observation

    Locate information from a variety of sources

    Compile, organize, and evaluate information

    Extract and interpret information

    Communicate orally and in writing

Intellectual Skills. Learning to:

    Compare things, ideas, events, and situations on the basis of similarities and differences

    Classify or group items in categories

    Ask appropriate and searching questions

    Draw conclusions or inferences from evidence

    Arrive at general ideas

    Make sensible predictions from generalizations

Decision-Making Skills. Learning to:

    Consider alternative solutions

    Consider the consequences of each solution

    Make decisions and justify them in relationship to democratic principles

    Act, based on those decisions

Interpersonal Skills. Learning to:

    See things from the point of view of others

    Understand one's own beliefs, feelings, abilities, and shortcomings and how they affect relations with others

    Use group generalizations without stereotyping and arbitrarily classifying individuals

    Recognize value in individuals different from one's self and groups different from one's own

    Work effectively with others as a group member

    Give and receive constructive criticism

    Accept responsibility and respect the rights and property of others

PARTICIPATION SKILLS

As a civic participant, the individual uses the knowledge, beliefs, and skills learned in the school, the social studies classroom, the community, and the family as the basis for action.

    Connecting the classroom with the community provides many opportunities for students to learn the basic skills of participation, from observation to advocacy. To teach participation, social studies programs need to emphasize the following kinds of skills:

    Work effectively in groups—organizing, planning, making decisions, taking action

    Form coalitions of interest with other groups

    Persuade, compromise, bargain

    Practice patience and perserverance in working for one's goal

    Develop experience in cross-cultural situations

SUMMARY

Every society prepares its young members to assume expected roles through some form of education. Using whatever educative process it chooses, the social group strives to ensure its perpetuation by passing on its heritage and traditions, laws and regulations, feelings of loyalty and unity, and values and morals. To achieve citizenship qualities is an enormous task, especially in a society as complex as that found in the United States.

This chapter has introduced you to several basic issues in social studies education, ranging from determining a definition of social studies to considering the characteristics of good citizens. We have examined a definition formulated by the NCSS Task Force on Early Childhood/Elementary Social Studies and some of the dynamics causing the social studies field to change from what it was at its inception to what it is today. We learned that the field is rife with disagreements about its very nature, but that there are three areas in which we can find general agreement today: (1) the content should be drawn from the social sciences, (2) the instructional objectives should be varied, but emphasize the acquisition of high-order thinking skills, and (3) the major goal of social studies education should be "citizenship." You were introduced to the six social sciences that are integrated into today's social studies programs (history, geography, civics, economics, sociology, anthropology) and learned that the tradi-

tional pattern of organizing them for instruction is called the *expanding environment* approach. You learned that the expanding environment approach, after remaining popular for over fifty years, has come under fire today, especially from advocates of history, geography, and civics who insist that these three social sciences should form the core of a social studies program for the 1990s. Citing low test scores and apathetic citizenry, these groups have rallied around the ideas of civic (or cultural) literacy and strong (or participatory) citizenship. We have examined the need to promote higher-order thinking skills (how to process information, analyze issues, make decisions, solve problems) by treating knowledge as part of a total educational process rather than as information to be added to living trivia libraries. Finally, we examined the three traditions of social studies education (citizenship transmission, social studies taught as a social science, and social studies taught as reflective inquiry) and considered how they appear to be moving together in today's social studies curriculum. The outcome of this alliance helps form a framework for contemporary social studies education that takes form around a framework of four objectives described as "Essentials of Exemplary Social Studies Programs" by the NCSS: (1) knowledge, (2) democratic beliefs, (3) thinking skills, and (4) participatory skills.

ENDNOTES

1. "Social Studies for Early Childhood and Elementary School Children Preparing for the 21st Century, A Report from NCSS Task Force on Early Childhood/Elementary Social Studies." *Social Education, 53,* no. 1 (January 1989): 15.

2. National Education Association, *The Social Studies in Secondary Education,* a report of the Com-

mittee on Social Studies, Bulletin no. 28 (Washington, DC: Bureau of Education, 1916), p. 5.

3. Robert D. Barr, James L. Barth, and Samuel S. Shermis, *Defining the Social Studies* (Washington, DC: National Council for the Social Studies, 1977), p. 1.

4. Arthur Bestor, *Restoration of Learning* (New York: Alfred A. Knopf, 1955), p. 126.

, 5. Barr, Barth, and Shermis, *Defining the Social Studies*, p. 57.

6. Shirley Crenshaw, et al., "Teaching History Across the Elementary Curriculum," *Social Studies and the Young Learner, 2*, no. 2 (November/December 1989): p. 1, special pullout feature.

7. Bradley Commission on History in Schools, *Building a History Curriculum* (Washington, DC: Educational Excellence Network, 1988), p. 25.

8. Joint Committee on Geographic Education, *Guidelines for Geographic Education* (Washington, DC: The Association of American Geographers, 1984), p. 2.

9. Ibid., p. 2.

10. Benjamin R. Barber, "Public Talk and Civic Action: Education for Participation in a Strong Democracy," *Social Education, 53*, no. 6 (October 1989): 355.

11. Ibid.

12. Walter C. Parker, "Participatory Citizenship: Civics in the Strong Sense," *Social Education, 53*, no. 6 (October 1989): 353–354.

13. Walter C. Parker, "How to Help Students Learn History and Geography," *Educational Leadership, 47*, no. 3 (November 1989): 42.

14. W. Lee Hansen, "Economics," in *Charting a Course: Social Studies for the 21st Century* (Washington, DC: National Commission on Social Studies in the Schools, 1989), p. 38.

15. Paul R. Hanna, "Revising the Social Studies: What Is Needed?" *Social Education, 27*, no. 4 (April 1963): 190–196.

16. Task Force on Scope and Sequence, "In Search for a Scope and Sequence for Social Studies," *Social Education, 48*, no. 4 (April 1984): 252–253.

17. Ronald G. Helms, "Reaction to 'In Search for a Scope and Sequence for Social Studies,' " *Social Education, 48*, no. 4 (April 1984): 264.

18. R. Freeman Butts, "Reaction to 'In Search for a Scope and Sequence for Social Studies,' " *Social Education, 48*, no. 4 (April 1984): 263.

19. Geraldine Hellman-Rosenthal, "Reaction to 'In Search for a Scope and Sequence for Social Studies,' " *Social Education, 48*, no. 4 (April 1984): 264.

20. Diane Ravitch, "Tot Sociology," *American Educator, 12*, no. 3 (Fall 1988): 39.

21. *A Survey of College Seniors—Knowledge of History and Literature,* Washington, DC: National Endowment for the Humanities.

22. E. D. Hirsch, Jr., *Cultural Literacy: What Every American Needs to Know* (Boston: Houghton Mifflin, 1987).

23. Diane Ravitch and Chester E. Finn, *What Do Our 17-Year-Olds Know?* (New York: Harper & Row, 1987).

24. Diane Ravitch and Chester E. Finn, in Paul Gagnon, "Content Counts," *American Educator, 11*, no. 4 (Winter 1987): 43.

25. Bradley Commission on History in Schools, *Building a History Curriculum* (Washington, DC: Educational Excellence Network, 1988).

26. William Bennett, *James Madison Elementary School* (Washington, DC: U.S. Government Printing Office, 1987).

27. *California History-Social Science Framework* (Sacramento, CA: California State Department of Education, 1988).

28. Gilbert Sewall in "Framework Will Force Textbook Changes," *ASCD Update, 30*, no. 1 (January 1988): 2.

29. Gilbert M. Grosvenor, "Geographic Ignorance: Time for a Turnaround," *National Geographic, 167*, no. 6 (June 1985): editorial page.

30. Bill Honig, keynote speaker, Conference on Geography in the California Curriculum, Los Angeles (UCLA), August 1986.

31. "Social Studies: Charting a Course for a Field Adrift," *ASCD Curriculum Update* (November 1989): 2.

32. Joint Committee on Geographic Education, *Guidelines for Geographic Education* (Washington, DC: The Association of American Geographers, 1984).

33. Geography Education National Implementation Project Committee on K–6 Geography, *K–6 Geography: Themes, Key Ideas, and Learning Opportunities* (Washington, DC: Geographic Education National Implementation Project, 1987).

34. Walter C. Parker, "Participatory Citizenship: Civics in the Strong Sense," pp. 353–354.

35. A. de Tocqueville, *Democracy in America,* trans. G. Lawrence, ed. J. P. Mayer (New York: Doubleday, Anchor Books, 1969), p. 506. (Original work published 1835–1839.)

36. Walter C. Parker, "Participatory Citizenship," p. 353.

37. Fred M. Newman, "Reflective Civic Participation," *Social Education, 53,* no. 6 (October 1989): 357.

38. John J. Cogan, "The Continuing Vigil for Democracy, Part II," *Social Education, 53,* no. 6 (October 1989): 341.

39. Walter C. Parker, "Participatory Citizenship," p. 353.

40. JoAnn C. Shaheen, "Participatory Citizenship in the Elementary Grades," *Social Education, 53,* no. 6 (October 1989): 361–363.

41. Peggy Cahoon, "Peer Mediation," *Social Education, 53,* no. 6 (October 1989): 363.

42. National Commission on Social Studies in the Schools, *Charting a Course: Social Studies for the 21st Century* (Washington, DC: National Commission on Social Studies in the Schools, 1989), p. v.

43. Walter C. Parker, "Both of the Above," *Educational Leadership, 46,* no. 3 (November 1988): 84.

44. Thomas H. Estes, Carol J. Gutman, and Elise K. Harrison, "Cultural Literacy: What Every Educator Needs to Know," *Educational Leadership, 46,* no. 1 (September 1988): p. 17.

45. NCSS Task Force on Early Childhood/Elementary Social Studies, "Social Studies for Early Childhood and Elementary School Children Preparing for the 21st Century," *Social Education, 53,* no. 1 (January 1989): 16.

46. Benjamin S. Bloom, ed. *Taxonomy of Educational Objectives—Cognitive Domain* (New York: Longman, 1956).

47. Roger Farr and Sam Weintraub, "Editorial: An Argument for Research," *Reading Research Quarterly, 9,* no. 2 (1973–1974): 131–132.

48. John H. Chambers, "Teaching Thinking Throughout the Curriculum—Where Else?" *Educational Leadership, 45,* no. 7 (April 1988): 5–6.

49. Walter C. Parker, "How to Help Students Learn History and Geography," p. 39.

50. National Commission on Excellence in Education, *A Nation at Risk: The Imperative for Educational Reform* (Washington, DC: U.S. Government Printing Office, 1983), pp. 13–14.

"When I die, I hope it will be my good fortune to go where Miss Blake will meet me and lead me to my seat."

—*Bernard M. Baruch*

2 Becoming a Social Studies Teacher

As you read, reflect on the following matters:

- What personality characteristics should effective social studies teachers display?
- Why are positive personality characteristics important?
- What professional characteristics do effective social studies teachers possess?
- How do professional preparation programs contribute to the acquisition of those professional characteristics?
- Why is it important to continually grow as a person and a professional once a person's initial certification requirements have been met?

Bernard Baruch's teacher obviously made a significant impact on his life. Like Baruch, we all hold precious memories of a special teacher who made some aspect of school gratifying for us, too. It may be that your own "Miss Blake" influenced you, perhaps even so much as to sway you to choose teaching as a career. Through their actions and attitudes, these memorable individuals exhibit the qualities of superior teachers. A group of confident, happy, active children reflect the masterful touch of a Miss Blake, someone who is able to pull together all the essential qualities of an educational program so that every child's special interests and needs are met through a wide range of stimulating learning experiences.

Despite the problems that face social studies education, there are examples of superb teaching everywhere. Many programs are excellent, built by teachers who have a sound knowledge of why they are teaching, whom they are teaching, what they are teaching, and how they are teaching.

Becoming a teacher is a momentous goal and a rewarding one. Special people work with children; they understand the long-range implications of their work not only as it affects children but also as it affects families, communities, and even the nation or world. That responsibility cannot be taken lightly, and the purpose of this text is to help you develop strategies and attitudes appropriate for establishing positive classroom practices. To achieve this goal, this book will fuse personal and professional components of teaching to show that teaching is done *with* children rather than *to* them.

At one time or another we all must have had at least one "Miss Blake" for social studies class: teachers who obviously enjoyed their work and the children they taught. They may have been *entertainers:* free enough to have fun with the children and bring a flair for the dramatic to their work. They may have been *intellectuals:* intensely interested in knowledge and its transmission to children. They may have been *directors:* shouting out, "You're in my classroom now and we'll operate by my rules." They may have been *recapitulators:* repeating everything taught until they were sure everyone understood. You may have had one of these teachers, unique individuals who found a special way of becoming successful at what they did. Who were those people? What special characteristics did they display? After thinking about these questions, you may wonder how there could be so many different yet successful teachers. The discussion of teacher characteristics is a routine topic not only for educators but also for parents and other concerned citizens. Each constituency is passionately absorbed in the quest to determine what makes one teacher better than another. As a teacher, you will be subject to this scrutiny—so much so that you will often become a topic of discussion around the family dinner table. Phyllis Naylor elaborates:

> Over our dinner table, we have heard about the teacher who threw chalk at the blackboard when he was angry, and the one who assigned as punishment a 500-word essay on fairness.
>
> They certainly made for interesting table conversation, much better than a prolonged discussion about meat loaf. But we have heard a large number of indirect compliments to teachers over our table as well. . . . To the primary teacher who never raised her voice, but got the attention of the class by lowering it instead. She had a marvelous calming effect on the nervous systems of beginning first graders . . .

To the teacher who helped Jeff realize that there have been many times in history besides our own when the world was in peril. When, during a discussion of international
problems, I said, "Don't you wish we could just sail to a tropical isle for the rest of our
lives?" Jeff replied, "You have to be a part of the solution, Mom, not the problem. That's
what my history teacher says."[1]

Whether discussed around the dinner table or debated in a formal educational
setting, the question of what makes a good teacher is still nearly impossible to answer.
However, general consensus exists that effective teachers have two fundamental traits:
good personalities and *sound professional competencies.*

PERSONAL CHARACTERISTICS OF GOOD SOCIAL STUDIES TEACHERS

People who choose to become teachers must view what they do as an extension of
their own lives. Because they are unique individuals they all bring something special to
teaching, be it helpful or harmful. Our personality differences ensure that no two
classrooms can ever be exactly alike.

Personality Differences

Many beginning teachers overlook this peculiarity and try on different personalities they
think are necessary for success. They may try to emulate a great teacher from their past
or a wonderful cooperating teacher from field experience courses or student teaching.
Thinking that there exists a magical mold into which all individuals should fit, these
beginners often try to teach as their model did. As a result they often flounder until they
eventually discover who they really are. Some are lucky; they are able to find their true
character and emerge as successful teachers. Albert Cullum offers this illustration from
his teaching career:

> When I first began teaching, there was Al Cullum the teacher and Al Cullum the person. I
> soon discovered that this split personality was not a healthy one for the children nor for
> me. I realized I had better bury Al Cullum the teacher and present Al Cullum the person,
> or else the school year would become monotonous months of trivia.[2]

A seventh grade teacher describes how his failure to find a true teaching personality
forced him to change careers early in his working life:

> In the beginning, I remember really wanting to be a teacher. Although my student teach-
> ing had been only a survival experience, I had lucked into a midyear teaching job right af-
> terwards. Maybe I should have taken more time to reflect on teaching before I jumped in.
> Anyhow, in January there I was, in River City Middle School with 125 seventh graders
> who would defy any one description. I never knew that the human body could come in
> so many different sizes and shapes, but they knew from the beginning that I was over-
> whelmed by their demanding presence. The rest of the year became a "me" versus

"them" battle for respect and control. I lost, or more appropriately, I finally surrendered. I had tried all angles: being myself (a once kind, warm-hearted, committed idealist), to being what I thought I should be (a cold, unemotional cynic) to what my principal encouraged me to be (a firm, no-nonsense disciplinarian). None of these approaches worked well for me. Thinking back, I realize now I didn't understand how to use the me most effectively in my teaching.[3]

Just as Jeff's teacher in our earlier example advised him that people cannot run away from their problems, teachers must face the fact that they need to examine themselves fairly by becoming students of their own personalities. This task is especially difficult, for at this time we have no single set of accepted personal characteristics associated with good social studies teaching. Yet a number of personal characteristics can be observed in individuals who, like teachers, deal with people as a major part of their work (see Figure 2–1). Kevin Ryan, Suzanne Burkholder, and Debra Hallock Phillips advise teachers to be "tough" while learning about themselves and to examine their attitudes toward young children. "[Good teachers] teach themselves how to be fair, friendly, and consistently firm, yet display a sense of humor and a warm, encouraging attitude in ways that are natural for them."[4] This book cannot deal in depth with

Smiling and accepting are signs of sincere affection toward children.

all the ways to examine your personality, but you may want to make the most of your professional program by following these suggestions.

1. Keep a written record of what you learn about yourself during your college training and how you behave in leadership situations with children.
2. Be open about your feelings and reactions during any experiences with young children.
3. Be willing to experiment with positive changes in personal behaviors and feelings as they relate to teaching young children.
4. Seek out and be receptive to feedback provided by those around you.

Allowing a positive personality to emerge, then, is a prerequisite to successful teaching. While no test can measure accurately whether your personality is of a type appropriate for teaching young children, past experiences, self-study, and feedback from others can provide the knowledge to stimulate your thinking about a career with elementary school children.

FIGURE 2–1
Personal Characteristics of Good Teachers

- I display a deep, affectionate regard for all the children I teach through my actions and words.
- I am freely and sincerely myself, not playing a role.
- I express realistic feelings of security and self-confidence.
- I offer genuine comments of concern; positive words and gestures communicate a warm regard for children.
- I get along well with people.
- I am a hard worker.
- I am willing to put in extra time to complete a job.
- I am punctual and dependable.
- I can keep secrets regarding confidential matters.
- I admit mistakes and work hard to correct them.
- I observe the rules of the groups to which I belong.
- I leave my problems at home and do not let them affect my work.
- I ignore rumors and refuse to gossip.
- I keep myself groomed and neat.
- I keep my work area in order.
- I use supplies and equipment as carefully as if I purchased them myself.
- I take pride in my work.
- I follow directions and respect the leadership of others.
- I have a good sense of humor; I can laugh with others.
- I am a flexible person; I can vary my approach if the situation calls for it.
- I am curious and want to explore new ideas for working with young children.
- I know youngsters are active, so I eat and sleep well and exercise in order to stay physically fit, energetic, and healthy.

Good teachers, then, must be among the best people we know; everything they do, even the most seemingly insignificant chore, makes a real difference in children's lives. Conversely, people without good intentions often display behaviors and temperament detrimental to a child's personal growth and learning. These people have no place as teachers.

Concern for Children

Good teachers always impress me with their marvelous concern for children. The special moments they describe and the spontaneous affection that grows from these special moments are what makes teaching so different from other professions. Let us look at the encounters teachers stress as those bringing them the most joy. Peter Madden[5] asked several dozen experienced teachers to share their "tales of joy" with future teachers such as you. Here are their major themes.

- The most frequently mentioned source of satisfaction was when the children finally understood or learned to do something they were not able to do before: "The expressions on their faces when they understand new concepts have been wonderful to see."
- Almost as important was the gratification in watching steady growth and development through the school year: "The progress the children make during the year makes me feel I'm in a worthwhile profession."
- Just being with children and sharing their open affection was mentioned by many teachers: "If they like me and they know that I like them, then I feel we can conquer the whole world in the nine months we're together."
- Many enjoyed the children's enthusiasm: "A child's ability to be so open about his feelings is the great pleasure in teaching."
- Teachers found great joy in the creative individual expressions that highlight each child's uniqueness: "Mark came up to me holding his finger as if it were hurt. When I asked him what the matter was, he replied, 'A camel bit my finger,' then turned and walked away!"

These are the special sources of satisfaction awaiting a teacher of elementary school children. You will find extraordinary joy, affection, excitement, and personal satisfaction as you meet challenges each day with your children. Such experiences are not only pleasurable, but they also help make our world. For, as Lloyd DeMause points out:

> The major dynamic in historical change is ultimately neither technology nor economics. More important are the changes in personality that grow from differences between generations in quality of the relationships between [adult] and child.[6]

Influence of Teachers on Children's Lives

Think of all the complex conditions that we regularly read or hear about when people discuss major social issues influencing our future: overpopulation, arms control, nuclear power, depletion of natural resources, economic factors, the explosion of technology, equal rights, racism, sexism, genetic engineering, drug abuse, pollution, crime, violence. All of these significant issues have been fervently examined by scholars for their potential influence on the future. Some of the resulting speculation has been so dramatic that "crash" programs or policies have been created either to heighten public awareness of present conditions or to check undesirable trends before they have a chance to escalate into a disastrous future.

DeMause's quote is significant because for the first time, the quality of children's lives has been so forcefully singled out from among all other pressing issues and trends as the major factor influencing social change. As individuals interested in teaching we certainly understand the significance of the elementary school years. But for them to receive such distinctive, singular prominence from among so many other factors influencing historical change is an extraordinary thought indeed. Such attention certainly underscores the significance of the task faced by all who assume major roles in children's lives. Good teachers realize this and use every approach at their disposal to bring a young child's world to life. They understand why the social studies program is so important. They tap its great promise for helping children reach their fullest potential by using techniques, activities, and strategies that grow from plentiful knowledge, creativity, and sensitivity. Good social studies teachers never become complacent with the job they do. They always have a spirit of inquiry: "There is so much more for me to know." Good social studies teachers make an intense commitment to teaching; they spend vast amounts of time and energy—physical and emotional—on the job. Whether they are planning a unit for their program or spotting something that would be perfect for a classroom display while on vacation, they are never completely off-duty. Elite social studies teachers earn their status through their commitment to students and their conviction that teaching is hard work. A good social studies teacher must sacrifice, but finds it's all worth the effort when, for example, a child suddenly declares, "Hey, social studies is fun. I like it this year!"

PROFESSIONAL CHARACTERISTICS OF GOOD SOCIAL STUDIES TEACHERS

Making sense out of the complicated world of teaching and finding your way as a teacher is a tough job—much tougher than it appears at first. Some, for example, may be so swayed by an individual's engaging personality that they categorize her as a "natural teacher." They imply that this individual's personality is so superior—she has such a natural ability to get ideas across to others and get them to respond positively to her requests—that it, by itself, could allow that person to achieve the same degree of success in teaching young children as a teacher who has received sound professional training. They understand the importance of a teacher's personality, but their perception of the value of professional training is narrow and uninformed. Graham and Persky, recognizing that both the untrained and the trained individual are well-meaning, provide examples of how the untrained person may lack the specific knowledge or skills necessary to maximize developmental opportunities for the very young.

The untrained person, recognizing the importance of establishing rapport and communication with a child, will show a book . . . and ask, "Do you like the pretty pictures?" She does not realize that a question asked in this way boxes the child into a "yes" or "no" response. The person who understands that there is a relationship between thought and language and that verbal interaction can promote thinking skills will word her comments so that they evoke a more thoughtful and complex response—e.g., "Why do you think the puppy is running after the little boy?" This can be the beginning a a conversation and an exchance of ideas rather than a simple question and answer episode.[7]

Importance of Your Professional Program

You will soon have a very special place in children's lives and be expected to deftly handle all the special encounters that occur in your social studies program with keen personal insight and astute professional skills. Consider, for example, a classroom situation where a third grade child gleefully approaches his teacher and hands her a book on penguins. It would seem natural for the teacher to open the book and share in the child's enthusiasm. Little advance planning seems necessary for this to be a warm, rich encounter. However, when six more children try to crowd in at the same time, the need to make clear decisions becomes evident. Should the book be used to encourage dialogue about related social studies activities, or should it be used in other ways? Should I simply praise the child without looking at the book, or should I glance through it with all the interested children? Should we look at the pictures, or would it be better to read a special part? Should I ask the child to share his book with the other children? Would it be better to wait for the child to take initiative in the situation before I make any response?

There are many different responses the teacher could make to this situation; some might be highly constructive while others could be ruinous. "Correct" responses, however, are relative; they are influenced by a maze of complicated professional decisions. The teacher in our example chose to acknowledge the child's discovery of a book related to a topic in the social studies program. She looked at the pictures with the child and asked the child to share his favorite parts. She defended her choice with the argument that her reaction would motivate the child and encourage more "finding out" activity. But when the other children gathered about, the teacher redirected them into other activities. When asked why, the teacher responded, "That's what they really needed at the time." On one hand, the teacher supported her actions with a professional explanation: she prized the child's interest in independent learning and discovery. On the other hand, she was unable to defend the redirecting effort with any cogent explanation. Making professional decisions is a difficult process, but it is often even more difficult for teachers to explain why they chose a particular option. As an elementary school social studies teacher you will regularly face conditions requiring immediate, informed, professionally sound tactics. How will you cope with those frequent demands?

Apprenticeship by Participation

Untrained individuals often look at such responsibilities and underestimate the colossal importance of the professional know-how necessary to accomplish them. They may say, in essence, "Anybody can teach social studies to elementary school children. What do social studies teachers do—ask the children to take out their textbooks? Read a few pages? Answer the questions? Why, even I can do that!" When faced with such an accusation, the best way to cope is to admit its validity. Anybody *can* ask the children to take out their textbooks, read a few pages, and ask them to answer the questions. The accusation is true, but there is one thing wrong with it—it misses the whole point of elementary school social studies education. Textbooks are not meant to be used that way; if they were, there would be no point in your taking this course. Anybody *can* teach elementary school social studies that way with little or no professional preparation.

You, however, will be a well-informed professional who thinks more deeply about what goes into your work. You will understand that there is much more to using the textbook or any other specialized learning tool in the social studies classroom than many would believe. Materials are but the substance of the program. By themselves, they are of little or no benefit; in the hands of a skilled teacher, they are the magical tools for developing happy, informed citizens. All the materials we use in the program involve the children in serious work and, with proper guidance, help them acquire important learning, skills, and sensitivities.

One major reason that many underestimate the value of a teacher's professional training is that a great portion of their lives has been spent in school classrooms. Some of their most stirring memories happened there: outstanding achievements, good friends, and all those experiences that have brought self-enlightenment. In fact, Dan Lortie has determined that, "the average student has spent 13,000 hours in direct contact with classroom teachers by the time he graduates from high school."[8] These direct experiences often make students feel as though they have completed an "apprenticeship by observation." They think that they have achieved all one needs to know about teaching just because they experienced twelve years of schooling. But, Lortie argues, this belief has definite limitations.

> The student is the "target" of the teacher efforts and sees the teacher front stage and center like an audience viewing a play. Students do not receive invitations to watch the teacher's performance from the wings; they are not privy to the teacher's private intentions and personal reactions on classroom events . . . [T]hey are not pressed to place the teacher's action in a pedagogically oriented framework [i.e., framework of acceptable teaching methods]. They are witnesses from their own student-oriented perspectives. . . . What students learn about teaching, then, is intuitive rather than explicit and analytical; it is based on individual personalities rather than pedagogical principles.[9]

Believing that one serves an apprenticeship for teaching simply by having spent a number of hours as a student is unreasonable. Would these same "apprenticeship by observation" advocates maintain their belief if asked whether an avid moviegoer is qualified to produce a movie, or whether being an ardent baseball fan is all the

Successful teaching does not happen automatically. It is a product of hard work and dedication.

qualification one needs to manage a major league baseball team? Observers in each of these situations most certainly lack the knowledge and insight necessary to reach informed decisions. If put into a classroom, believers in apprenticeship by observation are often shocked

> to realize that the spotlight is on them, that the initiative is in their hands, that they suddenly have responsibility for what happens, what will happen and what might happen. The classroom, which they saw previously as an unshakable . . . structure, suddenly becomes bewildering and problematic, fraught with difficulties at every turn. Many consequently exaggerate in their minds the degree to which the situation is "out of control" simply because they are unaware of the change in perspective brought about by the shift from the back to the front of the class.[10]

Your professional training is intended to furnish you with the knowledge and skills necessary to make the transition effectively from audience member to performer. It will help you act in ways that promote children's growth and learning within a stimulating social studies program. It will help you exercise sound judgment while selecting and defending teaching goals as well as methods of interaction and instruction. It will help you view teaching from a professional perspective.

Professional Standards for Social Studies Teachers

In 1988, the National Council for the Social Studies adopted a set of professional standards for the preparation of social studies teachers. Its standards urge that

> candidates for initial licensure as social studies teachers should have gained substantial understanding of the information, concepts, theories, analytical approaches and differing values perspectives, including global and multicultural perspectives, important to teaching

social studies. Problem-solving, critical-thinking, and application skills should be stressed.[11]

The standards recognize, however, that teaching social studies to children requires more. The standards further state that

> courses in social studies methods should prepare prospective teachers to select, integrate, and translate knowledge and methodology from history and social science disciplines in ways appropriate to students in the school level they will teach and give attention to the goals unique to the social studies and those shared jointly with other areas of the school curriculum. Students should also be able to teach social studies utilizing a variety of curriculum approaches and in different types of settings.[12]

Competency-Based Programs

These courses for elementary school social studies teachers are often referred to as *competency-based* courses. Competency-based programs are built on the idea that teachers-in-training best develop their skills by learning about them in the college classroom and then actually performing them in some meaningful context—usually the elementary school classroom as part of a field-based component.

Broad goal statements are developed first to give general direction to competency-based programs. Although numerous goal statements exist, those developed by the National Council for the Social Studies (Chapter 1) provide a good example of what is expected in social studies education in the elementary school. Once these broad goal statements are adopted, teacher preparation institutions organize and develop learning experiences that help students acquire specified skills and competencies important to successful teaching within each area. Because numerous competency statements would need to be detailed for each goal area, it is impossible to list them all in this book. However, the sample basic competencies developed by John Jarolimek (Figure 2–2) should serve as an excellent illustration of the specific behaviors expected in one program under the goal area related to "subject matter and planning."

Following a listing of competencies such as Jarolimek's social studies teacher-preparation programs identify the types of performance expectations that result from assigned readings, college classroom experiences, related field work, or any other supportive experiences. Some of Jarolimek's performance expectations include the following.

1. Explain the difference between a concept and a generalization and provide several examples of each that are appropriate to social studies.
2. Show by an example how concepts and generalizations provide organizing frameworks for planning and teaching social studies.
3. . . . [I]llustrate by specific examples (by defining the concepts to be developed and the subject matter to be used) how it could be presented at a level of difficulty suitable to the grade level in which you are teaching.
4. Using what you have done in number 3, show by specific example how the attitudes, values, and skills learned are built around the core subject matter selected for study.
5. Teach a concept or a generalization to the class to which you are assigned. . . .[14]

FIGURE 2–2
Basic Competencies—Social Studies

The intern teacher is able to

1. Identify, define, and explain key concepts and generalizations relevant to elementary school social studies education.
2. Use concepts and generalizations as organizing frameworks for planning and teaching social studies.
3. Convert subject matter into thought forms appropriate to elementary school pupils.
4. Select subject matter appropriate to the development of the main ideas and the development of related attitudes and values and skills objectives.
5. Use appropriate strategies for teaching various types of social studies learnings:
    a. Informational learning.
    b. Concepts and generalizations.
    c. Skills.
    d. Attitudes and values.[13]

These special capabilities help provide you with a professional identity. They enable you to examine social studies methods insightfully and choose what is appropriate for any given situation, not because they are "cute" or gimmicky but because they stand the greatest chance of contributing to the success of a specific learning objective. There are many methods for teaching social studies, but some are more appropriate for elementary school children. Not all contemporary methods are new, radical, or revolutionary; most are adaptations of older, standard methods. Regardless, the crux of successful teaching lies in the fact that *any* single method of instruction should be used sparingly with elementary school children; the younger the children, the greater the variety should be. As a person of many roles, your elementary school social studies program should reflect these ideals:

- Sometimes you will lecture to your children, but rarely; the younger the child, the less you talk.
- Sometimes you will hold discussion sessions with the entire class, using good questioning and discussion techniques.
- Sometimes you will lead whole-group learning experiences from the textbook or another common source of information; such experiences offer balance and proportion to the program.
- Sometimes you will encourage the children to work together in committees—the children learn a great deal from each other.
- Sometimes you will choose books, movies, slides, tapes, filmstrips, recorders, pictures, bulletin boards, and other learning aids—variety of materials is essential.
- Sometimes you will encourage children to solve problems and search for answers to their own questions; an independent quest for information is a lifelong necessity.
- Sometimes children will work alone; meeting personal interests and needs must assume high priority in all classrooms.

THE NEED FOR CONTINUOUS GROWTH

These are but some of the important skills that help make you a member of a unique, respected profession. They help establish the specialized abilities that make you as much of an expert in your work as physicians or lawyers are in theirs. Be proud, but not complacent, for your diploma and teaching certificate are only a beginning. You have reached only the first stage of what Lilian G. Katz[15] describes as a four-stage sequence of teacher development.

> *Stage 1:* You are preoccupied with survival. You ask yourself questions such as, "Can I get through the day in one piece? Without losing a child? Can I make it until the end of the week? Until the next vacation? Can I really do this kind of work day after day? Will I be accepted by my colleagues?" (first year)

During this period, according to Katz, teachers need support, understanding, encouragement, reassurance, comfort, and guidance. They need instruction in specific ways of handling complex behavior in children, especially since classroom management problems can cause intense feelings of inadequacy at this stage. Katz goes on to characterize the remaining three developmental stages of teachers:

> *Stage 2:* You decide you *can* survive. You begin to focus on individual children who pose problems and on troublesome situations, and you ask yourself these or similar questions: "How can I help a shy child? How can I help a child who does not seem to be learning?" (second year)
>
> *Stage 3:* You begin to tire of doing the same things with the children. You like to meet with other teachers, scan magazines, and search through other sources of information in order to discover new projects and activities to provide for the children. You ask questions about new developments in the field: "Who is doing what? Where? What are some of the new materials, techniques, approaches, and ideas?" (third and fourth years)
>
> *Stage 4:* This is the stage of maturity. You now have enough experience to ask deeper, more abstract questions calling for introspective and researched replies: "What are my historical and philosophical roots? What is the nature of growth and learning? How are educational decisions made? Can schools change societies? Is teaching really a profession?"

Katz's point is that the need to further your education and for exposure to new ideas changes as you gain experience. Administrators usually recognize this with a plan for staff development. Staff development programs generally address areas that need special attention, and include

- Orientation of new staff members to the school facilities
- Planned field trips, workshops, or speakers to gain new ideas
- Staff meetings for sharing concerns or ideas
- Financial assistance to enable faculty to take further course work or receive other kinds of in-service experiences

Membership in major professional groups will also help you keep up-to-date in the field. The primary professional organization for elementary and secondary school social studies teachers is the National Council for the Social Studies. For information, write to the National Council for the Social Studies, 3501 Newark Street, N.W., Washington, D.C. 20016. Two journals published by NCSS will be of particular interest: *Social Studies and the Young Learner* and *Social Education*.

You start your professional development, then, by fulfilling your state's requirements for certification. But your professional growth does not stop there. You must continually update your understanding and skills by carefully examining new knowledge. One teacher highlights the value of continuous learning:

> The biggest surprise of teaching, for me, was that I didn't know my subject matter. That was the one thing I had been most confident about. I had almost an "A" average in my major and felt really on top of my field. When I began teaching and had to explain concepts, I found that I had only a very superficial understanding of them. I knew stuff in kind of a rote way and when I had to explain it to someone else I kind of just fell on my face. I learned more about my subject in my first four months of teaching than I did in my four years of college.[16]

We all know that knowledge is important, but by itself, it does not ensure good teaching. Think of those outstanding scholars we may have admired. They learned facts and figures with ease, but they often failed in their attempts to communicate their wealth of knowledge to others. Teaching requires many skills that grow with us throughout each year of experience.

> Once I got my sea legs during the fall of my first year, teaching has really been interesting. I learn something new about teaching every day. I'm learning that there is an efficient and inefficient way to do everything. You can pass back papers so that it takes ten minutes and a third of the papers get lost, or you can do it perfectly in two minutes. You can give homework assignments in a casual way and end up getting only half of the assignments in, or you can really structure it for the students and get 100%. Sometimes I feel like an apprentice carpenter picking up tricks of the trade from master carpenters. It's a lot of fun and everyday I feel like a better craftsman.[17]

As you continually enhance the skills and knowledge initially brought to teaching, your goal will be to improve a quality social studies program that encourages inquisitive minds. Inspire your children to examine their world and prod them not only to learn subject matter but to think for themselves. A "geographer" bends down to study the effect of sand sifting through her fingers. An "economist" saves a portion of his allowance each week to buy a special skateboard. A "political scientist" petitions the principal for a new piece of playground equipment. An "historian" listens in awe as a grandparent describes life of the past. Children meet their experiences with unique outlooks, and they all have one thing in common—a teacher who helped them realize that the world is a fascinating place to live in and learn about.

By working hard to further your personal and professional growth, you will be bound for success. For the ambitious, mediocrity has no place. One consistent thread running through the careers of teachers who excelled is that they not only learned, but that they were also willing to take risks. They tried new ideas, spoke out for their beliefs, and tackled assignments with uncertain prospects for success. They demonstrated, without timidity, that they would rather be challenged than safe and bored. It's a good idea to accept as much risk as you can early in your career; succeeding in risky situations helps identify potential greatness more clearly than any other factor. Those who take risks have a high degree of self-confidence, and self-confidence is a distinctive quality of most outstanding teachers. As someone once said, having a positive sense of self-worth is worth fifty IQ points. So work hard, learn a lot, and muster up the intestinal fortitude to establish a point of view. But risks cannot, and should not, be taken unless your fundamentals are solid. Risks are never taken blindly by outstanding teachers; they are founded on a deep foundational core of knowledge and skill. Build that foundation in social studies education and take your risks there, for it is the one area of the elementary school curriculum that most openly invites the ideas of energetic innovators.

SUMMARY

How do individuals become good social studies teachers? They have worked hard to achieve their status and realize that progress toward good teaching is not rapid. Good teaching takes time and hard work to achieve, like completing a demanding race. Elite educators know that the race takes years to complete, but that once they reach the finish line the greatest rewards of teaching are theirs. Their satisfaction, however, comes not from basking in glory at the finish line, but from the race itself. Some teachers train for but never start the race; others begin but eventually determine that it takes more time and energy than they are willing to invest. Still others stride steadily and strongly toward the finish line until they break through as superbly talented teachers.

What are good social studies teachers like? They have examined their personal characteristics and have determined ways of doing things that are compatible with their own personalities. They understand that teaching is hard work, filled with joys, heartaches, satisfaction, frustration, and stress. Good teachers are good people who are dependable, honest, sincere, and self-giving. They know that good teachers must show affection and respect for their students. They are convinced, as is Lloyd DeMause, that the relationships they establish with their pupils may be the major dynamic in historical change.

Good teaching cannot be characterized by personality factors only. Good social studies teachers must be able to apply knowledge about teaching in designing effective instructional practices. The ability to do so is commonly referred to as a teacher's professional competencies. We understand that college or university teacher certification programs identify specific competencies (observable behaviors) and offer learning experiences directed toward their acquisition. The issuance of a teaching certificate verifies that an individual has attained the specific competencies required for satisfactory fulfillment of professional responsibilites. But the initial certificate does not imply that the receiver is a "completed product;" most beginning teachers are only at the first of what Lilian G. Katz describes as four developmental stages. A sound plan of continuous education will serve to enhance the skills and knowledge you initially bring to the social studies program.

ENDNOTES

1. Phyllis Naylor, "Over the Dinner Table," *Today's Education, 69,* no. 3 (September–October 1980): 19.

2. Albert Cullum, *Push Back the Desks* (New York: Citation Press, 1967), p. 19.

3. Kevin Ryan, Suzanne Burkholder, and Debra Hallock Phillips, *The Workbook* (Columbus, OH: Merrill, 1983), p. 144.

4. Ibid, p. 145.

5. Peter Madden, "Experiencing Joy in Teaching," *Childhood Education, 54,* no. 1 (October 1977): 12–14.

6. Lloyd DeMause, "Our Forebears Made Childhood a Nightmare," *Psychology Today, 8,* no. 11 (April 1975): 85.

7. L. B. Graham and B. A. Persky, "Who Should Work with Young Children?" in L. B. Graham and B. A. Persky, *Early Childhood* (Wayne, NJ: Avery Publishing Group, 1977), p. 336.

8. Dan Lortie, *Schoolteacher* (Chicago: University of Chicago Press, 1975), p. 62.

9. Ibid., p. 61.

10. Ibid., p. 62.

11. National Council for the Social Studies, "Standards for the Preparation of Social Studies Teachers," *Social Education, 52,* no. 1 (May 1984): p. 11.

12. Ibid.

13. John Jarolimek, *Social Studies Competencies and Skills* (New York: Macmillan, 1977), p. 45.

14. Ibid.

15. Lilian G. Katz, "Developmental Stages of Preschool Teachers," *Elementary School Journal, 73,* no. 1 (October 1972): 50–54.

16. Ryan, Burkholder, and Hallock, *The Workbook,* p. 177.

17. Ibid., p. 182.

"A teacher need not be a professional actor, musical artist, or scientist to present greatness to his students. He need only be aware of the creativity and excitement of the outside world and strive to bring that world into his classroom. If a teacher can show a principal the possible structure of a new project and the rules and regulations that will govern it, most administrators will agree to let him try the program. It will be a rewarding experience and not as difficult as it may sound."[1]

—Albert Cullum

3 *Planning for Social Studies Instruction*

As you read, reflect on the following matters:

- Why are individual differences among children central to effective planning in the social studies?
- What sources of planning help are available for social studies teachers?
- How does the textbook contribute to the eventual configuration of the social studies program?
- What options are available for teachers interested in planning a social studies program?
- What is a unit plan? How is it constructed? Why is it important?
- What is a lesson plan? How is it constructed? Why is it important?

Of all the qualities described in Chapter 2, which would you select as the most essential for success as a social studies teacher? Depending on your personality and style, one may stand out from among the others. To me, the teacher's enthusiasm toward her subject is of prime importance. She has to be excited about what she and her students are doing. Teaching is not only her job—it is her fascination. It leaves her virtually starry-eyed and supplies her with the eagerness and energy to devise experiences that activate children for learning. All children have to feel that their teacher is captivated by what she is doing. In the social studies, this means that teachers openly view their world with fascination and help children to look at their world as a never-ending mystery. To do this, teachers must plan to offer significant learning situations in which there is a little mystery, a bit of magic, and a dash of splendor to confront the children. Elementary school children respond to these things; that is what makes their classrooms different from those for any other age span.

PLANNING FOR INDIVIDUALS

Teachers achieve magic in the elementary school social studies program when they help each child become challenged by its activities and emotionally involved in its subject matter; they deliver the best for each youngster and make the most of their time with everyone in their classrooms. Therefore, the good social studies program is marked by a keen awareness and consideration of each youngster as a distinct individual. It is tailored to fit each and every child; the child with a solid store of information should be as challenged by the program as the child who has a narrower background. Knowledge background, however, is but one factor that accounts for individual differences in the social studies program. Sometimes the differences among children in the same classroom are so great that it seems the only thing they have in common is the great individual differences among them. What are some ways youngsters differ from one another? A typical class of fourth graders might differ in these ways:

Sex	Self-Confidence	Achievement Level
Age	Enthusiasm	Interests
Weight	Motivation	Values Orientation
Race	Social Adjustment	Intelligence Level
Height	Self-Perception	Ethnic Background
Creativity	Behavior	Socioeconomic Level
Learning Modalities	Life Experiences	Physical Health
Emotional Factors	Reading Level	Personality

Children differ from the time they come into the world and gradually become wholly unique as the environment and genetic factors combine to form individuals who vary in physical, creative, emotional, and behavioral characteristics, as well as in intellectual potential, social attitudes, interests, and special talents. They differ, also, in their ways of learning. No single system of instruction can possibly do justice to all these differences, but the variations among children are normal and contribute to the challenge we all face as teachers.

What does this all mean? Calvin W. Taylor[2] suggests that teachers view all children as *talented;* that is, each can be above average in at least one of the many important intellectual talents we can now measure. Furthermore, with major adjustments in our teaching styles, children can use their multiple talents to experience success in the social studies classroom. In fact, Taylor says they can exercise and develop every one of the known intellectual talents as they ponder and process knowledge in the social studies.

Taylor suggests grouping intellectual talents as in Figure 3–1. The grouping is based on world-of-school needs, specifying *academic talents* and six other extremely important types that are especially significant in the social studies classroom: *productive thinking, planning, communicating, forecasting, decision-making,* and *human relations.*

Let us assume that the child named Kathy is toward the bottom of the academic totem pole because she consistently obtains lower grades than her classmates and performs below average on achievement tests. When we begin to examine other characteristics, we also find that she has some trouble in activities where productive thinking is required. Extending Kathy's profile by following the line in Figure 3–1, we see that her ability to make sound decisions is high, especially in judging which information is valuable and which should be discarded. Kathy also displays talents in communicating her decisions to others. Choose any of the other hypothetical children and plot the pattern of talents. Each, like Kathy, will certainly have at least one talent strength and some weakness.

According to Taylor, talent searches should occur in the classroom, and children can experience greater success if they are encouraged to use multiple talents rather than

FIGURE 3–1

Multiple-talent Totem Pole (Adapted from Calvin W. Taylor, "Be Talent Developers . . . as Well as Knowledge Dispensers." Today's Education, 57, no. 9 (December 1968) 69. Reprinted with permission)

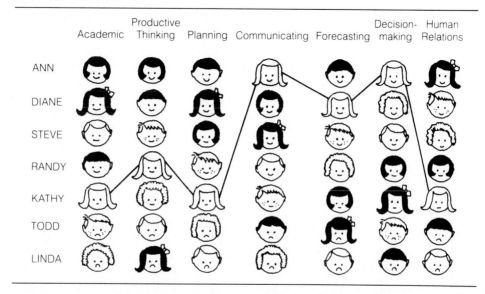

any single type. Multiple-talent teaching requires the selection of activities that work across a great number of children's talents. Of course, academic talent is valued, but we must augment the emphasis on this single talent with activities that encourage creative talent, decision-making talent, and all the rest.

INFLUENCES ON PROGRAM PLANNING

The implication is that you must develop personalized teaching plans that reflect an awareness of and responsiveness to the needs of each individual. Regardless of style, whether a strict no-nonsense approach or a highly personal, informal one, you must constantly search for self-improvement by combining your knowledge of teaching practices with your understanding of the uniqueness of each child in your classroom.

Curriculum Guides

Developing individualized teaching is hard work and requires much energy and expertise. It begins with knowing where to turn for help in choosing materials and activities designed for good instructional programs in the social studies. Most of the time *curriculum guides* are prepared by local school districts for the purpose of describing the objectives, content, materials, and activities expected to be offered at any particular grade level. Written by teachers and curriculum specialists of the district, these guides are not normally meant to be followed to the letter, but to be interpreted by the teacher and used in a personal, creative manner. Such local autonomy has been the cornerstone of a diversified social studies program over the years. However, recent trends have indicated increased influence from state and federal constituencies in curriculum planning. Former Education Secretary William Bennett's *James Madison Elementary School* and the Bradley Commission on History are but two efforts on a national scale designed to sway the direction of social studies programs. The *California History-Social Science Framework* is one example of how states have become active in curriculum development. In addition to state curricula, program influence may be exerted by requiring state adoption of textbook materials. In Texas, for example, an important reason for statewide adoptions is offered by Leroy Psencik, director of general education for the Texas Educational Agency. He says that common adoptions ensure that all schools have equal access to the "best materials."[3] Many states require state adoptions, but most permit local school districts to select the staple of most elementary school social studies programs—the textbook.

Textbooks

Textbooks provide most teachers with the foundation for planning and organizing their programs. Why are they so popular? The main reason is that, when elementary school teachers must cover art, math, reading, science, and spelling, textbooks greatly lighten the number of instructional decisions and reduce the pressures associated with comprehensive preparation in each subject area. Another reason is that they present a common core of knowledge organized as an orderly sequence of material from one grade level to the next. Each teacher from kindergarten through grade 8 knows what the children have covered in earlier grades and what they will experience in successive grades, eliminating gaps or repetition. Additionally, textbook programs are accompanied by well-formulated teacher's manuals that contain a wealth of recommendations for instructional activities. Elementary school teachers are often grateful for the comprehensive manuals that come loaded with unit objectives, lesson objectives, well-developed lesson plans, valuable follow-up activities, evaluation procedures, and suggested resources for further investigation. Finally, most new textbooks have made attempts to use conceptual-inquiry approaches to social studies teaching. They encourage active exploration into problem situations and organize learning experiences so that the text is but one of many sources of data for finding solutions to problems. Thus, social studies textbooks have remained popular over the years because they supply busy teachers with a sound, organized program and many suggestions for instructional activities to carry it out. Figure 3–2 will help you understand how the textbook contributes to a teacher's planning and organizing responsibilities. Study the suggestions this text offers teachers in carrying out a lesson related to reading material.

Despite these advantages, the use of textbooks in the elementary school social studies program has been criticized. However, if we examine the criticisms carefully, we often find that the problems associated with textbook use could be ascribed more readily to the teachers using them than to the textbooks themselves. For example, one criticism of the approach is that it stifles teacher creativity by causing dependence on the teacher's manual; however, manuals are not designed to be followed exactly, but merely to guide teachers.

Another criticism is that some teachers tend to treat the material in the textbook as the only reading material to which the children should be exposed. Obviously, children at all grade levels should have opportunities to be exposed to and explore many literary materials suitable to individual reading ability. Most children's texts even provide lists of materials for further reading, reinforcement, or enrichment.

The tendency of some teachers to expect all children at a certain grade level to be able to read a particular textbook is another criticism of the approach. This tendency certainly accounts for children's becoming disinterested in the social studies material and frustrated in the process of developing related skills and abilities.

A further criticism is the limited amount of material covered in the textbook. The teacher should realize that the textbook is not meant to be covered page-for-page and cover-to-cover throughout the school year, but to serve as a unifying force for whatever content is deemed appropriate for a given group of children.

PLANNING FOR INSTRUCTION

Of all the possibilities you may encounter as a beginning teacher, then, the textbook will probably be the single major source to guide and direct your planning. However,

FIGURE 3–2

Sample from a Social Studies Teacher's Manual (From SCOTT, FORESMAN SOCIAL STUDIES, Book 4, Barbara Parramore and Dan D'Amelio. Copyright © 1982, 1979 Scott, Foresman and Company. Reprinted by permission.)

Some people earn identity for the way they act. Did you ever say about someone, "He's a grouch" or "She's stuck up"? Have you ever heard someone described as friendly or outgoing? Grouch, stuck up, friendly, and outgoing are all kinds of earned identity.

Think About It

1. What two kinds of identity are there? How are they different from each other?
2. Which kind of identity do you think is more important? Why?
3. Take the "Who Am I?" quiz. Copy the quiz on paper and fill in the blanks. The quiz should be private.

Who Am I?

My name is _____

I live at _____

My favorite people are _____

My favorite things are _____

I like to play _____

I like to study _____

I would like to earn identity as _____

_____

169

As a **challenging activity**, students may divide the clippings into several file categories such as sports, bravery, social, business, government, and unlawful activities. (Students should learn that negative identities may be earned too.) Discuss why newspapers identify a person by giving information about the person as well as a report of what was done that was newsworthy.

Interested students could interview someone who has earned a special identity, such as an award. After the interview the students should report to the class on such things as what the earned identity is, how it was earned, and how the earner feels about it.

Have the **whole class** read and make reports on books about famous people. Ask the librarian to arrange a special display of books with content about "earned" identities.

As a **challenging activity**, have students look in the local newspapers for people in the community who are receiving recognition for contributions to community life. Then have students make reports to the class on the people being recognized and their achievements.

Answers to Think About It
1. Earned identity and given identity. Given identity is things a person is born with such as birth order and nationality. Earned identity is things a person must work to achieve such as good artist, nice person, or being stuck-up.
2. Responses will vary. Accept each response.
3. The "Who Am I?" quiz should be a private activity for students.

Related Materials
Have pupils complete page 42 of the workbook.

you will not want to use it as a cookbook; the needs, interests, and abilities of your students will require adjustment. Nevertheless, without its comforting help, how will you be able to plan and organize sequences of activities of most benefit to your children? This is where the heart of your professional role emerges: planning for instruction.

David F. Kellum offers some interesting ideas about the nature of planning:

> Teaching is an art form and the lesson plan is its working sketch. As the goal of art is unity, it is unity that becomes the key to effective lesson planning. Whether the impression to be conveyed is an emotional or an intellectual one, it must be a unified impression. Any effective lecture or inquiry lesson has a totality of its own which is the result of its unity. Most beginning teachers and not a few veterans collapse in hopelessly fragmented lessons . . . [ending] with . . . bewildered students . . . asking themselves, after thirty minutes of holding forth, "So, what?" . . . After twenty-five years of attending classes and ten years of watching colleagues teach, I can still count on one hand the number of teachers whose classroom presentation reflected some notion of unity.[4]

As Kellum says, facilitating children's learning in the social studies is largely a matter of organizing and manipulating the environment so that all learning experiences are characterized by some degree of *unity*. If we do not systematically plan what we offer to the children, we risk having random and chaotic lessons that cause children to wonder what they are supposed to be learning. The actual planning of a social studies program may take many different forms. It can happen at any point on a continuum where *children's choices* may be considered one extreme and *teacher's choices*, or a *preplanned series of learning outcomes*, the other.

Children's Choices

The social studies program may be organized in ways that leave most of the choices to the child. Such a program is based on trust—the teacher must have resolute faith that the children can learn most effectively if provided opportunities to make free, constructive, and appropriate choices. The teacher does not plan in advance for any particular content or activities, but does organize a stimulating environment in which children's choices can be made. The drive to popularize this form of education (I will refer to it as *informal* education) was led during the late 1960s and early 1970s by liberal educators such as John Holt and Carl R. Rogers. Holt insists that we must respect children:

> We do not need to "motivate" children into learning by wheedling, bribing, or bullying. We do need to keep picking away at their minds to make sure they are learning. What we need to do, and all we need to do, is bring as much of the world as we can into the school and the classroom; give children as much help and guidance as they need and ask for; listen respectfully when they feel like talking; and then get out of the way. We can trust them to do the rest.[5]

Rogers implored educators to redefine their major title as *facilitator* rather than *teacher*. He explains the differences in those two titles with his "mug and jug" theory.

> The teacher asks himself: "How can I make the mug hold still while I fill it from the jug with these facts which the curriculum planners and I regard as valuable?" The attitude of

the facilitator has almost entirely to do with climate: "How can I create a psychological climate in which the child will feel free to be curious, will feel free to make mistakes, will feel free to learn from his environment, from fellow students, from me, from experience? How can I help him recapture the excitement of learning which was his in infancy?"[6]

Within this view, much of what occurs in the social studies classroom depends on two major sources of inspiration for the children: *spontaneous happenings* or *advance arrangement of the environment.*

Spontaneous Happenings

Spontaneous happenings are those special events that grow from direct experiences encountered by the children themselves. An excellent illustration of a spontaneous happening is the experience of Dorothy B. (Debe) Holzwarth (now Hill) and her 26 third graders from the Highland Park Elementary School in Upper Darby, Pennsylvania. Through their intense interest in state symbols, Act 59 was passed on April 10, 1974—legislation that established the firefly as Pennsylvania's official state insect.

The project was born when the children in Mrs. Holzwarth's class read that Maryland had adopted the monarch butterfly as its state insect and asked their teacher if Pennsylvania had a state insect. After looking up the information in various resources, they found a state flower, a state song, a state tree, a state nickname, and various other official state symbols, but no official "state bug." The children then reasoned that they should write to the president of the United States to see if they could have one, but Mrs. Holzwarth explained that since this was a state matter, they should direct their inquiry to their district legislators in Harrisburg.

Before they did so, however, the children decided to conduct a regular democratic election to determine what the state insect should be. Several insects were nominated, each nominee the subject of intensive study by the class. They examined the pros and cons of such bugs as the dragonfly, ladybug, and grasshopper, but after weighing the advantages and disadvantages of each, a class vote settled the matter: the firefly gathered the most votes. Why? One reason was the scientific name—*Photuris pennsylvanica,* closely resembling Pennsylvania. Students also liked the fact that summer evenings often reflected the soft glow of hundreds of these insects.

Now that the children had designated their choice for state insect, the next step was to write to their district legislators. Both were impressed with the children's enthusiasm toward their special project and visited Mrs. Holzwarth's classroom. They discussed the procedure of initiating a law in the state legislature so that the children were informed of the procedures necessary to act further. The children learned that their next step would be to gain statewide support for their cause. They needed to write to every legislator to ask for his or her support. These 26 children responded by writing over 250 letters—203 to the House, 50 to the Senate, and two letters to the governor and his wife. In addition, the children learned that a petition would have to be circulated, bearing hundreds of adult signatures. The children learned how to draw up a petition; they obtained more than 2100 signatures, which they presented to the legislators.

At this point, they encountered a serious potential setback. Thinking they had fulfilled all the prerequisites to having their bill introduced in Harrisburg, the children now learned that they needed support from throughout the entire state, not only from the immediate area. Mrs. Holzwarth came to the rescue. She contacted the representatives of the state teachers' organization, telling them about the firefly bill. These representatives, of course, were dispersed throughout the state, and with their support, the bill would stay alive. Each representative canvassed his or her district and Harrisburg was deluged with more than 5000 letters from firefly fans throughout the state. The children were on their way—or so they thought.

Then came a second setback. The bill was introduced on the Senate floor for the first time (the children learned that it had to be read three times within ten days before a vote could be taken, or it must go back into committee). Then a very important tax problem came up, which superceded the firefly bill in importance. The children's bill was automatically put back into committee. The legislators, however, promised to reintroduce the bill once the tax matter was settled. In the meantime, the class continued their work, printing 600 luminous bumper stickers proclaiming "Firefly for State Insect." They also kept up their letter-writing campaign, asking legislators to vote YES when the bill came onto the floor once more.

Eventually, the Senate passed the firefly bill by an overwhelming vote of 37–11. The children were invited to Harrisburg two days later for the House Government Committee hearings on their bill. They went to Harrisburg armed with banners and an original song they wrote especially for this occasion:

> Oh firefly! Oh firefly!
> Please be our state bug.
> *Photuris pennsylvanica*,
> You'll fly forever above.
> Oh firefly! Oh firefly!
> You light up so bright.
> It's fun to see such a pretty sight.
> Oh firefly! Oh firefly!

Imagine the thoughts of the children as they arrived in Harrisburg to be met by crews from all major Philadelphia television channels and reporters from the major wire services. The hearing itself was held according to established decorum, the children testifying with all their knowledge about fireflies for a period of about two hours. The committee reported its unanimously favorable feeling toward the bill to the House of Representatives, and on April 2, 1974, the bill passed the House by a vote of 156–22. When Governor Shapp finally signed the bill (Act 59) on April 10, 1974, the children were again in Harrisburg to watch the creation of a new state law.

Photuris pennsylvanica takes its place alongside the whitetail deer, ruffled grouse, and Great Dane as official state animals. However, to Mrs. Holzwarth's class, this experience was much more than an exercise in choosing a state insect. It was a "children's choice" learning episode in which they learned about political action and legislative processes in ways that most of us have not been able to do. They learned about petitioning and writing letters to their representatives, and they saw firsthand how government works. As one child noted, "Now we have something to tell our grandchildren." Another, when asked if she would like to get another law passed, blurted, "Darn right! I'd like a law against homework. Homework gives you pimples!"

Advance Arrangement of the Environment

Since it is unpredictable which way the social studies program will go when it is based on spontaneous happenings, the teacher does not select content in advance. However, he does stand by to respond to the children with appropriate experiences designed to extend and support their interests and needs. Such social studies programs are difficult to manage; teachers simply do not know when a new happening will stimulate interest or even how long interest will be maintained in any particular area. For that reason, this approach calls for teachers who can make quick decisions and feel comfortable facing each class period with many unknowns. However, most teachers do not appear to feel at ease with a program based on spontaneous happenings. Consequently, their programs may be designed to exert a bit more control: a stricter time schedule, for example, and some specific activities or materials. Still, respect, trust, and autonomy in choice of activity remains. Ms. Boyer's class project illustrates advance arrangement.

Claire Boyer, a second grade teacher at the Media Elementary School, wanted to take the study of local government beyond the textbook. For a special midyear social studies project she placed her children in the position of creating a town for themselves and running it. To begin this special project, Ms. Boyer asked her children to pretend to be adult members of families driven out of Media by a severe pollution incident. The families, traveling together in search of a new place to settle, were led downstairs inside their school to a large, empty room made available for their project. In order to keep track of the victims of this unfortunate plight, the children were asked to fill out "official town survey sheets." Once this census was complete, the members of this new town ("Newmedia" by vote) built homes for themselves from large packing boxes saved from the past summer's shipment of new furniture. They painted and pasted until the boxes took on the appearance of houses and brought a sense of reality to the empty room. Streets were laid out and named: Dunlap Street, obviously a tribute to Mr. Richard Dunlap, the principal of Media Elementary School; but no one was quite sure of the inspiration for Grape Road or Ice Road. A town newspaper was begun to chronicle the daily progress of Newmedia's citizens and to keep its populace informed. "Pollution Sends Townspeople to New Land," blared the headlines on January 7, the first day of the project. A subsequent story read, "Townspeople Paint the Town," in reference to the construction of new homes.

The day after the families completed their homes, they met to discuss town problems, Ms. Boyer presiding. As is often the case with youngsters of this age, they could foresee no problems. However, Ms. Boyer was quick to suggest potential problems—fires, crime, and what would happen if she were not available to lead future town meetings. Discussion led to the establishment of a police department, fire department, and an election for mayor. The children quickly set up minimum qualifications for voter registration and went about soliciting candidates for the mayoral position. Seven candidates immediately announced their intent to run, but three dropped out of the race the following day—they were too busy to run. Campaigning and debating began as students formed their platforms: Alex promised low taxes, Curtis vowed gun control. Candidates then planned campaign strategies, directly learning that political make-believe can mirror political reality. There was, to be specific, the "great cookie caper," involving Alex and her closest opponent, Curtis. On the last day of campaigning, Alex distributed "Vote for Alex" pamphlets decorated with paper hands grasping real chocolate chip cookes. Curtis's followers quickly cried, "Bribery!", complaining that Alex was trying to buy votes. The matter went to the election board, which found that "No influence was obtained through the distribution of the cookies."

Following her 14–2 victory, Alex immediately appointed Curtis as chief of police and presented him with his first book of tickets. Using his tickets to control the breaking of laws such as speeding (running in the halls) and loitering (watching the classroom chess game), Curtis eventually learned the powers of his position. Through it all, Alex made new friends, was subject to pressures of old ones, and generally learned that a position of authority has its rewards as well as its pitfalls. "I learned I'm never gonna be the real mayor," she reflected. "Even just pretending to be the mayor is a tough job."

Leading Newmedia through its hectic early days, Alex and her council members provided leadership as the town began to grow. Other classrooms, for example, contributed to the new town. The first grade, studying the topic "Needs of People," contributed a food store and displayed the products themselves (Aisha's California watermelon: $20 a pound). The third grade, studying "What Towns Need," built an electric power station, stringing yarn lines from one paper light pole to another. The fourth grade, not involved in a relevant social studies topic at the time, demonstrated the interrelatedness of the physical and social sciences. They wired up street lights by connecting batteries to light bulbs, thus applying their knowledge of energy to making lives better for people. The fifth grade, studying "Community Services," and anxious to contribute with the rest, made a cardboard trash truck (complete with oatmeal box "trash cans" for the customers) and a bus from cardboard boxes. Finally, the kindergarten class spruced up the entire town with pink and red flowers.

The entire growing village remained on display for the remainder of the school year as the children shared their learning experiences with others. They simply served as hosts while the popularity of their venture grew.

Informal education exemplifies a teacher's belief that children learn most effectively when they have some say in how or what they will learn. Strategies emphasize learning as a *process*, not a *product*, that takes place in an environment reflecting these characteristics:

Respect for the children's right to pursue individual interests and activities

Provision for active exploration, manipulation, and physical action in the learning process

Encouragement of direct social contact with people whereby children acquire verbal knowledge from others

Realization that children learn efficiently when they proceed at their own pace and with their own learning style

Teacher attitude that learning should be exciting and enjoyable

Teachers assume the role of diagnosticians, guides, arrangers, and motivators

Teachers accept the role of facilitator. They prepare the classroom environment with a rich variety of materials and allow children to choose activities freely with one another and to pursue any one activity. Clearly, informal programs stress process over product and value such process goals and outcomes as problem-solving and discovery, as well as such skills as cooperation and self-expression. Informal programs are not planned according to any specific format or set of guidelines, but on the knowledge of children and what is of immediate interest to them. Because of the tremendous responsibility faced by teachers to make insightful, immediate decisions regarding those interests, most who use the informal approach are experienced professionals with rich backgrounds in arranging the environment and in selecting areas of expressed interest to be expanded upon.

Teacher's Choices

To the advocates of informal instruction, the suggestion of teacher direction brings to mind authoritarianism, rigidity, and lack of creativity. They view "child-centeredness" as allowing children to learn more effectively when they pursue their own interests as the moment arises. Critics of the approach, however, say that such an approach is impractical. They envision frustrated teachers throwing up their hands in despair when trying to arrange the environment or select which interest and need to emphasize. Additionally, they believe it is unreasonable to expect a beginning teacher to "have a bagful of tricks on hand at all times to skillfully capitalize on any new interest a young child may evidence."[7] Because of these beliefs, many advocate the organization of sequentially planned activities designed around a central theme.

Planning for teaching seems to have cycles of desirability. Only about twenty years ago, informal teaching was most widely acclaimed; formal plans were viewed as obstacles to originality and flexibility. Consequently, many teachers emphasized the child-centeredness of the informal approach in their social studies programs. The reverse is currently in vogue; there is a renewed emphasis on careful planning for selected teaching outcomes. This back-and-forth popularity of certain educational schemes is what I like to refer to as the pendulum effect. Robert Slavin likewise makes a pendulum comparison in describing the fickleness of American education:

American education tends to run from fad to fad, riding the pendulum from enthusiasm to disappointment and back. Part of the reason for this is the over-application of good ideas, pushing them so far and fast that they become bad ideas. If education is to make the steady progress characteristic of medicine or engineering, it will have to . . . learn better ways to enhance student achievement . . . And, even when truly effective programs are found, teachers need to be involved in choosing, implementing, and adapting them, as their judgment and professional skill are always required to make even the best programs effective.[8]

Successful elementary school social studies teaching today is considered to be based on the ability of teachers to carefully, deliberately, and systematically plan instruction. This teaching concept breaks subject matter down into a series of learning units in which a wide range of educational outcomes are clearly specified. Lack of careful planning is highlighted in a barrage of books, articles, and reports (see Chapter 1) as a major factor contributing to the fact that students in our schools have not learned as much as we might wish. As a result, teachers are advised to: (1) focus instruction on organized content, (2) supply appropriate objectives, (3) select teaching strategies that are compatible with those objectives, and (4) actively involve children in the learning process. Careful planning, then, is considered a process that allows teaching and learning to proceed purposefully, efficiently, and productively. It usually features both long-range and short-range designs for instruction. Long-range designs are commonly referred to as *unit plans;* short-range designs are called *lesson plans.*

UNIT PLANS

Unit plans are extended designs of systematic instruction created by teachers for the purpose of effectively implementing the social studies curriculum. They provide an organizational framework that allows teachers to adapt a school's written curriculum (whether based on a curriculum guide or textbook series) to the unique needs, interests, and abilities of their students. Unit plans are developed around a central theme; they contain an orderly sequence of lessons designed to provide a sense of cohesiveness, or unity, to classroom instruction.

Unit plans grow from a careful assessment of the abilities, needs, and interests of children. This knowledge helps teachers plan the specific content to be taught, the materials to be used for instruction, and the learning activities in which the children will be involved. A unit normally lasts from three to six weeks, so careful assessment is a must if you are to capture and maintain interest for that amount of time.

A helpful way to look at the process of constructing units is to put yourself in the position of a tour guide and imagine that your children are your passengers. You are about to help a group of human beings embark on a most thrilling journey—a happy, exciting excursion to wherever you choose. You have taken this trip in the past, or you may have dreamed about it, but whatever the case, your role is that of tour guide.

Selecting a Topic or Theme

Let us assume that we have three weeks for our special trip. The first decision must be, "Where should we go?" Interests, abilities, and resources will all affect the decision, so they must be considered first. Some people may be avid skiers and propose a trip to the mountains of Vermont. Others may be skilled surfers and voice their desire to visit California beaches. Many could be strongly interested in raw nature and suggest a hiking trip along the Appalachian Trail. But let us assume that you, like many other young college students in America, ultimately decide that a spring break journey to Florida would be the most attractive option. The teacher planning a social studies unit is much like a tour guide faced with similar considerations. She does not simply pull a topic out of the air and use it. All the talents and interests of the children must be considered because, in effect, she is asking the question, "Where do we want to go?" when she makes her decision. A teacher without a theme is often a teacher who wanders aimlessly, looking for direction or hoping for inspiration. The theme, however, allows the teacher to delve into a sequence of social studies activities tailored to each child in the room. Just as you are able to choose from among several desirable vacation spots, you can select from among hundreds or perhaps thousands of themes for your program and suit them to the needs and interests of your children. Here is only a small sampling of possibilities:

Abraham Lincoln	Mexico: Neighbors to the South
Canals and Early Railroads	Our Beautiful Blue Planet (Oceans)
Circus Magic	Our National Anthem
Clowns and Clowning	Penguins
Digging for Dinosaurs	Popcorn
Famous Cartoon Characters	Professional Baseball
Farm Animals	Protecting Endangered Wildlife
Games of Colonial America	Technology in the 1990s
History of Communication	Tools and Machines
Look at Me—I'm Special	Why People Have Laws
Manufacturing in China	Working People of Washington's Time

Although many teachers have complete freedom to choose topics for their classrooms, others are bound by recommendations from one or several different sources, including the most frequent sources—textbooks or districtwide curriculum guides. Check your college curriculum library for textbooks or curriculum guides for a grade level you might teach. Inspect the contents to analyze the various topics offered to teachers as directions for study. Some school districts demand that teachers sequentially cover each topic from either the curriculum guide or the textbook, while others encourage teachers to choose topics. Some districts want a coordinated schoolwide program in which all teachers are aware of each other's responsibilities; others value a program that responds to children's fluctuating needs and interests.

Choosing a theme for study is an involved, time-consuming procedure. Certain responsibilities of a new job may prevent you from giving the time and effort necessary to choose independently and carry out plans for a topic of instruction. Hanna, Potter, and Reynolds suggest an advantage of using prepared curricula for beginning teachers:

The choice for a beginning teacher is difficult. He will have problems of organization and must familiarize himself with many things before a suitable [theme] for his class may be chosen and initiated. In these cases, the principal, the curriculum coordinator, or the supervisor serve as integrating agents. Conferences on the choice of a [theme] for a particular group should be planned before school opens or early in the year. . . . If children are encouraged to continue with [their] interests until the teacher has had time to become acquainted with his group, leads for guiding the children into the selection of a new [theme] are usually perceived. The values of a curriculum framework for new teachers are evident. If a curriculum organization has been developed for a school, the choice can be made within the established framework with confidence and assurance. The fact that the framework has been built upon a careful study of the needs and interests of children means that the unit selected is considered . . . to be of value to children.[9]

Themestorming

Choosing a theme (or topic) calls for a great deal of expansive thinking. Jane Baskwill[10] calls the process "themestorming," a planning process that enables teachers to determine the potential of a particular theme as well as a planning structure that will allow the theme to be developed further. Virtually any topic can be themestormed (brainstormed) by a group (to stimulate each other's thinking) or by oneself. All that is required is to take a single idea and let your mind explore it freely. Through the entire process you must record your possibilities in an organized way—not in a list form, but in an expanding web. First, write the word or words describing your theme in the middle of a sheet of paper and draw a circle around it. Then, draw lines connecting to it anything that is related. It might be best to think in terms of asking "who, what, where, when, why, and how" questions. Let us suppose we chose "Our Beautiful Blue Planet" (Oceans) as our central theme. You might ask: "How big are the oceans? What lives in the oceans? Why is ocean water salty? What is the bottom of the ocean like? What makes the waves? The tides?" Dozens of other possibilities exist. The next step, naturally, is to try to answer some of these questions. As you locate answers, try to fit them into the web. A sample web has been started in Figure 3–3. Certainly, most of us do not know enough at this initial stage of the unit planning process to suggest all the content to be used. We are only brainstorming "launches," or ideas to help us judge whether our chosen theme has sufficient possibilities for use. If the theme seems too broad or too narrow in focus, it should either be adjusted or discarded altogether. If the theme seems appropriate, you will need to move on and select the ideas you wish to expand upon.

Should you wish to continue with the theme, the next step is to build the subject matter of the unit. Teachers of elementary school social studies must have much information at their fingertips, but they also have access to resources to supplement that knowledge. A good encyclopedia and dictionary should be commonplace in elementary school classrooms. They are good places to start. Other print materials, such as reference books or curriculum guides, are needed too.

Check with your school or public librarian for references on a theme you wish to pursue. It should be common for elementary school social studies teachers to admit they need more information: "I'll look it up," should be spoken many times a day. Books will provide most of the needed information, but resources need not always be books. Consult specialists either in person or by telephone, visit museums and other sites, view films or filmstrips, listen to audiotapes, and seek other opportunities to broaden your background. You will need to spend a great deal of time uncovering and organizing

FIGURE 3–3
A Unit Theme Web

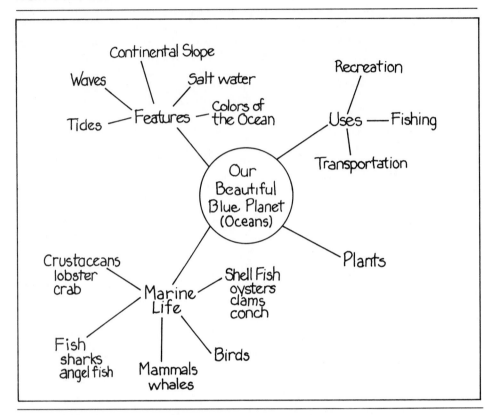

information: What is the key information necessary for a satisfactory understanding of this theme? What are the concepts and big ideas (generalizations) that can emerge? Do not be satisfied only with accumulating information; be sure the information is accurate. You must pass on true understandings, not careless misinformation.

The background material you uncover should be comprehensive in nature; you must be "tuned in" to knowledge. When you teach elementary school children you teach with all you can find out about, learning more than you can ever expect to cover in the unit. Many questions requiring information on specific points will come from the children. It certainly is permissible for a teacher to reply, "I don't know. Let's find out together," to children's questions each day, but the teacher who can answer a great many questions is the one who communicates greater preparedness. Study the key facts related to the theme; think about the concepts and important generalizations that should emerge. Constantly seek the major learnings that can arise from the planned instruction. That important background material should be outlined at the beginning of your unit. The outline is usually preceded by a short summary paragraph like the sample.

Summary Paragraph

When we view the earth from space, we see a large blue ball. That blue is water, covering more than 70% of the earth's surface; 97% of this water is in the oceans. The large expanses seemingly floating in the blue are the continents. The earth is a unique planet in our solar system because it is the only one that has water. Children have a natural curiosity about the oceans. This curiosity will be tapped as the students discover the many interesting features of the earth's fascinating oceans. The content to be developed includes:

I. Names of oceans
  A. Atlantic
  B. Pacific
  C. Indian
  D. Arctic
  E. Antarctic

(It is beyond the scope of this book to list additional content, but the list would be continued until the teacher thought there was sufficient background to develop a satisfactory understanding of the topic.)

Objectives

After settling upon the major theme of a unit and collecting accurate content, teachers are next confronted with a decision about what they want to do with it. Let us relate that decision to our vacation trip analogy, when we decided that Florida would be the most desirable spot to visit (our "theme"). Trip plans are not complete when we choose only the place where we wish to spend some time; we must go further and decide what to do when we get there:

- To visit Disney World and Epcot
- To swim, surf, and bask in the sun
- To visit Cape Canaveral, St. Augustine, the Everglades, or other points of interest
- To sample the possibilities at various night spots or parties
- To charter a boat for a pleasure cruise or fishing trip

Of course, other possibilities exist—shopping, dog racing, jai alai, water skiing, snorkeling, car races, and a variety of other choices. If we went to Florida without carefully examining what we wanted to do when we got there, we could find ourselves fluttering around from one activity to another without spending enough time on any single venture to get anything out of it. Or, we could devote so much time to one activity that we ran out of time for any of the others. In much the same way, teachers must choose from among the many possibilities and identify what they want to do with the theme chosen for their unit. *Objectives* are carefully constructed statements that identify what you want your children to accomplish from a planned sequence of instruction; they provide a focus that prevents the instructional sequence from wandering aimlessly or from becoming stalled in one place too long.

General Unit Objectives

When teachers plan objectives for their social studies units, they examine the range of possible outcomes for the learning experience: "How will children change their thinking, feelings, and actions as a result of the unit?" Objectives for social studies instruction commonly fall into the four categories of objectives that the NCSS considers essential for effective citizenship now and in the future (see Chapter 1). Each category is important, but the categories cannot be equally emphasized in all units because of the nature of the content itself. For example, skills objectives would be sure to dominate a unit such as "Learning About Latitude and Longitude," and knowledge objectives would seem most fitting for a unit entitled "How Laws Are Made." Some units, then, naturally lend themselves to a certain category of objectives, but most should incorporate a balance of objectives taken from all categories.

The selection of unit objectives is a matter of choice made by individual teachers after careful consideration of important information:

1. *Children*—What are their needs and interests? How do they learn most effectively? Can they perform the responsibilities they are likely to encounter?
2. *Nature of the Subject*—What are the types of learning that can arise from the subject matter? What contributions can the subject matter make in the lives of young children?
3. *Previous Experiences*—What has worked in the past? What relation does this new topic have to previous units or to other subjects?

Bloom's Taxonomy.   Teachers and curriculum planners have long utilized objectives in the planning process, but it was not until 1956 that a classification system was developed for the purpose of helping planners effectively state objectives that encompassed a wide range of learning possibilities. In that year, Benjamin S. Bloom compiled a series of recommendations generated by a committee formed by the American Psychological Association. The committee's responsibility was to organize and write a taxonomy (hierarchical classification system) of objectives for the three domains of learning: (1) *cognitive* (intellectual abilities and skills), (2) *affective* (attitudes and values), and (3) *psychomotor* (motor skills and coordination). The area that was most central to their work, and the one having the clearest definition of objectives, was the cognitive domain. The taxonomy was first presented in Bloom's 1956 book, *Taxonomy of Educational Objectives.*[11] It has been a highly influential reference for teachers and curriculum developers ever since. The taxonomy is described as hierarchical; that is, learning behaviors are classified from the simple to the complex. The simplest behavior becomes integrated with the next higher, those behaviors with the next, and so on until the most complex behavior is a combination of all classification units. Figure 3–4 summarizes the major components of Bloom's taxonomy. Notice that the simplest behavior is raw knowledge and the most complex is evaluation. Knowledge demands only the ability to recall facts, while evaluation demands the utilization of all other thinking skills. The objectives in Figure 3–4 have been related to our sample unit theme, "Our Beautiful Blue Planet."

One of the greatest problems faced by beginning teachers is to perceive the differences among the levels of Bloom's taxonomy. It takes time and practice to feel comfortable with them, so do not lose confidence if you are asked to apply your knowledge of objectives by formulating a set for a unit of your choice and find yourself floundering. Try to include as many levels as possible, though, for the traditional nature of elementary school social studies programs has been to focus only on the first two. Children must be offered opportunities to go beyond recalling or remembering knowledge by being involved in classroom activities that encourage higher-order thinking skills such as problem-solving and critical thinking.

Remember two important points when you write your unit objectives:

1. *State objectives in terms of the children.* An inappropriate objective would be one that described the behavior of the teacher; for example, "The teacher will furnish the children with information about our world's oceans." When you write objectives,

FIGURE 3–4
Major Components of Bloom's Taxonomy of Educational Objectives (Cognitive Domain)

Knowledge: This is probably the most common educational objective in American education. As the lowest level of cognitive functioning, this level involves only the recall of specific bits of isolated information. For example: "The students shall know the names of the five oceans."

Comprehension: This is the level at which students mentally organize and reorganize information for particular purposes, rather than storing it as received. Students not only know what is communicated, but are able to organize it sufficiently to restate it in a parallel form of communication. For example: "The students shall differentiate between the continental shelf and the continental slope." If the students read about these features—one form of communication—then they may express their understanding by drawing a diagram, writing a report, or by using any other type of communication that does not involve simply recalling some facts.

Application: This level encourages the use of information in new, concrete situations. You will often hear teachers say, "If Sally really comprehends this material, she can apply it." This means that if a student is given a problem in a context different from that where the understandings were developed, she will be able to transfer her learning to that problem situation; she will be able to solve it correctly without prompting. For example: "When presented with appropriate materials, the students shall prepare a miniature oceanic environment in a classroom aquarium." We expect that the students will apply their knowledge of oceans and ocean life to the preparation of the aquarium.

Analysis: This level involves the ability to break down the material into its component parts and to understand how thoughts or ideas are organized. Students are led to distinguish fact from opinion, identify whether conclusions are valid, see how one idea relates to another, and so on. For example, "The students shall examine the arguments of the proponents of ocean dumping to see whether their conclusions are valid."

Synthesis: This level involves a process of working with information and combining its component parts so as to create something that was not clearly there before. The students may be asked to produce a unique way to convey ideas or plan a set of operations to be carried out in order to fulfill a certain objective. For example: "The students shall create a short jingle for use in their campaign to clean up the dirty beaches."

Evaluation: This level requires students to make judgments about the accuracy or value of ideas, materials, objects, solutions, works, and so on. The student uses specific information to make these judgments; they must be backed up with sound evidence. For example, "The students shall decide whether or not garbage should be dumped into our oceans."

---

your statements must describe what you want the *children* to accomplish; *your* objective, of course, is to make sure the objectives are realized.

2. *List only a few objectives.* One problem in organizing objectives is to state too many. You can expect a topic of study in the primary grades to last one to three weeks, and in the upper grades, three to six weeks. That time limitation restricts you to choosing only objectives that appear most desirable. It is usually appropriate to list four to eight objectives for any topic of study.

Behavioral Objectives

Some educators think that the general nature of unit objectives makes it virtually impossible for others to understand fully what the unit developer wants to accomplish. For example, an objective such as, "The children shall understand that oceans are huge" lacks meaningful focus. For that reason, they prefer to state objectives in terms of direct, observable behaviors, called *behavioral objectives.* Behavioral objectives identify the specific behaviors children will demonstrate as they progress through the learning activities. Behavioral objectives are comprised of three parts: (1) identifying the input process; (2) describing what the student is to do; and (3) stating the minimum acceptable level of performance.

Behavioral objectives frequently give specificity to broader objectives. For example, a general objective might be, "The children shall understand that oceans are huge." Specific behavioral objectives for this general objective might include: "After viewing a film dealing with the physical conditions of oceans (input), the children shall be able to state (what the children are to do) that water covers 70% of the earth's surface and that 97% of that water is in the oceans (level of performance)."

You should state at least one specific behavioral objective for each general objective. Proponents of behavioral objectives believe they provide more direction to a unit because each general objective must be examined in greater depth. Depending on the philosophy of a school system, objectives need not always be stated in behavioral terms, but when they are, they are usually written within the separate lesson plans themselves. You will find that certain words or phrases cue in the three parts of behavioral objectives. To cue in the *input process,* these typical phrases would help:

- Given a topographic map . . .
- Given an encyclopedia . . .
- After examining the globe . . .
- After listening to a taped interview with a member of Greenpeace . . .
- Given five seemingly unrelated objects associated with oceans . . .

These phrases alert you to the *observable performance* (what the child is to do):

- . . . the children will use the legend to locate . . .
- . . . the children will write . . .
- . . . the children will orally list . . .
- . . . the children will identify . . .
- . . . the children will write . . .

Phrases like these cue in the desired *level of performance:*

- . . . three communities that are ocean ports.
- . . . a paragraph containing five accurate facts about oceans.
- . . . the five major oceans.
- . . . three statements of fact and three statements of opinion.
- . . . a minimum of two plausible hypotheses to describe their interrelatedness.

Test your ability to identify behavioral objectives by examining this list of five objectives.

1. The children will really understand the concept of exploration after they read five pages from the textbook.
2. Given a scrambled list of capital cities and states, the children will match each capital and its corresponding state with one hundred percent accuracy.
3. After reading a biography of any famous explorer, the children will write a paragraph of nine or ten sentences describing at least two major events in the person's life.
4. To gain insight into the lives of the Forty-niners.
5. Other than watching television, the children will write all of the things they could be doing on a Saturday morning. Discuss with your classmates the reasons for your choices.

I have selected statements 2 and 3 as behavioral objectives. Statement 1 lacks mention of observable performance and level of performance; statement 4 does not include input process, observable performance, or level of performance; and statement 5 does not specify the input process. Do you agree with me? Try rewriting each nonbehavioral objective to make it a behavioral objective.

Learning Activities

Objectives for a unit provide us with direction; they give us reasons for pursuing a topic and describe the outcomes we wish to attain. For that reason, the types of learning experiences we provide for the children should be closely allied with the stated objectives. Using our trip to Florida as an illustrative example, we must ask ourselves, "Now that we've determined where we're going and what we want to do when we get there, how can we get there most efficiently?" We can examine all the possibilities: airplane, boat, car, bus, motorcycle, pogo stick, balloon. Choices are numerous and varied. Some are ridiculous selections and would never allow us to satisfy our objectives; others are more realistic and reasonably suited to helping us accomplish our goals. A pogo stick would be useless in relation to the objective of getting to Florida as quickly as possible, but how would our attitudes change if we chose to break the *Guinness Book of World Records* entry for the longest trip by an unusual form of transportation? Likewise, learning activities that appear appropriate for one set of objectives may be totally useless in accomplishing another set. Too often, activities are chosen because they are "cute" or gimmicky and not because they have been identified as the best possibility for accomplishing particular objectives.

What should your children experience and what is your role in making that decision? If–then statements will help you choose classroom learning activities. For example:

> If we want to provide a quick general overview of oceans, then a common textbook reading assignment could be used.
>
> If we want the children to acquire skills of effective problem-solving, then they should examine town records and conduct interviews to produce a "living history" of their beachfront community.
>
> If we want the children to share their feelings about the problem of ocean pollution, then small discussion groups operating in an open, trusting environment could be appropriate.

Social studies educators classify learning activities or resources in many ways. Some classify those that are best for the *introductory phases* of unit development (pictures, map study, exhibits) and those that are best for the *developmental phases* (reading, writing, interviewing). Some label activities that are best for *research* (using references, collecting), and others as best for *expression* (murals, music). Still others classify resources or activities under labels such as *dramatics, audiovisual, oral expression,* and so on. A major fault with labeling activities or resources this way is that many are multipurpose; they easily fit into more than one category. For example, a resource such as a movie can be shown as an *initiating activity* at the beginning of a unit to create interest and enthusiasm as well as a common background of knowledge. Or, it may be a *developmental activity* when shown as a source of information. The movie could also be a *culminating activity* if it were shown to summarize main ideas at the end of the unit. Despite the limitations of categorizing activities, we will discuss unit activities as initiating activities, developmental activities, and culminating activities.

Initiating Activities

Initiating activities are stimulating experiences provided during the first day or two of a unit to arouse curiosity, introduce the topic to the children, and provide a common experience from which all the children can draw. Usually, you will want to arrange the environment during the launching phase so as to give the children exposure to the topic. Some teachers provide books, pictures, models, realia, clothing and other items for the children to explore and manipulate. As the children make comments and ask questions of each other, the teacher notes which might be elaborated during a subsequent discussion period. Other teachers may not plan an extensive initiating activity; they may simply show a film, read a story, take a field trip, or play a recording. Regardless, your concern is to establish interest, help the children relate the new material to previous experiences, and provide direction for subsequent learning.

Developmental Activities

After the introductory or interest-generating phase, you will begin other developmentally appropriate activities for achieving the unit objectives. Know what learning expe-

At the heart of social studies instruction lie enjoyable, productive learning experiences.

riences your class has had prior to entering your classroom. If they had been accustomed to problem-centered learning and group work, you can move on from there. If they have only whole-class instruction with a basic textbook and very little enrichment work, you should not plan for great changes during the first few weeks of school. Young children need the security of familiar experiences. Judge where the children are and move them cautiously to where you want them to be. A continuum of teaching methodologies commonly employed during the developmental phase of units is illustrated in Figure 3–5.

After you determine the level of the children's experience, start your instructional pattern there and move the students step by step toward the point you want them to reach.

Culminating Activities

Although units are usually planned for periods of two weeks or more, a unit should end when the children's interest begins to wane. Culminating activities bring a smooth conclusion to the study and pull together the learning gained through various activities. The culmination might be an assembly program to which all parents are invited, completing a map or mural, presenting a play, or visiting a historical site. Whatever you choose, all culminating activities should help children come to conclusions, draw generalizations, evaluate progress, and suggest areas for further study.

Not all units need to end with a culminating activity. Sometimes the unit that follows is such a natural transition that neither a culminating activity for the first unit nor an introductory experience for the second is necessary. If one unit deals with personal

FIGURE 3–5

A Continuum of Teaching Methodologies Commonly Found in Elementary Social Studies Classrooms

		TEXTBOOK (SUPPLEMENTED)	INQUIRY	
	TEXTBOOK (EXCLUSIVELY)	A basic textbook is supplemented with additional reading from other texts, reference books, and trade books. Children are given individual assignments and varied supplementary experiences such as field trips, resource persons, and audio-visual presentations. Higher thinking levels encouraged.	Variety of reading materials (including texts) and teacher-student planning. Problem-centered learning where children seek solutions to stimulating situations by using field trips, resource persons, audio-visual presentations, and so on. Considerable individualized thinking rewarded.	INFORMAL EDUCATION
LECTURE	Children receive information from one basic textbook. Very little enrichment reading, field trips, or audio-visual presentations. Emphasis is on content memorization.			Much individual and small group work emphasized. Children consult with teachers to pursue topics of interest. Inquiry techniques and learning centers promote rigorous thinking.
Children receive information from a speaker who tells the information they need to know. Very little enrichment activity.				

growth, perhaps "Belonging to Groups," stressing the interdependence between individuals and their groups, and the next unit, "Being Yourself," stresses the importance of uniqueness, the continuity need not be broken in the transition from one unit to the other. You will soon learn to judge whether to end a unit with a culminating activity.

You must carefully arrange the three major categories of activities, because each activity flows from preceding experiences and furnishes the foundation for those that follow. Arranging a meaningful sequence is like putting together a puzzle (Figure 3–6). Many teachers fit the pieces together by moving from the specific to the general, as illustrated in the teacher-directed sequence in Figure 3–7. These program designs demand a carefully planned beginning sequence, since all subsequent higher-level thought is based on clear understanding of the topic. The teacher thus deliberately controls learning experiences and sequences them to lead children in a cumulative way to eventual mastery of the whole. This list of activities illustrates how one teacher sequenced instruction for a unit on "Our Beautiful Blue Planet." Although they will not be directly linked to our unit theme, other options for organizing and implementing learning activities will be presented in Chapters 4–8.

Activity One. Set up a "Miracles of the Ocean" interest center; fill it with a wealth of information. Use a fishing net decorated with colorful paper shells and fish as a backdrop. Display books, pictures, shells, assorted model boats, diving or fishing gear, and similar treasures about the ocean for the children to explore. Allow them ample opportunity to ask questions and make discoveries.

FIGURE 3–6
Putting Together the Pieces of a Unit

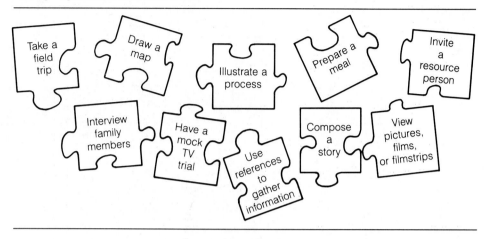

Upon the captain's signal (ring a bell), the children all take their seats and pretend to get ready for a trip on a submarine to discover and explore more about the fascinating oceans. Once the submarine has "submerged," show a film depicting various characteristics of oceans: location, area, depth, saltiness, waves, tides, underwater life, and so on.

Activity Two. Review the findings from the previous day. Lead the children in a discussion of the major ideas and record their contributions on the chalkboard. Divide the class into several small groups and help each group plan its contributions for a large mural of underwater life. Add shells, underwater features, plant life, even a sunken ship or buried treasure to the mural.

Activity Three. Help children identify animals that live in the ocean. Make a "fishing pole" by attaching a piece of string to a dowel stick. Tie a magnet to the end of the string to serve as a hook. Draw small pictures of sea animals (or cut them out of magazines, if possible), cut around their shapes, slip on paper clips, and put them into a large blue box. Children use their magnet "hooks" to catch a picture. The animal must be identified and researched. The children summarize what they discovered about their animals on index cards which are displayed next to the pictures in a "Sea World" classroom exhibit.

Activity Four. Play a "Who Am I?" game with your students to review the content uncovered in the previous activity. One child is chosen to come to the front of the room. The teacher selects one card from the "Sea World" display in full view of the rest of the class, but the child who is "it" cannot see the card. He or she must then ask questions that could help distinguish that animal from all others—the way it looks, walks, swims, hunts for food, and so on. For example, "Do I live in tropical waters? Do I have a shell?"

Activity Five. Read to the class the folk tale, "Why the Sea Is Salt." After reading it, tell the children why the oceans really are salty. Then ask them to hypothesize

FIGURE 3–7
*One Method of Organizing
Lessons Within a Unit*

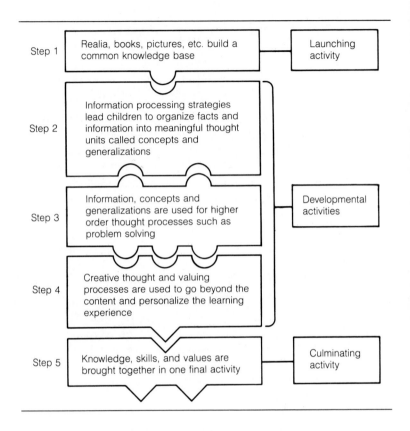

why the ocean looks blue. Record their answers. Ask them to spin a yarn entitled, "Why the Ocean Is Blue." After they finish and share their creations, explain that the ocean has no color, that the blue color is the reflection of the sky.

Activity Six. Show a videotape clip of a news show describing the misuse of our oceans—dumping garbage, oil spills, threats to marine life, and the like. If possible, invite an older citizen of the area to visit the class and speak about the changes in the local ocean environment during his or her lifetime. (We are assuming that this unit is happening in a coastal community.)

Activity Seven. Today the class will participate in an ecology field trip to a nearby beach area recently cited in the newspaper as particularly subject to ecological abuse. Ask each of the children to find two glaring examples of ecological abuse.

Activity Eight. Discuss the field trip, including "What did we see at the beach? What did we learn? How did you feel about what you saw?"

Ask the children to share the two examples of ecological abuse they found and to think about what can be done to eliminate them.

Activity Nine. Ask groups to plan their own "before and after" albums by drawing illustrations of the ideas shared in activities six to eight and putting them together in a booklet. As an extension, ask them to illustrate a scene depicting an ecological condition in the year 2100 if current habits do not change.

Activity Ten. This is the culminating activity. It should bring a satisfying climax to the unit. The children will compile the results of their study and present it as a dramatic skit to the other classrooms of the same grade.

Choosing the materials and activities for any unit can be an exciting challenge. It is a deeply personal process because the particular needs and interests of the students as well as the unique talents of any teacher all influence what is chosen. The sample activities described could be replaced by ten different activities and yet achieve the same objectives for the unit. To judge which set of ten is best would be a deep philosophical decision, open to strong debate. This is an engaging aspect of social studies instruction; perhaps no other part of the elementary school curriculum offers such flexibility in choice of methods and materials for instruction. Take advantage of this wonderful strength and allow yourself to create daily social studies programs full of significant activities. However, your activities should always be based on a premise that elementary school children do not have to sit down to learn the subject matter; they need not always be quiet; they should not always stay together as a large group; and they need not always locate information in a book. Social studies education must be enjoyable for both the teacher and the children. A sampling of the wide variety of instructional resources is presented in Figure 3–8. Many of them will be elaborated upon throughout the remainder of this book, as will the techniques and strategies for using them.

LESSON PLANS

Returning to our vacation trip anaology, you have now done all a good tour guide should do for your clients: you helped choose a destination based on interests and skills; you assisted in the development of objectives for the trip; and you helped your clients decide how they would get there. Now that everyone has reached the destination, it would be a good idea to establish a more detailed daily itinerary. We have the "big picture," but must now think about the specifics of our daily adventures. Much the same is true of our unit plan.

It is useful to think of our daily lesson plan as a unit plan in miniature. Lesson plans are outlines that identify exactly what we wish to accomplish during a specific day's experiences. They contain the same components as the unit plan, but in more detailed form: summary paragraph, objectives, and learning activities. See the sample lesson plan in Figure 3–9.

The *summary paragraph* explains the content to be stressed in the lesson. It is written for the teacher and explains information important for an understanding of the topics.

Objectives tell the teacher's purpose for the daily lesson. Usually, the teacher develops one, two, or three lesson plans to teach or reinforce one of the long-range objectives from the unit plan. You will often have to clarify your thinking by stating specific behavioral objectives for each long-term objective.

The *learning activities* section of the plan outline the procedure a teacher expects to follow to meet the lesson objectives and lists the teaching materials he will use. This section should fall into three parts:

1. *A good beginning,* in which you arouse curiosity, stimulate the imagination, relate the new content to past experiences, and establish a purpose for learning.
2. *An effective learning situation* (for which you should always have a contingency plan in case a learning activity falls flat) that provides significant situations in which the children can become involved.
3. *An effective finale* that achieves some sort of intellectual or aesthetic closure.

FIGURE 3–8
Instructional Resources for Social Studies Units

Albums	Field Trips	Pen Pals
Almanacs	Films	Photographs
Art Works	Filmstrips	Pictures
Atlases	Flags	Poetry
Biographies	Flannelboard	Postcards
Books	Free Materials	Posters
Bulletin Boards	Games	Products
Cartoons	Globes	Puppets
Cassettes	Government Publications	Puzzles
Chalkboard	Graphs	Questioning Strategies
Charts	Group Work	Radio
Checklists	Illustrations	Records
Coins	Inquiry	Reports (oral and written)
Collages	Interest Centers	Resource Persons
Collections	Interviews	Rewritten Materials
Community Action Projects	Learning Centers	Scrapbooks
Community Helpers	Literature	Sewing
Computers	Logs	Slides
Cooking	Magazines	Stamps
Costumes	Maps	Stories
Creative Dramatics	Marionettes	Study Prints
Dancing	Mobiles	Surveys
Diagrams	Models	Tape Recordings
Diaries	Mosaics	Television
Dictionaries	Murals	Tests
Dioramas	Museums	Textbooks
Directories	Music	Time Lines
Dolls	Newspapers	Tools
Drawings	Observation	Transparencies
Encyclopedias	Opaque Projector	Travel Brochures
Etchings	Oral Expression	Videotapes
Exhibits	Ornaments	Workbooks
Fiction	Overhead Projector	Written Expression

FIGURE 3–9
Sample Lesson Plan

LESSON NUMBER FIVE

Summary Paragraph

A central component of the study of oceans is sand. Sand begins as rock, which is gradually broken down by the forces of nature—wind, rain, and frost. The particles are eventually washed into the oceans and polished and ground by the waters into fine grains of sand.

In this lesson students will learn how sand is made in nature and investigate its properties in the classroom.

Objectives

1. The students shall describe how sand is created by the forces of nature.
2. The students shall discover the creative potential of working with sand.

Learning Activities

1. Begin by holding up a picture of a beach scene. Discuss the features with the students. Relate the discussion to the students' life experiences.
2. Inform the students that they will be viewing a filmstrip. Before it starts, motivate the children and share your purpose for showing it: "Who would care to guess how many grains of sand there are on the beach? How many are in this jar?" (Hold up a jar filled with sand.) "We may never know the answers to those questions, but we do know one thing—how sand is made. Watch the filmstrip to see if you can find out how it is done."
3. Divide the class into four groups of six students each; arrange the groups in circles. Give one student in each group a ball of yarn and explain that they will be starting a "deep sea yarn" (story) with the help of the ball. The student holds the loose end and begins a story: "I am a grain of sand. I began my life as a _____ ." The child finishes the story starter, holds onto the loose end, and rolls the ball to any other member of the group. That student must continue the story with another detail about the process of making sand. She holds onto her segment of yarn and rolls the ball to another student who continues the story. Repeat the procedure until everyone has had a chance. After the last student offers his contribution, wind the yarn backwards until it comes back to the starter. Make sure all the children repeat their contribution as the ball comes back.
4. Debrief the activity by asking:
   a. "From where do all grains of sand get their start?"
   b. "Which forces of nature help create sand?"
   c. "How does the ocean help make sand?"
   d. "What products do you know that are made of sand?"
   e. "How many of you have ever made something out of sand? What did you make? Where did you make it? When?"
5. Explain that the students will be making sand sculptures, just as many of them may have made at the beach. "This time, there will be a big difference: These sand sculptures will not wash away or crumble. They will actually last for quite some time." Use these materials:

   > 4 cups sand
   > 2 cups water
   > 2 cups cornstarch
   > pan, spoon, and hot plate

   Mix the ingredients and stir over low heat until the mixture thickens. When cool, the children can sculpt various sea creatures they have learned about. They will share their creatures with one another tomorrow.
6. Conclude by telling the students that their creations will become a part of the classroom interest center.
7. Review the day's activity by asking the children to tell you what they learned about sand.

EVALUATION

As we conclude each daily experience on our vacation trip we will have strong feelings about whether or not our plans were successful. Upon arriving home, we will again reconsider all of our activities to judge whether the trip as a whole accomplished what we set out to do for the entire vacation: "What was worthwhile? What was most enjoyable? Did we grow from the experience? If not, why not? Was there anything we didn't like about the vacation? What could we have done to make the trip more successful?" In a like manner, lessons and units must be continuously evaluated by teachers to judge what they actually accomplished. Evaluation is a somewhat more complex activity than we can explain at this point. A comprehensive discussion of evaluation in the elementary school social studies program is offered in Chapter 15.

Plan your program to fit your children's interests and needs. No single chapter can hope to give you a complete idea of the many factors that influence a teacher's choices while planning lessons and units. Central to the process, however, is an awareness of and sensitivity to the "real world" of children, one that includes careful, day-by-day observations and evaluations that serve as a basis for offering what is most meaningful and interesting.

SUMMARY

Successful teachers of elementary school social studies are good decision makers. They examine the recommendations of authorities in the field, weigh the benefits and shortcomings of each, and settle on a program that blends these influences with their own personality and style. Nothing is so professionally rewarding as watching children flourish in a dynamic program that grows and develops from your own initiative. No paycheck or other concrete reward can ever match the joy you'll experience when a wide-eyed child saunters up to you and declares, "You're a nice teacher. I really like school this year!"

This chapter has introduced important ideas about how to plan and organize your social studies program. You learned about the need to consider individual differences among the children and why, according to Calvin W. Taylor, each child must be viewed as "talented" in some way. We examined sources from which teachers are able to draw in order to address the individual differences—curriculum guides and textbooks. Next, we focused on the advantages and criticisms of using the most popular source for planning a social studies program—the textbook. Then, we examined a continuum of planning options available for teachers as they plan their own sequence of social studies activities—*children's choices* and *teacher's choices*. Attention was then given to unit plans (long-range designs) and lesson plans (short-range designs). The first step in designing a unit is to select a topic or theme, a process calling for expansive thinking. "Themestorming" enables teachers to determine the potential of a particular theme. A summary paragraph helps to describe the specific focus of the theme. An outline of the content to be stressed follows. Next, the task of formulating objectives (general and specific) faces the teacher. Bloom's taxonomy of educational objectives helps plan the general objectives, while concepts related to behavioral objectives help us write specific objectives. Once the objectives have been determined, teachers must choose appropriate learning experiences to accomplish them. Learning experiences are usually classified as *initiating activities, developmental activities,* and *culminating activities.* Each of these general categories of unit activities is then broken down into

separate daily lesson plans—unit plans in miniature. Finally, attention must be given to careful evaluation throughout each unit and lesson, a topic that will be discussed more thoroughly in Chapter 15.

ENDNOTES

1. Albert Cullum, *Push Back the Desks* (New York: Citation Press, 1967), p. 18.

2. Calvin W. Taylor, "Be Talent Developers . . . As Well as Knowledge Dispensers," *Today's Education, 57,* no. 9 (December 1968): 67–69.

3. Leroy Psencik in (no author) "Excuse Me, Got Change for a Scholar?" *What's Going On With the Three R's?* (Winter 1987 special curriculum issue of *Instructor* Magazine): 31.

4. David F. Kellum, "Presenting Subject Matter," in *Teaching Is . . . ,* ed. Merrill Harmin and Tom Gregory (Chicago: Science Research Associates, 1974), pp. 47–48.

5. John Holt, *How Children Learn* (New York: Pitman, 1967), pp. 185–189.

6. Carl R. Rogers, "Forget You Are a Teacher," in *Educational Psychology,* ed. Meredith D. Gall and Beatrice A. Ward (Boston: Little, Brown, 1974), p. 102.

7. Elizabeth M. Goetz, "In Defense of Curriculum Themes," *Day Care and Early Education, 13,* no. 1 (Fall 1985): 12.

8. Robert Slavin, "The Hunterization of America's Schools," *Instructor* (April 1987): 58.

9. Lavonne A. Hanna, Gladys L. Potter, and Robert W. Reynolds, *Dynamic Elementary Social Studies: Unit Teaching* (New York: Holt, Rinehart and Winston, 1973), p. 80.

10. Jane Baskwill, "Themestorming," *Teaching K–8* (August–September 1988): 80–82.

11. Benjamin S. Bloom, ed., *Taxonomy of Educational Objectives—Cognitive Domain* (New York: Longman, 1956).

Educators have finally arrived at the point that professionals in medicine achieved when the latter discovered that germs and not evil spirits were causing much of the problem. . . . [W]e can use . . . causal relationships to promote student learning in the same way the doctor uses his medical knowledge to promote health. . . . When the doctor prescribes, it is to increase the probability of the patient's recovery, not to guarantee it. In the same way. . . . teaching is now defined as a constant stream of professional decisions made before, and during and after interaction with the student: decisions which, when implemented, increase the probability of learning.[1]

—Madeline Hunter

Using Direct Instruction to Promote Thinking Skills

4

KEY CONCEPTS

As you read, reflect on the following matters:

- Is there one proven best way to teach social studies?
- Why and when should a teacher direct the children's learning?
- How does directed teaching help children master the content by forming concepts and generalizations?
- How have educational specialists such as Hilda Taba and Madeline Hunter helped define the process of directed teaching?
- What is the basic format a teacher might use as a guide to develop a personalized directed lesson?

Questions about the most effective way to teach elementary school social studies have obsessed educators since its introduction to the curriculum of our schools. We have heard disputes between distinguished rivals who were unwavering in their fervent claims: authority vs. democracy, discovery vs. expository, teacher-centered vs. child-centered, direct vs. indirect, and formal vs. informal, just to name a few prevalent positions. Despite their intensity, the clashes in various forums have failed to produce a clear victor in the effort to answer the burning question, "What is the best way to teach?" Out of the resulting smoke and rubble, Paul D. Eggen and Donald P. Kauchak offer this insightful observation: "Thousands of studies have been conducted in an attempt to answer this question in its various forms and the overriding conclusion is that *there is no one best way to teach.*"[2] Instead of being characterized by a magical teaching style accounting for success in all instructional settings, then, it appears that effective social studies teaching demands an ability to select and utilize alternative strategies. E. Paul Torrance observes that, "Alert teachers have always been intuitively aware of the fact that when they changed their method of teaching that certain children who had appeared to be slow learners or even nonlearners became outstanding achievers . . . star learners."[3] Changes in learning, then, are not brought about by teachers who steadfastly stick to one selected teaching style, but by those who conscientiously vary classroom procedures so that each child has an opportunity to be a classroom "star."

R. Murray Thomas and Sherwin G. Swartout are convinced that despite their best intentions, being able to vary instructional procedures is not easily accomplished by teachers:

> Every teacher wishes to be an excellent one. But each falls somewhat short of his aspirations. . . . There are varied reasons for this gap between a teacher's desired excellence and actual performance. In some cases the gap is caused by an inability to understand how students think. In others it is a result of a poor knowledge of subject matter or of an inability to maintain order in class. But often poor teaching is due to a lack of skill in selecting and using teaching methods.[4]

A major aspect of a teacher's job is making decisions. Every time you teach a social studies class, numerous decisions will need to be made: how much time should be allotted, what content should be covered, when the class should be scheduled, and how learning materials should be used, for example. As important as these decisions are, however, there is none more important than selecting the form of instruction to be used for the class. This decision affects not only student achievement and motivation for learning, but classroom behavior as well.

In the social studies there are two contrasting philosophical directions one might take while contemplating an approach to instruction. Each could be considered appropriate if used in a perceptive, skillful, and considerate manner. At one end of a continuum of teaching strategies is the "formal" classroom, where the teacher structures and directs learning, usually instructing the whole class at one time. "Informal" classrooms, on the other hand, involve student control, freedom of choice, exploration, discovery, and a focus on individual interests. We will examine the formal approach to social studies instruction in this chapter; informal strategies will be addressed in Chapters 5 and 6 (see Figure 4–1).

THE FORMAL APPROACH

The formal approach has been a popular teaching method for decades, being variously known as "expository," "mastery," "directed," or "reception" teaching. Since the teacher is in direct control of the entire classroom procedure, I have chosen to use the term "directed" teaching to describe it in this text. Whatever the term chosen, this style of instruction is based on the idea that the teacher defines the knowledge and concepts to be learned and carefully sequences instruction so that learnings progress from the simple to the complex. Supported by prominent authorities such as David P. Ausubel, teachers who use directed instruction view content acquisition as a flight of stairs where *facts* comprise the beginning steps, *concepts* the next, and *generalizations* the top. The development and organization of content thus proceed from facts to concepts and from there to generalizations (see Figure 4–1). *Facts* are discrete bits of information that we have verified as being true. These may include *dates* ("John Cabot claimed North America for England in 1497."); *events* ("The Gettysburg Address was delivered by Abraham Lincoln."); or *places* ("Columbus is the capital of Ohio."). Facts are important

FIGURE 4–1
Movement from Directed Learning to Child-centered Instruction

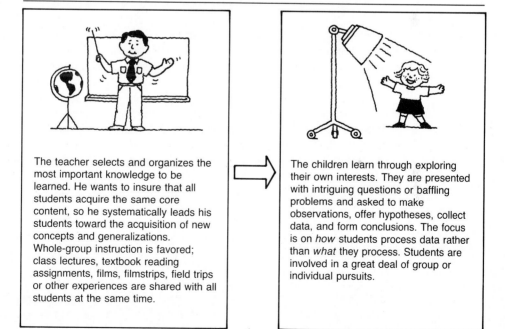

The teacher selects and organizes the most important knowledge to be learned. He wants to insure that all students acquire the same core content, so he systematically leads his students toward the acquisition of new concepts and generalizations. Whole-group instruction is favored; class lectures, textbook reading assignments, films, filmstrips, field trips or other experiences are shared with all students at the same time.

The children learn through exploring their own interests. They are presented with intriguing questions or baffling problems and asked to make observations, offer hypotheses, collect data, and form conclusions. The focus is on *how* students process data rather than *what* they process. Students are involved in a great deal of group or individual pursuits.

parts of the social studies program, for they are the building blocks upon which all higher-order thinking skills are based.

Concepts and Generalizations

Concepts are "ideas" that are based on an individual's ability to classify facts according to their common characteristics. A concept may be very simple—for example, *triangle.* It has two essential characteristics: three sides and three angles. Those two facts are all students need to know as they select triangular shapes from among all other shapes. The concept *triangle,* then, is an idea to which individuals attach personal meaning after repeated experiences. By contrast, a concept such as *justice* is much more difficult to understand because its critical attributes are much more numerous and abstract. The difficulty of a concept, then, depends upon two major factors: how concrete the related characteristics are and how many distinguishing characteristics a concept has. Organizing social studies content into concept categories benefits instruction because concept labels give us a mental filing system into which we catalog newly encountered objects, events, or ideas.

Generalizations are broader patterns of thought that help students link together concepts and discern their relationships. To illustrate, let us examine this generalization: "The more complex a society is, the more cooperation it requires of its citizens." In this statement, there is a relationship between *complex societies* (a concept) and *cooperation* (another concept). Look more closely at the generalization. It applies to all societies rather than to any single group. Each single instance of a society based on cooperation is a fact; a number of instances are still facts. However, when the observation is extended to a global description, it becomes a generalization. Some people become confused when comparing facts and generalizations; both appear to be accurate descriptions, but facts refer to one situation, while generalizations refer to a number of situations.

Ausubel and other direct instruction advocates believe that learning is best enhanced by helping children organize new information and place it in personal coding systems, or cognitive structures. The generalization at the top of Figure 4–2, for example, is called a *subsumer* by Ausubel, because it subsumes all other concepts and content under it. These facts, concepts, and generalizations are seen as best acquired when children's learning is directed by a teacher who has carefully selected and sequenced the content to be learned; the more organized and meaningful the presentation, the more the student will learn.

Directed Teaching as an Active Process

Those who prefer formal, directed teaching see it as an *active* process. Instead of being passively spoon-fed throughout a lesson, learners are mentally active as they seek out information and reorganize what they already know to achieve new learning. Active physical involvement through manipulating objects and other sensory or movement activities are not the only experiences we should classify as "active learning." Active

FIGURE 4–2
The Organization of Facts, Concepts, and Generalizations

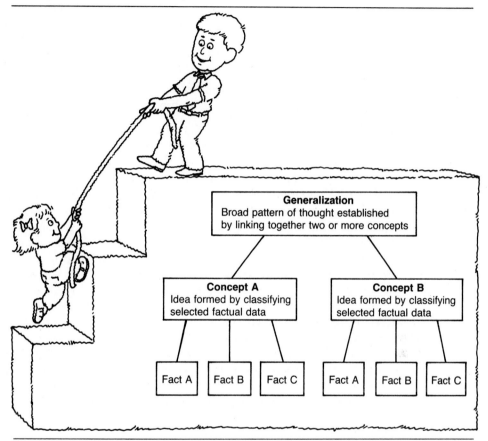

learning happens when students are participating mentally as well. When teachers offer stimulating mental and physical activity during social studies instruction, they help students develop basic concepts, important intellectual skills, and a flexible but organized way of thinking. Whatever concepts the students acquire are products of their own thinking. The teacher deliberately plans a sequence of events so that learners are able to retrieve their related past experiences and use them as a foundation upon which to build their own conceptual frameworks. Frank Smith asserts that concept formation is an active process in which students' new experiences are associated with what they already know or believe. He defines learning as "making sense of the world . . . by relating the unfamiliar to the already known."[5] David Ausubel affirms Smith's belief, declaring, "If I had to reduce all of educational psychology to one principle, I would say this: The most important single factor influencing learning is what the learner already knows."[6]

Teachers employ systematic procedures to guide and facilitate concept formation; the act of concept formation itself is performed by the learner. The ability to build structures and sense the connections among structures is crucial because social studies educators cannot expect to provide students with all the specific knowledge they will need to stay informed throughout their adult lives. Richard C. Remy maintains, "One of the most important attributes of competent citizens in a complex society is the ability to connect things that seem superficially to be discrete. Such an ability is a clear sign of higher order cognition . . . and is a highly prized goal of social studies education."[7] Mark Van Doren supports Remy's view of the importance of making connections:

> [T]he connectedness of things is what the educator contemplates to the limit of his capacity. . . . The student who can begin early in life to think of things as connected, even if he revises his view with every succeeding year, has begun a life of learning.[8]

Systematic, active instructional procedures help students acquire specific knowledge, sense connections among their learnings, and form key concepts. Support for this type of learning can be derived from the works of the renowned Swiss psychologist, Jean Piaget. Piaget explained the active psychological processes associated with a learner's inner drive to actively establish conceptual structures by matching what is known to the demands of a new learning task through the idea of *equilibration.* The state of equilibration (or equilibrium) is seen by Piaget as a basic human biological drive. He took the term from the field of physics and used it to describe an inner motivation to seek a balance between what is already known and what is yet to be understood. When something occurs to upset existing mental structures, there is a natural drive to restore equilibrium. As individuals strive to restore that balance, they reach a new level of equilibrium (intelligence). This movement from one level of intelligence to the next is called *adaptation,* a combination of the two processes of assimilation and accommodation. *Assimilation* is the process of dealing with the environment in terms of current mental structures. *Accommodation* is the process of changing existing structures when those structures do not allow us to deal effectively with the environment. This example dealing with the concept of communication illustrates the process of adaptation.

> Suppose that a first-grade teacher wished to develop the idea that all cultures rely on a system of language, but that some cultures use different forms of language. She gathered the children together, seated them comfortably on the floor, and asked one child to stand alone in a corner of the classroom. She then asked the others to think about ways they might be able to direct the lone child to walk from the corner of the classroom to where they were seated. The children offered obvious solutions by using their voices or printing a command on a large sheet of paper (*assimilation*). To extend the lesson, the teacher brought the children's attention to a drum, explaining that the drum is one of the oldest ways of communicating. She told the children they were to use the drum to tap messages to the child in the corner, each message identifying a different way to move from the corner to their circle: walking, running, dancing, and so on. The children had participated in rhythm and movement activities in kindergarten and first grade, and they needed to apply those experiences to the new problem (*accommodation*). Taking turns, the children tapped out fast rhythms to stimulate running, slower

rhythms to encourage marching, skipping, galloping, and other movements. The children learned through this direct experience that drums can talk to them without using words (*adaptation*).

The simultaneous processes of assimilation and accommodation, then, are *adaptation*. Equilibrium is achieved as the child adapts and moves from one level of understanding to a higher level.

In all his writings, Piaget stressed the importance of physical and mental activity, exploration, and direct experience as necessary ingredients of effective learning. From Piaget's viewpoint, then, the goal of education would be to stimulate children's curiosity by linking what is to be learned to past experiences. This motivates the greatest curiosity; the more curious they are, the more they will explore, the more discoveries they will make, and the more knowledge they will gain. It follows that the more knowledge they have, the more advanced the nature of their curiosity and the more mature their systems of exploration will be.

To help children form concepts, then, we must first be sure that they have one critical mental component—a previous exposure to a topic that serves as an internal "filing system" to help sort and classify new objects, events, or ideas into general categories of meaning. These categories help learners make sense of the vast amount of information they will accumulate throughout their social studies learning experiences. Smith contends that if learners do not have this conceptual filing system, they may opt for one of these methods of coping with the learning situation:

1. *Rejecting the information*—When the incoming subject matter content does not register and we cannot connect it to what we already know, we tend to discard or ignore it.
2. *Miscategorizing the information*—If we choose not to throw out the unperceived information, we may make some attempt to comprehend it. However, the tendency for children is to misfile it. They may place it into a wrong category or simply allow it to float "unattached," thinking that it must belong there someplace.[9]

Mastery Learning

A currently popular technique for directed teaching breaks subject matter down into a series of progressive experiences. Called "mastery learning," this approach contends that nearly all students can learn if they are given sufficient time and appropriate instruction. Benjamin S. Bloom elaborates:

> I find that many of the individual differences in school learning are manmade and accidental rather than fixed in the individual at the time of conception. My major conclusion is: "What any person in the world can learn, almost all persons can learn if provided with appropriate prior and current conditions of learning." However, I would qualify this by stating that there are some individuals with emotional and physical difficulties who are likely to prove to be exceptions to this generalization (perhaps 2 or 3 percent of the population). At the other extreme are 1 or 2 percent of individuals who learn in such unusually capable ways that they may be exceptions to the theory. At this stage of [my] work, it applies clearly to the middle 95 percent of a school population.[10]

Bloom contends, then, that up to 95% of students are capable of mastering most learning tasks in our elementary schools provided they are given appropriate instruction. "Appropriate instruction" was determined by Bloom to consist of such factors as clarifying the learning task, sequencing instructional materials, giving motivational support, matching the new learning task to previous experiences, and monitoring students' progress with effective use of evaluation techniques. This format is commonly referred to as *directed teaching*. Robert W. Gaskins defines directed teaching as "explaining to the students what they will be doing, why they will be doing it, how to do it, and when they can apply it. . . . This is followed by teacher modeling, teacher-guided application, and the teacher's gradual release of responsibility to the students."[11] We will examine two directed teaching formats: the *Madeline Hunter Approach* and the *Directed Learning Episode*.

The Madeline Hunter Approach

Recently the term "mastery learning" has become synonymous with the Madeline Hunter approach.[12] School districts around the country have enthusiastically accepted her theories of instruction, figuratively expecting to see "Madeline Hunter" evident in every lesson. The approach is so clearly orchestrated that for each instructional session teachers are advised to follow the "seven-step lesson." Here are examples of those steps.

1. *Anticipatory Set.* The suggested opening of a Madeline Hunter lesson creates an "anticipatory set," which is designed to focus the children's attention on the content of the upcoming lesson. The anticipatory set is also intended to hook into what the students already know about the topic. This gives teachers important diagnostic information; the children's "entry behavior" can be evaluated (what they already know or can do that will help them meet the demands of the new learning task).

2. *Statement of Objectives.* At the beginning of the lesson the teacher informs the students what they will know or be able to do at the end of the lesson. Students tend to learn better if they know what they will be learning and why it is important to them. For example, "Today we are going to write letters to Albany so you can get the materials you need to complete your social studies project."

3. *Instructional Input.* Information is considered the foundation of all learning; without information, we cannot build concepts, develop generalizations, or do higher-level thinking. The teacher must search extensively to find the information that can best accomplish the instructional objectives. That basic information must be organized so that it becomes the "magnet" to which children can add more complex information. All information must be presented in an organized way so that the students can progress from facts to concepts to generalizations, and eventually to more complex mental processes.

4. *Modeling the Information or Process.* We must help students see what we mean by providing a model of an acceptable finished product. The model may be concrete, such as a replica of a Native American tepee. It may be a replication, such as an illustration, chart, or map. Or it may be verbal, written, or spoken, such as a paragraph,

poem, or sample letter form. By offering a model, we turn a plea of, "Show me what you mean," into a satisfied, "I see what you mean."

It is important that the visual model be accompanied by verbal input about what is happening (or what has happened). For example, "Notice that the main character in my political cartoon has exaggerated features that help the reader to quickly identify who she is."

5. *Checking for Understanding.* The teacher must constantly observe the students' performance to make sure they possess the essential information or exhibit the skills necessary to achieve the intended instructional objective. Hunter says that we waste a great deal of instructional time with poor attempts to check students' understanding. The most common wasted effort is a teacher's ubiquitous "OK?" assuming that silence indicates understanding: "We're ready to move on to the next point, OK?" Such dysfunctional attempts to check students' understanding often result in the teacher marching blissfully through the lesson unaware that some students are lost. Hunter recommends that teachers use (1) *signaled answers* ("Thumbs up if the statement is true, down if false, to the side if you're not sure."); (2) *choral responses* ("Tell me whether this statement is fact or opinion."); (3) *sample individual response* (The teacher makes inferences based on a stratified sample of the whole class. For example, if a bright student is confused, we can assume most of the students do not understand; if a slower student responds correctly, the class is probably ready to move on.); and (4) *tests, papers, or observations of performance.*

6. *Guided Practice.* During this step of a Hunter lesson, students must answer short questions or solve problems. Teachers circulate among the students to make sure that they can perform all (or enough) of the task. If so, they can move on to independent practice. If not, needed remediation must occur immediately.

7. *Independent Practice.* Once the students can perform without major errors, they are ready to develop fluency without the constant presence of the teacher.

Robert Slavin examined Madeline Hunter's tremendous influence on instruction in contemporary classrooms and, despite its widespread popularity, finds little originality in her approach.

> Certainly, these elements of lesson design are hardly unique to Madeline Hunter. Many learning theorists call for a comparable sequence of activities. Besides, good teachers have used similar lessons ever since the first teacher had to teach more than one student at a time! That is, if asked, *What do you think you should do in an outstanding lesson?*, most teachers would give these steps never having heard of Madeline Hunter.[13]

Slavin's major reason for worry over the popularity of Hunter is that some will believe it is the only effective way to teach. Such a narrow conception could only lead to lack of spontaneity in teaching and eventually inhibit innovation. Hunter, on the other hand, counters Slavin's concerns by stating: "I believe teachers should be free to use their own creativity. Creative people have tremendous specific knowledge. Our model only tries to build that specific knowledge into a professional launching pad from which creativity can really soar."[14]

A Personalized Approach

Many teachers appreciate model programs such as Hunter's because they help make efficient use of time in the social studies classroom. Others are not comfortable with such prescriptive plans because they believe that opportunities to think creatively, to solve problems, and to make satisfying and productive decisions about how to teach young children are fundamental responsibilities of social studies teachers. They wish to help students achieve instructional goals, but are sensitive to the apparently prescriptive, formulaic nature of the Hunter approach. Such teachers are concerned that no single method can be appropriate or applicable to all situations. They prefer to take the basic tenets of well-founded instructional theories and modify suggested patterns of instruction to fit changing classroom conditions.

DIRECTED LEARNING EPISODES

Directed lessons for guiding the comprehension of any social studies learning experience involve four general steps:

1. Introduction
2. Learning experience
3. Information processing
4. Reinforcement and extension

We will call this four-step procedure a *directed learning episode,* or DLE. In the material that follows you will learn how to teach toward concept acquisition by using the DLE.

The Introductory Stage

For children to benefit most from a DLE, teachers must begin their lessons with an introduction that involves three critical instructional responsibilities:

1. Associating the children's previous knowledge to the new material
2. Introducing new terms
3. Setting a purpose for the activity

Associating Previous Knowledge

One fourth-grade social studies reading selection about a Native American Indian village, in which the major concept is "interdependence"—people's reliance on one another to survive—begins: "A long time ago, during the time of Thunder Moon, small children helped the people of the village meet their needs for food by collecting wild berries, nuts, and seeds."

Before presenting this reading to the students, the teacher needed to do something to help them understand the passage. He understood that there might be two possible problems with this selection. The first has to do with the reference to "Thunder Moon," and the second is the probability that not many fourth graders would understand that small children's contributions would be so crucial to a village's survival. He wanted to do a bit more with these ideas than tell the children that the old American Indian calendar was organized by "moons" rather than "months" and that the children's responsibilities in the Native American culture were different from those in the children's own lives. He began there, but went on to help them find out what the present month was in the old Native American calendar and how the Indians kept a record of days. The children then wrote that day's symbol and even used it in different contexts during their school day, writing it on their assignments or on the classroom calendar. The teacher displayed pictures from various cultures to show how different the world was in the past and how children contributed to the survival of other social groups, too. The important point, however, is that he previewed the selection to determine what unfamiliar areas might impede comprehension and provided help in those areas prior to the learning experience itself. This is old advice, but recent research adds support for this crucial teaching practice. Carver found that when children fail to adequately comprehend written

Many teachers believe that directed learning experiences are the most efficient and effective means for children to develop social studies concepts and generalizations.

material, it is primarily because they do not possess the necessary experiential background to relate to the new information.[15] There are a number of motivational techniques to help children bridge the gap between previous encounters and new experiences.

Motivational Techniques

Past Experiences/New Material.   Sometimes a brief question or comment will bridge the gap between what the children have already experienced and a new learning experience. For example, you may say, "Yesterday, you'll remember, we learned where Kenya was located on our globe. On which continent is Kenya located? Africa is right. See if you can locate Africa on the globe." Write the word *coffee* on the board. Show some coffee ads from newspapers and invite the children to smell a freshly opened can of coffee. Ask them, "How many of your parents drink coffee?" Tell them that coffee is grown in Kenya and that today they will be seeing a film about the Komu family, who raise coffee in Africa.

Predictions.   A second motivational technique is to encourage the children to hypothesize about what will happen. For example, one teacher wished to help children see how life in times past was different from life today. She chose to read *Ox-Cart Man*, written by Donald Hall and illustrated by Barbara Cooney. Before the book was read she asked the students, "How do you move heavy things from one place to another? How do your parents move heavy things from home to somewhere else?" Showing a picture of a scene from the colonial era, the teacher continued, "How do you suppose people living long ago did these things? Listen to the story to see if you can find out."

Real Objects, Pictures, or Other Materials.   A third motivational technique is to show something to the children. You know that children are full of questions as they continually attempt to discover the hows, whats, and whys of life. They are extremely curious, a characteristic that should be a highly motivational tool for classroom teachers. You could introduce a new learning experience by motivating children this way: Arrange on a work table a number of tools used by early American farmers. Ask questions about the types of tools the children see: "What are these tools? Are these hand tools or machines? These are tools used by early American farmers. What kind of tools are they?" The children can then be informed that a guest speaker will explain how these and other tools were used by early American farmers.

These are not rigid recommendations to follow to the letter before each learning activity. You must adapt your techniques to the type of material you will present. A relatively simple reading selection may require only a short discussion; a more difficult learning experience may require much more—real objects, pictures, chalkboard lists, or other types of background building. Each learning experience requires a different kind of advance preparation, depending entirely upon the difficulty of the selection and your knowledge of the learners' backgrounds. In preparing to guide your children through any learning experience, analyze the content, evaluate the children's backgrounds, then choose the appropriate strategy.

Introducing New Terms

Social studies learning experiences are more effective if teachers give special attention to explaining new terms before the children encounter them. You must learn to anticipate terms that could cause children difficulties with any learning experience. Introduce such terms carefully and deliberately before they occur in the experience. Here are some effective techniques to introduce new terms.

Direct Experiences. Provide real experiences that will establish a concrete background for understanding new words. Think how much more meaning the word *serape* would have if a real one were on exhibit alongside its word symbol. My college students are often skeptical at this suggestion and ask me how they would be able to obtain such items for their own classrooms. My response is simply, "Send a note home prior to studying a topic to explain to the parents that you need certain items related to that topic—and get ready." Through my own elementary school teaching experiences, I've always ended up with more than I could handle by using that technique. Edward W. Dolch illustrates the value of direct experience:

> The average adult tries again and again to tell children with words what things are. . . .
> The child asks, "What is a snake?" The adult says, "An animal that crawls along the
> ground." The child imagines such an animal and asks, "But his legs will be in the way."
> The adult says, "Oh, he hasn't any legs." So the child takes off the legs and sees a legless
> body lying there. "But how does he crawl around without legs?" "He wiggles," says the
> adult. The child tries to make the legless body wiggle. "How does that get him to go for-
> ward?" The adult loses his temper. The peculiar way in which part of the snake pushes
> the other part cannot be described. It has to be seen. Let us go to the zoo.[16]

Audiovisuals. Realistically, you will often not be able to show children the things they will learn about. When you need to, share the pictures in textbooks, other photgraphs, slides, or transparencies to illustrate key words. Much less time is needed to establish word meaning with a photograph and accompanying word label than with a verbal description.

Contextual Clues. Sometimes, when dealing with words of multiple meanings or figurative terms, you can best communicate a meaning with direct explanation. When a word such as *change* is introduced, for example, you should use it in various contexts. To illustrate, you may say, "Our new word for today is *change*. Who can tell me what *change* means when I say, 'The grocer gave me *change* for my quarter?' I'm going to use the word again, but this time it will mean something different. Listen to what I say and then tell me what *change* means. Here we go. 'The leaves *change* color in the fall.' What does the word *change* mean now?" Be careful in verbal explanations of new words, though, especially to primary-grade children; there are shortcomings to this technique:

> One difficulty with this procedure is the danger of relying on superficial verbalizations.
> Meanings that are clear to the teacher may be quite hazy to the child. Many of the classi-
> cal boners are due to superficial and inadequate grasp of word meanings. It is not suffi-
> cient to tell a child that *frantic* means *wild*, or that *athletic* means *strong*; he may try to
> pick *frantic flowers* or pour *athletic vinegar* into a salad dressing.[17]

Questions.   Use appropriate questions to stimulate word recognition skills. Mildred Fitzpatrick suggests four types:

> *Definition Question.* For example, "What does *school* mean in the sentence: He met a *school* of fish as he dove deeper into the water?"
>
> *Semantic Question.* For example, "List some other meanings for the word *school.*"
>
> *Synonym Question.* For example, "Look at the underlined word in the sentence: President Roosevelt began a program of *relief.* What other words can you substitute for *relief* without changing the meaning of the sentence?"
>
> *Antonym Question.* For example, "What words could you use for *relief* to make it have an opposite meaning?"[18]

Setting Purposes

The introductory phase of a DLE usually culminates in a purpose-setting statement, a "launching pad" from which children propel themselves into the reading selection, film, filmstrip, or other planned source of content. It stimulates awareness of the material and informs the students why a particular experience is about to be shared with them. A teacher who instructs, "Read pages 68–71 for today" fails to stimulate or guide the children. The students will be aimless in their reading; many "stumble read" their way through the assignment, wondering what is important for them to remember. Whether in reading from a text or in any other learning experience, nothing is more deadly. Such a technical blunder stifles any interest the children may have had in the topic and may turn off children to the learning process altogether.

Purpose-setting strategies may be either statements or predictions. *Statements* inform students why they are being asked to participate in the learning activity. "Read pages 89–90 to find out how the Incas used pieces of string to keep important records," cues the children that they will engage in a purposeful endeavor. Likewise, "Watch the filmstrip to discover why the Vikings are remembered as skilled craftspersons of ships," guides the students' viewing efforts. Their faces will virtually glow as the related information unfolds before them.

The second type of purpose-setting activity is encouraging students to make *predictions.* Most often utilized with printed matter, predictions are often stimulated through the use of picture clues, repetitive phrases, or headings. Ms. Kahn used picture clues to encourage personal involvement while introducing the story *Sarah, Plain and Tall* by Patricia McLachlan. She began by asking her fourth graders to examine the title of the book and to share their thoughts about the description "plain and tall." She then invited them to examine the cover art to predict whether the illustration depicted Sarah or someone else, what the character's thoughts and feelings appeared to be, and where and when the story took place. After examining the cover, Ms. Kahn offered a special prediction guide to help her students organize their thoughts throughout the story as they met new characters. The guide contained three columns; the first asked students to list the central characters, the second required them to predict what would happen to the character as the story progressed, and the third called for clues that supported their predictions (see Table 4–1).

TABLE 4–1

Prediction Guide

Character	Prediction	Clues
1. CALEB	will ask Sarah if she sings	misses his mother's singing so much
2. ANNA		
3. PAPA		
4. SARAH		

Mr. Burt chooses stories with social studies themes that have a great many recurring words and phrases. He realizes that while children are listening to the social studies-related content they are also acquiring a very basic reading skill—predicting what will come next. The repetitive words and phrases help children make those predictions. For example, Mr. Burt encourages the children to join in as he reads by pausing and waiting for the children to repeat phrases such as, " 'Not I,' said the goose," or " 'Very well,' said the Little Red Hen. 'I will do it myself.' And she did." The children learn not only about specific social studies concepts (cooperation, for example), but also about the reading process itself.

Ms. Bryan, on the other hand, regularly uses a book's headings to help her students make predictions. Her sixth graders habitually take out their notebooks and pencils each time their text is to be used. Ms. Bryan calls the students' attention to the main heading and tells the class that as she reads she always looks at the heading and thinks for a moment what the selection might be about. In this case, the main heading was "Life Before Humans." She asked the students to predict what the passage would be about and recorded their forecasts on the chalkboard. The students read the introductory paragraphs to verify their predictions. Ms. Bryan then directed the students' attention to the first minor heading, "Life in the Sea." She commented that she likes to look at the subheadings to get a specific view of what the rest of the selection will be about, and again invited predictions. Ms. Bryan continued in a like manner with each of the remaining subsections. In each case the predictions were used as discussion starters once the related reading was completed.

The purpose-setting activity closes the introductory phase of the DLE. The entire introduction is so important (first impressions are lasting) that prospective teachers often become confused over how much time to spend on it. That concern can easily be alleviated if we think of the introduction to a DLE in the same way as introducing two of our friends whom we want to like one another. You might say, "Carolyn, I would like you to meet Charles, who loves sports as much as you do." A brief introduction (if it is a good one) establishes a common bond between the two individuals by emphasizing past experiences and motivates them to explore that interest more deeply. A poor introduction—"Carolyn, I'd like you to meet Charles"—leaves both individuals unsure of where to go from there. If the introducer gets too long-winded, both parties will be mentally admonishing, "Hurry up and get it over with!" A good introduction to a DLE briefly introduces the material to your children by relating the new topic to previous experiences, helping them clarify new terms, and motivating them to pursue the subject matter that makes up the main body of the lesson. If motivated enough, your two friends may spend this first meeting talking and getting to know each other, asking questions of each other, and expecting direct answers in return. Learning experiences are similar; the children will have questions in their minds (purposes established by the teacher) and search the content to find answers to those questions. If your two friends decide to learn more about each other or to further explore common interests, they may agree to see each other again. Likewise, *follow-up* and *extension* activities give children a chance to reinforce what they have been exposed to or to explore an interest further.

The Learning Experience

Selecting sources of information for your social studies program and using the sources effectively are professional behaviors associated with any theory of learning. There are dozens of types of sources from which to choose. In learning about community workers, for example, there may be no substitute for visiting a firehouse to see the fire engines, to hear the chatter of the two-way radio, to try on the firehat, or to listen to firefighters explain their duties. At other times, objects such as kimonos, kinaras, or tabis might be brought to the classroom to enlighten children about other cultures. Bricklayers, craftspersons, artists, or musicians can visit the classroom to share expert skills or information. Movies and tape recordings offer valuable learning experiences. Children's literature offers information, emotion, and creative possibilities. All these sources of information appear in abundance in good social studies programs, but it has been estimated that up to 90% of all elementary school social studies content is communicated through social studies textbooks. Learning experiences receive in-depth discussion in later chapters.

Processing Information

Whether you engage the children in conducting a survey, reading a magazine article, interviewing a truck driver, viewing a film, or examining an historical document, they must ultimately face the task of processing and interpreting the raw data to which they were exposed. Over the years teachers have used various questioning strategies to help students achieve this skill. However, research studies have found teachers' efforts overwhelmingly unsuccessful. For example, Dolores Durkin[19] observed instruction in a number of fourth-grade classrooms and reported that "interrogation" rather than "instruction" best characterized what was going on. Practically no data-processing instruction was observed; out of a total of 4,469 minutes of observation, only 28 minutes were spent on actual instruction. The remaining 4,441 minutes were spent testing students' knowledge with rapid-fire, low-level, factual questions. Hilda Taba points out the difficulties of such limited instructional methodologies:

> A closed question such as, "When did Columbus sail?" permits only one child to respond. If the first student knows the answer that's the end of it. The teacher must then ask a second question to elicit another fact. A series of closed questions inevitably develops a teacher-student, teacher-student sequence. It also prevents the child who has a particular piece of information to offer from entering the discussion if the teacher does not ask "the right question." . . . A teacher whose opening question lacks focus may himself be unsure of the focus or the purpose of the discussion and his students will suffer accordingly.[20]

Unfortunately, closed questions permeate many classroom comprehension discussions. Some teachers repeatedly begin their approach with, "Let's answer a few questions to see if everyone understands what we've just read." To which Manning says, "If the students know the answer to the question . . . why ask? And . . . if the students do not know the answer to the question . . . why ask?"[21] Manning advises replacing such questioning sequences with more appropriate direct teacher instructional processes.

Realistically, teachers can ask many different kinds of questions, and good social studies teachers *must* use a variety of the right kinds of questions. The kinds of questions you choose, however, are primarily determined by the established *purpose* for the learning activity. When trying to determine whether children have grasped the main idea of a reading selection, for example, a teacher might begin discussion with, "Tell in your own words how the mountains affect the lives of the people in Peru." A crucial component of effective questioning is to tie the stated purpose for reading to the initial question. A teacher might state the purpose for reading this way: "Please read pages 195–196 to find out the three branches of the federal government." After the children have finished reading, she can ask, "What are the three branches of the federal government?"

The logic of the connection between *purpose* and *initial question* is apparent, but we sometimes neglect to make that connection. Be sure to keep in mind the necessity for this connection and ask yourself, as you develop your discussion sequence, "Why did I assign that reading?" Then, the process of framing your questions will become much easier.

The Taba Approach

Teachers often acquire help in designing information processing strategies from carefully formulated guides. One such prominent guide is the Taba model, which emerged in 1969 under the leadership of the late Hilda Taba at San Francisco State College. She and her co-workers were interested in formulating instructional practices that would balance emphases on content, learning processes, and the learner as an individual. Essentially the Taba model helps children develop certain mental operations as necessary ingredients for the acquisition of concepts and generalizations:

> Students can learn a specific date such as the discovery of America by means of straightforward presentation and recall of information, but learning to conceptualize or make war-

ranted inferences from data requires frequent practice over an extended period of time. Attitudes and feelings are not changed by studying facts alone; they are changed through participating in experiences, real or vicarious, which have an emotional impact.[22]

The Taba approach is centered on strategies that lead to three types of thinking outcomes: (1) concept development, (2) concept attainment, and (3) generalization formation.

Concept Development.   According to Hilda Taba and her associates, concept development begins with recognition of the special qualities of things and examination of characteristics or properties that separate one thing from another. From this knowledge base, the teacher helps children organize their thinking with a specified series of questions. To illustrate, let us suppose that a primary-grade teacher has just returned with her class from a field trip to the supermarket. She might help the children organize their thinking with a pattern of questions like these:

Teacher	Children
"What did you find at the supermarket?"	Recount items they saw at the store (factual data). Teacher lists information on chalkboard or chart.
"Do any of these items seem to belong together?"	Use colored chalk to group items (e.g., fresh vegetables, canned goods, meats, machinery, etc.).
"Why did you group these items together?"	Verbalize common characteristics of items in each group.
"What would you call each of these group?"	Decide on a label that encompasses all items in a group.
"Could some items belong in more than one group?"	Discover different relationships.
"Can you find a different way to group the items?"	Discover additional relationships (concept development).
"Can someone say in one sentence something about all these groups?"	Offer suitable summary of what transpired.

Children *develop concepts* as they respond to "opener questions" requiring them to:

1. list items
2. group similar items
3. identify similar characteristics of items in a group
4. label the groups
5. regroup and relabel items
6. summarize information.

Each one of these steps in concept development is a necessary prerequisite for the next one, and in all cases the students perform all thinking operations for themselves.

The teacher has very little control over the outcome; the concept labels are the children's own.

Concept Attainment.   Most of the time children are encouraged to manipulate data while forming their own concept labels, but there may be instances when teachers wish to label a group of items in a specific way. These concepts may be in the form of, for example, map symbols (a student learns to respond to a symbol for boundary line) or particular terms having a number of different characteristics (explorer, steamship, dinosaur, or hieroglyphics). The teacher would use the following script to help children learn a particular concept:

Teacher	Children
"Say these words after me: *forest animal.*	Repeat the word.
"This is a forest animal." (Shows picture to children.)	Look at the picture; listen to descriptions or stories.
"This is also a forest animal." (Shows picture to children.)	
"This is *not* a forest animal." (Shows a picture that is not a forest animal, e.g., fish or camel.)	Look at the pictures; listen to descriptions or stories.
"Show me a forest animal." (Shows three new pictures, one of which is a forest animal.)	Point to correct animal
"What is this? How do you know?"	Generate concept label and give summary description.

Children *attain concepts* when they:

1. are first given a concept word to say
2. are presented with a wide range of examples
3. are exposed to a number of nonexamples
4. are tested by being asked to point out an example of the concept from a group of examples and nonexamples
5. generate the specified concept label when presented with examples.

As children progress through such activity, their concepts become somewhat more sophisticated because the teacher (1) provides concrete experiences and (2) sequences questions to help organize the experience. The understanding of concepts will continue to grow and change as continued experiences become integrated into each child's life and into adulthood. Because it encourages children to think at levels beyond basic concept development, the Taba program extends the conceptual base through a process of developing *generalizations*.

Generalization Formation.   Concepts are most often represented by a word or phrase, such as *neighborhood, minority group,* or *inflation,* to help one organize or categorize information. Like concepts, generalizations are the products of grouping items that have similar characteristics, but generalizations indicate higher levels of thinking in that they state the relationship among two or more concepts. "Modern transportation and communication systems help to make possible easier lives for people in metropolitan areas" is a broad statement that contains two or more concepts and establishes a relationship among them. Can you name the concepts included in the generalization?

The generalizing process is among the most important goals of elementary school social studies instruction. You should capitalize on every opportunity to have students generalize about their social studies experiences, because the process demonstrates a sophisticated ability to gain deeper meaning from data. Children should have the freedom to express personal interpretations of shared experiences in a nonthreatening atmosphere, where no one is criticized for offering a "wrong" or "silly" statement. You must encourage them to offer interpretations and to support them by reexamining data from their experience so they will see how their ideas can change as they study the data more carefully. This example illustrates how one teacher conducted a discussion to help children recall important information, again following a trip to the supermarket, and to generalize beyond the data.

Skill in helping children organize and interpret social studies content enhances the learning process and generates enthusiasm.

Teacher	**Children**
Developing Concepts	
"What did you see at the supermarket?"	List items they saw at the store.
"Which of these things can be put together? Why?"	Group items into categories.
"What shall we call each of the groups?"	Generate labels as the teacher lists items beneath each label.
Developing Generalizations	
"What foods or supplies come from the neighborhood where the store is located?"	Generate list of items.
"What foods or supplies come from outside the neighborhood?"	Generate list of items.
"How do the stores get the things they sell?"	Children hypothesize (guess) solutions to the question as the teacher lists them on the chalkboard.
(At this point the teacher allows the children an opportunity to search for data to support or reject their hypotheses [library books, guest speakers, etc.].)	
"Which reasons were correct? Which reasons need to be changed? Why? Should we add some reasons?"	Children use their data to support or reject their hypotheses.
"What can you say about the supermarket and the ways it gets its food and supplies?"	Offer statements of relationship between workers and the services they provide; for example, "People in supermarkets need other people to furnish foods and supplies."

This example shows how a social studies program can promote development of higher-level thinking skills. Knowledge and details are the foundations to support these higher-level processes, not data for the children to commit to memory. A sample progression might look something like this:

> *Fact:* Columbus discovered America in 1492 (and other facts)
>
> *Concept:* Exploration
>
> *Generalization:* European rulers sought to extend their influence by exploring new continents.

The Taba approach provides a solid framework of sequentially ordered questions for promoting the mental operations necessary for development of concepts and generalizations.

The Taba program developers stress the importance of consistently following the questioning sequence described to this point. They believe that unless teachers adhere to the basic form, there is little chance that what is done in social studies will improve children's thinking skills. However, if children repeatedly go through the process of answering questions from a predetermined sequence, they will internalize the procedure and begin to create patterns on their own. Through such a process, we teach comprehension skills.

A Personal Pattern of Questioning

Many teachers enjoy the freedom of choosing a questioning sequence that matches their teaching style and individual student needs, while other teachers appear to be more comfortable leading group discussions when they are offered a specific format to follow. Morgan and Schreiber believe that teachers should be so skilled that they are able to engage young children in meaningful discussions by selecting their own classification schemes for questions. They comment:

> Any discrete categorization of questions is inherently artificial. It seems more reasonable to conceive of classroom questions as being on a continuum. One extreme of the continuum may be characterized by lower levels of mental activity such as pure recall . . . and questions which are likely to have one "correct" answer. The social studies classroom in which questions of this type predominate will tend to be teacher dominated, with minimal student involvement. . . . Conversely, questions at the other extreme of the continuum involve more complex, higher mental activity. . . . Student participation in class discussions would consume a greater proportion of class time.[23]

Figure 4–3 is an example of Morgan and Schreiber's advice. At which point of the continuum would you place each of the questions?

1. Who was the first president of the United States?
2. How would the world be different today if the Axis powers had defeated the Allies in World War II?
3. Do you think the Russian people are really as unhappy as the writer described?
4. Describe the operation of Henry Ford's first assembly line.

Whether or not we agree on our exact placements is immaterial; what is important is that you are able to sense what comprises a "lower-level" and a "higher-order" question. We both should have identified questions 1 and 4 as lower-level questions, though, because they deal with specific information. Questions 2 and 3 should have

FIGURE 4–3

Continuum of Personal Discussion Questions

been classified as higher-order questions because they require of the student more reflection, originality, and expression of personal feelings.

We can construct many questioning patterns, but the main consideration that should guide your thinking is knowing where you want to go with it. For example, one teacher who wished to draw on material the children had just finished reading to lead them toward developing a generalization used this approach:

TEACHER: Can someone tell me the name of a popular Mexican food?
CHILD 1: Tacos.
TEACHER: That's correct. And what are tacos made from?
CHILD 2: They're flat cornmeal cakes filled with chopped meat, cheese, and vegetables.
TEACHER: Has anyone here eaten a taco?

Several children relate positive experiences; plans are made to make tacos in class as a special project.

TEACHER: Tacos are a special Mexican food. Are there any special foods that children in the United States enjoy?
CHILDREN: Hamburgers! Hot dogs! Pizza!
TEACHER: My goodness. Does that mean you eat those foods every day?
CHILD 3: No. We just like them as favorites.
TEACHER: Just as the Mexican children like tacos?
CHILDREN: Yes. I don't think they eat tacos every day either.
TEACHER: What can you tell me about special foods?
CHILD 4: We all need food to eat, but people in different countries choose to eat special foods they themselves like to eat.
TEACHER: Very good. You did a lot of good thinking today.

Notice that the teacher led the children through a discussion of the data toward an appropriate generalization. Your guidance is important in this area, for you must guard against formation of generalizations that are too broad ("All Japanese wear kimonos") and against forming generalizations without sufficient evidence. John Dewey offered some important advice on questioning skills when he described the "art of questioning":

1. Questions should not elicit fact upon fact, but should be asked in such a way as to delve deeply into the subject, i.e., to develop an overall concept of the selection.
2. Questions should emphasize personal interpretations rather than literal and direct responses.
3. Questions should not be asked randomly so that each is an end in itself, but should be planned so that one leads into the next throughout a continuous discussion.
4. Teachers should periodically review important points so that old, previously discussed material can be placed into perspective with that which is presently being studied.
5. The end of the question asking sequence should leave the children with a sense of accomplishment and build a desire for that which is yet to come.[24]

Sustaining Classroom Discussions

Whether you choose a patterned approach such as Taba's or a less structured approach, the key is to organize classroom discussions so that they have a goal beyond the regurgitation of factual data. To achieve your goal, you will sometimes need to ask questions or offer comments other than those that form the major part of your strategy. *Probing* is a popular technique for sustaining classroom discussions. This process, mastered centuries ago by Socrates (and referred to as the Socratic method), remains a valuable teaching tool today. By probing, Socrates was able to prod students (offer them hints) if they were unclear in an answer or unable to answer a question at all. To understand the technique, you must realize that it is comprised of two subprocesses: *prompting* and *clarifying*.

Prompting.   Prompting utilizes short hints or clues whenever a child gives an incorrect response to a question, usually of the lower-level type. Several prompts or leading questions help the child organize his thinking patterns relative to the original question.

TEACHER: How does the process of gerrymandering work?
STUDENT: I'm not sure. I don't know.
TEACHER: How does an individual state establish voting districts?
STUDENT: The state is divided into sections, which have about the same number of people in each section.
TEACHER: That's right. Now can you tell me who is responsible for establishing those districts?
STUDENT: Oh, I see. The party controlling the state government at the time can use its power to set up districts unequally so that its voting strength will be as strong as possible, and the opposing party's strength will be as weak as possible.

Children are not told that their initial response is wrong; instead, they are led, reinforced, and encouraged. Since the teacher does not imply that a student's initial response is incorrect, prompting also helps to enhance the student's self-confidence.

Clarifying.   Clarification calls for enlargement or restatement of a student's original answer. The teacher uses clarification when an answer is correct but does not come up to expectations for accuracy and completeness, or when children are asked to defend a position when there may be differences of opinion. Thus, clarification can usually be applied to questions at the higher levels of thinking.

TEACHER: Would both Democrats and Republicans gerrymander in our state if they had the chance to do so?
STUDENT: Yes, I think so.
TEACHER: Can you explain your reasons for feeling as you do?
STUDENT: I think it's hard for people to be fair when so much is at stake.

The probing technique helps children express ideas individually and intuitively. It enables learners to operate on all levels of thinking while they develop solutions to problems. The success of your questioning technique, however, depends on your ability to adapt questions to the individual without expecting the same quality of response from all students.

Waiting. Your chances of eliciting thoughtful responses to appropriate questions are greatly enhanced by effective methods of framing questions. The basic approach for framing questions is: (1) ask the question, (2) pause, and (3) call on someone to respond. The process is grounded on the principle that students attend better to questions if a short pause follows. Donald C. Orlich and his associates offer several justifications for pausing.[25] First, *wait time* gives students a chance to think about their responses. Second, the nonverbal message (pause) indicates that any student may be selected for a response. Thus the attention level remains high. Third, a pause provides the teacher with a little time to "read" nonverbal clues from the class. With experience, teachers can readily observe such signals as pleasure, fright, or boredom. Fourth, teachers who pause after asking questions become more patient while awaiting student responses. The message, then, is not to expect rapid-fire exchanges during discussions. Make the decision to pause after you ask a question. You may discover that children make longer responses, offer more complex answers, dialogue more with one another, and gain more confidence in their ability to make worthwhile contributions.

Graphic Representations

Webbing. Although oral discussion strategies are critical teaching tools, *visual organizing strategies* often help children focus on major ideas and understand relationships among details. Graphic representations are visual depictions of information children gather from outside sources; they help children understand the content. One device for facilitating comprehension of social studies content is the *semantic web,* a technique introduced by Freedman and Reynolds.[26] A semantic web has four basic elements: core questions, web strands, strand supports, and strand ties.

The *core question* serves as the focus of the web. All the information generated in a discussion should relate to the core question, so the core question should create the possibility of several answers. An example of a core question is: "What words would you use to describe Martin Luther King, Jr.?" The core question is placed in the center of a growing matrix (Figure 4–4).

All subsequent information relates to this core question. The immediate responses to the core question are *web strands* and are placed systematically around the core question, as shown in Figure 4–5.

FIGURE 4–4
*The Core Question of a
Semantic Web*

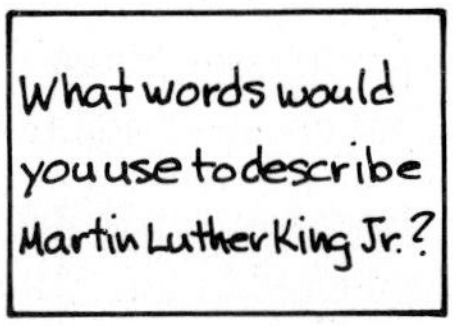

What words would you use to describe Martin Luther King Jr.?

FIGURE 4–5
The Core Question and Web Strands of a Semantic Web

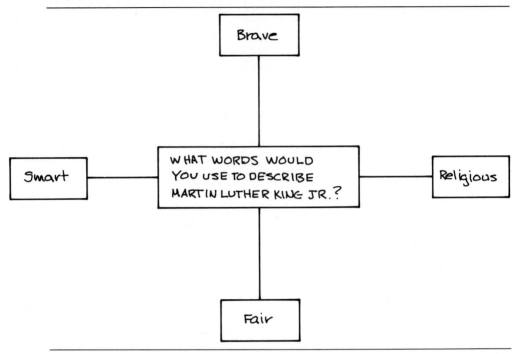

The facts or inferences the students use to support each web strand are *strand supports*. The strand supports extend from each web strand, as shown in Figure 4–6. The possible relationships among the strands are called *strand ties*. "Smart" and "fair," for example, may be related in that they describe Martin Luther King's personality characteristics. Likewise, each of the other characteristics is related to some degree. The teacher's responsibility is to probe and prompt the children until they discover some of those relationships.

Semantic webs can be constructed for many purposes. Here are some possibilities:

- How could the community best address its growing parking problems?
- How would Mexico be different today if it were settled by the French instead of the Spanish?
- Why did the United States become involved in the Vietnam conflict?
- What chores and crafts were performed by children during colonial times?

Because semantic webs can be used for such a variety of questions, it is quite a versatile technique. Teachers can also adapt the basic webbing technique in a number of ways. Rather than simply draw webs on the chalkboard or chart, you may wish to introduce your younger children to a stuffed toy spider called "Spike." Tell the children

FIGURE 4–6

A Semantic Web with Core Question, Web Strands, and Strand Supports

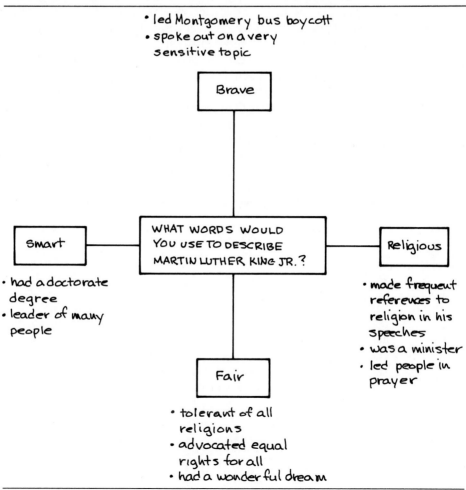

- led Montgomery bus boycott
- spoke out on a very sensitive topic

Brave

Smart

- had a doctorate degree
- leader of many people

WHAT WORDS WOULD YOU USE TO DESCRIBE MARTIN LUTHER KING JR.?

Religious

- made frequent references to religion in his speeches
- was a minister
- led people in prayer

Fair

- tolerant of all religions
- advocated equal rights for all
- had a wonderful dream

that Spike is a special spider because he always asks good questions and that he loves to stay in your classroom because the children are so helpful in answering his questions. Place Spike in the center of a circle of children next to a question printed on a sheet of construction paper (core question). Attach a long string of yarn to Spike, which you will use to construct Spike's "web." Request responses to Spike's question and, making sure each response is different, ask the children to print their answers on sheets of construction paper and display it for all to see (web strands). Then, pass Spike and the yarn to each child in turn and ask each youngster to explain the relationship between his answer and the question (web strands). Finally, encourage the children to offer ideas as to why each of their answers is connected by Spike's web.

Information Retrieval Charts.   The purpose of a retrieval chart is to help students categorize information into conceptual blocks. Retrieval charts typically consist of two interrelated elements: (1) the concept labels and (2) the information to be categorized. Table 4–2 shows these two retrieval chart components. After you have guided the children through a purposeful learning experience, display a chart and ask a main idea question, such as, "What did you find out about different neighborhoods?" As the children suggest information, ask them to identify the category into which their comments can best be organized.

When the children finish organizing the mass of information, you should use the retrieval chart to help them make generalizations. For example, you might ask, "What can you say about different neighborhoods and the things people do in them?"

Some teachers object to retrieval charts because they feel it offers too much "spoon feeding" of information. It's true that it isn't a good idea to lock students into any single system of information processing, but if retrieval charts are used wisely in combination with other devices, they can remain valuable teaching tools.

Guide-O-Ramas.   The guide-o-rama helps students process the major concepts of a reading selection. The guide-o-rama's six-step procedure provides a reading road map that emphasizes both comprehension and flexibility of reading rate. Wood and Mateja explain the process. First, determine the overall purpose of your reading assignment. In Figure 4–7, the teacher wants children to understand the events leading up to the Revolutionary War. Second, choose the essential sections that directly relate to the purpose. Third, develop questions or content statements to help children comprehend the selection. Fourth, design a novel, interest-capturing guide format to stimulate interest. Fifth, present the guide to the children, usually as a duplicated sheet or chart. Explain its purpose and "walk" the children through the guide to familiarize them with the procedures. Allowing the children to work in pairs or small groups helps promote

TABLE 4–2

Pattern of a Typical Retrieval Chart

	Buildings	*Traffic*	*Land*
City	Tall office buildings Large apartments Many stores	Many cars Buses Automobiles Taxis	Few trees Little grass Much cement and many roads

Suburbs	Houses for one family
	Shopping malls
	Shopping centers
		Shopping areas have
		   many cars
		Short streets have
		   few cars
			Many trees
			Grass
			Shrubs

Country	Houses for one family Barns	No busy streets Cars and trucks	Farmland grows crops Trees Grass

FIGURE 4–7

A Guide-O-Rama for Fifth Grade American History (From Dick Cunningham and Scott L. Shablak. "Selective Reading Guide-O-Rama: The Content Teacher's Best Friend." Journal of Reading, 18 *[February 1975]: 380–382.)*

The English Colonies

(Interview with a colonist) Purpose: Imagine that you were a colonist when Great Britain had control over America. Describe how you felt at each of the events on pages 159–164.

Start Here

Preface p. 159

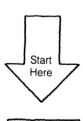

The Molasses Act 1733, p. 160

The Stamp Act, p. 161

The Boston Tea Party, p. 162

1. Why couldn't Great Britain pay its debts?

2. What did Great Britain expect from you and the rest of the colonists?

3. Why did you feel the need to smuggle molasses into the country?

4. What was the Stamp Act and what was your reaction to it?

5. In what ways was Patrick Henry either for or against your cause?

6. Why weren't you satisfied after the government repealed the Stamp Act?

7. By now, how are you and your fellow colonists responding? And what do you plan to do about it?

Closing of the Port of Boston, p. 163

Committees of Correspondence. p. 163

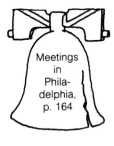

Meetings in Philadelphia, p. 164

Stop Here

8. What was King George's reaction to your "Tea Party"?

9. How did you communicate with other colonies?

10. Tell about those meetings in Philadelphia. What was requested and what was granted?

11. What do you suppose you will do next?

positive learning. Sixth, have the students share their guide-o-ramas and talk about their responses.[27]

The guide-o-ramas, as with other forms of information processing we have discussed, are direct teaching strategies for aiding comprehension. These content-based strategies help students take a greater step toward learning social studies materials.

Venn Diagrams.   You may have been exposed to Venn diagrams in mathematics classes; they are graphic techniques to compare two sets. Likewise, they can be used in social studies classes to compare two concepts. Let us suppose you have just read a selection dealing with people living in two different communities—urban and rural. Ask your students to complete a Venn diagram that compares the two different environments (see Figure 4–8). When students know how to use the Venn diagram, it can be used to guide comparisons of a variety of topics; for example, two children in the classroom, two forms of government, two communities, two nations, two religions, and so on.

Children's Own Questions

Simply asking questions and offering visual information-processing aids is not enough; children must be encouraged to initiate and discuss questions that are important to them. You can encourage them to ask their questions orally, set aside places where they can write questions whenever they wish, make tape recorders available, or simply encourage children to talk about things informally. In learning to listen to the questions children ask, you often find rich material for class exploration. Listen to these questions asked by elementary school youngsters and imagine the possibilities for discussion:

FIGURE 4–8
A Venn Diagram

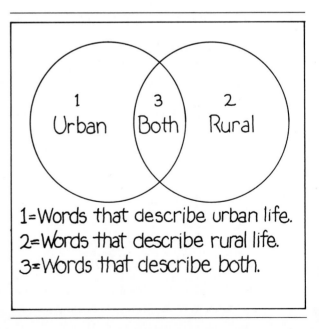

1=Words that describe urban life.
2=Words that describe rural life.
3=Words that describe both.

"Why are there so many fights and arguments on the playground?"

"Can a rocket ship get lost in the clouds?"

"Why is there no smoke from the fire on the sun?"

"Are elephants really afraid of mice?"

"Where does the trash go after the garbage collectors throw it on the truck?"

You can understand how teachers who feel pressure to get through the daily routine often neglect questions like these. Take time to listen to your children, though, because they need to be heard and to learn. Their understanding of their world is incomplete and their questions about the "unanswerable" often provide precious moments of innocence that we all enjoy remembering:

"Do the clouds have bones?"

"The vet said our cat has to go on a diet. He eats mice when he goes out. How many calories are in a mouse?"

"My father said that when someone is born, someone dies. I was born at 1:20 A.M. on June 8, 1981. How can I find out who died when I was born?"

Everyone agrees that good teachers should know how to ask good questions. Through good questioning techniques, we not only encourage effective thinking but we also help build positive relationships.

Follow-up and Extension Activities

Follow-up and extension activities are the culmination of the entire DLE procedure. They provide additional practice on certain skills through workbook or other seatwork assignments or through special projects or independent activities that encourage children to apply or extend concepts to a variety of situations. This list of the activities represents only a sampling of the hundreds of possibilities:

Have children illustrate major learning by drawing a picture, dramatizing, making a model, and so on.

Have special projects such as games or cooking going on around the classroom.

Make large table models of places from plasticene, clay, cardboard, or wood.

Have children pretend they are among the first Jamestown colonists, for example. Ask them to write a letter to a friend in England telling about life in the first year of the settlement.

Make a "fashion magazine" or "catalog" as it might have been published at another time in history.

Bring in foods described in the textbook and encourage the children to taste them.

Paint a mural to show the major characteristics of a culture.

Construct time lines to illustrate the sequence of important events.

Develop charts and graphs to summarize important data.

Go on a field trip or invite a resource person to speak in the classroom.

Show a film to reinforce main ideas from the text.

By reading professional journals and organizing an idea file, you will begin to accumulate ideas for experiences that will bring more meaning to reading assignments. *Remember, though, that these activities must be part of the total learning experience, not "extra busy work" or "icing on the cake" that gets done only because we have a few minutes to kill.*

A SAMPLE DLE

The following scenario describes the complete process of carrying out a DLE in a fourth-grade classroom. It pulls together all the sections of a DLE and illustrates a sound textbook-based social studies lesson.

MR. KURLAK: (Brings children's attention to a photograph on the opening page of the reading assignment. The photograph shows archaeologists examining a dig.) What do the television character Inspector Gadget and the people in this picture have in common?

BERNARD: Gadget is a detective who looks for clues to solve crimes. These people look like they're trying to find something, too.

MR. KURLAK: That's good thinking, Bernard. They both try to solve mysteries. These people are not called detectives, though. Does anyone know what they are called?

(None of the children answer.)

MR. KURLAK: People who study clues to solve mysteries of the past are called *archaeologists.* (He writes the word on the board.) They are like detectives who learn about communities of long ago. As we read this assignment, be good detectives, or archaeologists, and look for the ways people lived in the past. But, before we read, I'd like to ask a question: How many of you have ever been to a place where you were all alone, surrounded only by forest and wildlife?

INEZ: We went on a camping trip to the mountains. My brother and I went for a walk in the woods and we got lost. It was scary. (Other children offer similar experiences.)

MR. KURLAK: It sounds like many of you have been in far-out places in the country. If you have, you can begin to get an idea of what the world was like before people started settling in communities. I'd like all of you to read pages 118–21 to find out some ways people provided for food and shelter before there were cities.

(The children all read for the stated purpose.)

MR. KURLAK: Where did the early people get food, shelter, and clothes?

CHARLES: They moved around quite a bit to find animals to kill and to get wild berries and vegetables.

KATHY: When the food gave out in one place, they moved on to another spot.

MR. KURLAK: Very good. The people led what is called a gathering life. How would you feel to be constantly looking for food like that?

WILLIAM: I wouldn't like it. I'd be afraid of the animals or what would happen if there was a drought that killed all the plants.

MR. KURLAK: That's exactly how the early people felt, William. Suppose you were living back then. What kinds of things would you suggest to the other people to make your lives easier?

SONJA: I'd tell them to join together. That way people could grow their own crops.

REBECCA: And raise their own animals.

JOHN: Yeah. And then they wouldn't have to wander all around to get their food.

MR. KURLAK: Let's go back to our reading and find the place where one of the early people described his fear of being killed by an animal. Would someone read the part to show how that person felt at the time?

(Anita reads the part aloud with expression.)

MR. KURLAK: Thank you, Anita. The passage shows us that people had many enemies long ago. I'd like to have you think about the ways cities changed those problems. There is a chart on the board with two categories: "life before cities" and "life in cities." I'd like you to tell me how people got food before there were cities and then after there were cities. Then we'll continue down the chart. Ready?

	Before Cities	In Cities
Food		
Jobs		
Homes		
Transportation		

(The children complete the chart.)

MR. KURLAK: To finish our lesson today, I would like to ask you to group yourselves by fives. Pretend that you are planning an ideal city of the future where all of our present problems would be solved. What are some of our present problems? (He places this question on the board as a core question for a growing web.)

CHILDREN: Water . . . housing . . . pollution . . . too crowded . . .

MR. KURLAK: Your special project is to spend time discussing ways to solve these problems for our ideal city. Choose the problem you would like to talk about and think of all the ways it could be solved. You will have a chance to share your ideas when we start social studies class tomorrow.

SUMMARY

Learning can be accomplished in several ways. On one extreme we find teachers and children who are most comfortable in an environment that accommodates individual learning styles, small-group activities, and a great deal of self-direction and independence. At the other extreme are those teachers and children who require more structure to do their best work. They respond best to directed lessons presented to the large group, preferably with a textbook as the core of the program. They may choose models for directed teaching: Madeline Hunter's mastery teaching model and Hilda Taba's strategies for establishing concepts and generalizations are two popular programs that encourage teachers to improve their effectiveness. There is room for many variations in a social studies program; the main idea to keep in mind is that whatever approach you choose, make sure it matches your personality, philosophy, and area of competence.

In presenting directed lessons to the entire group from a textbook, teachers often desire more flexibility than that perceived in the Hunter approach; therefore, they follow plans such as the directed learning episode format. Regardless of how creative you become within the context of directed teaching, there are approximately four steps you will take to ensure adequate comprehension:

1. Introduce the lesson
   - Clarify terms
   - Relate past experiences to new material
   - Establish clear purposes for the activity

2. Offer the information-gathering experience
   - Offer developmentally appropriate activities

3. Teach information processing skills
   - Use a questioning guide
   - Compose your own questions
   - Utilize visual organizing strategies
     webbing
     information retrieval charts
     guide-o-ramas
     Venn diagrams
   - Encourage children's own questions

4. Relate follow-up and extension activities directly to the topic
   - Special projects to extend learnings
   - Reinforcement activities to strengthen concepts

Some of you may look at all that is involved in developing a DLE instead of just teaching page-for-page from a textbook teacher's manual and say, "Why bother? After all, the manual was written by experts in the field who really know the social studies." To an extent, you are correct. Manuals can be very helpful, especially for student or beginning teachers. As guides, though, they must be viewed as suggestions, not as prescriptions. Do the experts in the field know your fifth graders as well as you do? You will probably want to start your career by using the teacher's guide closely, but as you gain experience, adapt it to the changing needs of the different groups of children you will teach each year. The DLE allows you constantly to change your teaching ideas within a framework of sound planning.

ENDNOTES

1. Madeline Hunter, *Mastery Teaching* (El Segundo, CA: TIP Publications, 1982), p. 3.

2. Paul D. Eggen and Donald P. Kauchak, *Strategies for Teachers,* 2nd ed. (Englewood Cliffs, NJ: Prentice-Hall, 1988), p. 8.

3. E. Paul Torrance, "Cultural Discontinuities and the Development of Originality in Thinking," *Exceptional Children, 29,* no. 1 (September 1962): 2–3.

4. R. Murray Thomas and Sherwin G. Swartout, *Integral Learning Materials* (New York: Longmans, Green, 1960), p. 1.

5. Frank Smith, *Comprehension and Learning: A Conceptual Framework for Teachers* (New York: Holt, Rinehart and Winston, 1975), p. 92.

6. David P. Ausubel, "In Defense of Verbal Learning," *Educational Theory II,* no. 4 (January 1961), p. 16.

7. Richard C. Remy, "The Need for Science/Technology/Society in the Social Studies," *Social Education, 54,* no. 4 (April/May 1990): 204.

8. Mark Van Doren, in Ernest L. Boyer, "Seeing the Connectedness of Things," *Educational Leadership, 39,* no. 8 (May 1982): 384.

9. Frank Smith, *Understanding Reading: A Psycholinguistic Analysis of Reading and Learning to Read* (New York: Holt, Rinehart and Winston, 1982).

10. Benjamin S. Bloom, "New Views of the Learner: Implications for Instruction and Curriculum," *Childhood Education, 56,* no. 1 (October 1979): 5–6

11. Robert W. Gaskins, "The Missing Ingredients: Time on Task, Direct Instruction, and Writing," *The Reading Teacher* (April 1988): 751–753.

12. Madeline Hunter, *Mastery Teaching* (El Segundo, CA: TIP Publications, 1982).

13. Robert Slavin, "The Hunterization of America's Schools," *Instructor* (April 1987): 57.

14. Madeline Hunter, "Response to Robert Slavin," *Instructor* (April 1987): 60.

15. R. P. Carver, *Reading Comprehension and Reading Theory* (Springfield, IL: Charles C. Thomas, 1981).

16. Edward W. Dolch, *Psychology and Teaching of Reading* (Champaign, IL: Garrard Press, 1951), p. 309.

17. Albert J. Harris, *How to Increase Reading Ability* (New York: Longmans, Green, 1961), p. 409.

18. Mildred Fitzpatrick, in Miles V. Zintz, *The Reading Process* (Dubuque, IA: William C. Brown, 1970), p. 186.

19. Dolores Durkin, "What Classroom Observations Reveal About Reading Comprehension Instruction," *Reading Research Quarterly, 24,* no. 4 (1978–1979): 481–533.

20. Hilda Taba et al., *A Teacher's Handbook to Elementary Social Studies: An Inductive Approach* (Reading, MA: Addison-Wesley, 1971), p. 105.

21. John C. Manning, "What's Needed Now in Reading Instruction: The Teacher as Scholar and Romanticist," *The Reading Teacher, 39,* no. 2 (November 1985): 136.

22. Hilda Taba et al., *A Teacher's Handbook to Elementary Social Studies* (Reading, MA: Addison-Wesley, 1971), pp. 14–15.

23. Jack C. Morgan and Joan E. Schreiber, "How to Ask Questions," *How to Do It Series,* no. 24 (Washington, DC: National Council for the Social Studies, 1969), p. 2.

24. John Dewey, *How We Think* (Boston: D. C. Heath, 1933).

25. Donald C. Orlich et al., *Teaching Strategies: A Guide to Better Instruction* (Lexington, MA: D. C. Heath, 1990), pp. 203–205.

26. Glenn Freedman and Elizabeth G. Reynolds, "Enriching Basal Reader Lessons with Semantic Webbing," *The Reading Teacher, 33,* no. 6 (March 1980): 677–684.

27. Karen D. Wood and John A. Mateja, "Adapting Secondary Level Strategies for Use in Elementary Classrooms," *The Reading Teacher, 36,* no. 6 (February 1983), 492–496.

Teachers have always been somewhat ambivalent about what it is they do for a living. An excellent case in point concerns their conceptions of the human mind. For example, there is the type of teacher who believes he is in the lighting business. We may call him the Lamplighter. When he is asked what he is trying to do with his students, his reply is something like this: "I want to illuminate their minds, to allow some light to penetrate the darkness." Then there is the Gardener. He says, "I want to cultivate their minds, to fertilize them, so that the seeds I plant will flourish." . . . The Muscle Builder wants to strengthen flabby minds, and the Bucket Filler wants to fill them up.[1]

—Neil Postman and Charles Weingartner

Enhancing Thinking Skills Through Guided Problem Solving and Inquiry

5

As you read, reflect on the following matters:

- What do we mean by "active learning" in the social studies?
- How can guided problem solving encourage student autonomy, self-direction and responsibility while at the same time control the acquisition of subject matter?
- What is the teacher's role in guided problem solving?
- How do social studies teachers create situations that encourage children to initiate independent research?
- What is scientific inquiry? When should teachers introduce inquiry to elementary school children?
- How does open-ended inquiry contribute to mental growth in the social studies?

How do you view the teaching process? Should you scatter the seeds and apply the fertilizer? Or mold the child, as a sculptor would? Perhaps someone has advised you to become a builder—to provide children with a firm foundation and sturdy framework. It is not my intention to poke fun at teaching with these metaphors, but think how often we stereotype teaching as something we do *to* children. Surely, children are curious about the world they live in; they enjoy being taught about it by wise, helpful teachers. On the other hand, they also have a strong urge to be independent—to learn by themselves through trial, error, and experimentation. Finding out about things by themselves is a matter of profound importance; unmitigated pride flows from youngsters who master important skills or uncover meaningful knowledge with little or no help from "big people." Perhaps my most vivid illustration of this strong, natural spirit to learn was demonstrated by one first grader who was asked by his teacher what it would be like to know everything. "Awful," the little boy replied.

"Why?" his teacher asked.

"Because then there would be nothing to wonder about."

THE NATURE OF CHILDREN'S LEARNING

Children are exceptional learners. They radiate a sense of natural wonder for the world around them and look at life as a mystery to be searched and solved. Nothing is too small for their eager minds; nothing is so insignificant that it passes without generating curiosity. They are utterly infatuated with the mind-stirring phenomena that excite their eyes, tease their ears, tantalize their taste buds, awaken their nostrils, and stir their sense of touch. Observations of young children in their "child's world" would lead almost everyone to conclude that they are doers, thinkers, and natural scholars, delving naturally into happenings of interest to them. The best we can do for life's neophytes is to observe and facilitate; we turn the youngsters loose in their "child's world" of stimulation and stand out of the way to allow them to search for and discover all they need or want to know. Subject matter labels and compartmentalized experiences are not a part of their "child's world"; they exist only in adults' minds. Once children enter elementary school, however, adults compartmentalize their unique worlds into discrete subject areas because they believe that teachers can best help students accomplish optimal learning that way. Specific understandings and skills have become associated with each subject area, with the overall goal of helping future adult citizens assume productive roles in their shared culture. The elementary school teacher must walk a fine line—respecting the "child's world" but also tuning into the subject matter associated with each of the areas of specialty they will be teaching.

ACTIVE LEARNING IN THE SOCIAL STUDIES

Subject matter content and cognitive thinking processes are inseparable; they must work together in elementary school social studies programs for effective instruction to take place. Chapter 4 presented teacher-directed practices that systematically build selected social studies concepts through special processes that aid student thinking. Although the teacher was in complete control of the entire instructional process, learners were *active;* they were not deskbound listeners who simply received and retrieved information on command. It is important to clarify a distinction that has confused beginning teachers for years. When we speak of *active learning* in the social studies, we do not necessarily mean that the children always have something real to manipulate with their hands. If possible, they should have, but children can be actively involved without manipulatives. Their minds should be active even as they listen, read, observe, or speak. The key to successful teaching is not the style of teaching you choose, but how actively you involve the learners in whatever is being presented. Directed lessons, then, are active methods of instruction if the teacher stimulates cognitive thinking strategies as discussed in Chapter 4.

Skillfully prepared and competently executed teacher-directed lessons offer one teaching style which you may choose to bring about meaningful learning. Sequentially organized content in which learnings progress from the simple to the complex helps children perceive relationships among the subject matter to form concepts, and to build relationships among concepts to form generalizations. Being able to form concepts and generalizations from the subject matter involves the development of what Jerome Bruner refers to as mental "coding systems."[2] These systems develop as the children experience repeated learning opportunities and encounter subject matter at increasingly sophisticated levels. Being able to form concepts and generalizations with such coding systems makes it possible for children to go beyond the information given to answer intriguing questions, resolve interesting situations, or solve puzzling problems. To illustrate, botanists have developed a highly sophisticated coding system for classifying all the special characteristics of plants. When a botanist stumbles upon a plant species unfamiliar to her and her colleagues (a puzzling problem), she is able to learn quite a bit about it simply by comparing its features against the coding system. Bruner suggests that the social studies program should encourage similar processes; it must assist students to develop special coding systems and then allow them to apply those coding systems to many different situations beyond those in which they were learned.

Guided Problem Solving

When we extend teacher-directed instruction with situations that have potential for applicability of what was learned, we have a learning strategy called *guided problem solving* or *guided discovery.* The younger the children, the more you must present information and guide them through the process of developing coding systems; the older the children, the more you can begin to relinquish your director's role and function as a facilitator or guide for solving problems. Arthur A. Carin and Robert B. Sund advise that guided problem solving or guided discovery helps students become more autonomous, self-directed, and responsible for their own learning:

> Guided discovery teaching/learning tries to help students learn to learn. Guided discovery helps students acquire knowledge that is uniquely their own because they discovered it

themselves. Guided discovery is *not* restricted to finding something entirely new to the world such as an invention . . . or theory. . . . *It is a matter of internally rearranging data so your students can go beyond the data* to form concepts new to them. [Italics mine][3]

Because guided problem solving contains elements of both teacher-directed and student-centered learning, it can be considered a midpoint between expository teaching and inquiry. Problem solving and inquiry are often considered alike because they both involve the process of solving problems, but they will be considered as different processes in this text on the basis of these two areas: (1) the amount of teacher direction and (2) the emphasis placed on the children's previous mastery of related concepts. To illustrate how these two factors influence classroom practice, let us assume that a teacher-directed advocate, a guided problem solving proponent, and an inquiry supporter each choose to offer a lesson on the concept of investing money. Here is what you might expect to see:

Teacher-Directed Learning Advocate.   She could choose filmstrips, films, books, guest speakers, field trips, lectures, or a variety of other significant sources of information. Her role would be to structure the knowledge of investments in such a way that the students are sure to develop a mental coding system into which understandings related to investment options could be arranged. She could do this by using Hunter's mastery teaching strategies, the Taba approach, the DLE or any other suitable technique that would enhance active, meaningful conceptual growth.

Guided Problem Solving Proponent.   He could develop the concept in a fashion similar to the advocate of teacher-directed learning, but once he was convinced that the children had mastered the concept, deepen their understanding and extend their thinking by giving the children this problem: "Suppose a generous benefactor gave each of us $1,000 to invest in any way we wished. He is interested in seeing who has the greatest return on the money after one month. How would you invest your money?" The teacher's major goal is to see whether the children's previously acquired understandings of investments can be applied to a stimulating problem.

Inquiry Supporter.   She would not present information to the students as the other two teachers did. Instead, the teacher would start out by placing the students in the hypothetical investment situation and hope that it motivates the children to discover the underlying knowledge by themselves. The teacher mainly facilitates the students' efforts by supplying appropriate materials, support, and encouragement. The students are left on their own to test their hypotheses by simulating the investment of their money for one month and judging which was the most successful investment choice. Knowledge about investments is formed as the students strive to solve the problem.

As a midpoint of instructional methodology, guided problem solving is a technique to encourage student autonomy, self-direction, and responsibility while at the same time controlling the acquisition of subject matter. It is not a free, open-ended, do-as-you-want approach, but one that encourages children to use their own initiative to explore and discover after already developing a meaningful background. Guided problem solving forms a link between teacher-directed instruction and the openness of inquiry—a link that is essential for teachers desiring to move from teacher-directed toward inquiry-based classrooms. Many teachers over the past thirty years have attempted to achieve that goal by responding to the pleas of social studies educators who reasoned that the major instructional strategy to be used in elementary school classrooms should be inquiry because it was thought to be most effective in creating independent, critical thinkers and wise decision-makers. There were many attempts to describe the inquiry process, but little was offered to help teachers change from traditionally teacher-directed classrooms to student-centered classrooms. Teachers were left virtually alone to find their own way. Many who had never operated a student-centered program in their classrooms tried to change overnight from highly directed programs where all higher-level decisions were made by the teacher to programs requiring mature, responsible decision-making on the part of the students. As a result, aggressiveness, noisiness, confusion, and aimless activity often increased as the children moved from one set of expectations to another. The children could not change comfortably; the contrast was too great. As a result, many teachers found inquiry programs unworkable, children pleaded for a return to the "good old days," and most programs were abandoned after only short trial. For those few who persisted, an important lesson was learned: the thinking skills associated with inquiry do not happen automatically, or simply because we will them to happen. They are products of clear, deliberate, specific teacher guidance. Selma Wassermann describes the rationale for this guidance:

> We must not . . . make the mistake of expecting that . . . thinking for oneself will occur in the absence of classroom instruction and practice aimed at these specific goals.
>
> It may be a lot easier to teach children to read and spell than it is to teach them to . . . function on their own cognitive power. I have heard teachers give it up after a single attempt, saying, . . . "Children cannot think for themselves," and proceed thereafter to do children's thinking for them. But these very same teachers would *never* say, "These children cannot read by themselves," and thereafter remove any opportunity for them to learn to read. Nor would they deplore children's inability to add or multiply, or spell or write stories as the reason NOT to teach them to acquire these skills.[4]

Before you condemn inquiry teaching and all those associated with it by crying, "Bring back the textbook! Give me back my ditto sheets—this business of promoting autonomous learning just doesn't work," you must know that, even though new stimuli may be needed in your social studies program, children must move slowly. They must be given many opportunities to grow and learn—the skills needed for inquiry will not be achieved after a single experience. Time, patience, and your belief that the goal of autonomous learning is important are the key ingredients of a successful transition from teacher-directed instruction to inquiry. Here are some suggestions for increasing skills and interest in pursuing problem investigations—a beginning point for changing instructional emphases in the social studies classroom.

Encouraging Free Exploration

According to Jean Piaget, the foundation of all higher-order thinking skills is physical knowledge. Children discover properties of objects (color and shape, for example) as well as how objects respond to actions (bouncing or sliding, for example) through knowledge that comes from acting on objects with all their senses. Robert F. Smith advises, "As physical knowledge develops, children become better able to establish relationships (comparing, classifying, ordering) between and among the objects they act upon. Such relationships (logicomathematical knowledge, according to Piaget) are essential for the emergence of logical, flexible thought processes."[5]

Informal experiences that allow children to explore objects freely and discover relationships should increase the curiosity and thought processes necessary for problem solving and inquiry in the social studies classroom. Active exploration initiated by the students themselves should be offered as a means to motivate the children to cast themselves into their environment.

Exhibits, which E. Riley Holman refers to as "mini-museums," stimulate children to explore, comment, and ask questions. Whatever you call them, arrange exhibit areas in your classroom to surprise the children. Today's exhibit might be a ship's bell, origami, foreign coins, a butter churn, a cotton boll, shark's teeth, colonial tools, a tape recording of city sounds, or a sombrero. You can use the school resource center or ask parents for display items, but when they are placed in the "mini-museum," they are treated like exhibits in the best public, child-oriented museums—not with a "hands-off" policy, but one that invites touching and exploring. Good pictures also deepen interest in places or people the children are studying and stir them to ask more questions. Even kindergarten and first-grade children who cannot yet read words can read pictures. Exploit pictures as tools to encourage children to ask questions and to find new, more detailed information. Like a "mini-museum," the picture area can be decorated as a "Great Gallery." Finally, the books you make available for browsing as well as those you read to the children strengthen their real-life or school experiences and present new adventures that stimulate interests.

Children's natural curiosity must be allowed to surface in the classroom. By arranging opportunities for this to happen, you inform the children that you value and welcome their curiosity, which is a prerequisite to further inquiry. After arousing their curiosity, encourage children to tell what they already know about a topic on display— they will especially want to describe previous experiences. Then encourage them to express their ideas about the exhibit, picture, story, or whatever you have chosen by telling what they liked about the experience, asking questions, drawing a picture, putting a series of materials in correct sequential order, relating what they can remember about a story, or talking about the experience while you record comments on an expeience chart. All these activities stimulate a wish to discover new information and to describe what they find. The total process is a rudimentary form of inquiry, and a necessary initial step for further skill development.

Initially, it is up to the classroom teacher to bring in new materials to stimulate curiosity. One teacher, for example, brought in a stiff brush used by dog groomers and displayed it at her curiosity center. Almost immediately some of the more outgoing children began looking at it, touching it, and talking about what it might be. The teacher watched them and listened to their conversation, occasionally asking open-ended questions or making comments to encourage the children to talk and inquire more deeply about the item. One girl put the brush to her hair and tried to brush it. She was surprised to see just how stiff the bristles were. Naturally, the other children had to try, too.

Linda eventually identified the object. Her mother was a veterinarian and Linda often helped around the office. She was obviously thrilled to share her knowledge and experiences with her classmates. Interest in this one item led to several other social studies experiences: Linda's mother came to class to tell about her job; the children shared books about caring for animals; the teacher arranged a trip to the local SPCA; and the class explored recommended practices for animal care more deeply.

You can see from this example that it is a good idea to plan what you bring to your curiosity center rather than select items at random. You want interests to grow and concepts to develop and strengthen as you extend the activity based on the children's comments and questions. The follow-up activities you arrange are limited only by your own imagination and resources.

Keeping a Record of New Discoveries

Besides the curiosity center and related follow-up activities, what will help children practice the skills of inquiry? They must learn that scientists not only try to find out as much as they can about things that interest them but must also keep records of their findings. Suppose you wish to interest your young scientists in a collection of seashells as a curiosity experience leading to further activities for studying the seashore as a geographic area. You might begin by inviting the children to explore the seashells and asking an open-ended question: "What can you tell me about these seashells?" The children will examine them closely to compare colors, shapes, textures, and sizes. You might ask them to make separate collections based on these and other criteria. The more ways you encourage them to separate the seashells, the more sophisticated their level of beginning inquiry will become. You will want to keep a record of the children's investigations: a simple graph can show how many items were classified into each

FIGURE 5–1
An Information File Card

Name: Carlos Hernandez
Object: Seashell
Where found: Long Beach, California
When found: August 15, 1990
Description

Clam shell

Good classroom displays should be much like good children's museums—they both invite the students to "please touch."

group or an experience chart will summarize and record information. Children like to add to collections objects from home or things they find on the way to school. You may want to set up a special system of file cards like the one in Figure 5–1.

Depending on the children's ages, you may have to do the actual writing, but for the illustration, ask the child to trace the object and color it in. Recording information this way helps develop the more directed, purposeful observation and questioning techniques that are part of mature scientific inquiry.

Supplementing the Observational Experience

The observational experience, as important as it is, by itself does not guarantee meaningful acquisition of the skills necessary for higher-order thinking. Children need a teacher's skillful leadership through guiding questions or comments to help them gain meaning from the mysteries that confront them. With their relatively limited back-grounds of experience, young children often misinterpret new experiences. As Seefeldt says,

> Observing young children, talking to them, asking them questions about how they think engines work or why they think clouds move reveals to the adult the level of their scien-

tific thinking. Often the children have misconceptions that need clarification and revision. They may believe, for example, that the wind moves because it is happy or the shadows move to get out of their way. . . . Engines, air, the clouds, according to the young child, move because they want to. Often the young child's egocentricity influences his concepts: He may believe that the sun sets because he goes to bed or that the rain is falling because it does not want him to go outside.[6]

Skillful guidance can be an effective deterrent against formation of misconceptions when children observe new phenomena. You can guide their observations with questions like these:

"What do you see here?"

"How do you suppose it is used?"

"I wonder what would happen if . . . "

"Let's try it again to see if the same thing happens."

"Is this like anything you've ever (used, seen, tried out) before?"

"How can we find out about . . . ?"

"Maybe we can find out if we watch it carefully."

"What makes you think so?"

Some of these questions and comments help children look for specific things; others are more open-ended, to encourage higher thought processes such as predicting and discovering relationships. Through such experiences, children develop the rudimentary skills of scientific observation required for data collection in subsequent grades; your professional role continues to be that of guide as you stimulate thinking with questions such as those we listed, but with adaptations to particular cultural items:

"Who do you think might use this?"

"Where do they live? What makes you think so?"

"What can you tell about the people who use this?"

"What do you think of the people who use this?"

Our goal during direct observation is to lead the children toward unbiased observations that result in clear, accurate descriptions. Your questions and comments lead to deeper observations, and the children discover and record evidence. The situation is described, and the research question is partly answered but open to further research.

Direct observation is not limited to examining objects brought into the classroom. Observing people and processes, such as how postal workers speed letters through the post office or how a craftperson creates a patchwork quilt, also requires guidance so that children can attach accurate meaning to their direct experiences. Likewise, pictures, artifacts, books, maps, paintings, slides, film, and hundreds of other sources of raw data call for intensive inquiry, as children find solutions to problems they consider important and interesting.

Observation of objects, people, and processes thus comprises one important segment of elementary school social studies programs; another is encouraging children to ask their own questions about what is being observed. In addition to observing the behavior of construction workers at a building site near the school, for example, the children might want to ask some questions of the workers to clarify some concepts. Children must use care in creating and asking questions that will give them the information they want; this requires skill and practice. Usually the student determines a list of important questions to ask someone before the visit. Young children might decide they want to know how the backhoe operator learns to do his job, for example. The children might first compose specific questions they want to ask. They would probably decide on something like this:

> "How did you learn to work the machine?"
>
> "Where did you learn?"
>
> "How long did it take?"
>
> "What do you like about being a backhoe operator?"

Some teachers would ask the class to return to the construction site to interview the worker; others would invite the worker to school; still others might be able to encourage children to seek information by using telephones in the classroom. Whatever the approach, you should encourage children to compose a set of questions carefully so they can gather pertinent information. In the upper grades, teachers stress the process of composing good questions, but with different content. Here is an upper-grade example:

> "What is fifth grade like in France?"
>
> "What do the boys and girls study?"
>
> "What do the boys and girls do after school?"
>
> "What kind of music, TV, or movies do they like best?"

Questioning as a way of seeking information personalizes the social studies program and involves children in making decisions about what they learn. To be successful, however, teachers carefully guide the children in composing the questions they need to gather the necessary data.

Helping Children Make Discoveries

We hear a lot about discovery; it means someone has found or uncovered something of strong personal interest. It usually is accompanied by an intense feeling of elation. That is what drives people to explore: it feels good. Bello explains the feeling discovery brings even to adults:

> "I don't know how other people get thrills in life," says one outstanding physicist, "but to me the biggest thrill is seeing a new effect for the first time. It may happen only once or twice a year, but it's worth all the drudgery that precedes it. It's like shoveling dirt in a gold field and suddenly turning up a nugget. When this happens, it spoils you and you'll never settle for less."[7]

Discovery is creative and enjoyable. It feels so good that children will want to keep working hard at finding out. Jerome S. Bruner[8] recommends one way that teachers nurture insight into discovery through *intuitive thinking*. This can be done by encouraging children to make intuitive guesses based on incomplete evidence and then checking out the guesses systematically. For example, after learning about geographical factors affecting the development of cities, the students might be shown a physical map of a particular land surface with major cities deleted. They would be asked to decide where the largest cities would ideally be located. The guesses could then be checked through systematic research—a process that is usually of great interest as the children strive to find out if their guesses are correct.

Social studies discoveries do not need to be structured by the teacher in order to be valuable learning experiences. Discoveries are made whenever someone wants to know something badly enough to work hard finding out. Discovery is happening when David questions why two books offer different figures for the highest peak of the Andes Mountains. It is happening when Celeste figures out what makes Jello gel. It is happening whenever the children assume a detective's role as they are confronted by something puzzling and new. Young children are not content to leave things they do not completely understand; they will experiment, compare, dig into the facts. They are, in effect, "natural detectives."

Opportunities to discover provide springboards for questions or comments that eventually serve as the key motivators for inquiry. During these experiences, stay attuned to the children's enthusiasm so you can seize upon their interests and build on them. The beginning problem solvers will want to make significant learnings out of everything—a trip to the farm, a ride on a truck, a visit by a carpenter, cooking a pot of wonton soup, or breaking a piñata. They seek new "happenings" and strive to unlock answers to all the questions these experiences stimulate. This is problem-solving or inquiry time, it is planning time, investigating time, organization-of-ideas time—when children use their energies, minds, and skills to seek answers to all that enthralls them.

Initiating Independent Research

When children experience success with either informal explorations or discovery episodes, they are forming a pattern of thinking that will help them search for further knowledge. It is at this point that you may find it advantageous to help them move from observation-type experiences to a search for data that provide insight into personally meaningful problems. The first data-gathering technique most easily used by young or inexperienced learners is the *survey technique.*

Surveys

Surveys are one of the least complicated techniques enabling children to collect their own data. Young children enjoy collecting data, especially when the information they uncover helps them to find out about each other. Some survey topics might include birthdays, heights, weights, or a number of "favorites" such as each child's favorite books, games, toys, movies, television programs, school subject, sports star, or author.

The first step in a beginning survey is to select a meaningful problem (first problems should be closely associated with children's immediate interests) and design a set of good questions with which to gather information. The questions should be precise so they will yield the exact information being sought. Suppose your class has decided to conduct a survey on "Our Favorite Lunch" in the school cafeteria. A question such as, "What do you think of the food served in the lunchroom?" is too vague and would cause difficulty in categorizing the responses. On the other hand, "What is your favorite lunch served in the lunchroom?" and "What is your least favorite lunch served in the lunchroom?" target the responses and make the information easy to record. Once the questions are determined, the actual survey sheet must by constructed. Have the children write the lunches that are served most often in the lunchroom at the top of each column, as shown in Figure 5–2.

After they construct the survey sheet, the children must decide who to interview to gather their data. Do they need to ask every child in school to develop valid conclusions? Most surveys utilize some type of *sampling method.* They might choose to interview every third student who goes through the lunch line; if they want a boy/girl representation, they might ask every third boy, every third girl, and so on. If the school has 300 students, they may choose to select randomly any 30 students. Whatever the choice, the children must be sure to provide "fairness" in selecting the sample. As each child interviews someone, she indicates the response by making a mark or signing a name in the appropriate column of the survey sheet.

When the surveys are completed, the children tally the responses and organize the data. They count the responses in each survey category and, typically, record and communicate the findings on a bar graph. Young children may need to use blocks to make a concrete representation of the information (see Chapter 10), but older children

FIGURE 5–2
Sample Survey Sheet

OUR FAVORITE LUNCH					
PIZZA	TACOS	SPAGHETTI	HAMBURGERS	HOTDOGS	CHICKEN
⊮⊮ ⊮ ⊮ ‖	⊮ ⊮ ⊮ ⊮ ‖	⊮ ⊮ ⊮	⊮ ‖	‖‖	⊮ ⊮ ⊮ ⊮ ∕

can use a summary sheet to record results. Figure 5–3 shows a summary graph on which the children used a different color crayon for each column.

When they have recorded the information, the children must examine and analyze the data to draw accurate conclusions. Naturally, you don't impose a complicated statistical treatment that you learned in a college psychology course on the children, but you do want them to interpret the data accurately. The findings of the lunchroom survey might include these *interpretations:*

1. Most of the children like tacos for lunch.
2. Chicken is almost as popular as tacos.
3. Hot dogs are the favorite of the fewest people.

Each of the social science disciplines offers areas for survey research. For example:

> Should a shopping center be built near our school?
>
> What form of exchange (credit card, cash, check) do our parents use most often?
>
> From what countries did our ancestors emigrate?
>
> What is the most requested birthday present by fourth graders?

FIGURE 5–3
Sample Survey Graph

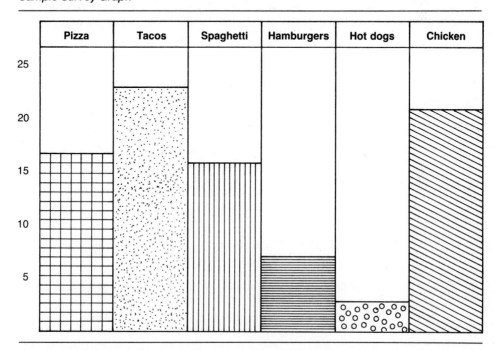

What kinds of books are most popular among the boys? The girls? Primary-grade children? Upper-grade children?

What is the most popular school subject?

The steps of the survey process are essentially the same at all grade levels; the teacher need only simplify the kind of problem and some aspects of the process (graphing, for example) for younger or inexperienced children. The basic survey pattern includes these steps:

1. Determine the problem to be solved.
2. Write the questions and design the questionnaire.
3. Determine a sampling method and administer the questionnaire.
4. Organize the data.
5. Analyze the data and form conclusions.

Observation

As the children develop an interest in asking questions and solving problems, you may wish to plan situations that help them create solutions to problems directly associated with social studies topics normally taught through a teacher-directed approach. Let us consider a classroom observational activity that was designed to enhance the students' historical understanding that "change occurs with the passage of time."

Mr. Jackson's third-grade class was involved in a series of lessons focusing on the principle of change relating to the passage of time. Mr. Jackson needed an activity to express the concept that as time passes, everyone learns to do more and different things. To prepare for today's activity, Mr. Jackson prearranged with two kindergarten and two fifth-grade teachers in his building to have several students spend some time observing children in each of their rooms. But before he sent the students to those rooms, Mr. Jackson asked the class these questions:

MR. JACKSON: What are some things you can do in school now that you couldn't do when you were in kindergarten?

CHILDREN: Read. Write. Tie our shoes. Draw better. Do harder math problems.

As the class continued to offer comments, Mr. Jackson recorded them on the chalkboard under the heading of *Third Grade (Present)*.

MR. JACKSON: What are some things kindergartners might do in school that most third or fifth graders would not do?

CHILDREN: Eat snacks. Play with blocks. Do puzzles.

Again, Mr. Jackson listed the children's comments on the chalkboard, this time under the heading of *Kindergarten (Past)*.

MR. JACKSON: What are some of the things you think you might do in the future—in fifth grade?

CHILDREN: Learn harder things. Learn French. My sister said fifth graders have more spelling words to learn each week.

Mr. Jackson continued to list the children's guesses, this time under the heading *Fifth Grade (Future).*

MR. JACKSON: Now I would like to divide the class into four groups. Two groups will visit kindergarten rooms and two groups will visit fifth-grade rooms. Those of you going to the kindergarten rooms will need to copy the "past" list from the board and those who will visit the fifth graders will copy the "future" list. You will spend one-half hour watching what the children are doing. Try to be quiet while you're there, but whenever you see someone doing anything on our list, put a check next to it. Also, add anything to the list that we did not think of.

When the children returned from their visits, Mr. Jackson asked each group to transfer the findings from their checklists to the chalkboard. He then led the children through an examination of the data by asking questions that encouraged the children to compare the observed activities with what went on in their own classroom.

This lesson shows how a teacher can motivate children with a personal problem, organize them to collect data through observation, and lead a discussion to examine the data for the purpose of developing the generalization stated at the beginning of the lesson. Many teachers, especially those in the earlier grades, choose single-day problem-solving sessions involving surveys or observation as the first exposure because it is a compact way to introduce children to a new mode of social studies instruction.

Inquiry

The guided problem-solving model as presented thus far is based on the idea of modifying the teacher-directed approach to increase the level of student thinking. By adapting the teacher-directed procedure slightly, the students are placed in problem situations that introduce them to the scientific method. As higher-level thinking skills evolve (some students take months, others require years), students gradually develop an ability to systematically perform inquiry tasks. As a teaching strategy, inquiry is often described as a four-step process:

1. The students confront a problem.
2. The students generate hypotheses, or unproven suppositions, that are tentatively accepted to explain the problem.
3. The students collect and analyze data for the purpose of testing the hypotheses.
4. The students form generalizations that can be applied to this problem and similar ones encountered in their lives.

The Inquiry Process

The inquiry process may look very similar to guided problem solving, and in many cases it is. What determines whether a particular strategy is inquiry or guided problem solving is primarily the way in which a problem is presented. Sound confusing? Well, you are not alone, for as R. Murray Thomas and Dale L. Brubaker contend:

> From time to time, a term intended to signify a new teaching procedure rapidly gains popularity among educators. In recent years, the expression *inquiry method* has achieved this distinction, particularly in the fields of science and social studies. However, as use of the term has spread, so has confusion about what it really means. Some people consider inquiry an approach to instruction that is indeed new. Others say it is at least as old as ancient Greece but has previously traveled under such names as the Socratic method, problem solving, critical thinking, scholarly investigation, scientific analysis, and the development of thinking processes.[9]

Teachers may mean completely different things when they say they use inquiry in their social studies programs. Despite these limitations, we will define inquiry as the four-step process described. Most teachers appear to prefer guided problem solving because it is efficient—it assumes a "readiness of the mind" necessary for attempting higher-level thinking. The method moves children from the path of a DLE to a particular problem situation in which they transfer concepts to new situations. This is the simplest problem-solving form; it requires only that the teacher adapt the teacher-directed format by presenting a question or problem and then arranging for groups of children to explore solutions based on the content. It is an easy procedure to implement.

Inquiry differs in that the strategy begins with a problem rather than the exposure to information. The children actively engage in gathering and working with data rather than having the data presented to them. The teacher does not systematically base the program on a textbook, for example, but the textbook can be used like any other source of information in gathering data. See Figure 5–4.

When teachers use the inquiry process in their social studies classrooms, they act as facilitators and assume the role of guiding children through the four inquiry steps described earlier. They assume that students have first developed skills at the guided problem-solving level and are now ready to perform the specific skills contained in the

FIGURE 5–4

Comparing Guided Discovery and Inquiry Formats

GUIDED PROBLEM SOLVING	INQUIRY
1. Students acquire knowledge, concepts, and generalizations under direction of the teacher.	1. Teacher may offer a problem or the students may express one of their own.
2. Teacher offers an interesting problem related to the content.	2. Students develop hypotheses that tentatively explain the problem.
3. Students solve the problem with previously acquired understanding.	3. Students search for their own informational data and analyze it for the purpose of testing the hypotheses.
	4. Students generalize their findings.

inquiry model, such as generating hypotheses and analyzing self-discovered data. The following suggestions will help you implement the inquiry process in your elementary school social studies classroom.

Selecting the Problem

In order for inquiry to work, students must first have an interesting, motivating problem to solve. The problem must hold a degree of mystery for the students in order to capture their interest. The major concern here is appeal—the children will not want to investigate anything they do not care about. There are three basic types of problems that serve to generate interest among students: (1) problems generated by the students, (2) problems generated by asking a stimulating question or presenting a perplexing dilemma, and (3) problems produced by arranging the classroom environment and encouraging exploration of various items on display.

Problems Generated by the Students.　To illustrate this type of problem, let's examine a social studies teacher's use of the model.

> The students in Mrs. Hernandez's fifth grade classroom came to school in an excited state. It seemed that the main topic of conversation involved the borough council's decision the night before to allow a local developer to build a shopping center in a neighborhood wooded area that many of the children played in. The debate involved a difference of opinion about whether or not the neighborhood residents wanted the shopping center.
>
> Mrs. Hernandez discussed the issue with her students and listened to their opinions about what the people "really wanted." Rather than have the children argue in class about this volatile topic, Mrs. Hernandez devoted the next few social studies periods to planning a survey that would discover what the people really wanted.

Problems Generated by a Stimulating Question or Perplexing Dilemma.　The following situation stimulated an inquiry episode that lasted for several class sessions.

> Mr. Greenberg, a sixth-grade teacher, read two conflicting editorials appraising Ronald Reagan's role as president. Since one editorial praised Reagan while the other criticized him, Mr. Greenberg asked the class how they could determine which was more nearly accurate.

Problems Produced by Arranging the Classroom Environment.　Often teachers prefer to "feed in" stimuli with attractive, thought-provoking classroom displays.

> Ms. Yu was beginning a unit on clothing in her fourth-grade social studies program. She began the unit by arranging different types of clothing on a large table and displaying a dozen photographs of diverse ways people dress themselves. She began her first lesson by saying, "Children, today we are going to begin studying how people all around the world clothe themselves. As a start, I'd like you to take a look at some actual clothing as well as some photographs of people to see what questions you might have about them."

The climate during this initial state of the inquiry process must be such that children are free to question and discuss. Ask open-ended questions that encourage children to think, imagine, and explore. These questions do not require right or wrong answers and are not threatening to the children:

"What can you tell me about this?"

"What else can you do with that?"

"How do you suppose that is used?"

"What do you think those people are doing?"

"I wonder what will happen next. What do you think?"

"Why do you suppose that happened?"

These questions ask children to examine ordinary situations with a new perspective. With open-ended questions, teachers initiate the process of scientific inquiry.

From the initial spark provided by the question or display, the teacher calls the children together for further questioning and discussion. The teacher writes the questions on the chalkboard or a chart so the children can refer to them throughout their inquiry. For the problem to be effective, we must also be aware of Bruner's advice that the problem must match what the children already know. If the children are confronted with a problem with which they have little or no previous experience, they often reject the problem because of its unfamiliarity. On the other hand, the problem should not be simply an opportunity for the children to "rehash" information they already know. Instead, the problem situation should be balanced between what children already know and that which is new to them. That balance seems to stimulate elementary school children's greatest need to explore and search for answers.

According to John Dewey, this first step of the inquiry process is crucial; if children cannot accurately define a problem based on previous experiences or if they aren't sufficiently motivated to pursue it, the subsequent steps of the process are futile.

Developing the Hypotheses

Once children know what the problem is and want to pursue it, the class is ready for action; it is ready to be led systematically and creatively toward a solution. Assuming that we meet the criteria for selecting a problem, the teacher might ask: "What do you already know about these items? What have you already learned that we might be able to use now? How could this information help us come up with answers to our problems? What are some answers you can suggest based upon what we've just discussed?" The purpose of these questions is to help children associate information they already know and to encourage them to offer assumptions, or *hypotheses,* about the solution to their new problem. Formulating hypotheses involves a certain amount of risk to the child, so teachers must be especially careful to value individual contributions. Remember that these assumptions are, in most cases, nothing more than predictions. Definitive solutions and opportunities to reject hypotheses arise when children become involved in carrying out their investigations and selecting the appropriate data that support or refute the hypotheses.

Gathering and Analyzing the Data

Having generated their hypotheses, students are now ready to gather data. The data can take several forms, depending on the nature of the investigation: *survey, historical, descriptive,* or *question-based.* The format selected depends upon the problem and its hypotheses. For example, in the case of the problem, "Should our neighborhood wooded area be replaced by a shopping center?" a *survey* of neighborhood residents would be in order. (We examined how surveys are conducted earlier in this chapter.) On the other hand, a problem such as, "How did the contributions of Chinese laborers influence the construction of the transcontinental railroad?" calls for more demanding and time-consuming *historical research.* (See Chapter 13 for an in-depth description of historical research.) Problems may call for descriptive or question-based data gathering, too; both of these forms of investigation will be described here.

Descriptive Research. Descriptive research is one of the most enjoyable of all data-gathering techniques used in the elementary school social studies classroom. It involves two major techniques: direct observation and indirect observation. *Direct observation* includes all the real-life experiences that involve children in touching, handling, trying out, and viewing objects or events. A trip to the commuter train station to observe the "crunch" of rush hour, a trip to a dairy farm to see how a cow is milked, and a visit by the town's mayor to question her about the need for a traffic light near the school are all examples of direct observational experiences offering data for the solution of problems.

Indirect observation involves the use of sources of information other than direct experiences. They may include, but not necessarily be limited to:

Books	Guides and timetables	Music
Magazines	Reference books	Paintings
Encyclopedia	Trade books	Radio
Almanacs	Advertisements	Television
Catalogs	Posters	Records
Dictionaries	Guest speakers	Objects
Government publications	Field trips	Artifacts
Travel brochures	Filmstrips	Movies
Pamphlets	Slides	Museums
Atlases	Photographs	Natural environment

Before you provide any of these materials, be sure the children know how to use resources independently. Most elementary school teachers try to involve their children in using direct data sources, but are hampered by the fact that they are time-consuming and costly. For that reason, ample indirect sources must be available so that students have satisfactory data with which to test their hypotheses.

Question-Based Research. One of the problems of using inquiry in the elementary school classroom is that it takes more time and effort than can be realistically extracted from an already crowded day. Richard Suchman[10] designed a data-gathering procedure that was aimed at alleviating that problem—a procedure that encourages students to seek information through questioning. Paul D. Eggen and Donald P. Kauchak offer this classroom scenario to illustrate the Suchman inquiry model. First, the teacher, Mr. Smith, presents a problem such as:

> In the mountains of the Southwest a number of years ago deer were quite numerous, although the population would fluctuate slightly. There were also wolves in the mountains. Some people from a small town witnessed a wolf pack pull down two of the smaller deer in the herd and were horrified. As a result, the people launched a campaign to eliminate the wolves. To the dismay of the people, the years following the elimination of the wolves showed a marked decrease in the population of the deer. Why, when the wolf is the deer's natural predator, should this occur?[11]

Once the problem is shared and the teacher is sure it is understood by all, the teacher encourages the students to question him while keeping two rules in mind: (1) the questions must be answered "yes" or "no" and (2) the answer to the question must be observable. Keeping those rules in mind, part of the questioning sequence went like this:

> "I have an idea, I think," Steve said tentatively. He went on, "After the wolves were eliminated, other predators such as bobcats, coyotes, and large birds, such as eagles, were able to prey more successfully on the deer, so their population went down."
>
> Steve then appeared to be finished for a moment, so Mr. Smith returned to Pam.
>
> "Jim and I have another idea," Pam suggested.
>
> "Excellent," Mr. Smith praised. "Go ahead."
>
> "After the deer's predator was eliminated, the population expanded so their habitat couldn't support them, and they became susceptible to starvation, and the population went down," Pam said.
>
> "OK," Mr. Smith said. "Can we gather some information to support your idea?"
>
> "Were more bobcats seen in the deer's habitat after the wolves were eliminated?" Ronnie queried.
>
> "No," Mr. Smith said.
>
> "How about coyotes?' Ronnie continued.
>
> "No again," replied Mr. Smith.
>
> "Were numerous barkless dead trees found in the region after the wolves were eliminated?" Sally continued.
>
> "Yes," Mr. Smith said.[12]

As you can see from the classroom dialogue, Mr. Smith's strategy began with a problem: "Why should a population of animals decline rather than expand when their primary predator was eliminated?" The students were then involved in seeking out data while testing their hypotheses. Obviously, the strategy cannot work with every topic you may consider for your social studies program; the problem must be stimulating and engaging. This process places great responsibility on the teacher; she must have a wide range of information to answer many questions on the topic.

When children attack problems and collect data, you must guide them through a thorough examination of the material so they can define and generalize accurately and objectively. Do this carefully and deliberately with questions such as these:

"What are some of the ways you've tried to find out about your problem?"

"How did you decide what to do to test your ideas?"

"Are there any other ways of testing that you might have tried?"

"How did you decide which ideas were correct?"

"Would you plan to do anything differently if we did this kind of lesson again?"

"How does your group feel about its findings? Are you satisfied?"

Children need to learn the skills for evaluating and extracting information from various sources:

- Searching for data from appropriate resources
- Recording relevant data
- Distinguishing between fact and opinion, or relevant from irrelevant information
- Comparing data from several sources, looking for variations and inconsistencies
- Judging whether data are useful or important
- Determining the reliability of a source
- Detecting bias
- Defining the relative strengths of arguments

This phase of the problem-solving process, extracting and evaluating data, calls for the use of several higher-level skills. Perhaps the ultimate skill in the independent research process is to think critically. Children must check materials for bias, prejudice, opinion, accuracy, and logic. They learn to ask questions such as: "Is the material relevant to what I am studying? Can the facts be verified? What are the writer's qualifications? Does the source seem to be omitting or suppressing any important facts? Are the statements expressions of facts or feelings? Should I revise my own ideas in light of what I have learned?"

When students address those concerns, they are involved as *critical thinkers.* Barry K. Beyer describes critical thinking thus:

> [C]ritical thinking is not problem solving. It is not decision making. It is not Bloom's taxonomy. It is not a cover-all term for all thinking skills. Critical thinking is, instead, the process of determining the authenticity, accuracy and worth of information or knowledge claims. It consists of a number of discrete skills, which one can use and is inclined to use, to determine such authenticity, accuracy and worth.
>
> If the consensus description of critical thinking outlined here could be communicated to all social studies educators and be accepted by them, we would dramatically improve student learning of this skill.[13]

Knowing that critical thinking is a crucial part of the inquiry process, teachers can help children acquire those skills by taking on the roles of resource person, guide, and authority.

Resource Person.   Children may often turn to you for help, especially when they have had limited experience with inquiry. They may need someone to help them answer questions—"Where do you find material on seeds?" or "This book says the population of our city was 1,500,000 in 1988, but that magazine says 1,400,000. Which is right?" You may want to give direct help at times, but remember not to steer the process away from the children. Eventually you want children to make decisions themselves.

Guide.   As children search through information and begin to select the most suitable data for solving their problems, guide them toward some important considerations. For example, a common problem during inquiry episodes is a child's strong need to prove his predictions or hypotheses correct. Children often choose only data that supports their predictions; they tend to feel they have failed if their predictions prove wrong. Watch for situations that block good data collection and interpretation. If you discover a major problem, a short class discussion on how to find and use data may be helpful.

Authority.   If unresolved conflicts emerge, you must be on hand to furnish direct action. You must be especially aware of situations that impede positive group work, such as inability to work with others, failure to share ideas, or misuse of materials. The results of a group's efforts may well be determined by how you divert negative forces.

The importance of developing independent research to solve problems cannot be overestimated. Well-educated students are much like detectives: their minds are flexible, yet disciplined enough to search between the lines or to discern implications. Children need to learn several methods of original data collection.

Forming Generalizations

In this final phase, children are led to test hypotheses and formulate final conclusions. They classify and categorize their information to defend their hypotheses, then summarize their findings and share what they have found with their classmates. Popular sharing techniques include maps, charts, bulletin boards, drawings, oral reports, written reports, dramatic skits, replicas, and demonstrations.

A Sample Inquiry Episode

As the children gain confidence and skill as inquirers, teachers gradually offer increasing freedom and time to pursue topics of interest. In the following episode, a fifth-grade teacher allows one week for collecting and reporting data.

On the first day of a two-week study on China, Mrs. Levenson arranged areas of interest in the classroom with boxes, cartons, desks, tables, and bulletin boards. Many materials were evident in the classroom—pictures, objects, newspaper clippings, books, reproductions of Chinese art, writing samples, and Chinese symbols such as those for yin and yang. She put a sign on one of the boxes: "Travel Agency." Arranged at the travel agency were flyers and brochures about China. While the children browsed, a record of traditional Chinese music played in the background.

This introductory activity took about thirty minutes. Mrs. Levenson provided this time because she knew that upper-grade children are often interested in contrasting cultures and spontaneously ask questions once their interest is stimulated. Mrs. Levenson encouraged questions and comments from the children and concluded that their major interest was: "How is life in China different from ours?" The children eagerly agreed to think of other questions that would help in solving the major problem. The next day the class met for a planning session. The teacher listed all the children's questions on the chalkboard:

How are East Asian values like mine? Different?

What is a dynasty? How is China ruled now?

What do the writing symbols mean?

Why are ancestors so powerful in Chinese culture?

What are yin and yang?

What kind of family life would we find in China?

What kind of life did the peasants lead?

Who was Confucius? Why was he so important?

What is the Great Wall? Why was it built?

What role did the Buddhist religion play in China?

How did China become communist?

Who were Marco Polo and Genghis Khan?

As she listed the questions on a chart, Mrs. Levenson reworded them for clarity. The class compared and contrasted the questions, finding many that could be placed into categories—clothing, family style, government, religion, people, the landscape, and so on. Mrs. Levenson provided separate sheets of chart paper for each category of questions and a different colored marking pen for each chart. Committees were appointed to separate questions on the charts into appropriate categories such as "food questions," "clothing questions," and so on.

The next day, the completed charts were displayed around the room. The children added new questions as they examined those from the previous day. Now the class was ready to explore means of solving the problems they had formulated. Mrs. Levenson informed the class that they were going on a simulated excursion to China to find answers to the questions, but to research the questions most effectively, the children would need to form committees. The teacher asked the children to decide what committees they wanted to work on and to sign their names on the appropriate charts.

"Our committees have been formed," announced Mrs. Levenson, "but before we go to China to find our answers, we need to find out a few things: How much will air fares, hotels, food, guides, tips, gifts, and other expenses cost? Do they use dollars in China? What clothing should we take? Where is China? How long will it take us to get there? Will we need shots?"

China's geography and economic system were brought into the study as the children prepared for these last-minute considerations. After "passports" were created, the decorated, brown-bag "luggage" was "packed" with pictures of clothing and other essentials, "Customs" processed the travelers, and the children were ready to take off! Committees were assigned plane seats by color and everyone was welcomed aboard. The flight attendant (Mrs. Levenson) welcomed them and explained about the plane, the exits, and the oxygen masks. Then a tape-recorded jet roar signaled takeoff and the children settled back in their seats. The room darkened while a film about China was shown. When the film was over, the plane landed, and the children were ready to begin.

The next day the children were taken to assigned meeting places in "China" to fulfill their research duties. Textbooks, trade books, films, filmstrips, slides, records, and other resources were available for each committee. Each committee knew that it had a responsibility to choose a chairperson, decide how to go about finding answers to its questions, and make plans to present what they found out to their classmates.

After three or four days of gathering and analyzing data the committees were ready to return to the United States and their classroom to share their findings. One group made a scrapbook of pictures depicting China's terrain, architecture, and other physical features. Another group planned a program of Chinese songs and dances. A third group presented a dramatic skit involving Marco Polo and the Mongols. To pull the entire learning experience together, Mrs. Levenson summarized what the class had learned on information retrieval charts next to each committee's question chart.

In this example, the children learned much more than subject matter. They learned to work together, to think critically, to accept responsibility, and to make individual contributions to a group's plans. An important facet of such experiences is their cooperative nature. Cooperative learning is an approach to solving problems that approximates democratic living, and thus reinforces an important purpose of social studies education. The goal of curiosity-stimulating experiences is to make children question and discover new ideas. Our intention is to motivate children to continually want to know about things and develop the logical thought processes they will use as functioning citizens in a democracy.

COGNITIVE STYLE AND THE INQUIRY PROCESS

In all inquiry episodes children are, theoretically, researchers who independently solve problems, much as a detective would. But in actual practice, few children approach a problem with similar investigative methods. Robert Sternberg, professor of psychology and education at Yale University, uses the following story to describe differences in approach:

A [insert the name of your college or university] student and one from [insert the name of your chief rival] were hiking in the woods when they came across a grizzly bear.

One student quickly calculated the mathematical differential between his speed and the bear's.

The other student simply traded his hiking boots for his jogging shoes and took off.

"Boy, you ARE stupid," the first guy hollered to the second. "You can't outrun a grizzly bear!"

"I don't have to," the runner yelled back. "I only have to outrun you!"[14]

The story demonstrates two types of intelligence or *cognitive styles* that people call upon when they are confronted with a problem. The two styles are generally referred to as *systematic* (the first student) and *intuitive* (the second student). Regardless of whether you are solving the problem of how to study for an exam when a big football game is scheduled for the weekend before, or where to get money for next year's tuition hike, you are likely to rely on one cognitive style to solve it. Think of a problem you faced recently and how you arrived at a solution. Which style is closer to yours?

Where do these differences in style come from? Research into the human brain has revealed that there are two sides, or hemispheres, each capable of processing information in a unique way—in effect, giving us two minds in our heads.[15] The *left brain* controls the logical, rational thought processes (as well as the right side of the body); the *right brain* controls intuitive, abstract thought (and the left side of the body). In most people, then, logic resides in the left hemisphere, intuition in the right. In early childhood, as with left- or right-handedness, one hemisphere becomes dominant. When confronted with a problem, most of us solve it in our preferred style. Before these breakthroughs, little was known about the right hemisphere. Since speech and language were functions of the left hemisphere, and most schoolwork called upon systematic rather than intuitive thinking, there was no way of communicating with the right hemisphere to find out what its contributions were. Therefore schools (and society in general) tended to overemphasize left-hemisphere skills at the expense of right-hemisphere skills, giving our children an apparently "lopsided" education.

Bruner examined the research into brain hemisphere characteristics and informed educators of its importance in *On Knowing Essays for the Left Hand*.[16] Bruner criticized the nearly exclusive emphasis on teaching toward systematic, rational (left-hemisphere) thinking in our schools and advocated teaching strategies that also encouraged exploration of innovative, experimental thinking (right-hemisphere). Edward de Bono looked at this "left-handed" (or right-hemisphere-controlled) thinking and found it to be quite distinct from logical thinking and more useful in generating new ideas.[17] He used the term *lateral thinking* to describe intuitive thinking and *vertical thinking* to denote conventional logical thought processes. De Bono explained that lateral thinking is easiest to appreciate when seen in action, as in the situation illustrated in Figure 5–5. Although this problem looks simple, it is actually quite difficult. As a matter of fact, only about one person in a hundred is able to solve it the first time around. There are four volumes of Shakespeare's collected works on the shelf. Each volume is exactly 2″ thick (pages only); the covers are each 1/6″ thick. A bookworm starts eating at page 1 of volume I and eats through to the last page of volume IV. What is the distance the bookworm covers? Try to work the problem before you look at the answer.

The answer is five inches. Remember that the bookworm started at page 1 of volume I. Put your finger on that point; do not count the back cover and all the pages in between. Are you catching on? Similarly, the bookworm ate only to the last page of the last volume, so do not count the front cover and all the pages of the last volume.

FIGURE 5–5
Bookworm Problem

What causes so many of us to generate incorrect answers by looking only at "obvious" solutions to problems? Torrance believes that a great deal of blame should be placed on the schools:

> Creative imagination during early childhood seems to reach a peak between four and four-and-a-half years, and is followed by a drop at about age five when the child enters school for the first time. This drop has generally been regarded as the inevitable phenomenon in nature. There are now indications, however, that this drop in five-year-olds is a man-made rather than a natural phenomenon.[18]

Some argue that this phenomenon occurs because schools limit children's freedom from kindergarten on. "You're acting like a first grader," or "Stop being so silly," and similar sarcastic put-downs often accompany original, adventuresome attempts at self-expression. Highly creative individuals such as Einstein and Edison were considered dunces and were forced to leave elementary school because they would not (or could not) conform to the rigid behavioral expectations of their teachers. Albert Einstein stressed his regard for creativity when he commented, "The gift of fantasy has meant more to me than my talent for absorbing positive knowledge." John Lennon, one of the great modern composers, was viewed by the headmaster at his school in England as a boy who was "up to all sorts of tricks, and didn't make life easy for the staff. I caned him once and he had been caned many times by my predecessor."[19] Einstein and Lennon had the persistence to fulfill their talents. But what has happened to the thousands of youngsters who surrendered their creative urges to conformity and were never encouraged or allowed to make significant creative contributions?

New, creative solutions to problems come from the ability to shift directions in thought: to move beyond the obvious to the subtle. The vertical thinker attacks a problem by first establishing a direction of thought and then digging deeper in that direction until he finds an answer or solution. The lateral thinker also attacks a problem by initiating a direction of thought, but when that direction appears to be leading nowhere, she feels comfortable taking new chances. Figure 5–6 characterizes the difference in vertical and lateral thinking.

Just as a person can become, with practice, more proficient with the nondominant hand, so can children become more novel problem solvers by looking at situations in

FIGURE 5–6
Vertical and Lateral Thinkers

THE VERTICAL THINKER   THE LATERAL THINKER

Digs one hole deeper to find   Abandons one hole and digs
a solution.   several experimental holes.

more ways than just the most probable—practicing with the right hemisphere of the brain in classroom activities. I do not mean to persuade you that all vertical thinking experiences are "bad," nor that all lateral thinking experiences are "good." The intention is to make you aware that a child's mind is capable of different thought processes, and that children may demonstrate greater skills in some processes than in others. Just as a child's physical realm may be characterized by greater skills in running than in hitting a ball, so his intellectual realm may be characterized by greater skills in lateral thinking than in vertical thinking. Teachers must be aware of this variability and plan classroom experiences that foster an assortment of thought processes. This perspective is especially important when we consider that the organization of the brain is quite plastic in young children. David Galin reports that lateralization is in flux up to about the age of ten.[20] Knowing this, we must develop classroom practices that encourage interaction between both sides of the brain.

Robert Samples, who worked on hemispheric functioning with Jerome Bruner at Harvard, designed educational strategies that bring both brain hemispheres into equal partnership. He found three characteristics in the resulting learning process: (1) higher feelings of self-confidence, self-esteem, and compassion; (2) wider exploration of traditional content subjects and skills; and (3) higher levels of creative invention in content and skills.[21] We must encourage in the social studies classroom not only systematic teacher-directed instruction, but also the inventive, intuitive thinking associated with *creative discovery.*

Planning for Open-ended Inquiry

Planning for creative thinking takes more time, more materials, more effort, and more thinking by both the teacher and the children. Is the extra effort worth it? It depends on what we want from the learner.

Basically, we must place children into two major problem-solving situations: (1) closed-ended and (2) open-ended. In the closed-ended situation, we plan a teaching/learning episode in which students solve problems through research or other experiences that provide data. Children explore the information, analyze its worth, and draw conclusions. These situations utilize the talents controlled by the left hemisphere of the brain. These are examples of directed problems:

- While studying the events that led to the American Revolution, students break up into three groups—loyalists, revolutionaries, and neutrals—to gather information and to form an argument by which they solicit new members for their respective groups.
- Students investigate a number of resources and prepare their own newspaper describing the daily activities of a particular historical period, perhaps pre-revolutionary colonial life.
- Boys and girls learn the concept of specialization of labor by comparing the time used to prepare peanut butter sandwiches individually and by an assembly line technique.
- Boys and girls trying to understand economics or the cost of providing for a family are allotted $200 or so and asked to prepare a weekly budget for a family of five.
- Children preparing to study a new country pretend they are going to make a trip there. Where is it? What type of transportation would be best to get there? What is the climate like—what type of clothing would they need when they arrived? What kind of people will they meet? What activities are popular?
- The class studies the effects of television advertising by polling students in the school to see how many buy a certain product because they have seen it advertised on television.

An open-ended problem differs from a directed problem in that children deliberately make themselves look at several solutions for each problem and offer their thoughts, no matter how absurd, to help originate unique, creative solutions. The social studies curriculum can encourage creative thinking in many ways, one of which is to offer stimulating discussion questions. When questioning, you must be aware of four basic steps:

1. Establish a creative climate in the classroom. You can stimulate creative thinking when you encourage children to think freely. Such an environment encourages a flow of ideas because it allows for the emotional characteristics of creative thinkers.
2. Present a challenging question or problem. Your role is to make children aware of a puzzling situation and to develop a personal concern for it. Pose challenges,

puzzles, and problems that do not have a correct answer and thus stimulate a wide variety of responses. Use these types of questions:

a. Quantity questions
- List all the ways you can use an empty beverage can.
- How many ways can you come up with to encourage people to stop polluting the environment?
- If a garbage heap were the only thing left of a civilization, what are all the possible things you might learn about the people?

b. Involvement questions
- How would you feel if you were the Mayflower?
- How would you feel if you were the football that scored the winning field goal in the Super Bowl?
- How would you have felt if you were one of the Wright brothers during the first airplane flight?

c. Supposition questions
- Suppose only women had the right to vote. What would happen?
- Suppose insects were more intelligent than human beings. What are all the things that might happen?

d. Viewpoint questions
- How would winter look to an Australian aborigine?
- How would a ship look to the fish in the ocean?
- How would the lush grasslands look to a herd of starved cattle?

3. Allow time to consider alternatives. During this phase, encourage the children to produce a large number of possible responses to your question. It is especially important to defer judgment as to the worth of each suggestion until a solution is called for. *Brainstorming* is a popular technique for this phase of creative production which we will discuss later. These are a few of the strategies that can be used when children consider alternatives to a situation:
- Confront the children with the familiar.
- Turn the familiar into an ambiguity or uncertainty.
- Ask provocative questions that require the children to think about things in a new way.
- Invite the children to explore new possibilities.
- Preserve open-mindedness during discussion sessions.
- Call for a sharing of constructive responses.
- Encourage several solutions to the same problem.
- Ask children to project their thinking into the future.

4. Encourage the children to put their ideas into use. The final stage of the creative process is to consider all possible consequences of each alternative and select the most acceptable. You can lead children to this goal through *attribute listing*. Table 5–1 is an example of an attribute listing activity. In this process, children list all the attributes of the problem in one column, generate ideas for improvement in the next, positive features next, and negative features in the final column. They can consider the positive and negative features of each alternative to reach the best solution.

TABLE 5–1
Attribute Listing Activity

Problem Area	Attribute	Possible Solutions	Positive Features	Negative Features
Swings on the playground	Too high for small kids	Lower them	Small kids can reach them	If too low, some kids can get hurt

Brainstorming

In the third step of encouraging creative thinking, you will find brainstorming an effective technique for helping children consider alternatives. Brainstorming works best in elementary classrooms when you limit the size of brainstorming groups to six or seven children. To begin, state the problem and encourage group members to think of as many new (and wild) ideas for possible solutions as fast as they can. One group member should record all ideas as they are offered. The children must be aware of the rules for brainstorming.

The main objective of the first part of the brainstorming session is to generate the greatest number of suggestions possible. Children should offer ideas for between five and fifteen minutes, depending on the size of the group and how long interest is sustained. One rule of thumb: The shorter the time available for discussion, the smaller the groups should be. The webbing or mapping techniques are effective when combined with brainstorming. Refer to Chapters 3 and 4 to review those processes. After this suggestion period, critical evaluation of ideas begins with restating the problem and inviting each group to narrow down its list of solutions to about four or five. They must address concerns such as: Will it actually solve this problem? Will it create new ones? Is it practical? Will we be able to use it in the near future? What are the strengths and weaknesses of each? Can any of our ideas be combined into one useful solution?

After the list has been narrowed down, the group should work toward a solution through discussion. The ultimate solution may contain one idea or a combination of ideas. Members are free to develop the ideas further so they can share them with the class as we discussed earlier: making diagrams, models, or designs of the idea or object; composing a letter to appropriate individuals or agencies; or offering a creative skit.

Perhaps your most valuable skill in guiding open-ended problem-solving experiences is to ask questions to spur the children's thinking while they are formulating ideas. Some sample questions follow:

- New ideas
    Can it be used in new ways as it is?
    Can it be put to other uses if it is changed in some way?
- Adaptation
    What else is like this?
    What other idea does this make me think of?
    What new twist could I add to the idea?

Could I change the color, shape, sound, odor, etc.?

- Enlargement

  What can I add?

  Should I make it longer, wider, heavier, faster, more numerous, thicker?

- Condensation

  What can I take away?

  Should I make it smaller, shorter, narrower, lighter, slower, thinner?

- Substitution

  What else can be used to do the same thing?

  What other materials or ingredients might be used?

One classroom teacher used brainstorming with his social studies class this way:

This brainstorming activity was intended to capitalize on an understanding of the concepts of past and future. The children had been investigating great inventions of the past and made comparisons between past and present ways of doing things. They were placed into a directed problem when Mr. Lacey, their teacher, asked them to spend some time looking through copies of an 1897 Sears, Roebuck catalog and a book of early American games for the purpose of arranging a turn-of-the-century birthday party for their room. The children were divided into groups to examine the resources and think about what they would have and do at their party. Mr. Lacey then led a discussion comparing and contrasting party activities in the past and in the present. The following day, he began the social studies class.

MR. LACEY: In the front of the classroom, I have two pictures. Take a good look at them. Tell me what you are looking at.

CINDY: One picture shows men using old-fashioned saws to cut down trees and the other shows a modern chain saw.

MR. LACEY: That's right, Cindy. Can anyone think of a way we can describe each picture?

JACQUES: The men look like they're working a lot harder in the old picture.

MARCIE: The man with the chain saw looks like he can cut more trees than the men with the saws.

MR. LACEY: Does it seem like the new chain saw is better?

CHILDREN: Yes!

MR. LACEY: Why?

VERNON: It makes the work easier.

LUCY: People can get a lot more done.

MR. LACEY: That's exactly right. Most modern inventions are good because they make work easier and help us get a lot more done. Can you see things around you that have changed? Now, I'd like you to think about something. What would be an invention you would like to have in the future to make work easier for you when you become adults?

Mr. Lacey then divided the class into groups of six.

MR. LACEY: It would be interesting to see what each group thinks it would like to see invented in the future. Spend a few minutes thinking up all the wild and interesting things you can.

The groups spent about fifteen minutes in uninterrupted brainstorming, after which Mr. Lacey asked them to narrow their choices to about five. Then he asked the recorder from each group to write its list on the chalkboard and led a discussion:

MR. LACEY: How will it work? How fast will it go? How might it be made?

After the class discussed each other's inventions, Mr. Lacey asked each group to illustrate (make a blueprint of) each of the things on the list of items it would like to see in the future. These were completed and displayed in an area of the room called "The Hall of Inventions."

SUMMARY

The major purpose of inquiry-oriented learning is to develop in children the curiosity and skills necessary for becoming independent problem solvers. Inquiry-oriented learning is usually based on an inquiry model explained as a four-step process: (1) problem awareness, (2) hypothesis formation, (3) gathering and analyzing data, and (4) developing conclusions. This process involves questioning and hard thinking about observable events.

Special instructional experiences help create readiness for inquiry in the primary grades: (1) directed lessons at the beginning of the school year; (2) guided problem-solving experiences; (3) exhibits, "mini-museums," and other curiosity-arousing areas around the room to present new adventures or stimulate interests; and (4) moving the children into situations involving inquiry.

The two major types of inquiry are open-ended and closed-ended. When children are challenged to solve unique problems with specific evidence, we refer to closed-ended inquiry. It is closed-ended because the solution must be based on the application and analysis of concrete evidence for the solution of the problem.

Open-ended inquiry differs from closed-ended in that children are not restricted to any particular set of data to solve their problem, but are encouraged to develop their own unique ideas as solutions. Given new scientific support as a teaching strategy by recent studies of brain-hemisphere functioning, open-ended inquiry is widely valued for stimulating creative thought. The social studies curriculum can encourage creative thinking in many ways, one of which is to offer stimulating questions that include these factors: (1) establishing a climate for creativity in the classroom; (2) presenting a challenging question or problem; (3) allowing time to consider alternatives; and (4) encouraging the children to put their ideas to use.

It is no exaggeration to say that today's knowledge explosion is a mere puff compared to what we can anticipate for the future. The ability to solve problems and to create will certainly be valuable for dealing with unknowns; thinking is not limited solely to the acquisition of knowledge. The purpose of this chapter is not to "sell" the inquiry method as the ultimate, nor as the preferred, instructional mode in social studies classrooms. Inquiry is an option for teachers that helps them explore and promote all the levels of thinking needed by an educated citizenry.

ENDNOTES

1. Neil Postman and Charles Weingartner, in *Teaching Is . . .*, ed. Merrill Harmin and Tom Gregory (Chicago: Science Research Associates, 1974), p. 57.

2. Jerome S. Bruner, *Beyond the Information Given: Studies in the Psychology of Knowing* (New York: Norton, 1973).

3. Arthur A. Carin and Robert B. Sund, *Teaching Science Through Discovery*, 6th ed. (Columbus, OH: Merrill, 1989), p. 94.

4. Selma Wassermann, "Children Working in Groups? It Doesn't Work!" *Childhood Education, 65,* no. 4 (Summer 1989): 204.

5. Robert F. Smith, "Theoretical Framework for Preschool Science Experiences," *Young Children, 42,* no. 2 (January 1987): 35.

6. Carol Seefeldt, *A Curriculum for Child Care Centers* (Columbus, OH: Merrill, 1974), pp. 176–177.

7. Bello, "The Young Scientists," in P. C. Ober and H. A. Estrin, Eds., *The New Scientist* (New York: Doubleday-Anchor, 1962), p. 81.

8. Jerome S. Bruner, *The Process of Education* (New York: Vintage Books, 1960).

9. R. Murray Thomas and Dale L. Brubaker, *Decisions in Teaching Elementary Social Studies* (Belmont, CA: Wadsworth Publishing, 1971), p. 239.

10. Richard Suchman, *Inquiry Development Program: Developing Inquiry* (Chicago: Science Research Associates, 1966).

11. Paul D. Eggen and Donald P. Kauchak, *Strategies for Teachers,* 2nd ed. (Englewood Cliffs, NJ: Prentice-Hall, 1988), p. 223.

12. *Ibid.*, pp. 223–224.

13. Barry K. Beyer, "Critical Thinking: What Is It?" *Social Education, 49,* no. 4 (April 1985): 276.

14. Robert Sternberg, comments made at a meeting of parents and teachers at the Episcopal Academy in Philadelphia, PA, March 14, 1989.

15. Robert E. Ornstein, *The Psychology of Consciousness* (New York: Viking, 1972).

16. Jerome Bruner, *On Knowing: Essays for the Left Hand* (New York: Atheneum, 1965).

17. Edward de Bono, "The Searching Mind: Lateral Thinking," *Today's Education, 58,* no. 8 (November 1969): 20–24.

18. E. Paul Torrance, "Adventuring in Creativity," *Childhood Education, 40,* no. 2 (1963): 79.

19. William Popjoy (John Lennon's schoolmaster at the Quarry Bank Comprehensive School), comments made during a newspaper interview shortly after Lennon's death in December 1980.

20. David Galin, "Educating Both Halves of the Brain," *Childhood Education, 53,* no. 1 (October 1976): 20.

21. Robert Samples, "Mind Cycles and Learning," *Phi Delta Kappan, 58,* no. 9 (May 1977): 689–690.

I have rarely been able to pinpoint an unequivocal right or wrong on my own, but at least when I was a child I felt secure that my mother and Franklin Delano Roosevelt could. Even as an adolescent, when almost all issues seemed up for re-examination, there were some moral truths which seemed unambivalent: . . . you shouldn't steal song sheets and makeup from the 5 & 10, and you shouldn't copy on an exam. (This last was becoming confusing because so many of my friends, of otherwise impeccable character, were doing it.)

In college, where a lot of useful un-learning takes place, my friends and I spent many long nights in passionate discussion of such old saws as who is permitted into the crowded lifeboat and whether any war is justifiable. . . .

I'm not sure whether my present moral uncertainties are the product of age or circumstance; but lately the issues seem infinitely more complex, and the people in decision-making positions are no help in clarifying where the [values] imperative lies.[1]

—*Lois Lamdin*

Thinking Skills Applied to Valuing Processes

6

KEY CONCEPTS

As you read, reflect on the following matters:

- Why do we treat the teaching of values differently today than we did in the past?
- What are values? How do values differ from attitudes and beliefs?
- What are the four major contemporary approaches to values education? What specific strategies are associated with each?
- What are the strengths of each approach?
- Why is a feeling of trust in the classroom essential to the effective use of any values strategy? What teaching practices help build feelings of trust?

In a simpler culture, societal issues seemed clear-cut; there was usually only one side for a good citizen to take on any issue. Schools, too, operated on the assumption that absolute values could be identified, so they carefully controlled teaching methodology and subject matter selection so as to transmit the values identified as "right," "desirable," or "good." Educators assumed that the best technique for transmitting values was *inculcation,* or direct instruction of specific values. In the 1800s emphasis was on reading, memorizing, and reciting value-laden materials, often of a religious flavor, as we see in this selection from *The Boston Primer* of 1808:

> Let Children who would fear the LORD,
> Hear what their Teachers say,
> With rev'rence meet their Parents' word,
> And with Delight obey.[2]

Values training also occurred in teachers' verbal interaction with the children, as in this recitation:

T: You must obey your parents.
S: I must obey my parents. (The pupils, at each repetition, place the right hand, opened, upon the breast.)
T: You must obey your teachers.
S: I must obey my teachers.[3]

At those rare times that children questioned their superiors about a behavior, the dialogue might have gone like this:

MASTER: You must not do so.
CHILD: And why must I not do so?
MASTER: Because it is naughty.
CHILD: Naughty! Why is that being naughty?
MASTER: Doing what you are forbid.
CHILD: And what harm is there in doing what one is forbid?
MASTER: The harm is, you will be whipped for disobedience.
CHILD: Then I will do it so that nobody will know anything of the matter.
MASTER: O, but you will be watched.
CHILD: Ah! But then I will hide myself.
MASTER: But you must not tell fibs.
CHILD: Why must not I?
MASTER: Because it is naughty.[4]

Educators of the time justified the process of inculcation with arguments like this: "Thus, we go round the circle: and yet, if we go out of it, the child understands us no longer. . . . I could be very curious to know what could be substituted in the place of this fine dialogue. . . . To distinguish between good and evil, to perceive the reasons on which our moral obligations are founded, is not the business, as it is not within the capacity, of a child."[5]

Young children were considered incapable of making personal decisions because it was believed that they had not yet acquired the ability to think rationally. The most popular practice thus required manipulating the environment or the experiences to which students were exposed to as to promote certain values outcomes.

Today's issues, however, are much more complex; the contrasts and changes we must deal with are overwhelming. Families are changing; the divorce rate in our country, for example, now tops the 50% mark. Many families consider two jobs necessary for economic survival; over 60% of married women with children are in the work force. The explosion of out-of-wedlock pregnancies and other alternative parenting patterns have contributed to a reexamination of traditional family values and beliefs. The lessons taught on television and in the movies are of major concern to many educators today. The rise of drug use, alcoholism, and crime create concern in adults and children alike: "We have freedom in this country, but it stinks," says one 11-year-old. "Drugs—alcohol—crime. There's no good news anymore. We need a president to come in and clean out America."

The task of building values has traditionally been assigned to our schools, although interactions with parents, peers, and the media all contribute to the acquisition of values. Concern about how values are fostered in our schools, however, has been strong over the years. You may have read about or been involved as a student or teacher in school-family controversies related to such value-laden topics as the content of books or sex, drug, and alcohol education. All these issues generate conflicting positions; the choices we make reflect our deep-rooted values.

WHAT ARE VALUES?

What are values? In order to consider values as an area of thinking abilities appropriate for the elementary school social studies program, we must understand what they are and how they can best be fostered. Carl R. Rogers defined two types of values:

1. *Operative values*—the tendency of individuals to show preference for one kind of objects or objectives rather than another. For example, a young child reaches out for a red ball instead of a blue one. The value choice, many times unconscious, is made simply by selecting one object and rejecting another.
2. *Conceived values*—the tendency of individuals to show preference for a symbolized object. Usually the individual involves conceptual thinking as he anticipates the outcome of such a symbolized object. For example, a choice such as "an eye for an eye" is considered a conceived value.[6]

Even the infant has a clear approach to values:

Hunger is negatively valued. His expression of this often comes through loud and clear.
  Food is positively valued. But when he is satisfied, food is negatively valued, and the same milk he responded to so eagerly is now spit out . . .
  All of this is commonplace, but let us look at these facts in terms of what they tell us about the infant's approach to values. . . . What is going on seems best described as an organismic valuing process in which each element, each moment of what he is experiencing, is somehow weighed and selected or rejected. . . . This complicated weighing of experience is clearly an organismic, not a conscious or symbolic function. These are operative, not conceived values.[7]

Rogers's "operative values" help illustrate a distinction that some make between "values" and "attitudes" or "beliefs." Operative values may not be values at all, but considered attitudes or beliefs. Attitudes or beliefs are the feelings we all have in response to our direct, sensory experiences with phenomena surrounding us. For example, some of us may prefer pepperoni pizza as opposed to plain cheese pizza. This is a judgment made after repeated sensory experiences—tasting, smelling, or looking at various combinations of pizza toppings. Those experiences provide us with the content upon which we base our decisions. Therefore, attitudes or beliefs are considered *cognitive* in nature; they are based on knowledge accumulated through direct experiences.

Like attitudes and beliefs, values are cognitive in nature, too. Actually, attitudes and beliefs often combine through repeated experiences to produce the beginning of values. Values are much more deeply held; they are based on extensive factual data gathered through a variety of resources and experiences. *Values contain both cognitive and affective components.* James P. Shaver explains:

> [V]alues have both affective and cognitive elements. That is, values evoke feelings in us (due process of law is "good," something we feel positive about) and so are affective. But values also have a cognitive component. They are concepts. We can define what we mean by due process, and argue about the appropriateness of each other's meanings and about the validity of proposed applications of "due process" in policy decisions.[8]

Because values have a cognitive aspect, their roots are established in content and experiences. The cognitive teaching strategies described in Chapters 4 and 5 help provide the bulk of such content and experiences in the social studies program. But the affective component of values implies that we must go beyond the cognitive aspects (definitions and applications) of attitudes and beliefs to encourage emotional attachment to any of a number of diverse views. Thereby, we extend our social studies thinking skills program into the valuing realm.

AFFECTIVE PREREQUISITES TO VALUES PROGRAMS

In order for any values approach to work, James Shaver advises, "Teaching . . . must be thought of developmentally."[9] At an early age, children must have teachers who look look at them as unique individuals and accept them for what they are. The teacher may say, for example, "Angela helped her social studies group today with all the nice pictures she found." Children feel accepted and know they belong to the group. They realize the teacher is happy to see them. For example, the teacher might say, "I'm glad you are back in school today, Warren. We missed you yesterday." The teacher allows children to learn by experience, sometimes by making mistakes, but mostly through successes. The child can say, "My adobe brick didn't harden because I didn't have enough dirt," and not feel threatened with punishment or ridicule. The teacher also helps children realize the effects of their actions on others: "Janie's tower tumbled because you bumped it. Is there something you could do to help her feel better?"

Openness to experience and acceptance leads naturally to value directions such as sincerity, independence, self-direction, self-knowledge, social responsivity, social responsibility, and positive interpersonal relationships.

Open, flexible teachers provide intensive group experiences that allow for freedom of personal expression, interpersonal communication, and exploration of feelings. Each child is encouraged to put aside defenses and facades and to relate directly and openly to everyone in the classroom. According to Rogers, the experience produces significant benefits:

> Individuals come to know themselves and each other more fully than is possible in the usual social or working relationships; the climate of openness, risk-taking, and honesty generates trust, which enables the person to recognize and change self-defeating attitudes, test out and adopt more innovative and constructive behaviors, and subsequently to relate more adequately and effectively to others in his everyday life situation.[10]

Feelings of trust can be communicated during daily routines or they can be extended through the use of special programs designed to promote self-confidence and comfort in expressing feelings. Two of the most popular programs are Magic Circle and DUSO.

The Magic Circle

Uvaldo Palomares and Gerry Ball[11] created a program for enhancing a child's ability to develop high self-esteem. This widely used Magic Circle program consists of 15- to 20-minute sessions with groups of five or more children that encourage interaction and acceptance. The Magic Circle involves cuing, encouraging active listening, varying procedures, and feedback.

Cues. Sitting in a circle with seven or eight children, the teacher gives a cue and waits for a child to respond. Discussion cues are grouped into three categories:

1. *Awareness* cues are the teacher's requests for a child to describe "Something that made me feel bad" or "What I like about my pet."
2. *Mastery* cues call for the child to describe "Some things at school that I can do for myself" or "Something I was afraid to do but I did anyway" or "Some things I can't do for myself."
3. *Social interaction* cues ask the children to talk about "A time we did something for each other" or "How I made someone feel good" or "Somebody did something that I didn't like."

Teacher encourages active listening. After a child talks about the subject of a cue, the teacher encourages active listening with questions such as "How did that make you feel?" or by paraphrasing a child's statement, such as "When you were telling us about the lake, you mentioned how much you like to swim. You said it as if it made you very proud." As each child talks, the teacher looks at her calmly and nods, smiles, or uses other gestures to indicate interest. When each child finishes contributing, the teacher thanks him for his idea.

TABLE 6–1

Illustrative Examples of Applications of Democratic Beliefs and Values

	Central Focus	Democratic Rights, Freedoms, Responsibilities, or Beliefs Addressed	Illustrations of Opportunities
KINDERGARTEN	Awareness of self in a social setting	1. Right to security 2. Right to equal opportunity 3. Respect of others' rights 4. Honesty	1. Explore how rules make a room safe for everyone. 2. Schedule every child to be a leader for a day. 3. Emphasize that when someone speaks we should all listen. 4. As teacher, reinforce honesty as exhibited by children.
GRADE 1	The individual in primary social groups	1. Impartiality 2. Freedom of worship 3. Consideration for others	1. When an altercation is reported, the teacher tries to find out exactly what happened before taking action. 2. Stress that each family decides whether or not or how to worship. 3. Make clear that everyone has a right to his/her turn.
GRADE 2	Meeting basic needs in nearby social groups	1. Respect for property 2. Respect for laws 3. Values personal integrity	1. Discuss vandalism in neighborhoods. 2. Demonstrate how laws protect the safety of people. 3. Explore the importance of keeping promises.
GRADE 3	Sharing earthspace with others	1. Pursuing individual and group goals 2. Government works for the common good	1. Explain how goods are exchanged with other places in order to meet the needs of people. 2. Discuss how government is concerned about the unemployed and works to reduce unemployment.
GRADE 4	Human life in varied environments	1. Respect for the rights of others 2. Respect for different ways of life	1. Stress the importance of respecting the right of individuals from other cultures to have different values. 2. Help appreciate that lifestyles of people in other places are different from ours.
GRADE 5	People of the Americas	1. Freedom to worship 2. Right of privacy	1. Point out that people came to the Americas because of religious persecution. 2. Explain that a home cannot be searched without a warrant except under most unusual circumstances.

TABLE 6–1

continued

Central Focus	Democratic Rights, Freedoms, Responsibilities, or Beliefs Addressed	Illustrations of Opportunities
GRADE 5 *(cont'd)*	3. Freedom of assembly	3. Make clear that there are no laws prohibiting people from getting together in groups for any lawful purpose.
GRADE 6 People and cultures	1. Governments respect and protect individual freedoms 2. Right to life 3. Right to justice	1. Compare the record of various governments in protecting individual freedoms. 2. Study societies in which individual human rights are not respected. 3. Examine various types of judicial systems.
GRADE 7 A changing world of many nations	1. Freedom to participate in the political process 2. Right to equality of opportunity 3. Government guarantees civil liberties	1. Discuss the anticolonial movement in parts of the world. 2. Discuss social class systems in various parts of the world. 3. Debate the status of civil liberties in various developing nations.
GRADE 8 Building a strong and free nation	1. Right to liberty 2. Participation in the democratic process 3. Freedom of expression	1. Discuss the injustices of slavery. 2. Analyze the voting record of Americans and particularly that of young people. 3. Study the debates and compromises reached in the development of the Constitution.

Source: Task Force on Scope and Sequence, "In Search of a Scope and Sequence for Social Studies," *Social Education* 48 (April 1984): 258.

Teacher begins to vary the procedure. The teacher can vary the procedure by reviewing what each child has said when conversation slows, perhaps by saying, "Let's see where we've come . . ." and then asking if anyone in the group can review what was said. She can focus on similarities and differences by saying, "Jim said something that sounds like what Amy was saying. Who can tell us what it was?" She can also encourage shy children with an invitation such as "Jane, would you like a turn today?" But the teacher should not force children to speak.

Teacher leads a roundup. At this point, all the contributions are summarized and the feelings associated with each event are identified. The teacher may say, "Let's go back and tell what each person did" or "Who can feed back just the feeling?"

A teacher who is sensitive to the Magic Circle technique would plan sharing and discussion sessions like this one described by Mary Olsen:

TEACHER: Some words people use make us feel bad or make us feel happy. Different words make different people feel bad. I don't feel happy when someone calls me stupid. Did someone ever use words that made you feel bad or unhappy?

BILLY: My sister calls me "stinky."

TEACHER: How does that make you feel? (No response.)

TEACHER: Do you like to be called "stinky"?

CHILD: No. It makes me feel bad.

TEACHER: Would someone else like to share a word?

SUSAN: It makes me feel bad when someone says, "Shut up."

TEACHER: I know what you mean, it makes me feel angry when someone says "shut up" to me.

JOHN: Big boys say, "Get out of here."

TEACHER: How does that make you feel?

JOHN: I don't like it.

SUSAN: My sister calls me "stupid."

CHRIS: "You can't play." I don't like it when they say that.

TEACHER: I can tell by your voice that you feel hurt when someone won't let you play. Alice, you look like you have something to say.

ALICE: My brother calls me "puny." I don't like it.

TEACHER: It isn't a nice feeling inside when a brother calls you "puny." Did anyone ever say some words that made you feel happy? (Two children start to smile but don't respond verbally to the questions.)

TEACHER: I can tell that you're thinking of something that makes you happy because you're smiling.

CHRIS: You get to ride a trike.

TEACHER: How would that make you feel?

CHRIS: I'd say, "Goodie," and I'd tell everyone.

SUSAN: (blurts out) I like you!

TEACHER: How does that make you feel when someone says, "I like you"?

SUSAN: It makes me feel good.

TEACHER: It makes me feel happy when my son says to me, "Mom, that pie was delicious." John, what did someone say to make you feel good?

JOHN: Someone said, "You're nice."

TEACHER: How did that make you feel?

JOHN: I liked it.

SUSAN: I like it when it's my birthday.

TEACHER: What do you like about your birthday?

SUSAN: The presents make me happy.

TEACHER: (smiles and nods) I like presents, too. Words can make people feel happy or sad. Different words can make people feel happy or sad. I'm going to say something that might make you happy. I think you did a very nice job of sharing how you feel.[12]

In this example the teacher encourages the children to talk openly about their experiences and emotions. The Magic Circle guidelines were not rigidly or mechanically followed, but the teacher's active and friendly leadership helped the children to recognize and accept each other's feelings. The Magic Circle program, under the leadership of Palomares, has lesson plans and teacher's guides to help improve children's self-confidence and awareness. Complete teacher's guides and session formats can be obtained from Human Development Training Institute, Inc., 7574 University Avenue, La Mesa, CA 92041.

The DUSO Kit

Another source for self-awareness goals is the Developing Understanding of Self and Others (DUSO) Kit, a program of activities to help children understand social-emotional behavior. The materials, contained in a large metal carrying case, include:

1. Teacher's Manual—contains a wealth of activities and special guidelines for their use.
2. Storybooks—contain theme-centered stories designed to catch the children's imagination. Each 10" x 12" storybook contains 41 stories and 200 full-color illustrations.
3. Records or cassettes—songs and stories to heighten the children's interest. They contain the "Hey, Duso" and "So Long, Duso" songs that mark the beginning and ending of each story.
4. Poster—More than 30 posters are included with the kit. Each poster summarizes in pictorial form a major point from a story.
5. Puppets—Two puppets make up the central characters in the program, Duso and Flopsie. Duso is a dolphin who helps lead children to a better understanding of behavior; Flopsie is an inquisitive flounder who provides a model for change. Other puppets are used in various ways.
6. Miscellaneous—Role-playing situations and puppet plays help children dramatize real-life situations.

The program follows this cycle: A stimulating story offers a problem situation. The story is followed up by positive discussions. A role-playing or puppet activity involves children in dramatizing a similar situation. The manual suggests several supplementary individual or group activities. For more information about the DUSO program, write to American Guidance Service, Inc. Publishers' Building, Circle Pines, MN 55014.

Using these types of programs develops the sensitivities required by both teachers and students to carry through a quality values program. As a result of these interaction skills, teachers find:

They are more able to listen to students.

They accept innovative, "troublesome" ideas from students, rather than insisting on conformity.

They pay as much attention to their relationships with students as they do to course content.

They work out problems with students rather than responding in a disciplinary and punitive manner.

They develop an equalitarian and democratic classroom climate.

The effects of the orientation on children's self-esteem and values acquisition skills have been demonstrated:

They feel freer to express both positive and negative feelings in class.

They work through these feelings toward a realistic solution.

They have more energy for learning because they have less fear of constant evaluation and punishment.

Their awe and fear of authority diminish as they find that teachers and administrators are fallible human beings.

They find that the learning process helps them deal with daily problems.

There are few who would argue that the outcomes associated with socializing strategies (importance of the individual, respect for others, recognizing the role of authority) are legitimate goals of a beginning values approach. Without such shared commitments, values discussions would not be likely to occur, much less be meaningful.

The central problem of values education lies not in whether values should be part of the curriculum, but in how they should be dealt with. At one extreme are people who believe that citizens' failure to understand certain democratic values would undermine the American political system. Proponents of this position do not give teachers license to project their own values preferences, but recommend direct instruction of certain values; they seem afraid to entrust the future to an emerging generation that is not completely instilled with unwavering pride in the American way of life. At the other extreme are those who believe all values are subjective, nothing is truly right or wrong, and all values are exclusively a matter of personal taste. More moderate types think the first position borders on totalitarian teaching—at best, an inconsistent approach to teaching democratic values: "How can you perpetuate democratic values such as freedom of choice without offering opportunities to examine and choose?" The other end of the continuum appears to them naive: "How can one generation expect to pass on its ideals to the next when, by definition of this approach, it has nothing to transmit?" The current thrust in values education appears to be a compromise between the two positions: giving students opportunities to identify and examine basic democratic values while at the same time familiarizing them with the process of examining personal values and beliefs. Some programs may lean more in one direction than the other, but all emphasize the importance of content and process. Currently, the four major directions of values education appear to be:

1. Values Inculcation
2. Values Clarification
3. Values Analysis
4. Moral Reasoning

VALUES INCULCATION

The primary aim of the values inculcation approach is to pass on a predetermined set of values to the young with the goal of molding them into good citizens. The approach is based on the selection of desirable character virtues and positive feeling about the American heritage. Systematic instruction to ensure their attainment is usually characterized by repetition of slogans, oaths, flag salutes, creeds, and pledges to instill the predetermined traits.

Advocates of this approach believe that such instruction is a necessary part of schooling because the perpetuation of our culture requires citizens who understand and accept its moral values. James P. Shaver supports this contention: "It is crucial that instruction in social studies be based upon an adequate conception of the role of values in our democratic society. Anthropologists have commonly noted that our shared commitments are critical to the survival of any society."[13] Table 6–1 shows how the National Council for the Social Studies apportioned various essential democratic values and behaviors according to grade level and suggested classroom procedures for teaching and reinforcing them. (The NCSS cautions that these are examples only and should not be construed as a recommended curriculum.) From this important base, teachers often choose to share stories from literature and historical accounts to give children positive feelings about their cultural heritage.

Critics of the values inculcation approach, such as S. Samuel Shermis and James L. Barth, "disagree with some [of their] distinguished colleagues who believe that some values are necessarily so overriding that they must be taken as a given."[14] When we identify values and teach them directly to the students, they argue, we are running the risk of producing narrow-minded students who blindly accept values rather than open-minded individuals who can make values choices for themselves. Shaver counters that schools have an obligation to society to perpetuate its values and are therefore justified to teach a commonly agreed-upon core of values basic to American society. He maintains, "It is reasonable and not in any way illogical to argue that we, and our students, should be committed to the basic values of our society."[15] What Shaver means is that we should accept society's values as givens (in the affective sense). "At the same time," Shaver adds, "we, and our students, [must] examine the meanings and applications of those values."[16] This means that students are taught core values such as freedom of worship, right to privacy, and equal opportunity, but in such a way that they do not accept values blindly. Students are encouraged to inquire into meaningful social issues and consider whether the values are valid and worthwhile. We cannot accept the position that *all* traditional values should be inculcated without question; otherwise racism and sexism would never have been challenged. By taking such a stance, Shaver has aligned himself more with a strategy called values analysis than with inculcation. For that reason, we will not elaborate on the inquiry strategy here but in the "Values Analysis" section.

THE VALUES CLARIFICATION APPROACH

Values clarification is an alternative approach to affective education. Rather than telling the students *what* to value, its major purpose is to teach them *how* to value. The values clarification approach is most often associated with Louis Raths, Merrill Harmin, and Sidney Simon, authors of *Values and Teaching*.[17] They believe that children acquire values only as they progress through the processes of choosing, prizing, and acting.

Seven Subprocesses

To Raths, Harmin, and Simon, a value is defined when seven subprocesses are satisfied:

Choosing
  1. freely
  2. from alternatives
  3. after thoughtful consideration of the consequences of each alternative

Prizing
  4. cherishing, being happy with the choice
  5. willing to affirm the choice publicly, when appropriate

Acting
  6. doing something with the choice
  7. repeatedly, in some pattern of life[18]

Choosing Freely. If a value is in fact to guide one's life whether or not authority is watching, it must be a result of free choice. If there has been coercion, the value is not likely to sustain one for long, especially when out of the range of the source of that coercion. Values must be freely selected for the individual to truly ascribe to them.

Choosing from Among Alternatives. This subprocess concerns values that are chosen by the individual; obviously, there can be no choice if there are no alternatives from which to choose. It makes no sense, for example, to say that one values eating; one really has no choice in the matter. One may value certain types of food or certain forms of eating, but not eating itself. Only when a choice is possible, when there is more than one alternative from which to choose, can a value result.

Choosing After Thoughtful Consideration of the Consequences of Each Alternative.
Impulsive or thoughtless choices do not lead to values as we define them. For something intelligently and meaningfully to guide one's life, it must emerge from weighing and understanding. Only when one clearly understands the consequences of each alternative can one make intelligent choices. There is an important cognitive factor here: a value can emerge only with thoughtful consideration of the range of alternatives and consequences in a choice.

Prizing and Cherishing. When we value something, it has positive associations for us. We prize it, cherish it, esteem it, respect it, hold it dear. We are happy with our values. A choice, even when we have made it freely and thoughtfully, may be one we are not happy to make. We may choose to fight in a war, but be sorry that circumstances made that choice reasonable. In our definition, values flow from choices we are glad to make.

Affirming. When we have chosen something freely, after considering alternatives, and when we are proud of our choice, we are likely to affirm the choice when asked about it. We are willing to affirm our values publicly; we may even be willing to champion them. If we are ashamed of a choice—if we would not make our position known when asked in an appropriate context, we would be dealing not with values, but something else.

Acting upon Choices. A value shows up in aspects of our living. We may do some reading about things we value. We are likely to form friendships or join organizations that nourish our values. We may spend money on a choice we value; we budget time or energy for our values. Nothing can be a value that does not, in fact, give direction to actual living. Someone who talks about something but never takes any action to support it is dealing with something other than a value.

Repeating. When something reaches the stage of a value, it is likely to reappear in a number of contexts in one's life. Values tend to have a consistency, to make a pattern in life.

What must the teacher do to help children develop values according to the values clarification theory? Raths, Harmin, and Simon say the process flows naturally from the described definition of values, that is, the teacher should:

1. Encourage children to make choices freely.
2. Help them discover and examine available alternatives when faced with choices.
3. Help children weigh alternatives thoughtfully, reflecting on the consequences of each.
4. Encourage children to consider what it is that they prize and cherish.
5. Give them opportunities to make public affirmations of their choices.
6. Encourage them to act, behave, live in accordance with their choices.
7. Help them to examine repeated behaviors or patterns in their life.[19]

Clarifying Responses

The most common technique of the values clarification approach involves a "clarifying response"—a way of responding to children that results in their considering what they have chosen, what they prize, or what they are doing. The comments should merely prod the child to think. Here are three classroom situations illustrating the use of a clarifying response.

MAURICE: I'd like to be president some day.

TEACHER: How long have you felt this way?

MAURICE: Gee, I'm not sure. I guess I felt that way after I read a story about John F. Kennedy.

TEACHER: What was there about the story that made you come to your decision?

MAURICE: I liked the way he fought for the rights of all people.

TEACHER: That's very interesting. Thank you for telling me, Maurice.

Charles complained to his teacher that it was too confusing in the classroom when groups were working on their social studies projects. When the class was all together for group time, the teacher guided this discussion: "How do you like our room when you're trying to work in groups? Should it be like that all the time?"

One morning, during a planning period at the start of a social studies unit, the teacher asked: "When you came to school in the morning and had a chance to look over all the things placed around the room, did you get an idea of what items interested you most? What do you like best? Why? What do you like least? Why? Would you like to work alone or with other children? All of the time?"

These are among the essential elements of composing effective clarifying responses:

- Do not criticize or evaluate the child's response.
- Put the responsibility on the child to look at his ideas and think about what he wants for himself.
- Do not try to do big things. The purpose of a clarifying response is to set a mood. Each response is only one of many, its effect is cumulative.
- Do not intend for the clarifying response to develop into an extended discussion. The idea is for the child to think, and he usually does that best alone. Allow for two or three rounds of dialogue and then offer to break off the conversation with some honest phrase, such as "Nice talking with you," or "I see what you mean now," or "Your idea was very interesting. Let's talk about it again some other time."
- Do not respond to everything everyone says or does in the classroom.
- Direct clarifying responses to *individuals* whenever possible. A topic in which Henry needs clarification may be of no interest to Mae. Issues of general concern may warrant a general response to the entire class, but even here the individual must ultimately do the reflecting for himself.
- Use clarifying responses in situations where there are no "right" answers, such as those involving feelings, attitudes, or beliefs. They should *never* be used to draw a child's thinking toward a predetermined answer.[20]

Clarifying responses are not designed to follow any mechanical formula, but must be used creatively and with insight. There are several responses, however, that experienced teachers have found useful with children. As you read through the list, try to elaborate upon the items and add to the suggestions.

"Are you proud of that?"

"Do you really like that idea?"

"Does that make you feel good?"

"Are you happy about your choice?"

"How did you feel when that happened?"

"Did you think of any other way to do it?"

"When did you first get such an idea?"

"Have you felt this way for a long time?"

"Did you do it yourself?"

"When might you use that idea?"

"What do you mean?"

"What would happen if your ideas worked out?"

"Would you really do that?"

"What other choices did (do) you have?"

"Should everyone go along with your idea?"

"Is that important to you?"

"Do you do that often?"

"Would you like to tell others about your idea?"

"Do you have a reason for doing (or saying) that?"

"Would you do the same thing again?"

"How do you know it's right (or good)?"

"Is that something that you like very much?"

"Would other people believe that?"

"Is this what I understood you to say?"

"Would you do that again?"

As you read through the list, you should have related each comment to the seven components of the Raths valuing process. Those seven criteria are valuable guides as you think of other useful clarifying responses. In one way or another, all clarifying responses should encourage children to choose, prize, or act as outlined by the value theory.

Raths recommends that the teacher (1) establish a climate of psychological safety, and (2) apply a clarification procedure.[21] These procedures help establish a climate of psychological safety:

> *Nonjudgmental attitudes.* Teachers must refrain from unnecessary comments, such as "That's good," or "That's bad," while responding to a child's idea.
>
> *Manifestations of concern.* Teachers should show interest in the children's ideas by listening carefully and remembering what they say. Students feel flattered by this recognition.
>
> *Opportunities for sharing ideas.* Teachers should encourage children to share their ideas and feelings in many different situations during the school day.

Values Clarification and Social Studies Content

You may draw from among these general situations to select strategies to help children think more deeply about their attitudes toward social studies content, about prevailing social conditions, or about their own lives. Raths, Harmin, and Simon suggest curriculum techniques.

1. *The Picture Without a Caption:* The teacher brings in a picture which involves a story of some kind . . . Students are asked to supply a caption describing what is going on. After various captions are examined in the light of the available evidence, an attempt is made to see what the students would have done in the same situation. As example, photographs of a street fight were used.
2. *A Scene from a Play or Movie:* A teacher obtains the script from a play, TV show, or a movie and duplicates a small part of it. Students act it out, but it is cut off before there is any solution to the problem. The students then take over and discuss what should have been done, how this situation was like something in their own lives, etc. Showing films which are cut prematurely can also lead to interesting discussions.
3. *Other Idea Sources*
   Briefly, here are other suggestions for sources of materials to spur discussion having a values clarification focus.
   a. Editorials
   b. Letters to the editor
   c. Literature passed around at election time
   d. Popular song lyrics
   e. Tape recordings of news broadcasts and other programs
   f. Tape recordings of interviews students have obtained from various persons in the community with strong viewpoints

   g. Excerpts from speeches
   h. Materials from embassies or foreign countries
   i. Advertising
   j. Cartoons, comic strips, etc.
   k. Films[22]

4. *Open-ended Questions:* An open-ended question is dictated or written on the board
   and students are asked to write responses either in class or at home. For example, "If
   I had twenty-four hours to live . . ." or "The purposes of my life are . . ." What comes
   out of such writing, usually, is a rather fruitful list of some of the child's interests,
   hopes, fears, the people he likes the most, and some things in his life which he considers worthy or unworthy. Here are some other open-ended questions which have been
   productive:
   a. With a gift of $100, I would . . .
   b. If this next weekend were a three-day weekend, I would want to . . .
   c. My best friend can be counted on to . . .
   d. My bluest days are . . .

5. *The Values Continuum:* The class or the teacher identifies an issue to be discussed in
   class. Then two polar positions are identified . . . (and) placed at opposite ends of a
   line on the board. . . . The task of the class, then, is to identify other positions in the
   issue and try to place them on the continuum, both in relationship to the poles and to
   the positions already placed. For example,

   Strongly _____ Strongly
    Agree └─────┴────────┴──────┴──────┴─────┘ Disagree
   There should be strict federal control of education.

6. *Voting:* To use the voting strategy, the teacher poses a list of questions . . . and students state a position by a show of hands. For example, the teacher might ask the following sequence of questions, pausing after each for a vote, the recording of the vote
   on the board, and a moment to reflect on the ideas generated by the question:
   a. How many of you have ever been seriously burned?
   b. Anyone here ever own a horse?
   c. How many think sometimes of dying or what death might be like?
   d. I'd like to see how much loneliness is in this group. Vote either that you feel lonely
   often, sometimes, or seldom. How many feel lonely often? Sometimes? Seldom?

7. *Devil's Advocate:* Too many discussions in value-related areas suffer from having only
   two positions in the room: a consensus and a "don't care" position. Especially in certain political and social topics, dissension is often absent. What often is needed is a persuasive argument *against* civil rights, *for* the use of profanity, *against* respect for
   elders, *for* revolution, *against* patriotism, and so on. . . .

   Each teacher does well to announce to the class that, from time to time, he will
   play a role that is not his real one, that he will do it merely to present a position that
   has not otherwise arisen. It is often fun to label this role as that of the devil's advocate
   and to announce what one is doing when it is played, but usually that is unnecessary.
   The extreme and dogmatic statements that characterize the devil's advocate signal
   that something is afoot.[23]

Many teachers have used a values clarification activity called "The Coat of Arms"
to help children explore issues. The procedure calls for the teacher to prepare an outline

FIGURE 6–1
*"The Coat of Arms" for Values
Clarification*

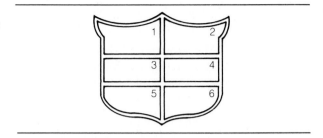

of a coat of arms, as shown in Figure 6–1. The students should draw a picture for each segment in response to a topic you suggest; for example, the contributions of George Bush as president of the United States:

1. Draw a picture to show what George Bush enjoys most about being president.
2. Draw a picture to show a time George Bush really laughed.
3. Draw a picture of a time when George Bush lost his temper.
4. Draw a picture to show George Bush's greatest accomplishment.
5. Draw what you think is George Bush's greatest problem as president.
6. Draw what George Bush most enjoyed doing when he was your age.

Students in small groups can share the drawings on their coats of arms, explaining the significance of symbols. A variation of the exercise might involve construction of coats of arms of popular news figures, figures from the past, or the teacher.

While values clarification strategies are recommended for use in all school situations, several materials have been developed specifically for social studies topics. Some resources for materials are:

> Casteel and Stahl, *Values Clarification in the Classroom: A Primer* (Pacific Palisades, CA: Goodyear Publishing Co., 1975)

> Raths, Harmin, and Simon, *Values and Teaching,* 2nd ed. (Columbus, OH: Merrill, 1978)

> Simon, Howe, and Kirschenbaum, *Values Clarification* (New York: Hart, 1972) (Seventy-nine strategies to help students build the seven valuing processes into their lives.)

> Volkmor, Pasanella, and Raths, *Values in the Classroom* (Columbus, OH: Merrill, 1977) (A multimedia program providing activities in values clarification; components include six sound filmstrips and text.)

VALUES ANALYSIS

The easiest way to describe values analysis is to say that it is based on the inquiry or problem-solving approach described in Chapter 5, except that the thinking processes are applied to values issues rather than to content-based problems. In essence, the values analysis approach follows this pattern:

1. Identification and clarification of the issue
2. Accumulation of the information related to the issue
3. Assessment of the validity of each alternative
4. Development of a position related to the issue

An excellent example of how the values analysis model can be used in the social studies classroom is the "Decision Tree."

Climbing a Decision Tree

One of the most effective programs for encouraging decision making in the development of values is that of Richard Remy and others at the Mershon Center of The Ohio State University. *Making Political Decisions* was planned as a supplement to a teacher's regular social studies program.[24] Several creative techniques help youngsters make political decisions, of which one of the most imaginative and applicable forms is "climbing a decision tree."

To begin the decision tree, ask how many students notice that they make decisions as they climb a tree or wall. Do they plan their attack by examining the obstacle, or seek alternative routes should their first choice fail? Do they foresee the consequences of a weak branch or a sharp point? Inform them that they are going to use their ability to see alternatives and consequences that grow out of an occasion for decision—they are going to help Sir Lottalance make a decision about fighting Dingbat the Dragon.

Tell the children to put themselves in the place of the knight, Sir Lottalance, as they listen to this story:

> One day very long ago, Sir Lottalance was riding along on his white horse minding his own business when he came across some very sad townspeople. They were sad because the mean old dragon, Dingbat the Dimwitted, had lumbered out of his deep, dark cave and carried off the beautiful princess from the king's castle. The king had offered a huge reward for anyone who could destroy the dragon and save his daughter's life. But the first knight to try had been barbecued by Dingbat's fiery breath. The second knight to try had tripped over his own sword and become the dragon's shish kabob. Sir Lottalance could hear the princess beating her fists fiercely against the dragon and calling him the nastiest names you ever heard. He could hear Dingbat's tummy rumbling as the dragon eyed Lottalance and eagerly waited for another tasty meal of fried knight. Sir Lottalance was the fastest, strongest, and bravest knight in the kingdom but he wasn't sure about Dingbat. What could he do?

Now point to a large construction-paper decision tree on the wall (as in Figure 6–2) so that the sign "Occasion for Decision," portraying Dingbat the Dragon, is exposed to view. For the children to climb the tree, they will have to think of Sir Lottalance's alternatives. Ask them for alternatives. When they have described fighting or fleeing,

FIGURE 6–2
Decision Tree

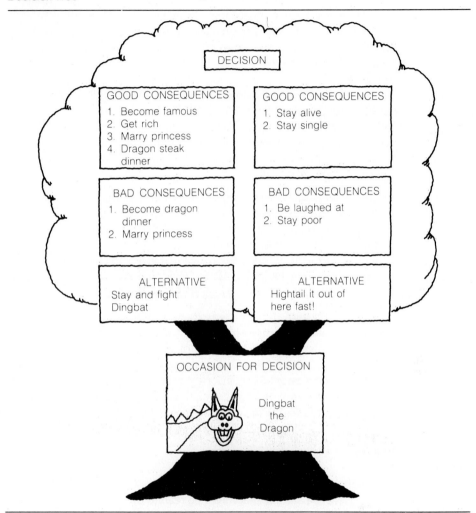

DECISION

GOOD CONSEQUENCES
1. Become famous
2. Get rich
3. Marry princess
4. Dragon steak
   dinner

GOOD CONSEQUENCES
1. Stay alive
2. Stay single

BAD CONSEQUENCES
1. Become dragon
   dinner
2. Marry princess

BAD CONSEQUENCES
1. Be laughed at
2. Stay poor

ALTERNATIVE
Stay and fight
Dingbat

ALTERNATIVE
Hightail it out of
here fast!

OCCASION FOR DECISION

Dingbat
the
Dragon

write the responses on the alternative branches of the tree and congratulate the children for doing such a good job of climbing a decision tree.

Lead the students to climb higher into the branches of the tree to look at the consequences of Sir Lottalance's decision by asking: "What would be a *good* (or positive) consequence of getting out of there fast?" and "What would be a *bad* (or negative) consequence of getting out of there fast?"

When the students have suggested ideas corresponding to "stay alive" and "be called Lottalance the Sissy," add them to the blank pieces of paper above the "getting out of here fast" alternative. Again, congratulate your students for a good job of climbing and remind them they still have an alternative branch to explore. Ask, "What would be a bad (or negative) consequence of fighting Dingbat the Dragon?" and "What would be some good (or positive) consequences of fighting Dingbat the Dragon?"

Again, list each contribution as it is offered. Examine the whole tree and look for the students' sense of accomplishment. Then, weighing the consequences, ask the class to vote on a decision. Then, place their decision high on the top of the decision tree.

The decision tree technique is useful whenever individuals or small groups face important decisions: what to do with friends on a free afternoon; who to invite to a birthday party; where to go on a field trip; what to do if your friends don't like each other; rules for a game with few players; who gets to play with what equipment or toys; how to raise money for a group; who's team captain; who gets to play. The teacher's role in a decision tree strategy is to:

1. Decide what question to examine and label it at the base of the tree
2. Abbreviate the decision in the "Occasion for Decision" sign
3. Encourage children to think up alternatives and write them in the boxes on the branches of the decision tree
4. Discuss positive and negative consequences of each alternative, one at a time
5. Write in the consequences, ask the children to weigh each, and write in their goal
6. Congratulate the children as successful decision makers

From these early decision tree experiences, you can lead children to examine more pressing social concerns: Should the planned sewage plant be built despite the taxpayers' protests? Should certain tuna nets be outlawed because they are killing so many dolphins? Should America's space program be escalated at the expense of federal programs for the poor? Should Congress continue the Social Security system? Should our community legislate leash laws for dogs? How should our class enforce the new regulations we added to the classroom constitution?

Using Stories

Presenting values conflicts in story form is a popular way to promote skills in analyzing values. Here is a sample that might be read to the children:

In Trouble

Willie Johnson was in trouble! In school this morning he had thrown his paint water at Sue Nelligan and the teacher had become angry with him. "Why did you do that, Willie?" she asked. Willie couldn't tell her, because he really didn't know why himself. He knew that Sue had teased him a little, but that wasn't the real reason. He just didn't know! The whole thing put him in a bad mood. From then on, the entire day just went to heck. In the afternoon, he had pushed Tommy Grigsley in the recess line. He also had stamped his foot and yelled at the teacher. The teacher had become angry with him again. But this time she put a note to his mother on his jacket with a pin.

That note! He knew it was about his behavior in class during the day. He knew that when he got home his mother would read the note and give him some kind of punishment. Then his father would find out about it and he'd really get it!

On his way home from school Willie was talking about what his father would do to him. "Wow!" he thought. "I'll get killed if I take this note home. I'd better take it off and throw it away."

He was just about to do that when he remembered what had happened to Billy Beatty when he was sent home with a note. Billy had thrown his note away and was sent to the principal's office about it. Then Billy was in double trouble!

Wow! He *was* in trouble. He couldn't throw it away. What should he do? He had a problem, all right. He had to make a choice, but how should he choose? No matter what he did, the outcome didn't look too good! What should he do?[25]

Upon completion of the reading, the teacher can ask the class the following questions:

1. "What things might Willie do?" (What alternatives are open to him?)
2. "What might happen to him if he does these things?" (Discuss each alternative.)
3. "How do you think he'd feel, in each case, if this happened?"
4. "If you were faced with this situation, what would you do?"
5. "How do you think you'd feel?"
6. "Basing your answer on how you've said you would feel and how you think Willie felt, what can you say about how people feel in situations like this?"
7. "Why do you think people have different feelings about things?"

The major assumption behind the values analysis strategy is that through empathizing with the feelings of another individual faced with unpleasant, conflicting alterna-

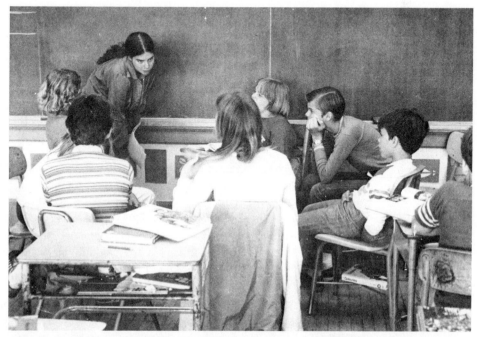

Thinking through and making choices about personal values is absorbing work.

tives, students will be making affective responses. This makes it possible for affective learning to occur. Several relevant teaching materials, including films, filmstrips, open-ended stories, and favorite stories of the children are being commercially produced and are available for classroom use.

You are the individual who will determine how values will be handled in the social studies curriculum. There is no absolute way to deal with values education. Children will face many different problems in their future that will call for different intellectual operations. You must thus consider alternatives for teaching values just as the children will need to examine alternatives while making decisions in your classroom. Learn about the alternatives and the consequences of using each alternative, then put your choices into action.

MORAL REASONING

In recent years educators have been guided by various stage theories of moral development. Although various degrees of compatibility appear among these theories, they all share the assumption that social behavior can be categorized in terms of a predetermined sequence of stages, referred to as *cognitive developmental stages*—cognitive because they recognize that moral education, like cognitive education, requires stimulation of active thinking about moral issues; developmental because each stage is a new structure that includes elements of earlier structures but transforms them to represent a more stable and sophisticated level of thinking.

Kohlberg's Cognitive-Developmental Model

Kohlberg became interested in moral development in 1955 and sought to validate Piaget's ideas by carrying out intensive studies throughout the world. Despite differences in cultural, social, economic, and religious backgrounds, Kohlberg found that all individuals move through the stages of moral development described in Figure 6–3. How can we encourage the moral growth of our future adults?

First let us examine some considerations of Kohlberg's stages:

> *The stages always occur in the same order.* Moral reasoning of the pre-conventional kind always takes place before conventional thought.
>
> *All movement through the stages is forward in sequence.* Once a child has begun to reason on the conventional level, for example, he or she will never return to the reasoning patterns associated with the preconventional level. Of course, often children will be half in and half out of a certain stage and will seem to be moving backward, but this characteristic only indicates a pattern of growth from one stage to the next.
>
> *The stages cannot be skipped.* They represent an "invariant developmental sequence," which means they come one at a time and always in the same order.

FIGURE 6–3

Kohlberg's Stages of Moral Development (Adapted from Lawrence Kohlberg, "The Claim to Moral Adequacy of a Highest State of Moral Judgment." The Journal of Philosophy, 70, no. 18 (October 25, 1973): 631–632.

Preconventional Level: Egocentric in Nature

Stage 1: To be "well-behaved" means unquestioned obedience to an adult authority figure. The child considers actions to be either good or bad solely because of the physical consequences involved (punishment, reward) or because of the desires of authority figures (teacher, parent, etc.).

Stage 2: The child is basically egocentric (self-centered) at this stage and regards goodness or badness on the basis of whether it satisfies personal needs. Children at this stage begin to consider the feelings of others, but elements of fairness and equal sharing are interpreted in a manner of "what's in it for me?" Children are out to make the best "deal" for themselves. Being "right" is viewed in a context of fairness: "You scratch my back and I'll scratch yours."

Conventional Level: Orientation to Conformity

Stage 3: Good behavior is that which pleases or helps others. Children conform to what they imagine to be a "good" or "nice" person and begin to see things from another's viewpoint for the first time (put themselves into the shoes of another person). Behavior begins to be judged on the basis of intent—a conscience is beginning to form. Children are strongly oriented to being labeled "good boy/nice girl."

Stage 4: The individual is oriented to obeying authority and following fixed rules for reasons of law and order. A good person does one's duty, shows respect for authority, and maintains the given social order for its own sake. One earns respect by performing dutifully, living up to one's socially defined role, and maintaining existing social order for the good of all.

Postconventional Level: Individual Moral Principles

Stage 5: Since laws have been critically examined and agreed upon by the whole society, they continue to guide decisions regarding goodness or badness. However, right and wrong begin to be characterized by personal feelings; the result is an emphasis upon the "legal point of view," but with an emphasis upon the possibility of changing laws, rather than obeying them as in Stage 4. One makes an internal commitment to principles of "conscience"; individuals are guided by a respect for the rights, life, and dignity of all persons.

Some individuals move farther and faster through the stages than other individuals. Differences in achieving various levels of moral reasoning can be compared to the differences in achieving various levels of cognitive skills.

The movement from stage to stage is not an automatic process. Individuals may stop at any given stage and apply the related reasoning processes to all moral situations encountered throughout their lives.

Involving Children in Moral Dilemmas

Kohlberg's approach to affective education is based on the assumption that growth through the stages can be stimulated by involving children in "moral dilemmas"—stories in which individuals face situations that involve issues of trust, fairness, or taking advantage. Children are encouraged to examine situations and make judgments about the various actions the characters might take.

An example of a moral dilemma suitable for upper-grade elementary school children is the case of Rosa Parks, a black woman in Montgomery, Alabama, who refused to give up her seat on a bus in defiance of the prevailing segregation customs in 1955. Here is a teaching plan to encourage children to think about the difficult decision Rosa Parks faced.

Warm-up Questions.   These questions should orient children to the situation: "How many of you have ever ridden on a bus? Were you able to sit anywhere you liked when you got on the bus? Did you ever hear of people being told that they couldn't sit on any section of the bus because of the color of their skin? their height? their sex? their religious persuasion?

Presentation.   Explain to the students that they are to read a short story about a woman who is told she cannot sit on a particular seat on a bus because of the color of her skin. She must decide whether to sit in that seat. Her name is Rosa Parks and the city in which the decision took place is Montgomery, Alabama. Tell the children to decide what they would do if they were faced with Rosa Parks's decision. Supply them with an account of the incident.

Follow-up Decision.   The first questions should help clarify the story. "Where was Rosa Parks before she got on the bus? How did she feel? Why was she asked to leave her seat? When did the story take place?"

Group Dialogue.   Split the children into groups and ask them to decide what Rosa Parks should do. Move from group to group and offer questions to guide the children's thinking. "Why do you think some cities had rules establishing separate facilities for blacks and whites? Did Rosa Parks have a right to break those rules? Were the rules fair? What could happen if she did not give up her seat to the white person?"

Follow-up Activity.   In this case, each group can be encouraged to role-play the scene on the bus, stopping at the point of Rosa's decision. Then, they should portray what Rosa should have done and what the consequences would have been. What other follow-up activities might be appropriate?

Enrichment.   The children will naturally be curious about the real outcome of this dilemma, and their questions will flow spontaneously: "What did Rosa Parks do? What happened to her?" The questions will indicate a perfect starting point for an inquiry session. You may wish to offer the information yourself or encourage the children to search for the answers in material you have collected for them. (For your information, Rosa Parks refused to give up her seat and was arrested. Her arrest touched off a bus boycott in Montgomery and was one of the major events in launching the campaign for black civil rights.) In 1980, Mrs. Parks received the Martin Luther King, Jr. Peace Award for the inspiration she provided to resolve racial differences through nonviolent means.[26]

When the children share their responses to story situations, they provide you with insight into the different levels of moral reasoning at which they are operating. The stages of moral reasoning are not defined by the nature of the decision itself, but on the basis of the reasons they give for each decision. For example:

> *Stage 1:* "Rosa Parks should get up from her seat because she would be in real trouble if she didn't. The bus driver would probably throw her off the bus." (People cannot disobey authorities or they will be punished.)

> *Stage 2:* "Rosa Parks should not go to the back of the bus because she is awfully tired and there wouldn't be anywhere else for her to sit." (Everyone has a right to do what he wants to fulfill legitimate needs.)

> *Stage 3:* "Rosa Parks should start to move to the back of the bus because if the white man sees how tired she is, he will be sure to understand and let her stay in her seat." (Children have a sense of fair play at this stage—what would a *good* person do?)

> *Stage 4:* "Rosa Parks should move to the back of the bus because she would be breaking the law if she didn't. People are expected to follow society's rules." (Established law emerges as a central value.)

Most elementary school children will not have gone beyond Stage 4 in their thinking. What do you think would be responses of individuals functioning at Stage 5?

Smooth Classroom Management

These suggestions ensure smooth classroom management of any moral dilemma.

1. *Focus on reasons.* Decisions are important, but they are not enough. Children need to examine their reasoning and the reasoning of others as they justify their solutions. "The process of stating, challenging, being challenged, defending, explaining, criticizing, and comparing highlights the existence of a gap between one's own stage of reasoning and the reasoning at the next higher stage. In time, students become conscious of this gap and move to close it."[27]

2. *Choose discussion groups with care.* Mix children at different stages of moral development in each group so that children at the lower stages of moral reasoning will benefit from exposure to the thinking of children operating at higher levels.

3. *Give direction and guidance.* Allow as many students as possible to respond to the dilemma. When shy students are reluctant to do so, simply ask students to react to another's comment: "Harold, do you agree with Marge, or do you have another idea?" or "Jane, many of your classmates think the boys should keep the kitten. What do you think?"

4. *Encourage undecided children.* Moral issues can be thoroughly perplexing, and decisions are not easily reached. Other children may attempt to exert peer pressure to

win over the undecided child to their side, and it becomes extremely difficult for some children to withstand the pressure. They fear that hesitation will be interpreted as a sign of weakness. To prevent children from "going along with the crowd," you should attempt to convince them that it's okay to remain uncertain until they have had enough time to make up their minds.

5. *Avoid giving your own opinion.* To move away from Stage 1 reasoning, children must be encouraged to see right and wrong from a point of view other than that of authority and must be led to understand that the most important products of moral discussions are personal ideas and feelings.

6. *Provide variety.* Children need a variety of conditions in which to consider moral issues. Use a variety of puppetry or other creative dramatics situations to improve and invigorate your program. Children develop a great sensitivity to others by "becoming" another person. Their imaginations take over and allow them to verbalize and act in ways they would not normally consider.

A strategy for guiding moral discussions, summarizing the roles of teacher and child, is presented in Figure 6–4.

Perhaps the teacher's most important role is to identify the children's reasoning levels and make sure the children are exposed to the next reasoning stage higher than their own. Children can easily understand the reasoning below their own level and reject

FIGURE 6–4
Strategy for Guiding Moral Dilemmas

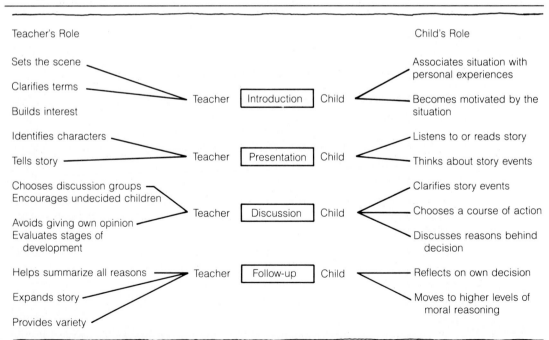

it as simplistic. But they grow in their abilities to reason only by listening to the arguments of those reasoning one stage above their own. They cannot understand the arguments of those who are reasoning more than one stage above their own. Figure 6–5 illustrates these concepts.

Young children enjoy a variety of stories containing moral dilemmas from their social studies program. Look for commercial materials such as films, filmstrips, and audiotapes or records, too. One company that specializes in the production of commercial materials appropriate for use with children of elementary school age is Guidance Associates. *First Things: Values* (Pleasantville, NY: Guidance Associates, 1972) is a filmstrip and record program presenting young children in various situations of moral conflict.

The type of control to which you expose children in normal classroom management needs careful consideration. Consider the typical scene in which two children are sent into the classroom for fighting on the playground. The first question usually fired at the children is, "Okay, who started it?" And to the guilty party, "Well, how would you like to have this sort of thing happen to you?" The question is met with a slight shrug and downward turn of the eyes. "Look at me when I'm talking!" demands the teacher. "Answer my question."

Tears well in the eyes of the "winner" as he desperately tries to answer the teacher's question, managing only a barely audible, "I don't know."

Angry by this time, the teacher retorts, "Okay, Smartie, you just sit in for one week during your outdoor recess periods and think about it!"

FIGURE 6–5
Principles of Movement Through Kohlberg's Stages of Moral Development

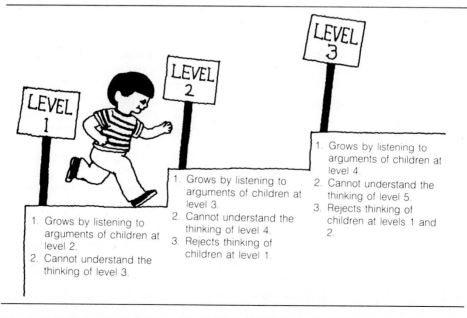

1. Grows by listening to arguments of children at level 2.
2. Cannot understand the thinking of level 3.

1. Grows by listening to arguments of children at level 3.
2. Cannot understand the thinking of level 4.
3. Rejects thinking of children at level 1.

1. Grows by listening to arguments of children at level 4.
2. Cannot understand the thinking of level 5.
3. Rejects thinking of children at levels 1 and 2.

If we analyze that fabricated situation according to Kohlberg's ideas we might assume that the "winner" was operating at Stage 1 of moral reasoning. He knows he has done wrong, but only because he has broken a rule established by the teacher—no fighting on the playground. In her disciplinary action, however, the teacher asked the child to reason at Stage 3—to put himself in another's shoes. Therefore, the child becomes frustrated and cries because he truly cannot understand the type of response the teacher wants. An important part of the teacher's use of Kohlberg's ideas is to help the child reexamine his actions before engaging him in new reasoning patterns that require reordering of thinking processes and seeking new ways to organize feelings. Every child needs to be aware that she is a member of a group and has a responsibility toward the group. For that reason, we usually have only a few restrictions in preschool settings, but they should be rigidly enforced. Prohibited acts are usually those that endanger the welfare or restrict the rights of others. The child must be aware that there are things he can and cannot do if the environment is to be safe. You must explain the reasons to him, at the same time understanding that his comprehension of your explanation may be extremely limited. He will usually listen and obey because you are the authority figure in the classroom and have gained his basic trust (Stage 1). In many instances, the child *demands* your limits.

Handling feelings is an extremely sensitive area. Guiding a child entails a great deal of personal insight. "Overdirection may distort his development; so may lack of direction. He needs time to learn through suitable experiences. He is sure to make some mistakes in the process of learning. . . . [I]f we deal calmly and confidently with unacceptable behavior, we will create the kind of climate in which the child is helped to master his impulses and to direct his own behavior. We will be using authority in constructive ways."[28]

SUMMARY

We live in a complex society today; very little appears to remain stable, especially the values choices people are expected to make. In this chapter we learned that *values* are strong beliefs having both affective and cognitive elements. They may be taught through either direct or indirect means, but before any technique is used, we must be sure to develop a healthy environment in which children feel free to make personal choices and sense the importance of social responsibility. The entire classroom environment contributes to these feelings, as do popular programs such as Magic Circle and DUSO. Once the children acquire appropriate personal and social sensitivities, it may be appropriate to involve them in specific social stud-

ies values experiences. Presently, there are four major directions of values education: (1) inculcation, (2) values clarification, (3) values analysis, and (4) moral reasoning. Each has its own particular pattern of instruction, but all appear to stress:

- examining important issues critically,
- sharing feelings with others,
- developing cooperative problem-solving skills, and
- applying values choices to one's own life.

The programs are based on the idea that if children are placed in a supportive social environment and encouraged to share their feelings with others, if they are taught to examine all sides of an issue, and if they challenge each other to support choices, then they will develop skills to make wise personal decisions throughout their lives. From this base individuals achieve the personal strength to address issues that involve controversy and commitment.

ENDNOTES

1. Lois Lamdin, "Moral Uncertainty," *Great Valley News 2*, no. 2 (October 1985): 3.

2. *The Boston Primer* (1808), cited in Richard H. Hersh et al., *Models of Moral Education* (New York: Longman, 1980), p. 16.

3. *A Manual of the System of Discipline and Instruction* (New York: Longman, 1980), p. 16.

4. Jean-Jacques Rousseau, selections from *Emilius* in Robert Ulich, ed., *Three Thousand Years of Educational Wisdom* (Cambridge, MA: Harvard University Press, 1971), p. 397.

5. Ibid.

6. Carl R. Rogers, "Toward a Modern Approach to Values: The Valuing Process in the Mature Person," in *Reading in Values Clarification*, ed. Howard Kirschenbaum and Sidney B. Simon (Minneapolis, MN: Winston Press, 1973), pp. 75–91.

7. Ibid., pp. 77–78.

8. James P. Shaver, "Commitment to Values and the Study of Social Problems in Citizenship Education," *Social Education, 49*, no. 3 (March 1985): 195.

9. Ibid., p. 196.

10. Carl R. Rogers, "A Plan for Self-Directed Change in an Educational System," *Educational Leadership* (May 1967): 718.

11. Uvaldo Palomares and Gerry Ball, *Grounds for Growth: The Human Development Program's Comprehensive Theory* (La Mesa, CA: Human Development Training Institute, Inc., 1969).

12. Mary Olson "It Makes Me Feel Bad When You Call Me Stinky," *Young Children, 26*, no. 2 (December 1970): 120–121.

13. James P. Shaver, "Commitment to Values," p. 194.

14. S. Samuel Shermis and James L. Barth, "Indoctrination and the Study of Social Problems: A Re-Examination of the 1930s Debate in *The Social Frontier*," *Social Education, 49*, no. 3 (March 1985): 190–193.

15. James P. Shaver, "Commitment to Values," p. 196.

16. Ibid.

17. Louis E. Raths, Merrill Harmin, and Sidney B. Simon, *Values and Teaching*, 2nd ed. (Columbus, OH: Merrill, 1978).

18. Ibid., p. 30.

19. Ibid., pp. 38–39.

20. Based on Raths, Harmin, and Simon, *Values and Teaching*, pp. 53–54.

21. James Raths, "A Strategy for Developing Values," *Readings for Social Studies in Elementary Education*, ed. John Jarolimek and Huber M. Walsh (New York: Macmillan, 1974), pp. 252–54.

22. Raths, Harmin, and Simon, *Values and Teaching*, pp. 117–20.

23. Ibid. pp. 127–55.

24. Richard C. Remy et al., *Skills in Making Political Decisions* (Columbus, OH: Mershon Center, The Ohio State University, n.d.).

25. Jack R. Fraenkel, "Value Education in the Social Studies," *Phi Delta Kappan, 50*, no. 8 (April 1969): 460.

26. Ronald E. Galbraith and Thomas M. Jones, *Moral Reasoning: A Teaching Handbook for Adapting Kohlberg to the Classroom* (Minneapolis, MN: Greenhaven Press, 1967), pp. 172–180.

27. Barry K. Beyer, "Conducting Moral Discussions in the Classroom," *Social Education* (April 1976): 197.

28. Katherine H. Read, *The Nursery School: A Human Relations Laboratory* (Philadelphia: W. B. Saunders, 1971), pp. 108–109.

Much of school life seems to be built upon . . . isolation. For example, what are teachers teaching children when they call for recitations with the preface, "Now, Johnny, I want to hear what you have to say. Don't anybody else help him!" Homework is given out with the admonition: "Make sure it's your own work.". . . *I realize that a purpose of this isolation is to enable the teacher to evaluate and rank her pupils. But every day? And at such a cost?*[1]

—*Rachel M. Lauer*

7 *Grouping for Instruction*

KEY CONCEPTS

As you read, reflect on the following matters:

- How have competitive pressures affected the social studies program?
- Why is whole-group orientation basic to all group work in the social studies? What are the components of a suitable whole-group orientation program?
- Why are subgroups important in the social studies classroom?
- What is cooperative learning? How do cooperative learning subgroups contribute to learning? How do teachers introduce, manage, and extend the responsibilities of cooperative learning subgroups?
- Other than cooperative learning subgroups, what additional grouping possibilities exist for the social studies classroom?
- What problems might complicate the use of subgroups in the social studies classroom?

It is a truism about teaching elementary school social studies that there is no one right way to teach it. That point was stressed in earlier chapters, but bears repeating because of the regularity with which educators declare that they have originated the most novel and best solution to our teaching problems. Their well-intentioned pronouncements try to convince others to jump onto a bandwagon headed for the education promised land.

By the late 1970s and early 1980s, that bandwagon was bedecked with an alluring "accountability" banner, although no one could really define accountability. The accountability movement was inspired by several influential, critical reports published during this era. *A Nation at Risk,* one of the most abrasive in describing our educational efforts, made searing statements such as: "If an unfriendly foreign power had attempted to impose on America the mediocre instructional performance that exists today, we might well have viewed it as an act of war."[2] In response to such shocking rhetoric, school boards established minimal competency levels of performance and state boards of education passed accountability laws, amidst rallying cries of "Bring back the basics." Back-to-basics programs generally had the following characteristics: (1) an emphasis on basic content and skills, especially in reading and mathematics; (2) an unrelenting use of quizzes and standardized tests; (3) repetitious drill and endless hours of paper-pencil seatwork; (4) the elimination of "frills" from the school programs. "Frills" were interpreted as anything not actually included in the "basics"; therefore, some subjects—particularly the social studies and arts—were deemphasized.

In 1984, John I. Goodlad noted that the nation's classrooms exhibited a "flatness"—they were places where little could be described as innovative, exciting, or dynamic.[3] Teachers were frustrated at being forced to compromise their child-centered philosophies with a rigid skills/content approach forced upon them by boards of education. One second grade teacher shares her discouragement:

> We must get them through workbook after workbook. We must make them produce on paper to be verified by all. We feel guilty doing an art lesson or having a wonderful discussion.[4]

Another teacher adds these thoughts:

> In the large, affluent suburb where I teach, the pressure is on the kids and the teachers from kindergarten through high school to get good grades, bring up the test scores, and be the best (on the test). Classroom teachers are locked into curriculum, scheduling, and test preparation that leaves little time for innovation, creativity or diversity in teaching. . . . Somewhere the meaning of education has been lost.[5]

Because most elementary school educators understood that excellent teaching is essential in the early years, they were distressed that the public did not share their views and had placed such competitive pressures on the schools and children. They decried the fact that most children left elementary school less eager and less excited about learning than when they entered. What could be done about this precarious situation? William Ayers suggested:

> The practical place to begin is to recall that children are whole people, with bodies, minds, cultures, and feelings. Furthermore, we can acknowledge that children want what all

human beings long for: love, support, respect, community, meaningful work to do, and real choices to make. . . .

Part of our task is to allow children to be children, to protect childhood, and to create spaces where children can interact productively with each other and with caring adults. This is our abiding responsibility to the development of whole human beings.[6]

Pleas such as this reflected the thoughts of many elementary school educators who deplored the trend toward rigidity and favored more humanistic, process-oriented instruction. These educators accepted the importance of content and skills objectives, but thought that instruction should be based on the developmental needs of children rather than on a demand for students to perform at a particular level on a standardized achievement test. Specific teaching recommendations for today's social studies classrooms reflect Ayers's philosophy—how children learn should determine how we teach. Children do not learn well by constantly being told, by taking tests, or by doing interminable dittoes and worksheets. It is possible and perhaps efficient to drill children until they correctly recite information such as historic dates; however, responses to rote tasks do not reveal substantive understanding. For children to understand the significance of their learning experiences, content and teaching strategies must be meaningful in the context of children's experiences and developmental characteristics. That is, experiences and content must be "developmentally appropriate."

Just as the phrases for the 1970s and early 1980s were "accountability" and "back to basics," the buzzword for the 1990s appears to be "developmentally appropriate practices" (*DAP*). We have examined developmentally appropriate ways of organizing and initiating whole-class, teacher-directed learning experiences. In this chapter we find that there is another approach to *DAP* that is of equal if not greater importance—the process of cooperative learning.

COOPERATIVE LEARNING

In traditional classes where whole-group instruction is the norm, most of the students' experiences with content are limited to interactions dictated by the teacher. Children, however, are by nature social beings; they are largely uncomfortable with the competitive nature of traditional classrooms—competing for grades, for the teacher's attention, and so on. Competition appeared to be more important than social cooperation during the 1970s and 1980s. Gunter, Estes, and Schwab state, however, that for the 1990s, "Working *cooperatively.* . . . may be the most critical social skill that students learn, when one considers the importance of cooperation in the workplace, in the family, and in leisure activities. If there were no other benefits, the importance of learning to collaborate would justify building a part of the school experience around cooperative learning activities."[7] Cooperative learning should be considered an important part of the social studies program for its contribution to children's social growth, but the benefits go beyond social considerations. Proponents stress its contributions to student achievement as well. They say that "when students support each other in mixed-ability groups they learn a lot more than just their lessons. They also gain self-esteem and are far more accepting of each other and of individual differences."[8] Cooperative learning is also particularly valuable in activating children's prior knowledge as they discuss and share ideas with each other, an important aspect of the comprehension process.[9] Additionally, cooperative learning presents opportunities for children to develop high-level reasoning and problem-solving skills as they present issues, clarify their thinking, and challenge others.[10] Finally, cooperative learning helps children extend their knowledge and awareness of different cultural groups as they work with children from different ethnic backgrounds.[11]

IMPLEMENTING COOPERATIVE LEARNING STRATEGIES

Two prominent advocates of cooperative learning, David W. Johnson and Robert T. Johnson, have identified five critical elements essential for successful implementation:

> The first is what we call "positive interdependence." The students really have to believe they're in it together, sink or swim. They have to care about each other's learning. Second is a lot of verbal, face-to-face interaction. Students have to explain, argue, elaborate, and tie in the material they learn today with what they had last week.
>
> The third element is individual accountability. It must be clear that every member of their group has to learn, and there's no hitchhiking. . . .
>
> The fourth element is social skills. Students need to be taught appropriate leadership, communication, trust building, and conflict resolution skills so they operate efficiently.
>
> The fifth element is what we call "group processing." Periodically, the groups have to assess how well they are working together and how they can do better.[12]

Before students are arranged into cooperative learning groups, they would benefit from stimulating whole-class experiences where individual importance and positive relationships are stressed. Good social studies teachers plan experiences with those goals in mind because they want children to leave school with a feeling of greatness. For most children, learning to be an effective member of a whole-class group is an important first lesson in personal awareness. For all too many, however, those first lessons end in failure. Studies have shown that children's self-esteem is lower in the latter part of elementary school than it was when they entered school; June Canty Lemke indicates that 80% of first graders have high self-esteem, 20% of fifth graders, and only 5% of twelfth graders.[13] That is why we must do all we can to establish a positive classroom environment where conditions of interaction promote effective group functioning. This does not happen automatically or by chance; it is a product of careful teaching.

Whole-Group Orientation

A major factor in establishing and maintaining effective groups in the social studies classroom is the children's and teacher's ability to get along pleasantly together. For both, this involves

- Developing a positive sense of self
- Understanding others
- Relating to each other positively
- Becoming comfortable and accepted in the classroom

Before children can begin to understand their roles in a new social group (the classroom), they must first acquire a positive sense of their own identities. They must feel good about themselves; only as children accept themselves as separate, unique, and worthwhile individuals can we expect them to enter into successful relationships with others. In the early grades, then, teachers must offer experiences that help children grow in self-confidence; those experiences begin on the very first day of school as teachers plan and organize the classroom environment for the children.

Coming to School

The first thing a child looks for in the classroom is *you.* Be at the door to welcome each child. Offer a cheerful hello and add something special as each child comes in: "I like your yellow shirt," or "You sure look ready for school today!" It is important for the child to be greeted by a warm and supportive teacher, for the initial impressions children have about their new classroom environment will be the lasting ones. Children will make further judgments about school as they walk into the classroom, so make it an inviting place by arranging bulletin boards, displays, and furniture in ways that show children the classroom is everyone's, not exclusively the teacher's. Is there a personal name tag on each child's desk? Are the seats arranged so the children can see each other, or are they all directed toward the teacher? Have you used dividers, screens, or bulletin boards to make the space inviting?

As the children enter the room, capitalize on their names to expand the development of self-concept and to create an understanding of the new social group. An excellent way to organize this part of your program is to choose a theme for introducing the children to each other. Before the first morning in a primary-grade classroom, you might, for example, decorate your room with pictures of popular, likable bears—teddy bears, Winnie-the-Pooh, Paddington, and Corduroy. Prepare simple bear-shaped name tags and arrange the tags, each not yet bearing a child's name, on a colorful bulletin board captioned, "A Beary Special Group." Introduce the children to a special bear puppet, "Bear the Magnificent—Beary for short." Have Beary greet the boys and girls with a nonthreatening roar and, "Good morning boys and girls. I am so happy to see you today and you all look so nice. I was lonely without you. We'll have fun each day playing, talking, and learning." Then, making Beary appear startled, call his attention to the bulletin board on which all the blank name tags are displayed. "Good gracious," roars Beary. "I've never seen so many bears in my whole life! A wall full of bears that all look the same! Quickly, bears, tell me your names." Then, making Beary appear to be talking to one of the tags, say, "Please tell me your name." The bear tag should respond, "Teddy." Then repeat the request ("Please tell me your name") and the response ("Teddy") for five more bears, with Beary appearing more frustrated each time: "Hold it—this just won't do," says Beary. "Are you trying to play games with me?" The little tags reply, "No, we're telling the truth!" The teacher can then turn to the children and say, "We have an awful problem. We must have new names so we can tell who is who. I know! We can use each of *your* names. How does that sound, Beary?" Beary eagerly agrees, but then becomes puzzled: "But I don't know their names yet." The teacher then asks the children to introduce themselves individually to Beary as she writes each name on the tags. (Remember to use upper- and lowercase letters.) Then pin each tag on the child's shirt and say, "Now this is better. All of the bears have new names." Then, Beary can repeat his request ("Please tell me your name") to each child and the child can respond. Happily, Beary responds, "Now the school year can begin!"

After this introduction activity, you may want to play a short action game with the children, keeping the bear theme central. Tell the children that bears are lots of fun and that school will be fun this year, too. Ask Beary if he is happy to be in this classroom and have him respond cheerfully, then encourage the children to join you in the action song, "If You're Happy and You Know It" using these phrases: ". . . say roar, roar . . . clap your paws . . . do them both . . . !" You can expand on this aspect of individual understanding on subsequent days with these suggestions:

Share popular children's songs such as "Thumbkin," inserting children's names in place of the normal lyrics:

Where is (*child's name*)?
Where is (*child's name*)?
There she is. (Child stands up)
There she is.
How are you today (*child's name*)?
Very well, I thank you. (Child bows)
Run away. (Child sits down)
Run away.

Play the "Police Officer and Lost Child" game. Select one child to be a police officer and another child to be the parent of a lost child. The parent requests, "Police officer, please help me find my lost child." The police officer asks, "What does your child look like?" The "parent" then describes one of the children in class. When they identify which child the parent is describing, the parent becomes the police officer and the child becomes the parent.

Construct a "talking book." Take a photograph of each child and mount it on a separate page. Begin a tape recorded narrative such as, "This is a picture of Caroline Montego." Invite the child to continue with information such as color of hair and eyes, age, home address, hobby, interests, and so on. Children will enjoy frequent replays of this book as they get to know one another.

Reserve a small area in the classroom for a "Me Display." Each week, let a different child take a turn making a bulletin board or other display about himself. Ask him to bring in pictures, toys, hobbies, or other things from home to show interests, skills, or other characteristics that help his classmates become aware of him as a unique individual.

From these and other introductory activities, you get to know the children and they get to know one another. As they gain initial confidence, children are eager to participate in other activities that help them understand their place in the group.

Birthdays. Part of the fun of going to school is the special recognition children get on their birthdays. Enhance that joy with a special bulletin board displayed on the first day of school. This display is valuable not only for the recognition it brings to children, but also for introducing them to the concept of days, months, and year. Cut construction paper to form the engine and cars of a train, making a car for each month. Print the name of a month above each car, insert a photo of each child in the windows, and print the birthdates below the pictures, as shown in Figure 7–1.

A highlight of the school year is the celebration of special days, but no party or occasion seems to bring as much excitement as the planning and execution of a birthday party. Most kindergarten or primary-grade teachers set aside a special time during the day when the birthday child is allowed to share her special day with the others. Here are some suggestions for these special days:

> Paint a chair with bright paint and decorate it; this "birthday chair" is for use by a child only on his birthday.

> Make a crown from construction paper, decorate it, and label it with the child's name, date, and age. The child can wear it during the birthday party and take it home as a souvenir.

> As a group sing "Happy Birthday" and/or "For He's a Jolly Good Fellow" to the birthday child.

Classroom Helpers. Individual contributions to group welfare can be effectively demonstrated by assigning helpers for specific classroom duties. You can decide who the helpers should be on a daily or weekly basis, but make it a consistent part of the schedule. There are several ways to organize this facet of your program; the following suggestions may prove helpful for kindergarten and first grade. All of them promote a sense of identity and of belonging to a group (see Figure 7–2).

FIGURE 7–1
Sample Birthday Chart for Primary-Grade Classrooms

FIGURE 7–2
Classroom Helpers Bulletin Boards

Begin the year using concrete materials to indicate individual responsibilities. For example, you can place a child's photograph and a sponge next to each other on the "Our Helpers" bulletin board to indicate who is responsible for cleaning the table after snack. A straw and a photograph indicate the straw arranger, a photograph and napkin the napkin passer, and so on.

As the children begin to recognize their names, print them on "smile faces" and associate the smile faces with the labeled concrete object. A "Happy Helpers" bulletin board is an attractive way to organize the materials.

As a final stage in this development process, organize a special "Helping Hands" bulletin board, on which one hand is labeled with the classroom responsibility and the other with the name of the child assigned to it. To avoid disagreements as to whose turn it is to do what job, print the completed job on the back of the hand with a child's name.

Children enjoy assuming responsibility in the classroom and enthusiastically meet their tasks each day, especially if they are motivated by colorful charts or bulletin boards.

Attendance Charts.   Charts that show who is present or absent each day help young children recognize that separate individuals comprise their group and help them learn to recognize each other's names.

Mount the children's photographs or small self-portraits on red construction-paper apples labeled with their names. Make a large apple tree from green and brown construction paper. As they arrive at school each day, the children find their apples and place them on the apple tree. During large-group time, the children can look at the chart to see who is absent.

FIGURE 7–3
Attendance Chart

Mount library book pockets on a bulletin board, each pocket illustrated with the child's photograph or self-portrait. Print each child's name on a card large enough so that the child's name can be read when the card is placed into the pocket. As the children come to school each day, they place their name cards into their corresponding library pockets.

To promote future graphing skills, make a series of cardboard dolls representing the boys and girls in the classroom. Label each doll with a child's name. As they enter the classroom, the children place their dolls in the "Here Today" row; when everyone has arrived, you take the absent children's dolls and place them in the "Absent Today" row. During group time, help the children count the number present, the number absent, the number of boys and girls present, and boys and girls absent (see Figure 7–3).

Activities like these show young children they are valued as individuals and as group members. The security that comes from a warm, accepting teacher gives young children the confidence to form relationships with others. Democratic classrooms must be firmly based upon a child's development of a positive sense of self. Without this clear perception, children will not see themselves as worthy persons capable of making personal decisions.

The First Day for Older Children

Older children require acceptance too, of course, but should be offered activities more suitable for their developmental needs, so you may need to vary their experiences. Here are suggestions for introductions on the first day of school.

Design posters with the twelve signs of the zodiac. Include the dates, characteristics, and symbols for each. Hang the posters around the room. Give each child two large sheets of tagboard and two pieces of string. Punch holes in the tagboard and tie the sheets together with string so they will hang over the children's shoulders like a sandwich board. Ask the children to divide each sheet into three equal sections and number sections 1–3 on the front and 4–6 on the back. They then complete their sandwich boards by illustrating information for each segment:

What is your favorite school subject?

What do you enjoy most outside of school?

What is one personal characteristic of yours that you are most proud of?

What do you admire most in other people?

What is one thing you do very well?

What do you like to do with others?

When the boards are finished, the children gather near the posters bearing their astrological signs. While they are there, ask them to compare their boards with others. Are they somewhat alike? Which of their characteristics are like and unlike those on the posters? What did they learn about the others in their group?

You can have the children make a "This Is Me" T-shirt collage. Pass out pieces of drawing paper cut into the shape of T-shirts. Ask the children to cut out from magazines pictures that show their interests, experiences, or favorite things and paste these clippings on the T-shirt shapes. Label each T-shirt with the child's name and attach it to an illustrated clothesline on a bulletin board captioned "We Hang Out in Mr. Robinson's Room."

The children will enjoy creating a classroom directory. Take individual photographs of all the members of your class. Mount the photographs in a booklet and label each. Ask the children to fill in data about themselves—family characteristics, address, phone number, hobbies, interests, abilities, favorites, and so on.

You can prepare a chart like the one in Figure 7–4 with the children's names listed down one side and categories of information across the top (hobbies, pets, etc.). Divide the class into groups and fill in the chart together. Take time to share responses and use the information for activities such as graphing or creative writing.

Children in the middle- and upper-elementary school grades enjoy the recognition associated with helpers' charts, birthdays, and other routines described for the early years, but you must adapt the classroom displays and patterns of interaction during the associated activity for the older child.

FIGURE 7–4
Classroom Chart of Individual Class Members

	COLOR OF EYES	COLOR OF HAIR	FAVORITE SONG	HOBBY	PET
MIKE					
JUDY					
STANLEY					
ROSE					
JEFF					
BRIAN					
MELISSA					
ELIZABETH					

After a period of well-planned, whole-class experiences, children usually acquire the self-confidence and skill to function well as members of the classroom group. This group orientation phase of a teacher's program is normally a very satisfying one. Most children come to school wanting to learn and will be cooperative within a secure environment that supports the dignity and respect of its group members. Establishing these whole-group characteristics early in the school year is an important responsibility because what happens at the beginning of the year affects the efforts of the group for the entire year.

Good social studies programs accept elementary school youngsters' absorption in themselves, an interest that very few of us lose throughout our lives. Young children are interested in themselves because they become more keenly self-*aware* as they move from the security of their families into various school groups. Children must feel they are as accepted by their teachers and peers as they are by their families. These youngsters must be helped to understand who and what they are—to become more accepting of their strengths and limitations within a program that recognizes several kinds of abilities and provides a wide variety of challenges so that all children can experience personal triumphs. We build intense competition into our program by forming competitive groups or groups that classify some students as "smart" and others as "dumb"—"the roses and the weeds," as one particularly insensitive teacher called them. It is devastating to be a "weed," ruinous to come in last. Instead, James Hymes, Jr., advises, children need to identify with someone they know likes them, someone who will build an intimate bond with them:

> Every youngster has to feel: This is *my* teacher, as if that one child alone was the apple of the teacher's eye. It is no simple job for a teacher to convey this sense of caring to each one. Some lucky youngsters are magnetic—they immediately attract a teacher's warm feelings. But often a teacher must go to extra lengths . . . to reach other youngsters who are less quickly lovable . . . Everything about a well-loved teacher gets under a child's skin; her patience, her humor, her reasonableness, her kindness . . . her helpfulness.[14]

Helpful teachers know not only that young children crave attachment to a caring teacher but that once such a hunger has been satisfied, children become eager to meet new, rich challenges. They will want to leave their dependency behind, just as they will want to look ahead to chances to satisfy their deep-rooted curiosity.

Informal Experiences with Small Groups

Regardless of how smoothly your whole-class routine is going, a quick move from whole-class instruction to small group activity with little or no preparation can be disastrous. Teachers often find that children have trouble functioning—children will not focus on tasks; some wander, others complain, "I don't know what you want us to do"; a few become involved in power struggles for group control. Frustrated teachers often conclude, "Bring back the text! Run off the dittoes! Put the desks back in rows—this doesn't work!"

Children often find unique ways to express new interests when included in cooperative learning.

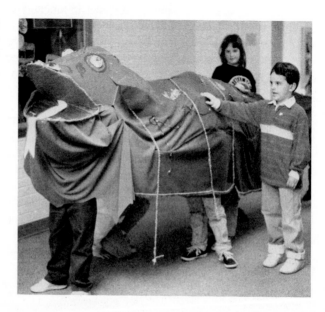

Selma Wassermann addresses those feelings from her own experience:

The behaviors children exhibit during the first attempts at cooperative, independent group
work may scare us into retreat. That behavior is likely to be noisy, aggressive, random. It
is certainly unproductive, in terms of any clear product-result. When we see this behavior
emerge, our nerve-endings are set a-buzz. All our nightmares about "losing classroom
control" surface. We want to restore order, gain control immediately, put the lid back. . . .
If teachers want to beat a hasty retreat from this experience, I can certainly understand
the reasons, with great compassion.[15]

Despite these serious start-up concerns, many courageous teachers find ways of
moving children from whole-class instruction to effective small group functioning. It
may take from September until November or December, but the move must be
deliberate and based on classroom strategies that help with the transition. As Lori Fisk
and Henry Clay Lindgren advise, "Introducing [new ways of working] all at once
produces a situation in which the children's cognitive systems collapse under an
'overload of input,' as my computerized friends and colleagues would say."[16]
Teachers must be willing to take risks; establishing small group skills demands a
lot from teachers. Teachers must be convinced that cooperative learning is an important
goal—sure enough that they will endure months of trial before the groups eventually
function as productive entities. Children must be taught how to be reliable, to depend
on and and learn from others, to stand up for themselves, and to respect the contributions of all who offer ideas. With proper encouragement and support, students can be
led to discover the skills and develop the interest necessary for cooperation in a group
setting. Ideally, they will master the skills of group behavior in practical ways by actually
using them in exemplary situations. To get an idea of good group membership, the
children need to conceptualize how individual behaviors contribute to group effectiveness. Students must be prepared for small-group cooperation in much the same way
they were oriented to whole-group membership: they must be involved in situations
that help them internalize norms of behavior. The first step in small-group orientation
is to prepare students for cooperative work situations with direct experiences.
An experiential approach to learning group skills and attitudes is necessary to help
children develop expected behaviors. We cannot expect children to function effectively
in groups unless they first experience what groups are all about. The following activities
will help you to introduce and develop group work skills. To start, make sure all
members of the group can see each other; tables with two chairs on a side work very
well.

The Button Game

Arrange your class into groups and give them these directions: "I am going to give you
a job to do as a group to see how well you work together. Each group has a box that
contains buttons of different colors, sizes, and shapes. You must work together as one
group and decide upon one way to group the buttons. Remember, you must agree on
one answer. When you have finished, choose one person to give your results to me."
Make sure all the children understand the directions, then step back and watch them
go to work. After the groups offer their answers to you, ask them to discuss the process

they used to arrive at their solution. Ask these questions: "How did you get organized? What slowed the group down? What helped you work faster? Did your group choose a leader? How? In what way did each member contribute? What would you do differently next time? What would you do the same?" Conclude the discussion by constructing a large chart listing the behaviors the groups considered important to working together on a joint task. The value of this activity is that the group members themselves construct standards for their behaviors rather than having those standards imposed upon them by an authority figure. Such direct activity helps children achieve a degree of "psychological ownership" of their standards and will more often result in acceptance by the group.

Puzzle Squares

Puzzle squares, a simple nonverbal game, creates an environment for understanding the limitations of achieving a group goal when all communication is prohibited. As the children attempt to reach their goal without communication, you will observe reactions of anxiety, frustration, fear, aggression, hostility, and indifference. After the activity, you should discuss these feelings and their causes at length.

Materials
1. Cut out five heavy tagboard squares, each about five inches. It is advisable to begin with five because the recommended group size for elementary grades is four to seven members per group.
2. Cut each square into three segments following the patterns in Figure 7–5.
3. Scramble the fifteen pieces and put them into a large manila envelope.
4. Repeat the procedure for each set of five children in your classroom.

Goal
Each child in a group must use the puzzle pieces to complete a five-inch square consisting of only three pieces.

Procedure
1. Place children into groups of five and have them select a group leader.
2. Give each group leader an envelope containing fifteen puzzle pieces.
3. On signal, the group leader opens the envelope and randomly passes three puzzle pieces to each group member.

FIGURE 7–5
Patterns for Puzzle Squares

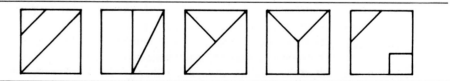

4. Direct the students to examine their puzzle pieces and try to make a square from them. Signal the students to begin. Allow approximately thirty to forty minutes of working time. If the students discover their segments will not form a perfect square, they may exchange pieces with other members of their group, but only under these rules:
   - No talking. The game must be played in complete silence.
   - No eye signals, hand signals, or gestures. Communication of any kind is discouraged.
   - No taking another puzzle piece from another player, unless he or she first offers it to you.

When the time is up and several puzzles have been completed, discuss questions such as: "How did you feel when you first started working with the group? Did you find it difficult to cooperate with others as you kept working? What were some of the problems that resulted from not being able to communicate? What feelings did you have toward the other members of your group? What made you feel that way? How would it help to be able to communicate with the others in your group? What are some ways you would have used to communicate with them? What would happen to our city, state, country, or world if people followed the same rules for communication that you had for your game?"

You would be wise at this point to ask the children to think about and suggest any additional rules they think would make their group projects effective experiences. Students will show greater insight into the mechanics of effective communication and cooperation after these direct experiences. If you really want to develop the concept of good communication and cooperation in groups, involve your students.

The Gossip Game

This game is designed to show that the level of each individual's involvement and interest affects the quality of communication within a group.

Materials
1. A short story containing many details that can be composed by a small group.
2. Tape recorder.

Goal
The children can see how stories change as they are heard and retold to other people.

Procedure
1. Select three or four students to leave the room for ten to fifteen minutes on a "special errand."
2. Have a group or the entire class secretly construct a short story full of many details and incidents. Copy it on paper for later reference.
3. Call one of the students back and have the story read to him. Tape record the reading.

4. After the student hears the story, the second student who left on the "special errand" is called back to the room and listens as the first student tells her the story as he heard it. Record this version also. The progression is repeated until all the pupils who have left the room are back and have recorded their versions of the changing story.
5. Play back all four taped versions of the story. The class listens to hear how each version varies from the way the story was written.
6. Discuss with the class why the original story changed as each individual told his or her version.

Paper Skyscrapers

Collect as much scrap paper as possible—index cards, file folders, and old tagboard or construction paper are all fine. Clear a large area of the room and divide your class into four or five equal groups. Each group gets a pile of paper to build a tower. Only the paper may by used—no tape, glue, staples, or other type of fastener. Papers can be folded to reinforce construction, but the tighter the folds the smaller the paper gets. Likewise, loosely folded papers provide large building parts but the construction becomes more fragile. Such considerations provide excellent opportunities for cooperative problem solving.

The object of the activity is to build the highest skyscraper. You will certainly want to recognize the group achieving this goal. However, be sure to recognize the efforts of other groups, too—the cleverest, the most unusual, the widest, and so on.

Peer Pressure

Peer pressure often is irresistible when the opinions of the whole group differ from one's own. Children must be able to cooperate in groups, but they must also maintain their own strong beliefs in certain circumstances. This activity illustrates the value of sticking to one's convictions.

1. Choose four of five children from your class and send them on a short errand.
2. Divide the class into the same number of groups.
3. Place this problem, or a similar problem appropriate to the general ability levels of your children, on the board: $(8 \times 15) - (25 \div 5) - 3 = \underline{\hspace{1cm}}$. Decide on the correct answer. (In this case, the answer is 112.)
4. Instruct the groups that when your errand runners return,
   a. The groups will be asked to come up with a single solution.
   b. Everyone will give a deliberately wrong answer. In this example, they could agree upon 16.
   c. No one should laugh or act suspicious.
   d. Each group member will give his or her answer in turn, with the errand runners last.

   After a short time, inform the errand runners what happened and ask: "How did you feel when everyone gave an answer different from yours? Did you feel uncomfortable going against the others? How important is everyone's personal opinion while working in a group?"

Now is an excellent time to encourage the children to suggest ways that group efforts can be made effective. Suggestions can be compiled and illustrated in a chart or on a bulletin board to refer to whenever difficulties in group efforts arise, as in Figure 7–6.

For teachers interested in grouping children for specific social studies communication purposes, a variation of the Gossip Game technique may be appropriate. The same game procedure is followed, but instead of sending three or four students out of the classroom, send three groups of the same size. After a story is constructed, bring each group back and have the students listen to the story. Then have each group decide how to retell the story. This can be an excellent transitional activity; the children can discuss the similarities of their rules for good discussion and the characteristics of good group work.

Now that the children have experienced good group work, you can initiate grouping techniques in the classroom. Chances for successful group work are enhanced when the children have been prepared for it. By participating in group activities that illustrate the value of cooperation and responsibility, students can more effectively develop these essential understandings:

1. Groups must establish and understand their goals.
2. Members must not feel threatened while sharing their ideas and feelings with the group.

FIGURE 7–6
Sample Group Work Guidelines

OUR RULES FOR GOOD GROUP WORK

1. Talk clearly so others will understand.
2. Listen carefully when others speak.
3. Follow our leader's directions carefully.
4. Sometimes we may write what we want to say instead of talking to one another.
5. Cooperate with others to get the job done.
6. Take care of our work materials and supplies.
7. Respect the contributions of others.
8. Support ideas with good evidence.
9. Everyone should participate.
10. We should all agree on an answer.

3. All members should share ideas and feelings accurately and clearly.
4. Leadership and participation should be equally shared.
5. Group responsibilities vary according to the group's purposes.
6. Conflicting solutions are to be encouraged because they promote creativity and decision making, but excessive competition and pressure should be avoided.
7. Group cohesion is important. Work toward a high level of acceptance and trust among group members.

When we initially guide children into group work specifically designed for the social studies, we must be sure to offer projects that do not involve complex responsibilities. Making an illustration, map, information retrieval chart, graph, model, or chart that organizes or represents materials they have already studied helps the children build cohesiveness and moves them toward increasingly sophisticated group work skills. Such activities are often planned to follow guided, whole-class instruction. As the children establish suitable group behaviors, you can gradually offer them more complex responsibilities: creating dramatic skits, organizing an antilittering campaign, designing a classroom flag, or illustrating an aspect of life in the twenty-first century. These possibilities call for expression of different information or contrasting points of view about an idea, theme, or topic; therefore, greater cohesion and skilled work habits are necessary. Group work thus offers children the opportunity to process information or explore ideas in ways that otherwise would not be possible.

Cooperative Learning Groups

Cooperative learning groups are often limited to four members each. Jay McTighe and Frank T. Lyman, Jr.[17] advise that those four members initially form two-member teams teacher guidance and necessary cooperation involved preclude such common abuses of group work as "coasting" by some while others do all the work; children become true "partners in learning."

Think-Pair-Share

Cooperative learning groups are often limited to four members each. Jay McTighe and Frank T. Lyman, Jr.[17] advise that those four members initially form two-member teams to participate in cooperative discussions called *think-pair-share* as a foundational experience in partnership learning. Think-pair-share is a discussion cycle in which all students are presented with a question and given time to think individually, talk with each other in pairs, and finally share responses with the larger group. Each phase is special, with distinct responsibilities required of the students. The teacher signals children to switch from observing some type of presentation to the *think, pair,* and *share* modes by using cues. McTighe and Lyman suggest hand signals similar to those illustrated in Figure 7–7. Printed cards labeled with the four cues or illustrated cartoon figures may also be used.

Cuing has enabled teachers to manage the efforts of the group more effectively by focusing the children's attention on a response process, rather than encouraging the

FIGURE 7–7
Hand Cues for Think-Pair-Share Experiences

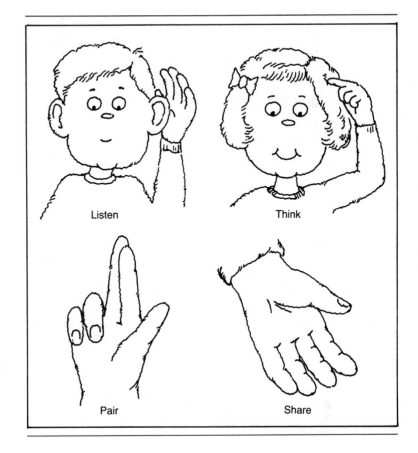

impulsivity that normally surfaces when children respond to questions in traditional recitation models of instruction. A basic script for the think-pair-share procedure follows:

1. Children witness a presentation.
2. The teacher poses a question while giving the listening cue.
3. The teacher signals the children to think silently by using the thinking cue.
4. The children are given 3–10 seconds of silent thinking time after the question has been posed.
5. The teacher offers the pairing cue and encourages the partners to share their thoughts with one another.
6. The children are given a sharing cue and raise their hands on that signal to give a response.
7. A "wait time" (3-second pause) after each response is recommended as a means to encourage deeper listening and thinking.
8. Students may write, diagram, or express their thoughts in a number of other ways.

The strengths of the think-pair-share approach are: (1) it involves all children in a response mode to a discussion starter rather than only one or two at a time; (2) it promotes student involvement and increased verbal interaction; and (3) the cuing system helps the teacher to manage classroom learning effectively and efficiently.

Numbered Heads Together

Spencer Kagan has created a *numbered heads together* approach to cooperative learning. It involves a simple, four-step cooperative structure:

1. The teacher has students count off within groups, so that each student has a number: 1, 2, 3, or 4.
2. The teacher asks a question.
3. The teacher tells the students to "put their heads together" to make sure that everyone on the team knows the answer.
4. The teacher calls a number (1, 2, 3, or 4), and the students with that number can raise their hands to respond.[18]

Kagan reports that positive interaction and individual accountability are both included in this approach since "the high achievers share answers because they know their number might not be called, and they want their team to do well. The lower achievers listen carefully because they know their number might be called."[19] Other cooperative learning structures are useful in the social studies program. A list of major structures and their functions are contained in the following resource:

> Spencer Kagan, *Cooperative Learning Resources for Teachers* (San Juan Capistrano, CA: Resources for Teachers, 1989).

Jigsaw

The *jigsaw* model is most effective when students are given a great deal of narrative material. The teacher starts the jigsaw process by assigning students heterogeneously to groups of four members each. After the students are assigned, the teacher allows a short meeting, during which the group members select a team name. Each team then constructs a display chart indicating their team name and membership. The teams then follow these procedures:

1. Students are given books to read, stories to listen to, videotapes to watch, or other highly narrative content learning experiences.
2. After completing the learning experience, each member of the study team is assigned an "expert topic." Jamaal, for example, was assigned to be his "Giants" team's expert on the topic, "How did the steam engine help bring about rapid changes in the Industrial Revolution?" The other three members of the Giants were assigned different topics related to the Industrial Revolution. The same four topics are assigned to each of the members of the other jigsaw teams.
3. All students with the same topic leave their base group and meet together to devise the best response to their questions. Jamaal, then, would leave his Giants team to join with experts from each of the other teams. When the experts achieve a clear

understanding of their topic, they work together devising a plan to present their information to the members of their respective base teams.

4. When all experts master their topics, the base teams are reassembled and the experts teach their group members about their special topics.

Determining Group Composition

The two-person groups should be given many opportunities to work together on common experiences. Eventually, they will be combined into four-member *heterogeneous* teams, set up according to the students' abilities (see Figure 7–8). List the students according to ability in the social studies and assign numbers according to how many teams you want. To ensure variety of exposure, you will need to reshuffle some of the names to balance gender, race, or ethnic backgrounds and to avoid combinations of children who may create discipline problems.

It is wise not to allow the groups to stay together for the entire year; most teachers prefer to change teams every month. Keep records of your changes, however, for most children appreciate the opportunity to be teammates with everyone in the class.

Behaviors in Cooperative Groups

Numerous interpersonal skills affect the success of cooperative learning groups. Among the most important are what David W. Johnson and Roger T. Johnson refer to as *forming* skills. According to these authorities, forming skills are those skills directed toward organizing the group and establishing minimum norms for appropriate behavior. Some of the important behaviors in this category are:

1. Move into cooperative learning groups without undue noise and without bothering others: Work time in groups is a valuable commodity, and little time should be spent rearranging furniture and moving into learning groups. Students may need to practice

FIGURE 7–8

A Strategy for Establishing Heterogeneous Groups According to Social Studies Ability

	Student	Group			Student	Group
1.	Darcee	1		11.	Jeff	1
2.	Warren	2		12.	Inez	2
3.	Holly	3		13.	Patrick	3
4.	Ahmad	4		14.	Greg	4
5.	Johnny	5		15.	Linda	5
6.	Penny	5		16.	Mack	5
7.	Mike	4		17.	Bobby	4
8.	Luis	3		18.	Eugene	3
9.	Nate	2		19.	Robin	2
10.	Carla	1		20.	Felicia	1

the procedure for getting into groups several times before they become efficient in doing so.

2. Stay with the group: Moving around the room during group time is nonproductive both for the student doing it and other group members.

3. Use quiet voices: Cooperative learning groups do not need to be noisy and can learn to work very quietly. Some teachers assign one student in each group to make sure that everyone speaks softly.

4. Encourage everyone to participate: All group members need to share their ideas and materials and be part of the group's efforts to achieve. Taking turns is one way to formalize this.

5. Other necessary social skills include:
   a. Use names.
   b. Look at the speaker.
   c. No "put-downs."
   d. Keep one's hands (and feet) to one's self.[20]

Assigning Roles

In order to promote involvement in the actual cooperative learning group, you might want to assign specific roles to the students. One child may be the group *captain,* responsible for organizing and coordinating the group's efforts. The *recorder* keeps the official written record of the group's work. The *reporter* informs the rest of the class of the group's actions or decisions, and the *monitor* assumes responsibility for gathering and replacing supplies or equipment. Naturally, they all operate as a team, embracing the "sink or swim together" concept.

A Sample Cooperative Learning Episode

Cooperative learning can be easily adapted to any social studies learning objective, whether it involves textbook comprehension or problem solving (see Chapters 4 and 5). Here is how one teacher used cooperative learning groups to enhance his textbook program.

Mr. Stanchak established four-member groups prior to reading the textbook selection. He arranged each group around a table, making sure they could see each other. Mr. Stanchak introduced the reading selection according to the DLE procedure explained in Chapter 5. The selection was an account of the exploits of Harriet Tubman as she led slaves to freedom with the help of the underground railroad. The students were asked to read only the first half of the selection silently and then stop. Mr. Stanchak then posed the question, "How will Harriet Tubman lead other slaves to freedom in the North?" while giving the children a "listening cue." The children were then given a "thinking cue" and provided with ten seconds to predict the solution. Mr. Stanchak followed with a "pairing cue" and encouraged group members to share their ideas, reaching consensus on the ones they considered most plausible. They were then given a "sharing cue" which signaled them to share their predictions with one another. A wait time of 3 seconds was given to encourage deeper thought. Then the students completed the reading selection and compared the actual events to their predictions.

Tom Bernagozzi has used cooperative learning groups quite extensively in his elementary school classroom. He points out these pitfalls and benefits of the approach:

> Of course, cooperative learning can intensify personality conflicts. At first, some children hold on to their prejudices and don't want to work with their teammates. Loners can find it hard to share answers. Aggressive children try to take over. Some bright students tend to act superior. But these problems are typical of any classroom and needn't be barriers to cooperative learning . . .
> Then there are the benefits. Watching students adjust to cooperative learning must be something like watching survivors on a life raft. Students quickly realize that they'll either sink or swim together. They learn to be patient, less critical, and more compassionate. If they see a teammate in need, they go to his aid . . . Many times I'd stand back, watch the teams, and think: *This is what good teaching and learning should look like.*[21]

There are no firm answers on how far and fast to go while implementing cooperative learning in your classroom. You must trust your own judgment and expand the approach to meet your own needs and style.

Group work skills develop over an extended period of time through much practice. Working with others for special purposes is a developmental process that needs carefully sequenced experiences throughout the elementary school grades. Beginning in the early grades you will want to plan gradual transitions from whole-class projects to coordinated small-group activities established for special purposes. Inherent in such a scheme is a gradual transformation of classroom space arrangements and work habits to encourage greater individual emphasis in the social studies program. Movable tables, desks, and chairs offer much flexibility. Figure 7–9 shows classroom arrangements for accommodating group projects. There are many variations of these examples, but the point is that the physical arrangement of the classroom should be such that children can easily discuss, share materials, and carry through projects in comfortable, stimulating work areas.

Cooperative learning is certainly a valid purpose for grouping students for social studies instruction, but there are other worthwhile reasons to group youngsters. As your teaching objectives change to meet the special needs and interests of your children, so should your approach to grouping change. In other words, effective grouping involves *flexibility*. More suggestions for effective cooperative group functioning are offered in these books:

David W. Johnson and Roger T. Johnson, *Learning Together and Alone: Cooperation, Competition, and Individualization* (Englewood Cliffs, NJ: Prentice-Hall, 1987).

David W. Johnson and Robert T. Johnson, *Circles of Learning: Cooperation in the Classroom* (Alexandria, VA: Association for Supervision and Curriculum Development, 1986).

Robert E. Slavin, *Cooperative Learning* (New York: Longman, 1983).

FIGURE 7–9

Classroom Arrangements Designed to Accommodate Group Projects

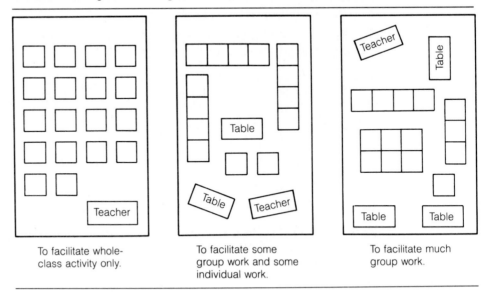

| To facilitate whole-class activity only. | To facilitate some group work and some individual work. | To facilitate much group work. |

Robert E. Slavin et al., eds., *Learning to Cooperate, Cooperating to Learn* (New York: Plenum Press, 1985).

Robert E. Slavin, *Student Team Learning* (Washington, DC: National Education Association, 1986).

Interest Groups

One of the benefits of cooperative learning is that students who have opportunities to work with others on areas of common interest become more personally involved in social studies instruction. Common interest binds the members together and creates a high level of motivation and self-direction. Generally, children who have similar interests in a subject come together and supplement the ideas found in their textbook by preparing a group project. One teacher, after using the DLE format to lead his class through textbook readings on various communities, decided that specialized group work would help establish the generalization that people work together to get things done. The following illustration describes how that teacher, Mr. Long, organized interest groups following textbook reading with his second graders.

First, the children read about different kinds of communities (urban, suburban, rural) and about the ways that people work together in communities to get things done. Mr. Long sensed a great deal of remaining interest in the topic and knew the children enjoyed working together on special projects dealing with social studies topics. So he planned a whole-class discussion about what projects the children might be interested in doing.

MELVIN: We could build a model of our community showing where all the houses and buildings are.

ANEATRA: I'd like to do a big painting to show how a large town gets its bread.

ROBERT: I've been collecting pictures of people doing different jobs in the community. Could we make a bulletin board showing all the special community workers?

As the children contributed their ideas, Mr. Long wrote them on the chalkboard, guiding the whole group as they became involved in the process of planning together. Intermittently, Mr. Long reinforced ideas with supportive phrases such as, "I think that's a great idea," or "You're really cooking today." In this way, he not only received a great number of ideas, but he also encouraged the others to listen to the ideas as they were offered.

MR. LONG: We have some wonderful ideas here. I'm proud of the exciting projects you suggested. Now take a few minutes to think about the project you would most like to work on.

After allowing the children a short time to plan, Mr. Long listed children's names beneath each project title he had written on the board.

MR. LONG: How many of you would like to work on the model of our community? (and so on).

After all the interest groups were formed, they examined the room to decide where they would need to work. One group chose the large worktable for their community model; the group collecting pictures of community workers pushed together a group of desks to form their work area near the large bulletin board; and the group planning the large painting decided to tape a large sheet of butcher paper to a blank wall along the back of the room. The next day, the groups planned their work and selected materials to begin their projects. They collected boxes, colored paper, scissors, paste, thumbtacks, old magazines, and other items.

MR. LONG: Now that each group has organized itself and is ready to begin work, I'd like to have you think about using the next two social studies class periods to finish your projects. I'll walk around from group to group to help if you have any problems.

Mr. Long visited each group for a short period during this planning day to see that each boy or girl had a fair amount of work to do. He was pleased to see that the community model group had divided itself further into downtown, park, and residential subgroups. The work progressed satisfactorily as the children shared their ideas and tried to make each project successful. On the second day, however, an important problem surfaced within the community model group: the children from the residential area subgroup had made their streets from white construction paper, while the downtown subgroup had chosen black. When both parts were put together on the second day, the difference was apparent. The teacher asked both subgroups to talk to find out what could be done to solve their problem. Finally, after a short deliberation, the residential subgroup decided that "dark is more like what streets really are."

As with the community model group, the children on the bulletin board group worked cooperatively to complete their project. They searched through magazines in the classroom and at home to find pictures that best illustrated the types of communities and people they read about in their textbooks. They cut out the pictures, mounted them with paste on colorful construction paper, and tacked them to the bulletin board. They worked well together, combining their efforts and ideas.

All of the interest groups worked together to complete their special projects. When they were completed, Mr. Long brought together the entire class and invited each interest group to share its results.

Mr. Long successfully used interest grouping for purposes directly related to textbook reading: (1) he helped reinforce the information presented by involving children in the projects, (2) he deepened the idea that things are done better when everyone works together and helps one another, whether in a community or a classroom, and (3) he provided a "hands-on" experience through which children were able to learn more readily and able to channel their creativity.

You should form interest groups according to these general criteria:

- Discuss the topic of study with the children to see what interests have developed (plan together).
- Invite the children to associate themselves with the group in which they have the most interest.
- Allow the groups to participate in a planning session to decide where they will work on their projects and what materials they will need.
- Give the groups enough time to complete their projects.
- Serve as a facilitator during the project work periods: be available to talk with children about special problems, offer suggestions, give verbal support, and so on.
- Bring together the entire class for each group to share the results of their efforts.

Research Groups

Grouping children for research on special topics is similar to interest grouping. Under research grouping, though, children are brought together to collect and organize information beyond that provided by their textbooks for the purpose of sharing it with others in oral or written reports, art or construction activities, creative skits, and so on. Research groups can also be formed when children become especially interested in studying a specific topic. Somewhat related to *inquiry* and *problem solving* (Chapter 5), special research groups delve into supplementary materials to deepen their understanding of the general textbook information or to compare sources of information to judge whether the textbook was accurate in its interpretations.

Here is an example of one teacher's approach to grouping children for research purposes.

Ms. Javier led her fifth-grade children through several lessons from their textbook focusing on change within urban society. Yesterday in this suburban schoolroom, the class read about and discussed how modern technology brought about new forms of city transportation—especially the role of automobiles in the rise of suburbs. To review yesterday's lesson, Ms. Javier asked this question:

Ms. JAVIER: How did new transportation technology affect life in the cities?

BETH: It gave people a chance to spread out and move to the suburbs.

Ms. JAVIER: That's good, Beth. The automobile, especially, meant that people could move to the suburbs if they wanted to. But we're facing a problem in our country today that makes it harder for people to live in the suburbs and causes many families to move back to the cities. Can anyone tell me what it is?

RUSSELL: The high cost of gasoline. I hear my parents talking about it all the time.

Ms. JAVIER: Yes, Russell, you're correct. Let's keep in mind that gasoline is expensive but that some families would rather live in the suburbs than move back to the city. What could they do?

(Children give no response, but are obviously interested.)

Ms. JAVIER: Let's look at the map and find our community, Oakdale. Suppose you want to go from Oakdale to Stuart's Department Store in downtown Metropolia. Who will come to the map and find Oakdale? That's it, Juanita, keep your finger on the place. And now, we need someone to locate Stuart's in the center of Metropolia. Very good, Robin. Now, Juanita, mark Oakdale with your red crayon and Robin, mark downtown Metropolia with your green crayon. We must find out about traveling from Oakdale to Metropolia.

At this point, Ms. Javier established three research groups. Research Group 1's role was to study the large map to determine whether any public transportation was available for their trip. If so, the children were to name the various forms (train, bus, etc.), describe the routes, compare travel times of each with the automobile, examine the differences in cost, and decide which route they would take, evaluating advantages and disadvantages of each. Ms. Javier helped the children by providing brochures, timetables, and the like. Research Group 2's role was to design a survey questionnaire to use while interviewing citizens of Oakdale to determine what places in the city are traveled to most regularly and how the people get to those places. These are sample questions:

Oakdale Elementary School
Transportation Survey

1. Where do you go?
   ☐ Park
   ☐ Movies
   ☐ Shopping

2. How do you get there?
   ☐ Bus
   ☐ Car
   ☐ Walking

The children were to tally their results to identify the means of transportation used most often. Research Group 3's role was to predict and hypothesize about future transportation innovations. The group was challenged to consider the current energy situation and to create new ways to travel from their suburban community, keeping in mind that all gasoline-powered vehicles would be banned for public transportation.

Each group was given three class periods to collect its data and plan a method of sharing them with their classmates. This type of sharing brought together all aspects of the problem examined by the children.

Research groups using textbook study should be formed along these guidelines:

- Establish a firm foundation of information from the textbook.
- Create a puzzling dilemma related to the topic so the children will be motivated to explore ideas beyond the textbook.
- Group children to explore various phases of the dilemma.
- Supply research materials or encourage the children to uncover their own data through interviews and survey techniques.
- Allow the children ample time to complete their separate areas of research.
- Be available for each group during the research time. Talk with children, offer encouragement, stimulate thinking, and so on.
- Ask each group to share the results of its work with the rest of the class.

Ability Groups

Grouping children according to mastery of skills or understandings is a popular practice, especially for subjects such as reading or arithmetic. In social studies, ability groups are formed by dividing children into groups of somewhat equal ability in performing certain skills such as reading maps. Children who have been evaluated as better map readers are placed in one group, and the others in one or more additional groups. The organization we often find in ability grouping is this:

1. Children who are ready for grade-level work.
2. Children whose ability exceeds grade-level work.
3. Children whose ability is much below grade-level expectations.

Because these children require different instruction as well as different materials, teachers often divide their classes into three groups whenever appropriate instructional goals dictate. This group plan gives the teacher a valuable framework upon which to develop meaningful, individualized instruction. Used properly, ability groups narrow the range of differences teachers face during any instructional period and help to focus on the needs of specific children.

Despite these advantages of ability grouping, there are serious objections to the way grouping methods are used. For example, once three ability groups are established at the beginning of the school year, there is rarely any change in composition of groups throughout the year. The slow child is quick to discover his place in class, as is the superior child. Year-long membership in relative groups often stigmatizes the slower child and encourages snobbishness in the faster learner. Teachers often attempt to minimize stereotypes by labeling ability groups with names such as "Hummingbirds,"

"Bluebirds," and "Canaries," or "Steelers," "Cowboys," and "Rams." Despite such attempts, children *always* find out what their classification is. This fact gives rise to the major objection to ability grouping. Another serious objection is the tendency of teachers to use the same books to cover the same material with the children, but at a quicker pace (with enrichment activities to take up the extra time) for the faster children and a slower pace for the slow learners.

When grouping on the basis of ability, the key idea to remember in preventing these shortcomings is *flexibility*. As we recall from Taylor's talent totem pole (Chapter 3), children have different academically oriented characteristics and are above average in at least one. Therefore, if we are flexible in our reasons for grouping, we will find that a child may be in a low group for reading textbook assignments, but in a high group when designing a construction project, or vice versa. This point brings to mind a former sixth-grade student of mine named Robert, classified by all his previous teachers as "slow" and "disinterested." Predisposing Robert to a life as a dropout was incomprehensible to me, so I sought every avenue to get him interested in schoolwork and in school. How to do that with a 14-year-old sixth grader reading on a primer level? As it turned out, by involving Robert in projects where he experienced success rather than repeated failure, he soon became more spirited and involved in his work. Even though he had trouble with the easiest first-grade basal readers, Robert could read directions for construction activities and make things expertly—an outstanding craftsman. Assuming leadership in these kinds of social studies group projects brought great pride and joy to Robert while helping him win the respect and admiration of his classmates. Years after losing contact with Robert, I returned to visit the community and saw this ad in a local newspaper: "Robert _____ 's Construction Company." Robert now owned one of the most successful businesses in the area!

Of course, not all your slow learners will become as successful as Robert (and neither did mine), but should they not at least be given a chance to exploit their strengths rather than simply cope with their special needs? Whenever you group by ability in the social studies, keep the groups flexible and disband the groups once the needs have been addressed.

Here is one teacher's approach to ability grouping.

Mrs. Grego consistently observed her fourth-grade children to evaluate their map reading abilities and to discover, at their earliest stages, any problems in this skill. She tabulated her information on a large class summary sheet (Figure 7–10), and on the basis of her information, developed special instructional groups.

Her summary sheet shows that Mrs. Grego could put Margaret and John (among others) into a group in which material for promoting skills in *reading cardinal directions* (north, south, east, and west) would be used. John, Theresa, Margaret, and Everett would be among those grouped for the purpose of reinforcing understanding of *map scale,* while David and Sara have indicated appropriate mastery of all necessary map reading skills and are ready for new, challenging encounters with enrichment activities. To facilitate success with appropriate materials, Mrs. Grego planned this activity for Group 1: Before being exposed to this direction reading activity, the entire class worked on points of direction in relation

FIGURE 7–10
Skill Mastery Summary Sheet

Longlake Elementary School
Class Summary Sheet

Student Name*	Recognizing Map Symbols	Locating Places	Reading Cardinal Directions	Understanding Map Scale	Reading Special Purpose Maps	Special Notes
Sara	✔	✔	✔	✔	✔	Plan enrichment project
Elnora	✔	✔	✔	✔	✔	
John	✔	✔				
Theresa	✔	✔	✔			
David	✔	✔	✔	✔	✔	Plan enrichment project
Margaret	✔	✔				
Everett	✔	✔	✔			

*Check indicates no need for special attention.

to the earth. In a series of outside lessons, the children's attention was called to the different positions of the sun at different times of the day until they understood the concept of east and west. North and south were established with a compass. Children played directional games such as "Simon says . . . girls take two steps south . . . boys turn to the east . . ." and so on. After these activities and some additional simple map work, Margaret and John still had difficulty reading directions on maps. To give them extra practice, Mrs. Grego prepared a "secret code map" which the two children were to follow until they found their special treat (Figure 7–11).

At the bicycle rack, John and Margaret found a note that read, "Go *east* to the sandbox. Read your next direction on the note in the pail." As the children went from location to location they were required to chart their course on the map Mrs. Grego provided. The last direction read, "You are here. The big round surprise is a basketball hidden behind the basket support. You may each shoot baskets for three minutes." Mrs. Grego checked their "secret code maps" to see if the directions were correctly plotted.

Keeping direct involvement in mind for the other children, Mrs. Grego provided each of the other groups with activities designed to reinforce or extend important social studies map reading skills. Other skills areas within the social studies should be reinforced and extended similarly: specialized reading skills such as word recognition or comprehension, reading charts and graphs, or independent study skills.

FIGURE 7–11
Map Reading Activity

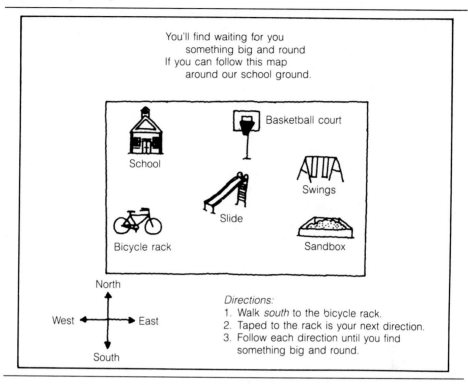

You'll find waiting for you
something big and round
If you can follow this map
around our school ground.

School

Basketball court

Swings

Slide

Bicycle rack

Sandbox

North

West ◄──────► East

South

Directions:
1. Walk *south* to the bicycle rack.
2. Taped to the rack is your next direction.
3. Follow each direction until you find
   something big and round.

When teachers use ability groups with textbooks, they should follow this basic format:

- Assess the special needs of your children.
- Group children on the basis of their needs.
- Disband the group once the needs are addressed.
- Establish a flexible grouping pattern.
- Be available for special help as each group works on its assignment.

Grouping children as a means to deal with individual differences can be a major contribution to the successful social studies program. Remember you must be flexible in your approach. A child may be in one group based on skills needs and in another organized for pursuing individual interests. A group experience must match its purpose, and the purpose is determined only after carefully observing the children.

Know your children well enough so that you can tell who are the most self-directed in their work. These should be the first to try a small-group project.

Start deliberately. Wait until you have established the appropriate rapport with and among the children.

Select a simple, well-defined task that the group can assuredly complete successfully.

Offer individual assignments for the rest of the class.

While the rest of the class is working, meet with the small group. Designate a leader and explain what learning resources the group members can use to complete their task.

Gradually introduce the small-group technique to one group at a time until the whole class is familiar with working that way. Acclimating the entire class to a pattern of small-group activity can take up to two months.

Since group work is to be as independent as possible, supervise only as needed. Be prepared to answer questions or redirect efforts, but resist the temptation to overdirect.

Evaluate group progress continually. As their work progresses, involve the children in class discussions about their abilities to follow group work standards. Keep a watchful eye on those who may not yet demonstrate an appropriate sense of responsibility. After you move these children into groups, it may be a mistake to remove them entirely for unacceptable behavior. You may want to cut back on the amount of time they spend in groups or even move the child to another group, but removing them eliminates the opportunity to learn the skills and behaviors they do not have.

DIFFICULTIES OF GROUP WORK

Group work in the social studies can present a few difficulties at any grade level. Recognizing these problems will help you stop them before complicated situations arise.

Initiating Grouping

Children who have never participated in grouping activities do not understand the techniques. Therefore, you must promote understanding by introducing the children to the procedure they will follow.

Children's Readiness for Group Work

Remember that some children, especially in the early primary grades, will not have the maturity necessary for sharing responsibilities and getting along with others. Functioning as a group member is a learning experience, so do not force children into it until they have shown appropriate readiness. For the reluctant child, plan individual activities but constantly encourage group orientation.

Dominating the Group

Often, one or two children seem to take over the group. These youngsters are forceful in their wishes and feel secure in speaking their minds on every issue, expecting the others to follow their lead. You should not attempt to quench the spirit of these leaders even when their viewpoints do not conform to the majority. Instead, encourage all children to speak their minds and to arrive at a decision on the basis of one of these three methods.

> *Consensus.* Perhaps the most appropriate technique for social studies groups, all members offer suggestions so that the group as a whole can agree on a common plan of action.
>
> *Compromise.* This technique is a form of "give and take" where members of a group with sharply conflicting ideas each modify their positions so that agreement can be reached.
>
> *Voting.* Perhaps the most popular decision-making process among children, this technique simply decides the direction of a group by moving toward the wishes of the majority of its members.

To illustrate how each of these techniques could be used to solve an impasse, consider the following:

> A sixth-grade class, while building a model of a Navajo Indian village, argued over the shape of the Navajo houses, called *hogans.* Some said the shape of the hogan under construction was right; others argued that something was wrong. The group decided to clear up the controversy by taking a vote. The vote ended up three to two in favor of the shape under construction, resulting in unhappy losers. The teacher joined the disagreement at this point and asked whether a satisfactory solution was arrived at through voting. "No," was the response, and further discussion ensued. The three children showed their teacher a picture of a crude brush and mud hut they had been using as their model. "But we saw other pictures of hogans showing much larger houses," argued the contenders. The teacher encouraged a library visit to relocate the pictures, and the group agreed to wait until the skeptics could compromise. Soon they returned, book in hand, ready to prove their point. Indeed, they found that the hogan under construction was like those from the primitive Navajo civilization, while the hogans researched by two children—large, permanent structures of earth-covered logs—were from a more advanced Navajo civilization. After a short discussion, the group agreed that their model village should show both types of hogans, one labeled "primitive" and the other "advanced." So in a very short time, the children moved from *voting* to *compromise* to *consensus.*

You should encourage children to handle their own problems in group settings, but be near to furnish appropriate guidance. In this way, children not only learn about social studies content in their group work, but also get firsthand experience in the operation of a democratic system of decision making.

SUMMARY

Effective group work in the social studies does not happen by chance; it involves special skills that need to be learned through experience over a period of time. Teachers need patience and understanding to help children develop group work skills; it is not until third or fourth grade that some children are socially mature enough to handle it. For that reason, the early primary grades provide many "readiness" experiences: a social climate in which children develop a positive sense of self, learn to understand others, relate to each other, and become comfortable and accepted in the classroom. Social learning activities (such as "puzzle squares") help children "try out" the roles of group members who work together to achieve a common goal. These direct learning aids help them construct their own guidelines for effective group membership. Eventually, the children learn to participate in special, flexible social studies groups such as whole-class groups, cooperative learning groups, interest groups, research groups, or ability groups that promote interaction and democratic action. These behaviors are important for many reasons, but they especially contribute to successful use of special social studies instructional techniques involving action learning and independent inquiry or problem solving where children must work individually or in small groups.

Group situations are valuable experiences for either directed instruction or discovery learning. They reflect the teacher's sensitivity to individual differences by adjusting the instructional program to children's needs and interests. Group work as a supplement to large-group instruction enhances children's achievement potential.

ENDNOTES

1. Rachel M. Lauer, in Mary Greer and Bonnie Rubinstein, *Will the Real Teacher Please Stand Up?* (Pacific Palisades, CA: Goodyear, 1972). p. 144.

2. *A Nation at Risk: The Imperative for Educational Reform* (Washington, DC: National Commission on Excellence in Education, 1983).

3. John I. Goodlad, *A Place Called School* (New York: McGraw-Hill, 1984).

4. Ernest L. Boyer, "What Teachers Say About Children in America," *Educational Leadership, 46*, no. 8 (May 1989): 74.

5. Ibid.

6. William Ayers, "Children at Risk," *Educational Leadership, 46*, no. 8 (May 1989).

7. Mary Alice Gunter, Thomas H. Estes, and Jan Hasbrouck Schwab, *Instruction: A Models Approach* (Boston: Allyn and Bacon, 1990), p. 169.

8. Tom Bernagozzi, "The New Cooperative Learning," *Learning, 88* (February 1988): 39.

9. James Flood, "The Text, the Student, and the Teacher: Learning from Exposition in the Middle Schools," *The Reading Teacher, 39* (April 1986): 784–791.

10. Roger T. Johnson and David W. Johnson, "Student-Student Interaction Ignored but Powerful," *Journal of Teacher Education, 36* (July–August 1985): 22–26.

11. Robert E. Slavin, *Cooperative Learning* (New York: Longman, 1983).

12. Ron Brandt, "On Cooperation in Schools: A Conversation with David and Roger Johnson," *Educational Leadership, 47,* no. 3 (November 1987): 14–25.

13. June Canty Lemke, "Developing Confidence: How Can We Help?" *The Journal of Early Childhood Teacher Education* 10:2, no. 31 (Spring 1989): 17.

14. James L. Hymes, Jr., *Teaching the Child Under Six,* 3rd Ed. (Columbus: Merrill, 1981), p. 97.

15. Selma Wassermann, "Children Working in Groups? It Doesn't Work!" *Childhood Education, 65,* no. 4 (Summer 1989): 205.

16. Lori Fisk and Henry Clay Lindgren, *Learning Centers* (Glen Ridge, NJ: Exceptional Press, 1974), p. 58.

17. Jay McTighe and Frank T. Lyman, Jr., "Cueing Thinking in the Classroom: The Promise of Theory-Embedded Tools," *Educational Leadership, 45,* no. 7 (April 1988): 18–24.

18. Spencer Kagan, "The Structural Approach to Cooperative Learning," *Educational Leadership, 47,* no. 4 (December 1989/January 1990): 13.

19. Ibid.

20. David W. Johnson and Roger T. Johnson, *Circles of Learning* (Washington, DC: Association for Supervision and Curriculum Development, 1984), pp. 45–46.

21. Tom Bernagozzi, "One Teacher's Approach," *Learning, 88* (February 1988): 43.

The opening day of elementary school is like an opening night on Broadway, with celebrities gathered to look one another over and then to see what the play is all about. As an audience waits expectantly for the opening curtain, so children enter classrooms in September with the hope that something is going to happen.[1]

—*Albert Cullum*

Enriching Instruction with
8 *Learning Centers*

As you read, reflect on the following matters:

- What is a learning center? How can learning centers contribute to the elementary school social studies program?
- For what purposes can social studies learning centers be created?
- How can centers be introduced and managed in the social studies program?
- How can teachers encourage children to make choices and assume responsibility for their own learning?

The elementary school social studies teacher uses movies, slides, books, bulletin boards, pictures, and many other teaching aids that contribute to the overall learning process. The strongest emphasis, however, is on the use of real things. You search for situations that involve direct experience and stimulate the children to ask "What is that? Where did it come from? What is it used for? What is it made from?" The answers need not always come from us, but from the children themselves as they explore and discover. We can make our classrooms places that provoke curiosity by nurturing children's natural responsiveness to life around them. The independence and activity of learning centers often meet this need.

"Learning center" is a loose term used to describe any area in the classroom where students can manage their own learning. Such centers represent educators' most recent efforts to individualize instruction. In England you will find entire classrooms organized into learning centers where students pursue individualized activities, but in the United States learning centers are most commonly used as additions to the traditional classroom setting.

TYPES OF CENTERS

Different purposes demand different types of learning centers in a social studies classroom. The centers may be designed: (1) to reinforce skills previously learned; (2) to acquire information through problem solving and inquiry; (3) to stimulate creativity; or (4) to examine attitudes and values. Most learning centers, though, can serve more than one purpose at a time. For example, a creativity-oriented learning center may have been designed to focus on the colonial art of quilting, but because of the nature of the activities, the center provides not only for creative expression but also for skills development (reading and following directions), research (finding out how quilting fit into the colonists' lives), and attitude response (reacting to a part of early colonial culture). This multipurpose aspect of center design should be considered as you organize social studies learning centers.

Reinforcement Center

Teacher A wanted his students to have many follow-up experiences with map symbol recognition after he introduced several new symbols to the entire class. He designed independent learning activities to provide extra practice; for example, one activity in his map skills reinforcement center consisted of a cigar box divided into two equal sections with a tagboard divider. In one section, he placed a number of "symbol cards"—cards on which map symbols were drawn. In the other section, he placed a number of "picture-word cards"—cards with drawings or photographs of each symbol along with the printed word. The teacher pasted two colorful hands on the inside cover of the cigar box, and put a drapery hook into each. The children were to hang a "symbol card" on one hand and the corresponding "picture-word card" on the other.

New Information Center

Teacher B wanted her pupils to explore on their own the advantages and disadvantages of working individually versus working cooperatively at different kinds of jobs. She set up a center that instructed students to perform a variety of tasks such as erasing the chalkboard, illustrating a story, drawing a picture, and moving a desk—first alone, then with another classmate. The children first recorded how long it took to complete different tasks by themselves and with a partner's help. Then they shared their reactions and conclusions.

Creativity Center

Teacher C wished to deepen her students' interest in poetry as an expressive medium of the Japanese culture. She introduced several forms of Japanese poetry to the class. They enjoyed interpreting the ideas and the techniques of each form. Then the teacher planned an independent learning center. She displayed pictures of Japan's scenic beauty and encouraged the children to compose haiku or tanka about them. The children drew their own illustrations for their poems and hung their finished products in the center.

Attitudes Center

Teacher D hoped to capitalize on the children's desire to talk about their personal wishes, hopes, and dreams. He constructed a "wishing well" by covering a large coffee can with construction paper and drawing lines to make the base look as though it were made of stone. He then made a canopy out of construction paper attached to dowel sticks that he taped inside the can. A series of sentence starters were written on slips of paper and placed inside the wishing well; for example, "When my friends talk about me, I wish they would say . . ." or "I wish the president of our country would . . ."

The children were to reach into the well and pull out a wish, then complete the sentence with a story: serious stories, funny stories, fantasies, or anything the child chose. The children had a choice of posting their stories, signed or unsigned, on a wishing well bulletin board or putting them into folders to show the teacher.

CONSTRUCTING LEARNING CENTERS

After establishing the purposes for a social studies learning center, you must plan the center. There is no magic formula for defining learning center patterns, but two key elements for establishing successful centers are the methods of putting together the center and presenting directions for students.

Pupils' Needs and Interests

Direct observation of children at work or play, some simple pretesting techniques (your own or standardized tests, skills analysis checklists, attitude surveys), and careful consideration of the children's cumulative records will help determine the children's needs and interests. Most important is direct feedback from the children in terms of their reactions to the materials you select for each learning center.

Activities and Materials

Appealing activities with *concrete materials* (*realia*) can provide exciting learning experiences for children (Figure 8–1). A variety of *audiovisual materials* can also be used to accomplish specific learning center purposes. Tape recorders, film loops, instructional kits, and so on may at times be the most appropriate means to present, reinforce, or enrich a concept. Children enjoy working with learning center materials such as these and, given proper instruction and guidance, can soon be trusted to use the machines independently.

Children prefer *manipulative activities* when they work independently. Materials for these activities may include commercial, teacher-made, or "junk" items. Teachers and children can find tools for learning in the home, school, and community. Some materials for designing various manipulative activities are tin cans or film containers

FIGURE 8–1
Appealing Activities with Concrete Materials

with lids, tools (e.g., hammers, saws, nails), yarn and cloth scraps, broken appliances, styrofoam of all kinds, clean milk cartons, frozen food trays, egg cartons, lumber scraps, shoe boxes, old telephone directories, plastic buckets.

Game boards stimulate children; teachers frequently comment on how much children enjoy game-oriented center activities. Games give children the same practice they get through traditional drill or worksheet activity, but in a more enjoyable form. Game boards are generally used in reinforcement centers, since they involve activities that promote reinforcement of previously taught ideas or skills. You must carefully evaluate achievement levels within the class with respect to a particular skill so the game is neither too hard nor too easy. If the game is too easy, there is probably no need for practice in that skill (unless the purpose is to build independence or self-confidence). If the game is too hard, it will be frustrating, and constant failure will kill the children's motivation. Ideally, a game should be designed so that winning or losing depends on the children's ability to employ effective strategy to contend with the vagaries of chance. When games combine luck and skill, they keep competitiveness in balance; while motivating children to use their best skills, they also allow children to accept defeat graciously and realistically.

I will mention a few basic formats in board games that seem to be exceptionally popular with elementary school children. Each of these boards can be used for any area within the social studies curriculum. You can print the tasks on the game board squares or prepare a deck of cards with content questions or skills activities. For example, the cards may require the child to identify pictures, furnish definitions for words, or associate states and capitals. To differentiate between easier and harder tasks, you can have the card specify the number of spaces a player can move, with answers to harder questions allowing children to move more spaces. Or place movement may be left to chance, with spinners or dice determining the number of spaces to be moved. For example, a child could roll a die and draw a card from a deck. If the child can do successfully what the card asks, he gets to move the number of spaces shown on the die. If he can't, the card is placed at the bottom of the deck and the child must remain where he is until his next move. The game continues until one player reaches the finishing point. In this way, children may get a second chance to remember the right answer for the missed question if it comes up again later. To help sustain interest in game boards, you can include reward and punishment cards as well as skill cards in the deck; a spaceship race game board might contain cards like those shown in Figure 8–2.

Hundreds of start-finish game board ideas are possible for the imaginative teacher. How many can you add to this list?

Reach a pot of gold at the end of a rainbow

Have a cat catch a mouse

Shoot a rocket to the moon

Have a magnetized ladybug climb a stem to reach a flower

The same basic format can be followed to design game boards for soccer, football, baseball, tennis, volleyball, or other popular sports. Questions or tasks can be printed

FIGURE 8–2
Sample Reward and
Punishment Cards

in the circles or squares on the board, which gives the game a limited life span, or the teacher can write rewards and punishments on the board and put questions and tasks on separate cards that can be changed as needed.

Imaginative teachers have created interest and enthusiasm among their children by designing novel *independent written activities* as shown in Figure 8–3. Commercially prepared materials can also be used in learning centers. Many good learning center games and activities are being marketed; take advantage of them.

Number of Activities

The particular content of the learning center, as well as the special needs and interests of your students, dictates the number of activities you will need for the center. Don't overwhelm the children by planning more than they can handle and don't provide them with such unattractive or unchallenging activities that interest in the center soon wanes. Don't hesitate to change or drop an activity if it seems indicated. Experience in using a learning center approach and observing children at work in centers will show you what constitutes an appropriate number and variety of activities.

Successfully Completing a Task

Build into the learning center some means or device so the children can tell immediately whether they have completed a task successfully. Provide a special answer key at the center for immediate reference, or place the answers on the reverse side of the activity card. Another approach to feedback is to use a code. Letters or numerals can be placed on the reverse side of the activity cards, and matching symbols on the bottoms of cans, cartons, or boxes into which the cards are to be sorted. Symbol or color codes can also be used. Children match colors or pictures to check their answers. Some activities are self-correcting by design; for example, when puzzle pieces fit together, they show the student she is correct.

Center directors may correct the children's work, or teacher's aides, parent volunteers, older students, or classmates who have completed the activity can do it. Teacher-student conferences are often used in addition to self-evaluation. They are especially useful as feedback for creative activities that have no one correct answer, or when the teacher wants to know more about the children's attitudes toward the activities in the

FIGURE 8–3
Sample Surprise Cards

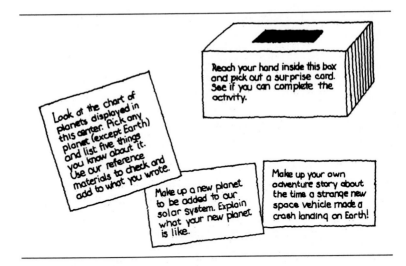

centers. Of course, diagnostic information about the child's growth in skill or concept development also emerges as the teacher asks questions or observes pupil performance in activities.

Directions

Giving clear directions enables the children to use the learning center activities independently. In addition to carefully introducing the children to each center activity and thoroughly explaining how to use it, clear directions should be displayed so the children will be constantly aware of the center's organizational patterns and can function independently.

Carefully print or type the directions. Be economical with your words. The nature of a learning center requires that children work independently, so make sure all of them understand the vocabulary. Avoid unnecessary words; for example, don't say, "Get some crayons. Find the stack of drawing paper. Take a piece of paper and draw a winter scene." Instead, say, "Draw a winter scene." The materials should be provided right at the center. Underline or highlight key words that are essential for completing an activity; for example, "*Draw* a picture of . . ." Whenever possible, use action words to begin directions; for example, "*Look* carefully at the picture . . ."

Enumerate the directions in proper sequence; for example, "*First,* ask fifteen classmates to name their favorite rock stars. *Second,* list the names of the stars in order so that the most popular star is first, etc. *Third,* compare your list with a classmate's list. Are your lists the same or different? Why do you think this is so?" Include pictures or hand-drawn illustrations to help students who may have difficulty reading printed directions. A drawing of a pencil can illustrate a writing task or a picture of scissors a cutting task. Tape record the learning center directions for the very young child or the child who has extreme reading difficulties.

Providing examples in the directions is helpful. Whenever possible, try to make the directions open-ended; that is, encourage the child to extend the activity into a new area of interest; "How would the results be different if . . ." or "Compare your results with a friend. Why are they the same? Different?"

Explain in the directions how the finished work will be evaluated: an answer key? Answers on the reverse side of the material? Covered answers? Tell them what will be done with the finished work.

Attractive Backgrounds

Children respond favorably to unique packaging techniques. Capitalize on this by providing a colorful background picture accompanied by a catchy caption to attract attention. Place the directions in a strategic spot on the center background. If you are not a great artist, don't despair; you can obtain pictures for center backgrounds from several sources. Commercially prepared transparencies can be projected on a sheet of oaktag. Trace around the image with a marking pen and color in the areas with other marking pens, crayons, or paint. You can also prepare your own transparencies by running a favorite picture through a thermofax machine or tracing it on a sheet of clear acetate. Use an overhead projector and follow the preceding procedure. Pictures can also be projected onto a sheet of oaktag with an opaque projector. Instead of projecting an image for tracing to create your center background, you can simply cut out illustrations from magazines and newspapers, store displays, advertising circulars, and coloring books and paste the pictures on heavy tagboard.

In addition, plan to create centers in a variety of shapes and place them in different spots in the classroom (see Figure 8–4). Learning centers should contain a number of activities necessary to complete an objective, that are multilevel in nature when the children differ in achievement levels. Three decisions you face in using a learning center format in the social studies classroom are (1) familiarizing students with the organization and management patterns; (2) deciding when the centers will be used; and (3) assigning students to the centers.

INTRODUCING CENTERS

Since children need careful guidance with any new classroom procedure, an introduction to learning centers is no place to hurry. Introducing children to this new classroom learning arrangement all at once by setting up a room full of centers and expecting each child to work independently with little or no introduction may be devastating to both teacher and child. The analogy of the tortoise and the hare is apropos; staring out quickly with learning centers, you may find that the children do not understand what to do with them, even though they are enthusiastic and all too willing to rush headlong into them—just like the hare in the race. Instead, slow the children down and give more careful guidance to introduce the bridge between what may have been a formal classroom environment and the new learning center environment. To introduce learning centers, it is better to adopt the tortoise's gait rather than the hare's, establishing a starting point and proceeding very slowly while clearly explaining every step to the

FIGURE 8–4

Sample Learning Center Locations

children. Gradually, you will find that your classroom is operating smoothly and efficiently, without the setbacks that befall an impulsive and hasty teacher.

Inform students about how the learning centers are to be used. Don't get involved with detailed educational jargon, but explain these points simply:

■ What kinds of activities are available at each center
■ When the centers are to be used
■ How each center is to be used

- How the children are to be assigned to the various centers
- What responsibilities the children who are working at the centers have
- What is to be done with the work that has been completed

Tell the children of your availability for the social studies time slot. You will need to divide your time among activities such as giving individual or group assistance, holding conferences, special teaching to small groups, and guiding whole-group projects. Making your plans known to the children helps them in self-direction and in formulating their own plans for the class time.

Since no single way of introducing learning centers has proven best, all decisions should reflect the children's needs as well as the teacher's experience. Howes[2] suggests three possible variations:

1. The teacher introduces and explains the new way of working to a few of the more mature students. Others are invited to participate as the teacher forms new groups, with the experienced children serving as leaders. Gradually, the entire class makes the change to the open classroom.
2. The teacher divides the class into four equal groups on a heterogeneous basis. The fourth group is introduced to the new program as the other three pursue their usual studies. The teacher rotates the pattern so that each group works part of the day in the new pattern and part in the old pattern. Gradually, the time is lengthened for each group to work in the new program.
3. The whole class is introduced to the new way of working and the teacher continues the normal studies for those children who are more comfortable continuing in the traditional pattern. Gradually, more and more children begin to spend more time in the new way of working until a complete change is made.

USING THE CENTERS

Along with deciding how to introduce the new centers, you must identify when to use them most advantageously. Again, many different patterns have been tried successfully. You may decide, for example, to use the centers as a supplement to the social studies curriculum. Remember that slower-paced students are often unable to complete assigned work in time to use the centers and may feel frustrated when they don't have a chance to participate. By assigning realistic follow-up activities for meeting individual differences, however, the teacher can alleviate this problem. Your schedule might look like this:

9:00–9:20	Teacher-guided, whole-class activities (textbook assignment, resource person, film, etc.)
9:20–	Follow-up activities (workbook pages, special projects, etc.)
10:00–	Children work in learning centers

With this pattern, the children who finish their follow-up activities most quickly have more time to work in the learning centers. If you want all the children to work in the learning centers, you might schedule only teacher-guided activities for half an hour, then have all the children go to learning centers. Another alternative is to use the centers as the basis for all instruction in the social studies curriculum. A certain time of the day can be scheduled for the students to work individually or in small groups with concepts and skills introduced and reinforced in learning centers.

One word of caution: do not use learning centers as designated areas in which activities are isolated only for those who finish their assigned seatwork before the other children or for those who are ready for advanced enrichment activities. This limited interpretation contradicts the belief that children should take responsibility for their own learning. Pupil participation in the social studies learning centers should not be restricted to special times or to enrichment for the able learners. We risk a damaging blow to any interest the children may show to the approach by abusing centers this way.

The rate at which you can extend the use of learning centers will become apparent by the time you have followed some of these procedures. By thoroughly evaluating the children's capabilities for working with the centers, as well as observing their desire to work in a new classroom environment, you will begin to sense the amount of guidance necessary to move toward a completely decentralized approach to instruction.

When you have begun to introduce new centers and decentralize the surroundings, finding adequate space may pose a formidable problem. As shown in Figure 8–5, grouping desks may alleviate this problem and help you move to a less formal classroom setting. The transition from rows of desks to functional groupings of materials and equipment can be achieved in stages. Gradually, your room may evolve into an environment that encourages children to experience more and more physical and academic freedom. By removing some student desks, grouping others, bringing in

FIGURE 8–5
Formal to Informal

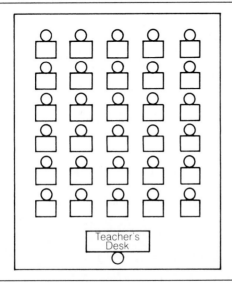 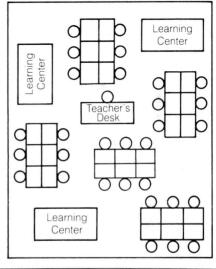

tables, placing bookcases and screens to serve as partitions, introducing a couch or pillows in a reading/research corner, the classroom atmosphere changes from a formal environment to an informal activity-oriented place where children have opportunities to work independently, by themselves or in small groups.

Organizing Routines and Student Assignments

The way you organize your classroom often affects to what extent the children will become absorbed in the learning center activities. It also determines the effectiveness of classroom management. You should:

>Separate areas that involve quiet activities from those that involve noisy activities
>
>Provide areas for individual work and areas for group interaction
>
>Reserve areas for displaying the children's work
>
>Make provisions for neat storage of supplies and materials
>
>Arrange adequate procedures for moving pupils to and from learning centers

The method of movement you decide on will closely reflect your personal educational philosophy, which will probably follow one of these patterns:

- Teacher makes all learning center assignments
- Teacher provides child with two or three alternatives and the child chooses from among them
- Teacher and children choose jointly from among all possible choices
- Children have free choice of all learning possibilities; teacher serves as a source for verification, classification, and evaluation

Scheduling

Among the scheduling procedures to consider are manipulative techniques, charts, and contracts.

Manipulatives

For younger children, planning guides should be as concrete as possible to help them understand what they are to do in the various centers. Having a manipulative visual plan also helps children use their work time appropriately. These are several concrete planning devices:

Coding.   Each center has an assigned number, color, and shape. Assigning a child to a center can be done with a ticket, necklace, badge, or other device that corresponds to the code.

Pictures.   Photographs of the children can be extremely useful in making center assignments. Take a picture of each child, mount it on a clothespin, and clip each to the center in which the child is to work.

Name Tags.   Write learning center titles on a large, sturdy cardboard circle. Place clothespins with the children's names on the corresponding centers for each time of the day.

Tickets.   Color code the centers. Use construction paper in corresponding colors to make tickets for admission to each center. The children match the colors of their tickets to the color symbol at the learning center.

Charts

As seen in Figure 8–6, charts are useful tools. Attach library book pockets to a firm sheet of tagboard. Place a child's name on each pocket. Print the names of the learning centers on card strips. Put the cards into the pockets to indicate the learning center at which each child is to work.

Contracts or Agreements

Contracts (some educators call them agreements) require students to sign up for the activities with which they will be working each day. With young children, the initial contract form should include pictorial symbols coordinated to symbols placed near or on the learning center. Gradually, the contract forms can become more abstract. Whatever the format for drawing contracts, the important outcome is that the children gain a sense of responsibility for following a daily or weekly planning guide.

Various formats for contracts progress from concrete to abstract representation of centers and from limited to greater student choice of which center to work in and of activities within a center. Also, as children gain experience in choosing and completing activities, they can take on greater responsibility for organizing their own time.

In Figure 8–7, the teacher assigns each child to a center. The child colors the circle with crayon to identify the center to which he has been assigned. The centers are color-coded.

FIGURE 8–6
Sample Chart

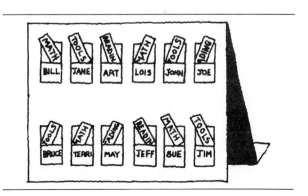

FIGURE 8–7
Color-coded Contract

FIGURE 8–8
Check-coded Contract

In Figure 8–8, the teacher puts checks in the circles to specify the one or two centers at which a child is to work. The child is free to choose one or two additional centers she would like to work in. The meeting box indicates a teacher- or pupil-initiated conference period.

The contract forms in Figure 8–9 are especially useful for project-oriented learning centers and call on the children to make long-range commitments to complete work in a chosen area of interest.

FIGURE 8–9
Project-oriented Contract

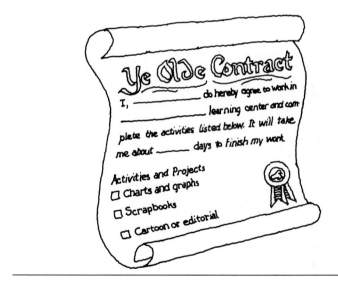

CONTRACT

I am interested in doing the following work in the

_____ learning center.

_____

_____

_____

I will spend about _____ minutes each day in
the center. It will take me about _____ days to
finish my work

SEAL
OF
APPROVAL

My signature

_____

Ye Olde Contract

I, _____ do hereby agree to work in
_____ learning center and com-
plete the activities listed below. It will take
me about _____ days to finish my work.

Activities and Projects
☐ Charts and graphs
☐ Scrapbooks
☐ Cartoon or editorial

Record Keeping

Effective record keeping is essential to the success of learning center-based instruction. With concise record-keeping forms, excessive paper work and hours of extensive review can be minimized. Forms of various design can be used to keep track of children's interests, involvement, skills, and deficiencies. Some of these forms can be completed by the children; others will have to be maintained by the teacher. A complete description of the many different individual and whole-class record-keeping instruments is beyond the scope of this book; however, a few general suggestions will stimulate your thinking toward formulating alterantive models.

Table 8–1 illustrates a whole-class record form. The *1* indicates that a child has contracted for the activity, while the + indicates that the activity has been satisfactorily completed.

Individual record sheets help the teacher develop a clear picture of each child's growth. Simple record forms prevent accumulation of volumes of information. Most of the data you record on the sheets are gathered from individual conferences. The conferences should be part of the teacher's daily work plan, with a definite time set aside for discussing each individual's progress.

In addition to formal conferences, a great deal of evaluation in the informal classroom occurs during planned group discussions. The teacher should schedule a short period (ten to fifteen minutes) to follow the use of learning centers for sharing ideas, comparing projects, talking about how children feel about the centers, and so on. Open discussion is an important and valuable experience in the classroom.

Besides planned and informal conferences with the children, various types of students record forms can be used to gather information about how meaningful, interesting, enjoyable, or appropriate the children find the centers. A sample student checklist is presented in Figure 8–10 for primary-grade youngers; for older children, you can use index cards and have them fill them in like this:

Another Day in the Life of _____		Date: _____
Center	Activity	My Personal Reaction

Initiating the Learning Center Experience

Trying something new is always a bit frightening. But you will know how effective you have been when you observe whether you are more relaxed, more stimulated, more excited about teaching and whether your children are more interested, more involved, and happier in school.

You will know whether it has been a profitable experience when you observe whether the children are developing proficiencies and skills in subject areas and whether they seem to be gaining self-confidence, initiative, and independence. You will know by their test scores, comments from their parents, and their motivation whether their achievement is the same, poorer, or better than it had been in a more formal learning

TABLE 8–1
Whole-class Record Form

Name	Map Center	Research	Construction	Games
Joe	1			+
Myra		1		+
Tom	1	+		
Jane			1	

environment. You will judge the impact of this approach on individual children. You will know which ones flourish in an environment that encourages responsibility for self-learning and which ones need more structure, more instruction, more outer controls. Eventually, you will be able to design a classroom flexible enough to meet almost all the children's needs.

Two learning center plans will help you begin to implement an informal approach to social studies instruction in your classroom.

Traveling Through Time

This learning center promotes concepts of colonial America. The center, designed to place the children in the role of problem solvers, requires them to research stimulating questions about colonial life. They record the information they uncover and design ways to share their findings creatively. The center should be stocked with a variety of books, maps, photographs, audiovisual aids, and any other learning resources that will help the students in their investigations (Figure 8–11).

Newspaper Notebook. Stock the center with appropriate reference materials about colonial America. Instruct the children to imagine that they have been taken back in history to the period of colonial America. To report back to their newspaper, they are to keep an accurate account of what happened on their time travels. The first four activities stimulate the creation of a newspaper story.

Map It Out. In your time capsule, there is a map that shows how America looked in the 1700s. Write the name of each of the thirteen English colonies on the map.

Take a Good Look. Children act as reporters and fill in the statement, "I landed at _____ . This is what I saw. . . ." Choose any place in colonial America where you imagine your time capsule landed. Draw the first four things you saw after you emerged from the time capsule.

Photo Album. You met a boy whose father was an important man in colonial history. Many people came to his house to meet with him. Draw a picture of the four most unforgettable people you met during your stay. Beneath each picture, describe the work that person was most famous for (Figure 8–12).

FIGURE 8–10
Primary-grade Student Checklist

FIGURE 8–11
Traveling Through Time

FIGURE 8–12
Photo Album

Newspaper Report. While your friend was doing his chores, he gave you a newspaper to look at. You realized that many important events were occurring in our country at that time. What events did you read about in the newspaper during your visit? Write the stories that go with the headlines and draw the picture (Figure 8–13).

Colonial Parade. Provide boxes, crêpe paper, tagboard, construction paper, clay, and other construction materials. The child is to select a scene, person, object, or event important in colonial history. She decorates a box with crêpe paper and construction paper to look like a parade float, as in Figure 8–14. She identifies her selection and constructs, mounts, or draws appropriate items on the box. Arrange the floats in parade fashion near the learning center display.

Colonial Hall of Fame. Create pedestals out of boxes mounted on heavy tagboard and display them at the learning center (Figure 8–15). The children each select a person who contributed a great deal to colonial life. They draw his or her picture, glue a tongue depressor to the back of the picture, and stick it in a pedestal. They write a short description of the chosen person's contributions and paste it on the pedestal below the picture. Add members to the "Hall of Fame" as children contribute their choices.

2100. Draw a large crystal ball on construction paper and mount it near the learning center (Figure 8–16). Instruct the children to imagine what their homes, city, or country will be like one hundred years from now. They write their ideas on circles cut out of construction paper and paste them on the crystal ball. Questions such as these will spur their thinking:

What will be the greatest invention?

Where will be the farthest place to which we will travel?

What will our school be like?

What will be the most popular sport?

What kind of transportation will be most popular?

What kinds of jobs will people be doing?

What kinds of foods will people eat?

What will have been done to cure hunger? Illness? Conflict among humans?

Look at Me!

A center like this one promotes creative self-expression and growth in values and attitudes. The activities at this center help children get to know themselves and each other better. They share facts, feelings, and experiences and become aware of how they see themselves, how they see others, and how others see them. They develop a sense of and a respect for the uniqueness of each human being. Some of the material that emerges is highly personal, and the teacher must exercise judgment about how to use and share it (Figure 8–17).

I Am Me.   Take a photograph of each child. Provide copies of a data sheet, as shown in Figure 8–18. Each child completes the information on the data sheet and pastes his picture at the top. The children hang their completed data sheets in the classroom for others to read and discuss. This activity must be completed before beginning the second activity.

Who Am I?   Provide a supply of white construction paper and marking pens. Instruct the children to use a strong flashlight or the light from the overhead projector to make a silhouette. To do this, one child sits in a chair between the strong light and a wall to which the construction paper has been tacked. Another child traces the silhouetted

FIGURE 8–13
Newspaper Headlines

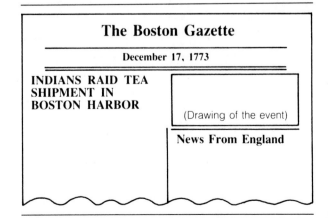

FIGURE 8–14
Parade Float

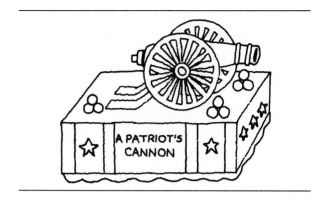

FIGURE 8–15
Pedestals

FIGURE 8–16
Crystal Ball

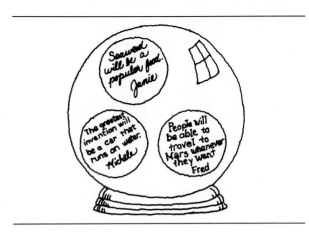

profile on the construction paper. Then they switch positions. When both have a profile, they draw or paste pictures on them to represent the information from their data sheets in the previous activity (Figure 8–19). Each day, display three or four completed silhouettes on the center background. Number them and have the children examine the silhouettes and guess who each one is. Guesses may be written on voting sheets. At the end of the day, reveal whose silhouettes were displayed and see how many correct guesses were made.

FIGURE 8–17
Look At Me!

FIGURE 8–18
Photograph and Data Sheet

I am _____

I am _____ years old.

My address is _____

My phone number is _____

My favorites:

Hobby _____ Color _____

Sport _____ Book _____

Food _____ Animal _____

My pet peeve is _____

FIGURE 8–19
Who Am I?

FIGURE 8–20
My Moods

My Mood Book.   In a box or envelope, put strips of paper identifying many different moods: happy, sad, angry, silly, afraid, disappointed, excited, nervous, frustrated. In another box, put a supply of white paper and cardboard picture frames. The child chooses a mood word and draws a picture of herself showing how she looks when she is in that mood. She pastes the picture in the frame, then writes a little story telling about a time she was in that mood. After the child has done a few mood stories, she can combine them into a book by punching holes and using paper fasteners or yarn, and making a cover, title page, and table of contents. Display the children's books in the classroom for everybody to read (Figure 8–20).

My Coat of Arms.   Prepare dittoed coats of arms, as illustrated in Figure 8–21. In each section, have children draw pictures or symbols, or write words, phrases, or sentences in response to questions you suggest. Display the finished products on an attractive bulletin board. Possible questions are "What three things are you good at in school? What is one thing you like to do most in our school? What would you like most to change

FIGURE 8–21
Coat of Arms

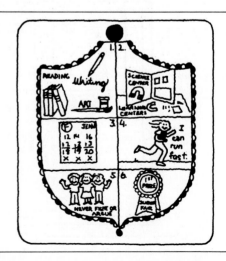

or improve about yourself at school? What is one thing your classmates admire about you? What one thing can your friends do to make you happy in school? What has been your greatest accomplishment in school?"

SUMMARY

There is no one definition that explains the term "learning center." Perhaps a major reason for this problem of definition is that learning centers are designed primarily to meet children's needs in unique ways. Because of this personalization, learning centers differ from one another much as children do, and it is as difficult to describe a typical learning center as it is to describe a typical child.

As they apply to the ideas in this book, learning centers are activities that organize individualized instruction in ways that encourage children to assume major responsibility for their own learning; thus, any independent activity in which the children provide major direction for their own learning is considered a learning center.

Different purposes determine what types of learning centers we find in a social studies classroom. The centers may be designed (1) to rein-

force skills previously learned, (2) to acquire information through problem solving and inquiry, (3) to stimulate creativity, and (4) to examine attitudes and values. After establishing the purposes for the centers, the teacher must plan their design. These guidelines will help in designing a social studies center: (1) analyze pupils' needs and interests; (2) choose effective, attractive activities and materials; (3) provide clear directions; and (4) create an attractive background display.

The activities and suggestions in this chapter reflect a step-by-step approach to changing the classroom setting; however, the sequence need not be followed slavishly. Choose the elements that are most appropriate to your children's needs and interests, and adapt or ignore those that do not appear to address individual needs adequately.

ENDNOTES

1. Albert Cullum, *Push Back the Desks* (New York: Citation Press, 1967), p. 13.

2. Virgil M. Howes, *Informal Teaching in the Open Classroom* (New York: Macmillan, 1974), pp. 197–198.

When you are ready to teach this child geography, you get together your globes and your maps; and what machines they are! Why, instead of using all these representations, do you not begin by showing him the object itself, so as to let him know what you are talking of? . . . [H]e will examine every new object for a long time. . . . He is thoughtful. . . . Be satisfied, therefore, with presenting objects at appropriate times and in appropriate ways. [Then, when] you see his curiosity fairly at work, ask him some . . . question which will suggest its own answer. . . . Leave him to himself, and he will be certain to think the matter over. . . .

In general, never show the representation of a thing unless it be impossible to show the thing itself.[1]

—Rousseau

9 *Selecting Instructional Resources*

KEY CONCEPTS

As you read, reflect on the following matters:

- What do appropriate learning resources contribute to the social studies program?
- Is there a classification system to aid teachers in selecting appropriate resources?
- How can teachers choose from among the abundance of social studies instructional resources those most likely to result in productive learning?
- What are the proper techniques teachers employ as they use various instructional resources?
- Why is it important to offer varied learning resources in the social studies classroom?

Τhis advice, offered by Jean-Jacques Rousseau hundreds of years ago, underscores the fervent interest people have maintained in providing meaningful learning experiences for children. That interest is still expressed in professional literature in words so similar to Rousseau's that it would be easy to surmise that his advice came from a current periodical.

INTAKE OF INFORMATION

Preparing children to cope with contemporary and future problems is an intriguing educational responsibility. An integral part of that responsibility is to help them develop the thinking skills necessary to take in, interpret, analyze, and evaluate social studies content. Learning materials help the teacher attain those goals by offering avenues for involving students in the instructional process. Figure 9–1 organizes the types of materials available for social studies classrooms into a cone of classroom experiences. The cone shows the most concrete, real-life experiences at its base and the most abstract at the summit. Social studies teachers usually begin instruction at the base— they provide many opportunities to examine the real and actual. Younger children especially need opportunities within this category, to see and do and explore. As they experience the concrete, the real, they begin to develop the solid base necessary for associating new ideas as they come along. With this foundation, children eagerly seek new ideas through alternative sources, and classroom teachers introduce learning experiences that move toward the top of the cone. With a concrete base, children gain a sense of more abstract learning experiences, including those that involve symbols, and are no longer locked into the world of their own experience. The urge to learn from others or from books quickly blossoms. A good social studies classroom, therefore, focuses on *balance*—the children see, hear, talk, taste, touch—*and* listen and read.

Most school districts encourage teachers to use a variety of materials in the social studies program because not all pupils learn in the same way, and different media appeal to different learning styles. Reading ranges among children in elementary classrooms are great, averaging three to five years in the lower grades and five to ten years in the middle and upper grades. Each of the media has particular strengths and limitations in the way it conveys messages; the impact of a message is likely to be stronger if more than one sensory system is involved in receiving it. Different sources can provide different insights on the same subject, while some discrepancies or inaccuracies may go undetected if a single source is used.[2]

Ways of Knowing

Jerome Bruner and his associates have identified three ways of knowing upon which I have based the cone of classroom experiences. These levels—*enactive, iconic,* and *symbolic*—describe the modes by which children organize and store concepts.[3] Children may need one type of experience as opposed to another for any given topic, or may need to use two or more of them together.

FIGURE 9–1
Cone of Classroom Experiences

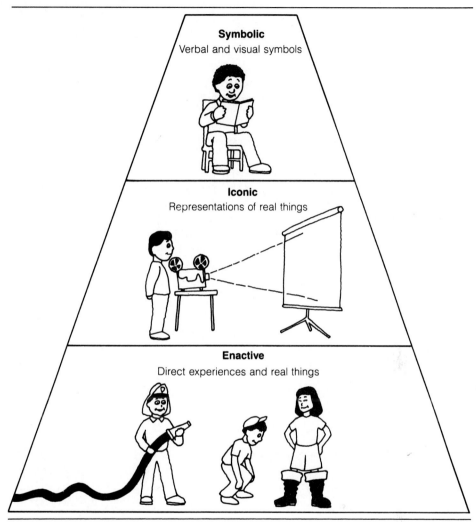

Symbolic
Verbal and visual symbols

Iconic
Representations of real things

Enactive
Direct experiences and real things

Enactive Mode

This mode of knowing involves all methods of *doing something,* whether making a recipe from Spain or playing a game from China. For some children, enactment is the best way of knowing. For example, if your objective is to develop concepts of how some Mexicans construct their homes from adobe brick, then the experience may begin with children actually mixing clay, straw, and water to make real adobe bricks (rather than using a less direct approach such as watching a film of the process).

Iconic Mode

This mode of knowing involves "imagery," or using representations of real objects when the objects themselves cannot be experienced directly. For example, your objective may be the same as with the enactive mode, but you realize that the children's concepts of an actual adobe house will not be accurately developed unless they can actually see a house constructed from the brick. Unable to travel to one, you may decide to bring in a scale model or even a picture of an adobe home or show photographs of an adobe home being constructed. Representations help children form concepts when real things are not available.

Symbolic Mode

This mode involves arbitrary symbols in written or oral form to communicate and store concepts. For example, the teacher might choose to reinforce the concept of an adobe home by asking the children to read a selection from their textbook that describes the advantages of living in an adobe home.

Understanding these three ways of knowing is important for planning and organizing learning activities for your social studies program. They help you recognize the need for *balance* among the activities you choose, so that there is not too much symbolism (workbooks, practice sheets, reading) and too little enactment (or vice versa) in your program.

ENACTIVE LEARNING

Young children learn by doing; they "mess about" and naturally get into or try out everything. They do whatever it takes to discover things—they strive to see, hear, touch, smell, and taste all the special things around them. They want to know all about the mysterious people, places, and things that confront them each day. They may come to elementary school knowing a little bit about a lot of things, but one characteristic they all share is a thirst for experiences that will help them find out more. When these enthusiastic, energetic youngsters come to school they expect to learn about all that interests them in much the same way, through activity and involvement. They are not greatly interested in memorizing information or in confining activities such as completing ditto sheets or workbook pages. They want to try things out. To understand how much direct involvement and personal activity affect us, take a few minutes to think about the three most powerful learning experiences you can recall from any context in your life. Write down the three incidents and consider these questions: Where did each occur? Was any in a school setting? Did you have a special need to learn at the time of each experience? What elements of the learning experiences made them so meaningful? Did any of the learnings fall under a "subject matter" heading or were they more personal in nature? If possible, share your answers with classmates. What generalizations can your group make about the conditions under which individuals learn best? Are "personal needs" and "active involvement" mentioned?

Children may receive direct, meaningful information in the social studies classroom from four major sources: (1) activities within the classroom, (2) realia, (3) field trips, and (4) resource persons. Regardless of the source, they are directly involved in actually *doing something real*—a learning principle aptly described in the Chinese proverb: "I hear and I forget. I see and I remember. I do and I understand."

Activities Within the School

A number of opportunities for direct experience are available in the school. Direct involvement in concrete experiences such as churning butter or making fabric dyes from berries enhances a child's understanding of life in colonial America. The election of classroom officials is an important experience for developing a rudimentary understanding of national election processes. Writing letters to the mayor or other elected officials helps children develop a positive attitude toward social action. By assuming classroom duties such as running errands or feeding the pets, young children develop job responsibility and an appreciation for an individual's contribution to the overall good of a social group.

Here are additional samples of real, direct experiences. Can you add to the list?

Having the children break a piñata and scamper for the prizes

Collecting cans and bottles for a recycling center

Polling children throughout the school to determine what new piece of equipment is most needed for the playground

Designing a school or classroom flag

Dancing the Virginia reel

Cooking a favorite ethnic recipe

Making a compost pile to produce soil for the class garden plot

Visiting a senior citizens' home during a holiday season to sing songs and exchange gifts

Realia

In addition to providing experiences in which children actually participate in doing something real, you should consider sharing real items or artifacts *(realia)* to elucidate difficult concepts. Typical items of realia might include:

Clothing (police uniform, Mexican serape, Alaskan parka)

Money (rubles, yen, marks, Confederate money)

Documents (wills, letters, mortgages, newspapers)

Household items (old candleholders, antique eating utensils, old furniture, butter churns, cooking supplies)

Tools (farming tools, blacksmith's tools, carpenter's tools)

Weapons (old rifles—be sure they *cannot* work, powder horns, clubs)

Foods (authentic cultural, national, or ethnic foods)

Toys (toys of ethnic, cultural, or historical interest)

School items (books from other nations or time periods, hornbook, globes or maps from the past)

Sports items (hockey equipment, soccer ball, fencing equipment)

These materials are excellent learning resources to help children more easily understand what life is like in other places or at other times. Of course, it is impossible to expect teachers to provide realia for every social studies topic; however, that does not excuse you from trying to provide as many real objects for your children as possible.

You will often find items related to specific topics of study at your local public library or museum. Some libraries and museums allow teachers to borrow items for short periods of time. If not, a field trip to the library or museum may be appropriate, especially if provisions are made for a tour guide to explain special items of interest.

Check your own materials for possible classroom value. If you have taken trips, reexamine souvenirs and other memorabilia that you may have stashed away or forgotten. Seashells, rock or mineral samples, surfboards, old clothing, records, and the like are often taken for granted; think about those things and also about bringing back interesting items from future trips.

In most instances, parents or other adults in the community will be your greatest asset for realia. Parents especially are willing and often eager to lend things once they know what you need and that their items will be properly cared for. A letter sent home with the children a few days before beginning study on a new topic will often result in a wealth of real classroom materials. A sample letter of this type is shown in Figure 9–2.

Don't shirk from bringing real items into the classroom. It is your job to search out items and get them into the classroom where they can be put to good use.

Field Trips

The world outside the classroom is rich in direct learning experiences. By organizing field trips outside the classroom, you help children explore and deal with the real world rather than representations of it. Trips are an important part of children's social studies learnings—children love the excitement, adventure, and new awareness of the world around them.

Kindergarten or first-grade children need to be in school for awhile (at least two weeks in most instances) and become familiar with their classroom environment and their teacher before taking trips. As they become accustomed to these new features in their lives, a short exploratory walk around the school building will help the children place their room in relationship to the other rooms in the building and familiarize them with your expectations in such settings. They can learn about their school by visiting the principal's office, kitchen, nurse's office, storerooms, heating plant, library, and gymnasium. After this first trip experience, you can take the children on a walk around the block, even though the sights may already be familiar to them. Point out even the

FIGURE 9—2
Sample Letter Requesting Realia from Parents

March 14, 1991

Dear Parents/Guardians,

    Our next topic of study in social studies will be *The Western States* (Washington, Oregon, California, and Arizona). In order to help the children learn about these places and about the people who live there, I am trying to locate and collect as many real items as possible in order to organize a classroom display. If you have any real items from those states that we could borrow, would you please let me know by returning this note to me?

    Thank you for your help in this matter.

                                             With appreciation,

                                           Mr. Woodburn

Parent/Guardian Signature _____

Phone Number _____

____ Sorry, but I cannot help at this time.

____ I have items you can borrow, and

       ____ they are fragile so please do not allow the children to handle them.

       ____ they may be handled with care by the children.

       ____ I will be glad to visit your classroom to show how the items are used.

---

most obvious things, as your goals should be to develop awareness of the environment and to help the children articulate about what they see and hear.

    During one episode, for example, a rabbit hopped out from among some short bushes as the children walked by. "Look at it hop," "Look how long the back legs are," and other comments ensued. The teacher encouraged their animated discussion and occasionally inserted questions to guide their observation: "Did you see its fluffy tail?" The children's interest was evident as several youngsters began "hopping" along the street to their next adventure. It is important to encourage dialogue at this age because it establishes the groundwork for active thinking about what the children will see on future trips. As you expand the walking trips, you will notice traffic lights, fire hydrants, mailboxes, bus stops, telephone booths, parking meters—all the sights and sounds of the streets. Loading and unloading of trucks, repair work on streets involving exposed pipes, open manholes, or large cranes are exciting to see. During the spring or fall months, pick a "class tree" or "class plant" and follow its progress for a few months. You might follow the route some of the children take to go home, stop and talk to a police officer, see the buildings where the children live, and on your return, try to find the windows of the classroom from the street.

You can visit, shop at, or just look at (1) stores (supermarket, pet shop, bakery, shoe-repair shop, florist, hardware store, open air market, automatic laundry), (2) building construction sites, and (3) community services (post office, fire station, police station, public library, subway station, health center, parks, factories, garages, lumber yards, housing projects).

Handle these first experiences away from the classroom carefully. You should be familiar with the location and be sure your visit has a distinct purpose. Be sure to establish a secure feeling by telling the children where they will be going, what they will see, and what they will hear or taste or smell. Don't be too informative, though, because you will want the trip to be a learning experience in itself. Before you prepare the children for the trip, consider these precautions:

Adequate supervision (at most a 5:1 child-adult ratio)

Toileting (everyone goes before you leave)

Emergency materials (bandages, tissues, safety pins, change for the phone)

Clothing (extra clothing for winter, rain gear)

Rules (walk in pairs, hold hands, walk with the teacher, stay on the sidewalk, cross streets on signal from the teacher, don't run)

When the children have had walking experiences of this type and feel comfortable in settings ouside the school, you can begin to locate worthwhile places that require transportation. Some school systems provide buses for transportation or offer a subsidy for trips. The same basic considerations for walking trips apply to transportation trips: finding a good place to visit, having a good purpose to visit, informing the children, and being aware of prerequisites. However, transportation trips require a great deal more preparation:

Arranging transportation

Scheduling the visit with those at the other end

Securing written parental permission (usually on a form provided by the school)

Planning for lunch (either packed at home or at school)

Arranging for admission costs to places such as the zoo

Maintaining a 5:1 child-adult ration (parents are usually willing to volunteer)

Establishing rules for behavior

Trips vary in kind, as we have seen, but regardless of the type, take a camera. Some young children may never have seen pictures of themselves, so take individual as well as group shots at the places you visit. If you mount them on a classroom wall at the children's eye level or use them for a group scrapbook, they will be a tremendous source of satisfaction as well as an important learning experience. The pictures come in handy to stimulate discussion long after the trip has been taken.

You can maximize the value of trips if you follow them up with a related activity after the children return to the classroom. An experience story is one good approach;

A good field trip should encourage participation among the children.

illustrations, discussions, creative skits, and comparing the experience with information from reference books are others. Whatever you choose, the trip will not be valuable unless you lead the children through activities that help to summarize their experience and apply it to the topic of study. You and the children should also evaluate the trip by asking questions like these: "Were we able to answer our questions? Did we develop any new interests (e.g., hobbies, ideas)? In what ways did our behavior affect the trip? Would we recommend this trip for others? Why? What suggestions could we give to make the next field trip better?"

In addition to careful planning of all phases of a field trip, it is advisable to extend courtesy and appreciation by sending group-dictated letters of thanks to everyone involved—chaperones, resource people, bus driver, school nurse, and principal. You can handle letter writing in the early years by asking the children to express their thoughts to you; as they dictate their message, write it on a chart. If any of the children are able to write, they can copy the letter and send it to the designated person. People especially enjoy receiving letters the children have handwritten.

An additional point to remember is that it is helpful to compile a schoolwide file of successful field trips. This file can be kept in the principal's office or in the teachers' room for reference. Information should be compiled in summary form and stored on a file card like the one in Figure 9–3.

These are good sites for field trips in the elementary years:

Farm	City Hall	Public library
Museum	Supermarket	Truck terminal
Department store	Post Office	Concert

FIGURE 9—3
Field Trip Information Form

Place name:

Address:

Phone:

Name of person to contact:

Best time to call:

Admission charge:

Number of people accommodated:

Time required:

Experiences available:

Historical site	Campground	Cultural event
Airport	Public building	Zoo
Railroad station	Bus terminal	Repair shop
Factory	Shopping center	Bakery
Newspaper building	Planetarium	Construction project
Fire station	Children's theater	Restaurant

This checklist summarizes the major considerations to address before, during, and after field trips.

Pretrip evaluation

I am familiar with the location to be visited.

This trip is suitable for the maturity level of my children.

Teacher preparation

My principal has been notified of the trip.

Administration approval has been secured in writing.

Parental permission slips have been signed.

Transportation has been arranged.

Proper supervision has been planned (a 5:1 child-adult ratio is ideal).

Toilet facilities are present at the location to be visited.

Clothing requirements have been communicated to the parents.

Safety rules have been communicated to the children:
   Stay together in a group
   Walk with a friend
   Stay on the sidewalk
   Cross only with the direction of your teacher

Teacher-child planning

The children are familiar (but not *too* familiar) with where they are going.

Points of interest have been shared.

Individual and group responsibilities have been assigned.

The trip

All children can see and hear.

I offer cues and comments to stimulate the children's interest.

I am constantly aware of special problems or emergency situations.

Follow-up activity

Informal discussion of the trip

Art projects related to the trip

Group experience charts

Creative dramatics

Bulletin board display

Resource Persons

Resource persons are individuals within or outside the school who have certain expertise, experience, skill, or knowledge in a field of special interest to the class. Generally, children enjoy contact with outside visitors and the interesting materials they share. In studying topics related to the neighborhood or community, for example, much insight can be gained from people who provide goods or services in the area—police officer, firefighter, farmer, delivery person, construction worker, doctor, nurse, and so on. When introducing children to different cultures or ethnic groups, people with appropriate backgrounds can provide information and answer questions. When studying remote cities, countries, or regions, people who live or have traveled there are good resources. As with field trips, careful planning is essential for a successful visit by a resource person:

1. Determine whether inviting a visitor is the best way to get the intended knowledge and information.
2. Determine whether the speaker's topic and style of delivery are suitable to the children's maturity level.
3. Inform the speaker about the children's age level, their needs, the time allotted for the presentation, and the facilities available.
4. Provide follow-up and discussion related to the speaker's presentation; discussion, reporting, art projects, dramatization, creative writing, and further reading will summarize and extend the information.
5. Ask both the children and the speaker to evaluate the presentation.
6. Write a letter of thanks.

Merely having someone visit your classroom does not guarantee a successful learning experience. Two examples will show the benefits of thoughtful planning.

One day Mr. Perry overheard a spirited discussion about construction machinery among a small group of children as they examined books on the reading shelf. He listened as the children expressed wonder at the size and power of backhoes, bulldozers, and other machines. Seizing the moment, Mr. Perry suggested inviting a construction worker to come to school to talk about his work.

"Would he really come to see us?" asked Michael.

"I'd like to see him come here," added Meghan. "Can we ask him to come?"

Mr. Perry had no doubt that the children's intentions were sincere, so later that day, he called the local construction company to see if a visit could be arranged. Learning that the company was working on a project nearby and was willing to send out not only a worker but also a piece of heavy equipment, Mr. Perry prepared the entire class for what would take place the next day. He told the children about what they were going to see, why they were going to see it, and how to conduct themselves safely.

The next day the children eagerly waited at the school parking lot for the construction machinery to arrive. Their anticipation grew into excitement as a bright yellow loader motored up the winding entrance. Keeping the children well in control, Mr. Perry reminded them to stay behind him until the vehicle came to a complete halt. When it did, the children gingerly approached the huge piece of machinery. The construction worker came out to show the children how the loader worked and to explain her related job responsibilities.

"The loader is so big," remarked Michael.

"Yeah, and listen to it beep when it goes backwards!" shouted Jeffrey.

"The construction worker is a lady. Wow, a lady loader driver," commented Ashley, all agog.

The children watched, listened, commented, and asked questions as they sat on the stopped loader, touched its huge tires, and tried on the worker's hard hat. All of this wonderful activity culminated in a well-supervised, short trip around the parking lot on the loader as the children took turns sitting in the high seat with the driver. Mr. Perry was rewarded by the children's enjoyment and by their learning a great deal about heavy construction machinery.

After the construction worker left the school, Mr. Perry gathered the children together and invited them to share their thoughts. As the children spoke in turn, he recorded their comments on an experience chart. Later, the children dictated a thank-you note to the worker.

Mrs. Orlando, on the other hand, assumed quite a different posture in providing her class with a visit by a resource person. To deepen the children's study of colonial America, Mrs. Orlando invited to the classroom a personal friend who was particularly skilled at weaving. When the weaver arrived, Mrs. Orlando called for the children's attention.

"Quickly and quietly, children, put away your math work and clear your desks. Show Mr. Quinlan what good boys and girls you are."

Promptly and efficiently, the children put away their materials, folded their hands on the tops of their desks, and directed their attention to the front of the room.

"Weren't they just terrific?" commented Mrs. Orlando, as if attempting to convince her friend of her superlative classroom control. The children, who had not been prepared beforehand, listened to a lengthy introduction of the visitor without completely understanding why he was there. When the resource person eventually got a chance to speak, he explained his craft in such minute detail that even the most mature child's attention wandered. Nervous glances from Mrs. Orlando informed fidgety children of her displeasure over their actions. At the end of the long presentation, Mrs. Orlando eagerly thanked the speaker for visiting and warned the children of the danger of going too close to his weaving loom for fear of damaging it.

"Stay in your seats, children," she admonished. "Work on your math papers until our speaker packs up his materials. First, we'll all show how much we enjoyed his visit. Everyone clap now." Dutifully, the children followed Mrs. Orlando's instructions.

Compare Mr. Perry's and Mrs. Orlando's techniques. What were the apparent strengths in Mr. Perry's approach? What were the obvious flaws in Mrs. Orlando's technique?

Schools or parent-teacher organizations often keep a centralized card file of community members who are willing to share their expertise and people who can help break down stereotypes—senior citizens with special skills or hobbies, women carpenters, male nurses, and so on. The card file can be organized by subject for teachers to use as a ready reference (see Figure 9–4). Care must be exercised, though, in soliciting possible classroom speakers. The practice of sending request forms throughout the

Individuals in the community who have specialized knowledge and skills can provide informative and enjoyable classroom experiences.

community, for example, is questionable, since a small number of persons who have little or no immediate usefulness may volunteer. Public relations problems can result if these persons are never called upon to speak. The safest approach seems to be to request recommendations from other teachers, involved parents, and other school personnel. This will enable you to select speakers who will inform and motivate your children about a variety of new jobs and experiences.

Enactive experiences offer students opportunities to learn by doing and by watching what others do. This mode of direct experience is crucial to a social studies program, especially when children encounter something new. It furnishes the essence of meaning that will be represented internally and stored as mental images or concepts. We all rely on enactive experiences to enhance our learning; we never outgrow it. Take, for example, the time when you first learned to run a word-processing program on the computer or play a musical instrument. You certainly had to do it several times before having a good mental picture of the process. You could have watched a film or videotape lesson (iconic stage) or read an instructional book (symbolic stage); they were or could have been very helpful, too. But neither experience would have meant as much if you didn't experience using the computer or playing the instrument itself. The message for teachers is apparent: iconic and symbolic learning can be very helpful in the elementary school social studies classroom, but enactive opportunities are most likely to help children develop a broad, realistic view of the world.

ICONIC LEARNING

Models or Replicas

There are many instances when you will not be able to bring realia to the classroom or take your children on a trip to see it. For example, in studying modes of transportation during the westward movement, it's unlikely that you can provide an experience with a real covered wagon—but you could bring in a *scale model* of a covered wagon. The model may be authentic in every detail except size. Similarly, *replicas* are actual reproductions of realia that duplicate the original object in every way, including size.

FIGURE 9–4
Special Speaker Questionnaire

Area of knowledge:
Preferred age level:
Name:
Address:
Phone:
Days available:
Hours available:
Is it best for us to visit you, or are you willing to come to our classroom?

Use these items when problems of size (the original item may not be transportable), time (many original historical items are too fragile), or expense (the original may be too valuable) prohibit sharing a real thing.

Collections of models or replicas can be displayed in the classroom in special *exhibit areas*. In a study of Mexico, you might arrange replicas, models, and realia on a large table for the children to see and touch. You can stimulate the children's attention to the exhibit area with a large, attractive bulletin board displaying pictures and documents. Exhibits not only help clarify desired concepts but also bring authenticity and motivation to any topic of study.

When choosing models or replicas, be aware of their many uses:
- To introduce a topic of study:
  1. Allow children to view and handle the materials to motivate interest in further investigation.
  2. Encourage the children to ask questions and make comments about the materials.

- To enrich understanding during development of the topic:
  1. Use the materials as models to clarify vocabulary or build concepts.
  2. Use the materials as guides for construction activities.
  3. Use the materials as stimulants for discussion either before or after reading assignments, films, field trips, or other learning activities.
  4. Encourage children to use the materials to add realism to skits or other dramatizations.
  5. Prepare an arrangement so the children can view the materials in a realistic setting.

- To culminate a topic of study:
  1. Encourage children to show real objects as they deliver oral summaries.
  2. Use a display of real objects in realistic settings to summarize major learnings.

Simulation Games

Simulation games are realistic representations of actual life situations that involve the children's ability to consider alternatives while making decisions people actually face under similar conditions. Roles, rules, and material for simulation games present a simplified representation of reality. In simulation games, scoring and reward systems are used to evaluate the *correctness* of a player's decisions. These results closely approximate those in real life situations and form the element that determines winners and losers. In other creative dramatics exercises, the player merely acts as he thinks the person being portrayed would act and does not directly experience the immediate consequences of the actions. The "Stores and Shoppers" game illustrates the major features of simulation.

Stores and Shoppers is probably best used to teach the following social studies objectives to primary pupils.

1. To help the children discover that people may prefer to buy for any of several reasons—lower prices, better goods or services, convenient location, customer confidence.

2. To help children understand that owners of stores earn income from the production and sales of services and goods, and that from income they must pay for goods and materials to replace what they have sold, wages for their workers and selves, rent and utilities, repair and replacement of tools and equipment, taxes.

3. To help children understand that the income left after the business owner has paid his expenses is his profit. He earns this profit by the risks he takes since he can't be sure that his customers will buy the goods and services he sells.

4. To help the child discover that business owners compete to attract customers with better goods and services or prices.

5. To show how stores use advertising to tell what they are selling and what are their prices and to help children understand how advertising can help people make choices.

The Situation

The players are divided into two groups: shoppers and store owners. In a class of thirty, there might be four stores with three owners per store. Each store selects an owner to be the treasurer. Pupils are score keeper, resource keeper, and card dealer. Others are shoppers.

Resources for Players

Each shopper has some sort of medium of exchange, which can be play money or a simulated medium such as red paper circles. Each shopper receives an equal amount of "money," and all shoppers receive identical shopping lists of items to be obtained at the stores. All the stores have equal amounts of the exchange medium but their amounts are not equal to that of the shoppers. The stores are also provided with goods for the shoppers to buy, but the quantity and prices vary among the stores. Goods are represented by different colored paper squares, triangles, and rectangles. Prices are set by the teacher; for example:

> *Store 1:* 2 green triangles sell for 3 circles;
> *Store 2:* 6 green triangles sell for 1 circle;
> *Store 3:* 1 green triangle sells for 5 circles;
> *Store 4:* 1 green triangle sells for 5 circles.

The card dealer has small cards which designate amounts of exchange medium that must be paid by store owners at different intervals. For example, "Pay rent—5 circles."

The resource keeper is only used in a more complex game for a middle grade. He sells goods to stores when they want to use their profit to buy more goods.

Goals for Actors

The shoppers try to buy all the things on their shopping lists. The shopper who completes or comes closest to completing his list in the given time is the winner. If two shoppers tie, the shopper with the most exchange medium left is the winner.

The store owners try to sell all their goods at the prices the teacher has set. The store with the most profit is the winner.

The score keeper is in charge of counting the stores' profits and determining the winner among the shoppers.

Special Rules and Limits
1. When the card dealer blows the whistle, each treasurer of a store must draw a card and pay to the dealer what the card says.
2. All sales are final.
3. Shoppers cannot resell goods.
4. Stores cannot trade goods; shoppers cannot trade.
5. Playing time is set by the teacher—approximately twenty minutes to one-half hour.

Follow-up
The most important part of a simulation game is the follow-up. Leading questions asked by the teacher help children verbalize the objective of the game and the meaning of the game symbols. Such a question for this game might be, "Why did you buy green triangles at Store 2 instead of Store 1?" Hopefully the answer would be that the price was lower at Store 2.[4]

Teachers often wish to construct simulation games that more closely address particular concepts than do commercially prepared games. To do so, follow these key construction guidelines:

1. *Decide what you want the game to teach.* Clearly define the skills, concepts, or attitudes that will be reflected in the objectives.
2. *Identify the real-life situation you want the game to simulate.* Be sure the situation involves competition or conflict.
3. *Outline the broad details of the situation to be simulated.*
4. *Specify the roles of the players.* Each player must be faced with decisions so that he or she has an effect on the outcome.
5. *Identify the resources* (money, raw materials, machinery, military arms) *available to each player.* Determine the relative value of each resource and its influence on the outcome of the game. Specify the method of resource distribution to each player.
6. *Determine the interactions of the participants.* Players may face interactions based on group or individual actions; for example, if store owners group together to limit the amount of a product to be sold, individual consumers will be faced with higher prices. Consumers then have a choice to boycott or to buy anyway.
7. *Determine the sequence of events.* A simulation game is normally played in well-defined cycles. Action in each cycle begins with a crisis of some kind. Cycles may be defined in terms of a certain amount of time (hours, days, months), a certain number of repetitions, or in terms of achieving a certain score.
8. *Write the directions for carrying out each phase of the simulation game.*

A simulation game in the social studies classroom is easy to play. Its success or failure depends upon your preparation. Sound preparation involves these strategies:

1. *Preplanning.* Know the game yourself by carefully studying the rules and materials. If possible, play the game with several students in advance. Divide and organize

game materials in advance, and introduce the game by *briefly* telling the students what it's all about. Divide the players and assign roles, giving students a clear description of each role.

2. *Playing the game.* Do not help the players with their strategies, but be available to answer questions concerning rules. Keep the players informed of the scores throughout. Permit students to play the game several times, since they may be interested in trying alternate strategies or other roles.

3. *Follow-up discussion.* Discuss decisions the players faced and the strategies each chose. What were their reasons for choosing specific strategies? How can the decisions and strategies be applied to real life? Discuss how the game could be modified to make it better.

Simulation games have a number of strengths and weaknesses. They vary greatly in style and appeal, so what works for one group of children may fail with another. The key to success is to follow the suggestions on these pages and give the game a chance to show what it can contribute to your social studies classroom.

Because children have a natural love for games, simulation games capitalize on a child's self-motivation. They actively involve children in social studies learning; because the game situations represent real-life circumstances, the students view the games as relevant. An advantage for teachers is that many concepts can be developed with one activity. In addition, the slow learner or emotionally upset child has an equal chance to compete with faster learners in the same acrivity. A final advantage of simulation games is that children work cooperatively.

On the down side, most simulation games are too expensive for the classroom. Commercially prepared games cost from $15 to $100. Yet constructing one's own game requires an overwhelming amount of time. The games can be lengthy; many take at least a half day to play completely, and some children may lose interest toward the end of an exceptionally long game.

Motion Pictures, Videotapes, Slides, and Filmstrips

Like many of the activities treated in this chapter, motion pictures, videotapes, slides, and filmstrips are representations of reality. But because children are generally not *directly* involved in preparing these media, they are less concrete than other learning experiences we have discussed. They do, however, have many unique contributions to offer social studies teachers.

The success of motion pictures, videotapes, slides, and filmstrips in a social studies classroom depends on how you use them.

1. *Preplanning.* Preview the medium so you can analyze it. As a result of previewing the material, you can create questions to guide discussion before and following the class viewing, thus establishing a *purpose* for viewing, and relating your follow-up questions to that purpose, as we discussed regarding the DLE in Chapter 4.

Another important aspect of preplanning is to determine the most advantageous place in the unit for showing the medium. You can introduce the topic or theme with it, use it as the study progresses to supply or clarify related details and concepts, or summarize or review the material at the end of a topic.

2. *Class preparation.* Prepare the class for viewing by asking a few key questions that the medium will answer. Without clear purposes to guide them as they watch, children may wonder what the teacher expects. Guiding questions remove that doubt and establish thought direction. Don't ask too many questions, however; they may be as confusing as not asking any at all. Three or four questions should be a maximum. Vary the types of questions; the most appropriate are those that ask the student to identify main ideas, analyze thoughts and feelings of others, look for relationships, or evaluate the film's truthfulness. Purpose-setting questions that ask the student to recall facts and details should rarely, if ever, be used. Discourage notetaking; overemphasis on factual purpose-setting questions may lead students to take notes during the viewing and perplex and distract them from the continuity of the presentation.

3. *Viewing.* Prepare the class for viewing the material as an *educational experience* rather than as a "movie show." Children should look forward to each and every learning experience in the social studies classroom as a specific educational outcome.

4. *Follow-up.* The follow-up portion of the lesson evaluates how successful the viewers were in finding answers to the purpose-setting questions. Encourage the students to relate their experience to a discussion of the previously established purpose.

Some films, videotapes, slides, and filmstrips may be interesting to view for a second time. The second showing can be made during the same period if the film or tape is short, or on another day if it is especially lengthy. When showing it the second time, you could have the students explain the action as it plays silently, or students could supply the voices of characters in each scene. Use stop-action or slow motion to emphasize certain points.

Films or tapes can be used in a variety of creative ways. You can use a camera or camcorder to record the major characteristics of your local environment and set up an exchange program of films, slides, or tapes with schools in other areas.

Computers

In addition to all the possibilities for traditional learning materials, you must become knowledgeable about the computer. With its general acceptance as an important teaching tool, the computer has become an ally for social studies instruction. Teachers use computers primarily for drill and practice and for educational games, but new uses such as simulation and problem solving are supplementing those activities in social studies classrooms.

Computer technology appears to be altering the character of instruction in our schools. Commercial developers have produced computer-based instructional materials, and some textbook publishers supplement their textbooks with materials for computer use.

Software Learning Programs

In the most common type of computer program, the child begins by typing in her name from a keyboard. The machine usually responds with some kind of welcome, such as a smile face and the word "hello" printed on the screen. Problems—perhaps matching capitals and states—appear on the screen, and the child works them out. If the decision is correct, the smile face appears and enters the next problem or task on the screen. If the response is incorrect, the machine notifies the child in either script or an alternate symbol and invites the child to select another response. If the child gives a second incorrect response, the computer automatically shows the correct answer. This type of program, designed primarily to teach social studies content, would normally take 10 to 15 minutes to complete.

Some educators criticize this pattern of computer-aided instruction as nothing more than an expensive form of teaching with a drill-and-practice emphasis. Proponents of computer-aided instruction counter that computers were never meant to replace teachers, but simply as a tool to help them in their teaching. For students who need remediation, or who learn best from an individually paced program or lack the background for understanding new material, or for those who simply enjoy the stimulation of electronic games, judicious use of drill-and-practice programs may be the key to effective instruction.

Computer usage in the social studies, although primarily drill-and-practice, has other valuable uses as well. Glenn and Rawitsch identify these uses for the social studies instructional program.[5]

1. *To deliver content.* Types of activities for delivering content include *tutorial,* in which new information is imparted; *drill,* in which knowledge of previously imparted information is tested; and *simulation,* in which students learn by experiencing a model of a real-life situation.

An exemplary *tutorial* program in geography is *States and Traits,* developed by Designware. In one learning option, the outline of a state appears on the right of the screen, and the child must move the state to its correct position on an outline map of the United States. Students learn a great deal about the states, including their capitals and major products.

One of the most noteworthy simulations available for elementary school children is *The New Oregon Trail,* developed by the Minnesota Educational Computer Consortium (MECC). It presents a series of decisions pioneers faced in 1847 as they set out in wagon trains to find new homes in the Oregon Territory. They stock up with provisions at the beginning of the five- to six-month journey, but heavy rains, wagon breakdowns, illness, and robberies eventually deplete their supplies. Children must make decisions along the way, but if they choose to hunt for food or stop at a fort, for example, they lose precious time and could suffer starvation or illness, or fail to pass the western mountains before the freeze and blizzards. The computer mathematically determines the outcome of the children's decisions and gives the decision makers immediate feedback about the consequences of their choices. Although most simulations involve only one user per computer, *The New Oregon Trail* assumes a small-group approach by engaging a student family of four or five children to make the difficult decisions.

2. *To receive and analyze information.* Computers can tally numerical amounts, as in analysis of a sample opinion survey. They can select information based upon chosen characteristics. For example, a data collection for all countries can be created showing location, type of political and economic system, and so on. Students can then use the computer to investigate questions such as, "Are there common characteristics among countries that are governed by dictatorships?"

3. *As an example of the use of technology in society.* In a world increasingly dependent on technology, understanding social implications becomes more important. Computers are at the heart of this new information technology. Having computers available facilitates teaching students about the technology that will influence their lives and helps them more directly comprehend conflicting issues related to a technological society.

4. *To develop thinking skills.* Most subject areas are concerned with developing children's thinking skills, but the goals of logic and problem solving appear to apply most directly to social studies learning. Computer activities can contribute directly to the development of these skills.

As the children experiment with the computer, they often experience the process of problem solving that is essential to upper-level thinking abilities. Just a few of the motivational programs available for elementary school social studies are described here.

Where in the USA Is Carmen Sandiego? (Grades 4–8). Students become crime-fighters as they search the USA for Carmen Sandiego (an ex-secret agent turned thief) and her gang of criminals, who are out to steal our most precious natural treasures. The venture starts with one of the 16 thieves hiding in a city and leaving a trail of clues for student "detectives" to decipher. The students read descriptions of various cities, visit clue locations, and check possible destinations, all the while using their problem-solving and analytical skills. Along the same principle, the program developer has added *Where in the World Is Carmen Sandiego?*, *Where in Europe Is Carmen Sandiego?*, and *Where in Time Is Carmen Sandiego?* (Broderbund Software)

Map Skills (Grades 2–8). Students get behind the steering wheel and follow directions as they maneuver through five imaginary towns. Designed to reinforce and teach map skills, the program allows users to take 100 trips at ten levels of difficulty. The trip begins with a map displayed on the screen, followed by directions to get from the point of origin to a destination. The students touch a key to begin the trip about the map, maneuvering a cursor according to instructions including mileage, direction, distance to travel, and route numbers. (Optimum Resource-Weekly Reader Software)

Galleons of Glory: The Secret Voyage of Magellan (Grades 4 and up). The children imagine the world of 1519 by taking the place of Magellan and trying to sail a galleon around the globe. They are confronted with problems ranging from nature's fury to shipboard politics as they react to changing circumstances that arise during the voyage. Calm seas give way to vicious storms and a frightened crew comes close to mutiny, challenging students to make decisions based on real historical events. (Broderbund)

Oh Deer! (Grades 5–9).   Students become members of a town council charged with the responsibility of dealing with a swiftly growing herd of deer in a residential area. How can they maintain a herd size that is in balance with the natural environment and human tolerance? Should they shoot some of the deer? Poison them? Ship them to another area? This simulation allows children to experience the social pressures of dealing with such a real-life dilemma. (Minnesota Computer Consortium)

Elementary Volume 6 (Grades 2–6).   In each program, children take a trip to a different time and place where they must develop whole new sets of survival skills. "Furs," for example, is a simulation of the North American fur trade of the 1770s. "Voyageur" transforms students into early eighteenth century woodsmen in the forests of northern Minnesota. This is a fascinating "time machine" in which children experience history. (Minnesota Computer Consortium)

Meet the Presidents (Grades 6–12).   A series of portraits of American Presidents is "painted" on the screen as the child is given brief factual statements at the bottom of the screen. The object of the game is to identify each President by typing his name on the keyboard before the portrait is complete. The teacher has an option of changing or adding to the facts presented. (Versa Computing)

Pictures and Study Prints

A valuable project all beginning teachers should initiate as early as possible is collecting a picture file for each topic they will teach, from sources such as magazines, newspapers, calendars, and advertising brochures. Pictures help children visualize people, places, processes, or feelings they cannot experience directly. The dress, home, and family composition of people in different regions of the world can be clarified and enlarged through pictures. Geographical terms, such as *plateau, tundra,* and *desert,* can be visualized much more clearly. The processes of irrigation, moving through canal locks, extracting ore from a mine, making bread, and so on become more meaninfgul through pictures. Abstract concepts such as fear, trust, or love can be perceived more tangibly by examining pictures that reflect selected moods and feelings.

Teachers at the various elementary-grade levels should realize that children vary in their ability to read and interpret pictures just as they vary in their ability to read and interpret verbal symbols. Chase and John describe pupils at the *low level* as being able to name, list, and enumerate objects being viewed.[6] Children at this stage tend to focus on the upper left-hand quadrant of the picture until they are encouraged to do otherwise. The pupils at the *middle level* are able to detail meaning and describe what is happening. The students at the *high level* are able to draw inferences, see relationships, interpret, and think critically. You should strive to provide questioning and discussion at each of the levels to give children of varying abilities the chance for success at their individual levels at the same time they are exposed to higher levels of interpretation through the comments and observations of their peers.

You can encourage children to look for different things in a picture by guiding their observations.

- Low level: "Tell how many . . ."
                 "Tell me what you see . . ."
- Middle level: "What are _____ doing?"
                 "What kind of _____ do you see?"
                 "Describe the _____ ."
                 "What color (how large, how far, etc.) is the _____?"
- High level: "What kind of _____ do you think _____ is?"
                 "What will _____ do next?"
                 "Why did _____ happen?"
                 "What title can you give this picture?"

To lead a group picture discussion, design a sequence of questions appropriate for the range of the children's interpretation abilities.

Some publishing companies have organized sets of pictures around central themes or problems for study and discussion. The study prints are placed on durable, attractive mounts and indexed for easy reference. They include a teacher's guide in the form of a manual or printed on the backs of the pictures for ease in guiding discussion. You should examine catalogs and samples of study prints since they vary a great deal in quality and price.

Graphic Materials

Tables and graphs represent lengthy information in summary form, allowing students to gather information, visualize relationships, and make comparisons much more easily than with narrative materials. All forms of graphics appear in social studies materials, but to make maximum use of graphic materials, children must be able to comprehend on three levels: literal, inferential, and critical.

At the level of literal comprehension, one leads children in locating specific factual data with questions such as "How many . . . ?" or "What are . . . ?" Literal comprehension is the basic level of understanding and is essential to the thinking required on the next two levels.

At the inferential level, children compare and contrast factual data to form generalizations and draw conclusions. Guided interpretation of the graphic material through thoughtful questions is the best way to develop inferential comprehension: "In what ways is _____ similar to (or different from) _____ ?" "Explain what is meant by . . . " or "Why did _____ happen?" These questions require the student to project beyond the immediate factual data in more abstract ways than in answering literal questions.

Developing critical comprehension of graphic materials helps children examine and recognize biased or inaccurate information. Questions that guide critical thinking might be in these forms: "For what reasons would you favor . . . ?" or "Which of these _____ would you consider to be of greatest value?" or "Do you agree with these conclusions?" or "Is this information useful or valuable?" In all cases, the student must indicate the basic criteria and supply the appropriate data that caused her to make a decision.

Just as we apply developmental learning principles to all phases of children's skills acquisition, we must also introduce graphic materials to a child by means of something he has experienced. Young children grasp the relationships shown in graphic representations only if they first go through the process of representing things graphically themselves.

Tables

Tables present numerical data concisely in columns and rows for quick comparisons. Tables in social studies materials may represent comparative data on exports, imports, rainfall, income, mountain elevations, population, and dozens of other concepts. Since children need to become familiar with tables before they can understand and interpret other graphic materials, the teacher should plan early learning experiences that will help the child clearly understand how to make them.

TABLE 9–1
Boys and Girls in Second Grade

Room	Boys	Girls
2-A	17	10
2-B	12	15
2-C	11	15

TABLE 9–2
Class Attendance

Day	Absent	Present
Monday	3	21
Tuesday	2	22
Wednesday	4	20
Thursday	3	21
Friday	1	23

The children's first tables should be short lists of figures related to daily classroom experiences. For example, the children may compare the number of boys and girls in the three second-grade classrooms, favorite pets, favorite colors, favorite times of the day, attendance for each day of the week, and so on (see Tables 9–1 and 9–2).

You can then ask the children to find a table of data in the newspaper. This could be anything from weather reports to sports scores to import and export data. Record the data in a table like Table 9–3. Similar tables can be used to record and analyze data from other sources and experiments. The resulting lessons can be extended as we help children practice the social studies skills of drawing conclusions from data ("Our population has grown in each decade.") and predicting ("The population in 2000 will top 270,000,000.").

TABLE 9–3
Population of the United States

Year	Population
1900	76,212,168
1910	92,228,496
1920	106,021,537
1930	123,202,624
1940	132,164,569
1950	151,325,798
1960	179,323,175
1970	203,302,031
1980	226,547,082
1990*	250,000,000

*1990 Census figure not available; figure represents projection.

Gradually, children will move to tables similar to Table 9–3 that are common in social studies materials. Be sure, though, that the children can read large numbers before they meet them in social studies tables.

Graphs

After the students experience the construction and interpretation of several tables, you should show them how best to display the kinds of data visually. Create several graphs from the data.

Graphs present quantitative information that can be read and interpreted quickly. In elementary school social studies, this is accomplished with pictorial graphs; bar graphs; circle, pie, or area graphs; and line graphs. Generally, the pictorial and bar graphs are the easiest to interpret, the others may be more difficult for elementary school children.

In the children's earliest experiences with graphs, you should make instruction as concrete as possible. Use blocks, books, or other stackable materials to help children understand how factual data can be represented with graphs. Bring an empty table to the front of the room and choose a topic on which the children might have a variety of responses—favorite foods, sports teams, flavors, colors, and so on. Construct labels for about four of the most apparent choices and tape them on the edge of the table so all can see. Then ask the children to name their preference and, one by one, place their blocks above the appropriate label. When everyone has done so, you can easily compare and contrast columns by asking, "Which food has the most blocks? What does our class enjoy as its favorite food? Which food has the fewest blocks? What is our least favorite food? Do any foods have the same number of blocks? Do you think the results would change if we asked the children next door to tell us *their* favorite foods?" You may want to repeat this experience several times using different categories.

From these initial experiences, provide a transition activity before the children try to interpret graphs in books or other sources. This transitional activity begins by once more choosing a topic of personal interest for the children. Rather than pass out blocks, give each child a rectangular piece of colored construction paper (about 1" x 2"). Following a procedure similar to the concrete graphing experience, ask the children to make their choices and to glue their rectangles on a large sheet of chart paper (or tack to the bulletin board) above their choices. Children can see summaries of data in a graph that evolves before their eyes (Figure 9–5). Follow the graph construction with ques-

FIGURE 9–5
Transitional Graph Activity

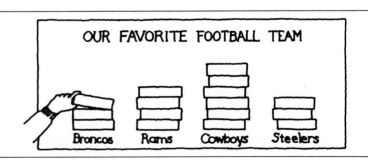

tions like those in the concrete graph discussion. End your questioning sequence with an evaluative-type question to encourage *critical comprehension* of graphs: "How might our graph be different if it were done in Pittsburgh rather than Denver?"

Now, you can begin to show children how closely graphs and tables are tied together. For example, you might use your table of class absences and ask the children to transform it into a graph by placing pictorial symbols on corresponding sections of the graph (a *pictorial graph* or *pictograph*), as in Figure 9–6.

In the later grades, picture graphs can be used to illustrate such factual data as natural resources, exports, imports, manufactured goods, population, methods of transportation, comparisons of population, and so on, like the graph in Figure 9–7.

Picture graphs appeal to children because of their simple presentation of data. The symbols are more concrete than those of any other graphic form, and the children can interpret their meaning fairly easily. They must learn to construct them carefully; carelessness in counting may account for inconsistencies in the data, especially when large numbers of symbols are necessary. In addition, picture graphs can be ineffective either because the information is difficult to illustrate pictorially or because pictorial symbols give an inexact representation of certain data.

As the children progress, they will encounter *bar graphs* such as Figure 9–8. To read these data successfully, children must have had prior experiences gathering and summarizing data in simple picture graphs and bar graphs relating to the children's personal interests. Eventually they will be able to comprehend the summary information presented in graphs quickly and use more sophisticated thought processes to compare two or more graphs.

Circle graphs (also called *pie* or *area graphs*) are most appropriate for showing how a total amount is divided into parts. Because children have a difficult time interpreting fractional parts or percentage of area in the primary grades, circle, pie, or area graphs are recommended for use only later in the intermediate grades. Figure 9–9 illustrates the typical use of area graphs in elementary school social studies materials.

Line graphs constitute the most accurate form of graphing. They are especially useful for showing changes that occur over a period of time. Because young children have relatively poor time concepts, and because line graphs are the most abstract form of graphing, they should not be introduced until the intermediate grades. Line graphs

FIGURE 9–6

Numerical and Pictorial Graphs Showing Class Absences

Monday	3		Monday	👤 👤 👤
Tuesday	2		Tuesday	👤 👤
Wednesday	4		Wednesday	👤 👤 👤 👤
Thursday	3		Thursday	👤 👤 👤
Friday	1		Friday	👤

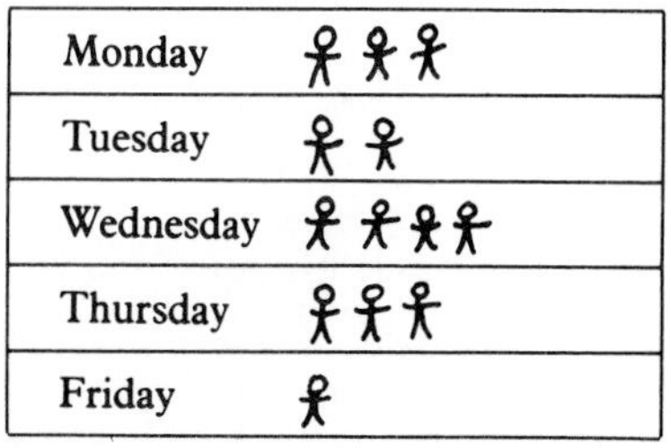

FIGURE 9–7
*States Having the Same State Tree**

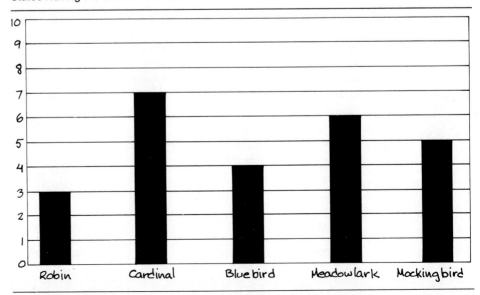

OAK	🌳🌳🌳
DOGWOOD	🌳
SPRUCE	🌳🌳
PINE	🌳🌳🌳🌳
ELM	🌳

* Each 🌳 means two states

FIGURE 9–8
States Having the Same State Bird

	Robin	Cardinal	Bluebird	Meadowlark	Mockingbird
Value	3	7	4	6	5

FIGURE 9–9
A Circle Graph Showing How
Much of Every City Tax Dollar
Is Spent for Different Services

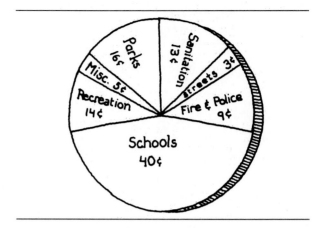

are especially valuable to show changes in temperature during the year, rainfall changes, population changes, or production changes (Figure 9–10).

Discuss the content of the graphs, with students drawing conclusions from the data presented. Line graphs show trends, so they often present interesting situations for the children to predict what might happen in the future. One class, for example, projected the growth of population in the United States through the year 2020. Their results are shown in Figure 9–11.

Tables and graphs are comprehensive representations that allow students to gather information, visualize relationships, and make comparisons much more easily than through the use of narrative materials. Like conventional reading, these symbolic

FIGURE 9–10
Population of the United States

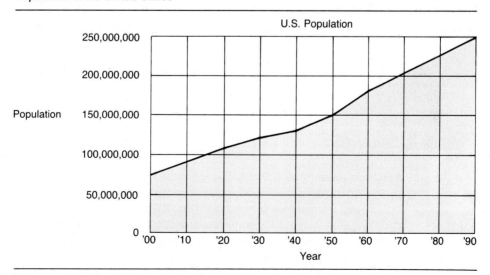

FIGURE 9–11
Population Projection

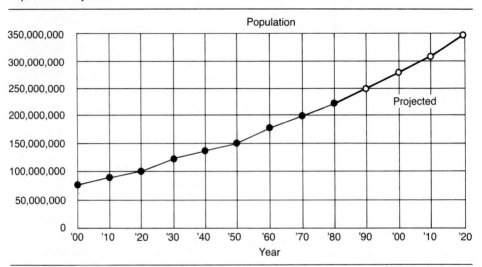

systems attain maximum usefulness when children become able to comprehend them on three levels: literal, inferential, and critical. As with map and globe instruction, children learn best about tables and graphs through direct, meaningful instruction and by becoming involved in situations in which they actually use the skills.

Enactive and iconic learning experiences are two important sources of social studies content for elementary school children. Enactive representations involve all the sources of direct experience in which children can be involved. Iconic representations are those that are provided when children may not be able to observe or interact with the *original* objects or events, but they may be able to observe or interact with reproductions or models, whether produced by others or by themselves. These activities are somewhat like the enactive stage in that they are highly realistic and closely tied to actual physical involvement, but they differ because they are not "the real thing," only accurate reproductions. Both of these levels help create distinct growth in the students' thinking processes by allowing them to interact with objects, people, and ideas.

SYMBOLIC LEARNING

Symbolic learning deals with the different kinds of abstract experiences teachers provide to communicate social studies concepts: textbooks, reference books, literature books, and lectures. Each of these forms of communication is an integral part of our daily lives, but they may be considered the most highly abstract means of sharing ideas because they involve a system of arbitrary, abstract *symbols* (printed and spoken words) that stand for *real* ideas or objects. Each is a social instrument to help people understand things they want to communicate to each other. The written and spoken word is the foundation of the school curriculum, and teaching these abstract forms of communication is perhaps your most important task as a social studies teacher. We discussed the proper way to share textbooks with young children in Chapter 4 and will examine the use of literature in Chapter 10; here, we consider the positive and negative features of lectures so we can determine their proper role in the social studies classroom.

Lectures

Lecturing is the oldest instructional technique. Before the invention of the printing press, those few individuals fortunate enough to read and own a book would share their knowledge by reading from their book while others listened. (The word *lecture* derives from the Latin word *lego* (*legere, lectus*), "to read," and the process of teaching others by reading to them became generally described by the term *lego*.) Because the technique eventually became so popular, the word *lego* took on the expanded meaning "to teach." Even when books became more readily available after the invention of the printing press, teachers continued to base instruction on reading texts to students. After years of abuse, the technique fell into disfavor among critics of social studies education, who characterized the teacher as a stern autocrat lecturing in front of a class, with his or her words going into the students' notes without passing through the minds of either. Despite these negative connotations, the lecture method, when used correctly and sparingly, can be a valuable addition to the social studies program. Although the lecture technique (or any other technique) should never be used as the exclusive instructional method, there are occasions when it can be used to advantage.

Determining When to Lecture

Presenting Information.   You will sometimes find that books and other reference materials used in class do not present points that need to be developed or lack up-to-date information. A lecture can fill in gaps and smooth over rough surfaces. In these cases, the teacher must be careful to emphasize that the lecture is only one viewpoint and must be evaluated as critically as any other source of information used to gather data.

Integrating Information.   You will sometimes find it necessary to explain difficult ideas to the children. In this type of lecture, the teacher shows the students the process of logically ordering information to arrive at a clear explanation. Students can be encouraged to repeat the process in explaining individual areas of interest.

Giving an Overview.   You may wish to use the lecture technique to relate a new topic of study to a previous topic or to place a topic in perspective. This type of lecture is concerned less with providing specific information than with providing an overall idea or general picture of a topic.

Sharing Personal Experiences.   If you or a fellow teacher have had an interesting experience such as a trip to an important place or a visit with a well-known person, you will want to share it with the children. They are interested in their teachers' lives and may be motivated to find out more about the people or places associated with your experiences.

If you find that a lecture is the only or best possible technique to achieve your goal, then you must present the lecture articulately, enthusiastically, and interestingly. Often, beginning teachers are tempted to memorize the content they wish to share with the children. Try not to do that, because it often leads to a stiff and stilted performance. Of course, you should know the content well and organize the important points in your mind. From there, you must realize that lecturing is a very personal skill; there is no special formula to ensure its success. The technique one person uses may work magic, whereas the same technique might fail terribly for someone else. Nevertheless, some general guidelines will help you deliver an effective lecture.

Rehearse your lecture several times before delivering it to the children. In the "rehearsal" stage, consider these suggestions:

> Rehash it silently to get an overall idea of the presentation.
>
> Say it aloud so you can develop a "feel" for its mood. Read it on a tape recorder and analyze your style. Try to eliminate "uh," "ah," and "you know."
>
> Sit or stand in front of a mirror. Try to use body gestures and facial expressions to emphasize major points or to communicate moods and feelings.
>
> If you can, practice your presentation in front of a friend and ask for an honest critique of your technique.
>
> Determine how long your presentation will take. Children's attention spans vary from topic to topic, but a good rule of thumb is to stay within a time frame of five to fifteen minutes.

Lecture Technique

Introducing the Topic.   Your enthusiasm can be contagious, so a major objective of the lecture must be to arouse interest in a topic. Transferring enthusiasm to students, however, is a difficult skill for teachers to attain.

Give the children an idea of what your presentation is going to be about, but don't provide a highly detailed description of the topic. Avoid dry statements such as, "Today I want to tell you about oil drilling." Instead, try to capture their attention with statements such as: "How many of you have ever thought a 'grasshopper' could be used to pump oil? Let me tell you how."

Presentation.   Your physical presentation influences your ability to maintain the children's attention. Be conscious of your eye contact, use of gestures, and voice. Speak naturally, modulating your tone and enunciating clearly. Observe your audience to assess whether your volume and speed are appropriate. Be prepared for unsolicited questions or comments by the children, and anticipate ways to direct attention back to the lecture topic.

Use Audiovisual Aids. Illustration of major points helps the children understand what you are telling them and brings realism to information that might otherwise be difficult to imagine. A photograph of an oil pumping "grasshopper," for example, shows children how this large pump got its name from its resemblance to an insect. In short, remember that "a picture (or other audiovisual aid) is worth a thousand words."

Summarize the Main Points. After your presentation, ask children to summarize the content or share their feelings about it.

Using a Variety of Activities

The following episode describes one fifth-grade teacher's approach to using many of the activities suggested in this chapter. Of course, there are many possible variations to this approach. What are some *you* would suggest?

Ms. Lawrence's social studies program reached the point where the children were ready to move from a single-text approach to one that would present information from several sources (still using the basic text as one of those sources). So, for this unit on Africa, Ms. Lawrence chose to use *three* textbooks for exposure to basic information before branching out into individual or group projects. Also, individual differences could be met and the reading might lead to good class discussion comparing the different accounts.

Ms. Lawrence, realizing that some *vocabulary building* was needed before good reading could be expected, addressed this concern by examining new terms during the initial phase of reading on the topic of the Ibo culture of Africa. She wrote words such as *tunic* on the board and pronounced them. Ms. Lawrence had prepared a display of pictures and artifacts so the children could read for the purpose of identifying each item on the table. Lois found a paragraph in her book describing tunics which she read to the rest of the class who were not using the same text: "A tunic is a long slip-on robe or gown." Lois took the card with the word *tunic* printed on it and placed it by a robe at the display. This, however, was only a partial definition, and further reading would enlarge the concept of *tunic*. Rose and Jerome discovered that their book described much more elaborate tunics: "The king of Mali wears a fancy red tunic made of expensive foreign cloth." Rose and Jerome found the picture at the display that illustrated the fancy red tunics and contributed their part to a growing concept. In the same manner, the children identified the rest of the items at the display.

Following the introduction, Ms. Lawrence encouraged the children to discuss things they might like to learn about the Ibo culture. They suggested some ideas, and Ms. Lawrence wrote them on the chalkboard. Typical queries were: "What kind of clothes did they wear?" "How did they live?" and "What did they eat?" Ms. Lawrence used these questions as the purpose-setting part of her teaching procedure and directed the children to read further in their texts to see if they could locate appropriate information.

After the children had studied their texts for two days, Ms. Lawrence demonstrated to them how a trade book could help them find even more information about the ideas they had listed on the chalkboard. She read a short selection about ceremonies, from Sonia Bleeker's *The Ibo of Biafra* to show the beautiful rituals that are part of the Ibo culture. The children expressed strong interest in finding out more about ceremonies and traditions celebrated by Africans and Afro-Americans, so Ms. Lawrence pointed to a table of other trade books, magazine articles, newspaper stories, and pictures and suggested to the class that these resources might help them find information about their interests.

One group was motivated to study a relatively new African American holiday, *Kwanzaa,* which means celebration of the "first fruits of harvest" in Swahili. It is described as the only true African American holiday and lasts for seven days at a time coinciding with the Christmas holidays. After much reading, planning, and locating information, the Kwanzaa group was ready to begin the actual work of collecting and constructing materials to help them tell their story. The search for information gave the children practice in considering many sources of information, evaluating each source, and selecting the most important for their purposes. Once the information was collected, the groups were responsible for reporting their discoveries to their classmates. The boys and girls found that Kwanzaa activities begin on December 26 with a *mkeka* (straw mat) on which all items for the celebration are placed. Ms. Lawrence helped the children make the mkeka and listened as the children explained to their classmates that the mkeka is placed on a low table or on the floor because it represents the land. The children had built a *kinara* (candleholder) to hold seven candles, and brought *muhindi* (fruit and corn) from home to place on the mkeka. They then presented the story of Kwanzaa.

> One candle is lit each day until the seventh, when the center and final candle is lit. Each one is labled with one of the seven principles of *nguzo saba* (blackness) that serve as guidelines to follow all year:
>
> - 1st day (*Umoja*—unity)
> - 2nd day (*Kujichagulia*—self-determination)
> - 3rd day (*Ujima*—collective work)
> - 4th day (*Ujamaa*—cooperative economics)
> - 5th day (*Nia*—purpose)
> - 6th day (*Kuumba*—creativity)
> - 7th day (*Imani*—faith)
>
> The kinara represents the original stalk from which all people spread, and each muhindi represents a child. The kernels are the children and the stalk represents the father. At each meal during Kwanzaa, a candle is lit, its meaning is discussed, and everyone drinks from a unity cup.
>
> Kwanzaa is primarily a children's holiday begun during the 1970s as a way to help them place true value on their cultural heritage and to prepare them for adult responsibilities.

Pleasurable experiences like this fostered deeper interest in cultural celebrations. Ms. Lawrence, with help from the school librarian, located other reading material that, when arranged with books, artifacts, and other materials already discovered, comprised an attractive exhibit of the things the children had all enjoyed learning about.

SUMMARY

An abundance of materials and activities is essential for successful teaching in the social studies. Most school districts encourage teachers to use a variety of media for instruction. Obviously, though, they reward teachers not only for the materials they use, but also for using them skillfully. Whether they are intended to promote knowledge, skills, or values objectives, learning experiences can be classified into two major types: (1) information intake activities and (2) expressive activities. Although probably no single material or activity falls exclusively into either realm, this chapter has dealt primarily with those that promote intake of information.

One method of describing reliable social studies learning resources is the cone of classroom experiences. Based on Bruner's theory of how children organize and store concepts, the cone specifies three categories into which all learning materials can be classified:

1. Enactive mode (involves all methods of doing something)
   Activities within the school
   Realia
   Field trips
   Resource persons
2. Iconic mode (involves representations of real objects)
   Models or replicas
   Simulation games

   Motion pictures
   Narrated slides and filmstrips
   Computers
   Pictures and study prints
   Maps, globes, graphs, and other graphic material
3. Symbolic mode (written or oral symbols to communicate concepts)
   Social studies textbooks
   Lectures
   Reference books
   Children's literature

Whereas teachers should use a variety of activities for the social studies program, the overwhelming practice is to rely primarily on the textbook. This is not to imply that textbook usage is bad and that a multimedia approach is good, for you do not want to engage children in activities simply for the sake of making it appear as if the children are "doing something." Have a specific purpose for your social studies lesson; if a textbook best helps achieve that purpose, fine. But if the specific purpose can best be achieved by taking a field trip, choose that experience for your children. What is important is that you identify the desired outcomes of your lesson beforehand and consciously select and offer the most practical and valuable learning material to ensure that outcome.

ENDNOTES

1. Jean-Jacques Rousseau, *Emile, or, A Treatise on Education*, B. Foxley, trans. (London: Dent, 1911). (The first French edition was published in 1762.)

2. John Jarolimek, *Social Studies Competencies and Skills* (New York: Macmillan, 1977), p. 32.

3. Jerome Bruner et al., *Studies in Cognitive Growth* (New York: John Wiley, 1966).

4. John Twoler, Lisa Montgomery, and Judy Waid, "Simulation Games: How to Use," *Instructor, 68*, no. 7 (March 1970). Reprinted from *Instructor*, copyright © March 1970 by The Instructor Publications, Inc., used by permission.

5. Allen Glenn and Don Rawitsch, *Computing in the Social Studies Classroom* (Eugene, OR: International Council for Computers in Education, 1984), pp. 8–12.

6. Linwood Chase and Martha Tyler John, *A Guide for the Elementary School Teacher* (Boston: Allyn and Bacon, 1972), p. 195.

Teachers tell us that many of their school systems are moving toward the integrated teaching of various subjects in the elementary curriculum, and that they are searching for information on integrating social studies and other subjects. Social studies, it turns out, is a logical area for blending subjects previously taught separately.[1]

—Huber M. Walsh

Integrating Social Studies with the Language Arts

10

As you read, reflect on the following matters:

- What do we mean by "integrating" the elementary school curriculum?
- How does the concept of "cultural literacy" help support the idea of integrating social studies and the language arts?
- How can teachers enrich their social studies program through the use of children's literature? What types of literature are most useful in the social studies classroom?
- What special techniques do teachers use to read/tell children good stories?
- What is meant by the term "writing-across-the-curriculum"?
- How do teachers apply the writing process to the social studies program? What kinds of writing experiences are appropriate?
- How can teachers give students public recognition for their writing efforts?

Integrating content and ideas drawn from across all subject area lines has become a major trend in elementary education today. Putting things together in ways that make sense to young children is an idea that centers education in a true "child's world." A child's world is one that supports questioning minds by offering a variety of "doings" designed to satisfy and extend a child's natural sense of wonder. It is not a world fragmented into subject areas in which learning is dispensed in discrete dosages. An integrated program is one that is simply a way of examining our educational mission and looking for new curricular combinations that make the children's learning experiences more closely attuned to their unique world. Subject matter lines may be critical for adults' administrative and organizational purposes, but the child's world is not bound by such thinking. James L. Hymes invites us to consider, for example, the teacher who takes her children to the farm

> to learn where milk comes from. If you make the teacher put one label on the experience, she will probably call it science. . . . But what about the conversation in connection with the trip: before, during, and after? That should be called the language arts. The stories before and after the trip are literature. The singing—"Old McDonald Had a Farm" is fated to be sung!—must be called music. Rules for conduct are developed. This is what civics, government, and politics are all about. The teacher recalls what happened the last time the group took a trip: "You remember how we all crowded around and some people could not see." The lessons of the past are usually labeled history. A child misbehaves; the teacher's response is a lesson in psychology. Someone counts the children to be sure no one is left at the farm: arithmetic. The trips costs money; that is when the four-year-olds take a brief course in economics. The cow is probably pretty, even if the farmer and the highway are not. The presence of beauty and the absence of it are matters of aesthetics. When the teacher soothes a disappointed child—"Things don't always work out the way we want"—the lesson is one in philosophy. And if, on such a trip, the children drink some milk, that experience is labeled nutrition. Yet the whole trip is labeled science [or social studies]!
>
> The best place for labels is in the teacher's mind. Knowing the organzation of knowledge helps her to focus on what there is for her to teach. But the children do not have to sit down to learn subject matter. They do not have to keep quiet to learn subject matter. They do not have to stay together as a whole group to learn subject matter. They do not have to read subject matter out of a book. And the label does not have to show.[2]

Knowing content and how to organize knowledge helps you focus on what you teach, but no real educational opportunity can be limited to one subject matter label—learning comes in big packages. When educators speak of combining learnings from several disciplines into one package, they refer to *integrated learning*.

A SOCIAL STUDIES-LANGUAGE ARTS CONNECTION

Marlowe Berg examined the trend of integrating the elementary school curriculum and commented about the place of social studies in such a scheme:

> Where does social studies fit in this resurgence of interest in integration? Right in the middle! A major goal of the social studies is to help students understand the myriad interac-

tions of people on this planet—past, present and future. Making sense of the world requires using skills that allow one to read about the many people and places that are scattered about the globe; to use literature to understand the richness of past events. . . . The story of humankind well told requires drawing from all areas of the curriculum.[3]

Cultural literacy (see Chapter 1) has become a battle cry of those who point to major educational problems of our day. You learned that the concern for cultural literacy arose during the late 1980s as critics concluded that American youth were grossly ignorant in history and literature. But what does cultural literacy have to do with integrating the curriculum? Jeri A. Levesque examined the term and concluded:

> The terms *culture* and *literacy* are complex and need to be defined before pursuing this discussion any further. *Culture* generally refers to a way of life. It embraces all that is learned including different ways of behaving, feeling, believing, and communicating. Literacy addresses a way of communicating which utilizes language. . . . [L]iteracy has been analyzed as either a skill, a state or an action. Research focusing on literacy as a set of skills involves the decoding and thinking associated with written language. When literacy is viewed as a state of being, it is hailed as the hallmark of an educated or cultured person. Literacy as an action takes place in the mind and makes writing an essay about Manifest Destiny possible.[4]

Literacy and social studies, then, appear to be an inseparable partnership in the process of education. A truly literate person is one who can communicate with members of our society with well-developed language arts skills: reading, writing, speaking, and listening. Integrating the social studies curriculum must begin with the language arts. The *English-Language Arts Framework for California Public Schools, K–12,* has been incisive in this aspiration, calling for "subject area teachers who ensure that students read widely, write frequently, and use language effectively, rather than subject area teachers who give to reading and English teachers the whole responsibility of guiding students in acquiring effective language arts and skills."[5] The social studies is an ideal subject matter area to help achieve this ambition; it offers the content that connects children to the reading, writing, speaking, and listening acts.

UTILIZING CHILDREN'S LITERATURE

Most of us shared our childhood with an engaging array of storybook characters. Some we recall with smiles and special fondness. Their adventures and misadventures were sources of much delight, and the thought of missing out on the likes of Peter Rabbit, Curious George, Winnie-the-Pooh, or the Cat in the Hat is almost inconceivable. The narratives and illustrations filled us with delight. Powerful learning resulted from those books, too; prior to the advent of the expanding environment approach, children's literature was a valued part of the social studies program. Diane Ravitch recalls how literature was used in the past:

> Until expanding environments managed to push historical material out of the social studies curriculum, children in the early grades in most public schools learned about . . . myths, biographies, poems, . . . fairy tales, and legends. The story of Robinson Crusoe

and the study of Indian life were particular favorites. Stories about explorers, pioneer life, American heroes . . . , and famous events in American history were the staples of the first three grades. The line between historical literature and general literature was virtually non-existent. Teacher guides emphasized the importance of telling stories.[6]

Ravitch goes on to describe the status of literature in today's classrooms:

Today, children in most American public schools do not read fairy tales, myths, folklore, legends, sagas, historical adventure stories, or biographies of great men and women unless the teacher introduces them during reading period. And we know from recent studies of reading instruction that current reading methods depend almost entirely on basal readers, a species of textbook containing simple stories of ordinary children, families, and neighborhoods.[7]

Gilbert Sewall, an educational researcher, believes that this trend is destined to change in the immediate future, especially if the new history-social science framework adopted in California (see Chapter 1) affects social studies curricula to the degree most authorities think it will. Sewall reasons that since the California framework emphasizes the use of clear, exciting, informative writing as found in quality children's literature, and "[l]iterary shortcomings in textbooks seem to contribute to the broader problem of teaching [social studies] to students,"[8] great changes in the type of reading material to which students are exposed will need to be made. Those changes would appear to involve reintegrating literature with the social studies: more fairy tales, myths, legends, biographies, and historical fiction.

Reading and Telling Stories

Children enjoy having stories read or told; most have been exposed to them since they were babies. The pleasurable experiences they delighted in at home should be extended in school through varied, ongoing, positive story-sharing experiences.

A key to developing an exciting early grade social studies program is to replicate as closely as possible the learning conditions most children bring from home—going places and hearing good stories. Read to the children several times a day; it doesn't have to happen during social studies class to be social studies: Is *Katy and the Big Snow,* by Virginia Lee Burton, a "reading class" book or a "social studies class" book? It is both—books must be *about something* and they must be *read.* Therefore, when you read to children, you are not only reinforcing important literacy skills but are also introducing them to people, places, and things that are commonly categorized as social studies.

Read aloud from books such as *Katy and the Big Snow,* Lois Lenski's *The Little Fire Engine,* Virginia Lee Burton's *Mike Mulligan and His Steam Shovel,* Hardie Gramatky's *Little Toot,* and Donald Crews's *Harbor and Freight Train* to present the children with examples of how machines work to make our lives easier. Youngsters can be transported by their imaginations to visit exciting places such as the seashore in Claude Clayton Smith's *The Gull That Lost the Sea;* the Maine countryside in Robert McCloskey's *Blueberries For Sal;* the top of a city apartment building in John and Lucy Hawkinson's *Little Boy Who Lives Up High;* a deep, dark, wintry forest in Jane Yolen's

The surest way to bring children and books together is to indicate a joy in reading aloud.

Owl Moon; the arid Kapiti Plain in Verna Aardema's *Bringing Rain to the Kapiti Plain;* the North Pole in Chris Van Allsburg's stirring Christmas book, *The Polar Express,* or a Chinese fishing village in Marjorie Flack's *The Story of Ping.* They can return to times past in Donald Hall's *Ox-Cart Man,* or examine the deep emotions of childhood in Bernard Waber's *Ira Sleeps Over,* Judy Blume's *The Pain and The Great One,* or William Steig's *Doctor DeSoto.*

Good stories can provide valued sources of instructional material to teach social studies; you can't teach social studies if you don't have a good book to work with. It is difficult to say which books will be enjoyed by any particular group of children, though. Some will like stories that somewhat mirror their own lives, and others want to imagine what they have not yet experienced. Some want adventure and fantasy; others delight in humor and nonsense. Most, however, will enjoy a wide variety of children's literature if the stories are chosen carefully and the story-sharing session is made as enjoyable as possible.

You can locate quality literature for children of all grades by examining several different sources of information:

1. Follow the annual children's book awards. Some of the most influential awards are
   - the *Caldecott Medal,* for the most outstanding picture book
   - the *Newbery Medal,* for the most significant book in children's literature
   - the *Carter G. Woodson Book Award,* for books that deal accurately with minorities
   - the *National Book Award,* for the most significant juvenile book published in the United States
   - the *Carnegie Medal,* for the most distinguished book written in English and first published in the United Kingdom
   - the *Kate Greenaway Medal,* for the most outstanding illustration of children's books
   - the *Canadian Library Award,* for the most distinguished book authored by a citizen of Canada

2. Take time to read the children's books. Develop a spirit of appreciation and love for children's books. Teachers should never outgrow the enjoyment children's books bring. A wise person once said, "There are good books which are only for adults because their comprehension presupposes adult experiences, but there are no good books which are only for children."

3. Examine children's book reviews in professional journals such as *Social Education* (the journal of the National Council for the Social Studies), *Social Studies and the Young Learner* (the elementary journal of NCSS), or *Language Arts* (the journal of the National Council of Teachers of English).

4. Probe handbooks that recommend books for children according to ages. Jim Trelease's *The Read Aloud Handbook* (New York: Penguin, 1985) is one source; *For Reading Out Loud!* by Margaret Mary Kimmel and Elizabeth Segal (Delacorte, 1983) is another fine guide for locating books to share with children.

5. Talk with experienced teachers or librarians. They often create their own lists of favorites based upon the stories children have enjoyed over the years.

Marjorie V. Fields and Dorris Lee advise that, despite all our diligence in choosing good books, the final arbiter is the individual teacher:

> Teachers cannot possibly find an expert opinion on every book, nor should they. Instructors must develop their own criteria for what constitutes a good book and then form an opinion about which books are right for certain children and in which specific situations. One simple guide is to decide if you like a book yourself. Good children's literature isn't just interesting to children; it is timeless. Have you picked up a child's story book and found that you couldn't put it down until you finished it? That's definitely a good book.[9]

The magic and wonder of books capture the children's wide-eyed, wondering spirit, and their variety often leaves them spellbound. When we choose books that help children explore the real world, we must be careful of two very important considerations. A major concern in choosing books is to select those free of unfair racial, ethnic, or cultural stereotypes. Black, Hispanic, Native American, or Asian characters should be portrayed in realistic settings. Second, steer clear of books perpetuating sexist stereotypes—the story with a little girl in a frilly dress running to a boy to have her doll fixed or a "brave" boy who cannot express emotions such as fear. Remember that male roles as well as female roles have been traditionally stereotyped in children's stories. Try to avoid establishing such stunted role expectations; choose stories that portray people in roles free of racial, ethnic, cultural, or sex stereotypes.

Children's Literature in Broader Contexts

A major aim of an integrated social studies-literacy program is to produce not only readers who *can read* but ones who will continue to read throughout their lives. To accomplish this goal, children should not only listen to good stories but also have ample opportunity to read good literature.

Like adult literature, good children's literature offers variety. Those seemingly most appropriate for the social studies curriculum include folk and fairy tales; fables, myths, and legends; biographies; and historical fiction. These and other kinds of literature are commonly called "genres." You should be sensitive to this broad variety of literature available for children in the social studies program so you can help them learn from it.

Folk and Fairy Tales

Handed down by word of mouth for generations, folktales are wildly imaginative stories that have enraptured people since the beginning of language. Originating wherever people gathered—in marketplaces, during tasks such as weaving or sowing, in taverns, or around the hearth—the stories were told not only for the entertainment of the listener but often as an expression of the philosophies and living conditions of the masses of illiterate people. The rich oral tradition of these stories was kept alive for generations by storytellers; the tales eventually found their place within printed literature.

The deep reservoir of folktales is a source of abundant social studies reading material. *The Arabian Nights,* for example, is a collection of tales that reveal much about early life in India, Persia, and North Africa. "Aladdin and His Wonderful Lamp" is one example of these tales that originated in the Moslem world. The folktales of France may be quite familiar to you: "Cinderella," "Puss in Boots," "Blue Beard," "The Sleeping Beauty," and "Red Riding-Hood." They were all created by Charles Perrault in 1697 and greeted by French children with the same enthusiasm children bring to their reading or telling today. In Russia, children delight to tales such as "The Mitten" and "Peter and the Wolf." "Ananse," the clever spider, and other tales of animal heroes have fascinated African children with their charming explanations of natural phenomena. When people speak of Scandinavian folktales, they often refer to *East o' the Sun and West o' the Moon,* one of the most popular collections of folktales the world has known. Another traditionally celebrated source of folktales is the work of the Brothers Grimm in Germany. "The Golden Goose," "Hansel and Gretel," and "Rumpelstiltskin" are three favorites from this source. When English folktales are mentioned, "Mother Goose" rhymes normally come to mind. But "The Story of the Three Bears," "The Story of the Three Little Pigs," "Henny Penny," and "Dick Whittington and His Cat" will be remembered for generations, too. In Japan, "The Dancing Kettle" makes a fortune for a junk dealer. The Native American Indians of Wisconsin tell the story of how "Little Bear" threw the sun back into the sky after it was stolen by an old woman. A popular Yugoslavian tale, "Nail Soup," has evolved into the children's favorite, "Stone Soup." Legendary heroes such as Paul Bunyan, Pecos Bill, John Henry, Joe Magarac, Mike Fink, Tony Beaver, and Casey Jones all have become a part of North American folklore. "Tikta Liktak" is a brave and skilled Eskimo hunter who triumphs over the forces of nature.

Scholarly investigators since the nineteenth century have examined the sources of folktales and have found that versions of the same story appear around the world, even in locations far removed from one another. For example, scholars have found variations of "Cinderella" in England, Iceland, and China.

Mrs. Gilland, a third-grade teacher, used this phenomenon to enrich her unit on China. To begin, Mrs. Gilland read two books to her students: the Charles Perrault version of *Cinderella* (retold by Amy Ehrlich and illustrated by Susan Jeffers [Dial, 1985]) and the Chinese version, *Yeh-Shen* by Ai-ling Louie and illustrated by Ed Young (Philomel, 1982). She then constructed a large chart which had the titles of the books across the top and the areas for comparison along the side (see Figure 10–1).

FIGURE 10–1

Chart Comparing Two Versions of Cinderella

	Cinderella	*Yeh-Shen*
Characters	Stepmother, 2 stepsisters, prince, fairy godmother, and beautiful Cinderella	Stepmother, stepsister, king, and beautiful Yeh-Shen
Setting	"Once upon a time" long ago in Europe	Long ago in China
Problem	Stepmother and stepsisters mistreat Cinderella. She is not allowed to go to the ball.	Stepmother forces Yeh-Shen to do the heaviest work. She kills Yeh-Shen's pet fish. Yeh-Shen is not allowed to go to the big festival.
Magic	Fairy godmother turns a pumpkin into a gleaming coach and rags into clothes, including glass slippers.	The bones of Yeh-Shen's dead fish give her a dress and slippers.
Events	Cinderella goes to the ball, loses a glass slipper while rushing to return by midnight; prince finds the slipper, Cinderella tries it on, and marries the prince.	Yeh-Shen goes to the festival, loses a slipper, returns home. King finds slipper and searches for owner; Yeh-Shen tries on the slipper and it fits. Her rags become a gown. Yeh-Shen marries the king.

To help the children fill in the information, Mrs. Gilland asked timely and appropriate questions; for example:

"Who were the main characters in the stories? How were they alike? Different?"

"Where do the stories take place? When?"

"How are the settings alike? Different?"

"What problems did Cinderella face? Yeh-Shen?"

Mrs. Gilland's overall goal was to help the children understand that, despite many differences in cultures around the world, similar problems often motivate people to generate similar ideas. (Did you recognize the pattern of Mrs. Gilland's lesson as the DLE, described in Chapter 4?) Mrs. Gilland brought this phase of her China unit to closure by having her students dramatize the events of both stories. To work with folktales in a similar way, it is important to know the characteristics of this literary genre. Folktales have these characteristics:

- enchanted people (a long sleep, for example)
- people, animals, or objects with magical powers (magical lamp, magical kiss, hen that lays golden eggs, for example)
- special tasks and trials (return by midnight, guess the name of Rumpelstiltskin, for example)
- a clever hero ("The Hare and the Tortoise," for example)
- absolute character portrayal (good people are altogether good, wicked people are completely wicked)

Children enjoy hearing folktales and find their exciting action most appealing. In their enjoyment, children can perceive a sense of their own culture and appreciate the cultures of others.

Fables, Myths, and Legends

Fables, myths, and legends, like folktales, belong to the great component of literature we refer to as "folklore." They were created by illiterate people, with no scientific knowledge of the mysteries of their natural world, as an attempt to create explanations for those mysteries.

Fables are short, moralistic stories that were intended to serve as guides for a society's behaviors. They take contrasting ideas of good and bad and attempt to make them meaningful enough to be remembered, usually by assigning animal characters such qualities as greed, vanity, or wisdom. A moral is normally tacked onto the end of the fable: "Do not count your chickens before they are hatched." In our culture, fables are usually associated with the name Aesop, a Greek slave who is said to have lived about 600 B.C. "The Tortoise and the Hare" is one of Aesop's fables that you may remember ("Slow and steady wins the race."). Do you recall "The Grasshopper and the Ants" ("No one has the right to play all the time or he will have to suffer for it.") or "A Lion and a Mouse" ("Little friends might prove great friends.")?

Myths and legends involve simplistic explanations of some aspect of nature that mystified people of the past. Usually these stories involve the exploits of superhuman beings cast in the image of humans or beasts. Greek and Norse myths are the prime sources of mythology for the Western world, but they are too difficult for children to read in their original forms. Elementary school children become too confused with the Greek and Norse gods that dominate these stories. If myths and legends are used, they should be chosen as representative of ethnic groups contributing to American folklore.

Olaf Baker's *The Story of Jumping Mouse* (Warne, 1981) and Paul Goble's books *The Girl Who Loved Wild Horses, Star Boy, Buffalo Woman,* and *The Great Race* (Bradbury 1978, 1983, 1984, 1985) are beautifully written and illustrated myths and legends that offer insight into Native American Indian culture.

Fables, myths, and legends, as with folk and fairy tales, offer children a source of insight into other cultures. For that reason, they should be included in the social studies program. However, they also serve as themes for the children to create their own stories for today. Students would be interested in selecting a moral for a fable and using their imagination to write a story to illustrate it. At the beginning of a unit on "Islands," you may ask your students to write a myth or legend about how islands came into being. Then, compare their accounts to actual scientific explanations as the unit progresses. Explain to the students that myths and legends represented truths before the advent of modern science.

Biographies and Historical Fiction

Biographies are original, written stories detailing the lives of interesting people. As history, biographies must be rooted in fact.

Children meet Harriet Tubman, Paul Revere, Debora Sampson, Sam Houston, Abe Lincoln, George Washington Carver, or Maria Tallchief in their social studies texts, but reading about their real lives presents a vividness difficult to attain through other means. Biographies impress children with a sense of historical reality. Even early primary-grade children can become interested in biographies if you give them picture biographies such as those by Ingri and Edgar Parin d'Aulaire (*Abraham Lincoln, Benjamin Franklin, George Washington, Pocahontas, Columbus, Buffalo Bill*). Gradually, you can move on to many excellent biographies suitable for children at each age level: Fernando Monjo's *The One Bad Thing About Father* gives a son's view of Teddy Roosevelt; James T. DeKay's *Meet Martin Luther King, Jr.* is a picture essay describing King's early childhood and growth into adulthood; Dan D'Amelio's *Taller Than Bandia Mountain: The Story of Hideyo Noguchi* tells of a Japanese doctor's efforts to combat serious obstacles while achieving success in bacteriological research; and Evelyn Lampman's *Wheels West: The Story of Tabitha Brown* describes a 66-year-old woman's wagon train trip to Oregon, where she became a famed educational pioneer.

Historical fiction is a category of realistic stories set during an historical period that is convincingly true to life. It often includes actual historical figures such as Peter Stuyvesant or Abraham Lincoln, but normally uses fictional characters in settings that are historically accurate. The work of Esther Forbes provides an excellent comparison of a biographical story and historical fiction. In 1942 Forbes won the Pulitzer Prize for her adult biography, *Paul Revere and the World He Lived In*. While she was researching the book, she uncovered many fascinating stories about Boston's apprentices. As a result, she created a book for children, *Johnny Tremain* (Houghton Mifflin, 1943) that won the Newbery Medal in 1944. The book is about a silversmith's apprentice who lived in Boston in the days leading to the American Revolution. It remains one of the most popular pieces of historical fiction to this day. Joan W. Blos's *A Gathering of Days* (Scribner's, 1979), also a Newbery Medal winner, is a contemporary example of quality historical fiction. It describes in diary format what it was like to grow up in New Hampshire during the 1830s.

Storytelling Techniques

Good literature and the social studies are inseparable. Through various genres of literature, students are able to recognize concerns that unite people of all ages, places, and times. Your social studies program will be enriched by "using material that engages the hearts as well as the minds of your students."[10]

Sometimes all the children will have copies of a story you wish to share and will be able to read it silently, but most often you will either read or tell it. Be familiar with the story before you share it with your students. You will be able to share it more effectively by knowing it well. Your expression and pacing will be more natural and you will be able to skip any long passages that might cause children to lose interest. In general, these guidelines should help you plan a profitable story-sharing session with your students:

1. Be prepared—know the story well.
2. Sit on a low chair or on the floor.
3. Introduce the children to the main characters of the story as well as to the setting in which it takes place. A small cloth drawstring bag decorated with relevant characters helps motivate the children for the story. Place an object in the bag that represents a key character or theme in the story to be read; for example, a piece of inexpensive sterling silver could be used for Esther Forbes's book *Johnny Tremain*. Have the children touch the bag and try to guess what it contains. After everyone who wants to try gets a chance, open the bag and reveal the object while relating it to the story to be read. This technique helps capture the children's attention and motivates them to listen for the significance of the object in the story. Johnny Tremain, of course, was an apprentice silversmith.
4. Encourage the children to ask questions about the pictures and to relate the picture content to their own experiences. Keep this part of your introduction brief, however, for if you extend it unreasonably, you run the risk of losing their attention before the story even starts.
5. Use your voice effectively. Speak naturally, but be aware of the ways in which volume, pitch, and speed can affect the mood of a story.
6. Keep good eye contact with the children. A good storyteller looks directly at the audience in order to gain and hold their interest.
7. Use appropriate gestures to add to the vividness of the story being told.
8. Anticipate questions and minor interruptions during the reading or storytelling period. Handle children's questions or comments tactfully, so the flow of the story is not interrupted. For example, one child became so absorbed in a story that he blurted out just before the climax, "Aladdin finds out that the woman isn't holy. She's a wicked magician; Aladdin kills her." Although the storyteller could have become flustered at the revelation of the story's ending, she remained composed and simply commented, "Your idea was very good, Robin, but let's all listen and see if you were right." The children in this case were drawn right back into the story.
9. Share pictures throughout the story if they help clarify or illustrate the evolving sequence of events. Use a variety of visual aids. (*Flannel-boards* have traditionally been used by early childhood teachers for this purpose.)
10. After the story is completed, you will want to discuss the major characters and events to make sure the children understood the essential nature of the story. (Review Chapter 4 for appropriate techniques.) There is no particular number of

recommended questions to ask following a story. Sometimes children will want to talk about a story for five or ten minutes; at other times they will only want to reflect on it quietly. Don't ruin a discussion by prolonging it with too many questions.

Not all these considerations will need to be examined before each story time. However, all must be emphasized because your ability to plan and execute a story-sharing experience is so important to the success or failure of the children's total social studies program. Your preparation is central to making literature a delightful and rewarding experience for both your children and yourself.

WRITING IN THE SOCIAL STUDIES CLASSROOM

The term *writing-across-the-curriculum* is often used to label the approach to planning that offers children purposeful writing opportunities in the social studies. Their writing may be either realistic or fanciful, but it must present information accurately. In

TABLE 10–1
Purposes and Forms of Writing in the Social Studies

Purpose	Writing Form
To record feelings	—Personal letters —Science reports —Poems —Jottings of sensory impressions from observations, stories, drama, music, art —Diaries, journals
To describe	—Character portraits —Reports of a sequence of events —Labels and captions —Advertisements, e.g., wanted to buy or sell, lost and found
To inform or advise	—Posters advertising coming events —Scripts for news broadcasts —Minutes of meetings —Invitations —Programs
To persuade	—Advertisements and commercials —Letters to the editor —Notes for a debate —Cartoons
To clarify thinking	—Note-taking for research topics —Explanations of graphs, science diagrams, etc. —Jottings

writing-across-the-curriculum, students view writing as a means to (1) communicate information and (2) organize their thinking. Terry Salinger describes how this can be accomplished in the social studies:

> A unit on Thanksgiving, for example, could lead to a factual report on the Pilgrims or Indians, a letter from Plymouth colony, a description of the first Thanksgiving dinner (with drawings), a thank-you note to Squanto, a script to reenact the first Thanksgiving dinner, a report on Thanksgiving celebrations in other nations, or a recipe for cooking turkeys. A few children may find some of the assignments "silly"; others may have trouble handling a full "research report"; but because there are varied opportunities for writing, the whole class—avid story writers to meticulous fact seekers—can accomplish something. Through assignments like these, children gain valuable practice writing in different modes, for different purposes, and to different audiences.[11]

Jo Ann Parry and David Hornsby charted the wide range of possibilities available for functional writing experiences in the social studies. Table 10–1 summarizes their collection. You can see that there exist many useful purposes for writing in the social studies. The social studies program encourages children to experiment with as many as possible.

TABLE 10–1
continued

Purpose	Writing Form
To explore and maintain relationships with others	–Letters –Requests –Greeting cards –Questionnaires
To predict or hypothesize	–Speculations about probable outcomes in health, science, social studies topics –Endings for stories –Questions for research or interviews
To make comparisons	–Charts –Note-making –Diagrams, graphs –Descriptions
To command or direct	–Recipes –Instructions, *How to make a* –Stage directions –Rules for games, safety, health, etc.
To amuse or entertain	–Jokes, riddles, puzzles –Scripts for dramas, puppet plays –Stories and poems –Personal anecdotes

Source: Reproduced with permission from Jo Ann Parry and David Hornsby, *Write On: A Conference Approach to Writing* (Portsmouth, NH: Heinemann Educational Books, 1985).

The Writing Process

To help children learn effectively in a literacy-based social studies program, there must be ample opportunity for reading and writing. Before you begin any such program, however, you need to think carefully about what is meant by the writing process. Figure 10–2 illustrates the major phases involved in the writing process. It is not intended as a rigid pattern for procedural steps that every child must follow, but as an organizational guide to help you plan appropriate classroom experiences.

Recognizing Children's Writing Efforts

Children may receive public recognition for their written work in several ways. Three methods that I have found to be most beneficial for social studies programs are bulletin board displays, book publishing, and class newspapers.

Bulletin Board Displays

Seeing their work exhibited on an attractive bulletin board is a proud moment for elementary school students. Be sure to include the work of all authors on the board, except for those who are somewhat timid about sharing. Children should not be forced to exhibit their work publicly. Mount the writing at the children's eye level so they can read each other's work without straining. Choose a theme for the display that will attract everyone's attention (see Figure 10–3).

FIGURE 10–2
Phases of the Writing Process

EXPERIENCING
–Direct experiences provide ideas for incubation: "Maybe I can write about that."

PREWRITING
–Discussing ideas with others, interviewing, researching, reviewing events, taking notes, and brainstorming help children generate and organize ideas.

DRAFTING
–Getting ideas and feelings down on paper in the form of a rough draft; children should not be overly concerned with spelling, punctuation, or style at this point.

EDITING
–Sharing the draft with a peer and planning changes to strengthen it.
–Proofreading the revised product to check on details such as spelling, punctuation, grammar, and handwriting.

PUBLISHING
–Writing the final copy to be shared with an intended audience.

FIGURE 10–3
Sample Bulletin Board Display

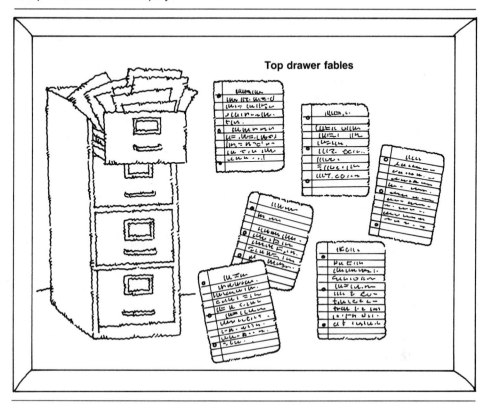

Book Publishing

Any collection of individual or group written works produced by the students could be compiled and published in the form of a book. First books can simply be the pieces of paper stapled between two sheets of construction paper. Eventually, students will prefer a bound copy including a title page, preface, and table of contents. A guide to group publishing was effectively organized by Jo Ann Parry and David Hornsby; the process is shown in Figure 10–4.

Newspapers

Classroom newspapers help provide a stimulating publishing medium. Children can write about what's happening on the local, regional, national, or world scene, a special social studies activity, a new classroom animal, field trips, classroom visitors, or new books of particular interest; they may even include an advice column, a lost and found column, want ads, or advertisements.

FIGURE 10–4

A Guide to Group Publishing (Source: Reproduced with permission from Jo Ann Parry and David Hornsby,
Write On: A Conference Approach to Writing *(Portsmouth, NH: Heinemann Educational Books, 1985).)*

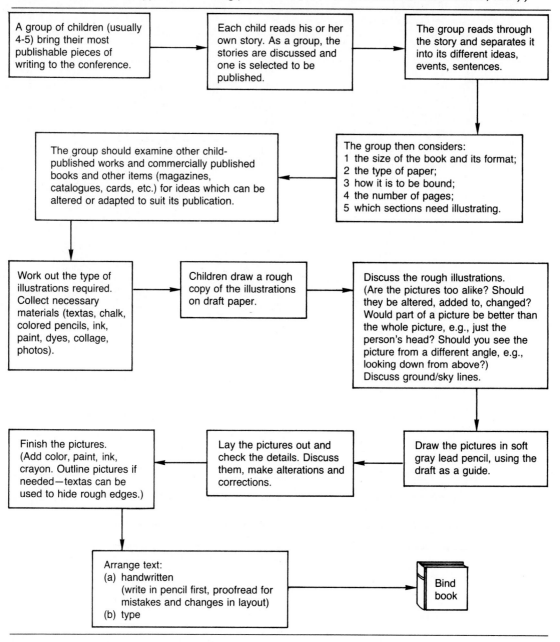

Children benefit most when their classroom newspaper is based on what they know about real newspapers. A trip to a newspaper publisher can help the children understand how newspapers are planned and produced. Although newspaper publishers differ in organizational arrangements, some responsibilities of newspaper people can be simulated in the classroom; for example:

> *Publisher*—owner or person who represents the owner; responsible for the overall operation of the newspaper. (The teacher usually assumes this position.)
>
> *Editors*—responsible for several facets of newspaper production, such as deciding what goes into the newspaper, assigning reports to cover events, determining where to position the stories, or writing their opinions of significant events (editorials).
>
> *Reporters*—cover the stories; columns to which reporters can be assigned include class news, school news, local, state, national, and world news, sports, or special events; reporters can interview others as primary sources for gathering their news or use secondary sources such as radio, television, newspapers, or magazines.
>
> *Feature writers*—produce special columns such as jokes and riddles, lost and found, a version of "Dear Abby," recipes, and so on.
>
> *Copy editors*—read stories for mistakes and adjust length to meet space requirements.

After assigning several students to the news gathering and processing activities, you will want to get the rest of the class involved in these "behind the scenes" departments:

> *Production department*—put pictures and stories together and get them ready for printing. (Children who know how to use the typewriter, or have a desire to learn, make special contributions here.)
>
> *Art department*—create ads (with pictures) that highlight coming events, special sales, parent meetings, special assemblies, or other important school functions.
>
> *Mechanical department*—run the ditto machine or copier, collate the newspaper pages, staple them, and get them ready for distribution.
>
> *Circulation department*—deliver the newspaper to the principal, other teachers, and classmates.

By simulating a real newspaper, children bring more interest and excitement to their work. Be careful, though, to make sure that all children have an equal opportunity to assume as many different newspaper responsibilities as possible. Let them try the various jobs so they develop a complete understanding of the many duties performed on a real newspaper and enlarge their interests in the different areas. Figure 10–5 is an example of an elementary class's newspaper.

FIGURE 10–5

Newspaper (Adapted from a creative classroom newspaper program developed by Dr. John Heaps when he was a laboratory school teacher at Mansfield (PA) University.)

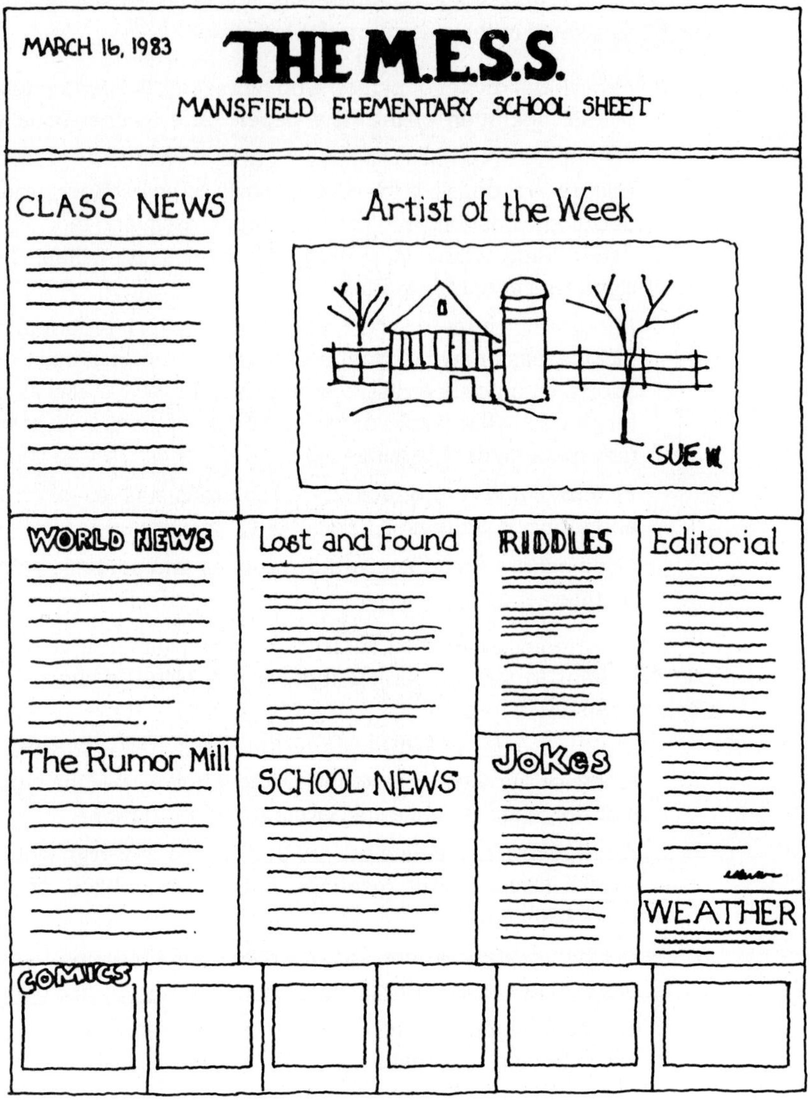

It is not until children publish their work that they become fulfilled as writers. Publishing should not be considered a boastful process where only the "best work" gets chosen for public sharing; it should be an integral part of the writing process for everyone.

Types of Writing in the Social Studies

James Britton[12] suggests three categories into which all writing could be divided:

1. *the expressive voice,* in which children write about themselves, usually in the pattern of "I + (action verb)."
2. *poetic writing,* which includes stories, plays, poems, jokes, and other creative expressions that have a basic structural pattern.
3. *transactional writing,* where information, directions, advice, or persuasion are expressed.

The Expressive Voice

Children are quite comfortable with the expressive voice and instinctively use it in their writing. Very little teacher direction is required to encourage children to write about themselves. One teacher, valuing a strong interpersonal component of her social studies program, passed out a sheet like the one illustrated in Figure 10–6. She invited the children to bring in a photograph that they could glue to the bottom and encouraged them to complete several variations of the "I + (action verb)" statements.

Poetic Writing

Writing poetry demands that students use language in unique ways, creating vivid word pictures to describe the world around or within them. Ideally, teachers should not use an analytic approach to writing poetry, in which children are required to dissect words and phrases extensively. Instead teachers should introduce poetry by encouraging personal visualization of an image that a poet has sketched with words. Choose a good poem and read it aloud as the children listen with eyes closed. Many poems' themes can be related directly to specific social studies topics under study. Zena Sutherland's *Children and Books,* 7th edition (Glenview, IL: Scott, Foresman, 1985) is a highly useful source of "visualizing poems." Children can be encouraged to translate the poet's verbal images into an art medium after the listening experience.

Teachers have discovered that art media are natural companions of poetry. Students can begin to sense the relationship by using relaxing art media such as fingerpaints, clay, and watercolors. They might be taken outdoors to depict a scene, for example, or simply be asked to express their thoughts and feelings freely. In either case, their artistic depictions can then be used as structures to be translated into words. These first translation efforts are commonly referred to as *free-thought experiences.* Free-thoughts are simply one- or two-line, unstructured word pictures associated with an artistic expression. Here is one fourth grader's free-thought expression associated with

FIGURE 10–6
Activity Sheet to Encourage Writing in the Expressive Voice

I am __Laura_____.
I am __7__ years old.
I have __green__ eyes and __brown__ hair.
In my spare time, I love to __read__.
My favorite school subject is __Social Studies__.

A picture of me.

a scene depicting a polluted landscape: "The world will be no more unless people learn to protect it."

In order to use forms of poetry other than free-thought effectively, teachers often find it useful to offer specific demonstrations or models. By observing models, students can easily see what can be done and how. This is an important consideration, especially since specific patterns of poetry have unique ways of generating images. It should be emphasized, however, that the act of writing poetry is a creative process and that the *form* and not the specific *wording* serves as the model. Louise Rosenblatt describes this personal aspect of poetry: "[The writer] marshalls his resources and crystallizes out from the stuff of memory, thought, and feeling a new order, a new experience, which he sees as the poem. This becomes part of the ongoing stream of his life experience, to be reflected on from any angle important to him as a human being."[13]

Forms of poetry appropriate for expressing thoughts and feelings in the social studies include the following.

The Haiku. This highly structured form of Japanese poetry consists of three lines of seventeen syllables—the first and third lines have five syllables each and the second line has seven. These poems usually describe nature, and appeal to children of all ages.

The rain is falling
Soon the flowers will burst out.
Spring is beautiful.

The Senryu.　This form of Japanese poetry is structurally similar to the haiku, but expresses ideas about human beings rather than nature.

The strong ox-cart man
Trudges down the lonely trail.
His cart is his life.

The Tanka.　Tanka are extensions of haiku; they add two lines of seven syllables to the haiku and contain a total of thirty-one syllables.

Big puffy white clouds
Floating across a blue sea.
A white castle there?
Maybe a giant white ship?
What do you want them to be?

The Cinquain.　The cinquain is not a form of Japanese poetry, but is often thought of as such because of its similar structural pattern. Cinquains consist of five lines following this syllable pattern:

The ships	(two syllables)
remarkably	(four syllables)
slip across the ocean	(six syllables)
seeking a new discovery.	(eight syllables)
Land ho!	(two syllables)

Some teachers have chosen to simplify this form, using numbers of words instead of syllables per line: one word, two words, three words, four words, one word.

The Simile.　Similes are comparisons made between two things or ideas that people normally tend not to associate. The words "like" or "as" often signal the associations, as in, "as quiet as a mouse." Here is an example of a fourth grader's simile, written in response to the teacher's suggested title, "How Brave Can You Be?"

I can be as brave as a tree in a thunderstorm.
I can be as brave as a seed sprouting under the dirt.
I can be as brave as writing this poem!

Persona.　Here is an example of how one upper-grade teacher extended the study of tribal societies by guiding her group through the use of "persona" as a writing technique.[14]

To begin, the students had just learned that in many tribal societies a person has a "bush soul" as well as his or her own. The bush soul can take the form of an animal, tree, rock, or some other existence in nature that might give one strength and courage. This characterization aspect can be applied to writing poetry—putting oneself in the place of someone or something else (real or imaginary) to say what might not normally be revealed.

The teacher started her class by displaying a large poster print of a young African woman adorned in ceremonial attire, gazing wistfully into a brilliant sunset. The teacher asked her class to extend their imaginations and become that young woman.

At this point, the students were asked questions about the scene. For example:

"Who are you?"

"What are doing in the picture?"

"Where do you live?"

"How do you feel?"

"What is it like to be you?"

"What changes have you been through in your life?"

The teacher wrote the children's responses in a few short lines of prose:

There was a young woman
Adorned with jewels
And painted with earthen ashes.
It seemed like only yesterday
When she frolicked freely in the fields.
Now she prepares for a wedding ritual.
What lies ahead is invisible.

The teacher began her writing sequence with a direct experience and used oral activities to create a written product. The model product was then kept in full view as the students each received their own photos depicting tribal life cut from old *National Geographic* magazines. They were to write their own "persona poetry" using the writing process techniques described earlier in this section. Once completed, the poems and photos were mounted on colored construction paper to be displayed for all to enjoy.

Objects.   Bring in intriguing objects related to a topic of study and encourage children to write about them. Perhaps the children could pretend to be that object and describe a typical day as the object.

Historical Transplants.   Describe the reactions of famous people of the past if they were to come back to life today. What do they see or experience that would make them happy? Unhappy? Afraid?

Character Transplants.   Take someone who has assumed a strong stance on a particular issue (like Jane Fonda) and place him or her into a new situation—for example, as a colonial housewife. Of course, the character's personality and attitudes must remain unchanged.

Someone I Admire.   Invite the children to write about the most impressive character they ever met.

Unusual Questions.   Put a series of unusual questions about a social studies topic on the board and invite the children to write about one:

What does Paul Revere's horse think of him?

What is it like being a skyscraper?

How would you like to yabber with a jackeroo?

How did bees get such small waists?

Story Starters. Provide beginnings to stories and ask the children to complete them. For example:

> The storm lasted two days and two nights. I never saw waves so high or the wind blow so hard. Our ship was thrown against huge rocks and was smashed to bits. We held onto our lifeboats for longer than I could remember and finally spotted some land. . . .

Diaries. Use popular situations (such as Columbus's journey to America) or famous personalities as a stimulus to write daily diary entries. For example, a diary can be used to extend the story starter.

> *Day 10.* Fresh water is disappearing. Captain Jones divided us into four groups. Each group was to go in a different direction to search for fresh water. In midafternoon the fourth group found a freshwater spring on the west side of the island.

Endings. Ask the children to write stories that end with a sentence you provide for them, such as:

> I'll never do that again!

> And that's how the state of Texas got longhorn cattle.

> "Mrs. Jackson is right, Melissa. There is a city law against keeping a horse in your backyard."

> And, even though Lake Michigan still faces other problems, fish are finding it a safe place to live again.

> We held onto our lifeboats for what seemed like forever!

Transactional Writing

Transactional writing is the form of personal expression by which we communicate information or directions or attempt to influence others by offering advice or presenting persuasive arguments. Some children experiment readily with transactional writing, while others need encouragement and instruction. Be watchful of those children who feel comfortable writing in the poetic voice, for they are the ones who will most eagerly undertake the risk of writing in the transactional voice. John Kerrigan, for example, made the move when he became deeply interested in his principal's decision to remove the door from the boy's restroom in order to curb vandalism. See Figure 10–7 for John's effort.

Letters. Letters comprise one type of transactional writing possible for the social studies classroom. Children can write letters for many real and imaginary purposes:

- To thank people involved in field trips or resource persons
- To request information from companies, travel agencies, and the like
- To personalities being studied—George Washington, Abraham Lincoln, Jefferson Davis, and so on
- To complain to or congratulate authors or editors of books and magazines

FIGURE 10–7

John Kerrigan's Sample of Transactional (Persuasive) Writing

"Are bathrooms private anymore

Mr. Towson has a great scence of hummer, his last joke was the funnyest of of all. You better sit down for this Ready? Okay - He took... you sure your ready for this... Well, he took the bathroom door off See! I tould you should sit down. Now you propally think all the resonibillaty has gone to his head. Well for once I think he's absolutely almost right. Heres his side. Someone took three rolls of tolite paper in the toilet and flush it. It flooded the bathroom and the boys locker room. But taking the bathroom door off is to much. I mean you ever try and go in the bathroom with about 50 girls standing in front. But, there is a good part, the vandalism has gone down.
Now Mr. Towson has something to worry about that is weather the school board impeaches him and if the health board calls the school a health hazid.

Har! A litel town with a litel school has there own Watergate. I can see the head of linds now "First Princepal to be Impeached," I thought Mr. Towson is a nice guy (sometimes). But the health hazard is yet a nother thing. But don't worry Mr. Towson will figure out some and we hop bathrooms are still private

                                        Chris

OH The Bathroom, first open Door on the right

- To invite people to visit the classroom
- To a sick classmate or one who has moved

Informational Writing. Another major type of transactional writing commonly employed in social studies classrooms is informational writing—written reports. To understand how the writing process can be applied to informational writing, let us visit a classroom where students are planning an informational report on mountains.

> The students in Mr. Jackson's fourth grade class were in the final week of a unit on the topic of mountain regions around the world. Today, Mr. Jackson divided the class heterogeneously into cooperative learning groups to summarize what they had learned. He began the review by asking the groups to think about any words or facts about mountains that they recalled from their previous study. A scribe from each group listed her group's points on a sheet of chart paper as they were mentioned. When the groups had exhausted their data, Mr. Jackson led a discussion to help them see relationships within the data. He began by asking the scribe from each group in turn to list the first five items from the group's chart on the chalkboard so that a cumulative list could be gathered. As each group listed its data, scribes from the other groups crossed off the duplicate items from their group charts so no data would be repeated on the class chart. Once the cumulative list was completed, Mr. Jackson led the students to seek relationships among the data. He underlined the words "Andes" and "Himalayas" in red chalk and asked, "What do both of these words tell us?" The students responded, "They are both names of mountain ranges." Mr. Jackson extended their thinking in this direction by asking, "What other words are names of mountain ranges?" At that point, students came to the board and underlined in red words such as "Rockies," "Alps," and so on. Next, Mr. Jackson directed a similar sequence by asking each cooperative learning group to gather the remaining data into categories and to give each category a name. The students suggested various categories such as "animal life," "plant life," and "human conditions." (You may recognize Mr. Jackson's strategy as the Taba approach discussed in Chapter 4.)
>
> When the categorizing activity was complete, Mr. Jackson helped his students broaden the data collection into the construction of a written informational paragraph. He began by saying, "There appear to be many facts on our list. What do you suppose it is telling us?" Silence dropped over the class, for this was a tough question. Mr. Jackson allowed some wait time; shortly, Sheena suggested, "Mountains are found all over the world." "Yeah," agreed Brody. "Some are really high and others aren't."
>
> "That's a nice start," replied Mr. Jackson. "Let's write your ideas here on our chart." He continued until all the children's ideas were recorded. Now, Mr. Jackson conducted a review of what was recorded. He asked the students to examine the first two sentences to see if they could be combined or expanded to form one sentence. Each group toyed with the words; the whole group eventually settled on "Large and small mountains are found all over the earth." Progressively, the students edited and rewrote the other sentences recorded earlier.

The next day, the cooperative learning groups became writing teams. Each team was assigned a data category and was asked to generate a web (see Chapter 4) indicating relationships among the data. They used the web as a basis to organize their thinking about what should be said in the paragraphs. Mr. Jackson also encouraged each group to use the helpful hints for informational writing chart that was on display in their classroom (see Figure 10–8). Mr. Jackson carefully guided their efforts in editing and revising what was written during group and individual conferences.

The students' written paragraphs were displayed on a large bulletin board exhibit. What did the children learn from this exercise? Certainly, they learned about mountains; and, too, they learned how to write a series of informational paragraphs, each focusing on a main theme.

Mr. Jackson's information writing sequence followed these steps:

1. *Locating Data.* Either through teacher-directed experiences or independent investigations, students locate information that will serve as the data base for writing.
2. *Categorizing.* Student groups recall the information and arrange common data into categories.
3. *Charting.* A chart summarizing data from each group serves as an organizational tool for forming main ideas and supporting details.
4. *Teacher-Guided Writing.* The class constructs a model paragraph; the teacher guides them in writing, editing, and revising what they had charted.
5. *Independent Writing.* Small groups chart a category of data and draft paragraphs from the information organized on their webs or charts.
6. *Publishing.* Students become authors. Their writings are posted on bulletin boards, read orally, bound into a book, or shared with others in any of several forms.

Political Cartoons.   A third type of transactional writing in the social studies classroom is the *political cartoon.* Political cartoons are special ways of communicating ideas or feelings. Sometimes the message of a cartoon is just plain fun—an illustrated joke. Other times, however, cartoons carry serious messages intended to change a reader's opinion about an important issue, even though they use humor or sarcasm to make their point. The humor or sarcasm usually condones or rejects a stance on an issue by forcefully presenting a single point of view.

Most cartoons deal with one central idea and are fairly uncomplicated. Cartoons use few words to express ideas because the illustrations communicate most of the message. Cartoons often emphasize outstanding physical characteristics; George Washington's hair or Abe Lincoln's beard have been popular distinguishing characteristics used by cartoonists. Cartoons also use standard, quickly recognized symbols—Uncle Sam, the Russian bear, dollar signs, the Republican elephant and the Democratic donkey, or the hawk and the dove quickly communicate an idea or feeling. Cartoons also use exaggeration and satire. This characteristic can be a problem for social studies classes; if not handled properly, it can inspire unfair stereotypes of other people or other lands.

FIGURE 10–8
Special Hints for Writing a Good Report

HOW TO WRITE A GOOD REPORT

When we spend a lot of time writing about something. we want others to understand what we say. How can we do that? Here are some tips book publishers use that might help you.

WORDS

The first clue is to print, type, or write all of your words neatly. Sometimes you will want to bring attention to certain words. When that happens. use all CAPITAL letters or **boldface** letters, or underline the word, or even use a special color. You might also want to use *special* printing to make the title or other key words to stand out.

ILLUSTRATIONS

It is always a good idea to use photographs. drawings. charts. graphs. and other illustrations to tell about things and to capture the reader's attention. For best results, plan the overall appearance of your report: how many illustrations would be best? how big will they be? where will they be placed? Try different arrangements until you find one that is most pleasing to your eye.

SPECIAL HINTS

You can use many kinds of special ideas to help people become interested in what you write. Try to include riddles. questions. or special words. One of the best "tricks" is to make up an acronym (MESS for Mansfield Elementary School Sheet, for example). Another example of an acronym (a word made up of initials of key words in your report) is one that I made up to help you remember the ideas on this chart—WISH—which stands for Words . Illustrations. and Special Hints. So, next time you want to write a good report. WISH. and your wishes will come true.

In a study by Lawrence F. Shaffer, children in grades 4–12 were asked to interpret ten cartoons.[15] Children in grades 4 through 6 tended to describe the cartoon literally rather than to interpret its implied message. Not until later grades were children able to interpret cartoon symbolism. The researchers pointed out that this age (11 to 13) corresponds to Piaget's stage of formal thinking—the age at which abstract problem solving begins to emerge. For this reason, it is probably better not to introduce cartoons into the social studies program until the intermediate grades.

You should select only cartoons that convey the simplest of ideas in as uncomplicated a fashion as possible and allow time to analyze them. Have the children learn to identify the standard symbols and central characters; recognize the activity in which the characters are engaged; analyze the cartoonist's point of view; determine the cartoonist's purpose; and decide whether they agree or disagree with the cartoonist.

Figure 10–9 is a political cartoon. These are some questions you could ask children about this particular cartoon to help them understand the purposes of political cartoons in general:

1. "This cartoon contains illustrations of people you may know. Are these real people? Can you recognize any of the people in the cartoon?"
2. "Who are the men in the dark suits? Who are the others? Why are the four presidents in dark suits at the bottom while the others are in the clouds?"
3. "What is happening in the cartoon? Why are the presidents pointing to each other? Is there anything in the cartoon that can help you answer my question? What kind of a problem is an economic problem?"
4. "What are some economic problems faced by our nation today? What point is the cartoonist making about those problems?"
5. "Do you agree or disagree with the cartoonist? Why?"

Once children understand the nature of cartoons as a learning medium, they may want to draw their own cartoons in an effort to influence opinions on matters of immediate interest to the class.

Through questioning strategies, we help youngsters understand that cartoons are tools of communication that focus on one person's point of view and his attempt to sway others toward that line of thinking. Can you think of a time when you had a strong urge to communicate your feelings about an issue? Could that situation have been turned into a cartoon? Think of an issue in social studies education that you presently have strong feelings about. Make a serious point about that issue in a funny or sarcastic way by drawing a cartoon. Share your cartoon with your classmates.

Journal Writing.   The last type of transactional writing to be discussed is *journal writing*. In journals, writers make a personal record of their thoughts and feelings while describing meaningful school experiences. As such, journal writing is basically a student's dialogue with herself in which she is free to focus on her own thoughts and feelings rather than upon assigned topics for writing. Journals may be private or dialogues with the teacher. See a sample of the latter in Figure 10–10.

Keeping journals is a somewhat uncomplicated process: the children get their journals (notebooks) toward the end of each day or week, write the date at the top of

FIGURE 10–9
Political Cartoon (Paul Conrad © 1982. Los Angeles Times. Reprinted with permission.)

AFFIXING BLAME FOR OUR ECONOMIC PROBLEMS   10-11-82

the page, and compose their entry. Entries may include drawings as well as writing. The journals are returned back to the place where they are stored. If they are dialogue journals, the teacher must be sure to respond each day or week.

Randy Mills emphasizes the importance of journal writing to the social studies program:

> Although many social educators call for activities that make social studies personally meaningful to stimulate civic participation, the problem of how to accomplish this task remains.
>
> Having students keep personal journals may be one way to help students see the relationships that exist between their personal lives and civic activity. . . . Students' keeping personal journals can be a powerful way to achieve the goals of social studies education. It can help students take part in the process of dialogue that is essential to our democratic system.[16]

FIGURE 10–10
Sample Journal Page

June 8, 1989

I read the book the Titanic Lost. . . and Found.
The best part was when the Titanic sank. It
was awesome.

"Mike!"

Your interest in
historical research
is certainly growing.
I'm happy you enjoy it
so much!

Writing is easy for children if they write about what they know—something they have read about or lived. Regardless of the source of motivation, children have much to share in the social studies classroom. Throughout the social studies program, the children use reading and writing as tools to understand their world and communicate their knowlege of it.

SUMMARY

Integrating content and strategies from many curricular areas has become a major trend in education today. Putting learnings together in new and interesting ways is a rallying point in our nation's schools. The social studies/language arts combination fits nicely into this resurgent integration effort. Through the language arts students learn about humans and their environment.

In this chapter you learned that the "cultural literacy" concern in social studies education forms the basis for a social studies/language

partnership. A literate person is one who can communicate all that is learned about the culture. Therefore, the social studies program must offer students opportunities to read widely, write frequently, and use language effectively. We considered children's literature as a rich resource for social studies content. Folk and fairy tales; fables, myths and legends; and biographies and historical fiction are major types of literature that enrich the social studies program. These books may be read by the teacher or by the children; regardless of how they are experienced, good stories help students recognize concerns that unite people of all ages, places, and times.

In addition to reading, purposeful writing opportunities should be offered in the social studies program. Referred to as "writing-across-the-curriculum," this approach offers students occasions to organize their thinking for the purpose of sharing information. You read about many useful purposes for functional writing experiences in the social studies, each of which should be developed within the procedures of the writing process: (1) experiencing, (2) prewriting, (3) drafting, (4) editing, and (5) publishing. We stressed that all five phases of the writing process are critical, but for direct application to the social studies classroom, public recognition (publishing) is especially important. Teachers

can give public recognition by allowing children to see their work exhibited in any of these ways: (1) bulletin board displays, (2) book publishing, and (3) classroom newspapers. Their published works may be in any of the three categories into which all writing could be divided: (1) the expressive voice, in which the students write about themselves, (2) poetic writing, which includes stories, plays, poems, jokes, or other creative expressions having a basic structural pattern, and (3) transactional writing, where information, directions, advice, or persuasion is expressed.

Teachers can enrich the social studies program by integrating different content areas. Social studies teachers must use creative reading and writing strategies not only as means to stimulate a wider range of thought processes but also to encourage creative thought itself.

ENDNOTES

1. Huber M. Walsh, "Editor's Notes," *Social Studies and the Young Learner, 1,* no. 2 (January–February 1989): 2.

2. James L. Hymes, Jr., *Teaching the Child Under Six,* 3rd ed. (Columbus, OH: Merrill, 1981), pp. 80–81.

3. Marlowe Berg, "Integrating Ideas for Social Studies," *Social Studies and the Young Learner, 1,* no. 3 (January/February 1989): page 1 of the pull-out feature.

4. Jeri A. Levesque, "Integrating Social Studies with Reading/Language Arts," *Social Studies and the Young Learner, 1,* no. 3 (January/February 1989): 16.

5. Francie Alexander, "California Reading Initiative," in Bernice E. Cullinan, ed., *Children's Literature in the Reading Program* (Newark, DE: International Reading Association, 1987), p. 152.

6. Diane Ravitch, "Tot Sociology," *American Educator* (Fall 1978): 38.

7. Ibid., pp. 38–39.

8. Gilbert Sewall, in "Framework Will Force Textbook Changes," *ASCD Update, 30,* no. 1 (January 1988): 2.

9. Marjorie V. Fields and Dorris Lee, *Let's Begin Reading Right* (Columbus, OH: Merrill, 1987), p. 93.

10. Dianne Monson, "Characterization in Literature: Realistic and Historical Fiction," in Bernice E. Cullinan, ed., *Children's Literature in the Reading Program* (Newark, DE: International Reading Association, 1987), p. 110.

11. Terry Salinger, *Language Arts and Literacy* (Columbus, OH: Merrill, 1988), p. 258.

12. James Britton, *Language and Learning* (Harmondsworth, England: Penguin Books, 1970).

13. Louise Rosenblatt, *The Reader, the Text, the Poem* (Carbondale and Edwardsville, IL: Southern Illinois University Press, 1978), p. 12.

14. A technique shared with me by a gifted teacher and poet, Julia Blumenreich.

15. Ralph C. Preston and Wayne L. Herman, *Teaching Social Studies in the Elementary School* (New York: Holt, Rinehart, and Winston, 1974).

16. Randy Mills, "Personal Journals for the Social Studies," *Social Education, 52,* no. 6 (October 1988): 425.

We turned our sixth-grade classroom into a Renoir Room! . . . Slowly but delightedly the students hung . . . fifty-four reproductions of Renoir paintings . . . on the four classroom walls.

The purpose of this project was to have students enter the world of Renoir through the beauty of his work, to engage in independent research to discover the man Renoir, and to digest and share this newly found world with the rest of the school.[1]

—*Albert Cullum*

Integrating the Arts into the Social Studies Program

11

KEY CONCEPTS

As you read, reflect on the following matters:

- What are "the arts?"
- Why are the arts an essential component of a superior social studies program?
- What are three basic ways to handle arts instruction? Which is the most applicable to the social studies program?
- What are the four things people do with the arts that provide a focus for discipline-based arts instruction?
- How can the arts be integrated into the social studies program?
- Does the children's exposure to the arts stop with exposure to the arts of other cultures? If not, what else should they experience?

THE ARTS IN THE SCHOOLS

In this classroom, children reproduce Renoir paintings, perform dramatic interpretations of Edna St. Vincent Millay, and move freely to Bartok sonatas. Through these great works, the children become emotionally involved with social studies subject matter. They enjoy dancing, singing, strumming guitars, painting, and sculpting.

Their teacher has chosen to employ a social studies program that integrates the arts: music, drama (theater), dance, and the visual arts. His aim in doing so is to help students gain a sense of what a civilization's human spirit is by examining the great works of art created by its people. That idea is pure and simple, but the harsh truth is that arts education is denied most children in our elementary school classrooms today. In 1988, the U.S. Congress commissioned the National Endowment for the Arts to publish a report on the nature of arts education in American schools. Its extensive study found the arts to be in jeopardy: "They are not viewed as serious; knowledge itself is not viewed as a prime educational objective; and those who determine school curricula do not agree on what arts education is."[2] Elliot Eisner, an eminent scholar in both the arts and education, states, "I think people in this country—educators and the public at large—had viewed the arts, for young children at least, as having little value other than something to put on the refrigerator door. That conception of art can never compete adequately for time in the school program."[3]

Despite this sad status quo, William J. Bennett, then Secretary of Education, insisted that "the arts are an essential element of education, just like reading, writing, and arithmetic. . . . Music, dance, painting, and theater are keys that unlock profound human understanding and accomplishment."[4] Edith W. King believes that the social studies are an excellent elementary school context into which the arts could be integrated:

> Music, art, and literature know no national or cultural boundaries. The common expressions of human feeling found in these forms can be used effectively by the teacher to develop children's capacities to identify with other groups and other societies—indeed, the totality of mankind. . . .
>
> Aesthetic experiences, embodied in the arts and humanities, provide ways of giving the individual an opportunity to try on a situation—to know the logic and feeling of others—even though these others live thousands of miles away.[5]

ALTERNATIVES IN TEACHING THE ARTS

Elliot Eisner[6] explains that a systematic, sequential, carefully planned approach to teaching the arts is necessary for elementary school programs. He describes three basic ways to handle arts instruction:

1. Teaching each of the arts as a separate subject with its own particular characteristics, and assigning a block of time for teaching the arts as we do for any other elementary school subject,

---

Special encouragement for this chapter was provided by Dr. Arthur Mark, Professor of Elementary Education at East Stroudsburg (PA) University, valued friend, and respected proponent of integrating the arts.

2. Providing spaces in the classroom for children to pick up on their own individual work at various times during the week, and
3. Teaching the arts in relation to other subjects. This might be the best approach, according to Eisner, for then the arts would be taught in such a way as to allow for their parity among all the other subjects.

The first option is described by Eisner as a "discipline-based" approach to teaching the arts. Discipline-based approaches require specialists with professional commitments to their fields, a body of knowledge appropriate for arts education, and a particular style of teaching. Discipline-based instruction would focus on the four things people do with the arts: (1) make works of art, (2) appreciate art, (3) learn to understand art in relation to cultures, and (4) make judgments about the arts. Each will now be treated in greater detail in this text. The second and third options, however, appear most appropriate for the social studies classroom and are described more completely.

Providing Spaces in the Classroom

It is never too early to introduce children to the arts. Songs, rhymes, fingerplays, and chants elicit enthusiastic responses from the very young. Stories, pictures, books, arts and crafts, television, radio, films, stage plays, puppets, video- and audiotapes, dance, and other forms of creative expression add zest to childhood. Yet formal schooling often ignores the arts, and experiences in the creative fields are often limited to special, private training for but a few children. Children's arts experiences in school are usually limited to one or two classes a week with the art teacher and the music teacher. But children should understand that the arts reflect a culture, and one cannot fully *appreciate* the value of any art without some understanding of the cultural matrix from which it emerged. Conversely, one cannot fully appreciate a culture unless one respects and values the creative efforts of its individuals. Why wait until children go to the art or music teacher to learn about the world's great creative artists? The regular classroom can offer many opportunities to explore the arts.

Set up separate areas of the classroom for the different arts. One corner might be devoted to music and dance. Display large, attractive pictures or photographs of dancers, musicians, composers, and conductors, all woven together by a musical staff and bright-colored notes. A record player or tape recorder and a variety of music can be made available. First, you might offer a listening experience—Native American Indian or African *drum music* is considered a good place to start. Next, early American *folk music*, with its repeated verses and simple melodies should be shared. The bouncy rhythms of *jazz* artists such as Duke Ellington, Louis Armstrong, Thomas "Fats" Waller, Ella Fitzgerald, Count Basie, or Dave Brubeck, among others, should be added. The louder, faster-paced varieties of *classical music* are enjoyed by children, too. Bach, Beethoven, and Wagner are favorites—my experience is that children enjoy Bach's Brandenburg Concerto no. 2, for example, as well as Beethoven's Fifth Symphony. Don't limit your selection to only these, however; many others work just as well.

Play each artist's or composer's music for several days before moving on to another. Children need repeated exposure to benefit from their initial introduction.

Introduce the artists by calling the children's attention to their pictures and telling or reading little stories about their lives. Be sure to keep a globe nearby if you are introducing someone from another locality in the United States or from another country. You may also want to display a chart of musical instruments (or pictures of them) to refer to as you share information with the children.

Keep a box of props in the area to encourage free movement and dance. Brightly colored scarves or yarn can be used by the children in their dances. Rhythm instruments may be added to the center as the need dictates.

Similarly, the art corner which normally contains crayons, paints, and clay could be decorated with reproductions of the works of artists such as Picasso, Rembrandt, Van Gogh, Wyeth, Grandma Moses, or Mary Cassatt. Stories about each artist could be shared. Appropriate music adds a stimulating background for children who wish to express their own ideas through the use of available art media.

The possibilities for informal, open-ended arts activities are endless. They help to initiate the child's knowledge of artists, their works of art, and the circumstances in which the works were created. They help the child appreciate what is beautiful, and they offer children opportunities for their own natural creativity to flourish.

Integrating the Arts with the Social Studies

Proponents argue that the arts belong in our social studies programs because they make indispensable contributions to a child's total education. The arts help students improve the quality of their lives by challenging them to look at cultural beliefs, ideas, conditions, and problems in new ways. You need not be a professional musician, actor, or artist to present this segment of a culture's greatness to your students. You need only be aware of the beauty and excitement of the outside world and bring that world into your classroom. The arts belong in our schools because they are serious business, not frills. Teachers must treat them as essential parts of education because they help children understand human civilizations through examination of creative outlets for thoughts, emotions, and aspirations.

> One teacher took her class to an "Igbo Arts" exhibit of more than one hundred objects produced by the Igbo (or Ibo) people of Southeastern Nigeria. The objects in the exhibit included wooden totemic sculptures, pottery, textiles, examples of painting and body adornment, and a variety of masks. Wood predominated, as it does in most African art, but the exhibit included objects fashioned from bronze, iron, and ivory.
>
> The purpose of the visit was to stimulate interest in the Igbo through the beauty of their creative work. The teacher's goal was achieved, as the students returned full of questions ripe for research and discovery: "Why did the Igbo make the small totemic figures? What were the purposes of the elaborate masks on display?" The children ventured into the world of the Igbo through intensive reading and research in the school library, newspapers, books at home, and other references including informational pamphlets from the exhibit.

A whole new world opened up to them through the arts—the children learned that the Igbo art form was a direct expression of their culture. For example, the small, wooden totemic figures (*ikenga*) symbolized traditionally masculine attributes such as strength, courage, and aggressiveness. These carved figures were kept in the men's meetinghouse. Among women, body jewelry such as ivory and brass anklets symbolized prestige and social satisfaction. The masks played a major role in the Igbo's masquerades, in which male performers acted out various aspects of their spiritual beliefs. Other art forms—sculpture, drama, dance, paintings, music, and costumes—were also used in masquerades.

The Igbo culture became more meaningful each day. Their rich creativity came alive in the classroom. After they had accumulated all their data, the children chose ways to share what they had found out. One group recreated jewelry for a mini-display; another made a model of an Igbo mask; a third dramatized an Igbo spiritual celebration; a fourth made a model *ikenga*. Through their expressive activities, the children became creators of original art forms that communicated the discoveries they made as members of a social group.

In this example, the study of the culture was not taught through the presentation of information that historians or anthropologists established about the life of the Igbo people. The children studied not only what the culture accomplished but also *how* historians or anthropologists arrive at their conclusions about a culture. This teacher frequently brought examples of the arts and crafts of different cultures as the children studied them so they could better understand people's beliefs, ideas, and problems. The youngsters in this classroom left the social studies program with a developing consciousness of the relationship between culture and the form and content of art.

Those interested in integrating the arts and social studies should have a basic understanding of how to provide a meaningful experience for the children. Elliot Eisner's "four things people do with art" (make works of art, appreciate art, understand art in relation to cultures, and make judgments about the arts) should serve as one framework for guiding instructional decisions. Here is Eisner's illustration of how those four activities can be applied to a classroom situation:

> Let's say that a youngster is introduced to the coil method of constructing a clay pot. That activity provides opportunities for the teacher to help the youngster develop an awareness of things like proportion and technique and the expressive character of the vessel. That is, the shapes of different pots generate different kinds of feelings in viewers; pots can be delicate, they can be strong, they can be clumsy or graceful.
>
> The pot a youngster makes can be related to pots made in other cultures by other artists. The Greeks and the Aztecs made pots; the French, the Japanese, the Chinese make pots. So there are many opportunities to establish connections, to significantly broaden the kinds of things a youngster learns from the simple act of making a pot.[7]

Perhaps the most difficult part of Eisner's "four things people do with art" pattern of instruction, especially for teachers with little formal training in the arts, is to help children make judgments about the arts. He suggests that teachers do this by having children look at a painting (by a child or by an artist), for example, and talk about what they see—how it is organized, how the image makes the child feel, what the child likes best about it, and how it compares with other works of art. All children need not agree that the work of art is an excellent one; the major objective is to help the children recognize and react to the special qualities of art. Anne Meek offers this example from a third-grade classroom:

> Mrs. Wainner . . . moved to the comparison of *Evening at Kuerners* (Andrew Wyeth) and *The Old Oaken Bucket* (Grandma Moses). The Wyeth shows a dusky rural dwelling with a lighted window; the Moses, a cheerful primitive farmscape. Something exciting began to happen.
>
> Mrs. Wainner began by posing a question about the colors used by the two artists. "These are quiet colors," said one child, of the Wyeth.
>
> Another added, "It looks like a farm; the sun's going down."
>
> Another added, "It gives me a muddy feeling, like it's just finished raining."
>
> "There's a light on in the house," Ben observed.
>
> Mrs. Wainer moved on to the Grandma Moses farm, asking what kinds of colors these were and whether it looked like a real farm. Then Ben, his mind still on the Wyeth, told about going into his house and opening the curtains to make the house light. He was feeling emotions generated by light, the sweet security and aesthetic pleasure of coming home and letting in the light. I thought of Rembrandt's reply to the question about the most important person he had ever painted: "The most important person in any painting is light." I thought Ben had recognized intuitively the importance of the lighted window.[8]

These children offered completely personal and extraordinarily honest responses to the art. Their unschooled views—Ben's lighted house—were natural, yet so appropriate. Teachers must not only provide opportunities for the children to look at art but also encourage them to open their eyes and minds to see more in the world around them.

People have sent messages to each other in many ways during the history of humanity; some in print, others in dance, and still more in music. Whatever the form, children must have opportunities to examine how creative ventures have been influenced by or have influenced human behavior at different times in different places.

If you fear that exposing children to history or to the study of a particular culture will fail because they are insecure in their knowledge of facts, or because the information seems irrelevant to the children's lives, or because they might become bored and reject the study completely, try something new. Work together with your children to explore a culture's music, graphic art, crafts, drama or dance. You will be amazed at the amount of information they discover and retain as well as at the interest and eagerness they bring to their work. The National Endowment for the Arts[9] suggests that the consequences of a sound arts program are fourfold:

1. Arts education provides students with a more complete understanding of civilizations being studied.
2. Arts education provides opportunities to make critical assessments and evaluations.
3. Arts education offers students opportunities to express their own creativity.
4. The arts offer effective alternative means of communication—new verbal and nonverbal means of expressing thoughts and feelings.

We have considered classroom strategies to enhance the development of the first two consequences so far in this chapter. Now the third and fourth, both dealing with the children's own creative expression, will be addressed.

CREATIVE EXPRESSION IN THE CLASSROOM

Children's exposure to the arts should not stop with exploration. John Dewey once said, "A beholder must create his own experience." This thesis has become a contemporary theme. Children need to express what they learn about people through as many avenues as possible, and the arts are the most accessible way. Isadora Duncan, the renowned dancer, once said, "If I could tell you what I mean, there would be no point in dancing."[10]

Albert Einstein once commented, "The gift of fantasy has meant more to me than my talent for absorbing positive knowledge."[11] A recent report, *Performing Together: The Arts in Education,* states: "Studying the arts gives all students that gift. When they study drama, they can become someone else, if only for a few minutes. When they create a painting, they can see the world with fresh eyes. Research has shown that students who study the arts are also more likely to display originality and creativity in other subjects."[12] The report outlines several characteristics of a successful arts program, including incorporating arts activities into the regular classroom. For more information, write to Arts Alliance for Arts Education, 1801 North Moore Street, Arlington, VA 22209–9988.

Art Activities

Painting or drawing provides children with ways of thinking through new concepts and combining them with already familiar ones. After a trip to a farm, for example, children's art would reflect a variety of expressions. Carol might draw the barn and silo in such detail that it would look as if she could still see it before her; John might paint the farmyard full of farm machinery; Marie's picture would reflect her growing interest in farm animals; Mark's drawing might show a determined rider sitting on a large horse, with the caption, "This is me leading the cows to pasture."

Prerequisite to any art work in the social studies is a stimulating learning experience that has special meaning for the child. A significant *intake* of ideas through direct experience or intensive research must occur before ideas develop to the point where they can be expressed effectively in some art medium. For example, one teacher planned a trip to the circus and felt that it was a wonderful experience for all of the children. Maurice, however, became terribly frightened of the clown, cried, thrashed about, and withdrew from participating in the rest of the trip. When the class returned to school and was asked to express the things they best remembered from the trip, Maurice withdrew even further and failed to respond at all. His fright caused a lack of understanding of the trip, and he was thus unable to express his ideas effectively; he had no experience from which to draw.

Either simple or complex art activities offer inspirational means of translating and expressing social studies concepts.

Additionally, children need an *assimilation* period before they become ready to express their thoughts. For example, a teacher asked his students to draw a picture depicting the high points of a famous person's life immediately after he had read the biography to them. The children produced inaccurate and substandard drawings. A major reason may have been that the teacher did not follow up the story with a discussion of major events to help the children organize their thoughts. The original idea was a good experience, but the teacher did not give his students a chance to sort out and put together ideas to the point of creative expression. For these two personalized reasons—intake and assimilation—art related to the social studies must be done on a relatively organized basis.

Materials for art activities in the social studies are virtually limitless. A creative teacher sees the possibilities even in the "junk" materials all around her—cloth, straw, seeds, gift wrap, leaves, sand. Keeping this thought in mind, consider some creative extensions of these art activities.

Dioramas

A diorama is a three-dimensional model that depicts activities performed by people, animals, or objects. A cardboard box usually encloses the representation. Cut the lid from the box and paint the exterior or cover it with colored paper. Background scenery can be painted or cut from colored paper and pasted to the interior walls. People, animals, and other objects have a construction-paper tab at their base; this tab is folded and glued or stapled to the bottom of the box to keep the figure in place.

A variation of the diorama is the "peep show." Remove the lid from a cardboard box and place a mirror on the inside wall of one end. In the opposite end, punch a small hole. Construct the rest of the interior in the same way as the diorama. When you are finished, glue a sheet of translucent paper over the top of the box, thus making the scenery on the inside indistinguishable except through the peephole. The effect is extraordinary.

Murals

In many social studies units, a mural can summarize a group's investigation or pull together the contributions of several groups into one expressive product for the entire class.

Research is the first step in constructing an authentic mural, so as to develop the necessary background information for planning a theme. Once the theme is chosen, a list of the significant, contributing ideas should be cooperatively developed. A large, durable piece of wrapping paper is then laid on the floor of the classroom, and each committee is assigned a section of the mural. Each child on a committee is assigned to a portion of the mural and can make it at his own desk. Usually, individual contributions are made from paintings, sketches, cut paper, and similar art techniques. When the pupils finish, the sections are placed on the mural. When all of the pieces are in location, the teacher suggests the need for a background, usually a simple tempera-painted scene. When the background is complete, the children place their work back on the paper for gluing or pasting in final arrangement.

Mosaics

Begin a mosaic by having the children lightly draw their scenes on a 9″ x 12″ piece of construction paper. This will serve as a pattern for the mosaic work. Then use small pieces of colored paper, seeds, beans, rice, macaroni, eggshells, or other materials pasted on to form the mosaic pattern.

Collages

A collage is an arrangement of pictures or other materials. Abstract collages can be constructed by pasting pictures from newspapers or magazines within an outline in a free-form style. Realistic collages can be constructed by pasting scraps of materials in patterns. For example, a truck can be cut from construction paper, clouds can be made from chunks of cotton, foliage can be represented by green fabric, and a fence can be made from corrugated cardboard. Dried grass can be pasted in place to show a field. Encourage children to use their imaginations as much as possible while experimenting with collages, but they should not become so engrossed in novel materials that they forget the original purpose of the finished work.

Illustrations

Illustrating concepts related to field trips or research activities is probably the most popular art technique used in elementary social studies classrooms. Children may be asked to draw the details of the process involved in making linen from flax, to use crayon for indicating various areas on a state map, or to paint a picture of a landscape in the high Andes Mountains. Children like to illustrate group notebooks and decorative charts. There are literally hundreds of possibilities.

Construction Activities

Classrooms rarely contain *all* the real materials children need for exploration or for expressing the relationships they are learning. Some items are not made commercially, some are not readily available, and some are too expensive. In these cases, you can capitalize on the children's natural interest in construction and invite them to *create* original representations of their learning discoveries. For decades, educators have been telling us that when children are able to take information, work with it, and represent it in their own way through construction-type activities, they bring meaning to their learning and become intrinsically motivated to learn even more.

In *construction activities,* children use tools and materials to represent real people, places, or things, while clarifying social studies concepts and related processes. These activities provide meaning through motivation and interest and give purpose to reading and research. To illustrate, let us assume that a fourth-grade class is involved in a study of colonial living. The teacher may suggest that a group of students interested in colonial housing construct a model log cabin. Several purposes for this activity may be apparent to you. The teacher's purpose, for instance, is to have the children conduct research and select the appropriate information to help them construct an accurate representation of a log cabin. This enriches concepts and develops understanding as the children engage in a purposeful, creative activity. The children's purpose may be to learn as much as they can about a log cabin to enable them to build a model they can show to their classmates as they explain how logs are fitted and held together, what types of materials were used for roofs, and so on.

The value of this type of expressive activity is not in the aesthetic or "gimmicky" quality of the finished product, but in the process that contributes to the final structure. All too often, teachers unknowingly lose sight of their original purpose for an activity and place undue emphasis on constructing an impressive model. Use construction activities only if they:

>   Serve to achieve meaningful purposes
>   Follow careful planning and thinking by the children
>   Clarify concepts and understandings
>   Lie within the children's ability levels
>   Result in somewhat authentic (but not perfect) models

Creative Dramatics

A popular activity among all children, creative dramatics is considered a natural part of human growth. The wise teacher capitalizes on children's natural urge to imitate adult life by making creative dramatics an integral part of social studies instruction.

Creative dramatics can benefit the social studies program in many ways. Children enjoy it. Being able to do something they like enhances their interest in learning. The program also provides a purpose for gathering information. Children often need additional information to portray real-life circumstances in their dramatic representations accurately. This spontaneous motivation for new information can be capitalized on to expand the child's knowledge of other people's characteristics and actions. Dramatics can build the child's sensitivity to others' feelings. By the time a player has decided which character he is, what decisions he must face, and why he behaves as he does, he has gained a great deal of insight into understanding people in unique situations. Putting on a play is also a valuable opportunity for group cooperation. Social acceptance is often an extremely valuable outcome, as children develop a common bond of respect for a job well done. Plays can also be used to evaluate concept attainment. The situations the children portray reflect their knowledge of related information.

Children need teacher help to use creative dramatics effectively in handling increasingly difficult concepts about their world. Dramatic representation takes many forms, and children must be moved gradually from one form to another. Creative dramatics proceeds developmentally from the free-style play of preschool and kindergarten to the organized forms found in the upper primary and intermediate grades.

Dramatic Play

Dramatic play requires creative thinking when children enact roles or activities that are familiar to them. The process encourages growth in all areas of development:

- *Social:* sharing and planning with other children
- *Emotional:* savoring pleasurable experiences and expressing emotions such as anger, hostility, and agression
- *Affective:* exhibiting likes and dislikes; exploring and expressing feelings
- *Physical:* exercising muscular development and control
- *Cognitive:* expressing thoughts in play action (conceptual thought)
- *Creative:* bringing original thinking to the solution of problems

The dramatic play area is a popular setting for very young children. Various props encourage children to experiment at being mothers, fathers, babies, community members, teachers, animals—the list is endless. Whatever the design of the dramatics area at any one time, the furniture and equipment should be child-sized whenever possible. Many kindergarten classrooms contain a permanent housekeeping corner as well as a separate dramatic play corner that is changed periodically. The *housekeeping corner* generally includes a table and chairs; wooden kitchen equipment such as a stove, refrigerator, or sink; a wide selection of dolls; and cupboards containing cups, saucers, pots, spoons, pitchers, and so on. These materials do not need to be purchased—a little imagination turns orange crates into stoves or storage cabinets, and a little resourcefulness leads you to used and outgrown toys. The *dramatic play corner* offers children a wide variety of creative possibilities. Changeable items should be provided so that children can shift roles whenever they have the inclination. In this area children can explore people's lives in varying occupations and locations; they can use their equipment to pretend they are in many different places.

Creative possibilities for role-playing include: shoe repair persons, launderers, jewelers, service station attendants, firefighters, police officers, factory workers, secretaries, farmers, barbers, postal workers, race car drivers, and the like. Children want and need to play with each other. For that reason, play is perhaps the most potent vehicle in kindergarten and early primary-grade classrooms for encouraging social growth. Do your best to ensure ample opportunities for free dramatic play. Provide plenty of resources and abundant space.

Your role during this early part of the creative dramatics sequence is mainly that of observer and arranger. You must know the developmental sequence of play and use it as an index for selecting equipment and materials. Basically, children of ages 3 to 6 prefer play situations centering around familiar, adult living conditions in the home, school, neighborhood, and community. The opportunities for the child in an unstructured setting provide the readiness framework that will enable her to successfully participate in other forms of creative dramatics later on.

Piaget believes that the child does not move from unstructured play to directed, cooperative play until after the age of 7 or 8. When this state is attained, more direct guidance is required on the part of the teacher, and new dramatic opportunities can be offered in the intermediate grades.

Pantomime

Children of all ages enjoy using bodily expressions to convey ideas without words, and this is a good technique for introducing creative dramatics to the social studies program. Pantomime offers opportunities to characterize actions and personalities without having to furnish dialogue.

Pantomime is a logical extension of dramatic play because it helps youngsters become more sensitive to what is around them. Before that happens, children must become aware of how they can express their emotions and ideas, best described as *sensitizing.* To begin, gather the children in a large circle and have them cover their eyes or close them while you come around the circle with various objects for them to touch, smell, hear, taste, and see. For example, you would say, "Close your eyes and *touch* . . . a soft, snuggly teddy bear . . . rough sandpaper . . . a cold ice cube"; or "Close your eyes and *smell* . . . a fresh flower . . . a sour pickle . . . cinnamon"; or "Close your eyes and *listen* to . . . a sharp bell . . . a pencil tapping on the desk . . . paper being crumpled"; or "Close your eyes and *taste* (provide small samples) . . . sugar . . . salt . . . an apple slice"; or "Look outside the room and *see* . . . far away mountains . . . a cloud castle . . . a green grass carpet." Then ask the children to close their eyes once again and *think* about the things you will say to them even though the real items will not be in the classroom: "Close your eyes and touch . . . a hot stove; a sharp pin; a slimy jellyfish; a soft, furry kitten; a cold icicle"; or "Close your eyes and smell . . . hot cookies straight from the oven; soiled diapers; crisp bacon frying in a pan; dirty old garbage cans."

At this point you may want to say "Freeze." This technique, introduced to me by E. Riley Holman, is a signal for the children to keep their expression frozen on their faces and to open their eyes. Ask them to examine each other's expressions and to discuss how we would all know we had just smelled something awful. Intermittently use the "freeze" technique so that children become aware of how their faces communicate ideas and emotions without using words. Some other examples: "Close your eyes and *listen* to . . . your favorite popular tune; the crowd at a championship football game; a baby crying; chalk being scraped across the chalkboard; two cats fighting." "Close your eyes and *taste* . . . onions; a glass of fresh orange juice; the first food you've seen in two days; pizza with your favorite topping; a sour lemon." "Close your eyes and *see* . . . an old creaking house on a stormy night; two eyes looking back at you through the dark; a bright, colorful birthday package; a quiet beach with waves lapping the shore; a soft, gentle sunset."

As you share these and other sensitizing cues with the children, discuss each effect with the "freeze" technique and let the children describe the feelings or ideas they encountered during the experience. After you've suggested five or six cues for each of the senses, invite the children to suggest their own. You will be surprised at the creative responses they offer.

After the children become comfortable in the sensitizing phase, encourage them to explore the possibilities of communicating ideas and emotions with other parts of their bodies; for example, with parts of the body:

> "Say with your finger, 'Come here.' "
>
> "Say with your nose, 'I smell a skunk.' "
>
> "Say with your eyes, 'You're hopeless.' "
>
> "Say with your foot, 'I'm stuck!' "
>
> "Say with your ear, 'I hear beautiful music.' "
>
> "Say with your arms, 'It's heavy.' "
>
> "Say with your hands, 'Look at my acrobatic flea.' "

Then encourage them to communicate with the whole body.

> "You are now lifting the winning weight in the Olympics."
>
> "You are a peacock showing off for the people."
>
> "You are a tin soldier in Santa's toyshop."
>
> "You are a dish of Jello."
>
> "You are a caged monkey in the zoo."
>
> "You have scored the winning touchdown in a football game."
>
> "You are playing a musical instrument in a parade."

From simpler exercises, you can work up to presenting pantomime scenes. Use your imagination to determine stimulating situations for pantomime in the social studies classroom. One possibility is the popular *"What Am I Doing?"* or *"Who Am I?"* game. Many social studies concepts relate to people involved in making or doing something. Children enjoy imitating others' unique movements. They can be encouraged to portray activities of people in the unit under study and to challenge their classmates to guess who they are. Some suggestions: Pilgrims landing at Plymouth Rock, the first landing on the moon, Ben Franklin's kite flying experience, Henry Aaron's record-breaking home run, the type of work people do at home or in the community.

Your role in guiding social studies pantomimes begins with establishing a rich background of study trips, books, magazines, films, pictures, recordings, and other sources of information on which children build their pantomimes. After they share an experience, the children should discuss its characteristics and their feelings about the insights they gained. You may then divide the class into small groups and encourage each group to pantomime whatever they felt was their most meaningful recollection. Each group should then share their creative expression with the others, after which you should lead a follow-up discussion: "What persons are represented in the action? What helped you recognize them? Where do you think the action took place? What helped you know this? What do you think the people were talking about? What are some of the feelings you think the characters experienced? From what you know about the actual situation, do you think the actors accurately portrayed what really happened? What feelings did you have as you watched the action? What would you have done if you were any one of the characters in the same situation? Can you predict what might happen to the people after what was shown in the pantomime?

Improvised Skits

A charming characteristic of young children is their ability to use their creative imaginations in improvisations, unplanned situations where dialogue is necessary and characterized by scenes involving *no* learned lines, *no* costumes, and *no* sophisticated scenery. But improvisations can be difficult if the children have not had a great deal of practice in pantomime. With practice and a thorough knowledge of the story situation, however, dialogue begins to flow, and children further their understanding of a social studies condition by describing its characters more completely.

Many of the classroom situations described as pantomiming activities are also suitable for improvisation experiences. The teacher should also begin the initial improvisation experiences with simple situations. As the children gain confidence, they can attempt more challenging material.

Elementary school children enjoy acting out such scenes and often repeat the scenes to communicate different interpretations of the related information, to switch roles, or to create new endings to open-ended situations. Youngsters easily fluctuate between worlds of fantasy (witness the number of children who have "imaginary" playmates) and reality, and pantomime and improvisation give them opportunities to enter and leave new and different worlds at will. Even though spontaneity appears to be strongest during kindergarten and the early primary years and tapers off as children reach the later grades, a skillful teacher can bring it to the surface again in a relaxed, developmentally appropriate setting.

By mimicking words and actions as they have experienced them in other settings, children actually *feel* how tired the mail carrier becomes, how frustrated a teacher becomes when children act rowdy, or how elated a candidate is when he wins an important election victory. It is the power to help children empathize that makes dramatic experiences so valuable; children express and experience another person's viewpoint. This creative technique helps children understand people or events more fully.

Dramatization

Older children may wish to put on a formal play with script, costumes, and scenery. If the children have had sufficient experience with pantomime and improvisation, the most effective type of formal play is one in which the children are responsible for most of the planning. Your role is to guide the students in formulating the different scenes. As the children plan their script, ask them, "What are the most important things to tell? What are the people really like? What kind of place do they live in? What do the people do to make their lives interesting? How will you stage your play?"

The dramatization can result from many of the same sources described for pantomime and improvisation. The students' concern for elaborate scenery and costumes should not take precedence over the concepts or ideas the play is designed to convey. Simple objects can effectively represent more intricate objects; for example, a mural or bulletin board design can serve as a backdrop; a branch in a big can filled with dirt makes an excellent tree or bush; the teacher's desk becomes a cave; chairs placed in a straight line can be seats on a train or airplane; a pencil can become a hand-held microphone.

Sociodrama

Our examples of creative dramatics in the social studies classroom have dealt primarily with methods of summarizing or communicating highlights of learning experiences through pantomime, improvised skits, puppetry, or dramatization. Sociodrama is a specialized use of any of these techniques in a situation characterized by an affective, or human relations, dilemma. Children dramatize, unrehearsed, real problematical situations and offer suggestions for resolution through their dramatic interpretations. The topics should be fairly simple at first—schoolroom, playground, or cafeteria conflicts, for example. Later, children can play out problem situations they encounter in social studies class.

Leslie D. Zeleny names these steps for developing sociodramas in the elementary school classroom: (1) identify the problem; (2) assign roles; (3) discuss the situation; and (4) replay the situation.[13]

- *Identify the problem.* Through discussion and observation, you and the children identify problems that may be causing difficulties. For example, one young girl had been the target of ridicule in her classroom because she had recently tried out for her elementary school football team, until then exclusively the boys' domain. However, the adults in charge of the football program would not allow a girl, however eager or talented, to participate in the traditionally male sport. The boys in the classroom were unrelenting in their demeaning comments and actions and soon the girl withdrew from other activities. The teacher felt the problem had reached such proportions that sociodrama would be the best way to alleviate it. Frank discussions of the problem situation were then initiated, and the children were asked to share their thoughts.
- *Assign the roles.* Tensions in social situations usually arise because people do not understand the motivations and feelings of those involved. Therefore, children should be encouraged to imagine what others would say and do in the problem situation. After the problem has been discussed and the principal roles identified, volunteers are chosen to enact the problem spontaneously in front of the class, acting as *they* would in the situation, *not* as they think the real characters would.
- *Discussion.* By analyzing the sociodrama, the class can easily grasp a more complete understanding of the problem. The teacher should guide discussion by directing questions such as these to the players and audience: "How did each of you feel in your role? Do you think the treatment was fair? Why do you think the girl was treated as she was? Do you think people were fair to her? Why?"
- *Replay the situation.* At this point, the children may wish to replay the situation, to depict what they consider to be proper treatment or to suggest a fair solution to the problem. Replay may be done by the same group or by several different groups who may suggest alternative solutions. The various proposals can be discussed and an optimum solution decided upon.

Because sociodrama is an effective process for understanding feelings, some teachers extend its use from illustrating issues in the classroom to studying people's feelings as they face important decisions in contemporary life and throughout history. You can glean scenarios from newspaper stories, textbook readings, photographs or study prints, films, and the like. Some of the most popular of the commercially produced materials designed to encourage dramatic play with a focus on feelings are those of Fannie R. and George Shaftel.[14]

The major objective of the Shaftel sociodrama design is education for citizenship, using problem stories of day-to-day living that pose dilemmas of childhood in American culture. The intent is to help young people discover their own feelings, modes of action, and values, and learn to modify them objectively. Role playing and sociodrama are particularly appropriate to the young child's way of exploring ideas by playing characters and improvising action. In the Shaftels' program, for example, the children are given a situation where they find money on the classroom floor and must role-play what they would do—return it to the owner or pocket it. Besides such contrived situations, the Shaftels also use a number of study prints to encourage children to act out their approach to the illustrated dilemma—do bystanders have a responsibility to stop a fight between a bully and an obviously smaller child?

MUSIC AND DANCE

To develop a musical segment of your social studies program, consider the dimensions and directions organized by Alexander Frazier in Table 11–1.

In the social studies program, we do not formally teach Orff, Suzuki, or any of the other approaches employed by music teachers. Melody and rhythm as they express people's values and feelings, however, are excellent vehicles (along with the other arts) for understanding and expressing aspects of a culture that cannot be effectively communicated in any other way:

> People have sent messages across distances by pounding on drums. People have marched off to war to stirring music and down the aisle to the joyous strains of a wedding

TABLE 11–1
The Functions of Music

Function	Type of Music	
	Vocal	*Instrumental*
Communication (over distance)	Yodels	Drum messages Band music (at sports events)
Marching, parading	Marching songs	Marches: military, wedding, funeral, parade
Uniting together	War songs Patriotic songs	Dances: tribal
Working	Work songs and chants	Recorded music in stores and factories
Worshiping	Masses Oratorios Hymns	Processionals
Celebrating, rejoicing	Victory hymns and chants Holiday songs	Victory dances Festival music Folk dances
Grieving	Ballads Lamentations	Funeral marches
Romancing, courting	Love songs	Dances of many kinds
Playacting	Opera Operetta Musical comedy	Incidental music for plays and background music for movies
Pleasing self and others, entertaining	Art songs, popular songs Choral works	Chamber music Ballet Symphonies Solo works of many kinds

Source: Alexander Frazier, *Values, Curriculum, and the Elementary School* (Boston: Houghton Mifflin, 1980). Copyright © 1980 Houghton Mifflin Company. Used with permission.

march. People—great crowds of people—have raised their voices in national anthems. People have sung work songs or chants to keep their work rhythm straight as they pulled in nets or pried rails back into line. People have sung songs of worship in camp meetings and cathedrals, and they have celebrated harvests with festive dances. People have expressed their grief in tender ballads and their love in songs and dances both tender and gay. People have delighted in playacting that brought song and dance to the stage. They have been eager everywhere to listen to good music sung and played for itself alone. Wherever and whenever possible, people have gained satisfaction and joy in making music for themselves and for others.[15]

How can children be helped to understand all of this? Certainly, they must have experiences with many kinds of music. The primary aim is not to develop musical talent, but to think of music as an enjoyable art form and as a means of self-expression. Music and associated movements or dance can be used in the social studies program to enhance understandings of other cultures and for creative self-expression. Folk songs that reveal cultural or ethnic characteristics are a good example of the first use. But teachers cannot simply put a record on the record player and listen passively with the children. Elementary school children require more stimulation than that; they need a confident, expressive teacher who does not hesitate to get up and begin to dance. A folk dance, for example, encourages vigorous participation while helping children acquire individual responses to a creative art form.

A folk dance is a model the children must copy, and some teachers prefer not to use a patterned experience initially. Instead, they prefer to stimulate free movement during the first creative movement activities. Eastern and African music are outstanding sources for individual responses. The teacher encourages children to move according to how the music makes them feel. If the children seem self-conscious at first, try using colorful scarves, streamers, or balloons to start the dance activity. These accessories divert attention from the children and help minimize self-consciousness.

Both planned dance experiences and free movement activities are delightful activities to draw upon. They can be further enhanced by inviting resource people into the classroom to share their talents with the children or by allowing children to use musical instruments during the activity. Whatever the situation, combining musical experiences with other parts of the social studies program demonstrates to children that music is an integral part of all people's lives rather than a form of expression for only a talented few.

To see how music can enrich the social studies program, consider the use of choral singing to enhance the study of early American culture. A selection such as the traditional early American song *Poor Old Woman* is enjoyable to children. It is referred to as a "choral refrain," where a soloist sings the stanza (solo) and the group sings the refrain. At first, you may want to sing the solo parts, but eventually each stanza may be assigned to one group and the refrain to another. To add interest, you may want the children responsible for each solo to draw an illustration of the animal or bug mentioned and then hold it up as each stanza is read. Teach the selection according to this progression:

1. Ask each child to read the selection silently.
2. Sing the solo parts and ask the children to join you on the refrain.
3. Assign the solo parts to groups and try to put the entire selection together.

Poor Old Woman

SOLO:	There was an old woman who swallowed a fly.
ALL (dramatically):	Oh, my! Swallowed a fly!
(slowly)	Poor old woman, I think she'll die.
SOLO:	There was an old woman who swallowed a spider.
(said in an aside)	Right down inside her she swallowed a spider: She swallowed the spider to kill the fly.
ALL (dramatically):	Oh, my! Swallowed a fly!
(slowly)	Poor old woman, I think she'll die.
SOLO:	There was an old woman who swallowed a bird.
(said in an aside)	How absurd to swallow a bird!
(more quickly)	She swallowed the bird to kill the spider.
	She swallowed the spider to kill the fly.
ALL (dramatically):	Oh, my! Swallowed a fly!
(slowly)	Poor old woman, I think she'll die.
SOLO:	There was an old woman who swallowed a cat,
(slowly and deliberately)	Fancy that! She swallowed a cat!
ALL:	She swallowed the cat to kill the bird,
	She swallowed the bird to kill the spider,
	She swallowed the spider to kill the fly.
	Oh, my! Swallowed a fly!
	Poor old woman, I think she'll die.
SOLO:	There was an old woman who swallowed a dog.
(as if telling a secret)	She went the whole hog! She swallowed a dog!
ALL:	She swallowed the dog to kill the cat,
	She swallowed the cat to kill the bird,
	She swallowed the bird to kill the spider.
	She swallowed the spider to kill the fly.
	Oh, my! Swallowed a fly!
	Poor old woman, I think she'll die.
SOLO:	There was an old woman who swallowed a cow,
(slowly and carefully)	I don't know how, but she swallowed a cow.
ALL:	She swallowed the cow to kill the dog,
(with increasing momentum)	She swallowed the dog to kill the cat,
	She swallowed the cat to kill the bird,
	She swallowed the bird to kill the spider,
	She swallowed the spider to kill the fly.
(slowly and deliberately)	Oh, my! Swallowed a fly!
	Poor old woman, I think she'll die.
SOLO:	There was an old woman who swallowed a horse!
ALL:	She died, of course.

SUMMARY

Children wonder about different things in the social studies, including many kinds of artistic expression, and teachers must help them understand by providing a balance between content and experience. Children need, of course, to learn about Stephen Foster or Beethoven, but they are more motivated to learn if they can dance or sing. They must encounter art products of different cultures and be encouraged to let their own creative talents spill out—by illustrating a poem they have written or dramatizing jobs they have observed during a trip to a department store. Children can learn to paint, sing, or dance without learning about Pablo Picasso, Marian Anderson, or Martha Graham, but to really learn about and appreciate the arts, both content and experience are necessary.

Perhaps no area of the elementary school curriculum is so well matched to the normal creative tendencies of childhood as the social studies. So the social studies program should provide many experiences in the creative arts, including those that fall into these two broad categories: (1) sharing the creative arts of various cultures and (2) providing for children's creative arts expression within the classroom.

By sharing the creative arts of various cultures, teachers help children understand and appreciate a society's imagination and enthusiasm, for it is through the arts that a people's triumphs and failures are most vivdly portrayed.

Children's exposure to the arts should not stop with exploration; they also need to express creatively what they learn. Among the many creative opportunities in the social studies program are:

- Art activities—dioramas, murals, mosaics, collages, illustrations
- Construction activities
- Creative dramatics—dramatic play, pantomime, improvised skits, dramatization, sociodrama
- Music and dance

The arts provide valuable sources of new information about people and a good base for inquiry learning. In the process, the children not only learn content but broaden their understandings to a culture's "feeling dimension." As children express themselves through the arts, they not only present ideas vividly and forcefully but also tap the natural tendency to share with others through creative expression.

ENDNOTES

1. Albert Cullum, *Push Back the Desks* (New York: Citation Press, 1967), pp. 52–53.

2. Frank Hodsoll (Chair), *Toward Civilization: A Report on Arts Education* (Washington, DC: National Endowment for the Arts, 1988).

3. Ron Brandt, "On Discipline-Based Art Education: A Conversation with Elliot Eisner," *Educational Leadership, 45,* no. 4 (December 1987/January 1988): 7.

4. William J. Bennett, *First Lessons: A Report on Elementary Education in America* (Washington, DC: U.S. Department of Education, 1986): 35.

5. Edith W. King, *The World: Context for Teaching in the Elementary School* (Dubuque, IA: William C. Brown, 1971), pp. 5–6.

6. Ron Brandt, "On Discipline-Based Art Education," pp. 8–9.

7. Ibid., p. 8.

8. Anne Meek, "An Ordinary Lesson," *Educational Leadership, 45,* no. 4 (December 1987/January 1988): 58.

9. Frank Hodsoll, *Toward Civilization.*

10. Quoted in Patricia McCormack, "Are School Art Courses a Frill or a Staple?" (West Chester, PA:

Daily Local News, Wednesday, November 13, 1985), p. A15.

11. Ibid.

12. *Performing Together: The Arts in Education* (Arlington, VA: Arts Alliance for Arts Education, 1985).

13. Leslie D. Zeleny, "How to Use Sociodrama," in *How to Do It Series,* no. 20 (Washington, DC: National Council for the Social Studies, 1964), pp. 4–5.

14. Fannie R. Shaftel and George Shaftel, *Role Playing and Social Values* (Englewood Cliffs, NJ: Prentice-Hall, 1967).

15. Alexander Frazier, *Values, Curriculum, and the Elementary School* (Boston: Houghton Mifflin, 1980), p. 141.

To individuals lacking a global "mental map" the world must be little more than a confusing hodgepodge; places without location, quality, or context, faceless people and cultures void of detail, character, or meaning; vague physical features and environments for which terminology, mental images, causative agents and processes, and human patterns are lacking; temporal events that occur in a spatial vacuum; and a host of critical global problems for which they have no criteria on which to base analyses, judgments, or attempts at resolution. Such individuals are prisoners of their own ignorance or provincialism.[1]

—Charles F. Gritzner

12 *Incorporating Modern Geography into the Social Studies Curriculum*

KEY CONCEPTS

As you read, reflect on the following matters:

- What is meant by geographic literacy?
- What are the five themes that provide a blueprint for the scope of geographic study?
- Why are map reading skills crucial to a sound program in geography?
- What are the skills and understandings needed for success in reading maps? How do we help children acquire these skills and understandings?
- What six map reading skills need to be cultivated in a developmental approach to instruction?
- How is the map skills program in the primary grades like/different from the program in the succeeding grades?
- What kinds of maps and globes are appropriate for the elementary school social studies program?

GEOGRAPHIC LITERACY

Educators and geographers are cringing at survey results showing that today's American college and high school students are "geographically illiterate."[2] At no time on record has the level of geographic literacy been so low. Do *you* make the grade in geography? How well do you know your way around? Here are some questions that were put to high school and college students in various surveys; try them. If you and your classmates have trouble, it may help make the point that efforts to improve geographic literacy in the schools are important for the 1990s.

1. What mountain range stretches from Alabama to Quebec?
2. Define what is meant by a landlocked country. There are two landlocked countries in South America. Name one.
3. What country borders the United States to the south?
4. In what country is the city of Manila located?
5. Name the largest city in Africa.
6. From what Southeast Asian country did United States forces withdraw in 1975?
7. What are the seven continents?
8. What are the six New England states?
9. Name the smallest state in the United States in terms of area.
10. Name the two largest states in the United States in terms of area.

Answers
1. The Appalachians
2. One that does not border a major body of water and has no ports or access to international waters. Bolivia and Paraguay are landlocked countries.
3. Mexico
4. The Philippines
5. Cairo
6. Vietnam
7. North America, South America, Europe, Asia, Africa, Australia, Antarctica
8. Massachusetts, Connecticut, Rhode Island, Vermont, New Hampshire, and Maine
9. Rhode Island
10. Texas and Alaska

Although these questions required place names for answers, this quiz does not imply that geographic educators simply encourage memorization of facts. Certainly, they recognize that knowledge of one's immediate and world environments is an important characteristic of a geography program. But modern geographic literacy means knowing not only the location of the Persian Gulf but also its geopolitical importance; not only where Chicago is located but also the reasons it emerged as a major city. Salvatore J. Natoli and Charles F. Gritzner explain:

> Geographical literacy attempts to explicate the sentences of geography and distinguish them from the words (place names) that the public equates with geographical knowledge. Such knowledge cannot substitute for the coherence of thought and meaning in a geographically complete sentence ["Why is Boston located where it is?"]. Geographical

knowledge might diminish in our students a sense of wonder about the world in which they live. On the other hand, knowledge of geography should stimulate students' curiosities about the wonders as well as the problems of the world in which they live. It might also help to cultivate in them a sense of stewardship for the fragility of many of the earth's environments. Such knowledge about and appreciation of the world can lead students to satisfying lives and improve their participation as citizens in this democratic society and as partners in the world community.[3]

Promotion of Geographic Literacy

One of the most intensive efforts to revamp school geography programs to stress literacy rather than facts has been initiated by Gilbert M. Grosvenor, president of the National Geographic Society. He has toured the country and written in the society's magazine, *National Geographic,* to communicate the need for a modern geography program. In addition, the National Geographic Society has spent over $4 million per year on materials for teachers, workshops to improve instruction, and "alliances" of teachers, college instructors, geographers, and professional organizations to promote geography in the schools.

A second major effort to improve the quality of geographic education has originated with professional groups. The Committee on Geographic Education, in its *Guidelines for Geographic Education: Elementary and Secondary Schools,*[4] offers a blueprint of the scope of geographic study organized around five interrelated themes: *location, place, relationship within places* (human-environmental relationships), *movement,* and *regions* (how they form and change) (see Chapter 1). The Geographic Education National Implementation Project (GENIP)[5] has suggested a wealth of learning strategies appropriate for each theme. Let us look more closely at the five themes.

Five Geographic Themes

1. *Location:* Position on the Earth's Surface

Absolute and relative location are two ways of describing the positions of people and places on the earth's surface. *Absolute location* refers to a specific position on the earth's surface ("The Great Salt Lake is in northern Utah."), while *relative location* describes how geographic features are related ("Santa Fe is northeast of Albuquerque.").

2. *Place:* Physical and Human Characteristics

All places on the earth have distinctive tangible and intangible characteristics that give them meaning and character and distinguish them from other places. Geographers generally describe places by their physical or human characteristics.

3. *Relationships Within Places:* Humans and Environments

All places on the earth have advantages and disadvantages for human settlement. High population densities have developed on flood plains, for example, where people can take advantage of fertile soil, water resources, and river transportation. By comparison, population densities are usually low in deserts. Yet flood plains are periodically subjected to severe damage, and some desert areas, such as Israel, have been modified to support large population concentrations.

4. *Movement:* Humans Interacting on the Earth

Human beings occupy places unevenly across the face of the earth. Some live on farms in the country; others live in towns, villages or cities. Yet these people interact with each other: they travel from one place to another, communicate with each other, or rely upon products, information, and ideas that come from beyond their immediate environment. The most visible evidence of global interdependence are the transportation and communication lines that link every part of the world. Local, regional, and international trade demonstrate that no area is self-sufficient.

5. *Regions:* How They Form and Change

The basic unit of geographic study is the region, an area that displays unity in terms of selected criteria. We are all familiar with regions as political entities, such as nations, provinces, counties, or cities, yet there are dozens of ways to define meaningful regions depending on the problems being considered. Some regions are defined by one characteristic such as a governmental unit, a language group, or a landform type, and others by the interplay of many complex features. For example, Indiana, as a state, is a governmental region; Latin America, as an area where Spanish and Portuguese are major languages, can be a linguistic region; the Rocky Mountain range is a landform region. A geographer may delineate a neighborhood in Minneapolis by correlating the income and educational levels of residents with the assessed valuation or property tax rate, or distinguish it by prominent boundaries such as a freeway, park, or business district. On another scale we may identify the complex of ethnic, religious, linguistic, and environmental features that delineate the Arab world from the Middle East to North Africa.

The sequence of themes does not imply any order for instruction. Where appropriate they may be taught together or in any other manner dictated by the needs of the learners.

Geographic education at the elementary school level is based upon existing knowledge of the stages of children's cognitive, psychological, and social development as well as key geographic understandings. The rich and varied life experiences of children should be used as much as possible to illustrate and develop the learning opportunities selected for study. Use of the learning opportunities requires that they be adapted to meet local objectives at particular grade levels in ways that meet the needs of children with varying experiential backgrounds and differing language and intellectual abilities.

MAPS

Of all the materials essential for geographic understanding, maps are primary. Salvatore J. Natoli, a prominent geography educator, stresses, "In the sequence of geographic learning, maps are indispensable for collecting data by earth locations, analyzing areal and regional information, and formulating generalizations about spatial relationship. One cannot teach or learn geography without using a map or even several maps simultaneously. . . . Thus, desk and wall maps, globes, and atlases create distinctive requirements for classroom use . . . "[6] One of the major requirements is to help children learn the basic skills necessary to construct and interpret maps.

Learning to read maps, like learning to read other special symbol systems (such as the printed word), depends on an individual's ability to form concepts from previous life experiences and to attach arbitrary labels to those concepts so as to communicate them to others. For example, when learning to read the printed word *chicken,* the child associates the arbitrary printed symbol "chicken" with the actual animal only after she has first encountered a chicken in some way and has related the printed word to the object a number of times. The child is able to form a concept (idea) of the chicken because of her life experience; then she understands that the printed word represents that mental image.

Symbols are thus *arbitrary representations* that stand for other things. Basically, reading printed words is the process of attaching meaning derived from previous life experiences to a special printed symbol. Likewise, reading maps involves a similar process, but instead of attaching meaning to printed words, individuals must attach meaning to printed symbols that represent places in their environment.

PRE-MAPPING ACTIVITIES

Inherent in the acquisition of map reading skills is the formation of basic concepts of the physical world to which map symbols can later be associated. Preschool and kindergarten children acquire these concepts as they explore and manipulate objects in their immediate environment. As they participate in first-hand experiences, they are continually gathering, sorting, and storing the kind of information that subsequent map reading processes demand. Three important pre-mapping learning areas must be emphasized as children gather and assimilate knowledge about their physical world: (1) physical features, (2) the earth, and (3) representation.

Physical Features

Children continually "read their environment" for clues as to what the still undefined people, places, and objects in their young lives are all about. Teachers help children begin to make sense of their surroundings by directing them toward certain data or significant discoveries. This guidance does not stifle a child's interest in the experience, but provides the necessary direction to make the most of it. There are a variety of ways to help children inspect and identify physical features in their environment:

If your playground is comprised of several different surfaces (sand, dirt, grass, asphalt, concrete, etc.), have the children observe each carefully and decide which is best for riding a trike or running in bare feet. Discuss why the hardest surface is easiest for some tasks and the softest is easiest for others. Ask the children to find the area that would be best for digging, for tumbling, for resting, or for other uses.

Sand and water play can be used to help the children build model rivers, lakes, roads, mountains, farms, cities, and the like. Toy vehicles add additional fantasy to free play and help develop an awareness of the different types of geographical features on the earth's surface and how people use those features in their daily lives.

Take a walk outside the school and locate various physical features. Churches, houses, apartment buildings, trailers, row homes, stores, parking lots, and parks can be identified. You should lead discussions to help the children compare and contrast the ways people use these neighborhood features.

Take a trip to a more remote area than the one in which your school is located—to a rural area, for example. Encourage the children to look for different land formations and buildings, such as rivers, ponds, mountains, valleys, fields, farmhouses, or barns. Lead a discussion of the ways this environment differs from their own, especially regarding clothing, work, play, and living arrangements.

The Earth

Complete understanding of the earth and its features is certainly impossible for young children—consider, for example, the youngster who busily burrows with his shovel because he wants to "dig all the way to the bottom of the world." Despite maturational limitations, it is important for children to participate in experiences that focus on apparent features of the earth's surface:

When standing in the sun, ask the children to find their shadows. Explain that the sun's strong light makes the shadow. Move to the shade and talk about the differences.

Digging in the dirt and playing with water introduce children to the two basic features of the earth. Take the children to a lake or pond to help them more fully understand large bodies of water. Have the children classify objects or pictures of things that belong primarily on land or in the water.

Have the children look at the many varieties of cloud formations to learn that large, puffy, white clouds mean fair weather and large, dark, thick clouds warn of rain or snow.

During a windy day, point out the nature of the wind by asking the children to run into the wind and then turn away from the wind and run. Discuss the differences experienced during each effort.

Representation

The actual symbolic representations on maps are too abstract for kindergarten and early primary-grade children to use. This does not mean, however, that young children are incapable of using symbols of any kind; their oral language skills show that they are able to use verbal symbols. For that reason, a variety of informal representational activities will help children discover relationships between some physical aspect of their environment and its symbol. These activities help promote initial instruction in representation:

Encourage free play in the sand or water play areas with trucks, cars, boats, and the like. As children "build" roads, bridges, canals, and other geographic features, they begin to develop an understanding of how their miniature environment simulates the larger world.

Take a class trip around the neighborhood and photograph the buildings as you go. Mount the pictures on blocks of wood and encourage the children to use them as they would use regular blocks in their play.

Use photographs of the children to illustrate that familiar things can be represented by scale models. Point out to them, "The picture shows you, but the picture is very small and you are really much bigger." Take photographs or draw pictures of a variety of classroom features and ask the children to point to or pick up the real object. This leads children to understand that symbols represent real things or real places, but in much smaller ways.

Provide picture puzzles and map puzzles to help children develop accurate conceptualizations of real objects.

Some children use these experiences as springboards to successful map and globe consciousness, while others derive little benefit. What accounts for the variability? Perhaps the most reasonable explanation is that many children have not yet developed the ability to perceive the various spatial relationships required for understanding maps.

PERCEPTUAL FACTORS

Egocentrism and Conservation

Perceptual skills involve a child's ability to receive sensory input, interpret it, and respond to it. Two perceptual factors—Piaget's "egocentrism" and "conservation"—are

Special projects in which children illustrate familiar environmental features help them understand the use of symbols.

particularly important to successful map reading. *Egocentrism* refers to childrens' ability to see the world only from their point of view and their belief that everyone else sees it the same way. Children have difficulty imagining that a view of any physical feature changes if it is examined from a position other than their own. To test this characteristic, Piaget devised a square board with three distinctly different model mountains, arranged as shown in Figure 12–1. Interviewers ask children to sit at a table so that they see the view shown. Then the interviewers show the children drawings of the mountains as viewed from several different perspectives and ask the children to select the view they presently see. Next, the interviewers introduce a doll who "strolls" around the table along the edges of the model, stopping at each side of the square. The children remain seated and select pictures showing how the doll sees the mountains at each stop. Results showed that some children were able to make firm choices before the age of 8 or 10, but not until that age could most children answer with confidence.

In addition to egocentrism, Piaget found that children younger than about 7 or 8 have difficulty counterbalancing how things look now as opposed to how they looked a short while ago (*conservation*). Manifestations of the concept of conservation are illustrated in Figure 12–2.

Informal Play with Blocks

Because children before age 8 are egocentric in their view of the environment and have difficulty conserving, teachers of young children should learn to work *with* and not against these natural tendencies. Teachers of children 5 to 7 years old provide the foundation for helping the child conceptualize space by arranging blocks, boxes, and other construction materials in a variety of informal play situations. Children can build structures, large enough to play in, that represent neighborhood, school, shopping area, or airport. Although the emphasis is on creative play and not on constructing accurate representations, the children are making a symbolic representation of some real part of their environment, and in essence, that is what a map is.

Blocks are exciting materials for youngsters to work with. With blocks, children can make "real" things to touch, move, reach through, go around, and even to crash into on occasion. Children build, play, destroy, and build again as they gain mastery not only of their physical capabilities but also of their ability to represent some real place.

FIGURE 12–1
*Piaget's Arrangement of
Mountains on a Square Board*

FIGURE 12–2

Piagetian Tests to Estimate Children's Ability to Conceptualize Space

	Have the children agree that there are:	Then make this change:	And ask the children:
CONSERVATION OF LIQUIDS	two equal glasses of liquid. 	Pour one into a taller, thinner glass. 	Do the glasses contain more, less, or the same amount? Why do you think so?
CONSERVATION OF NUMBER	two equal lines of coins. 	Lengthen the spaces between the coins on one line. 	Do both lines have the same number of checkers or does one line have more? Why do you think so?
CONSERVATION OF MATTER	two equal balls of clay. 	Squeeze one ball into a long thin shape. 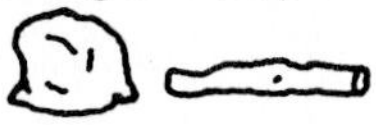	Which piece has more clay—the ball or the snake? Why do you think so?
CONSERVATION OF LENGTH	two pencils of equal length. 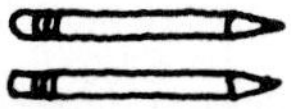	Move one pencil. 	Would two ants starting a hike at this end of the pencils and walking at the same speed both travel the same distance? Why do you think so?
CONSERVATION OF AREA	two identical pieces of green construction paper representing a field of grass on which are placed the same number of red blocks representing barns. Add a toy cow to each field. Establish that both cows have same amount of grass to eat. 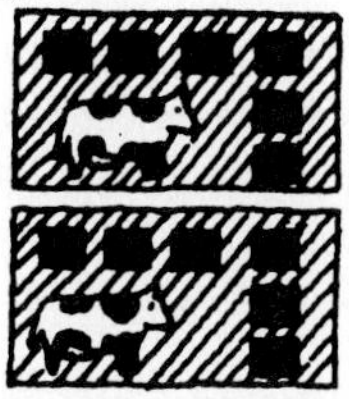	Rearrange the barns. 	Do the cows still have the same amount of grass to eat? Which has more? Why do you think so?

Watch a group of kindergartners or first graders strive to build a neighborhood with their blocks: cars, buses, and trucks maneuver up and down the streets, reacting to pedestrians and traffic signals or coming into a service station for a fill-up. The active involvement, role-playing, and mental exercise help make this a valuable initial learning experience.

Your role during this kind of activity is to *observe* and *encourage.* You may offer help and advice, but do not build or participate in the actual block construction. Maintain a lookout for safety reasons and interfere only if there is continued disarray or confusion, or physical danger. The atmosphere is one of independence and responsibility, encouraging the children to work hard toward their own purposes.

In addition to informal learning with block play, what specific map and globe skills can the teacher encourage in a more planned way? We can best answer this question if we think of a small group of children building with blocks who become aware they have made some structures and what appear to be streets. They have included toy people, animals, cars, and other "props" that were near the block area. Skillful teachers will interact with the children, asking questions that lead to the development of specific perceptual skills necessary for successful map reading. These are appropriate questions and comments:

> "Which automobile will fit through the garage door?"
>
> "How can you make this road longer?"
>
> "Does your road have curves or is it straight?"
>
> "Where would that car go if this road were closed?"
>
> "What made your building fall down?"
>
> "Let's see if that building is as tall as this tower."
>
> "Jimmy's foot is two blocks long. How many blocks long is my foot?"
>
> "How can you build a bridge so that the truck can get to the other side of the river?"
>
> "Are these blocks the same size?"
>
> "I wonder what would happen if you put a round block here."

By interacting in this way, teachers can encourage expansion of perceptual concepts such as size, shape, weight, measurement, classification, symbols, and categorization. These concepts, according to Piaget, are essential before formal map instruction begins.

Teachers can learn much about children by listening and watching. As the children investigate and discuss, the teacher may wish to introduce new materials unobtrusively or pull together random ideas. Do this carefully, because children's free experimentation and creativity can be stifled by teachers who fail to maintain the delicate balance between informal guidance and formal direction. The teacher's creativity, added in proper proportion to the children's, will bring interesting new aspects to the play. The teacher's role during this initial map reading experience includes these aspects:

- *Arranging the environment:* Provide blocks, boxes, boards, barrels, cardboard, spools from telephone cable, ramps, rugs, trucks, cars, fire engines, trains, boats, wagons, tractors, airplanes, rope, gas pump, traffic signs, barn, animals, family dolls, community worker dolls, and a variety of other equipment.
- *Informal guidance:* Allow children to experience the materials and to discover their dramatic possibilities. Creative play provides the necessary foundation for developing more sophisticated understandings.

■ *Evaluation:* Observe the children at dramatic play to pick up clues as to what areas need strengthening or which children are becoming ready for more formalized map instruction.

BEGINNING MAP INSTRUCTION

During children's experience with pre-mapping activities, skills and understandings will evolve at different rates. If you are in the process of building a truly developmental map reading program in the primary grades, children who do not have adequate experiential and perceptual characteristics should be given more opportunities for readiness-type activities. Children who are able to move ahead should be encouraged to do so with directed learning experiences that promote confidence and motivation to succeed, and that develop these map reading skills:

1. Locating places
2. Recognizing and expressing relative location
3. Interpreting map symbols
4. Developing a basic idea of relative size and scale
5. Reading directions
6. Understanding that the globe is the most accurate representation of the earth's surface

Planned instruction in map and globe skills is easy to begin with children identified as ready because of *direct involvement* and *concrete experiences,* two essential components of a program. Children learn best when they experiment with challenging materials that stimulate mental processes to organize and integrate new information into already present mental perceptions. This means that children can learn only if they have previously developed the perceptions necessary to make a logical progression to a new task.

Beginning Map Activities

Because of the importance of providing a continual, developmental approach to instruction, the experiences in the initial phases of planned instruction should remain concrete and not vary greatly from those of the pre-mapping period. However, the emphasis changes from informal play to planning and developing accurate representations of some real observed environment.

Siegel and Schadler advise us that the first environment to be mapped should be thoroughly familiar to the children.[7] To support this point, the researchers conducted an experiment to determine whether familiarity with the environment enhances young children's ability to produce spatial representations (map constructions) and found that increased experience in the environment to be represented (a classroom, in this instance) significantly facilitated the accuracy of the representations. Perhaps the most desirable environment in which to begin, then, is the classroom. In this way, children are able to constantly observe the environment they are to represent, enabling them more readily to make direct comparisons and contrasts.

Three-dimensional Maps

Begin this initial mapmaking project (it usually works best with second graders) by asking the children to bring back from lunch their empty half-pint milk containers. Clean carefully and cut off the tops of the containers at a point below where they meet so that you have a square-shaped, open-top box. Turn the box over and cut away parts of the sides with scissors so that the cartons appear to have legs and begin to represent the forms of the children's desks (see Figure 12–3). Discuss the representation with the children, pointing out that these model desks are to look like their real desks. Encourage the children to paint the desks with tempera paint, to glue construction paper books or pencils on top, and to put their name cards on the fronts of the desks.

When the desks are completed, ask one child to put his desk on a large sheet of cardboard or paper that has been placed on a worktable or on the floor. Show the child that the large cardboard represents the classroom on a smaller scale. Let him observe the room and then the cardboard to see where the desk should be placed. Once satisfied, you may ask for the child who "sits next to Mike" to place her desk. Actually, three basic map reading skills are being introduced as you continue to have the children place their desks on the cardboard.

1. Recognizing that their milk carton desks *stand for* their real desks (interpreting map symbols)
2. Finding where their desks should be placed (locating places)
3. Determining the placement of individual desks in relationship to the other desks (recognizing and expressing relative location)

To progress, ask the children to bring to school the next day empty boxes they might have around the house, from small jewelry boxes to boxes about the size of a toaster. Divide the members of the class who are able to work together into committees, each of which is responsible for constructing a classroom feature such as the piano, teacher's desk, learning center, and so on. Keep a careful eye on the children as they select the boxes most appropriate for their particular models. Often, the group responsible for the teacher's desk will select the largest box, even though that box is much larger than the relative size of the desk, because children view the teacher as an

FIGURE 12–3
Stages of Constructing Milk Carton Desks

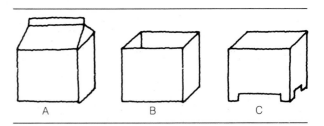

A   B   C

extremely important person in their lives and thus deserving the largest available box. But encourage the children to observe their own real desks in comparison to the teacher's so they can eventually select a box that represents the true relationship. Sometimes children create amusingly novel approaches to depicting relative size associations. For example, one teacher found that all students had completed their assigned tasks and were ready to place their features on the growing three-dimensional map, but Alice was still busy at the back of the room finishing her model wastebasket. When the teacher went back to watch he found that Alice's progress had been impeded by a sincere desire to represent the relative size as accurately as possible. Since the classroom wastebasket was full of paper scraps, Alice was folding and cutting dozens of tiny pieces of paper for her wastebasket in order to reproduce the real object with precision.

When all classroom features are chosen, they are decorated, painted, and ready for placement on the floor or table map. This phase of map reading instruction is crucial for its contribution to what Preston and Herman describe as the "bird's-eye-view" concept.[8] They found that a major reason for children's failure to read maps in the upper grades is the lack of ability to mentally view the environment as it would look from above, the way a map is constructed. You can help develop this key ability by encouraging the children to place their classroom features on the map and view them from above. That way, they will see only the tops of the desks, tables, file cabinet, and so on, and begin to understand that this is how a real map is constructed.

Notice that during this phase of construction, the three previous map reading skills are extended and reinforced, and a new skill is introduced: developing an idea of relative size and scale.

Once the classroom has been properly arranged, you can further extend and reinforce map skills with questions and tasks such as these:

Locating places
"Place your desk on the spot where it is located in our classroom."
"Where would you place the piano? The file cabinet?"
"Point to the box that shows the puppet stage . . . the work table . . . the teacher's desk."
"James, can you find Michelle's desk? Put your finger on it."
"Put your finger on the aquarium. Now trace the path you would take to answer the door."

Recognizing and expressing relative location
"Whose desk is closest to the coatrack?"
"Trace the shortest path from the reading corner to the door."
"Which is closer to the door, the science learning center or the teacher's desk?"

Interpreting map symbols
"Pick up the box that stands for the learning center table."
"What does the red box stand for?"
"How can we show the coatrack on our map?"

Developing an idea of relative size and scale
"Which is larger, the spelling center or the piano?"
"Which box should be smaller, the teacher's desk or the worktable?"
"Point to the smallest (or largest) piece of classroom furniture."

Class discussion of their three-dimensional representation affords children opportunities to understand that objects can be used to symbolize other objects. This skill is vitally important in a developmental plan of instruction, since Piaget tells us that children most effectively acquire understandings according to the three levels of representation illustrated in Figure 12–4.

Our beginning map activity moves through these levels by giving opportunities to construct symbols that represent real objects (index and symbol levels of representation) and to put their experiences into words (sign)—whereby we have provided an accurate language base for still newer ideas.

Constructing a Flat Map

After the three-dimensional classroom representation has been properly used, begin a transition from this concrete experience to one that is slightly more abstract. To move to the construction of a simple flat map, have the children look at their 3-D map from directly above and discuss their perceptions. Then ask them to put a piece of construction paper beneath each feature and trace around the outside of each with a crayon. As the 3-D features are removed and the outlines cut out with scissors, the children should label the remaining outlines, as "file cabinet" or "Bart's desk," and glue the outlines in their appropriate places. The 3-D map gradually becomes a flat map as outlines replace the models. For the children to perceive accurately how the flat map is similar to the 3-D map, you should ask questions like those suggested for the 3-D map. Effective discussion is as important for this flat map phase as for the 3-D phase.

FIGURE 12–4
Piaget's Three Levels of Representation

Concrete Experience	*Symbolic Representations*	*Language*

The child learns by experiencing the real thing. Meaning is attached only to the real object.	The child understands that another object, say a picture, can stand for something else.	The child attaches meaning to the spoken or written word.
1. INDEX	2. SYMBOL	3. SIGN

Reinforcing Map Symbol Recognition

To reinforce the concept of map symbol through activities that go beyond classroom maps, present the children with a few easily recongized symbols they might see every day, such as those in Figure 12–5. Ask the children what each symbol or sign means to them. What do they stand for? Emphasize that symbols represent real people, places, things, or ideas. Following the discussion, ask the children to pair up and each draw a secret symbol without allowing the partner to see. Then have each pair try to guess each other's picture. If they have difficulty getting started, offer suggestions such as road signs, punctuation marks, math symbols, and the like. Prepare a bulletin board display of their efforts after they have shared the symbols with each other.

Explain that a symbol is a sign that stands for something. Illustrate this idea by sharing a familiar object, such as a toy airplane. Ask the children to draw an airplane, say the word, and write the word on the chalkboard. Help children understand that some sounds are symbols, pictures are symbols, and printed words are symbols. The children should now be ready to understand that the special set of symbols a group of people commonly use to communicate ideas is called a *language.* In the United States, most citizens use the English language to communicate orally and in print. In school, we learn English as our main language, but we also learn other languages, such as the language of maps.

To move from this introductory lesson on symbols, write the word *tree* on the chalkboard, and ask the children what a tree looks like. After discussing their many interpretations, emphasize that the written *tree* stands for a real thing the same way a map symbol does. Ask the children to suggest what the symbol for *tree* would be in the special language of maps. Follow this procedure while helping the children make up their own symbols for houses, factories, stores, libraries, lakes, roads, mountains, and so on. Don't be overly concerned if their symbols are not the same as standard symbols for these things; at this point you are most concerned not with accuracy of representation, but with the overall concept of symbolization.

The children can practice their ability to make symbols and place them on "maps" with the following activity. Clear a large area of your classroom or take the children outdoors or to a multipurpose room. Outline the area as a diamond shape with a long piece of yarn, tape, or string. Have the children stand above the yarn and observe it from eye level. Show them a rough outline of this yarn shape that you have previously drawn on a large sheet of paper. Discuss how the drawn outline shows a real area as it would look from the ceiling. Then ask the children to draw their own copies with

FIGURE 12–5
Recognized Symbols

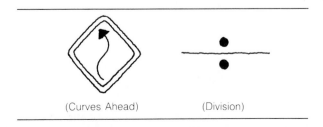

(Curves Ahead)   (Division)

crayon on sheets of drawing paper—a large, simple diamond is fine. Place a box on the floor near one corner of the large quadrangle and invite the children to stand over it and look at it carefully. Then, ask them to draw a picture of what they saw as they observed it from above and put a work label on it. Add several more objects to this activity, each time following the same procedure. Use objects such as books, chairs, blocks, toys,

Translating their three-dimensional model into a flat map helps children visualize the process of mapmaking.

and so on. Compare the relative size and distance of each item so children will see how position and proportion affect the accuracy of maps. Now split the class into groups of three or four. Have each group draw a special "map" showing how they would arrange the objects. The groups then challenge each other by exchanging and determining where the real objects should be placed on the floor within the large diamond. Now invite the groups to further challenge each other by having one group rearrange the objects on the floor and asking the others to make the map of the resulting configuration.

Standard map symbols can gradually be introduced now that the children are more familiar with the concept of "symbol." Remind the children that maps are symbols on paper—that they stand for real things. Show them photographs or slides of a railroad, a bridge, and a building. Then show the children the three corresponding map symbols. Ask them to match the symbols to their corresponding pictures and add the word labels. Follow this progression (photo or picture—symbol—word label) whenever new map symbols are introduced in your classroom. After the entire map transfer and symbol recognition procedure has been completed, the children will be ready for an introduction to a new map skill—reading directions.

Direction

The best method of introducing children to direction is to make the learning experience meaningful. Primary-grade children enjoy going outdoors with simple compasses to find the cardinal directions (north, south, east, and west). After they locate north on the compass, the children will soon learn that south is behind them, east to the right, and west to the left. If the children are outside at noon on a sunny day, they will find a new clue for determining direction—that, in our northern hemisphere, their shadows will point in a northerly direction. Once they determine north this way, the other directions will be easy to find. To help them remember the other directions, help the children search for outstanding physical landmarks. Have one child face north and select the first obvious feature, such as a large building. Give him a card labeled "north" and ask him to stand facing north with the card in his hands. Then select a second child to stand back-to-back to the northerly child. Ask the children what direction this child is facing. If no one says "south," tell them. Ask this child to find an outstanding physical feature to the south (such as a large tree) and give her a labeled card to hold. Repeat this procedure when explaining the east and west directions. The children can be encouraged to plot the position of the sun in the sky from morning through afternoon. By associating landmarks with directions, the children begin to understand that directions help us locate places in our environment. You may ask, for example, "In what direction must I walk if I want to go to that large hill?" To help reinforce these directional skills, provide a number of follow-up activities; for example, "Simon Says" can be adapted to a directional format—"Simon says, 'Take three steps west.' Simon says, 'Turn to the south.' "

After the children have had this fundamental introduction to direction, extend the learnings to their classroom maps. Ask the children to place their direction labels on the appropriate walls in the classroom after the outdoor experience is completed. Do not label the front of the room "north" and the back of the room "south" if these are not the true directions. After checking the classroom directions by using the compass or checking with the previously established reference points, teach the children always to orient their maps in the proper direction whenever they use them. This may involve turning chairs or sitting on the floor, but by always turning themselves and their maps in the direction of true north, children avoid the common misconception that "north" is the direction toward the front of the room.

The skill of reading cardinal directions can then be extended with the use of the children's classroom map and these questions or requests: "Point to the south wall. Put your finger on the worktable. Someone dropped a pencil near the chalkboard on the west wall. Show the path you would take to pick it up. Put your finger on the puppet stage. In which direction should you walk to get to the teacher's desk? In what direction would you go to get from your desk to the drinking fountain? True or false—Richard's desk is north of Marie's desk." You may also use the children's textbook maps to reinforce directions. Use "Who Am I?" riddles such as, "I am north of California and south of Washington. Who Am I?"

Scale

The idea of scale should be introduced in a relative way rather than in a mathematical sense in the primary grades. Children should be led to realize that maps need to be small enough to be easily carried and readily used. Give the children sheets of drawing paper in shapes that approximate their classroom and tell them to construct their own maps using the 3-D map as a model. Some children will immediately reduce the size of the classroom features proportionately. Others will have greater difficulty trying to reproduce the large classroom features on their smaller papers.

Children move toward an understanding of maps as they master the skills of locating places, recognizing and expressing relative locations, interpreting map symbols, reading directions, and developing the ideas of relative size and scale. These skills are best developed in a program that stresses activity and concrete experience.

The Globe

Since the early primary-grade child's view of the earth may be fairly restricted, planned instruction in globe reading skills is usually not recommended. But you should not totally omit globe-related activities from the primary classroom. With simplified 12" globes, the children can understand that the globe is a visualization of the earth much as their map was a model of their classroom. The globe should have a minimum amount of detail on it and preferably should show the land masses in no more than three colors and the bodies of water in a consistent shade of blue. Only the names of the continents, countries, largest cities, and largest bodies of water should be indicated. Globes that show more detail can confuse the very young child.

You should use the globe as a valuable, informal teaching tool. When reading stories, children may wish to find where their favorite characters live, and you can show them the geographical location. For example, if your second-grade class is in Philadelphia and you are reading the children a story about Los Posados in the city of Los

Angeles, you may want to show them where Los Angeles is in relationship to Philadelphia. However, even this would be a meaningless activity unless you relate it to the children's own experiences. You may ask, for example, "How many of you have ever taken a trip for a whole day in a car? Were you tired? If you wanted to go to Los Angeles by car, you would need to spend about eight days in a row riding in a car. That's how far Los Angeles is." Children who hear about the North Pole at Christmastime may want to know where this cold place is located. Television stories or newspaper articles may suggest places the children wish to find. The teacher can use instances like these to familiarize young children with characteristics of the globe and with the fact they can use the globe to find special places. The basic globe concepts for development in the primary grades are:

- To understand the basic roundness of the earth
- To understand the differences between land and water areas
- To begin to locate the poles, major cities, and the United States

These are some teaching suggestions:

> Use the names of large bodies of water and land masses, such as Atlantic Ocean, Pacific Ocean, North America, Africa, or the equator. Show the children where their home state is located.
>
> Have the children locate large land areas and bodies of water.
>
> Talk about how it would feel to be an astronaut and to be able to look at the earth from a satellite. Discuss how the land masses and bodies of water would look. Show a satellite photo and map of the earth.
>
> Have the children discover that the earth is composed of much more water than land. Also, most of the land is located north of the equator.
>
> When studying about families around the world, tape small pictures of people in traditional dress to their corresponding countries on a large papier-mâché globe constructed by the children. Discussion of the need for different types of clothing can lead to an awareness of warm and cold regions of the earth.

This list summarizes the teacher's role in developing map and globe skills in the early primary grades.

- *Prepare the environment.* Encourage the children to observe carefully the environment and compare the physical features of objects in the classroom for use in their map.
- *Plan a developmental sequence.* Reproduce the environment with an accurate three-dimensional model. Gradually transform this model to a flat map, substituting outlines for each feature. Finally, construct individual maps from the larger models. Make large "yarn maps" for the purpose of understanding map symbols. Use compasses and the position of the sun to teach directions.
- *Stimulate thinking.* Develop a sound questioning strategy that encourages children to think concretely and creatively throughout the entire map instruction sequence.

■ *Evaluate progress.* Observe the children at all times to see who is frustrated and who is bored. If either symptom is evident, you need to find the cause and adjust your instruction accordingly. Frustration occurs if you move too quickly with some children or present them with tasks for which they are not ready. If you fail to challenge gifted students or move too slowly for them, chances are they will become bored or apathetic. Remember that map instruction, like any other learning in the primary grades, must be developmental in nature and geared to individual needs.

Map and Globe Reinforcement

At the beginning of instruction, some teachers reinforce and extend map reading skills through commercially prepared map materials found either in social studies texts or practice booklets. Others create game-type activities to supplement and enrich early map programs.

In the primary grades, the globe should be used only as an informal learning tool. This teacher is pointing out the setting of a story she will read to the class.

Games and Activities

The children can find hidden surprises in a "treasure hunt" in the classroom. Hide a special prize somewhere in the room and encourage the children to find it by giving them map directions. Include directions such as "Walk north to the file cabinet. Turn in the direction of where the sun rises and take three steps. Look under the book for your next direction."

Use a game to reinforce directional skills. Give each child a sheet of primary graph paper and read these directions: "Start at the large dot on your graph paper and place your own dot at each location that I give you. Move 7 spaces east and place your first dot. Connect the two dots. Next, go north 10 squares and connect those two dots. Then, east 1 square. Then (pausing after each direction), north 4 squares, west 5 squares, south 3 squares, west 3 squares, north 2 squares, west 2 squares, south 2 squares, west 3 squares, north 2 squares, west 2 squares, south 2 squares, west 3 squares, north 3 squares, west 2 squares, south 1 square, west 2 squares, north 1 square, west 2 squares, south 4 squares, east 1 square, south 10 squares, east 7 squares, north 7 squares, east 8 squares, and south 7 squares." The result should be a castle outline. You can ask the children to draw a flag in the tower farthest west, damsel in distress in the tower farthest east, etc.

To arouse enthusiasm, use the children's names as labels for map features. Duplicate the map and add a sheet of questions covering the related map skills.

Use building blocks to help the children measure the distance from one classroom feature to another—the number of blocks from the teacher's desk to the file cabinet, the sink, bulletin board, and so on. How many miles would this distance be if each block were 1 mile? Most youngsters aren't sure how far a mile is. Take them on a walk and actually measure it out.

Using Children's Literature

Early primary grade children are not too young to begin developing a basic foundation of concepts and skills, provided they are actively involved in the process. Children's stories can extend the children's learnings by providing opportunities for creative skill-building activity.

Sandra F. Pritchard has developed a series of imaginative activities to accompany children's stories. There are many books describing the movement of characters through space; they can be excellent resources for teaching geographic concepts and skills. To illustrate, Pritchard took the five recurring themes identified by GENIP as central to geographic literacy (location, place, relationships within places, movement, and regions) and identified story-related activities appropriate for each theme. Here, for example, is a list of activities for *Katy and the Big Snow* by Virginia Lee Burton. Teachers are encouraged to read the book once for enjoyment, then read it a second time as children push a toy bulldozer along a teacher-made map indicating the streets Katy is plowing.

1. *Location: Position on the Earth's Surface*
   - locate buildings and streets;

- identify and locate the cardinal directions;
- determine in which direction Katy went from school to railroad station; from police station to fire station, etc.;
- describe the locations of buildings in relation to other buildings and streets;
- describe the location of places using cardinal directions and the intersections of two streets.

2. *Place: Physical and Human Characteristics*
   - discuss the changes between summer and winter in the little town and how the seasons affect people;
   - draw pictures of the deciduous and coniferous trees through the seasons;
   - describe the people who live in the little town in terms of their age, occupation, and recreational activities;
   - describe a walk along First Street or Third Street.

3. *Relationships Within Places: Human-Environment Interaction*
   - tell how snow affects the lives of people in the town;
   - tell what might have happened if Katy had not been available to plow out the town.

4. *Movement: Humans Interacting on the Earth*
   - identify and describe the various types of transportation in the story and on the map;
   - identify and describe the various types of communication in the story and on the map;
   - find symbols for buildings, roads, and airports on [road] maps;

5. *Regions/Neighborhoods: How They Form and Change*
   - identify residential neighborhoods and business areas in the little town.[9]

Stories other than *Katy and the Big Snow* appropriate for primary grade programs include *Little Black Bear Goes for a Walk* by Berniece Freschet, *Make Way for Ducklings* by Robert McCloskey, *Henry Explores the Jungle* by Mark Taylor, *Rosie's Walk* by Pat Hutchins, and *Harry the Dirty Dog* by Gene Zion.

Telling Stories

Donna E. Norton has created "The Mystery of the Kidnapped Chemist" as an innovative approach to reinforcing map skills for young children. The activity involves a map and a story, which can either be taped or read aloud by the teacher:

> You are going to have an opportunity to solve the case of the kidnapped chemist. The heroine in this story is a girl who invented a formula for turning people invisible. Two companies want the formula; one company is honest and the other one is not. When our heroine refuses to sell the formula to the dishonest company, they kidnap her, blindfold her, and put her in the back seat of a car. The kidnapper tells her she will be taken to a secret laboratory where she will be forced to make the formula. She cannot see where the car will be taking her. She wonders how she will be able to tell the police how to find the secret laboratory; she knows she will try to escape and she needs to know the location of that laboratory. The kidnappers have covered her eyes, but they have not covered her ears. She decides that if she listens carefully, she may be able to get enough clues to identify the route the car is traveling. She is afraid, however, that she will not be able to listen carefully enough to recognize all the sounds and to remember the order she hears them. The order is very important, since the sounds will form a sound road map, and provide the clues for locating the secret laboratory. When you finish listening to the clues, you will make her trip on a sound road map. Ready? The car is starting!
>
> The first sound she hears is a [church bell]. The sound is loud, so the car must be beside the sound. The car stops at the corner by the sound, and turns toward the right. She can hear a new sound off in the distance. The car is coming closer to [zoo animal

sounds]. As she rides past these sounds, she knows it is 8:00, because she can hear the [clock striking]. Many sounds are now heard in the sky. She can hear an [airplane] overhead. The road is getting bumpy, and she can hear [road construction noises]. Something big just passed the car. A pleasant sound is heard as the car travels on. She can hear [children laughing and talking] in the distance. She must be driving in the country, because she can hear the sound of [frogs].

She hears a [railroad crossing bell], and thinks the car is stopping at a railroad crossing. The car moves ahead, slows and stops. Her kidnappers tell her to get out, because she has reached the secret laboratory. She strains her hearing, and thinks she hears the sound of [turkeys gobbling]. Can you help her remember her trip? Where did the car travel? Where is the secret laboratory? To show that you remember the car's movements, draw the direction the car took on the sound road map [see Figure 12–6] in the listening center. After you have finished, listen to the tape a second time and check to see if you are correct. If you are not correct, draw in the right directions with a red pencil. [10]

FIGURE 12–6
Sound Road Map for ''The Mystery of the Kidnapped Chemist''

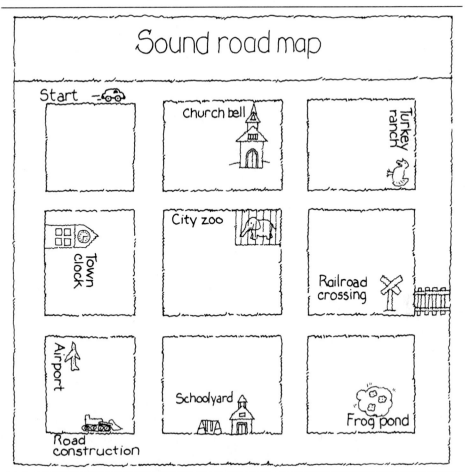

MAPS AND GLOBES IN THE SUBSEQUENT ELEMENTARY GRADES

The basic map and globe skills introduced and reinforced during the early grades are used in the later grades in more highly sophisticated contexts and for different purposes. Children in the early grades, developing concepts of what a map is and how to read one, primarily use maps in their textbooks and practice exercises that (1) are fanciful in nature (usually depicting *familiar places* such as a zoo, park, or neighborhood; or imaginary places such as Playland, Fantasyland, or Spaceland), (2) contain mostly pictorial or semipictorial symbols, (3) often represent a real environment shared by all the children, and (4) begin to introduce children to the locations of people or places under study in other contexts, such as in literature or reading books. In later grades, the skills are refined to include using maps to gather information and to solve problems. Children are expected to extend their basic skills to using detailed maps of areas well beyond their immediate location and direct observation. In short, the direction changes from *learning to read maps* to *reading maps to learn.*

Place Location

As the children progress through the elementary grades, they are still required to examine a map to find places. The major difference, however, is the level of sophistication of the map itself. Comparing this process to reading a book, you might say that children are taught to recognize words in first grade but only at a level appropriate for their stage of development. Later, as the children's skills mature, they are introduced to newer, more difficult words. Likewise, the maps early primary-grade children read gradually evolve into more specialized maps, many of which require skill in using grids. Middle- and upper-elementary grade children move toward the functional use of maps—employing maps, such as road maps, to acquire information for a specific purpose. As with the primary grades, children should be provided with varieties of activities that go beyond workbook or ditto maps designed to reinforce specific map reading skills.

Games and Activities

Guess What.   Give the children graph paper similar to that in Figure 12–7. Give them a clue, such as "I take you where you want to go." Encourage the children to find out what it is by coloring in squares; for example, the squares indicated in the figure would emerge as a bus figure.

Tic-Tac-Toe.   Divide your class into groups of three. For each of the following phases, designate two players and an umpire. During Phase 1, the umpire draws a regular tic-tac-toe grid and places *X*s or *O*s into the squares for each player. The players indicate the squares they want by pointing to the spaces only. Discourage any other form of communication. Play three games during Phase 1, alternating responsibilities so that each child has an opportunity to be an umpire and a player. For Phase 2, the umpire draws a regular tic-tac-toe grid but adds a new feature. On each row, she places the

FIGURE 12–7
Guess What

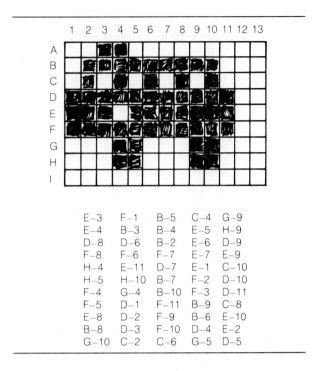

E–3	F–1	B–5	C–4	G–9
E–4	B–3	B–4	E–5	H–9
D–8	D–6	B–2	E–6	D–9
F–8	F–6	F–7	E–7	E–9
H–4	E–11	D–7	E–1	C–10
H–5	H–10	B–7	F–2	D–10
F–4	G–4	B–10	F–3	D–11
F–5	D–1	F–11	B–9	C–8
E–8	D–2	F–9	B–6	E–10
B–8	D–3	F–10	D–4	E–2
G–10	C–2	C–6	G–5	D–5

numerals 1, 2, and 3. Again playing three games, the players now indicate the *X*s and *O*s to the umpire by calling the numeral and then pointing to the appropriate square. The umpire writes in the proper mark. Finally, in Phase 3, the traditional tic-tac-toe grid is drawn with numerals for each row, and an added feature—letters for each column. Allow the children to play at least three games again, this time indicating their moves to the umpire by stating the row and column.

Tap-Tap. Arrange desks or chairs into rows. Tape a sheet of construction paper labeled with a different letter of the alphabet for each row to the first desk of each row so that it can be easily seen by someone standing in the front of the room. For each column, label a sheet of construction paper with a different numeral. Draw the names of five children from a hat and ask them to go to the front of the room and stand with their backs turned and eyes closed. Select five more children to sneak to the front, tap each child lightly, and return to their seats. Opening their eyes and facing the class, the original group of five must try to guess who tapped each of them by calling out the appropriate grid placement; for example, "The one who tapped me is seated at C-4." Alternate places so that everyone has a chance to participate.

Odd Town. Creative story writing and map skills instruction can be combined as an extension of the preceding activities. For example, encourage each child to look at a road map index and determine the oddest name of a town or city in the state. In Pennsylvania, for example, children have many from which to choose—Snowshoe, Bird-in-Hand, Potato City, and Conshohocken, to name a few. Using the coordinates specified in the index, the location of the city should be made and marked with an *X* on the map so it cannot be used again by someone else. The children are then encouraged to write an original story telling how the town they selected got its name.

Sports Map.   Get a large map of the United States and glue small metal washers near each city that has a professional football team. Buy a set of miniature magnetized NFL plastic football helmets (available in most mail-order catalogs for a reasonable price) and have the children attach the appropriate helmet to each metal washer. If you cannot get the plastic helmets, cut out the helmets from the catalog ads, paste them onto sturdy tagboard, and glue a small magnetic strip on the back of each. To extend this activity, supply the current season's schedule of the most popular professional football team in your area. Ask questions such as "Where do the Giants play their closest away game? What is the largest city the Giants visit? Going south from New York, what is the first city with a professional football team? What team must travel the farthest to play the Giants? What city on the Giants' schedule is farthest west?" Using energy conservation as a focal point, ask your children to consider the current alignment of divisions within the NFL. For example, Cleveland, Cincinnati, Pittsburgh, and Houston comprise one division. Ask whether divisions could be realigned so that teams in one region could be grouped together. One group of fifth graders eliminated Houston from the grouping above and came up with a Central Division of Cleveland, Cincinnati, Pittsburgh, and Indianapolis. As groups of children offer their alignment plans, many geographical concepts are brought out as support. The key idea, though, is that the children are beginning to understand how maps help us understand how people and the environment are closely dependent upon each other.

Map Display.   Display a large, colorful map on the bulletin board. Encourage the children to collect postmarks, business cards, matchbook covers, newspaper mastheads, clothing labels, etc. Pin them on the board and attach a piece of string to the location.

Latitude and Longitude

In the upper elementary grades, children extend their knowledge of grids as place location devices to the system of latitude and longitude. This system is comprised of east-west lines called *parallels of latitude* and north-south lines called *meridians of longitude* (see Figure 12–8).

The parallels of latitude, imaginary lines encircling the earth, measure distances in degrees north and south of the equator (designated as zero degrees latitude). The parallels grow smaller in circumference as they approach both poles. The meridians of longitude, also imaginary lines encircling the earth, converge at the poles and measure distances in degrees east and west of the prime meridian (designated as zero degrees longitude).

The importance of grids as means of locating places can be illustrated with a large, unmarked ball. Lead a discussion comparing the similarities of the large ball and the earth as represented by the classroom globe. Glue a small plastic ship to the ball and

FIGURE 12–8
The Earth's Grid System

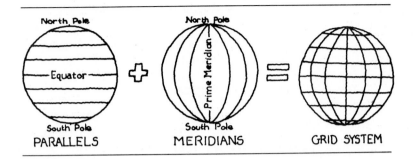

ask the children to describe its exact location, imagining themselves shipwrecked and needing to radio their location to be rescued (the ship marks their wreck). They will discover that this is nearly impossible, since there is no point of reference from which to describe an exact location. For example, if the children say the ship is located on the front side of the ball, you can turn the ball and the statement will be incorrect. If they say the ship is on the top of the ball, turn it back again to the original position. Gradually, the students will experience the frustration of locating places on a globe without agreed-upon reference points. After some deliberation, they will most likely suggest the addition of parallel east-west lines, and instruct the rescue squad to search an area "three lines down from the middle line."

On closer examination of this arrangement, and after prodding from the teacher, they will discover that the rescuers need to travel all around the world along the "third line down from the middle line" to find them unless given even more precise locations by devising *meridians,* or north-south lines. Then, the rescue squad only needs to find where the two points meet. Eventually, the children can be led to locate many well-known places in the world using latitude and longitude. Exact locations by actual *degrees* of latitude and longitude may be beyond the mental development of most fourth- and fifth-grade children. Guide them, however, in using latitude and longitude for locating general areas, such as the low latitudes (23 1/2° north and south of the equator), the middle latitudes (between 23 1/2 and 66 1/2° north and south of the equator), and the high latitudes (between 66 1/2° north and the North Pole and 66 1/2° south and the South Pole). Children can generalize about the climatic similarities within these areas. In which latitudes are most cities located? Where is the weather warm (or cold) throughout most of the year? They should be shown how to find places east or west or north or south of their location by using meridians. After careful scrutiny, they may be surprised to find such interesting facts as that Rome, Italy, is nearer the North Pole than New York is; Detroit is actually north of Windsor, Ontario; Reno, Nevada, is actually farther west than Los Angeles; the Gulf of California does not touch California at any point; and the Pacific Ocean is actually east of the Atlantic Ocean at Panama. All early grid instruction should be general and avoid as much as possible the use of degrees in place location.

In the sixth grade, after grid concepts have been firmly developed, children can begin to make increasingly precise locations. They can locate places they are studying, such as, "If you were at 20° south latitude and 20° east longitude, you would be in _____ ."

In addition to these activities, teachers may wish to reinforce the understanding of grid systems with other activities.

Games and Activities

Follow Directions Game. The teacher gives each child a sheet of paper that has a marked grid, as shown in Figure 12–9. The children start at the dot placed on the graph paper by the teacher. They make their own dots at each location given, such as, "Place a dot at the point 10° west." As they place the dot locations, the children connect them. An outline of an object, state, country, or continent results.

Destroy a Monster. The object of this game is for the player to capture an opponent's sea monster and to protect his or her own monster. Prepare two large tagboard squares as shown in Figure 12–10. Each large square is divided into a grid pattern. The rows and columns are numbered to represent degrees of latitude and longitude. Each player puts his game board in such a position that it cannot be seen by the other player. The players then place their monsters on the board in any position. Players take turns shooting at each other's monster in rounds. In the first round, each player may shoot at an opponent's monster ten times. A "shot" is taken by naming the square where a child thinks his or her opponent might be. For example, a child might guess the location 10° south latitude and 25° west longitude. The opponent must tell whether the shot was a hit or miss. Every time a shot is taken, it is marked on the game boards. The rounds continue until one player has hit any part of his or her opponent's sea monster five times.

FIGURE 12–9
Follow Directions Game

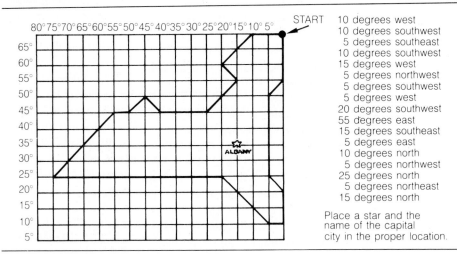

START   10 degrees west
10 degrees southwest
5 degrees southeast
10 degrees southwest
15 degrees west
5 degrees northwest
5 degrees southwest
5 degrees west
20 degrees southwest
55 degrees east
15 degrees southeast
5 degrees east
10 degrees north
5 degrees northwest
25 degrees north
5 degrees northeast
15 degrees north

Place a star and the name of the capital city in the proper location.

FIGURE 12–10
Destroy a Monster Game

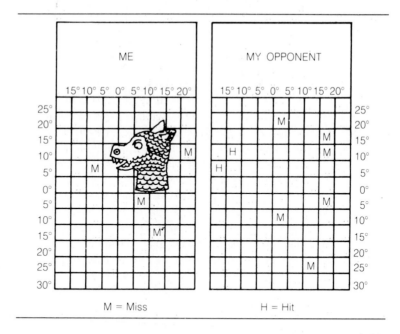

Coordinate Tic-Tac-Toe. Draw the diagram shown in Figure 12–11 on the chalk-board; use whatever successive numbers you wish to represent latitude and longitude. A child on one team gives a set of coordinates, for example, 10° east longitude and 20° north latitude, and places an *X* in that location. A child on another team gives another series of numbers. An *O* is placed on that spot. The teams continue in the same fashion as tic-tac-toe.

Relative Location

Place location, a significant map reading skill, must be expanded so that children perceive greater meaning from maps. Children must understand the influence of location on people's lives and how one physical feature may influence another. Recognizing and expressing relative location is a more sophisticated map skill because it involves not only finding places but also interpreting the interrelationships among geographical features, such as location, topography, and climate. For example, upon

FIGURE 12–11
Coordinate Tic-Tac-Toe

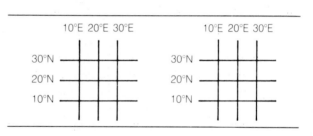

examining a rainfall map of an area such as Africa, shown in Figure 12–12, children should be able to determine the type of vegetation that might grow there and how its inhabitants use the land.

In the early primary grades, children can develop concepts of relative location by relating different places in the classroom ("Why do you think the science center is next to the sink?"). The concept is expanded in the intermediate grades as children develop the ability to interpret the significance of physical factors, such as mountains, deserts, valleys, and oceans, on human life. The effects of these geographic features should be discussed, along with humans' attempts to change conditions for their own benefit.

One way of doing this is to ask the children to participate in a simulation activity. Distribute a map of a community's downtown business section through which a new highway must be constructed. Assign each student a building in the section through which the highway must pass (bakery, florist shop, hospital, church, historic house, apartment building, department store, pizza parlor, movie theater, YMCA, auto dealership, supermarket, and so on). Construct a large master map and ask the children to write their names next to their respective businesses. Tell them that the highway must be completed with minimal delay, so the entire business community must meet to decide where to put the final route. How complex you get at this point is your decision, but insist that the children arrive at one solution. Tunnels or bridges are acceptable alternatives, but don't encourage children to choose them before they contribute those ideas by themselves. In similar ways, children can learn about other environmental interactions between humans and nature, such as the effect of a large shopping mall on an undeveloped rural area or the effect of a housing project on what had been farmland.

These experiences further develop concepts of recognizing and expressing relative location:

> Discuss the relationships among latitude and climate, temperature, land use, and living conditions.

FIGURE 12–12
Yearly Rainfall and Vegetation Maps of Africa

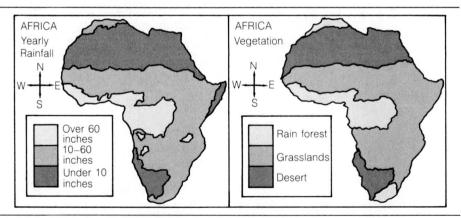

Discuss people's attempts to modify the physical characteristics of their environment. Locate dams, highways, cities, communications networks, and so on.

Have children locate areas of high population density in our country and cite possible reasons for growth.

Note relationships among topography and natural resources, population, vegetation, climate, and transportation.

Map Symbols

Maps and globes use symbols to represent a region's characteristics. In the primary grades, pictorial or semipictorial symbols are recommended; as a rule, the younger the child, the less abstract the symbols should be. As children move into the upper grades, conventional map symbols, as illustrated in Figure 12–13, can be used. Be careful to provide children with clear interpretation and visualization of newer map symbols. Present a picture of pictorial symbols (or the real thing). After discussing a new symbol, provide for review of the symbol without its label so children will learn the symbol and not rely on the label. Emphasize the importance of looking at the legend before using a map.

Many maps and globes use color or shading as a symbol, most commonly to show elevation of land from sea level. Color should be taught as a special kind of symbol. Children should understand that elevation is measured from sea level and that colors show the height above sea level. Discuss profiles of mountains and explain that color used in this way helps us determine elevation.

FIGURE 12–13
Common Map Symbols for Legends

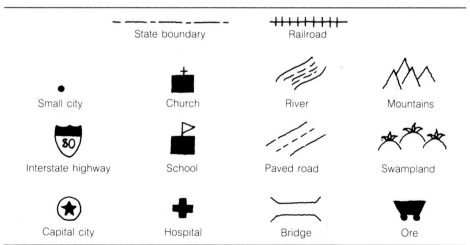

State boundary		Railroad	
Small city	Church	River	Mountains
Interstate highway	School	Paved road	Swampland
Capital city	Hospital	Bridge	Ore

Additional activities to help children grow in their ability to understand and use map symbols include these:

> Provide a blank "profile drawing" of the United States. Have children plan a trip from Maine to the Pacific Coast. As they proceed west, the children use crayons to color in mountains, valleys, and plains to represent proper elevations.
>
> Encourage children to look through magazines you provide for them, select pictures of outstanding physical features, and paste them next to the labels and map symbols you have organized on a chart.
>
> Examine *aerial photographs* to illustrate the relationship between an area's actual conditions and the symbols used to represent them.
>
> When studying world regions, children should be supplied with outline maps and encouraged to provide symbols to represent features such as main products, vegetation, population trends, elevation, and rainfall.

Direction

In the early grades, children learn the cardinal directions and participate in related map reading experiences. As they become more mature and learn to grasp the concept of cardinal direction, they can begin more complex map work such as intermediate directions (northeast, southwest, etc.). The ability to use directional skills is often combined with latitude and longitude skills for locating places on maps. Reexamine the reinforcement activities for place location, and notice that each activity includes directional knowledge that would also be appropriate reinforcement of latitude and longitude concepts.

An even more sophisticated skill than *interpreting* maps is the ability to *communicate* directions. An illustrative activity is to divide your classroom into teams of three. One student thinks of an easily accessible place somewhere in the school or around the school grounds but cannot tell the other members of the group what that place is. She must then take an easily carried object, hide it there, and tell the second group member (while the third cannot hear) how to get to where she's hidden the object. The "teller" describes which directions to go (north, south, northeast, etc.), what features he will pass (lavatory, drinking fountain), and how far he should go. Child 2, the "translator," translates the directions into a map showing the location chosen by Child 1. The map is given to the third team member, who must find the hidden object. Each team that finds the hidden object is a winner. When the activity is completed, discuss the problems encountered in translating verbal directions into accurate maps.

Scale

To portray geographic features of the earth on a globe or flat map, the concept of scale must be utilized to ensure accurate size and space relationships among the features. This is accomplished by reducing the size of every real feature in an equal percentage.

Very young children have difficulty conceptualizing that sizes and distances on maps actually represent some large, real geographical area. Therefore, the formal use of scales should not begin until a child is past grade 3 and then, instruction should be gradual. The children can be introduced to the concept of scale by comparing a class picture to the actual size of class members. They can be led to realize that the picture represents a real group of children, but in a much smaller way.

You must be careful to move forward gradually. Have the children measure the distances between prominent landmarks on walking trips around the school. They can make maps of their experiences and discuss the actual distances between the landmarks and the amount of space on their maps. Although their scale will probably not be accurate, have the children discover that although the walking trip covered a distance of 2,000 feet, it is represented by only 20 inches on their map.

Perhaps the most appropriate formal map scale to use at the elementary school level is the graphic scale. A scale of miles may be placed at the bottom of the child's map. Children can place a cardboard marker between any two points (Los Angeles and San Francisco) on their maps, place a dot for each city, and then lay the edge of the marker along the scale. The segments of the scale on Figure 12–14 are of equal length and represent miles on the map. Comparing the marks on their cardboard marker to the scale, children will see that the distance between Los Angeles and San Francisco is approximately 350 miles.

These additional activities will help children grow in their ability to understand scale:

> Show an aerial photograph of their city or neighborhood and have the children pick out recognizable landmarks. This will help them visualize that a small map can represent a large area on the ground.

> Using a camera, take a closeup picture of an object and then take another at a greater distance. Compare the amount of detail shown in each picture to develop the concept of scale.

FIGURE 12–14
A Graphic Map Scale

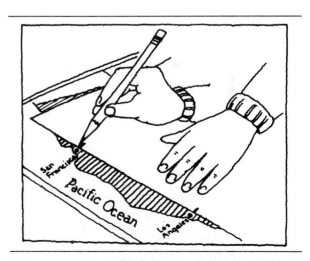

Have children compare two maps of the same area drawn to different scales. Discuss the likenesses and differences.

Reading a Globe

Recall the basic globe reading skills we discussed for the primary grades. Informal instruction aimed mainly to help the children realize that the globe is a model that represents the earth. Their major formal map reading experiences up to this time dealt with flat maps on which they located cities and other places of interest. They learned how to tell direction and how to compute the distance between one place and another. Now, they must learn that a globe, round like the earth, is the only accurate map of it, and an even better tool for studying locations, directions, or distances than is a flat map. To emphasize this fact, you may want to show a satellite photograph of the earth and compare it to a classroom globe. It is fairly easy to find satellite photographs, especially if you request them through the United States Weather Service.

After you compare satellite photographs to a classroom globe, illustrate just why the globe is more accurate than flat maps. Using a large, thin rubber ball or a globe made from papier-mâché, cut the ball in half and draw an outline of North America (or any random shape) on the ball. Have the children apply hand pressure to flatten the ball and discuss the resulting distortions. Then use scissors to cut through the ball along lines that represent longitude lines. Have the children try to flatten the ball again. Although the ball flattens more easily, the drawn outline still becomes distorted. Help the children discover that this is a major problem faced by mapmakers (*cartographers*) when they attempt to make flat maps of places on the earth (see Figure 12–15).

Globes help to show shapes of areas exactly as they would appear on the earth's surface. Unfortunately, maps are not able to do this. Representing a curved surface precisely on a flat map has confounded cartographers for years. The resulting distortion has been responsible for such honest comments as, "I didn't know Greenland was such a large country!" In fact, it isn't—although it appears huge on some map projections, Greenland is actually one-third the size of Australia. A classroom globe shows shapes and areas more accurately than maps and should be used in conjunction with the study

FIGURE 12–15
Globe as a Flattened Ball

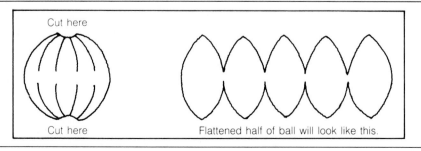

of wall maps. Because of this major problem, globes and maps should be used reciprocally while developing the skills outlined in this chapter.

As a third step in establishing the true characteristics of globes, lead the children to realize that the earth, a planet, is a large, spherical, solid body that moves through space around the sun and that it is from the sun that the earth receives its heat and light. Accompanying the earth as components of our solar system are eight other planets, the largest of which is Jupiter and the smallest, Mercury. Earth, the third planet from the sun, is a relatively small planet, which houses the only life of which we are aware. Establish that the earth *revolves* around the sun, making one complete revolution each 365 1/4 days. At the same time it is revolving, the earth makes another movement—it turns around or *rotates* in a west-to-east direction once every twenty-four hours. Point out that the earth turns on an *axis* which always leans a little (23 1/2°) from a true vertical line. The axis is an imaginary line that runs through the earth from North Pole to South Pole. Show how the earth rotates on an axis by spinning a gyroscope and having the children observe how it tilts to one side as it moves.

After familiarizing the children with these basic globe concepts, they should learn that the earth can be divided into *hemispheres* (*hemi* is a prefix meaning "half of"; thus, "half of a sphere"). If we live in the United States, we live in the northern half of the globe, or the Northern Hemisphere. At the same time, we live in the western half of the globe, or the Western Hemisphere. The *equator* and the *prime meridian* split the earth in half in each direction to form the hemishperes. Other significant lines that encircle the earth and run parallel to the equator are called parallels of latitude. Two important latitudes are the tropic of Cancer and the tropic of Capricorn. The region between these two lines, including the equator, is called the tropics. The tropic of Cancer is north of the equator; the tropic of Capricorn is south of the equator. Lead the children to discover that a combination of all these factors accounts for seasons. They have learned that the earth is tilted 23 1/2° on its axis and that the axis always tilts in the same direction. Note the angle shown on the four positions of the earth illustrated in Figure 12–16. As the earth moves around the sun, there are certain times when the Northern Hemisphere leans toward the sun and receives its direct rays and other times when it leans away from the sun and receives less direct rays. This gives us our summer season (when the direct rays are between the equator and the tropic of Cancer) and our winter season (when the direct rays are between the equator and the tropic of Capricorn). On what major parallel of latitude do the direct rays shine on March 21 and September 21? What seasons do we have in the Northern Hemisphere at those times? Why? It should be apparent to you at this time why the tropic of Cancer and the tropic of Capricorn are located 23 1/2° north and south of the equator. How could you explain this fact to your children? Regardless of the season, though, it is always hot in the tropics. The two zones that lie outside of the tropics receive less direct sunlight and have more moderate climate. It is in these regions that the seasons change. These are the northern mid-latitude region and the southern mid-latitude region. Seasons in the two regions are opposite because of the tilt of the earth's axis. As we move toward the North and South Poles, we encounter the polar regions, which receive little direct sun and are cold all year around.

FIGURE 12–16
Position of the Earth During the Four Seasons

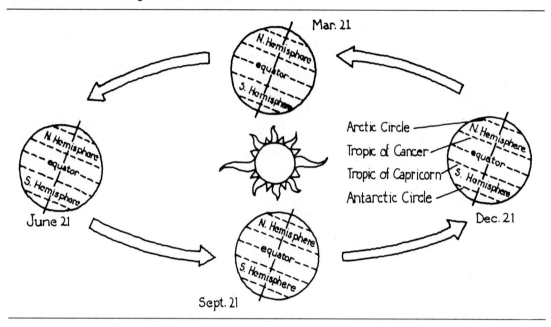

MAP SELECTION FOR THE CLASSROOM

Selection of appropriate maps and globes for the children's developmental levels is essential. Every school should be equipped with a large variety of maps, including wall maps, special purpose maps, outline maps, atlases, and globes. A variety of information can be shown on these maps, as in Figure 12–17. The *relief map* gives information about land elevation, the *vegetation map* shows what grows naturally, the *export map* shows what products are sold to other countries, and the *rainfall map* shows how much rain falls yearly in a region. These materials should be available in schools: physical-political maps of the home state, United States, each continent, and the world; plastic-coated washable maps of the United States and the world; plastic raised relief maps of the United States and each continent; outline maps of the home state, United States, each continent, and the world; physical-political globes; large markable globes; world atlases; pictorial charts of geographic terms; special purpose maps; and satellite photographs.

Besides using commercial maps in the classroom, children should also make their own maps. To be of value, however, these maps should directly relate to a specific topic or unit of study and suit the children's developmental level. As mentioned, initial mapmaking experiences should relate to the child's immediate environment and should be realistic and concrete. As children develop maturity, these activities can be extended to include areas beyond their immediate environment.

FIGURE 12–17

Special Subject Maps (Reprinted by permission of Scholastic Inc. from Scholastic Map Skills Book E *by Barbara Christensen. Copyright © 1978 by Scholastic Inc.)*

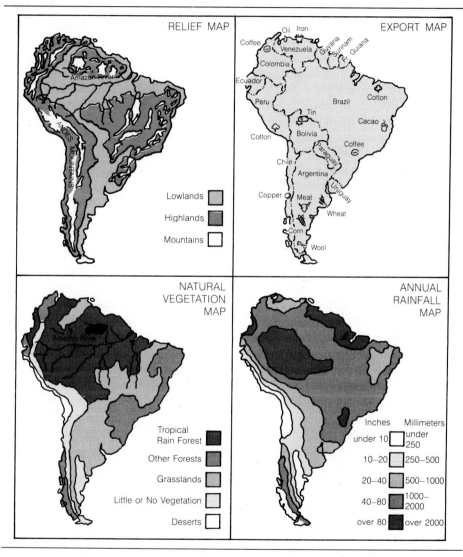

Outline Maps

Having children produce freehand map drawings of specific locations can be an unnecessary, time-consuming activity. When the need arises for an outline map, you should provide one as quickly and efficiently as possible. The opaque projector is one good source to use in constructing outline maps. Enlargements can be projected from textbooks, magazines, newspapers, atlases, or similar reference materials, and their outlines can be traced on the chalkboard or large poster paper. You can use an overhead projector if the necessary transparencies are available. If transparencies are not available, you can make tracings on clear plastic or glass. In the proportional squares technique, one covers the map to be enlarged with small squares. The same number of squares is then drawn on a much larger piece of paper, resulting in much larger squares. Match the outline shown in each small square with the corresponding large square, as shown in Figure 12–18.

Chalkboard outline maps can be made by punching large pin holes approximately one inch apart on an outline map. Hold the map up against the chalkboard and dust an eraser full of chalk over the holes. An outline of the map will appear on the chalkboard, which you can trace over with chalk.

Small outline maps can be made for individual student use by tracing original maps on a master for reproduction on a duplication machine. Commercial publishers also produce inexpensive printed outline maps.

Relief Maps

Maps that incorporate raised features are useful aids for visualizing topographic features and for determining the effects of those features on distance, travel, weather, terrain, and other conditions. One of the problems in constructing relief maps is the distorted vertical-horizontal relationship. Children must understand that the relationship of height to distance is highly exaggerated to show the topographic features more clearly. If true height-distance relationships were shown while scaling the earth down to the size of a large beach ball, the beach ball model would actually be smooth, and no actual topographical features could be shown. If relief maps are used, it must be understood that they show vertical distortion of topographical features.

Relief maps should be constructed on a firm base, such as plywood. Posterboard or similar materials are not strong enough to support wet modeling materials and can buckle and curl as the materials dry. An accurate outline for the relief map should be prepared carefully, and a second map should always be near to serve as a working guide as the modeling material is being placed over the outline. Rivers, lakes, mountains, valleys, and other features should be sketched where needed. After elevation and

FIGURE 12–18
The Proportional Squares Technique

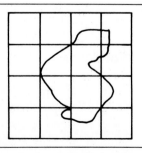

other land features have been identified, nails, pins, brads, and other materials can serve as supports for mountains, peaks, ranges, and hills. Color can be added to represent changes in elevation, to identify lakes and rivers, and to highlight other natural phenomena.

Several different recipes can be used to produce modeling materials; among the most popular are:

Papier-mâché. Cut newspaper or paper towels into strips about 1/2" to 3/4" wide and soak them overnight. Squeeze the paper and drain off excess water. Add wheat paste until the mixture assumes the consistency of dough. Surface features can be built by applying this mixture to the modeling surface. After drying for three to six days, the surface becomes extremely hard and is ready for painting.

Paste and paper strips. Cut paper towels into 1/2" strips and dip them into wheat paste. Place them over crumpled paper used to build up the surface features. Cover the entire surface with two layers of material. After this has been done, apply a coat of wheat paste over the surface. After the material is dry, paint can be applied.

Salt and flour. Mix equal parts of salt and flour with enough water to ensure a plastic consistency. The mixture can be added to a map outline and the terrain molded according to specifications.

Modeling dough. Mix together three cups flour and one cup salt. Stir and knead these materials together, gradually adding water until the mixture attains the consistency of dough. Dry tempera paint can be added to produce a bright-colored product.

Puzzle Maps

Puzzle maps can be made from cardboard, posterboard, or plywood. Trace the major features as you would on an outline map. Color in rivers, lakes, mountains, and other significant topographical features. Cut the map into a variety of shapes and encourage the children to reconstruct it.

Topographic Maps

Nearly everyone, at one time or another, has used a topographic map. In fact, the U.S. Geological Survey distributes more than seven million topographic maps annually. Chances are the children you teach will eventually have contact with a topographic map—as adults in jobs as diverse as fishing or engineering. Older children may use the maps for a variety of purposes in the classroom, including simulations involving highway and airport planning, selecting industrial sites and pipeline and powerline routes, making property surveys, managing natural resources, agricultural research, and planning recreation areas.

Topographic maps provide detailed records of land areas, showing geographic positions and elevations of both natural and fabricated features. They show the shape of the land (mountains, valleys, and plains) with brown contour lines; water features are shown in blue; woodland features are shown in green; roads, buildings, railroads, and power lines are designated by black markings; and urbanized areas are shown in a red tint. Other special features are shown by appropriate symbols.

The physical and cultural characteristics of the terrain are determined by precise engineering surveys and field inspections by United States Geological Survey personnel, who then record the data on a map. Topographic maps are published for each state and are free upon request from Branch of Distribution, U.S. Geological Survey, 1200 South Eads Street, Arlington, VA 22202.

Outdoor Maps

Some schools will allow construction of maps on hard-surfaced sections of the playground. Prepare the class by having them construct a paper model. Outlines, parallels, meridians, and/or significant topographical features can be drawn on the hard surface using the model as a guide. Many gallons of paint will be used to mark the selected countries as well as to designate the selected cities.

This list summarizes the teacher's role in developing and reinforcing map skills in the upper-elementary grades.

- *Prepare the environment.* Provide a wide variety of maps and globes, both commercially produced and child-constructed.
- *Plan an instructional sequence.* Continue with the developmental sequence begun during the primary grades. Reinforce and extend those skills with increasingly sophisticated maps such as relief maps or special purpose maps. Use concrete experiences to teach new concepts such as grids or those related to the globe. The emphasis has changed from learning to read maps to reading maps to learn.
- *Stimulate thinking.* Encourage youngsters to think logically and creatively while constructing and interpreting maps. Help them see how maps summarize and explain geographical phenomena and their influence on humankind.
- *Evaluate progress.* Remember that map instruction, like any other teaching task in the elementary grades, must be geared to each individual. Failure to challenge the gifted or meet the special needs of the slow learner will result in a classroom of disinterested, dissatisfied youngsters. Be constantly aware of the children's progress and adjust your teaching strategies accordingly.

Maps, globes, tables, charts, and graphs are summary techniques for representing information in clear, concise, symbolic form. The primary characteristic of each system is a pattern of scale, color, or shape that comprises its symbol scheme. The ability to use a map, table, globe, chart, or graph rests solely on a child's ability to unlock that symbol scheme, much as success in conventional reading rests on an ability to unlock the symbol scheme of letters and words. Like conventional reading, the ability to read maps, tables, globes, charts, and graphs is comprised of many subskills that need to be taught in a developmental sequence so the children will become skillful in their use.

Developing map and globe skills depends on the child's ability to perceive representations of her environment. Piaget's work shows us that up to about seven or eight years of age, children may be limited in their ability to unlock the map and globe symbol scheme because of the characteristics of egocentrism and conservation. Because of these characteristics, children younger than eight years may need "readiness" activities to promote geographic understandings such as representation, physical features, and the earth.

As the children indicate an ability to advance to actual beginning map instruction, you need to plan a developmental program that will promote each of these map reading skills:

- Locating places
- Recognizing and expressing relative location
- Interpreting map symbols
- Developing a basic idea of relative size and scale
- Reading directions
- Understanding that the globe is the most accurate representation of the earth's surface

Planned instruction in these skills should offer *direct involvement* and *concrete experiences,* for when children experiment with challenging materials that stimulate mental processes, they are best able to organize and integrate new information into existing mental structures.

GEOGRAPHIC SKILLS AND UNDERSTANDINGS

There is no common, established scope and sequence of map skills instruction. Expectancies differ widely among school districts. In some, first graders are expected to identify the major continents, while in others that may not be expected until third grade. There have been attempts to establish a common scope and sequence over the years, but none has become generally accepted. The pattern developed by GENIP, which relates the skills to the five themes outlined at the beginning of the chapter, is a recent example of such efforts.

Theme Activities for Various Grade Levels

1. Location
   - Kindergarten
     Map the relative locations of facial features using paper plates, paper, crayons, paint, and yarn.
     Draw pictures of the classroom and talk about objects that are near to or far from another.
   - Grade One
     Name the home city or town and point to it on a map and a globe.
     Name the directions north, south, east, and west in the classroom.
   - Grade Two
     Build models and draw maps to represent the location of places relative to other places.
     Place pins on a street map of the community to show the locations where students live.
   - Grade Three
     Locate places on a map that has a number/letter grid reference system.
     Make models of a "dream" community.

- Grade Four
  Locate the positions of continents and oceans relative to each other.
  Use latitude and longitude to identify the location of places on maps and globes.
- Grade Five
  Use maps and globes to classify locations in hemispheres.
  Trace the historical development of a populated area in North America in order to demonstrate the changing influences on the location.
- Grade Six
  Make inferences about the locations of major cities in each of the central focus regions (South America, Eurasia, Africa).
  Compare the locations of selected cities in South America (highland locations), with selected cities in Eurasia and Africa to note the geographic factors that influence the location of each city.

2. Place
   - Kindergarten
     Use a sandbox to make a model showing physical features.
     Use a globe to point out land and water.
   - Grade One
     Create a community with blocks, box sculpture, or a sandbox.
     Examine air photos of the school area.
   - Grade Two
     Use pictorial symbols and color to make simple maps.
     Make a key to show what the symbols represent.
     Create a country, as a whole class or in groups.
   - Grade Three
     Select pictures or diagrams that show the landforms and water bodies located in the community.
     Identify and describe the characteristics of the human landscape in the community, i.e., places people build.
   - Grade Four
     Define the characteristics of major landforms, e.g., mountains, hills, plateaus, and plains.
     Use a variety of sources to prepare advertisements designed to attract people to a place.
   - Grade Five
     Exchange drawings to compare and contrast perceptions of the same places.
     Design brochures or bus tours of North America.
   - Grade Six
     Use maps to determine relationships of human characteristics among and within each region.
     Choose the best place to live in designated focus regions. Defend your choice.

3. Relationships within places
   - Kindergarten
     Draw a picture of the ways people could improve the neighborhood, e.g., plant flowers or pick up litter.
     Make improvements to the classrooms, e.g., tidy up, plant flowers.

- Grade One
  Describe the seasons and how they affect people at work, at home, or at play.
  Observe, describe, and record changes in the local environment over time.
- Grade Two
  Compare ways students and other people use the physical environment to meet their needs.
  Decide whether empty land in your community should be used or left alone. If it is to be used, draw pictures to show how.
- Grade Three
  Explain how climate may influence the way people dress, what they do for recreation, and the types of houses they build.
  Compare ways in which people in urban and rural communities meet their needs from the environment.
- Grade Four
  Describe landforms using a map or aerial photo, and relate them to ways people may use the land to work and play.
  Describe, using maps and photos, how you would change the environment of an area for different types of activities.
- Grade Five
  Locate, on a map, the major resources found in North America.
  Examine maps, charts, and graphs to determine how a city has changed over time.
- Grade Six
  Evaluate land use in central focus regions.
  Define terms which describe the impact of technology upon the environment, e.g., pollution.

4. Movement
   - Kindergarten
     Name places outside the home community where family members have shopped.
     Use pictures to identify and describe different types of transportation.
   - Grade One
     Talk about how highways, railways, and airlines tie people together.
     Draw maps of trips from home to outside activities.
   - Grade Two
     Tell or paint a story about how people depend on farms for food and factories for products.
     Describe places family members travel to in order to do their work.
   - Grade Three
     Use a road map to trace and describe a route.
     Listen to a nightly news report on TV and locate places mentioned.
   - Grade Four
     Collect labels from domestic and imported products; graph and compare the findings.
     Locate places visited by students and their families and graph popular routes and travel destinations.

- Grade Five
  Explain why human activities require movement.
  Describe patterns of trade to demonstrate the routes of natural resources and manufactured products.
- Grade Six
  Trace movements of raw materials and manufactured products in the central focus regions.
  Evaluate migration patterns within and outside of the central focus regions.

5. Regions
  - Kindergarten
    Draw a picture or mural, or model a place with stores and offices.
    Tell ways that shopping areas and neighborhoods change.
  - Grade One
    Use a map to find symbols showing where people live and where they do not live.
    Use photographs to describe ways that the local area has changed.
  - Grade Two
    Draw pictures to show ways that students would like the neighborhood to change in the future.
    Compare ways in which the students' neighborhood is similar to and different from other neighborhoods in the community.
  - Grade Three
    Draw a boundary, or border, around a map of the community following the established political boundaries.
    Locate, on a map, where each student in the class lives and enclose all the places with a boundary to identify it as the residential or home region for the class.
  - Grade Four
    Locate examples of physical features that serve as boundaries between states/provinces and countries.
    Locate areas that can be classified as regions, e.g., forests, deserts, agricultural areas, or political units. Categorize them as physical or human regions.
  - Grade Five
    Distinguish ways that a neighborhood and a shopping mall are different/similar.
    Examine a variety of thematic maps to determine the criteria used to draw regional boundaries.
  - Grade Six
    Categorize subregions and regions of the central focus areas as "developed" or "developing."
    Assess the impact of change on the daily life of people in the central focus regions.

SUMMARY

Map and globe reading skills furnish children with the basic tools necessary for geographic literacy. Maps and globes, the primary tools of the geographer, provide accurate and orderly descriptions of the earth's surface. But geographic literacy also addresses the significance of places on the earth's surface. The GENIP committee's five themes provide a scope for geographical study: location, place, relationships within places, movement, and regions. The elementary school social studies program should focus on these themes through the use of abundant experiences in reading maps and globes.

The development of map and globe skills depends on a child's ability to perceive representations of the environment. Piaget's work shows us that up until about seven or eight years of age, children are limited in their ability to unlock the symbol scheme of maps and globes because of their *egocentrism* and *inability to conserve.* Children younger than eight, therefore, may need "pre-mapping" experiences that develop concepts of representation, physical features, and the earth.

As the students indicate readiness to move toward actual map instruction, they require a developmental program designed to promote each of these basic map reading skills:

- locating places
- recognizing and expressing relative location
- interpreting map symbols
- developing a basic idea of relative size and scale
- reading directions
- understanding that the globe is the most accurate representation of the earth's surface

Planned instruction in these skills should offer direct involvement and concrete experiences, for when children experiment with challenging materials that stimulate mental processes, they are best able to organize and integrate new information into existing mental structures.

ENDNOTES

1. Charles F. Gritzner, "Geographic Education: Where Have We Failed?" *Journal of Geography, 80,* no. 7 (December 1981): 264.

2. Gilbert M. Grosvenor, "Geographic Ignorance: Time for a Turnaround," *National Geographic, 167,* no. 6 (June 1985): unnumbered page; Charles F. Gritzner, "Geographic Education: Where Have We Failed?" *Journal of Geography, 80,* no. 7 (December 1981): 264.

3. Salvatore J. Natoli and Charles F. Gritzner, "Modern Geography," in *Strengthening Geography in the Social Studies, NCSS Bulletin 81,* ed. Salvatore J. Natoli (Washington, DC: National Council for the Social Studies, 1988), p. 9.

4. Committee on Geographic Education, National Council for Geographic Education, and Association of American Geographers, *Guidelines for Geographic Education: Elementary and Secondary Schools* (Washington, DC: Association of American Geographers, 1984).

5. *K–6 Geography: Themes, Key Ideas, and Learning Opportunities* (Indiana, PA: Geographic Education National Implementation Project, 1987), pp. 3–4.

6. Salvatore J. Natoli, "Implementing a Geography Program," in *Strengthening Geography in Social Studies, NCSS Bulletin 81,* ed. Salvatore J. Natoli (Washington, DC: National Council for the Social Studies, 1988), p. 98.

7. Alexander W. Siegel and Margaret Schadler, "The Development of Young Children's Spatial Representations of Their Classrooms," in *Contemporary Readings in Child Psychology,* 2nd ed., ed. E. Mavis Hetherington and Ross D. Parke (New York: McGraw-Hill, 1981), pp. 170–176.

8. Ralph C. Preston and Wayne L. Herman, Jr., *Teaching Social Studies in the Elementary School* (New York: Holt, Rinehart and Winston, 1974), pp. 405–406.

9. Sandra F. Pritchard, "Using Picture Books to Teach Geography in the Primary Grades," *Journal of Geography, 88,* no. 4 (July–August 1989): 126–136.

10. Donna E. Norton, *Language Arts Activities for Children* (Columbus, OH: Merrill, 1980), pp. 116–118.

History belongs in the school programs of all students. . . . It is vital for all citizens in a democracy, because it provides the only avenue we have to reach an understanding of ourselves and of our society, in relation to the human condition over time, and of how some things change and others continue.

We can be sure that students will experience enormous changes over their lifetimes. History is the discipline that can best help them to understand and deal with change, and at the same time to identify the deep continuities that link past and present.[1]

—The Bradley Commission on History in Schools

13 Examining the Role of History in the Social Studies Curriculum

As you read, reflect on the following matters:

- Why has there been strong support for more history in the social studies program?
- Can elementary school children learn history meaningfully?
- What sources of historical data are most useful and appropriate for elementary school students?
- How can we help young children develop a concept of time?
- How can we help children acquire a sense of historical consciousness?

What should be the status of history in the elementary school? This question engaged historians and educators at the beginning of the 1990s. The Bradley Commission on History in Schools, an influential committee created in 1987 in response to the inadequacy of history taught in American elementary and secondary classrooms, obviously believes that all children in our democracy need the knowledge and understanding that history imparts. The NCSS Task Force on Early Childhood/Elementary Social Studies, in its definition and rationale for social studies for young children, adds support for history in our schools: "The social studies equip [elementary school children] with the knowledge and understanding of the past necessary for coping with the present and planning for the future."[2] Furthermore, you read in Chapter 1 about the pleas to teach more history during the elementary school years. Despite this seemingly strong support, there are two key questions that have split educators on how history should be taught in the elementary school: (1) Are elementary school children mature enough to benefit from history instruction? and (2) Should history be taught to help children accumulate information or should emphasis be placed on the development of students' ability to think?

CAN ELEMENTARY SCHOOL CHILDREN LEARN HISTORY?

Matthew T. Downey and Linda S. Levstik undertook a survey of available research on these two key concerns and included these observations in their summary:

1. There is no evidence that delaying instruction in history is developmentally appropriate. . . . Research in . . . cognition suggests that children know more about time and history than has been thought. . . .
2. A shallow "cultural literacy" approach to concept development in history is not supported by the research . . .
3. The research . . . indicates . . . real engagement with history must be a pedagogical [effective teaching] as well as a content concern . . .
4. There is an inadequate body of research on instruction in history. We know little about how interaction among students, teachers, and others, whose influence is felt in the classroom affects how history is taught and learned.[3]

Reacting to these findings, Downey and Levstik comment, "We must not let proposals for reform become the mechanism by which teachers are reduced to technicians. Instead, reform should empower teachers, and support them in their efforts to engage children in the study of history."[4]

In recognition of similar concerns the Bradley Commission adopted the following resolutions for designing and implementing courses of historical study in our schools:

1. That the knowledge and habits of mind to be gained from the study of history are indispensable to the education of citizens in a democracy. The study of history should, therefore, be required of all students.
2. That such study must reach well beyond the acquisition of useful information. To develop judgment and perspective, historical study must often focus upon broad, significant themes and questions, rather than short-lived memorization of facts without

context. In doing so, historical study should provide context for facts and training in critical judgment based upon evidence, including original sources, and should cultivate the perspective arising from a chronological view of the past down to the present day. Therefore it follows . . .

3. That the curricular time essential to develop the genuine understanding and engagement necessary to exercising judgment must be considerably greater than that presently common in American school programs in history.
4. That the kindergarten through grade six social studies curriculum be history-centered.[5]

HISTORY SCOPE AND SEQUENCE

The Bradley Commission extended these resolutions by offering alternative scope and sequence plans that might improve social studies programs in the elementary grades. Their proposals are illustrated in Figure 13–1. Close examination of Figure 13–1 shows that Pattern A most closely parallels the traditional "expanding environment" approach, but adds a historical dimension to the familiar themes of families, neighborhoods, and communities. Notice the prominence of the study of geography during the 4th, 5th and 6th grades.

Pattern C is similar to the California History-Social Science Framework, which infuses historical, literary, and biographical materials into the elementary school social studies program (see Chapter 1). It represents the sharpest departure from the "expanding environment" pattern by concentrating on the study of history and geography through the use of biography, literature, and the arts. Certainly, the Bradley Commission proposals are but a start in the process of focusing on the effective teaching of history in the elementary schools. One useful trend, however, is the regular use of historical fiction, biographies, journals, diaries, and other forms of literature (see Chapter 11).

SOURCES OF HISTORICAL DATA

History is the study through a chronological framework of what has happened to humanity in the past. Historians study the human condition by gathering and evaluating relevant traces of people, places, and things past. Historical sources include physical remains and oral or written records of the past.

Physical Remains

Physical remains include artifacts, relics, and other "accidental survivors" of the past. By examining these sources, the historian is able to partially reconstruct the story of human life. I like to use the term "accidental survivors" because few historical artifacts or relics were planned to be preserved to describe a way of life to people in the future. Take a coin, for example. What do you think historians could learn from a coin? Suppose a recently unearthed coin had a figure of a person on one side and a series of fish on

FIGURE 13–1

Alternative Scope and Sequence Plans (Source: The Bradley Commission on History in Schools, Building a History Curriculum *(Washington, DC: Educational Excellence Network, 1988), p. 18.)*

Pattern A	
Grade	Course
K	Children of Other Lands and Times
1	Families Now and Long Ago
2	Local History: Neighborhoods and Communities
3	Urban History: How Cities Began and Grew
4	State History and Geography: Continuity and Change
5	National History and Geography: Exploration to 1865
6	World History and Geography: The Growth of Civilization

Pattern B	
Grade	Course
K	Learning and Working Now and Long Ago
1	A Child's Place in Time and Space
2	People Who Make a Difference
3	Continuity and Change: Local and National History
4	A Changing State
5	United States History and Geography: Making a New Nation
6	World History and Geography: Ancient Civilizations

Pattern C	
Grade	Course
K	Children's Adventures: Long Ago and Far Away
1	People Who Made America
2	Traditions, Monuments, and Celebrations
3	Inventors, Innovators, and Immigrants
4	Heroes, Folk Tales, and Legends of the World
5	Biographies and Documents in American History
6	Biographies and Documents in World History

the other, along with some words that could not be read. What could we tell about the people who used the coin? Ponder that question for a moment, then compare your ideas to these:

1. The people were advanced enough to use a monetary system.
2. They were advanced enough to use metal.
3. Their clothing and hairstyles can tell us something about their life-style.

4. The fish indicate something about their economy.
5. A stamped date would tell us how old the civilization was.

Oral or Written Records

In addition to examining artifacts and relics, historians study oral or written records. Historians put the most trust in primary witnesses who were close to an event and able to offer oral accounts. Suppose you attended the launching of a revolutionary new space vehicle. In the future, historians would most likely believe your account of that event rather than someone who heard about it from another (secondary witness). People who listen to the Super Bowl on radio every year and hear the announcer describe the action are secondary witnesses to the event. Written records in the form of diaries, wills, mortgages, government records, newspapers, magazines, and so on are witnesses for the historian to draw on. No source of information is insignificant to historians until they examine it and evaluate its usefulness. How many American colonial housewives thought their shopping lists or cooking utensils would be used by historians as evidence to explain colonial life, businesses, and activities in the home?

Regardless of the source, validity and authenticity must be checked. Much as detectives prepare a criminal case for court, historians must carefully gather information from more than one source and decide what is truthful. The historian's final responsibility is to write about the information without showing personal bias. This is perhaps the ultimate challenge, because historians see various meanings in the facts they uncover. For example, sometimes historians from different regions write conflicting accounts of an event. How might an 1860s Southerner's account of slavery differ from a Northerner's, or an English account of the American Revolution from an American one? In addition, historians often try to write about things they think will interest their readers, thereby choosing to report only the facts they believe to be of interest to the general population at the time. The Watergate activities of the 1970s, for example, provoked several conflicting accounts ranging from Richard Nixon's memoirs to those of legal prosecutors. In summary, the role of the historian is to:

Search carefully for facts

Use a variety of sources for evidence

Judge the evidence for accuracy

Write about the facts without showing personal bias

You will want to teach history in a way that allows children to investigate as historians. Provide situations where they can examine historical materials firsthand. Bring artifacts to the classroom, invite guest speakers to demonstrate items from the past, visit museums and historical sites to examine original written materials, compare written accounts of historical events to detect personal biases. Encourage children to make their own hypotheses about what they observe and give them opportunities to test their guesses. They should use the historian's methods of investigation to study a variety of local, regional, state, national, or international topics.

Conducting their own historical research gives children a taste of how actual historians collect and interpret data.

THE CONCEPT OF TIME

Basic to the study of history in elementary school classrooms is an understanding of the concept of time. Beginning with primary graders, listen for evidence of time-related comments: "I learned to roller-skate today, and I couldn't do that a long time ago when I was little!" "My new shoes are one size bigger than last time."

Young children often face rapid changes in their lives. Although change is exciting, children are often confused when trying to place less personal occurrences into an organized time frame, such as, "It is time to go outdoors," "It's Washington's birthday," or "I'll tell you a story in just five minutes." How long is five minutes to a 5-, 6-, or 7-year-old? It might be a fleeting moment spent outdoors during recess or an eternity waiting in line to get a physical from the school doctor. How long is an hour, a day, a month, or a year to a child?

Time concepts are interesting and challenging to children, but difficult to teach. Most time concepts, beyond those normally taught with clocks and calendars, are taught within the context of history—events that happened in the past.

I've found that children are eager to learn about the past, provided their learning activities are concrete and meaningful. Children must be led to discover that the consequence and evidence of the passage of time is *change*. Seasons change, friends change, clothes change, weather changes, and skills and capabilities change. Focusing children's attention on these natural events will help them discover how change affects everyone. Personal changes such as shedding a baby tooth and needing stronger eyeglasses are excellent opportunities to talk informally with children about physical changes that accompany the passage of time. Help children focus on other changes in their physical appearance by introducing simple comparisons. Ask parents to send their children's baby pictures, and have the children compare their appearances then and now. Have children bring their baby clothes, examine the clothes, and discuss why they do not wear similar clothing now. Compare baby food with food the children eat now. Keep a growth record on one classroom wall and mark the children's heights at the beginning, middle, and end of the school year. At the start of the year, when you first mark the children's heights, ask them to predict what their height will be at the end of the year. Record their predictions. At the end of the year, ask the children, "Did you grow as much as you thought? Why? Why not?"

Seasonal changes are the most obvious changes to talk about. When children notice the leaves turning red, ask, "Do you remember what color the leaves were in the summer? What will happen to the leaves in the winter?" Explore how seasonal changes affect clothing, plants, weather, and animals.

Emphasize that change can be regular, sudden, or unplanned—"If it's raining out, we'll have to play indoors," or "Jimmy has gone on a trip with his family and won't be back in school until next week." Comments like these help children learn that changes occur constantly whether or not we anticipate them.

The Time Capsule

The following activity helps students become familiar with the concept of passing time and the changes time brings. During the first week of school in September, have the children decorate a large box as a "Time Capsule." Discuss the concept of a time capsule and then follow with this series of activities:

1. Separate the children into three groups—tall, medium, and short—and take individual photos of the groups.
2. Have the children complete these individual tasks: writing their names, addresses, and phone numbers in their best handwriting; doing the "hardest" math problem they know how to do; spelling the hardest word they can spell; drawing a sample of their best art work; tracing their hands and feet on drawing paper.
3. Ask the children to write their answers to several of these questions on separate sheets of paper:
   - What is your favorite color?
   - What is your favorite food?
   - Who is your best friend?
   - What is your favorite TV show?
   - What singer or singing group do you like best?

- What animal is your favorite pet?
- What is your favorite subject in school?
- What is your favorite free-time activity?
- If you could go anywhere in the world, where would it be?
- Of all the people in the world, whom do you admire most?
- What is the one present you would like most for Christmas?
- What is your favorite sport?
- What do you like best about school?
- Do you ever cook? What is the best thing you ever made?
- What is one thing you are really good at doing?
- What time do you go to bed?
- Do you like school?

4. Gather each child's work in separate manila envelopes and have them sign their envelopes, seal them, and place them in the time capsule. Place the capsule somewhere obvious in the room and do not open it until the last week of school.
5. Repeat the first three activities during the last week of school. Have the children open the time capsule and lead them in comparing their initial work with their end-of-year work.

Children will react to the time capsule experiment in varying and exciting ways. Most will be amazed at how much they've grown physically or how much better they've become at math or spelling. There will also be discussions about who's missing from the capsule (newcomers to the class won't be in the original photo).

I remember one youngster looked at his work from the beginning of the year, crumpled it in his hands, and shouted, "This isn't mine. I was better than this before!" For some children change represents progress; for others it does not. Regardless, change surrounds children, and they should be led to an understanding that change is not something to fear.

Throughout the year, while you and your class wait to open the time capsule, provide other experiences that illustrate how things change with the passage of time.

Invite resource persons, especially senior citizens, to come to school to tell stories, share realia, or demonstrate skills that were important in the past.

Bring in objects from the past—butter churns, toys, clothes—and build an interest center around them. Encourage the class to manipulate the objects and discuss them.

Take a field trip to a local museum or an old building where children can observe things as they were long ago. Of course, the youngsters cannot completely comprehend the time period in which the objects were most commonly used, but they will be able to compare the use of objects with their newer versions.

Read or tell children stories of events that occurred long ago so they will learn about games, occupations, jobs, challenges, and accomplishments of the past. Develop a scrapbook of the school year. Place photos, souvenirs from field trips, samples of work from special projects, and other materials in the book. Save the scrapbooks from year to year so that succeeding groups of children can compare scrapbooks from the past to their own.

Arrange a drama center with materials representative of the past. Encourage the children to use the items—long dresses, old tools, lanterns, and other historical artifacts—in their creative play.

Investigate games and activities that help children understand how youngsters played in the past. Jump-rope chants, for example, provide a real window into the past.

You can make the concept of time exciting for young children by showing them that changing and growing are wonderful parts of being alive. Classroom routines hold tremendous potential for helping children develop increasingly sophisticated concepts of time, too.

Classroom Calendars

Because children experience great difficulty with the concept of time, we often unwittingly offer time and relation experiences in which children are forced to act as if they know something, when in fact they don't. Lilian Katz offers the following example:

> Imagine it's Thursday the 19th. The teacher asks her 5-year-old students what day it is. One child answers "Tuesday." Now that won't do. So the teacher asks, "What day was it yesterday?" This is not teaching, it is coaxing. "Can anyone point to Thursday on the calendar? What letter does it begin with?" The children have a one-in-seven chance of getting it right—and they eventually do. But 10 minutes are wasted, and the children still don't understand why it's Thursday the 19th. What does it mean when children have to behave day after day as though they understand something when they haven't got a clue?[6]

How do you translate such an abstract concept as "time" into the concrete, meaningful experiences required by young children? Certainly you don't do it simply by putting up a large calendar displaying clearly marked dates, the names of the month and days, and a colorful illustration appropriate for the particular month. Although this careful construction will attract the children's initial attention, it will not continue as a worthwhile learning activity. Young children may be able to adapt to a routine of selecting the numeral that stands for the day's date, but do so only as that numeral follows the previous one in sequence. It is doubtful that such a routine can help them acquire such basic time concepts as:

- Calendars tell us the number of days in a year—365.
- Calendars divide the 365 days into groups of 12, called months.
- Many of the months have the same number of days, but some do not.
- Calendars divide months into weeks; each week is made up of seven days.
- Days of the week are given special names.
- Calendars help us know when special days are coming.
- January 1 begins a new year. The last day of the year is December 31.

The following activities have been designed to help you translate abstract calendar concepts into concrete learning experiences for young children.

Daily Schedule

Because of the nature of calendars, it is best to approach the teaching of related skills by examining the sequential nature of the passage of time. A good way to do this is to illustrate and discuss the normal classroom routine. Make a chart of the daily schedule out of a long horizontal strip of tagboard. Divide it into sections and illustrate a major activity associated with each time block in the sections. Be sure to use simple, clear illustrations so they can be "read" by your children. Reading class, for example, can be a simple drawing of a book, math class can be illustrated by some numerals, while social studies class may be indicated by a globe (see Figure 13–2).

Discuss the illustrations to make sure that all the children understand what they depict. Each day, discuss the routines in sequence, pointing to the relevant sections of the chart. Be sure to stress activities that come "first," "next," and "last."

As the children internalize the daily routine, you may wish to cut apart the sections, shuffle them, pass them out so that each child gets a section, and ask the children to arrange themselves in sequence, explaining how they know the daily routine is correct.

Ask the children to draw their own illustrations whenever any changes in the classroom's daily routine are in store (field trip, guest speaker, rain cancelling outdoor recess, etc.).

Building a Calendar

To extend this beginning concept of sequence as it relates to time, it would be wise to capitalize on the personal routines of each child. Label a large sheet of rectangular oaktag with the name of the day—Wednesday, for example. Say the word while pointing to it, making sure to emphasize left-to-right progression. First talk about what goes on in school on Wednesdays by using the daily sequence chart. Then, talk about the things that make this a special day for your children. For instance, it is Francine's birthday; Arthur has an eye exam after school. As the children contribute, you may want to illustrate, print, or encourage the children to draw their own pictures of the special events (see Figure 13–3).

FIGURE 13–2
Sample Daily Schedule

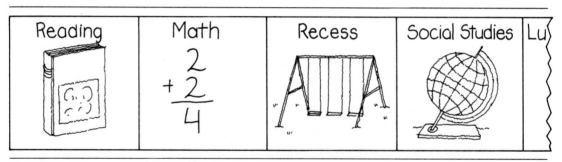

FIGURE 13–3
Daily Chart of Special Happenings

Kindergarten and early primary grade children will be able to help you construct a chart each day. Arrange the daily charts in sequence so that the children begin to sense the order of the days of the week and begin to understand that a week is a collection of seven days. Try to include the concepts of *yesterday, today,* and *tomorrow* in your daily discussions. Discuss what happened *yesterday* while recalling the significance of the illustration, focus on *today,* and determine what *tomorrow* will be called. When the children understand the days for each week, you may wish to introduce the numerals of each date at the start of a new month. Do so carefully, for when you're a child—so small and new to the world—even the most seemingly insignificant changes can be alarming (see Figure 13–4).

Cut out the numerals from colorful construction paper and paste them beneath the name of the day as you introduce the name of the day. Print the name of the month—let us say November—on a separate card and hold it in your hands so the children can focus on it. Pronounce its name and ask the children to do the same. Review that a collection of seven days is called a week and explain that now the children are going to make a collection of weeks called a month. But, because a month is made up of several

FIGURE 13–4
Weekly Chart of Special Happenings

SUNDAY	MONDAY	TUESDAY	WEDNESDAY	THURSDAY	FRIDAY	SATURDAY
① No School	② First Flower	③ Alice	④	⑤	⑥	

weeks, we give each day a second name (number name) so, for example, we can keep track of which Tuesday of the month we are talking about. Put the children in this situation: "Suppose a child was born six years ago, on a Friday. Someone asks him when his birthday is. He says, 'Friday.' Would that be a good answer? When is your birthday?" Children will typically answer with a month and date designation: "June 8th." Show how a week is a collection of days and how a month is a collection of weeks, both of which help people keep track of time. Use a page from a real calendar to show this.

Say to the children, "Today is Monday and it is also the first day of the month of November. We call it Monday, November one (or first)." Ask a child to place the numeral on the rectangle and continue your discussion in the manner previously described. Keep your daily chart collection up on the wall as the month progresses, making sure to arrange the weeks as a calendar.

Extending Time Concepts with Calendars

As the children construct calendars and understand the concept of day, week, and month, continue to provide concrete, meaningful activities. Introduce the name of each month with a separate printed card so the children can focus on it. Then it can be attached to a sturdy, attractive calendar base, as shown in Figure 13–5. The days of the week could also be placed on smaller cards and attached to the calendar base by the children themselves. Instead of using a rectangular sheet of paper each day, the numerals could be placed beneath the day names much as a regular calendar. The children see the calendar grow this way.

Many teachers prefer seasonal themes when making calendars, using numeral cards with acorns, pumpkins, turkeys, or Christmas trees. Others teachers choose to expose all the dates at the beginning of the month and ask the children to take turns

FIGURE 13–5
Calendar Chart

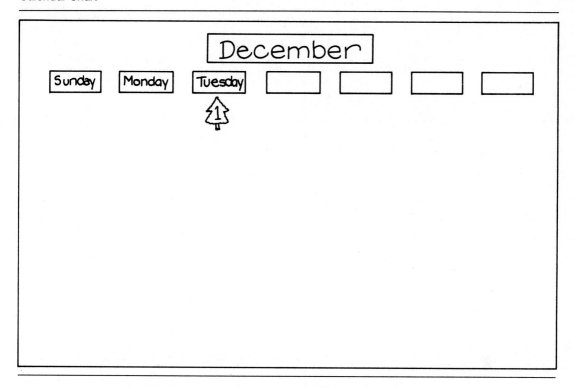

covering each as the days pass by with illustrative cards. Initially the entire month may be covered with identical shapes, but in order to develop other concepts, you may choose to vary your technique. You may alternate colors for each row on the calendar—red apples for the first row, green for the second, red for the third, and green for the fourth; or you may wish to alternate symbols for each column—corn shucks for one column, cornucopias for the second, pilgrims for the third, and turkeys for the fourth. Think of the patterning skills being developed as you take advantage of the calendar in these ways.

Calendar-Based Job Chart

For the purpose of illustrating the sequence of days, and especially the concepts of *yesterday, today, tomorrow,* and *week,* you may wish to associate your job chart with your early calendar activities. Attach library pockets to a large piece of oaktag, one for each child, as shown in Figure 13–6. Draw a picture and print the name of a particular classroom job on each pocket. Place a card containing a child's name in each pocket so that the name is visible. Each day, move the cards over one place, emphasizing what

FIGURE 13–6
Calendar-Based Job Chart

each child's job was *yesterday,* what it is *today,* and what it will be *tomorrow.* Some children may even want to count the days until they finally get a highly desired job.

To extend the children's time concepts from day to week to month to year, make a large circle outline on the wall, as shown in Figure 13–7. Divide it into twelve segments and label each segment with the name of a month, starting with January at the top. Make your winter month labels from white paper, spring from green, summer from yellow, and fall from orange. Illustrate a person standing in seasonal attire holding the name for each season next to its appropriate months. Have the children draw seasonal illustrations in each segment. Attach a smaller inner circle with a moveable arrow. Draw hash marks on the outside of the small circle, one for each week that begins during each month. Turn the dial each time a new week begins. This gives the children a good idea of the progression of weeks, months, and years as cyclical in nature.

FIGURE 13–7
Annual Calendar

Although the activities described have applicability to other subjects, too, their major contribution lies in their ability to establish prerequisite time concepts associated with history: change occurs with the passage of time. As John B. Poster suggests, an understanding of historical time requires a "sense of existing in the past as well as the present, a feeling of being in history rather than standing apart from it."[7] The developmental activities suggested to this point should help achieve that understanding.

HISTORY AS EXPERIENCE

As children mature and progress through the elementary grades, teachers must be careful to maintain the philosophy of history as experience rather than as facts. Events are bound by the child's experience; historical time is remote and unreal even for upper-elementary youngsters. We must remember that historical consciousness does not develop for many individuals until nearly adulthood and is found only in rudimentary form in the elementary years. Jenkins and Shacter tell us that during the elementary years, children's concepts of historical time are usually limited to days, months, and years, and they are trying to relate themselves to a past and a future.[8] They show an interest in things that happened "long ago," although they are often extremely confused about just when events occurred. They may think that grandmother lived in the time of the Pilgrims, used a spinning wheel, and was afraid of Indians. Upper-grade elementary children should be led to an awareness of the power of history in their own lives and of *themselves* as historical beings.

Biographies

Perhaps the most appropriate place to begin a search into the past is with the children themselves. After discussing the concept of *biographies* with her fifth-grade class, one teacher paired off the children and asked each to write the other's biography. Naturally, the children began asking each other questions that took them into the past: "Where were you born? Did you always live in this town? Where are your grandparents? What do you remember about when you first went to school?" The teacher asked the children to bring old photographs to illustrate the biographies; if children were not allowed to bring photographs, drawings were made. The result was a library of "historical biographies" that provided a year's worth of happy reading. This project provided a surprise for the teacher as the children became interested in moving from their biographies to the study of other cultures. One child from Vietnam stimulated initial interest and motivated other children to learn about the richness of Vietnamese culture, Vietnamese immigration to the United States, and the political events that shaped Vietnam.

Oral History

Oral history is often an interesting way to remove the remoteness of many historical concepts. Invite individuals, especially senior citizens, to spin tales of the old days. Don't be too surprised if those "old days" are all too clear to you, for the children will certainly consider things you grew up with to be old-fashioned. These items, for example, are real in my memory. How about you?

> Lassie (or Uncle Miltie or Howdy Doody) on television
>
> Green desk blotters with leather triangles on all four corners
>
> Burma-Shave road signs
>
> Charm bracelets
>
> Drugstores with a soda fountain

If these items are not familiar to you, you probably consider them "old-fashioned." They might be more interesting, however, if I were to share some of my experiences with them the way Mrs. Frazer, 83 years old, interested children in turn-of-the-century life. "When we got automobiles around here, you couldn't use them in the winter," Mrs. Frazer said. "My father had one of the first cars in town. It was one of those open cars with leather seats and brass lamps. I'll never forget one Sunday; we had eleven flat tires!"

Mrs. Frazer had the children in awe when she told what a dollar would buy in 1939: one dozen eggs, a loaf of bread, a pound of butter, and a half-pound of bacon. She also told the children about a whistle-stop campaign during which Teddy Roosevelt visited town in 1912 ("I can see him to this day") and the transfer of the Liberty Bell on flatbed car from Philadelphia to San Francisco for safekeeping during World War I. You should use such valuable sources of historical information both for the children's enjoyment and as a source for researching and recording details from the past. These experiences give them a clearer understanding of and appreciation for people and events of the past.

Historical Panorama

Moving from biographies and oral history experiences, the teacher might begin a historical panorama that would become a living history for classes to come. On one long, empty wall, secure a large sheet of tagboard, with the class name across the top of the sheet: "Fifth Grade Class, Main Elementary School (1991–92)." Beneath the title place individual class pictures of each child, with the names beneath. In succeeding rows, ask the children to fill in information such as this year's president, the most popular movie star of the year, the most popular song of the year, the winner of the World Series, the most popular hairstyle, the most popular clothing style, our class officers, and so on. Throughout the year, the children can complete the sentences with words or pictures. A teacher who used this panorama planned to have each succeeding year's fifth-grade class do the same for a growing history of the school and the times.

Field Trips and Historical Investigation

Children can increase their insight into history by taking field trips into the community to inspect buildings and other features from the past. One enterprising teacher, for example, took a group of children on a walk through their community for the purpose of listing as many interesting historical places as they could. The children found the local cemetery particularly fascinating and decided it would be an interesting place to study.[9] The teacher listened to the children's questions and comments as they examined the gravestones: "What is an epitaph? Why were they put on gravestones? How long did people live back then? What did they die of? Why did so many young children die? Look at the different names." In this context, the children became involved in the first characteristic of historical investigation: *identifying interesting problems*. When the class returned to school, the teacher encouraged further discussion and recorded the children's interests on the chalkboard as each contributed.

The next stage of historical investigation began with hundreds of gravestone rubbings the children made by placing large sheets of newsprint against the gravestones and rubbing crayons over the paper. Everything on the gravestone (names, dates, epitaphs) transferred to the paper and provided excellent research material for the classroom. Children were grouped according to interests and used their rubbings, along with a variety of library materials, for a variety of activities:

> Record the ages at death for any 20 men and 20 women. Determine the average for each group. Which group lived longer? Look through the material on this table (books and magazine articles were offered) and find as many reasons as you can.

> Record the average age at death for any ten men who died during each of the following periods: 1800–49, 1850–99, 1900–49, 1950–present. During which period did they live longest? Think of some reasons why this happened. Check the resources at this table to see if you were right.

> Look at the gravestones for epitaphs. Record the longest, shortest, funniest, most interesting, most religious, and so on.

> Examine the form of writing on the gravestones. Do any of the words or letters seem peculiar to you? List the ones that do.

> Suppose you were appointed to design a gravestone for the president of the United States (or other popular figure). Draw a picture of the gravestone and display it on the large bulletin board.

> How are the gravestones of the past like ours? How are they different? What changes can you predict for gravestones in the future? Use the large boxes to design a possible gravemarker of the future.

> Make a list of the most popular names on the gravestones. Are they popular today? What nationalities seemed most prevalent at the time? Why?

After the groups gathered their data and pulled them together to form conclusions, they shared their findings.

Family History

Mary E. Haas and Wilson Wylie[10] designed a "Family History Coat of Arms" activity based on the idea that history is not something written about distant people having no effect on anyone the students know. The activity was designed to show upper-grade students that their families were influenced by events chronicled in their textbooks and actually played a part in some of them.

To start, distribute a blank coat of arms to the students (see Figure 13–8). Have the students take the form home along with this set of questions to be asked of parents and grandparents:

1. What is the name and age of the person in your family who lived the longest?
2. What occupation was practiced by at least three members of your family?
3. What physical trait is common among members of your family?
4. What is the national origin of your family?
5. In what wars have members of your family fought?

FIGURE 13–8
Coat of Arms

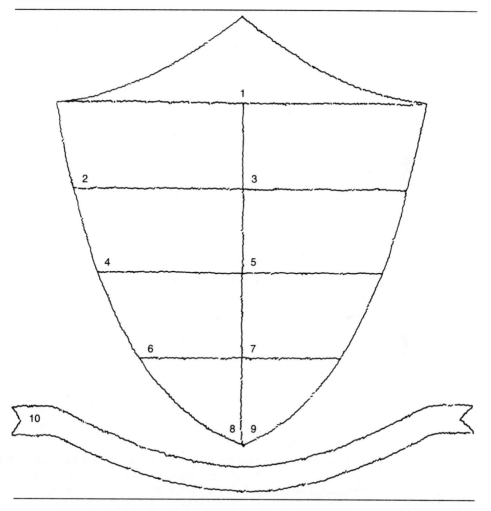

6. What is either the oldest or most important of your family's possessions?
7. What is the meaning of your family's name? If your family changed its name, what was the name before the change? What is a common first name among your family members?
8. Who is someone that everyone in your family (or almost everyone) admires and respects?
9. What tragedy or crisis did your family face?
10. What are some words of advice or sayings passed on from generation to generation in your family?

Encourage the students to draw symbols and use words to fill in the coat of arms, making it interesting and attractive. When the forms are completed, hold a brief discussion session with the whole class so students can share their reactions to the activity. Then, divide the class into groups of four to six students and ask each group to answer the following questions:

- What two questions received the largest number of similar answers?
- What two questions received the greatest variety of answers?
- Why do you think those questions received so many similar or so many different answers?
- What was the most surprising answer found by your group?

In a follow-up discussion with the whole class, list the answers on the chalkboard and compare the group lists by citing similarities and differences. Then ask whether the answers might be similar for other students in the school, in other schools throughout the district, or in other regions of the nation. Their ideas could be checked by comparing classes, reading biographies, or examining the text.

OTHER SOURCES OF HISTORICAL DATA

Children gradually realize that historians must find out about events of the past even when they cannot directly examine the evidence. If this happens, children can be encouraged to study different kinds of *written records* such as letters, diaries, wills, mortgages, and tax receipts, or interview either *primary witnesses* (those who were part of an event) or *secondary witnesses* (people who got information secondhand). A spacecraft launching illustrates these three sources of historical data. Thousands, perhaps millions, of people watch the launching on television and become secondary witnesses to the event, while newspapers carry accounts of the event and give us accurate written records for future reference. Who might be the primary witnesses to the event?

Children should understand that when secondary accounts must be examined, historians must carefully check the information. But even after they check their information for accuracy, problems remain. Like witnesses who offer conflicting testimony of a crime in court, even the most well-meaning primary witnesses interpret what they see differently. They tell what they *think* they saw, but did they *really* see what happened? To illustrate this point, one teacher arranged for a colleague to enter his room in the middle of the afternoon, disheveled, with the purpose of creating a minor disturbance while the children were quietly working at their desks. The fellow teacher was simply to enter the classroom to create a shock effect by yelling, safely throwing a chalkboard eraser, and leaving. After the colleague played her role and left the room, the regular teacher asked the children to write about what they saw and heard. When the children were finished, they compared individual accounts of the incident. Finally the teacher asked, "What does this tell you about witnesses?" In the same way, historians must carefully examine written accounts to decide if witnesses have reported them well.

Children should learn to compare historical accounts critically. Consider the following accounts of the Russian Revolution, one written for young children by a Russian author and the other by an American.[11]

> **The Soviet Story.** During 1917, a revolution took place in Russia. The working people overthrew the *czar* (zär), a Russian king. The czar and his family were killed. Everyone longed for freedom. They had never had it under the czar.
>
> Under the slogan, "All power to the Soviets," a new government was formed. It was a dictatorship of the people. At last the people had their own government. All land was owned by the government. Since the government was the people, the people owned all the land.
>
> The government also took over the banks, factories, mines, and stores. The people then owned everything.
>
> The Communist (käm-yə-nəst) party was the wise leader of the working people. It led the people along the right path. It led them to liberty and a classless life. The Revolution was a people's revolution. It threw out those who would make slaves of the workers. It established the dictatorship of the people.
>
> The Revolution brought a new life to all mankind. It brought them the victory of communism.
>
> **The American Story.** In 1917 the Russians revolted against their czar. The Communists cruelly killed the czar and his family. The Russians hoped to win freedom.
>
> Most of them hoped that the Russian Revolution would make their lives better. The Russian peasants hoped to divide the land among themselves. The workers wanted better wages. They wanted their living conditions improved.
>
> After the bloody Revolution, a new government was set up. It was a government controlled by Communists. It took over all the property owned by the people. The property became the property of the government. It took over factories, banks, and stores.
>
> The people did not get what they wanted. They did not control the government. The government was controlled by the Communist party. No one could disagree with the party. Those who tried to disagree were put in jail or killed.
>
> The Revolution made the Soviet people slaves of their government. It took away their religion. It took away their property. It took away their freedom.

Do you notice the similarities and differences in these accounts? For one, they report the same facts: (1) the Russian Revolution took place in 1917; (2) the czar and his family were killed; (3) the government owned everything after the Revolution; (4) the government was led by the Communist party. But the Russian historian and the American historian disagree about what the facts mean. Who was right? Both writers are convinced they are right, and it is here, when writers try to explain what facts mean, that the historian has trouble.

When children begin to understand the concept that an historian *interprets* facts, it is fun to place them into creative writing situations. Here is what one student wrote when the teacher said: "Just suppose that an Indian wrote the accepted account of the sale of Manhattan. What would it say?"

INDIANS GIVE US MAXI-HA-HA

A bunch of natives from Brooklyn paddled over to Manhattan in 1626 to eyeball the strange white guys who had landed and camped there. The Brooklyn Bridge wasn't built yet, but the natives of the land knew they had a bunch of yokels on the hook as soon as the settlers brought up the subject of buying an island no one was living on anyway.

Besides Manhatte's (that's what it was called back then) lousy reputation as a hunting land, the natives didn't have the white man's concept of land ownership—they figured the land was given by God to anyone who wanted to use it. So, when Peter Minuit kept heaping trinkets before them, the Canarsee Indians (the natives of Brooklyn), just stood straight-faced until they got enough loot to fill their canoes—about sixty guilders' (twenty-four dollars) worth of beads, needles, fabric, buttons, and fishhooks.

Then America's first fly-by-night real estate brokers paddled away hurriedly—probably to tell their friends about the easy "marks" the new neighbors were. It was later that Minuit realized he was swindled. Manhattan actually belonged to the Weckquaesgeeks who finally were paid for Manhattan, too. But, as businesspersons, the Canarsees had a way to go to catch the Raritan Indians. They sold Staten Island six times!

Notice that the creative experience was more than a "fanciful" activity. The student drew on his creative talents to produce something original, but still based his product on actual knowledge he had gained in the classroom. Through the use of historical research, teachers establish a basis of involvement that makes all inquiry an exciting learning process.

Original Documents

Examining original documents from the past also helps children personalize the study of history. Consider this excerpt from a newspaper advertisement in the early 1800s.

Ran away on the 1st of March instant, an indentured servant boy to the boot and shoemaking business, named Marble Laplant: he is between 16 and 17 years of age, dark complexion, has a scar on his right cheek, and is a remarkably ugly looking fellow.[12]

Among the advertisements in old newspapers, you will often find reward notices for runaway apprentices as interesting clues to 19th-century life. Young boys were commonly hired out to artisans to learn a craft. They were housed and fed at the craftperson's expense in return for training, working for free during their apprenticeship. Ads for runaway apprentices usually include such clues to early life as the clothing the runaway wore and comments on his appearance and temperament. With their "striped tow trousers," "gingham roundabouts," "brown flannel jackets," "old straw hats," or

Adorned in garb representing a particular historical era, these youngsters are representing real life and real-life acts.

"dark fustian pantaloons," these "remarkably ugly fellows" may have "lost two of their fore teeth" or "had three fingers cut off at the first joint on the right hand." These descriptions provide remarkable portraits of working class people of 150 years ago; they emerge as real individuals rather than as statistics or textbook portrayals when children read original accounts of their escapades.

It's fun for children to examine such documents, or to imagine the delegates leaving Independence Hall in 1787 to buy a newspaper. What would they have read about over 200 years ago? Consider even your own profession and the conditions your forerunners may have faced on the job at the turn of the century. Does the following list, distributed to female teachers in 1915, stimulate real interest in teachers of the past?

1. Do not get married.
2. Do not keep company with men.
3. Be home between the hours of 8 P.M. and 6 A.M. unless attending a school function.
4. Do not loiter downtown in ice-cream stores.
5. Do not leave town at any time without permission of the school board.
6. Do not smoke.
7. Do not get into a carriage with any man except your father or brother.
8. Do not dress in bright colors.
9. Do not dye your hair.
10. Do not wear any dress more than two inches above the ankle.
11. Always wear at least two petticoats.
12. Keep the schoolroom neat and clean. Sweep the floor at least once daily. Scrub the floor at least once weekly. Clean the blackboards once a day, and start a good fire at 7 A.M. daily.

Bringing Historical Figures to Life

Despite the fact that history can come alive for elementary school students, many teachers make it boring for children. The children may consider those long-gone people in their texts and their trials and tribulations insignificant, in light of such pressing daily concerns as deciding whom to sit with on the school bus or turning homework in on time. Textbook readings, worksheets, and memorizing names, dates, and events do nothing to remedy this unfortunate situation. A common antidote tried by many beginning teachers for a languid history program is to attempt elaborate recreations of historical times. Beverly Schreifels cautions, "The usual result is teacher exhaustion and pressure to increase the amount of material covered. Textbook readings, worksheets and discussions return."[13] Schreifels believes she has found a workable compromise: mini-simulations. She describes her approach thus:

> The day I discovered my fifth grade class had no idea who Vasco da Gama was—and cared less to find out—was the day I vowed to come up with some way to provoke interest in historical personalities. If da Gama and the rest of the early explorers were to become more than hard words to be stumbled over in a textbook, I realized, something drastic—and dramatic—had to be done.
>
> The next morning during social studies class, I slipped into the hall, plunked an old beehive hat on my head, swept a wraparound skirt over my shoulders and reappeared as an unreasonable facsimile of Vasco da Gama, fifteenth century sea captain. I introduced myself with my best Portuguese accent and invited questions.
>
> At first there were merely giggles, until I threatened to make every student walk the plank unless I got some proper, respectful questions. The first was about how I got there (via a time machine that just happened to look like a filing cabinet). Eventually someone wanted to know just who I was.
>
> "I'm Vasco da Gama, and I'm very famous."
>
> "For what?" they all demanded.
>
> I then proceeded to regale them with stories of my sailing prowess. Ever since that time, I've found I need only lean on the filing cabinet to get everyone's undivided attention. "Is the time machine going to bring us another mysterious person?" students plead. Quite often the answer is yes. And although these time machine visitors may have fuzzy historical memories, they serve to stimulate real interest in people of the past.[14]

As Schreifels advises, you need not "go overboard" to involve students personally and motivate them to learn. Some of the most effective techniques require very little extra teacher preparation time to organize. Here are some examples.

Historical Person of the Week.   Blank out the photo on the cover of a popular weekly news magazine such as *Newsweek* or *Time* and duplicate enough copies for all your children. Have groups choose a favorite person from the past, draw his or her likeness on the cover, and write a short description of the person's accomplishments, detailing why he or she was chosen as the "Historical Person of the Week."

Dear Abby.   Pair up your students. One student takes on the role of an historical figure writing a letter to Abby to seek advice on a significant problem. Each student's partner reads the letter and replies to it.

Historical Ballad.   Famous people such as Betsy Ross, George Washington, or Abraham Lincoln provide bountiful background material for student-originated ballads. Play the "Ballad of Davey Crockett" for your children and tell or read them a story about his exploits. Invite the children to choose a famous historical figure, research his or her accomplishments, and write a ballad that boasts of his or her courageous deeds.

Letter from Home.   Have the children choose a daring explorer or adventurer such as Christopher Columbus. Ask them to write a letter to the famous person from the point of view of his or her mother or father.

"Feinschmeckers."   A "feinschmecker" (a Pennsylvania Dutch word) is somebody who knows good food when he tastes it. Children are interested in learning about the foods eaten by people throughout history, especially if they learn why the food was important to the people. Take johnnycakes, for example. The word "johnnycake" was a popularized version of "journeycake," pancakes that could easily be made over a campfire while traveling during colonial days. Cornmeal, the base of johnnycakes, was often used for cooking in colonial America, along with buckwheat and rye flours. Wheat was more difficult to mill and therefore too expensive for most colonists. Johnnycakes were often served for breakfast, sometimes covered with apple butter. A typical breakfast was huge in order to ready workers for a hard day's work in the fields; it might also include sausage or ham, eggs, and bread. Here is the recipe one class found. It yielded about twelve 6″ johnnycakes:

JOHNNYCAKES

1 cup cornmeal
1 teaspoon baking powder
1 egg
1 1/2 cup milk
2 tablespoons oil
Mix dry ingredients together. Add remaining ingredients and mix well. Heat skillet until a drop of water placed in the skillet beads up and rolls to the side. Use a tablespoon of oil for cooking the cakes, adding more as needed. Turn johnnycakes with a flat spatula when bubbles appear, and cakes are golden brown underneath. Cook until golden on both sides.

Using Good Children's Literature

We discussed this topic comprehensively in Chapter 11, but using historical fiction and other forms of literature as vehicles to explore life in the past is such an integral part of contemporary recommendations for improving the social studies program (especially in history) that it must be re-emphasized. In their classrooms, teachers are choosing one of two approaches to integrate literature into their history programs: (1) abandoning the traditional "expanding environment" textbook approach and substituting literature to achieve the desired content, and (2) infusing as much literature as possible into their current course format. Whichever approach is taken, you can impart memorable content by engaging your students' curiosity and imagination through popular literature and engrossing storytelling techniques.

Donna E. Norton selected the story *Caddie Woodlawn* (New York: Scholastic Book Services, 1975) to show how good literature can launch a study of life during the early 1800s. Norton's excellent example begins with the teacher sharing information about the author, Carol Ryrie Brink:

> Carol Ryrie Brink had a very special reason for writing *Caddie Woodlawn*. The heroine of the book was Mrs. Brink's grandmother. When Mrs. Brink was eight years old, she went to live with her grandmother. Her grandmother, Caddie, told her many stories about growing up in Wisconsin in the 1800s. During Mrs. Brink's childhood, she amused herself by drawing, writing, reading, and telling herself long stories.
>
> When Mrs. Brink was an adult, she remembered the stories of Caddie's childhood, and thought other children would also like to read them. She wrote *Caddie Woodlawn* while her grandmother was still alive. She wrote letters to her grandmother to ask questions about details she could not remember.
>
> Carol Ryrie Brink says the facts in *Caddie Woodlawn* are mostly true. Some of the facts are changed slightly to fit the story. *Caddie Woodlawn* won the Newbery Medal for the best children's book in 1936.[15]

Following the sharing of information about the author, Norton suggests these highly appropriate activities:

1. Oral Language, Interviewing, Writing—Carol Brink wrote *Caddie Woodlawn* because she enjoyed her grandmother's stories. Ask the children to interview older relatives or other older people in the community. In their interviews, they should ask people to re-tell experiences they remember from childhood, or stories they heard from their grand-parents. During the interviews, the students can also gather information about what these people did for entertainment, how they traveled, where they got their food, how they dressed, and what toys they played with. Have the children share their informa-tion orally with the rest of the class, or write stories using the information. Develop a bulletin board to display the stories.
2. Creative Writing—Have the students choose a favorite chapter from *Caddie Woodlawn*. Ask them to pretend they are Caddie, and write a diary entry for that chapter.

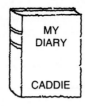

3. Reading for Details—After reading *Caddie Woodlawn,* have students complete the fol-lowing chart with drawings that show details for each category.

Life in Wisconsin in 1864		
Clothing	Transportation	Home furnishings
Entertainment	Education	Food

4. Evaluative Reading—Place in the learning center several reference and history books that give factual descriptions of the 1860s. Ask students to compare their readings about the historical period with the picture of daily life presented in the book. Are the historical facts accurate in *Caddie Woodlawn?* Make a list of accurate facts and a list of any inaccurate information.

5. Reference and Art—Caddie has a special friend named Indian Joe. Caddie even visits the Indian camp. Provide several reference books describing the Indians who lived in that part of Wisconsin. Students can read reference material about these Indians, then design and build a model of an authentic Indian camp.

6. Map Skills—Nero, the Woodlawn's dog, goes on a long trip with Uncle Edmund. They travel in a steamship all the way from Downsville to St. Louis. Nero runs away after he reaches St. Louis, and finally reaches his home in Wisconsin.

   a. Look at a map of the United States. Draw in the route Nero and Uncle Edmund followed to reach St. Louis.

   b. On page 53 of the Scholastic Book Services edition, there is a river named that is not near Downsville. What is the current name of the river on which Nero and Uncle Edmund started their journey?

   c. Now look at the map again. Imagine the route that Nero traveled on his lonely trip back to Wisconsin. What states did he go through? What was the country like? Draw in the route you think he followed.

7. Several types of transportation characteristic of the 1860s are mentioned in *Caddie Woodlawn:* Indian canoes, horses, steamships, horse-drawn wagons, rafts. Provide reference pictures and books describing these forms of transportation. Ask children to construct a mobile illustrating these early means of travel.[16]

Time Lines

A time line graphically represents a succession of historical events by dividing a unit of time into proportional segments showing important events that occurred in particular time periods. In the early primary grades, time charts might show events of the daily or weekly school schedule, important events in the community, major national observances, and personal experiences. An understanding of chronology can be developed in the early years by presenting children with large cards that illustrate steps of a familiar process in a jumbled sequence. The children must decide which card comes first, second, and so on, and hold the cards in front of themselves in proper sequence. Begin with a familiar series of events, such as the routine of a typical school day, and gradually apply the same teaching strategy to sequencing steps in a series of events in a social studies topic (see Figure 13–9).

Constructing time lines is similar to constructing other semiabstract or abstract learning aids in that initial experiences should be as concrete as possible. A wise way to begin the study of chronology is to start with the children's own lives. You can prepare large cards (and add appropriate photos, if possible) with the labels "Birth," "Learn to Walk," "Go to School," "Enter Grade _____ ," "Graduate from High School." Take the children to the playground and assign one card to each child. The child holding the "Birth" card would be the starting point for the time line. The children can next suggest the age at which they began to walk. The child holding the "Learn to Walk" card should pace from the "Birth" point the number of steps as years from birth to walking. Use the same process for each of the other cards. Relationships between the distances can then be discussed. In the same way, you may wish to develop time concepts related to other key events, such as important inventions, famous explorers, changes in transportation, notable events in the community, and the like.

This procedure can also be useful in showing the sequential development of historical events. The children can first be presented with a random number of cards listing events of history. They can go to the playground, organize the cards in sequence,

FIGURE 13–9
Sequencing Steps

and walk off one step for each year between events. This practice is especially appropriate in the upper grades, since history facts are difficult for most primary children to understand. Transferring this practice into the classroom, then, you would use a similar procedure, but the children will soon realize that if they take one step for each year between events, they will soon run out of room and not be able to complete their task. You can then direct them toward discovering that a smaller unit of measure will be needed—perhaps one inch to represent a year.

When working on smaller-scale time lines in the classroom, you should emphasize exactness and consistency. An inexact or inconsistent scale distorts time relationships and hinders true conceptualizations of chronology.

The attractiveness of the time line is also a major factor in its effectiveness as a learning aid. Pictures and illustrations add to the charm of the time line and encourage children to use it as an organized frame of reference. Figure 13–10 shows a fairly even span of time between events. If the periods between historical events are not even, you will need to choose an illustration that is not symmetrical.

On time lines such as the one in Figure 13–11 groups of children can be given a set of cards identifying events from a current topic of study. Ask the children to look up information about their assigned event and draw an illustration about it. From there you can direct the children to find the date for each event and place their illustrations in chronological order on the time line. After the time line is constructed, you may want each group to share pertinent information about the different events with the rest of the class. By the time this project is completed, your class will have constructed a master guide of the major events under study and will have begun to develop an historical perspective of particular events.

History had long been a valued part of schooling in America; it continues to exert a strong influence on social studies programming and practices. Many have praised its value over the years, but none more eloquently than Winston Churchill, who once said, "The further backward you look, the further forward you are likely to see." Statements like Churchill's underscore the importance of furthering historical consciousness in our schools. In a society steeped in triumphs and tragedies, knowledge of our past helps

FIGURE 13–10
Organized Frame of Reference

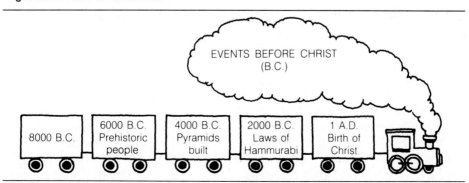

FIGURE 13–11
Group Work on Time Line

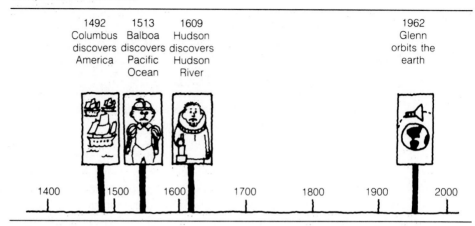

us to develop pride in our successes and discontent with our errors. We cannot, however, expect children to become interested in the study of history when all they are asked to do is memorize facts from a textbook. Surely, facts about the important people and events are an important part of history, but we must also be aware of the processes of history. Children must be given regular opportunities to *explore* history rather than simply be *exposed* to it. We must lead students to perceive the nature of history itself by helping them understand the concept of historical time, investigate their personal and family histories, and examine other sources of historical data. Such techniques of personal involvement will help students acquire a more balanced sense of history—it is not only something one *knows* but also something one *does*.

SUMMARY

Like the proponents of more geography in the schools, many today believe that U.S. students display an inadequate knowledge of history. The Bradley Commission on History in Schools has been instrumental in this cause, supplying alternative scope and sequence plans designed to improve social studies programs in the elementary grades.

Teachers are urged to recognize history as a compelling area of study for elementary school children, which can help them better understand the present by building bridges to the past. This historical bridge is constructed from two primary sources: physical remains and oral or written records. Basic to the study of the past is an understanding of the concept of time. This concept can be enlarged through the use of several creative activities: the time capsule, classroom calendars, resource persons, and objects from the past; visiting museums, sharing stories, examining old photos, playing games from the past, and so on.

As children mature, teachers should maintain a philosophy of *history as experience* by offering activities such as reading biographies or historical fiction, sharing oral history, taking field trips, studying family histories, examining original documents, integrating the study of history with other subject areas (especially language arts), and so on.

History is finding its way once more into the limelight of social studies programs. Although more research is required before we can understand how historical concepts develop in elementary schoolchildren, we know that historical study should be matched to the developmental level of the students and be offered in a meaningful context.

ENDNOTES

1. The Bradley Commission on History in Schools, *Building a History Curriculum* (Washington, DC: Educational Excellence Network, 1988), p. 5.

2. "Social Studies for Early Childhood and Elementary School Children Preparing for the 21st Century," *Social Education, 53,* no. 1 (January 1989): 15.

3. Matthew T. Downey and Linda S. Levstik, "Teaching and Learning History: The Research Base," *Social Education, 52,* no. 5 (September 1988): 336–344.

4. Ibid., p. 341.

5. The Bradley Commission on History in Schools, *Building a History Curriculum* (Washington, DC: Educational Excellence Network, 1988), p. 18.

6. Lilian G. Katz, "Lilian Katz: Let's Not Underestimate Young Children's Intellects," *Instructor, 92,* no. 3 (October 1987): 16.

7. John B. Poster, "The Birth of the Past: Children's Perception of Historical Time," *The History Teacher, 6* (August 1973): 589.

8. Gladys Gardner Jenkins and Helen S. Shacter, *These Are Your Children* (Glenview, IL: Scott, Foresman, 1966), p. 172.

9. See Edward Stranix, "The Cemetery: An Outdoor Classroom," *Teacher, 93,* no. 2 (October 1978): 66–67.

10. Mary E. Haas and Wilson Wylie, "The Family History Coat of Arms," *Social Education, 50,* no. 1 (January 1986): 25–28.

11. Frederick M. King et al., *Using the Social Studies 1970,* p. 262. (By permission of Laidlaw Brothers, a Division of Doubleday & Company, Inc.)

12. Douglas Harper, "Notices of Missing Servants in 19th-Century Newspaper Ads," Chester County Living Section of the *Sunday Local News* (West Chester, PA: June 4, 1989), p. 3.

13. Beverly Schreifels, "Breathe Life into a Dead Subject," *Learning* (March 1983): 84.

14. Ibid.

15. Donna E. Norton, *Language Arts Activities for Children* (Columbus, OH: Merrill Publishing, 1980), p. 317.

16. Ibid., pp. 317–319.

The notion that . . . social studies content should be drawn only from the social sciences is insufficient for a curriculum intended to demonstrate the relationship between knowledge and rationally based social participation. . . . Many kinds of knowledge are important contenders for inclusion in social studies. Ideally, . . . various sources of knowledge . . . would all contribute to the social studies program.[1]

—NCSS Social Studies Curriculum Guidelines

Utilizing Supplementary Sources of Social Studies Content

14

As you read, reflect on the following matters:

- Why are social studies educators frustrated at the amount of material they are expected to cover?

- In addition to the social sciences, what other major content considerations do social studies educators face?

- Why is current affairs instruction an important part of the social studies program? What kinds of related experiences are most appropriate for the elementary school classroom?

- Why is global education a priority in contemporary social studies programs? What should be the emphases of instruction?

- How has our current concern for the environment resulted in curriculum reform in the social studies? How can we help students acquire the knowledge and sensitivity to make constructive environmental decisions?

- Why is multicultural education perceived as a necessity in quality social studies programs? What experiences are most appropriate for elementary school students?

- How can career education contribute to the elementary school social studies program?

- How can the environment of the classroom help students understand the concept of law?

Most of our nation's social studies curricula are controlled at present by history and geography, although the content and methods of inquiry of civics and the other social sciences also contribute important elements. The social sciences are only part of what is included in contemporary social studies programs, however. There is another whole realm of special informational and procedural emphases associated with the social studies, but not normally included under the umbrella of social sciences: current affairs, global education, environmental education, multicultural education, career education, law-related education, and in recent years, AIDS and drug education. Marion Brady, in a satirical response to the volume of material assigned to the social studies, stepped into the role of a student and wrote this memo to the social studies establishment:

> It's difficult to believe you're serious. What you've summarized is . . . an incredible heap of miscellany you've been accumulating for decades—some odd pieces of the past held together by habit, a few bits of several social sciences (which are themselves in need of major rethinking), the remnants of a dozen ill-digested fads, an assortment of reactions to the demands of state legislators, and other odds and ends assigned to the social studies because they haven't seemed to fit anywhere else. During our formative years you have our attention (more or less) for a few hundred hours. In that brief span of time you apparently expect us to grasp a study which encompasses about two-thirds of everything known to humankind.[2]

The sheer mass of content to be included in the social studies program often causes even the most experienced teachers to grumble, "The administration sticks everything they don't know what to do with into the social studies. I just don't know how we're going to cover everything." When forced to cover topics they feel ill-prepared to handle, teachers often feel intimidated and frustrated. Those feelings frequently abate if teachers are given materials that provide structure and order to instruction, but for subjects outside the realm of the social sciences there is little available. Mike Bowler comments that even the social studies textbooks fail to handle special topics with any degree of depth or complexity, since textbook adopters generally want noncontroversial books stressing traditional values. They seek to avoid conflict (particularly family conflict), politics, sex, and violence—in short, much of the reality of children's lives. Strong pressures from the right and left—from conservative parents linked in an effective national network on the one hand, to African Americans, women, Hispanics, Native American Indians, "right-to-work" groups, and organized labor on the other—make it unsurprising that publishers are frantic or that their products are often considered bland.[3]

In any case, you can expect to assume greater responsibility for planning teaching strategies related to contemporary topics. In this chapter, nine such challenges are offered, and a number of teaching practices proposed for each. Use these suggestions to develop a growing file of ideas, for the topics are so responsive to society's needs that new ideas surface each day.

CURRENT AFFAIRS INSTRUCTION

AMENDMENT 1—UNITED STATES CONSTITUTION

Congress shall make no law respecting an establishment of religion, or prohibiting the free exercise thereof, or abridging freedom of speech, or of the press; or the right of a free people to peaceably assemble, and to petition the Government for a redress of grievances.

People over the centuries have argued that a *free press* (not only newspapers, but all broadcast media, too) is the keystone of a democracy and predict that without it our democratic form of government would fail. Likewise, it has been argued that a *free education* is the keystone of a democracy. Combining these two popular statements, we find that neither a free press nor an informed citizenry could exist without each other. The free press ensures the public's right to know; our schools have a responsibility to prepare citizens able and interested to understand the issues involved in their lives. With important issues changing as rapidly as they do in contemporary society, the matter of being well informed is now more important than ever. The foundation for developing such informed citizens should be established in the elementary grades as you present learning experiences designed to accomplish these objectives:

1. To develop skills in reading, viewing, and listening to news accounts.
2. To make critical evaluations of the sources and accuracy of news accounts.
3. To commit oneself to take a position on current problems or issues.
4. To anticipate future consequences in terms of current developments.
5. To develop a lifelong interest in current affairs.
6. To relate what happens in the study of the regular social studies program to the reality of the outside world.

To develop such worthwhile goals effectively, teachers must not treat news sharing as a "necessary evil" to get through before "real teaching" can take place. Perhaps this classroom scene will stimulate your memory.

MR. LOGAN: "Does anyone have a news article to report on this morning?" (He calls on Anthony, the only child with his hand raised.)

ANTHONY: (Walks to the front of the room skimming the article.) "This article tells about some people who are going out on strike."

MR. LOGAN: (Looks up from the attendance register.) "People going on strike? Why?"

ANTHONY: (Shifts his feet while looking at the floor.) "Yeah. I think because they aren't getting enough money. I heard my father talking about it at breakfast this morning so I cut out the article."

MR. LOGAN: "Does the article say where the people work?"

ANTHONY: "I don't know. I didn't read that far."

MR. LOGAN: "Well, sit down, Anthony. You can tack it to the bulletin board during recess so that the other children can read it if they are interested. Any more news? Okay, open your math books to page 81."

Think about that episode for a moment. On the positive side, Mr. Logan did recognize the news article and he did ask the children questions. On the negative side, however, just one child was really involved, his questions were not of top quality, and he did not radiate much interest.

This section provides you with suggestions to improve current affairs instruction. They will not guarantee perfect current affairs sessions, but will furnish you with some general ideas you may find helpful.

Reading Newspapers

Perhaps the best place to begin an effective current affairs program is to teach children how to read a newspaper. Children should be led to examine the various sections of the newspaper (world news, sports, community events, etc.) with special attention directed toward the sources of material for these sections—wire services, local writers, syndicated columns, and so on. Children can understand that a good news article answers four basic questions (*who, what, where,* and *when*) in the first paragraph or two and then should go on to state *why* and *how*. Lead the children through the literal interpretation of news articles by making copies of a news article, distributing it to each child, allowing them sufficient time to read it (for a *purpose*, of course), and then guiding their interpretation with questions such as these:

- "Who is the story about?"
- "What did the person do?"
- "When did the event take place?"
- "Where did the event take place?"
- "Why did the event come about?"
- "How can this event be extended (be prevented from happening again, teach us a lesson, etc)?"

News events are objective in nature; they present the facts with an absence of personal reaction. Encourage the children to share their feelings regarding any particular news article with questions such as:

- "How did you feel about the situation?"
- "What would you have done?"
- "Would you be willing to do the same thing?"
- "Do you agree with the central character?"
- "Is there any information you can add to the article?"
- "Do you think the story was written fairly (accurately)?"

Once the children have learned to interpret objective news articles, they should be led to distinguish among factual accounts (such as the articles on the front page) and opinionated accounts (such as on the editorial pages). Select sentences such as the following pair and ask the children to analyze whether they are fact-oriented or opinion-oriented:

The incredibly tiny 11-week-old infant entered the world weighing just 15 ounces.

The death penalty would have a deterrent effect in certain criminal cases.

After the children understand the differences between factual and opinionated articles, have them bring in editorials or letters to the editor and use them to support or reject feelings about certain contemporary events. Political cartoons (see Chapter 11) can also be used for this purpose. You may want to extend their understanding by inviting the children to write their own editorials and letters to the editor or draw political cartoons—all for classroom display.

Sharing News Items

Once the children gain interest in the newspaper they often wish to share news at regular or irregular intervals. Frequently, the teacher will set aside a 15-minute period early in the day for children to report on and discuss items of interest. Children in the early grades normally report on those events affecting them personally, but as they mature they expand their interests to topics of broader scope. The quality of the sharing period depends on the skill of the teacher. If you can generate the children's interest and enthusiasm through motivating classroom techniques during the sharing period, they will learn:

1. To develop an awareness of some of the most important news stories affecting people today.
2. To provide support for an individual's position on a current issue.
3. To compare news sources presenting conflicting points of view.
4. To develop interest in the events of the present.

The following activities are designed to supplement and extend sharing of current news items.

Develop a News Bulletin Board. These displays can be designed in a variety of ways. Separate areas can be set up for local, state, national, and world events, or for front-page, sports, weather, and entertainment news. Using a world map as a focal point, news items can be connected to their appropriate geographical locations with colorful yarn. Use catchy phrases, such as "A Nose for the News," to attract children to a general display of news items.

Publish a Class Newspaper. Assign reporters to different classifications of news topics: school news; the gossip column; the cartoon page; sports news; local, state, and national news (see Chapter 8).

Prepare Radio or Television Newscasts. Use audio and video tapes in much the same way class newspapers are prepared. The format of the show can be anything you like, but one that worked especially well for me was the music/news/talk show format: "My name is Lisa Forrest and this is radio station WOW right here in Cedar Elementary School." (Changing the host weekly generates more interest.) "Hope you're having a good day and are ready to listen to the top tune of the week as voted upon by the fifth graders of Cedar Elementary. Here it goes!" (Once the song is completed, you may wish to provide a teletype background for the news—an electric typewriter does fine. News items may range from actual current events to announcement of school events, special student accomplishments, or other local happenings.) Commercials may be interjected to promote items such as a school band concert, the school store, and so on. Some children enjoy creating parodies of actual commercials. The talk show format may conclude the broadcast as the host may interview a teacher who has taken an interesting trip, a student who has won a special prize, and so on.

Use Newspapers in Creative Ways.

1. Fictionalize a story about what happened just before and just after the moment captured in a selected newspaper picture.
2. Give students a newspaper headline and ask them to write their own news story based on it.
3. Take a student survey to find out what part of the newspaper interests them most. Divide the class into groups, each with a variety of interests. Each week assign a group to report to the class. Urge each "reporter" to read all he can find in the newspaper each day concerning his field. Each "reporter" then reads to the class one item in his field that especially interested him that week.
4. Read only the first paragraph of a news article, then make up the rest. Be original! Compare with the original article if you want.
5. Have each student study newspaper articles about different well-known personalities and each day, pantomime personality sketches as other students try to guess who is being portrayed. As students become skilled in mime techniques, have them scan the newspaper for simple situations to play out in pairs or small groups. Other students will enjoy guessing the actions.
6. Have a student assume the personality of a favorite cartoon character, such as Charlie Brown, and have classmates interview him. Remember, the student who assumes the character's personality must answer questions using the character's observed speech, attitudes, and mannerisms.
7. Have students write a nursery rhyme as a news story and give it an appropriate headline; for example, *Mr. Egg Fractures Skull.*
8. Have your students write letters to their favorite comic strip or newsmaking characters. Stress proper letter form and originality.
9. Let your students be advice columnists. Have them read letters to Ann Landers or Dear Abby. Pupils then write their own advice; check student replies with answers given by the advice columnists.
10. Clip headlines from stories, but keep one newspaper intact. Students read news stories and write their own headlines. Did students discover the main idea of the story expressed in the headline? Compare student headlines with the headlines in the uncut issue.
11. After identifying the main topic of an editorial, scan the paper to locate stories related to the topic and read them. Study how the editorial was developed and then have students write their own editorial on the same issue.

12. Children can write to other newspapers for an issue from a specific date, say, October 18th. When the newspapers arrive, pupils can compare major stories on the same event as reported in the different newspapers. What were the headlines? Where were news stories placed in the newspaper? What people were mentioned? What background interpretative data were included in the story? What can you conclude from this activity?

13. Most students know that the highest government official is the president. How many students can name the highest elected officials in your community? For one week, have students clip newspaper articles that mention government officials. Urge them to watch for news of officials of national, state, and local agencies, cabinet members, and members of the judiciary. Have them label three sheets of paper with titles: "Executive Branch," "Legislative Branch," "Judicial Branch." Students list each official they find and whether he or she is a local, county, regional, state, or national official and to what branch he or she belongs.

14. When Columbus discovered America, no reporters stood by to herald the event. Tell your students to pretend they are news reporters in 1492 and write a headlined story of Columbus's discovery of the New World. Have students also write editorials on the importance of Columbus's voyages and discoveries.

These are a few of the resons newspapers are an excellent classroom resource:

- They are an adult medium. No fifth grader with a reading problem likes to be seen carrying around "Six Ducks in a Pond," but he's proud to be seen reading the newspaper.
- They bridge the gap between the classroom and the real world.
- They contain something for every student: comics for the slow reader, editorials for the bright youngster; real math problems for the child who cannot tolerate the rigidity of textbooks; science as it happens.
- They contain practical vocabulary, words students will use throughout their lives.
- They can be marked, cut, pasted, colored—important to young children who learn by doing and seeing.
- They contain in their news stories the best models for clear, concise, simple writing.
- They are the perfect model for teaching students to write for a purpose and for a particular audience.
- They are the only really up-to-date social studies text there is.
- They are the only text the majority of children will continue to read throughout their lives.
- They are an influential and integral part of our free society. Freedom of the press is guaranteed under the Constitution; some have said that this freedom is "less the right of the newspaper to print than it is the right of the citizen to read."

Current Affairs Periodicals

Teachers often rely on current events magazines or newspapers published especially for elementary school children for most of their program in current affairs. This approach has several advantages and disadvantages.

This current events learning center encouraged children to pursue newspaper articles independently and guided their associated reading.

Advantages.   The school-oriented publications are graded; news items reflect varied developmental interests. The material is presented objectively, enabling teachers to plan ahead for fact-oriented activities. Finally, copies are available to each child. By developing a common background of experience, children are better able to contribute to class discussions. Periodicals offer teaching suggestions as well as recommendations for follow-up questioning and activities.

Disadvantages.   Some teachers become too dependent on a formal reading-reciting technique. Some periodicals fail to relate articles to social studies topics under study. Periodicals can present articles of world, national, or regional scope, but cannot deal with important local events.

I find current affairs periodicals an important educational tool. For one, these periodicals can motivate. They are written especially for children, and even reluctant readers respond positively to the nontext format and the comfortable reading levels. Second, the periodicals select interesting, contemporary topics. This week's big news, a special TV presentation, or the latest technological breakthrough help to make the classroom more current. Finally, periodicals are accompanied by comprehensive teacher's guides that describe creative teaching strategies. The magazines are used in thousands of schools around the country and are a valuable resource material.

Supplementing the Regular Program

Some teachers prefer to use current affairs as an integral part of regular social studies instruction. For studying a unit on highway safety problems, for example, one teacher asked the children to be on the watch for news items relating to highway safety. They would share and display the items on a bulletin board; the teacher hoped the children would be better able to associate classroom learning to the world outside the classroom. This kind of teacher concern and implementation is excellent; however, if this technique of current events instruction excludes other techniques, children rarely become motivated to examine current events that have no immediate bearing on the unit.

GLOBAL EDUCATION

Problems Shared by All People

An elegant blue planet encircled by swirling white clouds—a home for over 4.5 billion people. Regardless of nationality, race, or economic status, we are all passengers on this "spaceship Earth." All people share the responsibility to provide the support and care that will sustain the operation of their delicate, intricate space vehicle. The beauty of satellite pictures of our planet, however, belie the worrisome trends and complex problems simmering throughout the fragile environment in which we live. Some are political, others are social or economic, and many are environmental. Anne M. Blackburn separates these problems into three categories:

> The "D FACTORS" are observed negative trends. Examples include:
> —Desertification
> —Deforestation
> —Decimation of species
> —Declining water quality
> —Declining air quality
> —Depleted ocean fish stocks
> —Disappearing prime farm land
> —Declining ability to produce food
>
> The "I FACTORS" all relate to increases being observed, but, unfortunately, not the kind to be celebrated. Examples include:
> —Increased use of marginal lands for agriculture
> —Increased toxic contaminants
> —Increased flooding and erosion
> —Increased rural homeless/hungry
> —Increased urban densities

—Increased environmentally caused refugees

—Increased vulnerability to natural disasters

—Increased competition within and among countries for resources

—Increased potential for conflict within and among nations

The "M FACTORS" stand for Mother Nature: Unpredictable. Benign in some instances, harsh in others. . . . It is important to raise this point within the context of global environmental issues because—whether we like it or not—natural phenomena will occur that may throw off, by great margins, the estimates we make of the "resources available for human use."[4]

A global perspective becomes increasingly important as we focus our attention on the preservation of our planet into the twenty-first century.

Global Education Programs

Wherever people live on spaceship Earth, they share in a common destiny. Finding solutions for the Earth's problems is indispensable for the perpetuation of the human race. Social studies educators agree that global interdependence must be taken seriously in the social studies curriculum for the 21st century, and that is one of the most formidable challenges to social studies in the United States. Jan L. Tucker stated recently that a global perspective has the "potential for doubling and tripling our contribution to the global human condition."[5] The NCSS "Position Statement on Global Education" calls for a global education program that helps "develop in youth the knowledge, skills, and attitudes needed to live effectively in a world possessing limited natural resources and characterized by ethnic diversity, cultural pluralism, and increasing interdependence."[6] James A. Banks agrees with these goals, but cautions that "the search for solutions to global problems is complicated by the cultural, ethnic, religious, and national boundaries that divide, often sharply, the world's people into groups with conflicting interests. These groups consume highly disproportionate shares of the world's resources and exercise sharply different amounts of power in world politics."[7] Figure 14–1 shows, for example, that more than 75% of the world's population lives in poor or developing nations in Latin America and the Caribbean or on the continents of Africa and Asia. Banks comments, "Yet, the one out of three people in the world who live in the developed Western nations consume most of the earth's resources and exercise most of the political and economic power in the world."[8] Banks insists that a knowledge and skills base of global education is necessary, but not sufficient. He calls for programs that also help children become effective and committed civic actors: *"Helping students to acquire the competencies and commitments to participate in effective civic action to create equitable national societies is the most important goal for multicultural/global education in the twenty-first century."*[9] Banks admits that students

FIGURE 14–1
Distribution of World Population

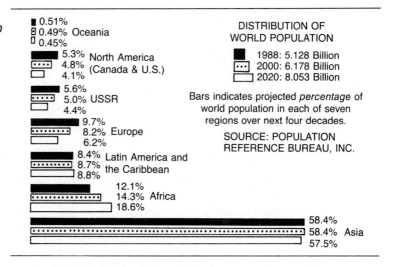

in the elementary school cannot remake the world with such an education, but believes that their attitudes and behaviors will help in a larger social and political context when they are adult citizens.

Jan L. Tucker agrees wholeheartedly that global interdependence must be taken into serious account in the social studies curriculum, but when teachers search for practical classroom suggestions they often come up empty:

> Very few of the major educational reform advocates . . . have offered serious proposals for upgrading the [global dimension] of the school curriculum. When the reform movement literature turns to [the global dimension], we typically find business as usual.
> This silence is deafening.[10]

Teacher's Role

The type of education that leads to a global perspective demands imaginative teachers willing to search for and develop interesting activities for their classes. Many specific activities can enrich your program, but the following considerations should guide your efforts:

1. *Present accurate information.* Too often children mistakenly believe that all Eskimos live in snowy igloos and every Australian owns two kangaroos. Such presentations only give children a distorted view of people in other countries.

2. *Use a variety of activities and materials.* The study of people around the world is more effective if the children participate in several different activities involving an assortment of teaching materials.

3. *Stress a global community.* All too often, social studies programs have stressed North America and Europe, to the near-total exclusion of the rest of the world. We need to widen our approach and introduce non-Western as well as Western culture.

4. *Emphasize likenesses as well as differences.* Children have traditionally been led to believe that if people lived in far-off lands, they were strange and exotic. Children need to be made aware of the commonalities in lifestyle of people throughout the world as well as the diversities.

5. *Begin with the immediate classroom situation.* Children must understand the characteristics of those children in the classroom and neighborhood who may differ in their social, cultural, religious, or ethnic backgrounds before they can extend this understanding to a world view. The program should be developed on a foundation of respect for the community and homeland before such respect can be extended to other countries.

Creative teachers should be aware of the types of motivating learning activities that lead children to an understanding of people of the world. Carol Seefeldt offers this valuable framework on which to organize your ideas.

Primary Grades

Art Forms.   Children who are encouraged to create their own poetry, paintings, dance, literature, or handicrafts can readily understand and appreciate the art of other countries. Art from all nations can help children discover people's common heritage. Children can:

- visit museums to observe the art of many cultures; you can display art from all over the world in the classroom.
- begin an exchange of their paintings, drawings, or creative writing with a school in some other land.
- invite foreign visitors to tell folktales from their nations; you can compare the folktales with those of the United States.
- listen to poetry from other lands—perhaps some haiku from Japan—and dictate their own poetry.

Group Rules.   As children begin to realize that rules are necessary to live together effectively, they can understand how groups function more successfully when the rights of each group member are recognized. Children can:

- establish their own rules for using playground equipment, allowing people in the housekeeping area, or walking to the cafeteria.
- use the rules of the school—walk in the hall, remain quiet while waiting for the bus—to illustrate the rules of a larger community. You can also help them compare classroom rules with their rules at home.
- explore the rules of the community such as the traffic rules. Do all communities have such rules? Why?
- determine what rules the nation has and compare these rules to the laws of other lands.

Social Organization.   Although the composition of families and social groups changes dramatically from place to place, all human beings live in some type of group or social organization. To comprehend the similarities among social groups, children in the primary grades can:

- graph their families' composition to show how many different kinds of family units are represented in their classroom. You will want to discuss with the children how these family units are the same.
- exchange letters with a family in some other nation to learn how it is like a family in this country.
- invite visitors from other countries to tell about their families, the things family members do together, and how they share work or celebrate holidays.

Common Needs.   Borrowing concepts from the field of economics, you can teach children that people the world over have common needs for food, shelter, and clothing. Children might be able to:

- taste food from other countries.
- examine different shelters from around the world. Ask them: "How are they just like our homes?" "How are they different?" "How many different kinds of homes do we live in?" "How are they alike?"
- compare the clothing of other nations. Question them: "How is it just like the clothing we wear?" "What things do we use that they do not?"

One kindergartner, after comparing shoes from seven different countries, made the statement, "The shoes are different, but everybody has feet."

Language.   People everywhere communicate both verbally and nonverbally. Verbal communication may involve many different languages; nonverbal communication is useful when you do not understand the verbal communication of others. Children can learn that both verbal and nonverbal communication skills are involved when they try to express feelings, ideas, attitudes, and knowledge. Children can:

- be given many opportunities to communicate in the classroom on a one-to-one basis or in large or small groups. Methods might include using a telephone or tape recorder or dictating to you. You can draw children's attention to their use of nonverbal communication and extend the concept by introducing Indian sign language or the sign language used to communicate with the deaf, role playing, or dramatizations.

- read or listen to the story, *Children of the World Say Good Morning,* and learn how to say "good morning" in some language other than English.
- listen to someone speaking another language; you or a visitor might teach the children a few phrases in the language. You could teach a few simple songs and let the children listen to music from other countries.

One element common to communication is that people everywhere have feelings. If we saw our homes being destroyed we would feel the way Vietnamese families did when it happened to them; Biafran parents watching helplessly as their children starve feel as we would if our children were starving; Brazilian children feel the same way the children in the United States do when they can go to the beach and swim in the ocean.

Children learn to express their feelings positively in the classroom, without hurting others; they learn to recognize that all people have the same feelings. When reading stories of people from other lands, such as *The Story About Ping,* you can ask the children: "How do you think the boy felt when he fell into the water?" "How would you have felt?" "Did anything like that ever happen to you?"

Many classroom experiences give children opportunities to clarify their feelings toward other people and understand the feelings of others. You can ask the children: "How did you feel when you hit him?" "How do you think he felt?" "How did it feel when they asked you to play with them?" "How did you feel when they called you a name?" You can also help children perceive the feelings of others: "What do you think she was telling you when she screamed at you?" "How do you think she felt?"[11]

Intermediate Grades

1. Exchange letters with pen pals in other countries. A good source from which to obtain information and addresses is:

   International Friendship League
   40 Mount Vernon Street
   Beacon Hill
   Boston, MA 02108

2. Plan to conduct a fund drive. Organize a special school program such as a bake sale and donate the money to CARE or UNICEF.
3. Invite resource persons to speak to the class. Foreign-born local residents, people returning from a trip, airline workers, or Peace Corps volunteers can add a great deal to enhance a child's understanding of a nation.
4. Children all around the world enjoy playing games. Allow your children to play games from around the world with each other. Here are two games enjoyed by the children of Africa:

Belenin or *Little Stone*

Two players collect fifty small stones, about the size of marbles. The first player tosses up the handful of stones and catches as many as possible on the back of his hand, then tosses them to catch them in the palm of his hand. The player chooses any two of the stones that have fallen to the ground, making sure they are far enough apart for him to get his finger between them. He draws a line between them with his finger and shoots one of the stones at the other, using the thumb against the pointer finger as the force. If the stone misses, he loses his turn. If his stone strikes the other, he may pick up the stone for which he was aiming or he may use the second stone to shoot at the first one, thereby being able to pick up the two stones. He continues to draw lines between and shoot at one stone with another until he misses the one at which he aimed or until there are no more stones with enough space between to draw a line with the finger. The opponent picks up the remaining stones and proceeds in the same way until she misses. The player with the most stones at the end is the winner.

Beleta or Take Stone (Similar to Jacks)

Players gather a number of stones, which are dropped together. One stone is used to toss into the air, and before it comes down to be caught the player must pick up one of the stones in the pile without causing any other stone to move or touching any other stone. Each player tosses the stone up and picks up stones until she makes the mistake of touching another stone, causing a stone to move, or not catching the tossed stone. The second player takes his turn, starting with all of the stones and proceeding in the same way until he misses. The player wins who succeeds in gathering the greatest number of stones.

5. The continuity of life is an important theme in cultures around the world. Africans, for example, celebrate pregnancy and birth enthusiastically. A large part of the celebration is the naming ceremony. Here is how it goes.

African Naming Ceremony

The child's parents announce the day of the naming ceremony. Female babies are named on the seventh day after birth and male babies on the eighth. The oldest living member of the family, male or female, performs the ceremony. He or she pours some wine (grape juice if you wish to re-enact the ceremony in your classroom) onto the floor and begins a narration of the family's history. Both husband's and wife's families are recited; the accomplishments of deceased members are particularly emphasized, enumerated, and praised. In this way the spirits of the ancestors are invited to join the celebration and bless the child. The baby is then formally introduced to the realities of life—wine (grape juice), water, honey, pepper, and salt. First the child is given a few drops of wine (grape juice) to symbolize the family's good wishes, hopes, and desires for a full and fruitful life. Next, the performer of the ceremony splashes a few drops of cold water on the baby's forehead, and then puts a drop or two into the baby's mouth when it cries. The water signifies its importance as the sustainer of life; at the same time, it tests the baby's alertness. The baby is wished a smooth sail through the seas of life but is warned of life's trials and tribulations as well. A drop of honey is placed on the baby's tongue to signify that life is sweet. A pinch of pepper is placed on the baby's lips to signify the spice of life. Finally, a pinch of salt is given the baby as a token of the flavor of life.

Reenactment of a Yoruba Naming Ceremony

Have the children participate by assigning a different child to bring in each ingredient for the ceremony. Use an Afro-American baby doll as the central figure, with each child giving it a name, or have one child act as the newborn in the ceremony and be given names by his or her classmates. Some sample names and their meanings follow:

Girls' Names	*Meaning*
Ayo (Ah-yo)	Joy
Ayoluwa (Ah-yo-loo-wah)	Joy of our People
Dara (Dah-rah)	Beautiful
Femi (Feh-mee)	Love me
Ife (Ee-feh)	Love
Nilaja (Nee-lah-jah)	Peaceful, Friendly

Boys' Names	*Meaning*
Adebayo (Ah-day-bah-yo)	Crown of Joy
Oba (Aw-bah)	King
Babafemi (Bah-bah-feh-mee)	Father loves me
Ola (Aw-lah)	Wealth, Riches
Olu (Oh-loo)	Highest among persons
Balogun (Bah-lo-goon)	Warlord

Compare and contrast this Yoruba naming ceremony with similar ceremonies in cultures around the world. Have the children research the genealogy of their families; ask them to find out from their parents why they were named as they are. Invite each child to adopt a name from the Yoruba list.

6. Keep one bulletin board in your classroom solely for the purpose of displaying current events from countries around the world. Use colorful yarn to connect the story to its location on an outline map.

7. Arrange for an "International Olympics," in which the participants dress in the traditional garb of their respective countries for the entrance ceremony.

8. Utilize the arts. As Edith W. King declares,

> Music, art, and literature know no national or cultural boundaries. The common expressions of human feeling found in these forms can be used effectively by the teacher to develop children's capacities to identify with other groups and other societies—indeed, the totality of [humanity]. . . .
>
> Aesthetic experiences, embodied in the arts and humanities, provide ways of giving the individual an opportunity to try on a situation—to know the logic and feeling of others—even though these others live thousands of miles away.[12]

ENVIRONMENTAL EDUCATION

Suppose that you were among the first group of settlers to arrive on the shores of this country. Your first strong impression would be of the incredible beauty of an unspoiled, vast land. You find fresh water; abundant natural resources, wildlife, and fish; no fuel-burning engines to pollute the air; no chemical processing plants to spew toxins into the environment. In just over 300 years, we have taken such a raw, pure land and turned it into a natural time bomb ready to explode into life-threatening catastrophe. A combination of humanity's disregard for its surroundings and a fantastic rate of unrestricted technological growth has produced an environmental emergency so great that some have predicted a disaster from which our planet could not recover. They point to such evidence as acid rain that harms crops, forests, wildlife, and fish; chemical and sewage pollution of our streams and lakes; contamination of our water and land with hazardous chemical or nuclear waste disposal; stripping of forests and mines with little regard for reestablishing the land; toxic pesticides that protect our crops yet threaten our physical health; and other major environmental depredations to back their claims.

Because these environmental concerns go beyond local or national borders, the topic of environmental education is often closely aligned with global education. To see why, refer once more to Anne M. Blackburn's three categories of complex global concerns. Most could be classified as environmental concerns. Cheryl Charles, recognizing this, advises social studies teachers that to stress only our human cultural heritage gives students an unbalanced program; *cultural roots* are important, but students must understand and appreciate their *natural roots,* too:

> When we recognize that this one earth is a habitat shared by people and other living things all over the planet, we begin to see things differently. We then put our teaching—whether civics, government, history, economics or geography—in the context of a living source. We remember that it all begins outside. The rivers, skies, oceans and breezes of this planet connect us to plants, animals and people all over the earth—in Saudi Arabia, Japan, Kenya, Brazil . . . all over, everywhere. Each day we are reminded that the planet is not the solitary domain of specialized academic disciplines. It is the living womb of cultural and natural systems.[13]

Learning About the Environment

Margaret Mead believed that learning about the environment is something children must accomplish in order to become responsible citizens:

> If children feel themselves as part of the living world, learn respect for it, and their uniqueness in it, they will have a foundation for growth into responsible citizens who will be able to discriminate and make decisions about science used for constructive purposes and the science used for destructive purposes.[14]

The present concern for sweeping environmental problems has prompted a strong push to include environmental education as a major topic of study in the entire K–12 school program. The National Council for the Social Studies moved to make environmental education a part of all social studies programs and stated that such an approach must be interdisciplinary, meaning that all areas of the curriculum must be combined to teach our students environmental awareness:

> We dedicate our cooperative efforts as educators to increasing our own and our students' understanding of the complexity of contemporary problems, and we accept the responsi-

bilities for restoring and preserving our natural and social environment. *The situation demands an interdisciplinary approach to environmental education.*[15]

Approaches to environmental education differ from teacher to teacher, but should be directed toward providing experiences that help develop these two major objectives: (1) to acquire basic understandings about the environment and about the causes and dangers inherent in our abuse of the environment, and (2) to develop positive attitudes toward and a respect for the quality of the environment. Such feelings should establish a spirit of personal commitment, a willingness to become active in efforts to help maintain and improve the environment.

Primary Grades

Teaching units in the primary grades should provide basic ecological knowledge relative to these topics: air, water, land, plants, food, and animals. In addition, studies of the home, school, neighborhood, and community environments should include concepts related to ecological quality.

Some specific activities for the primary-grade teacher include:

1. Collect samples of rainwater, ditch water, and river or pond water in separate jars, covering each and labeling according to source. Put the jars on a ledge for a couple of days and be careful not to move or shake them. Then check the jars and evaluate each as to color, smell, and sediment.
2. Prepare three small boxes of soil—one sand, one loam, and one clay. Label each according to soil type; plant an equivalent amount of grass seed in each box and water evenly. After about two weeks, compare the amount of growth in each box.
3. Constructing and maintaining both dry and wet terrariums is a helpful and interesting way to study animals and plants in their natural surroundings.
4. To demonstrate a concept of recycling, use a large box, topsoil, some small stones, and a collection of typical litter. Spread the stones evenly on the bottom of the box to a depth of about 1/2". Next, fill the box with about four inches of topsoil. Add a layer of common litter—strips of newspaper, broken glass, potato or apple peels, pieces of plastic, small chunks of wood. Cover the litter with another four inches of topsoil and water it well (don't soak). Finally, cover the box tightly with a sheet of plastic or other nonporous material. Allow the box to stay undisturbed in a warm, dry place for about one month. After the time has elapsed, spread the contents on a newspaper and sort it out. What has decomposed? What hasn't? What does this tell you about our trash problems?
5. Visit the community's water supply plant. Discuss where the water comes from and how it needs to be treated.
6. Invite older people into the classroom to discuss changes in the local environment during their lifetime. Discuss the effect of these changes on soil, animals, water, and people. Draw before and after pictures illustrating these changes.
7. Collect pictures from magazines or newspapers showing how people have caused environmental problems. Encourage the children to offer possible measures for improvement of the situation or suggestions as to how the situation could have been prevented in the first place.

8. The average American uses seven trees a year in paper, wood, and other products. Plant a tree with your children; it is not only fun, but it is one of the best things you can do for the environment.

9. Many plastic six-pack rings find their way into the ocean when people leave them on the beach or dump them into the water. In the water, they cannot be seen by sea creatures; as a result, animals hunting for food often get the rings caught around their necks or beaks. Encourage the children to snip each circle in their six-pack rings before they toss them into the garbage.

10. Each American throws away about 60 pounds of plastic packaging every year. Packaging accounts for about one-third of all the refuse in our landfills. Plan with your class to establish a recycling center in your school where all recyclable packaging can be collected.

11. Schools spend billions of dollars each year on school supplies. Write a class letter to the textbook publishers and ask them to use recycled paper. Ask the principal to order only recycled writing paper, paper towels, toilet paper, and napkins. Start working to change the world in the school.

Intermediate Grades

Teaching units in the intermediate grades should enlarge on the concepts developed in the primary grades and incorporate studies of special environments (urban, coastal, forest), nutrition, energy, and other ecology action projects.

Some specific activities for the intermediate-grade teacher include:

1. Take the students on ecology field trips to parks, woodlands, streams, or industrial areas. Provide guidelines or checklists for observation, and look for specified conditions of ecological abuse. Plan an action program to correct the most serious problems.

2. Encourage the children to keep a record of the times they encounter the words *pollution, ecology,* or *environment* during a one-week period. Have them record the source and context in which each word was used.

3. Use a simulation activity in which the class is divided into two teams of five children each. One team is composed of environment-minded citizens who wish to protect a marsh area from being filled in so an apartment complex can be built. The other team is composed of the developers who wish to build the complex. Each team should prepare its arguments to present to the rest of the class. The class members must vote for the team they feel best represents the interests of their community. Discuss reasons for the results of the vote.

4. Have the students conduct a household survey to determine the presence of products that hold the potential for harming the environment; for example, aerosol hairspray, non-biodegradable plastic beverage containers, toxic cleansers.

5. Have the students check the classroom trash can at the end of the school day. Define biodegradable and non-biodegradable; have the students sort the trash into the two categories. Ask the students to think of a replacement product for each of the non-biodegradable items.

6. Have the students find out how their community disposes of its waste. Is there a landfill? What do they think will happen when the landfill runs out of space?

7. Invite a member of a local environmental group to visit your class to talk about your community's environmental status: toxic waste disposal, solid waste disposal, water supply, recycling efforts, and so on.

8. Find out how materials are recycled. You may want to visit a recycling plant or conduct the following experiment dealing with recycled paper.

   Materials:

an old newspaper	plastic dishpan
blender	spoon
cornstarch	cup
bucket	blue food coloring
5″ square window screen	blow dryer (optional)

   Procedure:
   a. Rip several sheets of newspaper into small pieces and soak them in a half bucket of warm water for about one hour.
   b. Pour three cups of soaked paper into the blender and blend until mushy. This will break up the paper fibers.
   c. Dissolve two tablespoons (plus) of cornstarch and blue food coloring in a pint of water. Pour the mixture into the pulp. Blend slowly until thoroughly mixed.
   d. Pour the mixture into a dishpan. Dip the window screen into the mixture and move it around until you have a layer of pulp about 1/16 inch thick.
   e. Place the pulp-covered screen on several sheets of newspaper and place a sheet of plastic wrap over the pulp. Press down on the plastic with a sponge, lightly at first, until the excess water has been drained.
   f. Allow the pulp to dry for 24 hours, or speed up the process with a blow dryer (on slow speed at first).
   g. Peel off the fibers when they are dry. You have just recycled paper.

9. Use values activities to encourage children to think more deeply about environmental problems. For example:

   Proud Whip
   a. Seat the children in a circle.
   b. Announce an environmental topic such as "Something I have done to help avert an energy crisis."
   c. Encourage the children to take turns standing up and sharing something they are proud of. For example,, "I am proud that I turn the light out in my bedroom when I leave it."
   d. Remember that not all children need to participate; some may prefer to "pass."
   e. Reinforce each statement with comments such as "Thank you" or "OK."
   f. Ask the children to illustrate their contributions and arrange them in a large bulletin board display.

10. Read books that present strong environmental statements. *The Lorax* by Dr. Seuss is a good example. The story is about the greedy Onceler who had polluted the air,

cut down great forests, and committed a variety of other damaging acts simply because he had a strong desire to get rich. It is replete with possibilities for discussion about caring for the environment.

11. Plan some simple, concrete, revealing experiments to illustrate certain principles and problems related to the development, use, and conservation of energy. For example:

Draftometer

Make a draftometer: scotch tape a clear sheet of plastic wrap to a pencil. Check to see if your school is losing heat by holding the draftometer near the edges of windows and doors.

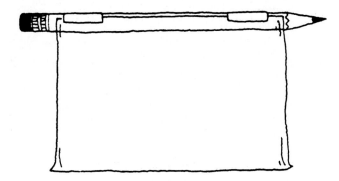

Colors and Temperatures

Paint four soup cans a different color (white, black, red, blue). Fill each can with the same amount of very hot (near boiling) water and put a thermometer in each can. Record the temperature every three minutes until the water cools and graph the results for comparison. (Crayon color for each dot corresponds to can color.) Discuss what color might be best to keep a house warm in the winter, and what would best keep it cool in the summer.

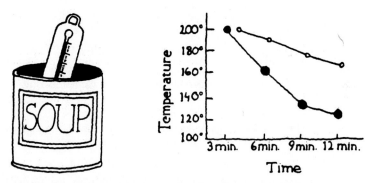

12. Start a school garden with many kinds of plants. The digging, weeding, and watering responsibilities add to the children's awareness of and respect for life within their environment.

MULTICULTURAL EDUCATION

Everyone has a culture—you, your students, your friends, the people in your neighborhood—all individuals who share a sense of group identification have a culture. Ina Corrine Brown defines culture this way:

> all the accepted and patterned ways of behavior of a given people. It is a body of common understandings. It is the sum total and the organization or arrangement of all the group's ways of thinking, feeling, and acting. It also includes the physical manifestations of the group as exhibited in the objects they make—the clothing, shelter, tools, weapons, implements, utensils, and so on.[16]

Culture is universal, but how a culture meets people's needs varies. Donna M. Gollnick and Philip C. Chinn illustrate this fact with foods; food is needed by all cultures to survive, but which foods are perceived as edible varies from culture to culture:

> Many Americans reject foods, such as horses, dogs, cats, rice, mice, snakes, snails, grasshoppers, caterpillars, and numerous insects, consumed by other cultural groups in different areas of the world. At the same time, other cultural groups reject foods that are normal to many Americans. Muslims and Orthodox Jews do not eat pork. Hindus do not eat beef, some East Africans find eggs impalatable, and some Chinese do not drink milk. . . . Do you remember the foods included on the Basic Four charts learned in elementary school? Often we find it difficult to believe that not everyone has a diet that includes the basic four foods seen on those charts.[17]

Kluckhohn offers this vivid example of the ways in which food habits of one culture are viewed with distaste by another:

> Guests who came her way were often served delicious sandwiches filled with a meat that seemed to be neither chicken nor tuna fish yet was reminiscent of both. To queries she gave no reply until each had eaten his fill. She then explained that what they had eaten was not chicken, nor tuna fish, but the rich white flesh of freshly killed rattlesnakes. The response was instantaneous—vomiting, often violent vomiting. A biological process caught in a cultural web.[18]

As with food, people often have a difficult time accepting the special practices and beliefs of other cultures; they often feel their culture is superior to any other. Understandably, culture becomes the filter through which its members judge the world. Gollnick and Chinn believe this is both a positive and a negative characteristic:

> It is an asset for the culture to be viewed by its members as the natural and correct way of thinking, acting, and behaving. At the same time it often solicits feelings of superiority over any other culture. The inability to view another culture through its cultural lens ["filter"] prevents an understanding of the second culture. This inability usually makes it impossible to function effectively in a second culture.[19]

Cultural insularity is especially dangerous today in light of the need for interdependence among countries and the importance of establishing positive ties among all cultural groups in the United States. Although America has been known as a great "melting pot," the virtues and achievements of the dominant Anglo-American sector of society were historically revered, while those of the African American, Native American, Hispanic

American, and Asian American populations were neglected. These four groups were consistently restricted from full participation in social, economic, political, religious, and educational life in the United States. According to Joyce, "Our nation's experiences in minority group relations demonstrate that the proverbial American melting pot has been a colossal fraud, perpetrated by a dominant majority for the purpose of convincing society at large that all cultural groups, irrespective of race or ethnic origin, were in fact eligible for full and unrestricted participation in the social, economic, political, and religious life of this nation."[20]

Reacting to concerns about unfair treatment of cultural groups in curricular content and school policy, educators conceived multicultural programs. Banks finds such programs flawed:

> Most of the programs that have been devised and implemented are parochial in scope, fragmented, and structured without careful planning and clear rationales. Typically . . . programs focus on one specific ethnic group such as Afro-Americans, Native Americans (Indians), or Mexican Americans. The ethnic group upon which the program focuses is either present or dominant in the local school population. A school district which has a large Puerto Rican population is likely to have a program in Puerto Rican Studies, but not one which teaches about the problems and sociological characteristics of other ethnic groups.[21]

Larry Cuban cautions educators against moving in such a narrow direction, stating that such programs and materials miss the point and create "black counterparts to the Nathan Hales and Molly Pitchers of the past."[22] Banks criticizes the programs on the basis that they "rarely help students develop scientific generalizations and concepts about the characteristics ethnic groups have in common, about the unique status of each ethnic group, and about why ethnicity is an integral part of our social system."[23]

Cuban offers perhaps the most realistic method of incorporating multicultural studies into the elementary school social studies program:

> Within the framework of the public school, the only legitimate goals for [multicultural] content that can be achieved are to offer a balanced view of the American past and present, including racism and democratic ideals, and to equip students with the skills to analyze the meaning of the [multicultural] experience in this country. Whether this combination of knowledge and analytical skills will raise self-esteem or invest youngsters with dignity is debatable, but both could help students to know and think about the many dimensions of the American experience, free of propaganda.[24]

How can you use this knowledge about multicultural education in your classroom? Edith W. King suggests this three-pronged approach:

1. *Knowing one's identity,* one's heritage and traditions. Who are *your* people? What are their practices, customs and ways?
2. *Knowing about other groups in the nation.* What groups other than your own are present in American society?
3. *Knowing about the relationships between these ethnic groups.* Are the relationships between various groups cooperative and supportive, or are they antagonistic and hostile? Have these relationships existed historically over centuries, over decades, or are they very current?[25]

The following sample activities are based on these three areas of exploration. They are meant only to exemplify the variety of instructional strategies available for promoting understanding among people in our country and are by no means a comprehensive list.

1. Edna Genise Lewis, a teacher in the West Chester, Pennsylvania, school district, has developed a technique called *Spotlight of the Week*[26] as a way to help children recognize individual similarities and differences. The activity is introduced shortly after school opens in September.

Spotlight of the Week

Introduce the activity by having students observe each other. Point out that every person in the class is different and equally important. Tell the students that everyone in the class will have an opportunity throughout the school year to be the most important person in the class for a day. Explain that although only one person will be spotlighted per week, all students will have a role in preparing for that day.

Have the students create press badges, microphones, and so on, and set up a podium. Have them list the special questions to be used for the interview, such as:

- "What kind of a person are you?" (boy, girl, tall, short, black, white, smart, pretty, athletic, etc.)
- "From where do your ancestors come?"
- "Are you Japanese, English, Mexican, Native American (etc.)?"
- "Are there any special foods you like to eat?"
- "What are some celebrations you enjoy?"

Select reporters who will do the spotlighting. Have the reporters interview the spotlighted student about his family life, customs or traditions, foods, pets, or likes and dislikes.

Have the entire class talk about what they have learned at the end of each interview.

Follow up by having the class choose a community person they would like to find out more about. Arrange an interview with that person.

2. Distribute a "family tree" chart to your children. Ask them to take the papers home and have their families help them fill out the chart. When back in the classroom, ask each child to tell a story about her family including the information presented on the chart (see Figure 14–2).

3. Discuss the children's first names and surnames. Begin by asking them how they got their first names—whether they are traditional names such as Matthew, for example, or invented names comprised of both parents' names, such as Donnelle (for Donald and Ellen). Bring in a book of suggested baby names. You might want to have a naming ceremony patterned after the Yoruba naming ceremony (see p. 432) and invite the children to name a doll that you bring into class. Ask the children to complete the statement, "If I had a baby, I would name it _____ because _____ ."

FIGURE 14–2
Ethnic Family Tree

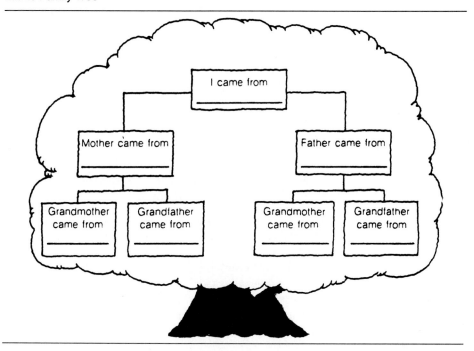

Discuss the children's surnames—their national origin, their length (some have one syllable, others are unusually long), and some distinguishing characteristics (for example, "son of" is conveyed by "Mc" or "Mac" in Ireland and Scotland, "-ez" in Spanish, "-tse" in Chinese, "-ov" in Russian). Many last names identify an ancestor's line of work—Smith or Baker. Books on surnames will help provide information on some common names and their origins.

4. Hang a large sheet of butcher paper on the wall and make a table summarizing the information the children gathered about their ethnic origins. Discuss that data, emphasizing that our families came from many different places. On a large world map, locate the nations from which the children's ancestors came and pin a small flag with the child's name on each nation.

5. Group the children according to their major ancestral background. Ask each group to cut out photographs from old magazines and paste them onto sheets of tagboard as a "cultural collage."

6. Explore regions and cultures. Throughout the country there are pockets of people with unique backgrounds; an in-depth study of one or more of these groups recognizes the special roles they played in the shaping of America. One group that particularly fascinates elementary school youngsters is Native Americans. The study of our first Americans has been largely overlooked; teachers often concentrate on

African American history, Spanish studies, or special units on Mexico, Japan, or India. While these are all valuable endeavors, we must also recognize the culture of the 850,000 native people who inhabited this country before the arrival of the Europeans.

Native Americans all have their own rich heritage, so it is not recommended that a general study of Native Americans be initiated. There are so many American Indian nations (16 in the Eastern Woodland area alone) that we recommend that you focus on no more than one group (California area, for example) at a time.

To begin, read a motivational story to your students. I have found Paul Goble's *Star Boy* to be an excellent starter book for the primary grades. Once interest in the study of early Native Americans is piqued, divide your class into several nations, the number of which is controlled by the total number of students in your room. Designate different areas of the classroom for each nation and guide their research with a variety of materials and questions such as:

- What were the major events in your history?
- What materials are used in your arts and crafts?
- What are some special beliefs of your nation?
- What special ceremonies do the people of your nation have? When and where do they take place?
- How does your nation communicate?
- How do the children of your nation become educated?
- What are the responsibilities of the family members?

Let us suppose that our study involves Native American nations of the Great Plains. Among those that might be highlighted are the Arapaho, Blackfoot, Cheyenne, Chickasaw, Choctaw, Comanche, Crow, Mandan, Pawnee, and Sioux/Dakota. Some activities might include:

1. *Making a Tepee* (Sioux *tipi*). The tepee was an ideal home for the Plains nations because most were nomads; they roamed the vast grasslands of the Midwest in search of buffalo. They lived in portable tents made of 8–20 tanned buffalo skins that women sewed together in a conical shape. The skins were draped over a structure of three long poles lashed together at the top to form a tripod and fortified with 12–17 additional poles. The overall structure was similar among all nations, but often the exterior design was distinctive; symbols of nature (sun, mountains, animals) as well as geometric designs offered variation.

   To make a classroom tepee, tightly roll batches of six full-size sheets of newspaper on the diagonal (see Figure 14–3). (First check fire regulations; the paper may need to be fireproofed.) To make a large tepee, roll six more sheets of newspaper around the first pole, overlapping the first set of newspaper. Continue to lengthen the pole until you reach the desired height (usually 7–8 feet). You will need to make about six poles.

   Tie the poles together at one end, then spread them so they stand up in a tepee shape. Piece together long sheets of kraft paper for the tepee cover. To determine the size, measure the length of the poles from the bottom to where they are tied.

FIGURE 14–3
Making Tepee Poles

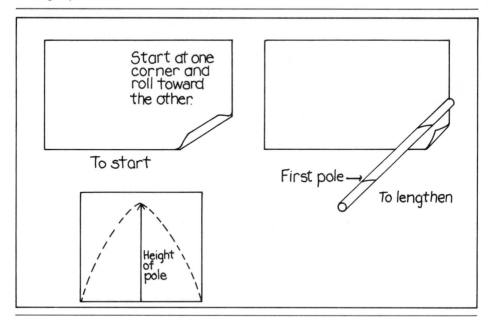

This will be the radius of a semicircle to be cut from the paper. Have the children decorate the semicircle with nature pictures or geometric designs using paints, crayons, or markers and cut it out. Drape the paper over the frame and use strong tape to hold the edges together. Leave a portion open to serve as a doorway.

2. *Picture Writing.* Important events in the lives of Plains Indians were passed on either by storytelling or picture writing. Accounts of important events such as a buffalo hunt or flood were painted onto dressed and tanned buffalo hides. The students can make their own pictographs on pieces of grocery bags torn in the shape of buffalo hides. Show the children some examples of pictographs; have them use the samples or create their own pictographs to tell a short story. If a child were to account for his after-school activities, he might do a pictograph such as that shown in Figure 14–4. A second "buffalo hide" should offer the translated version of the pictograph story.

3. *Native American Folktales.* Many of the Native American folktales explain why certain natural phenomena happened. The children could write their own "pourquoi" stories explaining, for example, why the deer is such a fast animal, or why the stars twinkle in the night sky.

4. *Indian Names.* Names such as Babbling Brook or Chief Stinking Saddle Blanket (who was always fighting and was too busy to change his sweaty saddle blanket!) are very significant to Native Americans. In most tribes, temporary names were given to babies, and when the child was old enough, he or she would receive a permanent name (age varied by tribe). Some tribes believed that a new name would be suggested by a spirit in a dream. In others, the name would tell something about

FIGURE 14–4
Sample Pictograph

the person's personality or actions, such as going to war or hunting an animal. Children might enjoy discovering how famous Native Americans such as Sitting Bull got their names, then selecting their own Native American names and writing legends about why they chose them.

5. *Religious Ceremonies.* Most religious ceremonies included dancing. The Plains Indians' buffalo dance was (and still is) performed each year to ensure hunting success. Dancing is done to the beat of a drum; the basic dance step is the toe-heel step. Have one or two children keep a steady beat with tom-tom drums; on the first beat, the children step forward on the toes of the left foot, On the softer second beat, they step down with the left heel. The step is repeated with the right foot and alternatively thereafter.

6. *Banish Indian Stereotypes.* Critique books by examining how Native Americans are depicted. Are they all wearing feathers, buckskins, or moccasins and living in tepees? Actually, these are valid depictions of Plains Indians. However, if educational materials treat all early Native Americans as one cultural group, they must not be used with your students. Avoid books, too, that depict Native Americans as fierce, war painted, "wild Indians" ready to pillage white settlements. Instead, select materials depicting Native Americans involved in natural, nonthreatening activities that accurately depict the rich cultural heritage of Native Americans.

Opportunities for children to build or create things enhance the study of important cultural and ethnic groups.

A strong multicultural component concentrates on the historical and contemporary contributions of various cultural groups, promoting appreciation of and respect for all Americans. For it to work effectively, programs must ensure that fair recognition of all groups is made throughout the social studies curriculum.

CAREER EDUCATION

During the early 1970s, a debate erupted among parents and educators about whether schools were doing an adequate job of preparing our nation's youth for the transition from school to the world of work. The overwhelming conclusion of that debate was a resounding "no." Resulting criticism spawned a new term, *career education,* and served as an impetus to create educational programs that went beyond *vocational education* (for youngsters planning to enter specific trades) toward programs informing children about career options. Differences of opinion about exactly what informing children about career options should mean and the stipulation by Sidney P. Marland, Jr., the U.S. Commissioner of Education in 1970, that career education be *"all encompassing"* added to the confusion. Out of the turmoil surfaced four basic approaches to career education.[27]

1. *Job.* The most basic view of vocational preparation is to provide vocational courses in which the students develop specialized skills for future employment—carpentry, typing, auto repair, etc.
2. *Work.* In this view, programs attempt to increase students' knowledge regarding the work associated with various jobs, the preparation necessary for the jobs, and the economic advantages associated with each.
3. *Self.* Neither job nor work should be the primary focus of career education. Instead, self-concept assumes primary importance in determining career choice. The program emphasizes that each person has potentialities for more than one occupation and that the power to fulfill one's future lies in knowing *how* to choose as well as *what* to choose.
4. *Life.* Those viewing career education in this light suggest that the entire school curriculum be restructured and directed toward *total education;* that is, for the different roles a person must play—work, leisure, family, and community *throughout life.*

Perhaps the most basic type of program emerging from this turmoil has been vocational/technical (vo/tech) education designed to teach students the skills to enter specific job markets—welding, auto mechanics, agriculture, secretarial sciences, child care. (The vo/tech education plan corresponds to the *job* approach to career education just enumerated.) These vo/tech programs are offered in nearly all school districts today. In addition to creating programs to address the specific skills needed by some students, the Office of Career Education (a branch of the Department of Education) has stimulated experimentation into programs that provide general skills that all individuals will need in considering future employment. The University of Minnesota program on career development, for example, takes the vo/tech philosophy further by combining features of the remaining three philosophies described earlier. The curriculum developers base their program on five major objectives:

1. To develop a positive attitude toward self through an awareness of developing values, talents, and interests as they relate to work roles;
2. To develop the student's awareness of occupational areas in terms of work roles, related life-style, and potential satisfactions and dissatisfactions;
3. To develop interpersonal skills required in work roles;
4. To develop decision-making skills and an awareness of the results of actions and decisions that give one a sense of destiny control;
5. To give students an opportunity to acquire respect for workers and the place of work in society.[28]

Some of the activities used to develop the objectives follow, based on material developed by Logacz, Laurich, and Hummel.[29]

Primary Grades

An awareness of workers with whom the children are familiar is emphasized during the primary years. Parents, school workers, community workers, and self-awareness are the primary topics. Some sample activities are given here.

1. "Getting to Know Me" presents self-concept activities in booklet form.
   - In one activity children look in a mirror and compare themselves with their classmates.
   - Children learn the term *abilities*. They try to discover their own abilities and those of others, eventually matching pictures of workers to a particular activity.
   - In another activity children draw a picture of what they can do well and what they would like to do well.
   - Keeping their own abilities in mind, the children look into the future and fantasize about the type of job they might have as adults. They draw a picture of the preferred job.
2. Changing work and family patterns are discussed. Emphasis is placed on eliminating stereotypes by viewing men and women in various work roles. The traditional idea that men become doctors and women nurses, for example, no longer applies. Boys and girls become aware that they can become what *they* want to become while developing as happy, fulfilled, productive individuals.
3. Another career education activity in the primary grades is to take field trips to various businesses in the local community. Children ask questions about the jobs at these places.
4. Dramatic play centers where children can role-play different occupations such as carpenter, nurse, auto mechanic, and doctor can be developed.

Intermediate Grades

Self-awareness is a direction of study continued through the intermediate age group. Additional objectives can be met by incorporating career development objectives into the existing social studies curriculum. Some examples follow.

1. Children can compile awareness booklets in which they draw pictures or complete sentences to tell specific things about themselves.
2. They can draw pictures of their parents at work. Each child explains his or her picture and categorizes it as a producer or service job. This helps the children learn about several different occupations.
3. Students can send a letter home to the parents inviting them to come to the classroom to tell about their jobs, the tools they use, and the education and training necessary for the job.
4. Children who are to be absent because of a vacation or a medical or dental appointment may be asked to complete a chart describing all of the different types of jobs they saw being performed.

Children become aware of their own abilities and interests when exposed to the talents of successful adults.

5. In a unit on mapping, children can locate major industries in the region or state. Personnel from these industries can be invited to speak to the class.
6. Children can act out the roles of community workers in the classroom. A public health official could check on cleanliness of the room, a newspaper reporter could do interviews for the class newspaper, and so on.

Career education can be incorporated into a variety of other classroom work. For example, a fifth-grade class might study how to run a retail business by establishing a classroom store where snacks, school supplies, souvenirs, or other items could be bought. They can learn about graphs by recording the jobs held by parents of the children in school. Another class might publish a school newspaper after inviting a reporter to speak to them about her work. Methods of instruction vary widely, but the principle of career education is to show children how their schoolwork relates to their future employment role in society and then to give them good, lifelong employability skills—good work habits, a positive self-concept, knowledge of various careers, and decision-making capabilities.

LAW-RELATED EDUCATION

Political decisions are choices individuals make about the actions of themselves, other individuals, or groups—decisions that influence a society's rules, goals, or social behavior. Political decisions can result in laws for groups. For example, allowing

16-year-olds to drive an automobile is a political decision, as is deciding that everyone must bring a signed permission slip from home before being allowed to go on a school field trip. Political decisions can also allocate things group members view as valuable or important. For example, establishing Head Start preschool programs for families of low socioeconomic status is a political decision, as is determining which classroom jobs are to be distributed to specific individuals during the week. Political decisions can also establish goals for a group. For example, setting the goal to balance the federal budget by a certain date is a political decision, as is deciding to have a class picnic on the last day of school.

Viewing law-related education as a decision-making process is a new direction for social studies education. In the past, it was connected to special courses in civics or government, which simply expected the children to store knowledge about the Consitution, define terms such as *electorate* or *ex post facto,* memorize the Bill of Rights, and absorb facts. Often, youngsters would tune out to such an approach and find the entire process of law and government confusing and unrelated to their own lives. Recent trends in the study of government and the law, however, have attempted to cure these problems. This is not to say that knowledge is viewed as unimportant, but to reestablish the proper perspective—that of aiding effective decision-making processes for good citizens. Many classroom experiences can be used to develop ideas about citizenship and law-related education.

Establishing Rules

Learning about rules and their role in helping govern personal conduct is an appropriate and convenient way to begin. Instead of making a rules chart or stating a set of predetermined, teacher-made rules, however, your program might begin with an understanding that rules are necessary for people's safe, orderly interaction. Unstructured literature experiences can help children establish concrete referents for that complex understanding. Marie Winn's book *Shiver, Gobble, and Snore* is a particularly useful resource.[30] The story focuses upon a funny king who made silly rules. In his kingdom lived three unhappy subjects: Shiver, who was always cold; Gobble, who was always hungry; and Snore (guess what he liked to do). Many of the king's rules adversely affected these characters, so they decided to move away to a place where there would be no rules. Alas, the three friends discovered that disputes could not be resolved in their new land—because they had no rules. They finally decided that to live peacefully, they must make rules. After reading them the story, you can lead the children through a discussion: "What are rules? Who made the rules in the kingdom? Did the rules make sense or were they foolish? Did all the people want to obey the rules? Why or why not? What did they decide to do? What else could they have done? What have you learned about rules?"

Another excellent literature resource is one of the episodes from *The Tale of Peter Rabbit* by Beatrix Potter, in which Peter is instructed not to go into Mr. McGregor's garden. Discuss the following: "What rule did Peter's mother give him? Why do you suppose she made it? Did Peter obey the rule? What happened to Peter because he did not follow the rule? Who makes rules in your family? Why are those rules made? What happens when those rules are not obeyed?"

The purpose of these questions is to encourage children to realize that rules are necessary to protect people's rights and to keep them safe from others' unacceptable behaviors. At this point, you may wish to introduce a classroom "guardian of rules"—a stuffed animal or a colorfully illustrated character—to help the children discuss these questions: "Do *we* need rules? Why? What are some problems we might have if there were no rules? Who should make the rules? What are some rules that are important for our classroom?"

Design a colorful display of these rules and place it in a prominent classroom location. When problems arise, you can pretend to consult your "guardian of rules" and let the character lead the children in an exchange of opinions about how to solve the conflict.

You can introduce older children to the need for rules and lead them to understand the essential nature of rules in the lives of citizens in a democracy through a game sequence like this one:

- *Phase 1.* Divide your class into equal-size groups. Give each group member a wooden block and tell them to play a game. Watch the children as they try to figure out what to do. When you notice the groups reaching a point of frustration, stop them and lead a discussion with these questions: "What took place when you started to design the game? Did you have any problems? Why? How did you decide to make the rules? Who made up the rules?"
- *Phase 2.* Ask each group to pass its blocks to one member. Declare that person the winner. Then discuss these questions: "Did this rule bother anyone? Is it important for you to share in making the rules? Why? How can we all share in decisions?"
- *Phase 3.* Follow the suggestions the children offer in their response to phase 2 and create rules for a game using the blocks distributed to each group. After the rules are written, have them play the game. Many will have designed a good sequence to follow, but some groups may have created rules that contradict each other or are too difficult to follow. Frustration will certainly result. At this point, the children can eagerly discuss their feelings about the problems that arise from unclear rules or too many rules.

After this game sequence, you may want to focus on these concepts:

1. What is a rule?
    (a guide that helps us know how to act)
2. Where are rules?
    (everywhere—home, school, community, etc.)
3. Why do we need rules?
    (they protect us and help us to live together in groups)
4. Who makes rules?
    (everyone can help make rules in our country)
5. Why should we follow rules?
    (people will find it hard to get along; it may be dangerous or unsafe; someone might be punished)

The Making of Laws

The rules the children live by in school are temporary; they serve a present purpose and will not likely be remembered throughout life. What will be recalled and expanded upon, however, are the *principles* behind rules—their functions and the responsibility of all members of a group to follow them. Many people use the terms *laws* and *rules* synonymously, but children should learn that a law is a rule made and enforced by a government. Societies have laws to ensure orderly behavior; to prevent someone from hurting others or infringing upon others' rights as citizens; and as convenient guides to customary behavior. In Britain people drive on the left side of the road; in the United States they drive on the right. Some laws are not as "customary," however. Consider how many people in Waterville, Maine, still use their handkerchiefs around others, even though an old statute stipulates that it is against the law to blow one's nose in public! In our society laws provide opportunities for voluntary obedience to established norms. Conscientious citizens should be motivated to obey laws willingly. Our society also values responsible reflection about behavioral norms. Citizens should freely criticize laws, suggest improvements, and elect representatives to make new laws.

How can these considerations be communicated to elementary school youngsters? The most effective techniques are those that exemplify the function of rules and laws in terms the children understand. Teachers must emphasize the broad concept of "courtesy" in the classroom—consideration for the needs, wants, and feelings of others. You can do this by emphasizing the need for good, clear, concise rules to help the classroom run smoothly. These rules should be appealingly illustrated and placed around the room for reinforcement. With personalized input from the children, they should follow the rules voluntarily—but when they do not, how should we handle conflicts in the classroom? Generally, teachers have these options:

1. Be a dictator. When conflicts arise, the teachers's position always prevails. You make the decision and the children follow your wishes. This type of teacher takes the position that "I'll never let these kids run over me; they've got to know who's boss!"
2. Be permissive. These teachers believe that children should have considerable freedom in their actions. Some dislike confrontation so much that they look the other way and pretend that a problem has not happened. Permissive teachers hope that children will enhance their self-respect through freedom of action and learn to like their teacher even more.
3. Be democratic. This pattern of teacher-child conflict resolution is based upon mutual respect. The democratic teacher employs a number of interpersonal interactions to encourage joint solutions to conflict situations.

Teacher Effectiveness Training

The democratic approach to conflict resolution is explicated in Thomas Gordon's Teacher Effectiveness Training (TET). Gordon's program is based on the resolution of two types of situations that often contribute to conflict in the classroom: (1) when the child has a problem, and (2) when the teacher has a problem.

A Child's Problem

Gordon believes that the most useful skill for solving another person's problem is the technique of *active listening.* TET claims that when children are upset or troubled, most teachers don't listen at all; instead, they tend to moralize, preach, criticize, or give advice. When children appear upset, a teacher's tendency is to talk: "Oh, come on. If at first you don't succeed, try, try again," or "Stop crying, you're no baby," or "That wouldn't have happened if only you were more careful." Gordon refers to these statements as "roadblocks to communication." The responses teachers make when children are troubled often block further communication by making children feel "bad," "stupid," or "untrustworthy." As a result they often withdraw completely, fight back, or become resentful and angry. These are some roadblocks Gordon describes:[31]

1. *Ordering, Commanding, Directing.* By giving children direct, forceful orders ("I don't care if it's snowing; sit down and finish your work") teachers often produce fear of their power.
2. *Warning, Threatening.* These messages are like commands, but consequences are added: "If you don't finish your work I'm going to keep you in for recess all week." Again, they allude to the teacher's use of power.
3. *Moralizing, Preaching.* These messages communicate to students that the teacher is always right and because of this wisdom, the children should rely on her judgment: "You have to learn one important thing; good boys never tell lies."
4. *Lecturing, Arguing, Giving logical arguments.* These methods try to influence students with lengthy, one-sided interpretations of facts or opinions.
5. *Judging, Criticizing.* Characterized as put-down messages, these statements denigrate students and chip away at self-esteem: "You're acting like a bunch of wild animals today," or "You are always the one who starts trouble around here."
6. *Praising, Agreeing, Giving positive evaluations.* While most teachers understand the terrible power of *negative* statements, they are often shocked to hear that praise is not always beneficial to children. A positive statement that does not match a child's self-image is often interpreted as a subtle attempt to manipulate; absence of praise in a classroom normally loaded with it may be interpreted as punishment; praise is sometimes embarrassing when given publicly ("Janie is the only one who got a perfect paper"). Students who are praised a lot may become overdependent upon it.
7. *Name-calling, Ridiculing.* These are forms of negative evaluation that have a devastating effect on children: "I never taught a class of babies before."
8. *Probing, Questioning.* Sometimes questions convey lack of trust or have the effect of putting a child in a corner: "How long did you work on that report? Only two class periods? Well, no wonder it was not what I expected."
9. *Sarcasm, Humoring.* When children have a problem, they need to talk about it and are generally serious about it. They need respect; if faced with distractions, they will take their problems elsewhere: "Are you a clown today, Al? Well, fold up your tent and take your act elsewhere."

Instead of roadblocks, Gordon recommends that teachers demonstrate *acceptance* through a willingness to relate to and listen to the children. When children have problems, they need and want to share them; they need teachers to *listen*—not talk—to them. "But I *do* listen to my children," most teachers claim. Surely, listening does help children open up and share their inner feelings, but TET promotes an even more effective strategy: *active listening,* a way of responding to a child that is new and at first strange to many teachers. To understand active listening, we must first examine the communication process.

Any message emitted by an individual can be interpreted as a coded effort to describe her inner state. What the listener hears is the listener's *personal interpretation* (decoding) of the sender's message.

In Figure 14–5, the teacher "hears" the child's statement as a neutral request for information. Actually, however, this student is feeling anxiety because he fears alligators and realizes he may have to look at the reptiles. Obviously, he must communicate this fear by going through the process of encoding, or selecting verbal symbols to describe an inner state. We are supposing he chose the verbal code represented in Figure 14–5a, the direct question: "Are we going to the zoo today?" The receiver of the coded message must then attempt to decode it—to understand the meaning of the message and respond accordingly (Figure 14–5b). While the receiver *infers* the meaning of the message, she cannot be sure whether she is right or wrong because the receiver "cannot read the sender's mind." Therefore, you need to determine the accuracy of your decoding effort. This determination is the heart of active listening. All you need to do is *feed back* the results of your decoding, as in Figure 14–5c. Paraphrased "feedback" of the child's message is intended to open up lines of communication by creating a safe psychological environment in which children realize their needs have been heard, you

FIGURE 14–5
Message Codes

(a) Encoder Decoder (b) (c)

want to hear more, and the concern will be dealt with. Hearing feedback (Figure 14–5c), the child would probably say, "That's right, but I'm afraid of alligators." Feedback, then, helped clarify the child's original reason for asking the question and might have led to a conversation like this:

TEACHER: Oh, you're worried that we'll stop at the alligators.
CHILD: Yes. I don't like to look at them. They're scary.
TEACHER: When we get to the alligator house you can stay with Mrs. Martin at the tigers. Is that okay?
CHILD: What a relief! I'm not worried now.

The skill of active listening takes much practice, but it is an extremely valuable technique of conflict resolution. It provides a model of joint problem solving within a democratic environment in which people are free to think, explore, and share feelings.

A Teacher's Problem

It is one thing to become effective in helping children deal with *their* problems, but what should be the democratic teacher's role when chidlren give *her* problems—when children are being noisy or disruptive, for example. When children have a problem, you communicate your willingness to relate to and listen to them. Now, when *you* have a problem—when your needs or rights are being violated—you must communicate to the children what you are feeling without sending a message of condemnation. The *wrong* way to communicate your feelings is by what Gordon calls "You-Messages":

"You're a real bunch of monkeys today."

"You better stop that right now!"

"You act so foolish when you do that."

"You better grow up and act your age."

These messages are predictably useless—they make the child resist change, damage self-esteem, and often lead to resentment. With TET, teachers learn to send different messages that maintain leadership responsibility, get the point across, and avoid hurting the child's feelings. Gordon calls these messages "I-Messages." Effective I-Messages have three basic elements:

1. Stating *what* (specific behavior) is creating a problem for the teacher: *"When the work materials are not returned to their proper places . . . "*
2. Clearly identifying the effect of the specific behavior on the teacher: "When the work materials are not returned to their proper places, *I have to waste a lot of my time putting them away . . . "*
3. Communicating the teacher's feelings that result from the condition or behavior: "When the work materials are not returned to their proper places, I have to waste a lot of my time putting them away and *often get frustrated.* "[32]

The sequence is important but not rigid. An I-Message in any order (or even with a part missing), if sincere, stands a good chance of being heard by the child as an honest and open statement. The intent is not to hurt or embarrass the child, but only to alert the child that you have a problem and are asking for help rather than inviting a confrontation. It demonstrates your trust in children and your acceptance of them as worthwhile individuals. Just as children understood your desire to help them with their problems through your active listening technique, they will learn to alter their problem behaviors out of consideration for your needs.

The techniques of active listening and I-Messages are foreign to teachers who view conflict resolution as win–lose confrontations. This approach implies a power struggle that builds resentment between teacher and children. One type of win–lose format is the teacher's constant use of a power-based authority role to reward or punish student behaviors; resentment flows from student to teacher as the teacher "wins" and child "loses." Other win–lose-oriented teachers look at conflict resolution as giving in to the children; teachers like this are manipulated and controlled by the children. When teachers, for whatever reason, are so permissive, they can be considered "losers" and the children "winners." Resentment then flows from teacher to children. These teachers eventually develop coping behaviors such as escapism, not associating with peers, or resigning. Instead of these two potentially damaging win–lose confrontations, Gordon proposes a *no-lose* conflict resolution method.

No-lose methods are employed whenever the I-Message or active listening techniques fail. When this happens, the temptation is often to moralize or lecture; instead, the teacher must change the approach. Gordon calls this approach Method III, or the no-lose process of working through a conflict from beginning to end, during which teacher and children put their heads together to search for possible solutions.

In this example, Mr. Marshall and his student, Alice, use Method III to resolve a classroom conflict:

MR. MARSHALL: Alice, when your group talks so loudly it makes it difficult for me to concentrate on helping Gary with his model, and I feel it's unfair to him. (I-Message because teacher owns problem)

ALICE: But you asked us to finish our project by next week and we have to talk so we can get our plans straight. (Expresses own problem)

MR. MARSHALL: I see. You're talking so loudly because you're concerned about the time you have left for completing your project. (Active listening)

ALICE: Yes. We have to finish up our research by Tuesday or we won't have time to plan our skit to show the rest of the class on Thursday.

MR. MARSHALL: It sounds like you're under some real pressure, but I also feel pressure to help Gary. We have a real problem. Do you have any ideas about how we can solve it?

ALICE: Well . . . would it be okay for our group to work in the library? It's always empty during this hour and the librarian said she is willing to let us work there by ourselves if she's there.

MR. MARSHALL: That would sure solve the problem. Alice, you go down the hall and check with Ms. Lawrence to see if it's okay with her.

Notice how the teacher used all the skills of democratic conflict resolution we have talked about so far. When both needs were known, it was not difficult for Alice and Mr.

Marshall to find a solution without forcing either party to resort to power. They both "won." Method III of conflict resolution is a six-step problem-solving process:

1. Define the problem (make sure both parties understand it)
2. Generate possible solutions (be open-ended; do not evaluate proposed solutions yet)
3. Evaluate the solutions (both parties state their opinions and preferences)
4. Make the decision (if steps 1, 2, and 3 are followed, step 4 usually results in a solution; if it does not, do not vote, but try to work toward consensus—invite both parties to try things out and, if they do not work, to reconsider and change)
5. Implement the decision (determine *who* does *what* and *when;* the failure of problem-solving efforts is usually attributable to lack of sound implementation)
6. Assess the solution (check on the effectiveness of your efforts: Has the problem gone away? Are we happy with our decision? How did our decision work out?)[33]

Skills in positive conflict resolution will help you as a teacher not only in the ways they contribute to effective classroom management but also in how they model the highest ideals of humanitarianism and democracy. You may want to do further reading in Teacher Effectiveness Training or other techniques for developing your skills as a democratic teacher. Become aware of workshops that teach these skills and explain their uses and abuses. Strive to become a model of the democratic processes you profess to your children. It will help you gain a new perspective on children and help your children gain a new perspective on their world.

Classroom Constitution

As children experience the dynamics of a democratic classroom, they should become involved in activities that help them apply their understandings to society in general. In a democratic society everyone is bound by the rules and laws fairly established by its members. To help make this connection, one teacher extended a discussion of the United States Constitution by encouraging the students to create their own classroom constitution (see Figure 14–6).

A democratic system gives us freedoms and, at the same time, limits our freedoms—rules and laws balance and protect personal or group interests and rights. To clarify children's ideas about democratic functioning, the classroom must reflect "regulated freedom." An appreciation for regulation within a democratic framework presupposes acceptance of the principles that underlie those regulations: (1) rules and laws reflect social values; (2) rules and laws are created to regulate human behavior; and (3) rules and laws assume voluntary compliance. Elementary school social studies programs should encourage examination of those principles through both direct activities and informal interactions.

Clearly, social studies is more than the sum of the social sciences. It is an area of the elementary school curriculum into which timely topics for learning about the world and its people should be introduced throughout the year. We should meet this responsibility with enthusiasm and become challenged to formulate policies that give all students a chance to learn about the problems and issues that, if properly resolved, have the potential for making our communities and nation better places in which to live.

FIGURE 14–6
Classroom Constitution

Grade Six Constitution

We the students of Grade 6, Room 14, in order to form a more perfect class, do establish this *Constitution of the Sixth Grade.*

ARTICLE 1. OFFICIALS

1. There will be two branches of our government: the *executive branch* and the *legislative branch.*
2. The executive branch is made up of the President, Vice-president, Secretary, and Treasurer.
3. The legislative branch is made up of all of the rest of the members of the class.
4. Two candidates each for the offices of President, Vice-President, Secretary, and Treasurer shall be nominated the Friday before the third Monday of each month.
5. Election of officers shall take place the third Monday of every month by secret ballot.
6. A student may hold a term of office only once.

ARTICLE II. QUALIFICATIONS OF OFFICERS

1. Everyone automatically becomes a member of the legislative branch when he enters Room 14 as a student.
2. Students must have these qualifications to be an officer:
   a. must be a member of Room 14 for at least two weeks.
   b. must be honest and trustworthy.

ARTICLE III. DUTIES OF EXECUTIVE BRANCH

1. *President*
   a. The President shall run all class meetings.
   b. The President shall take charge of the class in the teacher's absence.
   c. The President shall help the substitute (show him or her where things are).
   d. The President shall appoint class helpers.
2. *Vice-President*
   a. The Vice-President shall help the President when necessary.
   b. In the absence of the President, the Vice-President shall take over.
3. *Secretary*
   a. The Secretary shall take notes at all class meetings.
   b. The Secretary shall take care of all class mail (letters, thank-you notes, etc.).
4. *Treasurer*
   a. The Treasurer shall take care of all class funds.

ARTICLE IV. DUTIES OF LEGISLATIVE BRANCH

1. To approve, by majority vote, class helper assignments.
2. To approve, by majority vote, any decision for which the class is responsible.
3. To volunteer for class helper assignments:
   a. clean chalkboard
   b. feed fish
   c. water plants
   d. pass out papers
   e. take lunch count
   f. serve as class librarian
   g. greet room visitors
   h. keep art materials orderly
   i. check attendance
   j. run errands
4. To approve, by two-thirds vote, any amendment to this constitution.

continued

FIGURE 14–6
continued

ARTICLE V. PRESIDENTIAL VACANCY
The Vice-President shall take over if the President's office is vacant, followed by the Secretary, and then the Treasurer.

ARTICLE VI. CLASS MEETINGS
Meetings shall be held each Friday from 2:30–3:00 P.M.

ARTICLE VII. AMENDMENTS
1. An amendment may be proposed by any member of the class.
2. An amendment must be approved by two-thirds vote of the legislative branch.

Amendments

AMENDMENT 1.
An elected official shall temporarily give up any classroom helper jobs held during his or her term of office. (Approved: February 10)

AIDS EDUCATION

AIDS is clearly the most deadly epidemic we have faced in this century; as of May 1990 132,510 adults and over 2,258 children had contracted AIDS in the United States.[34] AIDS, which stands for Acquired Immune Deficiency Syndrome, is a disease characterized by loss of immunity against other infections. An individual may carry the HIV (human immunodeficiency virus) infection in his blood for a prolonged period without actually showing symptoms of the disease himself. An infected person can, however, spread the AIDS virus to others through certain forms of sexual contact (73% of current U.S. AIDS cases are homosexual or bisexual men), sharing intravenous needles (4% of classified U.S. cases), transfusions of contaminated blood (2%), and the birthing process (1% of cases were transmitted from infected mothers to their babies). Three percent of cases cannot be classified because of insufficient information[35] and the remainder were multiple risk exposures. At least 280,000 new cases of AIDS are expected by 1991, with the rate doubling each year.[36] Obviously, our nation is in the midst of an AIDS crisis; as educators, we must address the problem now. Our role is particularly important because there are no effective vaccines or drugs that cure AIDS; our only defense is to prevent and control the spread of the disease by offering concerted educational programs. Former Surgeon General C. Everett Koop has called for explicit, mandatory AIDS education beginning with 8-year-olds; many school districts have instituted educational programs. Several states including Rhode Island, Kansas, Oklahoma, and Pennsylvania already require AIDS education in their schools; others are likely to follow.

Teachers are faced with a great challenge in dealing with AIDS education. M. Patricia Fetter notes that many educators are unsure how to approach this challenge because

> [M]ost have limited formal sexuality education to prepare them to present information to pupils. . . . The language necessary for delivering accurate information about AIDS includes many words, phrases and behavior descriptors that adults may hesitate to use in a

classroom setting. Cognitive information is not enough. Focus must be on respect for life, dignity, decision-making and societal values.[37]

Carol Levine[38] advises that our uncertainty about AIDS education can be greatly alleviated by learning more about this deadly disease. Informative publications have been composed to help teachers learn more about AIDS so they are better able to pass on information to their students. The National Education Association's helpful handbook *The Facts About AIDS*[39] contains current information about AIDS and encourages teachers to educate students about avoiding behaviors that put them at risk. C. Everett Koop's *Surgeon General's Report on Acquired Immune Deficiency Syndrome*[40] is a comprehensive source of basic information.

Understandably, adolescents have a higher risk of contracting AIDS and are in need of direct education about the disease. Most elementary school youngsters are not yet sexually active, nor are most involved in the abuse of IV drugs, so the information we share with them must by carefully chosen. We do not want them to form serious misconceptions such as that "sex will kill you" or that a cut may "poison your blood"; children may be unable to understand concepts of sexuality and blood contamination. Indeed, the greatest exposure to AIDS among elementary school youngsters may be in facing the loss of a parent through AIDS, or in having an AIDS-infected classmate. In both cases, the teacher's role is primarily one of support and education. Patsy Sheen and Diane Hodson[41] examined these concerns and offer the following recommendations:

1. *Coping when a parent of a child in your classroom has AIDS.* We have learned that 85 percent of all people with AIDS will most probably face death unless a miracle cure is developed. Thus, the child faces the likely lingering death of the infected parent. Your role in such a case is primarily to give support. First, the child faces a strong possibility of being ostracized by other children. Educate your children about AIDS—it is not possible for others to get it from an uninfected relative of a patient.

Second, the child will experience the steadily failing health of the parent. Find out how much the child has been told, and if the child knows the parent's condition, help her cope with her feelings of sadness or anger. Take the first step and invite the child to talk—empathize with each feeling the child expresses.

2. *Dealing with a child thought to have been exposed to AIDS.* What are the risks of contagion in the school setting? According to the Surgeon General's report, no cases of AIDS have been attributed to skin contact or biting. Holding hands, hugging, sharing a water fountain, and sitting on a toilet seat are known to be safe. However, exposure of the mucous membranes to infected fluids may be contagious. Although it is difficult to prove absolutely that any given form of contact *cannot* transmit an infectious disease such as AIDS, to date, *no* cases of transmittal of AIDS through casual person-to-person contact have been reported.

The greatest risk of having AIDS-infected children in the classroom is to the infected children themselves. Because they have diminished immunity against a variety of common infections, school classrooms could be life-threatening to people with AIDS. Still, the risk to the patient of exposure to such infections must be judged by the child's physician. Parents and professionals must weigh the need for protection of the child against the emotional need to lead a normal life with children of his own age.

Effective AIDS instruction must rest on scientific, age-appropriate foundations. Tell children that AIDS is a serious disease; that, despite all they have heard about AIDS, their chances of getting it are very, very small. Few elementary grade children will ask for more than that. When young children ask questions about scary things, they do so mainly to be assured that they are safe. They don't want a lengthy medical explanation or a discourse on sex or drugs. If a child does press, inform her that AIDS is caused by a virus, a tiny germ.

M. Patricia Fetter[42] suggests that AIDS education can be addressed through immediate in-service training for all teachers. Workshops should be designed to disseminate information about AIDS, allay fears and misconceptions, dismiss bias and prejudice, and, in some cases, to change attitudes and behaviors. Fetter also advises that each school system appoint an AIDS educator responsible for coordinating educational programs throughout the district.

AIDS is a killer; the mortality rate of those diagnosed with the full syndrome is projected to be 100%. Health officials consistently warn that we cannot presently control the spread of AIDS without concerted educational programs and that one of the most critical settings is the classroom. Assume the responsibility to prepare yourself for this critical task, for your efforts may be influential in preventing a life of pain, anguish, and early death for one or more of your students.

DRUG AND ALCOHOL EDUCATION

Every community in our nation—regardless of size or economic status—has faced serious consequences related to drug and alcohol abuse. Children as young as nine years old are being treated for alcoholism;[43] teen drinkers account for nearly 50% of all fatal automobile accidents.[44] The United States had the highest rate of illicit drug use of any industrialized nation in the world.[45] The average American who does not have a drug problem will pay between $850 and $1000 next year to treat drug and alcohol abuse problems in taxes, health insurance, and increased costs of goods and services. In contrast, only about $1.75 will be spent in the same year on each child to prevent drug use.[46]

We are living in an era when politicians and educators have directed intense concern toward drug abuse prevention. A number of educational approaches have been developed to prevent drug and alcohol abuse. Several are directed toward children of elementary school age, the period when patterns of drug or alcohol abuse begin for many. William B. Hansen reports, for example, that the onset of substance abuse is predictable. Among preadolescents, the use of "gateway drugs" (tobacco, alcohol, and marijuana) commonly starts the pattern. About 10% of fifth graders drink alcohol during any given month; about 5% will have smoked or used tobacco; about 2% will have used marijuana.[47] These young people who begin on gateway drugs in elementary school are more likely to use "hard" drugs (cocaine, PCP, heroin) as they move into middle school and high school. This is why drug abuse prevention education is especially important in elementary schools. By high school, most young people who use drugs have established their pattern, and the opportunity for the most influential education is over. All 50 states now have laws requiring educational programs directed toward drug abuse prevention. The resulting programs include several crucial components:[48]

1. *Peer pressure resistance training.* The single best predictor of drug or alcohol abuse appears to be an inability to withstand peer pressure. To rectify this, programs explain the power of peer pressure and teach students how to cope with it.
2. *Normative education.* Students are presented factual information describing the true rates and effects of drug use. This is done to counter the misconceptions that "Everyone is doing it," and that drug use is an acceptable part of growing up. Programs attempt to influence perception of drug use as odd behavior and nonuse as desirable behavior.
3. *Inoculation against mass media messages.* Programs help students analyze the messages that advertisers use to promote the use of tobacco and alcohol. To a lesser degree, students are given opportunities to examine messages about drugs, tobacco, and alcohol communicated in movies, popular music, and television programs.
4. *Parent influences.* Many programs include information about parents' influence on children's drug and alcohol abuse. The message usually advises that children should not use drugs even if their parents do. In addition, some programs operate with an awareness that, because of the family's powerful role in determining children's behaviors, drug and alcohol abuse prevention must directly address family functioning (child-rearing skills). Education must be extended to the parents; they must learn techniques of positive, child-centered interaction that are likely to lead to more prosocial behavior throughout the period of preadolescence and adolescence.

The problem of drug and alcohol abuse is so pervasive that no single approach can hope to solve it. Each community and school must recognize the problem and courageously attack it with an all-out effort. We have found that one-dimensional or narrowly focused programs do not work. Those mainly emphasizing *information* about the harmful effects of drugs fail to change the behaviors of our youth. Young people operate with a conviction of "perceived personal immunity";[49] they deny that the harmful effects can happen to them personally. Those programs that mainly emphasize *self-concept* have used affective strategies to promote higher levels of self-esteem. The theory was that higher self-esteem would lessen the incidence of drug abuse; unfortunately, these types of school-based approaches have proved inadequate.

One comprehensive prevention program that encourages active school and community involvement has recently been evaluated and found successful in the often discouraging area of childhood substance abuse prevention. *Growing Healthy* was formulated by the American Lung Association and financed by the Centers for Disease Control. It has been adopted in 696 school districts in 41 states. Tracking students from kindergarten through grade 9, the study achieved the following results when students enrolled in the programs were compared to control groups:

- a reduced percentage of students used alcohol on a regular basis;
- students expressed stronger beliefs that they would not drink alcohol as adults;

- a reduced percentage of them had tried drugs;
- students expressed stronger beliefs that they would not try drugs as adults;
- a reduced percentage used tobacco products on a regular basis.[50]

Classroom materials are available for each grade level. For more information on *Growing Healthy,* contact your community office of the American Lung Association or the National Center for Health Education, 30 East 29th Street, New York, NY 10016.

Drug and alcohol abuse prevention must be central in the minds of teachers. We have compelling ethical responsibilities on behalf of all children and their families; our efforts through appropriate programs can make a difference in preventing drug and alcohol abuse. The happiness and perhaps the very lives of our children may depend on the successful implementation of sound substance abuse programs.

SUMMARY

The social studies program includes much more than the skills and understanding normally associated with the social sciences. Because it deals with all the factors believed to acccount for effective citizenship, the social studies curriculum is the logical place to include the challenges of topics especially meaningful to our culture. To present material on all of those possible topics is beyond the scope of this book, but several were offered as examples: current affairs instruction, global education, environmental education, multicultural education, career education, law-related education, AIDS education, drug and alcohol education.

In this chapter you learned that current affairs instruction provides learning experiences that help students interpret news accounts, make critical evaluations of them, commit themselves to a position on an issue, anticipate its future consequences, develop a lifelong interest in current events, and relate current topics to regular social studies topics.

Global education is emphasized because we are facing so many problems today that concern that whole human race, rather than isolated groups of people. Global interdependence must be taken seriously by social studies educators with overall program goals of (1) presenting accurate information about people around the

world, (2) using a variety of materials, (3) stressing a global community rather than just the Western world, (4) emphasizing likenesses as well as differences among people of the world, and (5) beginning with the immediate classroom situation.

Environmental education concerns the ruination of our physical environment through people's disregard of sound ecological practices. The emphasis of environmental education in the elementary school is on learning about the environment and its problems, as well as on developing respect for the quality of the environment.

Multicultural education seeks to go beyond the dominant Anglo-American focus of social studies education toward attention to the contributions and culture of the African American, Native American, Hispanic American, and Asian American sectors. This process must offer a balanced view of America's past and present that equips students with the skills of analyzing and appreciating the participation of all groups to the evolution of our society.

Career education has emerged as a result of concern that schools were not preparing our nation's youth for the transition from school to the world of work. Various approaches to career education have been proposed, but the most popular philosophy appears to center on these goals:

(1) developing a positive attitude toward self, (2) developing an awareness of work roles and related life-styles, (3) developing interpersonal skills, (4) developing decision-making skills, and (5) acquiring respect for workers and the workplace.

Law-related education centers on the development of an understanding that laws are political decisions that influence society's rules, goals, or social behavior. As such, the emphasis of classroom instruction is placed on decision making and involvement in the governing process.

Another serious social condition directly affecting our youth is AIDS. The spread of this deadly disease has become a subject of great attention and concern. The topic should not be avoided in elementary school classrooms, for most children have heard of AIDS and may be confused about its nature. Accurate information about the disease must be shared, and particular sensitivity must be present if AIDS affects children in a classroom in either of two ways: (1) a parent of a child in your room (or school) has AIDS, or (2) a child may have been infected by the AIDS virus.

The social consciousness concerning drug use has run deep in our nation; tobacco use and drug and alcohol abuse are in the news each day. The medical evidence about the harm done by these substances is overwhelming, but many of our youth are not convinced that *they* are vulnerable to the harmful effects. Our schools must, in their policies and practices, exemplify a healthful vision of society so that our youth are not hooked on fantasy and illusion, but develop an accurate concept of who they are, what they want to become, and how they might get there.

ENDNOTES

1. National Council for the Social Studies, "Revision of NCSS Social Studies Curriculum Guidelines," *Social Education, 43,* no. 4 (April 1979): 263.

2. Marion Brady, "Memo from Your Students' Minds," *Social Education, 49,* no. 2 (February 1985): 163.

3. Mike Bowler, "The Making of a Textbook," *Learning, 6,* no. 7 (March 1978): 40–41.

4. Anne M. Blackburn, "Teaching About the Global Environment," *Social Education, 49,* no. 3 (March 1985): 199–200.

5. Jan L. Tucker, "Social Studies for the 21st Century," *Social Education, 52,* no. 3 (March 1988): 213.

6. Chapman et al., "Position Statement on Global Education," *Social Education, 46,* no. 1 (January 1982): 36–38.

7. James A. Banks, "Education for Survival in a Multicultural World," *Social Studies and the Young Learner, 1,* no. 4 (March/April 1989): 3.

8. Ibid.

9. Ibid., p. 4.

10. Jan L. Tucker, "Social Studies for the 21st Century," p. 210.

11. Carol Seefeldt, *Social Studies for the Preschool-Primary Child,* 3rd ed. (Columbus, OH: Merrill, 1989), pp. 206–209.

12. Edith W. King, ed., *The World: Context for Teaching in the Elementary School* (Dubuque, IA: William C. Brown, 1971), pp. 5–6.

13. Cheryl Charles, "Using the Natural World to Teach and Learn Globally," *Social Education, 49,* no. 3 (March 1985): 213.

14. Margaret Mead, "Creating a Scientific Climate for Children," in Cheryl Charles and Bob Samples, eds., *Science and Society: Knowing, Teaching, Learning* (Washington, DC: National Council for the Social Studies, 1978).

15. Mary E. Hawkins et al., "Editors' Declaration on Interdisciplinary Environmental Education," *Social Education, 39,* no. 2 (February 1975): 72–73.

16. Ina Corrine Brown, *Understanding Other Cultures* (Englewood Cliffs, NJ: Prentice-Hall, 1963), p. 3.

17. Donna M. Gollnick and Philip C. Chinn, *Multicultural Education in a Pluralistic Society,* 2nd ed. (Columbus, OH: Merrill, 1986), p. 6.

18. C. Kluckhohn, *Mirror for Man: The Relation of Anthropology to Modern Life* (New York: McGraw-Hill, 1949), p. 19.

19. Gollnick and Chinn, *Multicultural Education,* p. 13.

20. William W. Joyce, "Minority Groups in American Society: Imperatives for Educators and Publishers," in *Readings in Elementary Social Studies: Emerging Changes,* 2nd ed., ed. Jonathan C. McLendon, William W. Joyce, and John R. Lee (Boston: Allyn and Bacon, 1970), pp. 289–290.

21. James A. Banks, *Teaching Strategies for Ethnic Studies* (Boston: Allyn and Bacon, 1975), p. 9.

22. Larry Cuban, "Black History, Negro History, and White Folk," *Saturday Review* (September 21, 1968): 64–65.

23. Banks, *Teaching Strategies for Ethnic Studies,* p. 9.

24. Cuban, "Black History, Negro History, and White Folk," pp. 64–65.

25. Edith W. King, *Teaching Ethnic Awareness* (Santa Monica, CA: Goodyear, 1980), p. 20.

26. Edna Genise Lewis, "Spotlight of the Week," in *Words into Action: A Classroom Guide to Children's Citizenship Education* (Philadelphia: Research for Better Schools, Inc., 1979), p. 41.

27. Lorraine Sundal Hansen and W. Wesley Tennyson, "Career Development as Self Development: Humanizing the Focus for Career Education," *Social Education, 39,* no. 5 (May 1975): 305.

28. Donald E. Super, "The Individual and His Environment," (paper presented at Ohio Conference on Guidelines for Implementing Career Development Through Curriculum, K–12, Ohio Department of Education, and The Ohio State University, June 6, 1971), in Lorraine Sundal Hansen and W. Wesley Tennyson, "Career Development as Self Development: Humanizing the Focus for Career Education," *Social Education, 39,* no. 5 (May 1975): 306.

29. Gregory Logacz, Suzanne Laurich, and Elaine Hummel, "Career Development: Applications to the Elementary Classroom," *Social Education, 30,* no. 5 (May 1975): 313–315.

30. Marie Winn, *Shiver, Gobble, and Snore* (New York: Simon and Schuster, 1972).

31. Thomas Gordon, *T.E.T.: Teacher Effectiveness Training* (New York: Peter H. Wyden/Publisher, 1974), pp. 80–87.

32. Ibid, pp. 142–144.

33. Ibid., pp. 227–234.

34. Centers for Disease Control statistics.

35. American Red Cross and U.S. Public Health Service, *AIDS, Sex, and You* (Latest Facts about AIDS Series), October 1986.

36. J. M. Ismach, "AIDS: Can the Nation Cope?" *Medical World News, 26,* (1985): 46–71.

37. M. Patricia Fetter, "AIDS Education: Every Teacher's Responsibility," *Childhood Education, 65,* no. 3 (Spring 1989): 150.

38. Carol Levine, "AIDS: Challenge to Science and Society." Symposium at the University of Georgia (November 1985).

39. N. Bauer et al., *The Facts About AIDS* (Washington, DC: National Education Association Health Information Network, 1987).

40. U.S. Department of Health and Human Services, *Surgeon General's Report on Acquired Immune Deficiency Syndrome* (Washington, DC: U.S. Government Printing Office, 1986).

41. Patsy Sheen and Diane Hodson, "AIDS: What Adults Should Know About AIDS," *Young Children, 42,* no. 4 (May 1987): 65–71.

42. M. Patricia Fetter, "AIDS Education: Every Teacher's Responsibility," pp. 151–152.

43. Lowell Horton, *Adolescent Alcohol Abuse* (Bloomington, IN: Phi Delta Kappa, 1985).

44. D. Sherhouse, *Adolescent Drug and Alcohol Abuse Handbook* (Springfield, IL: Charles C. Thomas, 1985).

45. L. D. Johnston, P. M. O'Malley, and J. G. Bachman, *Drug Abuse Among American High School Students, College Students, and Other Young Adults* (Washington, DC: National Institute of Drug Abuse, 1988).

46. William B. Hansen, "Effective School-Based Approaches to Drug Abuse Prevention," *Educational Leadership, 45,* no. 6 (March 1988): 9.

47. Ibid., p. 9.

48. Ibid., pp. 12–13

49. Ibid., p. 11.

50. David D. Moore, "Growing Healthy: An Effective Substance Abuse Preventive Program," *Educational Leadership, 45,* no. 6 (March 1988): 13.

In the United States today, standardized testing is running amok. Newspapers rank schools and districts by their test scores. Real estate agents use test scores to identify the "best" schools as selling points for expensive housing. Superintendents can be fired for low scores, and teachers can receive merit pay for high scores. Superintendents exhort principals and principals admonish teachers to raise the test scores—rather than to increase learning.[1]

—Lorrie A. Shepard

15 Evaluating Teaching and Learning

As you read, reflect on the following matters:

- What is meant by measurement? Standardized achievement tests? Norm-referenced tests? Criterion-referenced tests? Formative evaluation? Summative evaluation?

- How has "test consciousness" influenced school curricula and teaching practices?

- What are some abuses of tests? How should test results be used?

- What are some proper uses of teacher-made tests? How should teacher-made tests be constructed?

- What is the difference between assessment and testing?

- How can teacher observation be used as a valid source of evaluation in the social studies program?

- What special attention should be provided to children assessed as gifted?

- How should the program be adjusted for children assessed as handicapped?

Teaching involves evaluation—making hundreds of judgments based upon personal and professional values:

"Is my class ready for independent study projects?"

"Will Adam do better if I slow down the pace a bit?"

"Is this book a good choice to read to my class?"

"Should Melissa get an *A* or a *B* in social studies this marking period?"

"On what basis will I assign the grades—tests? Student projects? Improvement?"

Our consideration of these questions is aided by information from a variety of sources, the most dominant being *measurement techniques.* Measurement results provide the data for making decisions about assigning grades, motivating students, discovering learning problems, or deciding how to modify instructional practices to meet individual and group needs. Measurement can provide teachers with a wealth of objective data on which to base evaluative decisions. However, measurement processes have often been abused. Pearl M. Oliner[2] describes the proper use of measurement as its "overt functions"—doing with it what we say we are doing. The facilitation of learning and diagnosis of learning disabilities are examples of overt functions. However, measurement is often subverted to its "covert function"—inappropriate use. For example, labeling students and seeking to become the highest-scoring school in the district are covert functions. These covert functions are receiving considerable attention today, especially as they contribute to the fallibility of standardized achievement tests.

STANDARDIZED ACHIEVEMENT TESTS

Delivering quality social studies instruction involves evaluating student achievement before, during and at the conclusion of instruction. On the whole, tests that measure achievement are of two types: standardized and teacher-made. *Standardized tests* are those official-looking booklets purchased by school districts "in which the procedure, apparatus, and scoring have been fixed so precisely that the same testing procedures can be followed at different times and places."[3] Anita E. Woolfolk and Lorraine McCune Nicolich describe the standardization process:

> All items included in the test have been tried out on students, rewritten if unclear, and tried again. The final version of the test is then administered to a *norming* sample, a large sample of subjects as similar as possible to the students who will be taking the test in school systems throughout the country. This norming sample serves as a comparison group for all the students who later take the test.[4]

While norm-referenced tests compose an overall portrait of your students compared to a large national sample, they do not provide a valid measure of whether your students have mastered the understandings and skills defined in your specific social studies program. Nevertheless, because of the great weight assigned to standardized achievement tests by the public, tests often dictate changes in the curriculum. Carol Livingston, Sharon Castle, and Jimmy Nations describe the negative aspect of standardized testing on the curriculum:

> State-mandated standardized tests have a profound influence on the curriculum. . . . As one teacher put it, "Getting kids to perform well on the test is *the* top priority. In Georgia, test scores are published and schools and systems are compared by their scores." The message from the public, policy-makers, and the central administration has been to raise test scores. In short, the test "actually is the foundation of our curriculum."[5]

Standardized test pressures also affect the teachers. One first-year teacher described her experience:

> I was petrified that my class would do so poorly that I wouldn't be back next year. So I taught what the other teachers recommended to get them ready for the test. After the test I started teaching, *good* teaching. The class enjoyed it, and I think they learned more the last three weeks of school than they did the first six months, because I was more relaxed, the students were more relaxed, and I was able to hone in on those areas where they needed help.[6]

The demands felt by this teacher were so intense because of public pressure for *accountability*. Teachers at all levels are being pressured to prove that what they are doing produces significant results. That idea by itself sounds reasonable, but the underlying premise is that schools alone are accountable for a student's education. All other contributing factors—family, peers, television, movies, book publishers, and others—are not considered accountable. James L. Hymes, Jr., uses a medical analogy to make this injustice clearer:

> Imagine an automobile accident in which the driver is badly injured. Is it fair to hold the doctor alone accountable for whether the driver's life is saved? Does it make any difference how badly injured the victim is? Does the victim's previous health make any difference? . . . Does it make any difference whether the driver wants to live? Or whether the doctor can treat the patient in a well-equipped hospital or do the best that can be done at the accident scene?[7]

Hymes concludes that doctors, indeed, *should* be held accountable, but not for the *outcome*; there are too many variables involved. Instead, they should be held accountable for *input*—doing all that is possible for them to do. Likewise, accountability for teachers should be redirected to focus on input rather than outcome. Certainly, testing has an important role to play in providing a high quality social studies program to young children, but the sanctions or rewards placed on the test outcomes themselves are what concern most educators today. George F. Madaus explains:

> When important things like graduation, promotion from grade to grade, teacher evaluation, school district certification, and financial support—major aspects of accountability affecting teaching or administrators—depend directly on test scores, it corrupts the process you're trying to improve.[8]

Madaus refers to the process resulting in such sanctions or rewards as "high-stakes testing"; when the stakes are high, people will go to extremes to raise the scores. To make his point, Madaus shares a story involving airplane schedules:

> When the Federal Aviation Commission started to publish arrival times of airlines—who was late and who wasn't—within six weeks the airlines added a half hour to each schedule. I used to fly into Washington in 60 minutes; now it's scheduled to be an hour-and-a-half flight.[9]

Just as the airlines manipulate time schedules to make themselves look good, some educators will find ways to raise the test scores, too. That is what bothers many professionals today. Inevitably, teachers are pressured to teach to the test; the curriculum is skewed to ensure that students memorize facts and figures that can easily be measured on a standardized multiple-choice test. Challenging intellectual activities such as problem solving and creative thinking are deemphasized; learning centers, literature, art, and music are eliminated to make more time for daily informational drills. This pressure on teachers has resulted in what is popularly called the "dribble-down" disease, a condition where the curriculum becomes so concentrated that it is developmentally inappropriate. For example, much of what used to be taught in third grade is now found in second; significant portions of curriculum have dropped to a lower grade level for first exposure. As a result, failure rates have increased and children are subject to undue stress related to labeling ("You're in the dummy class," or "You have to be pretty dumb to flunk second grade.").

With the discussion so far, you may be ready to ask, "Is standardized testing ever appropriate for the social studies program?" The answer is a qualified, "Yes—if the tests are not asked to do too much." We must remove all incentives to "teach to the test" and not place undue emphasis on raising test scores. If a truly beneficial result for the child is not evident, tests do not serve a constructive purpose.

Criterion-Referenced Tests

Standardized tests are commonly classified into two major categories: norm-referenced and criterion-referenced. Norm-referenced tests help teachers, administrators, and parents compare their children's performance to the performance of other students around the country. Criterion-referenced tests, on the other hand, remove the comparison feature by describing only the extent to which an individual student has mastered any particular body of content or set of skills. Woolfolk and Nicolich offer this example of criterion-referenced performance:

> In deciding who should be allowed to drive a car it is important to determine just what standard of performance is appropriate to ensure that people who meet that standard will in all likelihood be safe drivers. In getting a license it does not matter how your performance compares to the performance of others. The important question is how does your performance compare to the standard specifying how good is good enough to be behind the wheel. If your performance on the test was better than that of 90 percent of the peo-

ple who took the test but you consistently ran through red lights, you would not be a good candidate for receiving a license, even though your score was high.[10]

Standards for criterion-referenced testing are very specific, usually having a direct link with behavioral objectives (see Chapter 3). When teachers state an objective behaviorally, they contend that it will be used as a standard by which achievement will be measured. For example, suppose a teacher listed this behavioral objective at the beginning of her instruction: "Given a list of ten states, the students will correctly identify their capitals with 90% accuracy." Following the instruction, then, the teacher could offer a fill-in-the-blanks or matching test to determine whether or not the criterion has been met.

Some social studies teachers prefer criterion-referenced testing because it evaluates the acquisition of content and skills particular to their social studies curricula, rather than making comparisons of their students with a norming sample on the basis of content they may or may not have covered in their programs. Through this form, some teachers believe that the true value of the social studies program can be tested.

Detractors of criterion-referenced testing cite the tremendous time and effort it takes to break down learning episodes into extremely specific objectives. With all the other time-consuming responsibilities teachers face daily, these critics believe it is unrealistic for teachers to specifically delineate each possible learning outcome for social studies instruction. In addition, it is very difficult to write specific behavioral objectives for higher-level thinking skills. As a result teachers often limit their test items to low levels of cognition rather than higher levels such as hypothesizing, analyzing, and predicting.

All things considered, standardized testing can be a valuable evaluative tool if used for the overt function of providing *input*. Beware of its covert abuses and use the results judiciously. You may find it interesting to examine standardized test items for elementary school students. Consider these:

> *Primary Social Studies Test* (Grades 1–3)
> Ralph C. Preston and Robert V. Duffey, developers
> Houghton Mifflin Company
> 2 Park Street
> Boston, MA 02107
>
> *Metropolitan Achievement Tests* (Grades 5–6 and 7–9)
> Harcourt Brace Jovanovich, Inc.
> 757 Third Avenue
> New York, NY 10017
>
> *Iowa Tests of Education Development* (Grades 3–9)
> Science Research Associates
> 259 Erie Street
> Chicago, IL 60611

Standardized tests, if used properly, offer valuable knowledge of student performance in relation to either normative data or an established set of specific objectives. Standardized achievement tests cannot, however, be used in social studies classrooms each time teachers need important evaluative information. Teachers must instead create their own tests.

TEACHER-MADE ACHIEVEMENT TESTS

Of all the paper-pencil varieties of tests, teacher-made tests are the most commonly selected evaluative procedure found in social studies classrooms. The reason for their popularity is obvious: when overworked teachers invest a great deal of time and energy to create meaningful social studies learning experiences, they want to know if their efforts are constructive. Teacher-made tests also serve other functions well. Pearl M. Oliner identifies these functions:

1. To enable pupils and parents to judge performance (grading)
2. To group students for more efficient learning
3. To retain or promote students in order to facilitate learning
4. To motivate achievement
5. To diagnose learning disabilities
6. To modify course objectives in accordance with student needs
7. To modify instructional strategies, techniques, and resources[11]

When used for these purposes, teacher-made tests can yield considerable information about your program and student achievement. This feedback can be measured in either of two basic ways: formative evaluation or summative evaluation. Benjamin Bloom and his associates[12] divided measurements of achievement into these two categories so that teachers could more readily visualize evaluation as an integral part of the entire instructional sequence rather than only something that comes at the end.

Formative evaluation occurs prior to or during instruction. When used prior to instruction, its purpose is to inform the teacher of the children's levels of knowledge, skills, interests, and attitudes before the instruction actually begins. Usually in the form of a *pretest*, the information helps teachers adjust their instruction to meet the students' prior needs and interests. When used during instruction (*diagnostic tests*), formative evaluation helps identify those students who are not progressing as expected, so the teacher can make appropriate instructional adjustments. Formative evaluation can be easily associated with its function, because its data help teachers *form* plans for instruction.

Summative evaluation takes place at the end of a sequence of instruction to document the educational progress that has taken place. It is considered a *summary* of student and teacher accomplishment, and because instruction has ceased, is more useful for assessing final achievement (usually a grade) than for initiating changes in instruction.

The distinction between formative and summative evaluation lies more in how tests are used than in their form. As a matter of fact, it is possible to use the same test for either purpose. If the test is used prior to or during instruction, it is considered to be formative; at the end of a sequence of instruction to measure achievement, it is a summative test.

Constructing Teacher-Made Tests

Despite the many benefits of teacher-made tests, they cannot provide you with meaningful data unless constructed properly. Your overall goal in test construction is to evaluate the students' progress toward or attainment of stated instructional objectives by linking the test items to the content, skills, and attitudes expressed in the course objectives. Overall, teacher-made tests come in two major varieties: *objective tests* and *essay tests*.

Objective Tests

Objective tests are short-answer tests that require little writing by the students, can be scored quickly, and permit numerous questions to be asked. Multiple choice, true-false, matching, and fill-in-the-blanks are all popular forms of objective test items.

Multiple choice. Multiple choice items are comprised of two major components, the stem and three or four alternatives. The *stem* is the part that asks the question; the *alternatives* are the choices available to the student. (The wrong alternatives are called *distractors*.) The student must read the stem carefully and select the best alternative. Here is where the real skill of test construction enters in: You must state the question so that the correct answer is the *only* or *best* alternative available. You have probably participated in many discussions with teachers or professors debating whether the "correct" answer was really correct. The guidelines in Figure 15–1 were developed by Woolfolk and Nicolich. They should facilitate your job of constructing multiple choice items.

True-false. True-false items offer students an opportunity to choose between two alternatives, only one of which is correct. Usually elementary school children respond best either to "true-false" or "yes-no" alternatives. Figure 15–2 presents true-false items that show common faults. See if you can pick them out before reading my explanations.

Matching. Matching items are comprised of a problem column and a response column. Students must select an item from the response column that correctly matches a problem item. Test your ability to perceive difficulties with matching items in Figures 15–3 and 15–4, as you did with true-false items.

In Figure 15–3 the first and most obvious problem is that items are heterogeneous; four items involve names (two in each column), one involves a song title (easily associated by a process of elimination), one refers to a city, and yet another to an object. We limit the range of potential responses with such a distribution. Another common error is to offer an equal number of items in each column. Again, students use the process of elimination to arrive at the last answer or two. Contrast the items in Figure 15–3 with those in Figure 15–4.

Fill-in-the-blanks. Fill-in items involve simple recall of important names, dates, places, and other discrete information. The test items are usually presented as statements with key missing words. See if you can detect the weaknesses in the samples in Figure 15–5.

FIGURE 15–1

Guidelines for Constructing Multiple Choice Test Items (Anita E. Woolfolk, Educational Psychology, 3rd ed., ©1987, pp. 528–529. Reprinted by permission of Prentice-Hall, Inc., Englewood Cliffs, NJ)

The stem should be clear, simple, and present only a single problem. Unessential details should be left out.

Poor *There are several different kinds of standard or derived scores. An IQ score is especially useful because . . .*

Better *An advantage of an IQ score is . . .*

The problem in the stem should be stated in positive terms. Negative language is confusing. If you must use words such as *not, no,* or *except,* underline them or type them in all capitals.

Poor *Which of the following is not a standard score?*

Better *Which of the following is NOT a standard score?*

Do not expect students to make extremely fine discriminations.

Poor *The percentage of area in a normal curve falling between +1 and −1 standard deviations is about:*

    a. 66%   *c. 68%*
    b. 67%   *d. 69%*

Better *The percentage of area in a normal curve falling between +1 and −1 standard deviation is about:*

    a. 14%   *c. 68%*
    b. 34%   *d. 95%*

As much wording as possible should be included in the stem so phrases will not have to be repeated in each alternative.

Poor *A percentile score*

    a. indicates the percentage of items answered correctly.
    b. indicates the percent of correct answers divided by the percent of wrong answers.
    c. indicates the percent of people who scored at or above.
    d. indicates the percent of people who scored at or below.

Better *A percentile score indicates the percent of*

    a. items answered correctly.
    b. correct answers divided by the percent of wrong answers.
    c. people who scored at or above.
    d. people who scored at or below.

Each alternative answer should fit the grammatical form of the stem, so that no answers are obviously wrong.

Poor *The Standford-Binet test yields an*

    a. IQ score.   *c. vocational preference.*
    b. reading level.   *d. mechanical aptitude.*

Better *The Stanford-Binet is a test of*

    a. intelligence.   *c. vocational preference.*
    b. reading level.   *d. mechanical aptitude.*

FIGURE 15–1
continued

Categorical words such as *always, all, only,* or *never* should be avoided unless they can appear consistently in all the alternatives. Most smart test takers know they ought to avoid the categorical answers.

Poor A student's true score on a standardized test is
a. never equal to the obtained score.
b. always very close to the obtained score.
c. always determined by the standard error of measurement.
d. usually within a band that extends from +1 to −1 standard errors of measurement on each side of the obtained score.

Better Which one of the statements below would most often be correct about a student's true score on a standardized test?
a. It equals the obtained score.
b. It will be very close to the obtained score.
c. It is determined by the standard error of measurement.
d. It could be above or below the obtained score.

The *poor* alternative given in the item above has a second problem. The correct answer is much longer and more detailed than the three distractors. This is a clue that *d* is the correct choice.

You should also avoid including two wrong answers that have the same meaning. If only one answer can be right and if two answers are the same, then these two must both be wrong. This narrows down the choices considerably.

Poor The most frequently occurring score in a distribution is called the
a. mode.   c. arithmetic average.
b. median.   d. mean.

Better The most frequently occurring score in a distribution is called the
a. mode.   c. standard deviation.
b. median.   d. mean.

Using the exact wording found in the textbook is another technique to avoid. Poor students may recognize the answers without knowing what they mean.

Overuse of *all of the above* and *none of the above* should be avoided. Such choices may be helpful to students who are simply guessing. In addition, using *all of the above* may trick a quick student who sees that the first alternative is correct and does not read on to discover that the others are correct, too.

Obvious patterns on a test also aid students who are guessing. The position of the correct answer should be varied, as should its length.

FIGURE 15–2

Guidelines for Constructing True-False Test Items

1. "Cooperstown is the home of the Baseball Hall of Fame and the Farmer's Museum."
   Fault: The truth or falsity should center on only one point.
   Improvement: "Cooperstown is the home of the Baseball Hall of Fame."
2. "Christy Mathewson was not a pitcher."
   Fault: Negatives should not be used; they are confusing to elementary school youngsters.
3. *"Players inducted into the Hall of Fame were deserving of the honor."*
   Fault: This is a value judgment. Values are not appropriate for true-false items.
4. "The annual Hall of Fame game at Doubleday Field is always a sellout."
   Fault: Words like "usually," "always," or "all" are usually signals that a statement is false.
5. "Lou Gehrig was one of the first ten players enshrined in the Hall of Fame in 1936."
   Fault: The statement contains three facts, two of which are false. Lou Gehrig was not in the first group; there were only five players enshrined that year. Do not mix true and false information in the same statement.
6. Avoid a pattern of responses; students discover patterns quickly. Your goal is to evaluate the students' knowledge and skills, not their ability to solve a pattern puzzle.

FIGURE 15–3

Guidelines for Constructing Matching Test Items

Directions: Select an item in Column B that goes with an item in Column A. Put the letter of your choice in the blank.

Column A	Column B
_____ 1. *Take Me Out to the Ball Game*	A. Abner Doubleday
_____ 2. "The Splendid Splinter"	B. home of the Baseball Hall of Fame
_____ 3. created the game of baseball	C. the "Doubleday Ball"
_____ 4. Cooperstown, New York	D. song played at first enshrinement
_____ 5. Babe Ruth	E. holds all-time homerun record
_____ 6. baseball's oldest known artifact	F. Ted Williams
_____ 7. Henry Aaron	G. elected as one of first five players to be enshrined in the Hall of Fame

---

FIGURE 15–4

Further Matching Test Guidelines

Directions: Select an item in Column B that goes with an item in Column A. Put the letter of your choice in the blank.

Column A	Column B
_____ 1. Amelia Earhart	A. first woman Supreme Court Justice of U.S.
_____ 2. Sandra Day O'Connor	B. earliest known black female poet
_____ 3. Clara Barton	C. first English child to be born in America
_____ 4. Elizabeth Blackwell	D. author of *Uncle Tom's Cabin*
_____ 5. Phillis Wheatley	E. first woman to make solo Atlantic flight
_____ 6. Virginia Dare	F. first woman doctor in United States
_____ 7. Harriet Beecher Stowe	G. Civil War nurse—Red Cross organizer
	H. Underground Railroad organizer
	I. Founder of the Girl Scouts of America

FIGURE 15–5

Guidelines for Constructing Fill-in Test Items

---

1. " _____ was a famous black American leader."
   Fault: The statement is ambiguous. More than one response can be accepted; there have been many famous black American leaders.
   Improvement: 1. "(Martin Luther King, Jr.) was a religious and civil rights leader whose national holiday is on the third Monday in January."
2. "Traveling with Robert E. Peary, Matthew Henson was the first black to reach the _____ _____ in 1909."
   Fault: Splitting a blank or varying the size of blanks gives students cues to answers.
   Improvement: 2. "Traveling with Robert E. Peary, Matthew Henson was the first black to reach the (North Pole) in 1909."
3. "A graduate of Penn State University, Guion Buford gained fame as an _____ ."
   Fault: Using "a" or "an" before a blank should be avoided.
   Improvement: "Guion Buford, a graduate of Penn State University, gained fame as America's first black (astronaut) ."
4. "At the start of the Civil War, the government refused to use _____ . This drew criticism from _____ as well as _____ ."
   Fault: The intended answers are "black troops," "abolitionists" and "black leaders," but the statement has so many words left out that it may not be understood.

Essay Tests

Objective test items are especially suited to lower levels of thinking. However, students should also be evaluated on their abilities to think and reason at higher levels—to apply, analyze, synthesize, and evaluate information. For that reason, they must be given opportunities to write unique answers to questions that involve more complex thought than is involved in answering short objective questions. As with objective items, though, essay questions are prone to problems in construction. Consider the examples in Figure 15–6.

A major concern when grading essay tests is to maintain objectivity; the evaluation of essay questions is often influenced by the bias of the teacher. A number of strategies can help you maintain objectivity.

1. Construct a model answer outlining the key criteria for evaluating the students' work. Apply the model to each response.
2. Elementary school students should rarely have more than one essay question on a test. Should they ever have more, correct all the responses to one question before moving on to another. This should prevent the quality of one answer from influencing your judgment on the same student's other answers.
3. Ask the students to choose a code to place on their papers instead of their names, or ask them to put their names on the back of the paper. This may reduce any bias you may have developed about a student's ability.

FIGURE 15–6
Guidelines for Constructing Essay Tests

---

1. "Describe how the contributions of Josiah T. Henson helped to improve the quality of life in America."
   Fault: The question is too ambiguous and general; the student may resort to recalling specific events.
   Improvement: "Josiah T. Henson was the inspiration for Harriet Beecher Stowe's *Uncle Tom's Cabin.* Give three examples of how the story of Josiah Henson converted many to abolitionism."
2. "What was the Underground Railroad?"
   Fault: The question requires only lower-level recall. Such information is more easily tested with objective items.
   Improvement: "Born as a slave in Maryland, Harriet Tubman ran away in 1849 to Philadelphia, using a series of safe houses called the Underground Railroad. Later, she led more than 300 slaves to their freedom, despite rewards offered for her capture. Why did Tubman return to the South time and time again to rescue as many slaves as she could?"

TESTING EARLY PRIMARY GRADE CHILDREN

So far, you have learned about several types of standardized and teacher-made tests appropriate for the social studies program. Most educators agree that if these tests are used *only* for the purposes for which they were designed, teachers could have valuable sources of information about their children and the curriculum. However, there is a great deal of concern about testing in kindergarten, first grade, and second grade. The National Association for the Education of Young Children (NAEYC), a highly influential professional organization for early childhood educators, recently asked, "Do we gain any new information about children from testing?"[13] Their response was emphatic: "[T]esting seldom provides information beyond what teachers and parents already know. The systematic observations of trained teachers and other professionals, in conjunction with information obtained from parents and other family members, are the best sources of information. *Most teachers and parents know that paper-and-pencil tests are not accurate measures of young children's development and learning.*"[14] [Italics mine]

A developmentally appropriate social studies program, then, should assess the K–2 children's learning through ongoing and systematic observation rather than by the regular administration of tests; many of the important outcomes of early primary grade social studies programs involve important skills and attitudes that are not easily measured on tests—self-esteem, social competence, self-discipline, motivation for learning. As a result, social, emotional, and moral development are assigned minor importance in schools with formalized testing programs. Young children are not driven to conform to "right answers," as adults are. Don't rush them; the rest of their lives will be filled with tests. Certainly, they must be taught about the real world and their mistakes must be corrected, but there should be no undue rush to get them through this charming period of life. It is a natural stage of development, one that is rich in enthusiasm and desire. Be careful not to squelch this natural eagerness by placing them in situations where their feelings about themselves or their perceptions about how others see them will be harmed.

If tests should be used sparingly, then, what can we do to ensure that our children are getting off to a sound start in the social studies? A number of techniques can—and should—be used throughout the elementary grades to evaluate performance. They include the observational strategies of *descriptive reports, checklists, time sampling, event sampling,* and *work samples.*

Sound observational strategies are essential to the success of elementary social studies programs. They help you understand how programs need to be changed, extended, or enriched in order to make each youngster's experience away from home personally rewarding and profitable. Jean S. Phinney summarizes the importance of this valued professional skill:

> The ability to understand children through observation might be compared to the ability to judge fine art. We all respond to art—positively, negatively, indifferently—but the person with experience and training can better assess the aesthetic value of a work of art. Similarly, we all form impressions of children, but for the inexperienced observer, the impression may be inaccurate, biased, or limited in scope. As we gain more skills and experience, we know better how to look at children, what to look for, and how to interpret what we see.[15]

Descriptive Reports

The observational technique most widely used by classroom teachers is the type of report in which an observer writes down in detail everything that a child (or small group of children) does over a given period of time. More specifically, the observer's role is to:

- Record all basic information (child's name, age, and sex).
- Describe the setting.
- Observe the behavior of the child and the behaviors of those who interact with the child.
- Report only the facts. Stay away from interpretive judgments ("Arnie's social skills will cause him problems in kindergarten.") and evaluative terms such as *angry, sad, happy,* or *friendly.*
- Organize all events in chronological order.
- Limit observations to brief episodes, usually five to ten minutes. Since you are responsible for recording everything you see, an extended observational period can result in volumes of paperwork. Take a break after a short episode, gather your thoughts, and then begin another episode.

A descriptive report sounds easy, but observers making their first attempt soon find out how difficult it is. Teachers frequently find it difficult to stay away from interpretive statements as they describe their observations: "The child is bashful," "The teacher was insensitive," or "The child thought . . ." While these explanations may be accurate, they are not *observable behaviors.* Good observers learn to separate behaviors (knocking over own sand castle) from the inference (the child is angry). As an experiment (if you have an opportunity to work with children), pair up with another student and write your separate observations of the same children. Independently develop your interpretations of what you saw and compare them. You will probably find that you came up with two quite different results—where one finds shyness, the other sees good behavior; where one finds aggressiveness, the other sees leadership. For example, one teacher placed this comment about a child in his permanent file: "Arnie created a disruption with his social studies group today by refusing to share a library book with Arlene. His social skills are much below those of the other first graders and will certainly cause him problems as he enters the higher grades." By recording your opinion, especially in reacting to some negative aspect of a child's behavior, you run the risk of stigmatizing that youngster for the rest of his school years. If you must enter negative observations, make every effort to balance them with positive comments so that future teachers will be aware of the child's strengths as well as weaknesses. A descriptive report is shown in Figure 15–7.

Notice how the sample avoids inferences and provides only clear, concise descriptions of the behaviors. The descriptive report is an excellent way to guide your observation of young children, but the process takes great concentration and repeated practice before it is mastered.

Checklists

Some teachers prefer to use checklists as tools for observing patterns of children's behavior. Checklists are particularly handy when you wish to investigate a child's achievement of certain skills, competencies, or concepts. To determine the degree to

FIGURE 15–7
A Descriptive Report

Children Observed:	Michael (age 5 years-6 months)
	Scott (age 5 years-8 months)
Setting:	School Playground

Observation Report: Michael is tossing a foam rubber boomerang. He flings it vigorously and says, "Watch it come back to me!" The boomerang flies off and lands about ten feet from Michael. Scott says, "Let me try it once, Michael." They both run to the boomerang, Michael reaching it first. Scott grapples with Michael and they both fall to the ground giggling. Both boys roll over a few times, still chuckling as they play. Finally, Michael gets up with the boomerang in his hand and hands it to Scott. "Okay, Scott," says Michael, "let's see if you can make it come back to you." Scott hurls the boomerang. It flies off, hovers in the air, and lands at least fifteen feet away. "Ha-a-a," says Michael, "yours didn't come back either. Let *me* try again!" They both scurry to the boomerang and tumble to the ground once more.

Personal Comments: Michael and Scott spend much time playing with boomerangs and each other. They are physically active young boys. They exhibit a high level of social maturity—they share toys and amuse themselves during play with no unfortunate consequences.

which children have achieved the goals, you must first define the behaviors to be observed and then record the occurrence of each of those behaviors. A sample checklist of social-emotional skills and behaviors a child is likely to develop between the ages of three and six years is shown in Figure 15–8. Each item is a sample of many related skills or behaviors, and in that sense, serves as an indicator of more general characteristics of development. There is usually room at the end of the checklist for observers to add their own opinions and observations about the child's development.

Checklists are particularly useful observational tools in that they direct the observer to specific behaviors or characteristics. The checklist in Figure 15–8 exemplifies specific goals of social studies education; other checklists are based on broader goals and can be several pages long.

Time Sampling

This observational technique is perhaps the most commonly used technique for formal research purposes, but it also has a degree of applicability for teachers. In using the time sampling technique, the observer records behaviors of a child during regularly recurring

FIGURE 15–8
Sample Checklist for Social-Emotional Behavior/Characteristics

SOCIAL-EMOTIONAL CHECKLIST

The child:

	Sometimes Present	Mastered
1. separates comfortably from parent		
2. talks easily with other children		
3. participates willingly in group activities		
4. does not interrupt others; takes turns		
5. plays cooperatively with other children		
6. relates positively to adults		
7. understands consequences of own behavior		
8. demonstrates pride in accomplishments		
9. persists until tasks are completed		
10. is eager to try out new activities and experiences		

Directions:

( ) Place a "check" in the "Sometimes Present" column if the behavior or characteristic is present but has not been firmly developed.

(+) Place a "plus" in the "Mastered" column if the characteristic or behavior occurs repeatedly as a regular part of the child's behavior.

( ) Make no mark if the behavior or characteristic does not occur.

Evaluating these students' accomplishments cannot be done with paper-pencil tests.

intervals (for example, 30 or 60 seconds) and records a check for each occurrence of a particular behavior during that time period. For example, let us suppose you wish to examine the preferences for activity of a youngster or small group of youngsters during an informal social studies class. A sample of the recording instrument you might choose to use is shown in Figure 15–9. Details about the specific observable behaviors could be filled in after the sample time period has elapsed. By using this technique, observers can make reasonable inferences about a child's typical pattern of behavior.

Event Sampling

After using either of the observation techniques discussed to this point, you may become interested in some recurring behavior or characteristic that you would like to examine further. Wait for an incident to occur and record all the relevant behaviors or characteristics. Let us suppose that you've become interested in a child's readiness for map skills instruction. You would need to watch for any indication of relevant actions pertaining to map reading and then compile a clear, complete written record of what you observed. A sample event sampling description (often referred to as an *anecdotal record*) is shown in Figure 15–10. These brief, written descriptions directed toward specific behaviors must accumulate over several observations to be meaningful.

FIGURE 15–9
Time Sampling Example

CLASS-TIME PREFERENCES

Dates __November 12–16__

Record at one minute intervals for 15 minutes daily.

Child's name	Books	Reinforcement Center	Group Project	Creative Writing	Unoccupied/ Other Activities
Sean	✓✓✓ ✓✓✓✓✓			✓✓✓✓ ✓	✓
Allison		✓✓✓✓✓	✓✓✓✓✓ ✓✓		
Delena	✓✓✓✓✓ ✓✓✓	✓✓✓✓			✓

Work Samples

Teachers find it useful to observe special characteristics or behaviors of children by periodically collecting samples of their work. They organize files containing samples of artwork, writing assignments, research efforts, or other indications of children's growth. Some teachers prefer to take weekly, biweekly, or monthly samples, which they date and place in the folder. In this way, they are able to keep a running record of how the child is progressing and use that knowledge as a base to extend or reinforce areas of particular interest or need.

FIGURE 15–10
Sample Anecdotal Record

October 23

Brit (boy, age 7) is sitting alone looking intently at a globe. He spins the globe a few times and points to water and land masses each time the globe stops. He gets a toy airplane and "flys" it from land mass to land mass, not naming any of the places he stopped. Brit appears to have developed a budding interest in learning about maps.

INTELLIGENCE TESTS

One of the most famous standardized tests, the Stanford-Binet IQ test, has been left for next to last because it has less direct applicability for the social studies program. But because they describe a level of cognitive ability, IQ tests are often used as guides to explain why certain children perform better in social studies (or other subjects) than do others. IQ scores are used for a variety of purposes, one of which is to identify children needing special help and those with superior cognitive functioning.

The Gifted

Exceptionally talented or intelligent children were given little attention in our schools until the 1970s. To single out and provide special classroom instruction for these youngsters was considered elitist, somewhat un-American. "Why," people asked, "should we channel extra money and resources toward these youngsters' education when others, particularly the handicapped, need them so much more?" We began to realize, however, that our concern for so-called un-American schooling was paradoxical. We realized that our schools were in most instances meeting the needs of handicapped learners but failing to meet the unique needs of gifted students. In effect, the gifted were prevented from reaching their fullest potential.

At the same time educators sought to define characteristics of gifted students and to describe the most suitable classroom experiences for them. We consider gifted children those who are exceptionally intelligent, creative, or talented in some special way, such as in music, art, or even sports. Originally, though, giftedness was defined primarily in terms of rank on a standardized intelligence test, most frequently the Binet scale. Some specialists identified those with IQ scores of 120 or more as gifted because they made up only 10% of the population. Others suggested a 130 IQ score because only 2.27% had scores that high; still others suggested an IQ score of 140 or over because it would restrict giftedness to only 0.5% of the total population. Since IQ tests are somewhat inaccurate in these upper ranges, however, psychologists and educators searched for other definitions of giftedness. Eventually, Martinson suggested a well-rounded, practical definition:

1. A score in the top 3% of the child's ethnic or cultural group on an individual intelligence test (a score of 130 or better for white, native-born Americans).
2. The results of a teacher's observation. Walton found that when teachers were asked the following questions, they were often able to select gifted individuals from their classroom: Who learns easily and rapidly? Who uses a lot of common sense and practical knowledge? Who retains easily what he or she has heard? Who knows about many things of which other children are unaware? Who uses a large number of words easily and accurately? Who recognizes relations and comprehends meanings? Who is alert, keenly observant, responds quickly?
3. Previous accomplishments in an area of special talent. Experts in the field are usually called in to judge the quality of a child's artistic, musical, dramatic, or other creative talent.
4. Creativity test scores. Not all children with high IQs are necessarily the most creative individuals. Tests of creativity may help identify gifted youngsters normally not selected by standard IQ measures.[16]

Gifted students have special learning needs, much as any other distinctive group that differs from the norm. Joyce Van Tassel-Baska[17] contends, however, that many school districts do little to meet the needs of the gifted. She notes that efforts to deliver appropriate services to the gifted are hampered by four mistaken beliefs common among educators:

1. A "differentiated" curriculum for the gifted means anything that is different from what is provided for all learners.
2. The experiences provided for gifted students must be centered on creative, open-ended processes.
3. One curriculum package will provide all that is needed for the entire gifted population.
4. Acceleration is harmful because it pushes children socially and leaves gaps in their knowledge.

Van Tassel-Baska believes that these misconceptions must be remedied in all areas of the elementary school curriculum, including the social studies. She describes an appropriate program for the gifted as having these equally important dimensions:

(1) a content-based mastery dimension that allows gifted learners to move more rapidly through the curriculum;
(2) a process/product/research dimension that encourages in-depth and independent learning;

(3) an epistemological concept dimension that allows for the exploration of issues, themes, and ideas across the curriculum areas.[18]

The special learning needs of gifted students and general curricular implications are shown in Table 15–1 and Table 15–2. Van Tassel-Baska sees the direct application of these concepts to the social studies curriculum as having far-reaching implications, for

TABLE 15–1

Curriculum Implications of Characteristics and Learning Needs of the Gifted

Characteristics	*Learning Needs*	*Curriculum Implications*
Ability to handle abstractions	Presentation of symbol systems at higher levels of abstraction	■ Reorganized basic skills curriculum ■ Introduction of new symbol systems at earlier stages of development (computers, foreign language[s], statistics, etc.)
Power of concentration	Longer time frame that allows focused in-depth work in an area of interest and challenge	■ Diversified scheduling of curriculum work ■ "Chunks" of time for special project work and small group efforts
Ability to make connections and establish relationships among disparate data	Exposure to multiple perspectives and domains of inquiry	■ Interdisciplinary curriculum opportunities such as special concept units, humanities, and the interrelated arts ■ Use of multiple text materials and resources
Ability to memorize well and learn rapidly	Rapid movement through basic skills and concepts in traditional areas; economical organization of new areas of learning	■ Restructured learning frames (i.e., speed up and reduce reinforcement activities) ■ New curriculum organized according to its underlying structure
Multiple interests; wide information base	Opportunity to choose area(s) of interest and to study a chosen area in greater depth	■ Learning center areas in the school for extended time use ■ Self-directed learning packets ■ Individual learning contracts

Source: Joyce Van Tassel-Baska, "Appropriate Curriculum for Gifted Learners," *Educational Leadership, 46,* no. 6 (March 1989)

TABLE 15–2

Appropriate Adaptions of Curriculum, Instruction, and Materials for Gifted Learners

Curriculum

- Compression by using a diagnostic-prescriptive approach for basic skill learning
- Acceleration of content
- Reorganization of content according to higher-level skills and concepts
- Infusion of higher-order thinking skills into content
- Development of advanced products related to the content area
- Integration of content area by key ideas, issues, and themes
- Integration of ideas across related content areas

Instruction

- Faster-paced instructional pattern
- More frequent use of inquiry techniques
- Use of varied questioning strategies that include convergent, divergent, and evaluative
- Use of cooperative learning groups for problem solving and special projects (cluster by ability/interest)
- More frequent use of discussion
- Greater use of independent contract work and study
- Use of a variety of instructional strategies

Materials

- Advanced reading level
- Organization by concepts rather than isolated skills
- Higher-level questions for discussion
- Ideas for group and independent student investigation
- Problem sets, exercises, and activities organized from simple to complex and including examples that extend 2–4 years off level
- Extension activities that allow students to pursue a topic in-depth
- Idea connections to multiple areas of the curriculum

Source: Joyce Van Tassal-Baska, "Appropriate Curriculum for Gifted Learners," *Educational Leadership, 46,* no. 6 (March 1989).

gifted students will most likely constitute the leadership of the future. She recommends a social studies program with an emphasis on increasing awareness of other cultures, language (two languages in addition to English are recommended), global interdependence, multinational interests, and the importance of being competitive in the world trade market. Teachers would employ faster-paced instruction; frequent use of inquiry techniques; group and independent investigations; varied questioning strategies that include convergent, divergent, and evaluative discussions; and a variety of instructional strategies.

A sound social studies program for the gifted should include varied and challenging experiences for individuals who, barring tragedy, will live most of their lives in the twenty-first century. Their future world will be built on the foundation laid in elementary school. It is imperative that this experience be fruitful, for the children are America's insurance policy for a bright and promising future.

Students Requiring Special Help

> There are more than eight million handicapped children in the United States today, and the special educational needs of these children are not being met. More than one-half do not receive appropriate services . . . and one million are excluded entirely from the public school system—Introduction to PL 94–142 (1975)

The *Education for All Handicapped Children Act* (Public Law 94–142) was passed by Congress and signed into law by President Gerald R. Ford on November 29, 1975. PL 94–142 is primarily a funding bill offering fiscal support to the states in return for their compliance to its provisions. The law, implemented in steps over a 5-year period, required that by September 1, 1980, each state must provide a free, appropriate public education for every handicapped child between the ages of 3 and 21 years.

The law affects all schools and calls for educating handicapped children in "the least restrictive environment," often requiring regular classroom teachers to accommodate handicapped children in their classroom. Therefore, the money provided through PL 94–142 is made available to help schools make needed changes for these children and provide in-service training so that regular classroom teachers can more effectively integrate children with special needs into the established classroom routine. Moving handicapped children from a special setting into regular classes for their education is called *mainstreaming.* Although PL 94–142 calls for educating youngsters in "the least restrictive environment," it does not specify that such an environment be the regular classroom. Mainstreaming became the accepted practice for implementing PL 94–142 through the efforts of the Council for Exceptional Children (CEC), which identified the regular classroom as the most appropriate educational setting for all children, exceptional and nonexceptional. Underlying this philosophy is a recognition that when handicapped and nonhandicapped children learn, grow, and play together, they develop the sensitivities and understandings necessary for creating interpersonal relationships.

You should know as much as possible about PL 94–142 because as more and more handicapped children become integrated into the regular classroom, your entire program, including social studies instruction, will most likely need to be adjusted to provide appropriate experiences for all. A number of teaching competencies are necessary to make those adjustments; those that follow are specified by the Commonwealth of Pennsylvania from *Guidelines for the Preparation of Teachers in Compliance with U.S. Public Law 94–142* (Pennsylvania Department of Education, 1980). Does your state have a similiar listing?

> The prospective teacher will
> 1. Understand the legal basis for educating students with handicaps in the least restrictive environment.
> 2. Understand the implications which handicapping conditions have for the learning process.
> 3. Recognize students who may be in need of special services.
> 4. Make use of appropriate resource and support services.
> 5. Confer with and report to parents on educational programs for students with handicaps.

6. Facilitate the social acceptance of persons with handicaps by encouraging positive interpersonal relationships.
7. Use individual, group, and classroom management techniques for effective accommodation of students with handicaps.
8. Assess the educational needs of students with handicaps.
9. Modify instructional strategies to provide for the individual needs of students with handicaps.
10. Evaluate classroom progress of students with handicaps.

Special Handicaps

Elementary school teachers agree that every child is unique and special. For that reason, all of education should be *special education,* and all educational practices should be directed toward meeting each individual's unique needs. Some children, however, have mental or physical difficulties that cause them to differ markedly in behaviors or characteristics from the typical child at a particular age level (see Figure 15–11).

Planning an Instructional Design

PL 94–142 mandated that schools develop an individualized educational program (IEP) for every child mainstreamed into the regular classroom. The IEP is a written statement developed jointly by a qualified school official, the child's teacher, the child's parents or guardian, and, if possible, the child. The written statement must include:

1. Analysis of the child's present achievement level
2. Listing of long- and short-range goals—the expected outcomes to be achieved
3. Statement of specific services that will be provided to help the child reach the goals
4. Indication of the extent to which the child will become involved in regular school programs
5. Schedule for evaluating the progress experienced with the IEP and recommendations for revisions

Mainstreaming

Since our mission in social studies education is equal opportunity for all, the concept of mainstreaming physically and mentally handicapped children should be met enthusiastically. In mainstreaming children, we build on all we know about the importance of the elementary school years to all aspects of the child's development.

- *View the child as a whole child with strengths as well as weaknesses.* Do not assume that the mainstreamed child is different in that regard.
- *Learn all you can about the mainstreamed child's specific disability.* Become aware of therapy techniques and technical terminology.
- *Involve parents in dealing with their child both in the school and at home.* They should learn what you are doing in school so that your practices can be reinforced and extended in the home.
- *Maximize interactions between the handicapped and nonhandicapped children.* Give simple explanations about a child's handicap, when needed. Youngsters are curious;

FIGURE 15–11

Categories of Handicapped Children: Public Law 94–142 (U.S. Office of Education, "Education of Handicapped Children" Federal Register, part 2 [Washington, DC: Department of Health, Education and Welfare, 1977])

Public Law 94–142 defines categories of handicapped children as including the following:

Deaf means a hearing impairment which is so severe that the child is impaired in processing linguistic information through hearing, with or without amplification, which adversely affects educational performance.

Deaf-blind means a concomitant hearing and visual impairment, the combination of which causes such severe communication and other developmental and educational problems that such children cannot be accommodated in special education programs solely for deaf or blind children.

Hard-of-hearing means a hearing impairment, whether permanent or fluctuating, which adversely affects a child's educational performance but is not included under the definition of *deaf* in this section.

Mentally retarded means significantly subaverage general intellectual function existing concurrently with deficiencies in adaptive behavior and manifested during the developmental period, which adversely affects a child's educational performance.

Multihandicapped means concomitant impairments (such as mentally retarded-blind, mentally retarded-orthopedically impaired, and so on), the combination of which causes such severe educational problems that these children cannot be accommodated in special education programs solely for one of the impairments. The term does not include deaf-blind children.

Orthopedically impaired means a severe orthopedic impairment which adversely affects a child's educational performance. The term includes impairments caused by congenital anomaly (for example, clubfoot, absence of some member, and so on), impairments caused by disease (for example, poliomyelitis, bone tuberculosis, and so on), and impairments from other causes (for example, cerebral palsy, amputations and fractures, or burns which cause contractures).

Other health impaired means limited strength, vitality, or alertness, due to chronic or acute health problems, such as a heart condition, tuberculosis, rheumatic fever, nephritis, asthma, sickle-cell anemia, hemophilia, epilepsy, lead poisoning, leukemia, or diabetes, which adversely affects a child's educational performance.

Seriously emotionally disturbed means a condition which exhibits one or more of the following characteristics over a long period of time and to a marked degree, which adversely affects educational performance: (a) an inability to learn, which cannot be explained by intellectual, sensory, or health factors, (b) an inability to build or maintain satisfactory interpersonal relationships with peers and teachers, (c) inappropriate types of behavior or feelings under normal circumstances, (d) a general pervasive mood of unhappiness or depression, or (e) a tendency to develop physical symptoms or fears associated with personal or school problems. The term includes children who are schizophrenic or autistic. The term does not include children who are socially maladjusted, unless it is determined that they are seriously emotionally disturbed.

Specific learning disability means a disorder in one or more of the basic psychological processes involved in understanding or using language, spoken or written, which may manifest itself in an imperfect ability to listen, think, speak, read, write, spell, or do mathematical calculations. The term includes such conditions as perceptual handicaps, brain injury, minimal brain dysfunction, dyslexia, and developmental aphasia. The term does not include children who have learning problems which are primarily the result of visual, hearing, or motor handicaps, or mental retardation, or environment, culture, or economic disadvantage.

Speech impaired means a communication disorder, such as stuttering impaired articulation, language impairment, or a voice impairment, which adversely affects a child's educational performance.

Visually handicapped means a visual impairment which, even with correction, adversely affects a child's educational performance. The term includes both partially seeing and blind children.

---

they want to know about a new child and will be satisfied by an open, honest exclamation. ("Jeannie's legs don't work well so she needs a wheelchair.") Read books or tell stories about children with differences. Encourage the handicapped child to share strong capabilities. For example, the wheelchair-bound youngster can help another child in a project that demands manual dexterity and soon gain that child's appreciation for outstanding manual skill.

- *Individualize your program.* Start where the child is and plan a sequential program to encourage him to build one skill upon another. Build on continuous success.
- *Visit classrooms where exceptional children have been successfully mainstreamed.* Look for ways teachers individualize their instruction. How is peer interaction stimulated? Are parents involved in the classroom activities? Are peer questions about a child's disability answered openly and honestly?
- *Attend special conferences, workshops, or other in-service training sessions* designed to assist you in IEP writing and/or designing special learning materials and teaching techniques.
- *Talk to handicapped children's parents and previous teachers.* They can offer valuable suggestions and advice.
- *Seek special assistance through publications—Exceptional Children* or the *Journal of Learning Disabilities* are two examples—and nonprint media (speakers, films, and so forth) from local, state, or national agencies, such as the Council for Exceptional Children.
- *Look for special programs designed to introduce regular students to the special needs of the handicapped.* Barbara Aiello has developed a special program called "Kids on the Block," which includes puppets with different types of impairments. Each puppet displays a vibrant personality. "The Great Renaldo," for example, jauntily announces that he "sees nothing and knows all," carrying his white cane and happily describing how he can tell time with his Braille wristwatch. Mark explains how his wheelchair ("cruiser," as he calls it) helps him enjoy life—he once went to a Halloween party as a tractor (only a "handicapped kid" can do that!). Children can ask the puppets questions. Mark, for example, is often asked how he can go to the bathroom. He explains that bathrooms are equipped with special rails to help him get up and down. Life-sized and dressed in real clothes, these puppets become ideal educators in every way. For more information on this complete curriculum on disabilities, contact Kids on the Block, Inc., Suite 510, Washington Building, Washington, DC 20005.

Mainstreaming requires changes in attitudes, behaviors, and teaching style. Since you will be part of this movement, you must gain the skills and attitudes necessary to help all children function effectively in society. What better place to start this process than in a social studies classroom?

Plan your program to fit your children's needs. No single chapter can give you a complete idea of the innumerable factors that influence your planning. If you truly want to be a successful teacher, you must build an awareness and sensitivity to the *real world* of children, one that includes careful, day-by-day observation and evaluation to serve as a basis for effective instruction.

SUMMARY

Inherent in the process of teaching is evaluation. Although teachers receive information for making evaluative judgments from many possible sources, *measurement techniques* appear to be especially dominant today. One measurement technique particularly favored by school districts is *standardized tests.* Standardized tests may be norm-referenced or criterion-referenced. Norm-referenced tests compare students' achievement to a large national sample. Criterion-referenced tests measure whether students have mastered a particular content area or skill; they do not compare students' results with a large sample.

Teacher-made tests comprise a second major measurement technique, perhaps the most popular of all evaluative procedures used in the social studies. Teacher-made tests may be either "formative" (helping teachers plan for instruction) or "summative" (helping the teacher evaluate the success of instruction). Teacher-made test items are of two basic types: objective questions and subjective questions. Multiple choice, true-false, matching, and fill-in-the-blanks are popular forms of objective items. Although teacher-made tests are popular and effective forms of evaluation, they should not be used as the exclusive source of evaluative data.

Observational techniques including descriptive reports, checklists, time sampling, event sampling, and work samples furnish valuable data for the social studies teacher. It takes practice to use these techniques effectively. Avoiding bias while observing and recording behavior requires strong mental discipline. The results, however, provide teachers with valuable information about how their children are progressing.

Intelligence tests are not used directly in the social studies program, but they help identify children in need of special attention. Gifted children require program adjustments including the following: (1) they must be able to move more rapidly through the content dimension. (2) they must have opportunities for independent learning, and (3) they must explore issues, themes, and ideas across the curriculum areas. Children classified as "handicapped" under PL 94–142 must be educated in the "least restrictive environment," often requiring regular classroom teachers to accommodate handicapped children in their classrooms. PL 94–142 defines eleven categories of handicapped children and requires that those entering the regular classroom receive instruction within the guidelines of an individualized educational program (IEP).

Good social studies programs must be planned around student needs. Through sound evaluation procedures, we can discover these needs, make adjustments to our program, and judge the success of our efforts.

ENDNOTES

1. Lorrie A. Shepard, "Why We Need Better Assessment," *Educational Leadership, 46,* no. 7 (April 1989): 4.

2. Pearl M. Oliner, *Teaching Elementary Social Studies* (New York: Harcourt Brace Jovanovich, 1976), p. 280.

3. Lee J. Cronbach, *Essentials of Psychological Testing,* 3rd ed. (New York: Harper & Row, 1970), p. 27.

4. Anita E. Woolfolk and Lorraine McCune Nicolich, *Educational Psychology for Teachers* (Englewood Cliffs, NJ: Prentice-Hall, 1980), p. 440.

5. Carol Livingston, Sharon Castle, and Jimmy Nations, "Testing and Curriculum Reform: One School's Experience," *Educational Leadership, 46,* no. 7 (April 1989): 24.

6. Ibid.

7. James L. Hymes, Jr., *Teaching the Child Under Six,* 3rd ed. (Columbus, OH: Merrill, 1981), pp. 106–107.

8. George F. Madaus in an interview with Ron Brandt, "On Misuse of Testing: A Conversation with George Madaus," *Educational Leadership, 46,* no. 7 (April 1989): 26.

9. Ibid.

10. Woolfolk and Nicolich, *Educational Psychology for Teachers,* p. 437.

11. Oliner, *Teaching Elementary Social Studies,* p. 281.

12. Benjamin S. Bloom et al., *Handbook on Formative and Summative Evaluation of Student Learning* (New York: McGraw-Hill, 1971).

13. No author, *Testing of Young Children: Concerns and Cautions* (Brochure #582) (Washington, DC: National Association for the Education of Young Children, 1988).

14. Ibid.

15. Jean S. Phinney, "Observing Children: Ideas for Teachers," *Young Children, 37,* no. 5 (July 1982): 16–24.

16. R. A. Martinson, "Children with Superior Cognitive Abilities," in *Exceptional Children in the Schools: Special Education in Transition,* ed. L. M. Dunn (New York: Holt, Rinehart and Winston, 1973), pp. 580–84.

17. Joyce Van Tassel-Baska, "Appropriate Curriculum for Gifted Learners," *Educational Leadership, 46,* no. 6 (March 1989): 13–15.

18. Ibid.

SOME FINAL THOUGHTS

You are now at the point of your professional development where you are expected to make personal, informed decisions regarding the principles and practices most appropriate for teaching the social studies to any group of elementary school children. The decisions you make and the skill with which you carry them through make you one of the most important people in the lives of the youngsters with whom you are entrusted. This is a tremendous responsibility and one that must not be taken lightly. You will need to think and act on your own, without the immediate aid of Jerome Bruner, Jean Piaget, your instructor, your classmates, or your textbook. Don't feel alone, though—every teacher must go through this growth process: "How do I do that? If only I had a chance to talk with my college instructor again! Where can I get help for that special topic they've asked me to teach?" These questions and concerns are very important—don't ever stop searching for solutions to them. Make your future the brightest possible by constantly growing in the field. Strive toward self-improvement and for increased professionalism. Although your career will be filled with hard work, your sincere efforts in the classroom will be rewarded with smiling faces, enthusiastic efforts, and hugs aplenty.

As you progress through your career, you may become interested in journals or professional organizations specifically recognized for their contributions to elementary school social studies instruction. The most popular of these organizations is:

The National Council for the Social Studies
3615 Wisconsin Avenue, N.W.
Washington, DC 20016

Journals: *Social Education*
Social Studies and the Young Learner

Best wishes for a long and fruitful career!

Index

Aardema, Verna, 289
Ability learning groups, 214–18
Accommodation, 92–93
Active learning, 124–46. *See also*
    Enactive learning; Learning
    methods
  and guided problem solving,
    125–33
  and inquiry, 137–54
Active listening, 161, 452–54
Adaptation, 92–93
Affective learning domain, 72
Affective values, 160
Africa
  Ibo culture, 281–82, 320–21
  Kwanzaa holiday, 282
  naming ceremony, 431–32
  rainfall/vegetation maps, 368
  Yoruba culture, 432
Agreements for activities, 235–37
AIDS education, 458–60
Aiello, Barbara, 491
Alcohol/drug education, 460–62
American Historical Association, 23
American Lung Association,
  461–62
American Psychological
  Association, 72
Anecdotal records, 482, 484. *See
  also* Record keeping
Anthropology, 14–15

Antonym questions, 100
Archaeology, in directed learning
  episode, 118–20
Assimilation, 92–93
Association of American
  Geographers (AAG), 21
Attendance/name charts, 194–97,
  235, 275
Attitudes learning centers, 225
Attribute listing, 151–52
Audiovisuals, 99, 226, 266–67,
  421–22. *See also* Visuals
Ausubel, David P., 89, 90, 91
Ayers, William, 188–89

Baker, Olaf, 293
Ballads, 409
Ball, Gerry, 161
Banks, James A., 427–28, 439
Barber, Benjamin R., 11
Barr, Robert D., 6
Barth, James L., 6, 167
Baruch, Bernard, 36, 38
Baskwill, Jane, 69
Behavior (student), 480–81
  behavioral objectives, 74–75
  descriptive reports, 479–80
Bennett, William J., 20, 58, 318
Berg, Marlowe, 286–87
Bernagozzi, Tom, 209
Bestor, Arthur, 6, 7

Beyer, Barry K., 26, 27, 143
Biographies, 294, 400. *See also*
  Children's literature; History;
  Story reading/telling
Birthdays, 193
Blackburn, Anne M., 425–26, 433
Bleeker, Sonia, 282
Bloom, Benjamin S., 26, 72,
  93–94, 472
  *Taxonomy of Educational
    Objectives*, 26, 72–73, 84,
    143
  components, 73
Blos, Joan W., 294
Blume, Judy, 289
Book publishing, 299–300
Boston Primer, The (1808), 158
Bowler, Mike, 418
Boyer, Claire, 64
Bradley Commission on History
  in Schools, 7, 8, 19–20,
  23, 58, 384, 386–88, 414
Brady, Marion, 418
Brain hemispheres
  lateral vs. vertical thinking,
    147–49
  right vs. left, 147
  systematic vs. intuitive thinking,
    147
Brainstorming, 151, 152–54
Brink, Carol Ryrie, 410

Britton, James, 303
Brown, Ina Corrine, 438
Brubaker, Dale L., 138
Bruner, Jerome S., 125, 133, 140, 147, 149
  cone of classroom experiences, 250–52
Bulletin boards. *See also* Charts/ graphs/tables; Creative arts; Learning centers
  attendance/name charts, 194–97, 235, 275
  birthday charts, 193
  current affairs, 421
  helper charts, 194
  map displays, 364
  students' writing, 298–99
Burkholder, Suzanne, 40
Burton, Virginia Lee, 288, 359
Butts, R. Freeman, 17

Cahoon, Peggy, 22
Caldecott Medal, 289
Calendars, 393–400
  calendar making, 394–400
  daily/weekly/monthly/yearly, 394, 395–97, 398–99
  and job charts, 397–400
  Native American, 97
  personalized, 394
California History–Social Science Framework, 20, 23, 58, 387
Canadian Library Award, 289
Cardinal directions, 355–56, 370. *See also* Map-reading skills
Career education, 445–48
Carin, Arthur A., 125–26
Carnegie Medal, 289
Carter G. Woodson Book Award, 289
Cartoons (political), 310–12, 313
Carver, R. P., 97
Castle, Sharon, 469
Chambers, John H., 27
Charles, Cheryl, 433
Charts/graphs/tables, 111–16, 272–78

attendance/names, 194–97, 235, 275
  birthdays, 193
  helpers, 194
  information retrieval, 114
  jobs, 397–400
  learning center tasks, 235
  semantic webbing, 111–13
  talent totem, 57
  Venn diagrams, 116
Children's literature, 287–96. *See also* Story reading/telling
  awards, 289
  biographies, 294
  and history, 294, 409–12
  and map reading, 359–61
  resources, 288–94
China, 144–46
Chinn, Philip C., 438
Cinderella, 291–93
  Chinese version, 291–92
Cinquain poetry, 305
Citizenship. *See also* Democratic beliefs
  and curriculum, 4
  and sociodrama, 332
  as teaching objective, 28–29
Civics, 9–11, 21–23. *See also* Democratic beliefs
  classroom activities, 64–65
  classroom constitution, 456–58
  current affairs, 419–25
  Oh Deer computer software, 270
  Pennsylvania's state insect project, 62–64
Civil rights, and moral reasoning, 180–81
Clarifying
  as probing method, 110–11
  of responses, 169–71
  of values, 171–73
Classroom activities, 75–81, 117–18. *See also* Cooperative (group) learning; Creative arts; Learning centers
  activity contracts, 235–37
  birthdays, 193

calendar making, 394–400
  and career education, 447–48
  and civics, 64–65
  and computer software, 268–70
  cooperative (group) work, 202–4
  creative arts, 323–26
  dance/music, 319–20, 333–35, 409
  drama, 327–32, 447
  and ecology, 434–37
  and enactive learning, 253
  first school day, 191–92, 196
  games, 199–202, 227–28, 263–66, 359, 362–64, 366–67, 393, 430–31
  and global/multicultural education, 428–32, 440–45
  historical panoramas/guide-o-ramas, 114–16, 401
  and lesson/unit plans, 75–81, 82–83
  map making, 374–78
  and newspapers, 421–23
  paper skyscrapers, 202
  publishing, 299–302, 421
  seating arrangements, 210, 233
  and symbolic learning, 281–82
  tepee building, 442–43
  time capsules, 390–93
  time lines, 412–14
  time machines, 408
  and valuing processes, 171–73
Classroom constitution, 456–58
Classroom discussions, 110–11
  Magic Circle program, 161–65
  and moral reasoning, 180–84
Classroom helpers, 193–94
Closed-ended inquiry teaching method, 150
Coats of arms, 246–47
  and family history, 402–4
  and valuing processes, 172–73
Cogan, John J., 22
Cognition
  cognitive-developmental values model, 178–84

cognitive learning domain, 72
and inquiry teaching method,
    146–50
intuitive vs. systematic thinking,
    147
lateral vs. vertical thinking,
    147–49
and values, 160
Collages, 325
Committee on Geographic
    Education (of NCGE), 7–9,
    21, 341
Committee on Social Studies (of
    NEA), 4–5
Community living, 210–14
Competency-based programs (for
    teachers), 47–48
Computers/computer software,
    267–70
Conceived values, 151, 159–60
Conceptualizing skills, 27
    and directed teaching, 90–93
    Taba approach, 104–5, 107
    spatial concepts, 347
Cone of classroom experiences
    (Bruner), 250–52
Conservation
    of energy, 437
    as perceptual factor, 345–47
    recycling, 434, 436
Construction activities, 202, 326,
    374–78, 442–43
    learning centers, 225–31
Content acquisition skills, 26
Contracts for activities, 235–37
Cooney, Barbara, 98
Cooperative (group) learning,
    188–220
    and ability groups, 214–18
    and cooperative learning
        groups, 204–10
    jigsaw approach, 206–7
    numbered heads together
        approach, 206
    think-pair-share approach,
        204–6
    difficulties, 218–20
    and interest groups, 210–12

and research groups, 212–14
resources, 206, 209–10
sample episodes, 208–18
seating arrangements, 210
and small groups, 198–204
and whole groups, 190–98
Core questions, 111–13
Council for Exceptional Children
    (CEC), 488
Creative arts, 323–26. *See also*
    Bulletin boards; Classroom
    activities
    calendar making, 394–400
    coats of arms, 173, 246–47,
        402–4
    collages, 325
    construction, 202, 326,
        374–78, 442–43
    dance/music, 319–20, 333–35,
        409
    dioramas, 324–25
    drawing, 173, 246, 326
    and global/multicultural
        education, 428–29, 432
    map making, 374–78
    modeling materials, 377
    mosaics, 325
    murals, 325
    paper skyscrapers, 202
    and valuing processes, 172–73
Creative writing, 303–7, 406,
    410. *See also* Writing skills
Creativity learning centers, 225
Crenshaw, Shirley, 7
Crews, Donald, 288
Critical thinking skills, 26, 27, 143
Cuban, Larry, 464
Cullum, Albert, 39, 54, 222, 316
Cultural literacy, 19, 287
Cunningham, Dick, 115
Current affairs, 419–25. *See also*
    Civics
Curriculum, 2–32
    and AIDS, 458–60
    and alcohol/drugs, 460–62
    career education, 445–48
    and citizenship, 4, 28–29
    content organization, 15–25

expanding environment
    approach, 15–18
by grade level, 13, 17, 18
interdisciplinary approach,
    15, 16
controversies over, 3–6
creative arts, 318–35, 428–29,
    432
    language arts, 286–314
current affairs, 419–25
ecology, 432–37
for gifted students, 485–87
global/multicultural education,
    425–32, 438–45
for handicapped students, 491
law-related education, 448–58
reform, 23–25
resources, 23, 58–59
social sciences, 6–25
    anthropology, 14–15
    civics, 9–11, 21–23, 419–25,
        456–58
    economics, 11–13
    geography, 7–9, 10, 20–21,
        340–82
    history, 7, 8, 18–20,
        386–414
    sociology, 12–14
    teaching objectives, 28–32
    and thinking skills, 25, 26–28,
        31–32
    values clarification, 171–73

D'Amelio, Dan, 60, 294
Dance/music activities, 319–20,
    333–35, 409
Data collection/analysis skills, 27,
    32, 102–17
    and inquiry teaching method,
        141–44
D'Aulaire, Edgar Parin, 294
D'Aulaire, Ingri, 294
De Bono, Edward, 147
Decision-making skills, 32
    decision trees, 174–76
Definition questions, 100
DeKay, James T., 294
DeMause, Lloyd, 42, 43

Democratic beliefs, 11, 28, 30, 31, 419. *See also* Citizenship; Civics application, 162–63 and classroom constitution, 456–58

Developing Understanding of Self and Others (DUSO) program, 165
Dewey, John, 24, 140, 323
Dioramas, 324–25
Directed learning episodes (DLEs), 96–120
  data collection/analysis skills, 102–17
  follow-up, 117–18
  introduction, 96–102
  learning experiences, 102
  motivational methods, 98
  and new words, 99–100
  purpose setting, 100–102
  sample episodes, 118–20
  Taba approach, 103–8, 110, 120, 126, 309
Directed teaching, 88–120, 126
  directed learning episodes, 96–120
    Taba approach, 103–8, 110, 120, 126, 309
    mastery learning, 93–96
    Hunter approach, 94–96, 120, 126
Discovery *See* Research/ discovery/exploration
Discussions. *See* Classroom discussions; Questioning
Dolch, Edward W., 99
Downey, Matthew T., 386
Draftometer, 437
Drama activities, 327–32, 447
  dramatic play, 327–28
  improvised skits, 330–31
  pantomime, 328–30
  sociodrama, 331–32
Drawing, 173, 246, 326
Duffey, Robert V., 471
Durkin, Dolores, 102
DUSO program, 165

Ecology, 432–37
  energy conservation, 437
  for primary/secondary grades, 434–37
  recycling, 434, 436
  waste disposal, 435–36
Economics, 11–13
  basic concepts, 12, 13
Education for All Handicapped Children Act (Public Law 94-142), 488–90
Eggen, Paul D., 88, 142
Egocentrism, 345–46
Ehrlich, Amy, 291
Einstein, Albert, 148, 323
Eisner, Elliot, 318–19, 321
Elementary Volume 6 computer software, 270
Enactive learning, 251, 252–62. *See also* Active learning
Energy conservation, 437
English-Language Arts Framework for California Public Schools, K-12, 287
Equilibration, 92
Essay tests, 477–78
Essentials of Exemplary Social Studies Programs (of NCSS), 30, 31, 33
Estes, Thomas H., 25, 189
Evaluation, 84, 468–91. *See also* Tests
  of behavior, 479–81
  of comprehension, 468–78
  of cultural literacy, 19
  event sampling, 482, 484
  of geographic literacy, 340
  of gifted students, 484–87
  of handicapped students, 488–91
  of intelligence, 484–87
  of primary grades, 478–84
  time sampling, 481–82, 483
  work sampling, 483
Evaluative thinking skills, 26
Event sampling, 482, 484
Expanding environment approach, 15–18

Exploration *See* Research/ discovery/exploration
Expository teaching. *See* Directed teaching

Fables, 293–94
Fairy tales, 291–94
Family history, 400, 429
  coats of arms, 402–4
  family trees, 440–41
Farr, Roger, 26
Fetter, M. Patricia, 458–59, 460
Fields, Marjorie V., 290
Field trips, 254–59, 392, 435
  and historical investigation, 401–2
Fill-in-the-blank tests, 473, 477
Finn, Chester E., 19, 23
First Amendment rights, 419
Fisk, Lori, 199
Fitzpatrick, Mildred, 100
Flack, Marjorie, 289
Folk tales, 291–94
Foods
  cultural differences, 438
  johnnycakes recipe, 409
Forbes, Esther, 294, 295
Frazier, Alexander, 333–34
Freedman, Glenn, 111
Freschet, Berniece, 360

Galin, David, 149
Galleons of Glory: The Secret Voyage of Magellan computer software, 269–70
Gallup Organization, 19, 21
Games, 199–202, 393. *See also* Classroom activities
  board games, 227–28
  computer software, 267–70
  and global/multicultural education, 430–31
  map reading, 359, 362–64, 366–67
  simulation, 263–66
  stores and shoppers, 263–65
Gaskins, Robert W., 94

Generalization skills and directed
  teaching, 90
  and inquiry teaching method,
  144
  and questioning, 109
  and Taba approach, 105–7
Geographic Education National
  Implementation Project
  (GENIP), 21, 341, 379, 383
Geography, 7–9, 20–21, 340–82
  conservation vs. egocentrism,
  345–46
  geographic literacy, 340–42
  map reading, 342–79
  organizational themes, 7, 10,
  341–42
  States and Traits computer
  software, 268
Geography Awareness Week, 21
Gifted students, 484–87
Glenn, Allen, 268
Global/multicultural education,
  425–32, 438–45
  classroom activities, 440–45
  creative art activities, 428–29,
  432
  folk/fairy tales, 291–93
  foreign games, 430–31
  for primary/secondary grades,
  428–32
  problematic trends, 425–26
  verbal/nonverbal communication, 429–30
  world population, 427
Globes. *See* Map-reading skills
Goble, Paul, 293, 442
Gollnick, Donna M., 438
Goodlad, John I., 188
Gordon, Thomas, *Teacher
  Effectiveness Training*,
  451–56
Graham, L. B., 43–44
Gramatky, Hardie, 288
Graphs. *See* Charts/graphs/tables
Gritzner, Charles F., 338, 340–41
Grosvenor, Gilbert M., 20–21, 341
Group learning. *See* Cooperative
  (group) learning

Growing Healthy program,
  461–62
Guided problem solving teaching
  method, 125–37
  vs. inquiry, 137–38
  observation, 130–32, 136–37
  research/discovery/exploration,
  127–29, 132–37
  record keeping, 129–30
  surveying, 133–36
*Guidelines for Geographic
  Education* (of AAG and
  NCGE), 21
Guide-o-ramas/panoramas,
  114–16, 401
Gunter, Mary Alice, 189
Gutman, Carol J., 25

Haas, Mary E., 402
Haiku poetry, 304–5
Hall, Donald, 98, 289
Handicapped students, 488–91
  categories, 490
Hanna, Lavonne A., 68–69
Hanna, Paul R., 15–16
Hansen, William B., 460
Hansen, W. Lee, 12
Harmin, Merrill, 167–69, 171–72,
  173
Harrison, Elise K., 25
Hawkinson, John, 288
Hawkinson, Lucy, 288
Heaps, John, 302
Hellman-Rosenthal, Geraldine,
  17
Helms, Ronald G., 17
Herman, Wayne L., Jr., 351
Hill, Dorothy B. (Debe)
  Holzwarth, 62, 63
Hirsch, E. D., Jr., 19, 23
History, 7, 18–20, 386–414. *See
  also* Family history
  artifacts/relics, 387–89
  children's literature, 294,
  409–12
  Elementary Volume 6
  computer software, 270
  experience vs. facts, 400–404

historical guide-o-ramas/
  panoramas, 114–16, 401
historical investigation, 401–2
historical personages, 408–9
Meet the Presidents computer
  software, 270
oral/written records, 389,
  400–401, 404–7
organizational themes, 8
primary vs. secondary
  witnesses, 406
scope/sequence, 387, 388
of students' families, 400,
  402–4, 429, 440–41
time concepts/calendars/time
  lines, 270, 390–400,
  412–14
Hodson, Diane, 459
Holman, E. Riley, 128, 329
Holt, John, 61
Holzwarth, Dorothy B. (Debe),
  62–63
Honig, Bill, 21
Hornsby, David, 297, 299, 300
Hummel, Elaine, 446
Hunter, Madeline, 86, 95
  mastery learning approach,
  94–96, 120, 126
Hutchins, Pat, 360
Hymes, James L., Jr., 198, 286,
  469
Hypotheses, and inquiry teaching
  method, 140

Ibo African culture, 281–82,
  320–21
Iconic learning, 251, 252, 262–78
I-messages, 454–55
Individualism, 22
Information processing skills. *See*
  Data collection/analysis
  skills
Inquiry teaching method, 137–54
  brainstorming, 151, 152–54
  and cognition, 146–50
  data collection/analysis,
  141–44
  generalization skills, 144

vs. guided problem solving,
    137–38
hypotheses development, 140
open-ended, 150–54
    vs. closed-ended, 150
problem selection, 139–40
sample episodes, 144–46
Inquiry, as teaching objective, 29
Intellectual skills, 32
Intelligence tests
    for gifted students, 484–87
    for handicapped students,
    488–91
Interdisciplinary approach, 15,
    16
Interest learning groups, 210–12
Intern teachers, 47–48. *See also*
    Teachers
Interpersonal skills, 32
Intuition, and brain hemispheres,
    147
Intuitive thinking, 147

*James Madison Elementary
    School: A Curriculum for
    Elementary School*, 20,
    23, 58
Jarolimek, John, 47–48
Jenkins, Gladys Gardner, 400
Jigsaw cooperative learning
    approach, 206–7
Job charts, 397–400
Johnson, David W., 190, 207–8,
    209
Johnson, Roger T., 190, 207–8,
    209
Joint Committee on Geographic
    Education *See* Committee
    on Geographic Education
    (of NCGE)
Journal writing, 312–14. *See also*
    Writing skills
Joyce, William W., 439

Kagan, Spencer, 206
Kate Greenaway Medal, 289
Kauchak, Donald P., 88, 142
Kellum, David F., 61

Kimmel, Margaret Mary, 290
King, Edith W., 318, 432, 439
Kluckhohn, C., 438
Kohlberg, Lawrence
    cognitive-developmental values
        model, 178–84
    stages of moral development,
        178–79, 183, 184
Koop, C. Everett, 458, 459
Kwanzaa (African American
    holiday), 282

Lamdin, Lois, 156
Lampman, Evelyn, 294
Language arts, 286–314
    children's literature, 287–96
    writing skills, 296–314, 406,
        410
Lateral thinking, 147–49
Latitude/longitude, 364–67
Lauer, Rachel M., 186
Laurich, Suzanne, 446
Law-related education, 448–58.
        See also Civics
    and classroom constitution,
        456–58
    law/rule making, 449–51
    teacher problem solving,
        451–56
Law-/rule-making skills, 429,
    449–51
Learning centers, 224–47
    constructing, 225–31
    introducing, 230–32
    and new information, 225
    organizing/scheduling, 234–38
    record keeping, 237–38
    samples, 239–47
    seating arrangements, 233
    types, 224–25
Learning domains, 72
Learning methods, 124, 250–82
    active learning, 124–46
    cooperative (group) learning,
        188–220
    directed learning episodes,
        96–120
    enactive mode, 251, 252–62

iconic mode, 251, 252, 262–78
    mastery learning, 93–96
    symbolic mode, 251, 252,
        278–82
Learning skills
    conceptualizing, 27, 90–93,
        104–5, 107, 347
    content acquisition, 26
    data collecting/analyzing, 27,
        32, 102–17, 141–44
    decision making, 32, 174–76
    generalizing, 90, 105–7, 109,
        144
    intellectual skills, 32
    interpersonal skills, 32
    law/rule making, 429, 449–51
    listening, 161
    map reading, 214–18, 269,
        342–73, 378–82, 411
    moral reasoning, 178–84
    participation, 32
    problem solving, 26, 27,
        125–33, 139–40. *See also*
        Inquiry teaching method
    self-awareness, 161–66, 447
    thinking, 25, 26–28, 31–32,
        88–120, 124–54
    values analysis, 173–78
    writing, 296–314, 400, 406,
        410
Lectures, 279–81
Lee, Dorris, 290
Left/right brain hemispheres, 147
Legends, 14, 291–94. *See also*
        Children's literature; Story
        reading/telling
    Native American, 293
Legends (map), 293–94
Lemke, June Canty, 190
Lennon, John, 148
Lenski, Lois, 288
Lesson plans, 81–83
    activities, 82–83
    objectives, 81
    sample, 83
Letter writing, 307–9, 430. *See
    also* Writing skills
Levesque, Jeri A., 287

Levine, Carol, 459
Levstik, Linda S., 386
Lewis, Edna Genise, 440
Lindgren, Henry Clay, 199
Listening skills
    of students, 161
    of teachers, 452–54
Livingston, Carol, 469
Logacz, Gregory, 446
Logic, and brain hemispheres,
    147
Lortie, Dan, 45–46
Louie, Ai-ling, 291
Lyman, Frank T., Jr., 204

McCloskey, Robert, 288, 360
McLachlan, Patricia, 100
McTighe, Jay, 204
Madaus, George F., 469–70
Madden, Peter, 42
Magic Circle program, 161–65
Mainstreaming, 489–91
Making Political Decisions
    program, 174
Manning, John C., 103
Map-making skills, 374–78
    modeling materials, 377
    outdoor maps, 378
    outline maps, 375–76
    relief maps, 376–77
    topographic maps, 377–78
Map-reading skills, 342–73,
    378–82, 411
    cardinal directions, 355–56,
    370
    children's literature, 359–61
    computer software, 269
    in cooperative learning
        episode, 214–18
    flat maps, 352
    games, 359, 362–64, 366–67
    global maps, 356–58, 372–73
    by grade level, 379–82
    latitude/longitude, 364–67
    legend symbols, 353–55,
    369–70
    perceptual factors, 345–49
    prerequisite activities, 343–45

rainfall/vegetation maps,
    367–68
scales, 356, 370–72
and story reading/telling,
    359–61
three-dimensional maps,
    350–52
Map Skills computer software,
    269
Marland, Sidney P., Jr., 446
Martinson, R. A., 485
Mastery learning, 93–96. *See also*
    Directed teaching
    and directed learning episodes,
    96–120
    Hunter approach, 94–96, 120,
    126
Matching-item tests, 473, 476
Mateja, John A., 114
Mead, Margaret, 433
Mediator program, 22
Meek, Anne, 322
Meet the Presidents computer
    software, 270
Mills, Randy, 313
Modeling materials, 377
Monjo, Fernando, 294
Moral reasoning skills, 178–84
    and civil rights, 180–81
    and classroom discussions,
    180–84
    developmental stages, 179, 183
Morgan, Jack C., 108
Mosaics, 325
Motion pictures, 266–67
Motivational methods, 98
Multiple choice tests, 473,
    474–75
Murals, 325
Music/dance activities, 319–20,
    333–35, 409
Myths, 293–94. *See also*
    Children's literature; Story
    reading/telling

Names
    African naming ceremony,
    431–32, 440

name/attendance charts,
    194–97, 235, 275
name tags, 191–92, 235
and national origins, 440–41
Native American, 443–44
National Association for the
    Education of Young
    Children (NAEYC), 478
National Book Award, 289
National Commission on Social
    Studies in the Schools, 23,
    24
National Council for Geographic
    Education (NCGE), 21
National Council for the Social
    Studies (NCSS), 4, 23, 30,
    33, 167, 433
    *Position Statement on Global
        Education*, 427
    as professional organization,
    50, 492
    Task Force on Early
        Childhood/Elementary
        Social Studies, 4, 25, 386
    Task Force on Scope and
        Sequence, 16–18, 163
    teachers' professional
        standards, 46–47
National Education Association
    (NEA), 4–5
National Endowment for the Arts
    (NEA), 318, 322
National Geographic Society
    (NGS), 21
Nation at Risk, A, 30, 188
Nations, Jimmy, 469
Native American culture,
    442–45
    calendars, 97
    in cooperative learning
        episode, 219
    in directed learning episode,
    96–97
    legends, 293
    name origin, 443–44
    pictographs, 443
    tepees, 442–43
Natoli, Salvatore J., 340–41, 342

Naylor, Phyllis, 38–39
Newbery Medal, 289
Newman, Fred M., 22
New Oregon Trail computer
    software, 268–69
Newspapers.
    and classroom activities,
        299–302, 421
    and current affairs, 420–23
    and First Amendment rights, 419
Nicolich, Lorraine McCune, 468,
    470–71, 473
Norton, Donna E., 360–61, 410
Numbered heads together
    cooperative learning
    approach, 206

Observation
    direct vs. indirect, 141
    guided problem solving
        method, 130–32, 136–37
Oh Deer computer software, 270
Oliner, Pearl M., 468, 472
Olsen, Mary, 164
Open-ended inquiry teaching
    method, 150–54
Operative values, 151, 159–60
Orlich, Donald C., 111

Palomares, Uvaldo, 161, 165
Panoramas/guide-o-ramas,
    114–16, 401
Pantomime, 328–30
Papier-mache, 377
Parallels of latitude, 364–65
Parker, Walter C., 11, 21–22, 25,
    28
Parks, Rosa, 180–81
Parramore, Barbara, 60
Parry, Jo Ann, 297, 299, 300
Participation skills, 32
Pennsylvania's state insect
    project, 62–64
Pen pals, 430
*Performing Together: The Arts in
    Education*, 323
Periodicals, 423–25. *See also*
    Newspapers

Perrault, Charles, 291
Persky, B. A., 43–44
Persona writing technique, 305–6
Phillips, Debra Hallock, 40
Phinney, Jean S., 479
Piaget, Jean, 92, 93, 127–28, 178,
    312, 328, 348, 352, 378
    egocentrism/conservation,
        345–47
Political science. *See* Civics
Population, 273, 277–78, 427
*Position Statement on Global
    Education* (of NCSS), 427
Poster, John B., 400
Postman, Neil, 122
Potter, Beatrix, 449
Potter, Gladys L., 68–69
Preston, Ralph C., 351, 471
Pritchard, Sandra F., 359
Probing, 110–11
Problem solving skills. *See also*
        Inquiry teaching method
    problem selection, 139–40
    of students, 26, 27, 125–33
        Mediator program, 22
    of teachers, 451–56
Professionalism, of teachers,
        43–51, 492
    NCSS standards, 46–47
Professional journals/
        organizations, 49–50, 492
Prompting, as probing method,
    110
Psencik, Leroy, 58
Psychomotor learning domain, 72
Public Law 94-142, 488–90

Questioning
    antonym/definition/semantic/
        synonym questions, 100
    and brainstorming, 152–53
    core questions, 111–13
    and directed learning episode,
        103–8
    and observation, 130–32
    personal pattern, 108–9
    and probing/waiting, 110–11
    and semantic webbing, 111–13

by students, 116–17, 141–43
Taba approach, 103–8

Raths, Louis E., 167–69, 171–72,
    173
Ravitch, Diane, 17, 19, 23,
    287–88
Rawitsch, Don, 268
Realia, 98, 226, 253–54, 255
Reception teaching. *See* Directed
    teaching
Record keeping. *See also*
    Evaluation
    anecdotal records, 482, 484
    behavior checklists, 480–81
    behavior reports, 479–80
    and learning centers, 237–38
    and new discoveries, 129–30
Recycling, 434, 436
Reflective inquiry, as teaching
    objective, 29
Reinforcement learning centers,
    224
Remy, Richard C., 92, 174
Report writing
    by students, 309–10, 311. *See
        also* Writing skills
    by teachers. *See* Evaluation;
        Record keeping
Research/discovery/exploration,
    127–30, 132–37
    cooperative (group), 212–14
    descriptive, 141
    historical investigation, 401–2
    observational, 136–37, 141
    question-based, 141–43
    resources, 141
    surveys, 133–36, 141, 435
Resource persons, 143–44,
    259–62, 392, 430
Resources, 82, 250–82. *See also*
    Teaching media
    children's literature, 288–94
    cooperative (group) learning,
        206, 209–10
    curriculum, 23, 58–59
    for handicapped students,
        491

map-reading skills, 359–61
and research/discovery/
exploration, 141
standardized tests, 471
valuing processes, 173, 183
Response clarification valuing
process, 169–71
Reynolds, Elizabeth G., 111
Reynolds, Robert W., 68–69
Right/left brain hemispheres, 147
Rogers, Carl R., 61–62, 159–60,
161
Rosenblatt, Louise, 304
Rousseau, Jean-Jacques, 248, 250
Rule-making skills, 429, 449–51
Russian Revolution, 405
Ryan, Kevin, 40

Salinger, Terry, 297
Samples, Robert, 149
Sampling
evaluation methods, 481–84
survey method, 134
Scales (map), 356, 370–72
Schadler, Margaret, 349
Schliemann, Heinrich, 14–15
Schreiber, Joan E., 108
Schreifels, Beverly, 408
Schwab, Jan Hasbrouck, 189
Seating arrangements, 210, 233
Seefeldt, Carol, 130–31
and global/multicultural
education, 428–30
Segal, Elizabeth, 290
Self-awareness skills
and career education, 447
DUSO program, 165
and valuing processes, 161–66
Semantic questions, 100
Semantic webbing, 111–13
Senryu poetry, 305
Seuss, Dr, 436
Sewall, Gilbert, 20, 288
Shablak, Scott L., 115
Shacter, Helen S., 400
Shaffer, Lawrence F., 312
Shaftel, Fannie R., 332
Shaftel, George, 332

Shaheen, JoAnn C., 22
Shaver, James P., 160, 167
Sheen, Patsy, 459
Shepard, Lorrie A., 466
Shermis, S. Samuel, 6, 167
Siegel, Alexander W., 349
Simile, 305
Simon, Sidney B., 167–69,
171–72, 173
Simulation, 263–66, 368
Skits, 330–31
Slavin, Robert E., 66–67, 95, 209,
210
Slides, 266–67
Smith, Claude Clayton, 288
Smith, Frank, 91
Smith, Robert F., 128
Social organization, 429
Social studies. *See also*
Curriculum
and citizenship, 4, 28–29, 332
and social sciences, 28–29
teaching objectives, 28–32
as term, 4
for twenty-first century, 23, 24
and values clarification, 171–73
Sociodrama, 331–32
Sociology, 12–14
Socrates, 110
Special education, 488–91
Spotlight of the Week program, 440
States and Traits computer
software, 268
Steig, William, 289
Sternberg, Robert, 146–47
Stores and Shoppers game,
263–65
Story reading/telling, 287–96
biographies/historical fiction,
294, 400
folk stories/fairy tales/legends,
291–94
for map reading, 359–61
methods, 294–96
and valuing processes, 176–78
Story writing, 305–7
Native American pictographs,
443

Subsumers, 90
Suchman, Richard, 141
Sund, Robert B., 125–26
*Surgeon General's Report on
Acquired Immune
Deficiency Syndrome*, 459
Surveys
and ecology, 435
and guided problem solving,
133–36
and inquiry, 141
sample taking, 134
steps, 136
Sutherland, Zena, 303
Swartout, Sherwin G., 88
Symbolic learning, 251, 252,
278–82
Synonym questions, 100
Systematic thinking, 147

Taba, Hilda, 103–4
directed learning episode
approach, 103–8, 110,
120, 126, 309
Tables. *See* Charts/graphs/tables
Talent totem, 57
Tanka poetry, 305
Task Force on Early Childhood/
Elementary Social Studies
(of NCSS), 4, 25, 386
Task Force on Scope and
Sequence (of NCSS),
16–18, 163
*Taxonomy of Educational
Objectives* (Bloom), 26,
72–73, 84, 143
components, 73
Taylor, Calvin W., 57, 84, 215
talent totem, 57
Taylor, Mark, 360
*Teacher Effectiveness Training
(TET)* program, 451–56
Teachers, 38–51, 66–67
competency, 47–48
continued education/growth,
49–51
developmental stages, 49
fundamental traits, 39

NCSS professional standards, 46–47
personality characteristics, 39–43
problem solving skills, 451–56
professionalism, 43–51, 492
Teacher Effectiveness Training program, 451–56
Teaching media. *See also* Learning centers; Resources
audiovisuals, 99, 226, 266–67, 421–22
computers, 267–70
visuals
charts/graphs/tables, 57, 111–16, 193–97, 235, 272–78, 397–400
models/replicas, 262–63
pictures, 98, 270–72
realia, 98, 226, 253–54, 255
Teaching methods, 47–48. *See also* Learning methods
directed teaching, 88–120, 126
facilitating, 66, 138
and global/multicultural education, 428–32
guided problem solving, 125–33
inquiry, 126, 137–54
mastery learning, 93–96
multiple-talent teaching, 57–58
problem solving, 451–56
and values. *See* Valuing processes
Teaching objectives, 28–32
Bloom's taxonomy, 26, 72–73, 84, 143
citizenship transmission, 28–29
of lesson/unit plans, 71–75, 81
reflective inquiry, 29
social science emphasis, 28–29
Teaching skills
analyzing/clarifying/inculcating values, 166–78
brainstorming, 152–53
listening, 452–54

problem solving, 451–56
questioning, 100, 108–9
probing/waiting, 110–11
Taba approach, 103–8
semantic webbing, 111–13
Tests. *See also* Evaluation
comprehension, 468–78
essays, 477–78
filling in the blanks, 473, 477
for gifted students, 484–87
for handicapped students, 488–91
of intelligence, 484–91
matching items, 473, 476
multiple choice, 473, 474–75
resources, 471
standardized, 468–72
criterion-referenced, 470–72
teacher-created, 472–78
Texas Educational Agency, 58
Textbooks, as planning tool, 58–59
Themes
geography, 7, 10, 341–42
history, 8
selecting, 67–71
and unit plans, 68–71
Thinking skills, 25, 26–28, 31–32
and brain hemispheres, 147–49
critical thinking, 26, 27, 143
and directed teaching, 88–120
evaluative thinking, 26
and guided problem solving/ inquiry, 124–54
intuitive vs. systematic, 147
lateral vs. vertical, 147–49
types, 26, 27, 32, 147–49
and valuing processes, 158–84
Think-pair-share cooperative learning approach, 204–6
Thomas, R. Murray, 88, 138
Time concepts, 390–400
calendars, 97, 393–400
Elementary Volume 6
computer software, 270
time capsules, 390–93
time lines, 412–14
time machines, 408

Time sampling, 481–82, 483
Tocqueville, Alexis de, 22
Torrance, E. Paul, 88, 148
Transactional writing, 307–14
journals, 312–14
letters, 307–9, 430
political cartoons, 310–12, 313
reports, 309–10, 311
Trelease, Jim, 290
True-false tests, 473, 476
Tucker, Jan L., 427, 428

Unit plans, 67–81
activities, 75–81
objectives, 71–75
themes, 68–71

Valuing processes, 158–84
affective vs. cognitive values, 160
classroom activities, 171–73
conceived vs. operative values, 151, 159–60
and decision trees, 174–76
and ecology, 436
how vs. what to value, 167
and moral reasoning, 178–84
resources, 173, 183
self-confidence development programs, 161–66
and story reading/telling, 176–78
values analysis, 173–78
values clarification, 167–73
values inculcation, 166–67
Van Allsburg, Chris, 289
Van Doren, Mark, 92
Van Tassel-Baska, Joyce, 485–87
Venn diagrams, 116
Vertical thinking, 147–49
Videotapes, 266–67
Visuals. *See also* Audiovisuals
charts/graphs/tables, 57, 111–16, 193–97, 235, 272–78, 397–400
models/replicas, 262–63
pictures, 98, 270–72
realia, 98, 226, 253–54, 255

Waber, Bernard, 289
Walsh, Huber M., 284
Wassermann, Selma, 127, 199
Waste disposal, 435–36
Webbing. *See* Semantic webbing
Weingartner, Charles, 122
Weintraub, Sam, 26
Where in the USA Is Carmen Sandiego? computer software, 269
Winn, Mary, 449
Wood, Karen D., 114

Woolfolk, Anita E., 468, 470–71, 474–75
Work sampling, 483
Writing skills, 296–314
  biographies, 400
  creative writing, 303–7, 406, 410
  forms/purposes, 296–97
  steps, 298
  transactional writing, 307–14
    journals, 312–14
    letters, 307–9, 430

political cartoons, 310–12, 313
reports, 309–10, 311
Wylie, Wilson, 402

Yolen, Jane, 288
Yoruba African culture, 432
You-messages, 454

Zeleny, Leslie D., 331
Zion, Gene, 360

About the Author

George W. Maxim is a professor in the teacher education program of the Department of Childhood Studies and Reading at West Chester University where he specializes in social studies methods and early childhood education. He is an experienced classroom teacher, having held positions at both the elementary and preschool levels. As an active member of the National Council for the Social Studies (NCSS), he has served on the Educational Publishing Advisory Committee and has chaired the Early Childhood/Elementary Advisory Committee. Currently, he is a member of the Editorial Advisory Board of the NCSS journal for creative teaching in the elementary school, *Social Studies and the Young Learner*. He has consulted with several school districts in the development of social studies curricula and has been a conference presenter on many occasions. His teaching and professional leadership efforts have led to numerous awards. In addition to *Social Studies and the Elementary School Child*, Dr. Maxim has authored *The Very Young* (3rd edition) and *The Sourcebook* (2nd edition) for Merrill, an imprint of Macmillan Publishing.